BENTHAM
AND THE ETHICS OF TODAY

Bentham

AND THE ETHICS OF TODAY

WITH BENTHAM MANUSCRIPTS
HITHERTO UNPUBLISHED

BY DAVID BAUMGARDT

1966

OCTAGON BOOKS, INC.

New York

Reprinted 1966
by special arrangement with Princeton University Press

OCTAGON BOOKS, INC.
175 Fifth Avenue
New York, N.Y. 10010

Library of Congress Catalog Card Number: 66-28381

Printed in U.S.A. by
NOBLE OFFSET PRINTERS, INC.
NEW YORK 3, N. Y.

TO

LADY CLARKE HALL

"His dry coolness was enemy only to melodrama, and . . . deflating its falsity, he allowed the real drama to emerge." —Dorothy Canfield Fisher, *The Deepening Stream*, 1930, p. 227.

"Having bought truth deare, we must not sell it cheape . . . least of all for the bitter sweetening of a little vanishing pleasure, For a little puffe of credit and reputation."— Roger Williams, *The Bloudy Tenent, of Persecution, for cause of Conscience, discussed, in A Conference betweene Truth and Peace*, 1644 (200 copies reprinted and ed. by Samuel L. Caldwell, 1867, p. 13)

PREFACE

JUST as Hitler came to power, in 1933, I published the first volume of a history of modern ethics, *Der Kampf um den Lebenssinn unter den Vorläufern der modernen Ethik*. In this volume, I gave a detailed analysis of the ethics of Kant and his contemporaries on the European continent. I had planned, at that time, to continue my work with an examination of the world-wide influence of Fichte's, Schelling's and Hegel's ethics. This plan had to be altered in consequence of—my changed residence. But the critical attitude I had already assumed in Germany toward the moral philosophy of Kant and his followers is unaltered. As I tried to explain in 1930 in my treatise *Über einige Hauptmethodenfragen der Ethik*, what is of true and great value in the metaphysical speculation of the nineteenth and twentieth centuries, especially in the German, is in need of a far more solid "positivistic" substructure than has yet been found. A complete re-evaluation of Bentham's critical method in ethics points the way, in my opinion, to such a new and sounder basis for any type of ethical reflection, even though Bentham's moral philosophy, taken by itself, doubtless requires essential supplementation and refinement.

Again and again, metaphysics has pronounced the death sentence on positivism and vice versa. But English Hegelianism could not prevent the revival of positivistic thought in Henry Sidgwick and Ludwig Wittgenstein. Fichte, Schelling and Hegel, with all their contempt of empiricism could not undo the international impact of Ernst Mach's, Mill's and Spencer's positivism, nor could De Maistre, Chateaubriand and Victor Cousin detract from the triumphs of Comte. Neither could Comte, despite his strict prophecies to the contrary, stop the most successful "return" of Bergson and Sartre to the "metaphysical age" nor Husserl and the "Wiener Kreis" the return to metaphysical ontologies in Germany and France. It seems to me time, therefore, to abandon all such mutual sectarian anathemas and to remember that from the days of the aged Plato and of Aristotle the great masters of thought took both metaphysics and positivism most seriously.

There is no doubt of the profound respect for empirical facts even in the marked metaphysical speculations of Descartes, Spinoza, Leibniz and Kant. Of course, this must never mean the praise of a cheap mixture of the two seemingly irreconcilable philosophical tempers; but it means the highest desirability of their integrated cooperation. Any light-minded eclecticism is, in my opinion, more dangerous in philosophy than even the most pronounced but honest one-sidedness. It is for this reason that I have tried to make fruitful for the ethics of today the consistent ethical positivism of Jeremy Bentham, which has been almost universally misjudged from the day of its birth by friend and foe.

I do not, because I feel I cannot, address myself to the reader who wishes to see the wisdom of Bentham presented in a nutshell, no matter how enlarged a nutshell. It is with deliberate purpose that I have refrained from giving no more than a systematic transverse section through Bentham's moral philosophy, a systematic extract from the ethical ideas which he developed during sixty years of intense and subtle thinking. If I had tried to offer such a digest of his system, I might have given the impression of showing his main argument in high relief. But this would have been possible only by omitting numerous characteristic changes which took place in the development of his doctrine of motives, his theory of fiction, his criticism of bills of rights and the like.

After a great deal of thought as to the best way of presenting my complex material, I have chosen the genetic method, showing as clearly as possible the inner development of Bentham's thought in its main phases. In fact, as I have tried to demonstrate, Bentham's *Fragment on Government*, his *Comment on the Commentaries*, his *Introduction to the Principles of Morals and Legislation*, his *Traités de législation civile et pénale*, his later juristic writings and his *Deontology*—all these approach practically the same problems from different angles. Each of these versions, in which Bentham expounded his ethical theory, has its merits and its defects. But each of these expositions is a comparatively independent whole in itself and deserves to be pondered over by itself.

If, nevertheless, a reader wishes to get hold of a compressed but comparatively comprehensive summary of Bentham's ethics he may best turn to my critical commentary on the *Introduction*, to the extracts which I give from the later juristic writings, or to my brief epilogue. I should like, however, to caution the reader that in doing so he will miss essential parts of Bentham's teaching and its confrontation with the ethics of today. I thought it proper to present the comparison with related modern doctrines on those points of Bentham's works on which he comes nearest to, or is instructively opposed to, contemporary ethical ideas; and these points are best understood only in their original context. Perhaps there is something to the "time saving" tendency to listen only to a summary of the best movements of the symphonies of a great composer or to take the overture or the finale of a composition as a substitute for the whole. It seems to me that the virtues of such a procedure are over-compensated by its vices, even if the vices are not visible to the quick scan of a critic.

In any case, what I considered my principal duty and what, I think, should have been done a long time ago, is to blaze a path through the wilderness of Bentham's widely scattered published and unpublished writings, to show their connections with pre-Benthamite thought, and to comment in detail on their importance for contemporary systematic ethics. What I most urgently request from the reader is what is, naturally, rarest in these excited times: patience, and freedom from too loose and too rigid preconceived opinions.

For what I owe to my English and American friends no expression is too strong, no thanks can be warm enough: it is more even than intellectual life-saving. One name I have already mentioned in my dedication. I further wish to thank particularly my friend H. P. Adams of Birmingham University, England, who, with infinite patience, revised the stammering English of my lengthy first draft; to Professor L. J. Russell, Birmingham University, who gave me most careful advice and showed a never tiring interest in reading and correcting the first part of my work; to my friends Stephen and Rosa Hobhouse, Broxbourne, Herts; G. D. Hornblower, London; Margaret Worsdell, Woodbrooke College; to the late Douglas Owen, Manchester, England; the late Professor Sigmund Freud; and the late Adolphe S. Oko, Ridgefield, Connecticut; to Dr. and Mrs. Howard H. Brinton, Pendle Hill; Norma Jacob, Jamaica, Vermont; Marcus Fraenkel, Rose Di Cecco, New York; Dr. Kurt Rosenwald and Ernest Sternglass, Washington, D.C.; Henry J. Dubester and Donald H. Mugridge, The Library of Congress; Dr. William Gerber, The State Department, Washington, D.C.; Professor Charles A. Baylis, The University of Maryland; President John W. Nason, Swarthmore College; Professor Charles W. Everett, Professor John H. Randall, Jr., and Professor Herbert W. Schneider, Columbia University; The Honorable Felix Frankfurter, Justice of the Supreme Court of the United States; Dr. and Mrs. John R. Fisher, Arlington, Vermont. Each of them has read at least parts of my manuscript. The literary taste of my friends Joseph and Rachel Frank, Washington, D.C., came to my rescue throughout my work and I am, therefore, under an even greater obligation to them. None of these generous helpers, however, bears any responsibility for the ideas presented or for any shortcomings of the book.

I am, further, greatly indebted to several libraries: to the Library of University College, London, England, and to the British Museum Library for having both generously granted me the right to publish hitherto unpublished MSS; to M. Jean Graven, Professeur à la Faculté de Droit, Université de Genève, Switzerland, for having kindly sent me photostats of marginal notes by Dumont and allowing me to quote them; to the Library of the University of Birmingham, England; the Library of the Law Court, Birmingham; the Selly Oak Colleges Library; the Library of the University of Pennsylvania, Philadelphia; The Martha Canfield Library, Arlington, Vermont; and especially to Dr. Luther H. Evans, Librarian of Congress, Washington, D.C., and numerous members of his staff.

Last but not least, I wish to express my lasting gratitude to the Society for the Protection of Science and Learning, Cambridge, England, for its generous financial support, for most helpful research grants given me by the American Philosophical Society and the American Committee for Emigré Scholars, Writers and Artists and for all the encouraging support I received from Mr. Datus C. Smith, Jr., Director of the Princeton University Press as well as from the Press' most conscientious editor, Miss Gladys Fornell.

December 30, 1949

DAVID BAUMGARDT
Consultant of the Library
of Congress in Philosophy
Formerly Professor of Philosophy
at the University of Berlin

CONTENTS

THE MAIN THEME

xii

CONTENTS

PROLOGUE

*The Injustice Done To The Moralist Bentham. Reasons
For The Low Estimate Of Bentham's Ethics*

PROLOGUE

The Injustice Done To The Moralist Bentham. Reasons For The Low Estimate Of Bentham's Ethics

———

DID any other European of the eighteenth century do as much as Bentham did for the clarification of great issues which are still vital in 1949? He contributed to the organization of a permanent international peace, as well as to social and economic reforms of manifold types, to the emancipation of the colonies, to the creation of a league of nations and of a non-coercive arbitral tribunal for settling of international disputes, to the codification of English and American Law, to the improvement of prisons, to the limitation of capital punishment, to the exclusion of corporal punishment from school discipline, to the prevention of cruelty toward animals, to the enlargement of public health legislation, to the emancipation of women, to the establishment of savings banks, to the creation of an international language, to the theory of language and analysis of its impact on philosophical thought in the sense of modern semantics, to the founding of one of the greatest institutions for higher secular learning, to the promoting of encyclopedic education and, last not least, to the laying of a new, critical foundation of ethics. I know of no one, particularly of no one on the European continent, who could in this respect rival the greatest reformer of English Law.

To pass from Kant and Friedrich Heinrich Jacobi to their contemporary Jeremy Bentham involves a journey, not only into another country, but into another world and another epoch. It is to travel from the ducal estates and the last phases of continental absolutism to the first industrial centers of Europe and the beginnings of modern democracy.

England was, even before Bentham, the classical land of philosophical empiricism; and if one wishes to indulge in what Bentham calls "aerial" speculations, one may say that there is, perhaps, a common tendency in English horticulture (which made such a deep impression on European aesthetics in the eighteenth century), in British empire policy, English epistemology, English common sense ethics and even in English cooking or love for open fireplaces. In all these comes to the fore the will to leave things, facts, as they are. The scenery of the parks, the cultural

3

life of colonies, the vegetables, meat and other food are preferred in their pure substance, in their own shape, without too many artificial ingredients, garnishings and modifications. In the ceremonies of political life, as well as in the extremely conservative love of the open fire, there is the same love of the natural form and color of things as they are.

In England, generally speaking, even metaphysical minds such as Coleridge or T. H. Green are more tinged with empiricism than the great German speculative philosophers; and in Germany, on the other hand, even thinkers with very marked empiristic tendencies, such as Herder or Feuerbach, have a far more intimate connection with metaphysical thought than have the English positivists. This may perhaps suffice to explain why F. E. Beneke, the only outstanding admirer whom Bentham has found among German philosophers, sought to tone down many too "sensualistische" statements in the Bentham-Dumont *Traités de législation*;[1] and in Dumont's edition itself, Bentham's thought and expression had already been recast in less radical and more religious form.

[1] See Friedrich Eduard Beneke, *Grundsätze der Civil- und Kriminalgesetzgebung aus den Handschriften des engl. Rechtsgelehrten Jeremias Bentham, herausg. von Etienne Dumont, nach der 2. verbesserten und vermehrten Auflage für Deutschland bearbeitet und mit Anmerkungen von Dr. F. E. B.*, 1830, vol. 1, pp. xi, x. Beneke deplores here the fact that Bentham is a "moralischer Sensualist," that he "zieht nur *sinnliche* Interessen in Betracht"; he goes on, however, to say that Bentham is not an "egoist," but a very "edel" personality (compare p. 46). Similarly an anonymous German author defends Bentham in 1836 in a work entitled *Der Moralist Bentham und die Geldaristokratie der Zeit. Etwas in die Wagschale des gesellschaftlichen Wohls.* This apparently young writer who mocks at Hegel only five years after his death and is interested in St. Simon and Fourier (p. 6 f) vindicates Bentham's doctrine also against the reproach that it is "ein Evangelium der Sinnenlust" (p. 71). "Der vernünftige Zusammenhang des Lebens liegt bei Bentham viel mehr in den Worten 'nütze und es wird Dir genützt werden'" (p. 67). Beneke and this anonymous critic both regret, "dass ein solcher Mann (namely Bentham) gerade bei uns kosmopolitischen Deutschen weniger bekannt ist als bei allen übrigen gebildeten Völkern" (p. 9, cf. Beneke, I, 4). And Beneke adds some conclusive reasons, "weshalb Bentham . . . so wenig bei uns bekannt geworden ist": first, in France and in England there is a common conviction that only by close contact with interior and exterior experience can sound knowledge be won, while in Germany it is thought in "speculation" (p. vi). And, second, in Germany "sind seit Kant . . . alle materialen Prinzipien d. h. alle Erwägung der durch Handlungen und Gesetze erstrebten Gegenstände oder Zwecke aus der sittlichen und rechtlichen Beurteilung verbannt" (p. vii). "Man findet seit Kant bei uns Deutschen in der *wissenschaftlichen Theorie* eine ganz wunderliche Scheu vor dem Begriff des Nutzens, während man in der Praxis demselben nicht selten . . . aus nur zu beschränkten Gesichtspunkten huldigt. Es ist beinah, als fürchte man, dass durch die Kontrolle einer *aufgeklärten* Wissenschaft diese Beschränktheit werde gemissbilligt werden und zöge

eben deshalb vor, unter *unklaren formalen* Ausdrücken sich zu verhüllen" (p. ix). Bentham, on the other hand, has according to Beneke often "die Notwendigkeit der *reinen Form* der Beurteilung übersehen" (p. x).

As a matter of fact, besides Beneke and this anonymous writer, hardly anyone in Germany mentioned Bentham's *ethics* in Bentham's lifetime or for some time after his death. (Beneke himself could exercise no influence in this epoch of German metaphysics and probably the persecution under which he had to suffer —after Hegel had expelled him from Berlin University on account of his positivism—hastened his death, see M. Lenz, *Geschichte der Königl. Friedrich Wilhelms-Universität*, 1910, vol. II, pp. 296 ff.)

Even among German jurists of Bentham's lifetime I could trace only the following references to him: Hanns Ernst von Globig, *System einer vollständigen Gesetzgebung für die Kaiserl. Russ. Gesetz-Commission*, I, Teil 1815, Allgemeine Einleitung, p. 4: "Die scholastischen Träumereyen des Engländers *Jeremias Bentham*, welchen der Franzose *Dumont* mit vielem Enthusiasmus übersetzt und nachgebetet hat, verdienen kaum in die Reihe wissenschaftlicher Versuche gestellt zu werden." In "*Hermes oder kritisches Jahrbuch der Literatur*," 3. Stück für das Jahr 1822, pp. 316 ff, "Über die Philosophie des Rechts und der positiven Gesetzgebung," a bitter antagonist of Hegel, N. L. says: "Es ist zu verwundern, dass . . . Bentham's Werke in Deutschland wenig bekannt geworden sind und in unserer Literatur kaum genannt werden"; *ibid.*, 2. Stück für das Jahr 1823, p. 189: Herr Bentham, "durch dessen Werke so viel Licht über die Kriminalgesetzgebung verbreitet ist"; Mittermayer in *Kritische Zeitschrift für Rechtswissenschaft und Gesetzgebung des Auslands*, 1829, I. Heft, pp. 31 f, praises the jurist Bentham, but criticizes his "Reformationswut" (Das Englische Criminalrecht); cf. *ibid.*, Zachariä in an essay "Die Regeln der Logik über den gerichtlichen Beweis von Jer. Bentham, kritisch dargestellt," Heft II, pp. 252-270; *ibid.*, Zachariä, 1831, Heft III, pp. 88-97.

Also Goethe in his talks with F. J. Soret obviously has the radical jurist Bentham in mind in calling him several times a "höchst radikalen Narren" (see J. P. Eckermann, *Gespräche mit Goethe*, of February 3, 1830, and March 17, 1830). In any case, Goethe's self-praise of his own more balanced liberalism and his censure of the greatest law-reformer of his century throws no favorable light on Goethe, particularly considering Goethe's own far more passive political attitude. In his conversation with Friedrich Jakob Soret of February 3, 1830, Goethe went even so far as to express his amazement at the fact that Etienne Dumont, the uncle of Soret, the popularizer of Bentham's ideas and certainly a far inferior mind could "se déclarer le disciple et l'admirateur constant de ce fou de Bentham," see *Goethes Gespräche, Gesamtausgabe*, ed. by F. v. Biedermann, 1910, vol. IV, p. 203. Compare *ibid.*, p. 244: Bentham, "ce grand fou de radical"; and compare *ibid.*, p. 271.

It is extremely significant that Eduard Gans, the leading jurist of the Hegelian school, a personal friend of Hegel, refused at first to accept an invitation to dine with Bentham who was at this time the greatest jurist of England and a personality of world-wide reputation. See E. Gans, *Rückblicke auf Personen und Zustände*, 1836, pp. 198 ff: "Ein Besuch bei Jeremia Bentham," p. 199: Abraham Hayward, "Advokat von der Genossenschaft des Tempels," translator of Savigny's *Vom Beruf unsrer Zeit für Gesetzgebung und Rechtswissenschaft* and of Goethe's *Faust*, informed Gans on October 20, 1831, that Bentham would like to meet him. "Nun, ich bin alle Tage bis 12 Uhr zu Hause . . . Bei diesen Worten sprang Herr Hayward einige Schritte zurück, und nachdem er zuvor wie erschreckt

Along with this, it remains a strange fact that, while Bentham was greatly admired in Greece, Spain, Portugal, South and Central America, Tripoli and Russia,[2] especially in the last epoch of his life, he had

gewesen war, konnte er endlich das Lachen nicht unterdrücken. Sie erwarten, sagte er etwas spöttisch, dass Bentham Sie aufsuchen wird . . . dass Sie ihn wieder besuchen können, wann es Ihnen beliebt. Nein, mein Herr! Bentham geht weder aus, noch empfängt er Besuche." Gans thought "die Philosophie der französischen Encyklopädisten in einem englischen Exemplar wiederzufinden, hätte ich nie für wünschenswert gehalten." But he accepted Bentham's invitation; and Bentham greeted Gans with the words: "Ich . . . freue mich, den eifrigen, beständigen, und wie ich hoffe, auch nicht unsiegreichen Gegner der historischen Schule kennen zu lernen." Hence Bentham assumed that Gans as the adversary of the so-called historical school was a kind of German Bentham. In fact, Hegel and Gans were much more connected with historical thought than Bentham.

[2] On Greece see Bentham, *Works*, ed. by Bowring (1843) part VIII, pp. 185 ff. On Spain see G. H. Borrow, *The Bible in Spain*, 1908, vol. II, p. 327, chap. XII. Compare *Biblioteca de autores españoles, Obras publicadas é inéditas* de Don Gaspar Melchor de Jovellanos, tom. II, 1859, pp. 319 f (I owe this reference to the kindness of Dr. Edith Helman, Boston). On Portugal see Bentham, *Works*, part VIII, pp. 573 ff; on Central and South America, *ibid.*, part XX, p. 533b, part VIII, pp. 192 f, part XIX, p. 17a; Ambassador Rafael Heliodoro Valle in *La Prensa*, Buenos Aires, May 25, 1947, Sección Seconda, p. 2, emphasizes the strength of Bentham's influence mainly in the fields of constitutional law and prison reform, the Panopticon ideal. Further, see R. H. Valle in *La Prensa*, Nueva York, December 27, 1949, and compare K. *Lipstein's* essay, "Bentham, Foreign Law and Foreign Lawyers" in *Jeremy Bentham and the Law*, ed. on behalf of the Faculty of Laws of University College, London, by G. Keeton and G. Schwarzenberger, 1948, p. 209; *ibid.* on Greece, pp. 211 ff; on Spain, pp. 214 ff; on Tripoli, Bentham, *Works*, part XVI, p. 555.

On Russia, see *ibid.*, part XX, pp. 406 ff, 473, 478, further see E. Salkind, "Die Dekabristen in ihrer Beziehung zu Westeuropa" in *Jahrbücher für Kultur und Geschichte der Slawen*, 1928, pp. 534, 537 f and Anatole G. Mazour, *The First Russian Revolution, 1825; the Decembrist Movement*, 1937, p. 27. One of the leaders of the first Russian revolution of December 1825 staged by the Russian guards confessed at his trial that, of all the French and English political writers, Bentham exercised the strongest influence on him; another of this group who worked out one of the first constitutions for the Russian Empire was accused by his fellow conspirators of being too much under the spell of Bentham. Alexander I had sponsored the translation of Bentham-Dumont's *Traités* soon after their appearance; see *Vosstanie dekabristov* published by Tsentrarkhiv, Moskva, 1925, I, pp. 430, 520 and compare A. N. Pypin's essay about the Russian followers of Bentham in *Vestnik Evropy*, 1869, February, pp. 804 ff (I owe these references to the kindness of Dr. Sergius Yakobson). Further compare the letter sent to Bentham by the Emperor Alexander I in April 1815, the letter of General Sabloukoff (Bentham, *Works*, part VIII, p. 515, part XX, pp. 412 f) and the fact that Dumont-Bentham's *Traités* were "admired" in Russia and "as many copies" of the *Traités* were sold in Petersburg as in London (*ibid.*, part XX, p. 406).

On U.S.A. see Bentham, *Works*, part VIII, pp. 467 ff, 577 f, part XXI, p. 23. Compare C. K. Ogden, *Jeremy Bentham 1832-2032*, 1932, pp. 90 ff. P. A. Palmer

practically no influence in Germany and, according to William Hazlitt, very little even in England.[3] Nevertheless, considering Bentham's total influence on the nineteenth century, it is almost the repetition of a truism to call him the "prophet" of the whole age of "democratic citizenship" in England, and also the philosopher of the new industrial era.[4] Or if not as a *political* theorist, at least as the democratic reformer of English law, his overwhelming influence on the nineteenth and twentieth centuries is today scarcely disputed.[5] "In no language does

---

in his essay on "Benthamism in England and America" in *The American Political Science Review*, 1941, pp. 855 ff, tries to explain why on the whole Bentham's influence in U.S.A. was slight. Compare C. W. Everett's essay "Bentham and the United States of America" in *Jeremy Bentham and the Law* ed. by George W. Keeton and G. Schwarzenberger, 1948, pp. 185-201.

[3] See W. Hazlitt, *Complete Works*, ed. by P. P. Howe (1930 ff) XI, 5: Bentham's "name is little known in England . . . best of all in the plains of Chili and the mines of Mexico" ("The spirit of the age," 1825). Compare Macaulay, "Mirabeau," 1832, *Miscellaneous Writings*, 1889, pp. 268 f, and G. de Ruggiero, *The History of European Liberalism*, 1927, p. 98. Cf. in the British Museum in a "Collection of Newspaper-Cuttings and printed Announcements Relative to J. Bentham" the following poem by Bowring:

"I have travelled the world and that old man's fame
Wherever I went shone brightly
To his country alone belongs the shame
To think of his labours lightly."

[4] See for instance John MacCunn, *Six Radical Thinkers*, 1907, p. 215 or C. B. R. Kent, *The English Radicals*, 1899, p. 167: nobody "ever did so much to democratise our institutions"; or see W. I. Jennings in J. Macmurry, *Some Makers of the Modern Spirit*, 1933, p. 125: Bentham "had nineteenth-century ideas in eighteenth-century surroundings"; and cf. E. Spranger, *Volk, Staat, Erziehung*, 1932, p. 114: "Die Wohlfahrtsethik hat ihre klassische Gestalt in der englisch-amerikanischen Geistesarbeit empfangen. Dieser grosse Prozess . . . steht . . . seit Bentham in unverkennbarem Zusammenhang mit dem Industrie-und Handelsgeist, der sich zu einem Weltevangelium erweitern möchte."

[5] As with everything in this world, even Bentham's importance as a jurist is not completely undisputed. J. M. Zane in John MacDonell's and E. Manson's *Great Jurists of the World*, 1913, p. 532, states that "Bentham is not a jurist at all," obviously because Bentham was "little versed in the history of English law" and "profoundly ignorant of Roman and Continental law" (see *ibid.*, p. 431). Whether this estimate can be maintained, particularly after the publication of Bentham's *Comment on the Commentaries*, I wish to leave to the judgment of the jurists. Zane even states that "a Cleon or a Bentham are far more convincing than an Aristotle or a Burke, because men are more easily satisfied with words than with facts" (*ibid.*, p. 542). This pronouncement is indeed astonishing, because it is certainly difficult to see how the poetically impressive orator Burke —as a theorist—can be placed on the side of facts and Bentham on the side of empty words. Moreover it is manifestly a partial judgment when Zane (as an avowed adherent of the historical school in jurisprudence) reproaches Bentham because Bentham "never seems to have discovered" that "Bauer, Weiss

7

any other such monument of the legislatorial labour of one mind exist."[6] But can Bentham claim the same or even comparable importance as a moralist? This claim is almost universally contested at present not only in Germany or France, but also in England and America; and even if occasionally granted, it certainly has not been demonstrated hitherto with sufficient detail and comprehensiveness.

Madame de Staël thought Bentham greater than Napoleon;[7] Macaulay, in spite of his general criticism of the utilitarians, placed him in the same rank with Galileo, the founder of modern exact physics;[8] J. M. Guyau drew a parallel between his method and that of Descartes.[9] Stendhal called him the Epicurus of his time and generally

---

and Savigny were living and writing" (*ibid.*, p. 533). For Bentham evidently knew of the existence of the German historical school, see E. Gans, *Rückblicke auf Personen und Zustände*, 1836, pp. 198 ff; and cf. a letter of E. Chadwick, hitherto unpublished in which Chadwick writes to Bentham on June 24, 1831: "I send you for your perusal if you think proper a translation of Von Savigny's work against codification. It is deemed in Germany, as you are perhaps aware, the decisive book on the question." (I am much obliged to Mr. S. E. Finer and Mr. R. A. Lewis for having informed me of this passage in a manuscript first deciphered by them.) For other derogatory judgments on Bentham's juristic work, though not as severely critical, see e.g. in W. G. Miller, *Lectures on the Philosophy of Law*, 1884, p. 417; and A. Kocourek and J. H. Wigmore, *Evolution of Law*, 1915, vol. II, p. 176.

[6] J. H. Burton, "Introduction to the Study of the Works of Jeremy Bentham" in Bentham, *Works*, 1843, part I, p. 12a. Compare C. Phillipson, *Three Criminal Law Reformers*, 1923, p. 109: Bentham's "herculean efforts . . . the creation of one man . . . occupies no mean place by the side of the whole collected body of kindred works produced by hosts of continental writers . . . like Montesquieu, Beccaria, Voltaire and the Encyclopedists."

[7] *The Atlas, a general newspaper and journal of literature, on the largest sheet ever printed*, vol. III, Nr. 89, p. 57, Sunday January 27, 1828, on "Bentham's Writings on Jurisprudence-Rationale of Judicial Evidence": "Madame de Staël said that the eventful times in which we have lived would be described by posterity not as the age of a Bonaparte or a Byron, but as the age of Bentham." "Mr. Bentham is indeed the Father of Jurisprudence in this country." "His own countrymen . . . have been the last in the enlightened world penetrated by the great truths which he has promulgated in his works. . . . He is now grey in age and but just green in his glory. . . . The remark that no man is a prophet in his own country is as ancient as human injustice and for many years of inestimable and unappreciated toil it was applicable to the case of Bentham" (The British Museum, Newspapers Library, Colindale, London).

[8] Macaulay, *The Miscellaneous Writings and Speeches*, 1889, "On Mirabeau," p. 268.

[9] J. M. Guyau, *La morale anglaise contemporaine*, 1879, p. 5. According to J. S. Mill, Bentham "earned a position in moral science analogous to that of Bacon in physical" (*Dissertations and Discussions*, Boston, 1865, vol. III, p. 144, "Dr. Whewell on Moral Philosophy"); and John Neal, the American journalist,

spoke of him with special esteem and wit.[10] In Spain, he has been compared with Solon;[11] Aleksandr Ivanovich Hertzen placed Bentham at the head of those classical writers whom the romanticism of the nineteenth century could not easily discard; and some historians list him, together with Kant and Goethe, among the most original thinkers of his epoch.[12] On the whole, however, his greatness has seemed to be founded exclusively on his achievements in the sphere of law, as a philosopher of jurisprudence.

Dicey thinks that "Bentham was primarily neither a utilitarian moralist, nor a philanthropist: he was a legal philosopher and a reformer of the law."[13] And a similar line is followed by E. Halévy in his standard work on *La formation du radicalisme philosophique.* Halévy combines, as Lujo Brentano and many others did later, an emphasis on Bentham's juristic work with the delineation of his influence upon the legal side of the economic and the political life of the nineteenth century.[14] And so in various forms from the time of the first essays on Bentham, from John Stuart Mill and Théodore Simon Jouffroy down to the present day, we find the same commonplace repeated: Bentham "holds a position in the history of legislative theory rather than in *philosophy* proper."[15] But is this estimate of

reports that also by Samuel Parr, Bentham's *Principles of Morals and Legislation* used to be compared with Bacon's *Novum organum* (see Neal's biographical notice of Bentham, attached to J. Neal, *Principles of Legislation from the MS of Jeremy Bentham,* by M. Dumont, Boston, 1830, p. 11).

[10] See Stendhal, *Oeuvres complètes,* ed. by Paul Arbeleet, 1939, vol. II, p. 133: les préceptes d'Epicure "éclaircis de nos jours par Jérémie Bentham." Compare *ibid.,* pp. 3, 53, 133, 226. Arnaud Caraccio, the editor of Stendhal's *Promenades dans Rome,* 1939, vol. II, p. 370, however, says: "Bentham a plus de valeur comme publiciste que comme philosophe."

[11] G. H. Borrow, *The Bible in Spain,* vol. II, ch. XII, 1908, p. 327: "The most universal genius which the world ever produced, a Solon, a Plato and a Lope de Vega" said the Alcalde of Finisterra on Bentham.

[12] See A. I. Herzen, "Der Dilettantismus in der Wissenschaft," second essay, in *Ausgewählte Schriften* ed. by Alfred Kurella, 1949, p. 36; in Herzen's "Letters to an old friend," Mikhail Aleksandrovich Bakunin, the motto is a quotation from Bentham's letter to Alexander I concerning the secondary relevance of motives, see *ibid.,* p. 599. See further J. T. Merz, *A History of European Thought in the 19th Century,* 1924, vol. IV, p. 139.

[13] A. V. Dicey, *Lectures on the Relations between Law and Public Opinion in England during the 19th Century,* 1924, p. 127.

[14] L. Brentano, *Eine Geschichte der wirtschaftlichen Entwicklung Englands,* Bd. III, 1. Hälfte, 1928, S. 60 ff; S. 66 brings even the victory of the free trade and economic consequences of the abolition of slavery into relation to the work of Bentham.

[15] See A. Seth Pringle Pattison, *The Philosophical Radicals,* 1907 (written

9

Bentham just? Did not the Duke of Leeds at the time of Bentham's youth show more insight in nicknaming the boy "the philosopher"?[16]

Obviously, different successive phases in the evaluation of Bentham's work have to be distinguished. The period in England from about 1825 till the death of J. S. Mill (1873) could be called simply the period of Benthamism.[17] Then, during the last third of the nineteenth century and the beginning of the twentieth, after the immediate disciples had finished their work, a strong movement of collectivism took the place

1901), p. 17; and compare J. S. Mill, "Bentham," in *Works*, vol. IV (The New Universal Library), p. 298: "It is fortunate for the world that Bentham's taste lay rather in the direction of jurisprudential than of properly ethical inquiry"; p. 300: in the department of law "he accomplished his greatest triumphs." Compare Th. S. Jouffroy, *Cours de Droit Naturel*, 1843, p. 376: "Bentham n'est pas un métaphysicien, mais un légiste"; p. 378: "Bentham . . . est éminemment légiste et pas du tout philosophe"; Th. S. Jouffroy, *Introduction to Ethics*, translated from the French, vol. II, 1840, p. 7: "Bentham was not a philosopher, but a jurist." Leslie Stephen, *The English Utilitarians*, 1900, vol. I, p. 271: Bentham "did . . . in the theory of legislation . . . very well without philosophy," but "he is clearly not satisfactory in ethics" (p. 270). A. V. Dicey, *Lectures on Law and Public Opinion in England*, 1924, p. 137: "The principle of utility is far more easily applicable to law than to morals." C. B. Kent, *The English Radicals*, 1899, p. 185: "Bentham was before everything a law-reformer." E. Albee, *A History of English Utilitarianism*, 1902, p. 190: "Bentham contributed almost nothing of importance to Ethics considered strictly as such." Stephen Ward, *Ethics, an Historical Introduction*, 1924, p. 75: Bentham's first aim was not to write an ethical theory but to reform the law. Compare P. Janet and G. Séailles, *A History of the Problems of Philosophy*, 1902, vol. II, p. 76. J. L. Stocks, *Jeremy Bentham*, 1933, p. 19: "Bentham . . . can hardly be reckoned a philosopher at all." C. R. Morris in Alfred Barrat Brown, *Great Democrats*, 1934, p. 41: "The real moral or philosophical insight contributed to mankind" by Bentham "was negligible"; A. K. Rogers, *English and American Philosophy since 1800*, 1922, p. 53: "While Utilitarianism is on one side a hedonistic theory of life for the individual man, it is not as such that Bentham is mainly interested in it, but as a program, rather, of legal and political reform." Even in his later work, *Morals in Review*, 1927, where Rogers comes to an interestingly greater appreciation of Bentham's ethics, he repeats, p. 310: "While as a social and political method Benthamism is a more defensible philosophy than its rivals, one cannot call attention to these merits without at the same time suggesting qualifications"; Bentham's "interest in the more inclusive field of private morality tends to stop with . . . still a legislative question." A. G. Fuller, *A History of Philosophy*, 1938, vol. II, p. 511: "Bentham was not interested so much in the strictly ethical implications of his doctrine as in its economic and political bearings. Utilitarianism is most closely associated with the name of John Stuart Mill." Miguel de Unamuno, *Del sentimiento trágico de la Vida*, 1931, p. 108: "Stuart Mill, éste el más consecuente y logico de los positivistas."

[16] Bentham, *Works*, 1843, part XIX, p. 31a.

[17] A. V. Dicey, *Law and Public Opinion*, 1924, pp. 496, 126-210, 259 ff. Compare H. S. Maine, *Ancient Law*, 1930, p. 90 on "the secret of Bentham's immense influence in England."

of Benthamite individualism; and in philosophy an epoch of idealism followed the predominance of utilitarian positivism. So that about the year 1900, the work of Bentham was regarded by philosophers as of historical rather than of systematic interest; and nearly all the most distinguished historical works on Bentham and the philosophical radicals appeared between 1899 and 1902. From the systematic standpoint, according to Graham Wallas, it was only the average unphilosophical Englishman of that day whose intellectual life was "spent among the ruins of utilitarianism."[18] Today, it seems, only a hopelessly small number of voices insist that Bentham's thought still has a great future. C. K. Ogden prophesied, as recently as 1932, "that Bentham's greatest triumphs are still to come" in the second century after his death, that is, between 1932 and 2032;[19] and Ogden himself tried to elucidate the special significance which he attributes to Bentham's theory of fictions.[20] In support of this new evaluation of the great jurist, the present study aims at showing the value which Bentham's ethical method still has today.

It was, however, not only his reputation as a lawyer that stood in the way of an appreciation of Bentham as a philosopher. Perhaps even more prejudicial was the quite common assumption that Bentham was, at most, a kind of intellectual inspirer of his more philosophically gifted successors, James Mill and J. S. Mill;[21] and it is very character-

[18] G. Wallas, *The Great Society*, 1924, p. 95. In Robert Louis Stevenson's "The Story of a Lie," written in 1879, an old English Squire uses the term "a Benthamite" as a gross invective, see Stevenson's *Works*, 1925, vol. x, p. 179.

[19] C. K. Ogden, *Jeremy Bentham 1832-2032*, 1932, p. 14. Cf. e.g. Victor Cohen, *Jeremy Bentham*, 1927, p. 18: "If his psychology was premature, he nevertheless made potent a method of submitting every institution and every belief to the pitiless searchlight of utility."

[20] See *Bentham's Theory of Fictions*, edited and with a detailed introduction published by C. K. Ogden, 1932, and C. K. Ogden, *Jeremy Bentham*, 1932, pp. 35ff.

[21] See e.g. W. R. Sorley, *A History of English Philosophy*, 1920, p. 215; James Mill "was less of a jurist than Bentham, but more of a philosopher, and better equipped for the defence of . . . fundamental principles on psychological and general grounds." Cf. E. Albee, *A History of English Utilitarianism*, 1902, p. 267: "Seldom . . . has a personality counted for more in the whole history of Ethics" than J. S. Mill; p. 165: I "dissent from . . . the opinion that Bentham contributed anything essentially new to ethical theory." Compare W. Fite, *An Introductory Study of Ethics*, 1903, p. 56: "The classical document of hedonism is J. S. Mill's Utilitarianism . . . Bentham . . . is a loose, unphilosophical, yet entertaining writer"; R. A. Tsanoff, *The Moral Ideals of Our Civilization*, 1942, p. 491: J. S. Mill "retained for Bentham a gratitude which . . . preserved a spirit of solidarity beyond the required."

istic that, in Muirhead's collection of intellectual autobiographies written by the leaders of "contemporary British philosophy," 1924-25, the name of Bentham is not mentioned at all, while that of J. S. Mill is mentioned extremely often. It was hardly ever remembered that, as Henry Sidgwick and Eugène Dupréel[22] observed, Bentham is at least a more "exact . . . thinker"[23] than any of the other utilitarians. It is still very rare that anyone holds the view of René LeSenne that Bentham is "le plus original et le plus pénétrant des utilitaires"[24] or the view of C. K. Ogden, who says: "The more . . . I read of the older Benthamites (particularly of that intrepid, but somewhat monolithic, ratiocinator, James Mill) the more I feel it essential that one should first have read the humorous and very human Bentham."[25]

But the question is not only: who was the greater thinker, Bentham or James Mill or J. S. Mill? It is still more important to ask: Were Bentham and the Mills actually occupied with quite identical problems? Is there not a difference between Bentham's and J. S. Mill's thought, as clear and wide as the difference between the thought of Kant and his successors, not only as regards their answers to certain questions but even as regards those questions themselves? It is true that we are accustomed to speak as if there were a uniform creed of the utilitarians, or as if there were one single characteristic expression of German idealism. But if it is unsafe to look at Kant with the eyes of Hegel, is it less a mistake to see Bentham solely through the eyes of J. S. Mill?

At any rate, I think, it should be asked first: which are the ethical problems of Bentham himself? This has to be done before a doctrine common to all utilitarians is presupposed. Perhaps we will discover then that many of Bentham's most fascinating questions have been veiled by inquiries of the later utilitarians; while they have much in common with them in sound, they have far less in substance.

Certainly, James Mill and J. S. Mill represented themselves much more specifically as philosophers than did the master of the utilitarian school; and so Bentham shares the fate of many thinkers who have worked inspiringly in more than one field of intellectual life. Their names are often better known than their work because, for further explanation of their greatness, the philosopher refers to the jurist, the

[22] E. Dupréel, *Traité de Morale*, 1932, vol. 1, p. 52, sees in Bentham even "l'un des génies les plus systématiques que le monde ait connus"; but he dissociates himself from Bentham's utilitarianism far more than Sidgwick.
[23] H. Sidgwick, *The Methods of Ethics*, 1874, p. 68, 1901, pp. 41, 94.
[24] R. Le Senne, *Traité de morale générale*, 1942, p. 216.
[25] C. K. Ogden, *Jeremy Bentham, 1832-2032*, 1932, p. 17.

lawyer refers to the philosopher, and the political scientist refers to the philosopher *and* the jurist, while the overlapping parts of the activity of such intellectual leaders are commonly lost sight of.

Besides this, the larger public prefers to study movements such as utilitarianism in the works of those who bring them to completion rather than in the writings of their inspirers; and such a consummator was, in nearly everyone's opinion—including his own—John Stuart Mill. Bentham was hardly ever credited with having completed the utilitarian system.

Finally, a third danger of blurring one's vision exists in the often deplored state of the publications of Bentham. Perhaps nobody in the modern literary world was more careless in his way of communicating his ideas. Spinoza did not publish his chief work before his death, and did not wish that his name should appear on the title page; but he himself most carefully revised and completed this principal work before he died. Kant waited for the fifty-seventh year of his life before publishing any of his important philosophical writings. But Bentham, with quite unique unconcern, in his later years generally left the final shaping of his ideas and their selection for publication to his friends and pupils, while he himself was only interested in filling up page after page. About 75,000 sheets are stored in 173 boxes in the cellars of University College in London; and several big volumes of Benthamiana in the British Museum also contain numerous manuscripts of Jeremy Bentham, apart from papers concerning his family. Only a relatively small part of Bentham's writings, together with the reprint of his first books, a collection of letters, and extracts from diaries, have been published (and that in a somewhat revised form) in an edition of 11 volumes or 22 parts by John Bowring, 1843. But the whole of the anonymous writings of Bentham on religious topics, his *Deontology* and the French text of the treatises first published in French by Etienne Dumont are not to be found in the only edition of Bentham's collected works. F. Jodl has, therefore, spoken with some reason of a "babylonische Verwirrung"[26] which has necessarily to be overcome before the original edition of a number of Bentham's writings can be found. Siegwart wrote a whole book in 1910 for the sole purpose of clearing up these bibliographical questions.[27] And today, first publications

[26] F. Jodl, *Geschichte der Ethik als philosophischer Wissenschaft*, 1912, vol. II, p. 703.
[27] A. Siegwart, *Benthams Werke und ihre Publikation*, 1910 (Aus dem Politi-

of Bentham manuscripts are dispersed in still more scattered places.[28]

Yet, by the utilization of this greater number of original publications and of unpublished manuscripts, it is today possible to give a far more extensive and precise account of Bentham's ethical ideas and of their fundamental importance for the ethics of today. This is the task of the present work.

---

schen Jahrbuch der Schweizerischen Eidgenossenschaft, ed. by C. Hilty and W. Burckhardt).

[28] The most complete bibliography of Bentham's works has been compiled by C. W. Everett in the appendix of the English translation of E. Halévy's "La formation du radicalisme philosophique," *The Growth of Philosophic Radicalism*, 1928, pp. 527 ff, supplementing similar catalogues published by Leslie Stephen in vol. I, of his *English Utilitarians*, 1900, pp. 319 ff, and by A. Siegwart, *Benthams Werke und ihre Publikation*, 1910. Arnold Muirhead, "A Jeremy Bentham Collection," in *The Library*, Oxford, Fifth Series, vol. I, No. I, June 1946, pp. 6-27, contains also a great number of important bibliographical notes. In *The Library of Congress Quarterly Journal of Acquisitions*, vol. I, No. 20, 1944, p. 40 f, I reported my finding the only copy of volume II of Bentham's *Constitutional Code*, 1830, which is now known to exist.

PRELUDE
Bentham's Earliest Writings

PRELUDE

Bentham's Earliest Writings

THE ANONYMOUS ESSAYS IN *THE GAZETTEER* AND THE PREFACE TO THE TRANSLATION OF VOLTAIRE'S *LE TAUREAU BLANC*

EVEN Bentham's early writings, which were published in part for the first time only a few years ago, are, I believe, of considerably greater interest than has generally been realized. In the first small essays which Bentham sent anonymously to *The Gazetteer*,[1] there are already to be found some striking critical observations of the young philosopher who was only about twenty-three years of age when he made them.

John Bowring and C. H. Atkinson assume that the first essays of Bentham were some letters addressed to the *Gazetteer*, signed Irenaeus, which were written to repel an attack upon Lord Mansfield and printed in 1771.[2] But C. K. Ogden has been able to show that Bowring and even Bentham's own memory were at fault on this point:[3] Bentham's first publication, signed Irenius (not Irenaeus) had already appeared on December 3, 1770, several months before these letters; and it concerned quite another topic, namely, a criticism of a document which appeared over the signatures of Wedderburn, Glynn and Dunning on November 26, with the heading "Inlisting of Seamen for his Majesty's Service" (see Appendix III of the present volume).

This very short essay has, indeed, a kind of symbolic significance. For it already contains indications of one of the most characteristic and

---

[1] From these essays only parts have been recently reprinted by Ogden in his *Jeremy Bentham 1832-2032*, 1932, pp. 52 ff. As my quotations from the first of these pieces are not to be found in Ogden, I give its full text as Appendix III of the present work.

[2] See C. H. M. Atkinson, *Jeremy Bentham, His Life and Work*, 1905, p. 26 and J. Bowring in "The Works of Bentham," 1843, part XIX, p. 67 f.

[3] C. K. Ogden, *Jeremy Bentham*, 1932, p. 53; compare C. W. Everett in his bibliography of *The Growth of Philosophic Radicalism* by E. Halévy, 1928, p. 544. But Everett, *The Education of Jeremy Bentham*, 1931, p. 46, is obviously mistaken in assuming that Bentham's letters defending Mansfield were "his first essays in print" and that they were written in 1770. Also J. H. Burton in Bentham's *Works*, ed. Bowring, part XXII, p. ccxxiii, is wrong on this point.

meritorious tendencies of Bentham's ethics and jurisprudence: his "censorial,"[4] critical attitude toward all reasons given for accepted moral valuations and their unquestioned acceptance.

In this first publication, Bentham has already distinguished with precision between all questions concerning the inquiry as to "what the law *is*" and the quite different questions concerning "the *new laws*" which have to be "woven from the cobweb-materials of ancient barbarism."[5] The subsequent attacks on Blackstone and other moralists which occupied his whole life are already foreshadowed in his polemic against the "Serjeant-at-Law" John Glynn, whom he reproaches as a "Janus" with a "double countenance." According to Bentham, Glynn constantly confused the inquiry into existing laws with the inquiry about laws which ought to exist, and he liked as a "Counsellor to his clients to sell them another judgment, when they pay him for his own."[6]

In short, in this essay Bentham is already assailing the same type of jurists and moralists he attacked later on, men to whom he cries with all the youthful freshness of his language: "with loudness you proclaimed that pressing was illegal: in silence you affixed your seal to its legality"—lawyers with a "double countenance . . . one facing the higher world, the other working contrary intimations to the gaping populace below,"[6] men who identified "what the law is" with the "new laws" which ought to be. Thus, this short essay, with its striking ethical zeal, is an extremely fitting opening note to the career of a great moral theorist and a reformer of the law. It certainly deserves to be made more accessible than in the single copy of the *Gazetteer* in the British Museum Library.

The second publication of Bentham, which also appeared in the *Gazetteer and New Daily Advertiser* on Friday March 1, 1771 and Monday March 18, 1771, consists of two letters written for the purpose of vindicating the honor of Lord Mansfield which had been attacked by a writer who signed himself Touchstone; but for the history of ethics these essays seem to me of less interest than the polemic

[4] See Bentham, *A Fragment on Government*, ed. F. C. Montague, 1891, pp. 98 ff, 106.

[5] *The Gazetteer and New Daily Advertiser*, Monday December 3, 1770, p. 2, column 1 (British Museum, State Papers Reading Room, Burney Collection).

[6] *The Gazetteer and New Daily Advertiser*, Monday December 3, 1770, p. 2, column 1.

against John Glynn, though from the political and historical point of view the defense of Lord Mansfield is perhaps more relevant.

It remains, however, significant of Bentham's general attitude that in his defense of Lord Mansfield he protests again, in the style of the great reformers of the eighteenth century, against "the rubbish of antiquity." He demands that a careful distinction be drawn between the "two *sources* from which *literary* as well as other *productions* derive their value totally opposite and unconnected . . . these are *merit* and *rarity* to which latter *antiquity* may be referred."[7] But in his view, it would be absurd to believe that "an author must have a *great deal* of merit because he wrote a *great while* ago at a time when nobody else wrote upon the subject."[8] Therefore, the main advice he gives to his opponent Touchstone (who "retailed" to us in his attack on Lord Mansfield the "nonsensical" old "story about 'judges,' hanging, and 'King Alfred' ") is to make of [sic] the rubbish of antiquity to pack up his *black letter books* with honest Andrew among the rest and . . . to dispatch them away to Jackton's or to Wagstaffe's.[9] For, as he finally

[7] *Ibid.*, Monday March 18, 1771, p. 2, column 1. This passage is not reprinted by Ogden. Touchstone's answer to Bentham's first letter of Friday March 1, 1771, p. 1, is no longer to be found in the British Museum Library.

[8] *Ibid.*, Monday March 18, 1771; Ogden, *Jeremy Bentham*, 1932, p. 57. How far Bentham goes in his fight against antiquity may be inferred from another remark of these essays in which he apparently intends to express the conviction that all early art must as art be of lower value than that of modern times (see Ogden, *Jeremy Bentham*, 1932, p. 56). This would be another proof of a rather undeveloped understanding of art which is noticeable in Bentham. He once showed some interest in the painted glass of Fairford Church mentioned in a letter to his father on August 24, 1766, Add. MSS British Museum 33, 537, p. 161, published in C. W. Everett, *The Education of Jeremy Bentham*, p. 42; but in general he lacked any understanding of the problems of medieval painting (see e.g. *ibid.*, p. 162, *Works*, part xix, pp. 157b, 158a). We are told that Bentham had some interest in good music (see *Works*, part xix, p. 32: "To the end of his days the music of Handel was delightful to him"). Only John F. Colls, *Utilitarianism Unmasked*, 1844, p. 17, denounces him for the habit of singing vulgar songs such as those from *The Beggars Opera*—a taste which today, however, would be reason for much less censure. As we shall show later, in psychological and historical questions demanding artistic sensibility, Bentham's limitations can be clearly seen.

[9] "Two booksellers who deal in that kind of literature," see *The Gazetteer and New Daily Advertiser*, Friday March 1, 1771, p. 1, column 4. This passage is not printed in Ogden. The story to which both Touchstone and his authority "honest Andrew Horn" refer is, in fact, not considered authentic. Historians doubt that King Alfred of England in the ninth century ever ordered the hanging of judges. Bentham, therefore, advised his opponent Touchstone to give up all these references to ancient English law, to such questionable authorities as Andrew

remarks pointedly, "moderation" should never be confounded with "dullness."[10]

After the printing of these three letters in the *Gazetteer* only one other publication came out before the appearance of his first book in 1776: this was his translation in 1774 of Voltaire's *Taureau Blanc*, anonymously edited as *The White Bull, an oriental history from an ancient Syrian manuscript communicated by Mr. Voltaire cum notis editoris et variorum: sc., the whole faithfully done into English.*

The long preface Bentham wrote to this translation of Voltaire is characteristic in that here he already attacks Blackstone's *Commentaries on the Laws of England*,[11] and that he praises Barrington's "Observations on the Ancient Statutes,"[12] as he does later on. It is also of some interest that he quotes Adam Ferguson's *Essay on the History of Civil Society*,[13] and that he ironically calls "Bishop Butler's Analogy: one of the profoundest books that ever was written in behalf of the system of unaccountables"[14]—apart from other rather satirical remarks on religion.[15]

Horn, and to sell all the "black letter books" from which he quoted to the junk dealer.

Andrew Horn, a fishmonger and chamberlain of the City of London who died in 1328 is said to be the author of *The Mirror of Justices* which was printed in 1642 in the black letter. It is interesting to see how little historical and juristic value Bentham attributes to *The Mirror of Justices* in 1771, more than half a century before Francis Palgrave's analysis in the *Quarterly Review*, 1826. See further details on Andrew Horn's work, e.g. in W. S. Holdsworth, *A History of English Law*, 1923, vol. II, pp. 327-333; Sir Frederick Pollock, *Law Quarterly Review*, vol. XI, pp. 395 ff; H. Potter, *An Introduction to the History of English Law*, 1926, p. 35.

[10] *The Gazetteer and New Daily Advertiser*, Monday March 18, 1771, p. 2, column 1.

[11] See *The White Bull, an Oriental History*, 1774, for instance p. xli: "as bad as Dr. Blackstone's Commentaries" and compare *ibid.*, pp. xxxiv, xxxviii, lxxviii, lxxxviii.

[12] *Ibid.*, p. xxxii.   [13] *Ibid.*, p. xlviii.   [14] *Ibid.*, p. 40.

[15] *Ibid.*, p. xxv: "In an inspired work, as everybody knows, morality is an affair of very inferior consideration." A. Muirhead, "A Jeremy Bentham Collection" in *The Library*, June 1946, p. 9, mentions two further translations published by the young Bentham: part of a novel by Jean François Marmontel, and in 1783 the famous Swedish chemist Torbern Olof Bergman's essay *Anledning til Foreläsningar öfver chemiens beskaffenhet och nytta, samt naturlige kroppars almännaste skiljaktigheter*—a work apparently first published in 1779 by Henrik Theophil Scheffer. But as Mr. Muirhead kindly informed me, he cannot give more detailed information about these two publications.

A FRAGMENT ON GOVERNMENT

It is, however, certainly not from these first small journalistic attempts that we can today gain a larger insight into the tendencies of the freshest and most vivid works of Bentham's youth. This can be reached only by the analysis of the first sizable book written by the young jurist, a criticism of William Blackstone's *Commentaries on the Laws of England*, of which the larger part was first printed in 1928 by Charles Warren Everett from the manuscripts of University College; only a small part of this work was known until then, viz. *A Fragment on Government*, published anonymously in 1776.

I shall therefore start with an explanation of the *Fragment on Government*—that part of the book which was published by the author himself—and then supplement this analysis by the contemplation of the whole work, which was unknown before 1928 and has not hitherto been subjected to any detailed ethical analysis. To this we shall add a brief series of Bentham's notes, selected from his manuscripts in University College, London, and not published before, but obviously written about the same time, and lastly some memoranda mentioned in Bowring's biography which also have relevance in this connection.

Wherein lies the special significance of Bentham's *Fragment on Government* and of his *Comment on the Commentaries*, these "slashing attacks"[16] on Sir William Blackstone, one of the most respected authorities in the history of English law? What is the importance of these two works? Not, certainly, Bentham's criticism of any juristic details of Blackstone's famous commentaries. Rather, it is the masterly and profound analysis of the moral background of this well-rounded exposition of English law. Blackstone was, beyond all doubt, a most able interpreter of the existing English law; and Bentham himself never intended to deny this. Yet, as a moral and legal theorist or philosopher, Blackstone was the prototype of an eclectic, by no means consistent mind. He tried primarily to give a graceful, eloquent exposition of the law, borrowing arguments from different leading theories rather than using any original reasoning. So Bentham's polemic is, in truth, much less concerned with the specific teaching of Blackstone than with all

[16] J. L. Stocks, *Jeremy Bentham*, 1933, p. 8.

21

the older legal and moral theories eclectically combined in Blackstone.

Like Nietzsche's controversy with David Friedrich Strauss, Kant's polemic against Eberhard, or Pascal's "Lettres provinciales," Bentham's criticism of Blackstone is less directed against one person or a group of persons than against whole systems of thought. Even what seems to be personal hostility in such writings has actually more general and systematic value than is apparent at first sight.

As in Helvétius[17] so in Bentham, ethical and juristic problems are most closely connected. But we must here separate these questions from each other; and especially in analyzing the *Fragment on Government*, we have to renounce all detail concerning the political and juristic aspects of Bentham's deductions, particularly since these arguments are clearly enough developed by the author himself and are in general sufficiently known. Bentham himself concentrated his discussion in the *Fragment* on general principles, and limited his polemic to the criticism of Blackstone's introduction to the *Commentaries on the Laws of England*. Moreover, even of this first introductory chapter of Blackstone's work, Bentham analyzed only the second and third sections. But it is precisely in the fundamental arguments of this early work that we observe how much more original and fascinating is the ethical discussion than the juristic and political one.

The Parallel between Ethics and Natural Science

In the *Fragment on Government*, Bentham starts the preface by an interesting parallel between the natural sciences and moral philosophy —an assumption of correspondence between the natural and the ethical world which has been, in general, flatly denied by philosophers down the ages and only the other day again by Ortega y Gasset.[18] But Ben-

[17] Claude Adrien Helvétius, *Oeuvres complètes*, 1818, tome I, p. 219, "De l'esprit," discours II, chapitre 24: "Je regarde . . . la morale et la législation . . . comme une seule et même science." Compare discours II, chap. VI, p. 74.

[18] See José Ortega y Gasset, e.g. *Teoría de Andalucía y otros ensayos*, 1942, p. 208: "En la mente, al revés que en el mundo presentado por los sentidos, ningún hecho se da de hecho aislado, sino que tan hecho como él mismo, tan patente y primario como él es el hecho de su conexión con otros." And as Ortega adds (see his *Concord and Liberty*, 1944, p. 179): "My willing something always points back for its motive to a value feeling that has prompted me to adopt" certain ends. "And this valuation in turn presents itself as founded on, or mo-

tham insists on the necessity of such a presupposition throughout his ethical thought. And this is a characteristic and, as I think, a very valuable feature of his philosophy of morals, a leitmotif which is more original and goes much further than the old doctrine of the *jus naturae*, the assumption of a so-called law of nature in ethics.[19] Bentham himself admits that the supposition of a parallel between natural and moral philosophy is certainly not a common one; on the contrary, it is nearly everywhere rejected. But he declares from the very outset that, though it seems to be "a common notion . . . that in the moral world there no longer remains any matter for discovery," he is convinced that "reformation in the moral world . . . is . . . correspondent to *discovery* and *improvement* in the natural world."[20] And reformation in the moral world is just as necessary as discovery and improvement in the world of nature.

In alluding to the most important chemical and geographical research of his epoch, Bentham sums up his first formulation of the claims of ethics in the following impressive words: "If it be of importance and of use to us to know the principles of the element we

---

tivated by, my perceptions and ideas of things. . . . An authentic and radical positivism resolved to accept mental facts as they are" takes this into account.

Perhaps the most conclusive argument hitherto developed against the contradistinction between the knowledge of nature and that of values is to be found in C. I. Lewis' *An Analysis of Knowledge and Valuation*, 1946—a work which in its preface and by its whole structure "points out the extended parallel between valuation and the more commonly considered types of empirical knowledge," see *ibid.*, p. viii, and compare p. xi: "We cannot finally escape the fact that ethics and epistemology and the theory of meaning are essentially connected." Compare further Richard von Mises' protest against the establishment of any "Normwissenschaft" in opposition to "Seinswissenschaften" in his *Kleines Lehrbuch des Positivismus*, 1939, pp. 380 ff.

[19] Compare for instance *An Introduction to the Principles of Morals and Legislation*, New edition Oxford, 1879, chap. xvi, 58 note, chap. vi, 5 note, chap. vii, 27 note, preface, p. xiii (*Works*, part i, p. iv), chap. viii, 5 note, chap. xiv, 8 note, chap. xi, sect. 42, explanation of rule iv; MSS, University College, London, Portfolio 32, quoted in E. Halévy, *La formation du radicalisme philosophique*, 1901, tome i, p. 289 f; *Comment on the Commentaries*, ed. Everett, 1928, p. 234 f note; *Works*, 1843, vol. viii, pp. 245b, 246a, note ("Essay on Logic"); *Works*, 1943, vol. iii, p. 273b ("Nomography," chap. vii, §3); *Works*, 1843, part ii, p. 304b ("Principles of the Civil Code," on the moral thermometer); *Works*, 1843, vol. vii, p. 393 ("Rationale of Judicial Evidence"); *Works*, 1843, vol. vi, p. 239a ("Rationale of Judicial Evidence"), *Works*, 1843, part iv, p. 454a ("Book of Fallacies"); *Deontology*, ed. Bowring, 1834, vol. i, p. 316, vol. ii, p. 52 f.

[20] *A Fragment on Government*, by J. Bentham, ed. by F. C. Montague, 1891, p. 93 (*Works*, 1843, vol. i, p. 227a).

breathe,[21] surely it is not of much less importance nor of much less use
to comprehend the principles, and endeavour at the improvement of
those laws, by which alone we breathe it in security . . . if it be a
matter of importance and of use to us to be made acquainted with
distant countries, surely it is not a matter of much less importance, nor
of much less use to us, to be made better and better acquainted with
the chief means of living happily in our *own*."[22] And how central the
wish to extend the methods of physics to ethical research always was
in Bentham's mind may, perhaps, best be illustrated by a remark in
one of Bentham's manuscripts, probably written about the time of the
publication of his first book and first quoted by Halévy: "The present
work as well as any other work of mine that has been or will be published on the subject of legislation or any other branch of moral science is an attempt to extend the experimental method of reasoning
from the physical branch to the moral."[23] Certainly, some attempts to
apply the methods of physics to ethics had already been made before
Bentham, for instance by Helvétius;[24] and the very title of Hume's
Treatise of Human Nature contains the addition: "being an attempt to
introduce the experimental method of reasoning into moral subjects."
Today any epistemological comparison between the methods of science
and those of ethics doubtless stands in need of still greater refinement
than Bentham could give these difficult questions. But, as we shall see
later, on this and on other points he is certainly more radical and consistent than his predecessors and most of his successors.

The "Censorial" Problem in Ethics

Equal consistency is to be recognized in the *Fragment on Government* with regard to a second distinctive tendency of Bentham's whole
work, viz. the radically "questioning spirit" of his philosophy.

As to this, John Stuart Mill went right down to the marrow of Ben-

[21] *Ibid.*, p. 94 (*Works*, vol. I, p. 227a). In 1774—only two years before the
publication of Bentham's *Fragment*—Priestley had discovered oxygen, his "dephlo-
gisticated air."
[22] Bentham, *A Fragment on Government*, ed. by Montague, 1891, p. 94 (Bentham, *Works*, 1843, vol. I, p. 227a).
[23] E. Halévy, *La formation du radicalisme philosophique*, 1901, vol. I, p. 289 f.
[24] See C. A. Helvétius, *Oeuvres complètes*, tome I, 1818, "De l'esprit," preface,
p. vii: "On devait traiter la morale comme toutes les autres sciences et faire une
morale comme une physique expérimentale." Or compare *ibid.*, discours II, chap.
2, p. 49: "Si l'univers physique est soumis aux lois du mouvement, l'univers
morale ne l'est pas moins à celles de l'intérêt."

tham's ethics and theory of legislation in stressing that nowhere can be found a deeper "questioning spirit," a more profound "disposition to demand the why of everything"[25] than in Bentham, the "father of English innovation, both in doctrines and institutions."[26] Bentham was, indeed, the greatest "questioner of things established . . . in this . . . country."[25] Or, again to quote J. S. Mill, "in the language of continental philosophers": Bentham was "the great critical thinker of his age and country."[26] Today, however, a hundred years later, considerable opposition would be encountered if one still counted Bentham among the finest critical minds which the last two centuries of European culture have produced.

During nearly the same years in which Bentham wrote his *Fragment on Government* and his *Comment on the Commentaries*, Kant also was preparing a critical theory of nature, of ethics and of law, a *Critique of Pure Reason*, a *Critique of Practical Reason*, and a critical jurisprudence in the first part of his *Metaphysik der Sitten*. But it seems to me that, in his ethics at least, Kant showed himself a far less consistent "critic" than Bentham. For Kant never actually called into question the results of common ethical valuation as Bentham did. On the contrary, he acknowledged them and, in the preface of his *Critique of Practical Reason*, he affirmed explicitly that the commonly accepted rules of morality are not in need of any reform. He aims only at finding a new, more exact formula embracing all possible cases of existing, acknowledged moral imperatives;[27] and for this purpose alone he criticized the ethical formulas developed in the theories of moral sense—theories that assumed the existence of a particular moral faculty.

But Bentham critically examined on principle even the *results* of *common* ethical belief. In this respect, I think, J. S. Mill has underrated Bentham's radicalism. For, in order to illustrate the radical character of Bentham's ethics, Mill characteristically quotes a statement from the "Essay on the Promulgation of Laws" which is, in truth, in

[25] J. S. Mill, *Works*, vol. IV (The New Universal Library), p. 271 (*Dissertations and Discussions, Political, Philosophical and Historical*, 1861, vol. I, p. 357).

[26] *Ibid.*, p. 273.

[27] Kant's *Critique of Practical Reason*, transl. by Th. K. Abbott, 1883, p. 93: "Who would think of introducing a new principle of all morality and making himself as it were the first discoverer of it, just as if all the world before him were ignorant what duty was or had been in thoroughgoing error? But whoever knows of what importance to a mathematician a *formula* is which defines accurately what is to be done to work a problem, will not think that a formula is insignificant and useless which does the same for all duty in general."

comparison with other statements of Benthamite radicalism, particularly moderate; and Bentham himself in his manuscript did not formulate his argument in as moderate terms as his editors Dumont and Bowring, and his interpreter Mill. Unfortunately, Mill did not take the reference in question from Bentham's original text but from the English translation of Dumont's first French edition of the *Traités de législation civile et pénale*.[28]

[28] It is, I think, worth while illustrating by this one example how Dumont and, in this particular case, Bowring and J. S. Mill as well softened down the meaning of Bentham's sentences, even when Bentham was quoted relatively accurately in French and then translated into English. The four texts in question are the following:

Bentham writes in a MS not yet published (University College, London, Portfolio 100. Folder 3, sheet 43, p. 11, written about 1790):	*E. Dumont* publishes this in his *Traités de Législation*, 1802, tome III, pp. 294f; 1820, tome III, pp. 86f:	*J. Bowring* prints this in his edition of Bentham's works, 1843, part I, p. 161b:	*John S. Mill* quotes and interprets in his essay on Bentham (*Westminster Review*, April-August 1838, p. 424) in the following way:
"Il y a des vérités maximes qu'il faut prouver non pas pour faire recevoir ces mêmes vérités, (pour les faire recevoir elles-mêmes), mais pour en faire recevoir d'autres, mais pour faire recevoir d'autres vérités" [Very carelessly written, as the repetition shows. Then with pencil in the margin: Vérités palpables à prouver pour faire recevoir celles qui ne le sont pas]. Telles (sic) sont la mauvaise qualité de certaines actions/tout le monde en convient et le besoin qu'il y a de les faire punir. L'assassinat est une mauvaise action, tout le monde en convient: la punition en doit être sévère: tout le monde en convient de même. *Si donc il faut s'attacher à faire voir la mauvaise qualité* de l'assassinat et le besoin qu'il y a d'y attacher une peine	"Il est des vérités qu'il faut prouver non pour elles-mêmes, puisqu'elles sont reconnues, mais pour conduire à d'autres vérités *qui en dépendent*. Il faut démontrer les vérités palpables pour faire adopter celles qui ne le sont pas. C'est par elles qu'on parvient à faire recevoir *le vrai principe*, qui, une fois reçu, prépare les voies à toutes les autres vérités. L'assassinat est une mauvaise action, tout le monde en convient: la peine en doit être sévère, tout le monde en convient encore. Si donc il est besoin d'analyser les *funestes effets* de l'assassinat, ce sera comme un degré nécessaire pour amener les hommes à trouver bon que la loi distingue entre différens assassinats, qu'elle en punisse les différentes espèces selon la malignité relative, qu'elle ne punisse pas ou	"There are truths which it is necessary to prove; not for their own sakes, because they are acknowledged, but that an opening may be made for the reception of other truths *which depend upon* them. It is necessary to demonstrate certain palpable truths, in order that others, which may depend upon them, may be adopted. It is in this manner we provide for the reception of *first principles*, which, once received, prepare the way for the admission of all other truths. All the world acknowledges that assassination is an evil action: its punishment ought to be severe: everybody is agreed again. If it is necessary to analyze the *mischievous effects of assassination*, it will be necessary as a step towards bringing men to acknowledge the fitness of the	"There are truths which it is necessary to prove, not for their own sakes, because they are acknowledged, but that an opening may be made for the reception of other truths which *depend upon them*. It is in this manner we provide for the reception of *first principles*, which, once received, prepare the way for admission of all other truths." To which may be added, that in this manner also do we discipline the mind for practising the same sort of dissection upon questions more complicated and of more doubtful issue.

plus ou moins sévère, ce ne sera pas pour que les hommes trouvent bien qu'on défende l'assassinat et qu'on lui attache cette peine; c'est pour qu'ils trouvent bon qu'on en punisse les différentes espèces selon la malignité relative; qu'on leur aura prouvé c'est pour qu'ils trouvent bon qu'on laisse impuni (sic) ou punisse d'une peine moindre telles autres actions qui ayant les caractères extérieurs de l'assassinat n'en ont (portent) pas les fruits amers qui composent

qu'elle punisse d'une peine moindre des actes qui ont les caractères extérieurs de l'assassinat, mais qui n'en ont pas les fruits amers; par example, le suicide, le duel, l'infanticide, le meurtre après une provocation violente."

law which distinguishes between different species of assassination, that it may only punish them according to their respective degrees of malignity that those actions which bear the exterior characters of assassination, but do not produce its bitter fruits, may either not be punished, or only punished in a less degree: for example, suicide, duelling, infanticide, murder after violent provocation."

la partie essentielle de ce crime: je veux dire le suicide, le duel, l'infanticide. [this last passage is written in very thin ink, hard to read even with magnifying glass] . . . . Briser le sceptre toujours doux de l'instinct pour y substituer le joug souvent importun de la raison, voilà une tâche qu'il faut remplir . . . Si l'instinct et le préjugé pourroient tenir lieu de la raison et de la vérité . . . si seuls ils suffiraient pour indiquer à l'homme tout ce qu'il lui importait de savoir, la raison ne feroit que déraisonner en se mettant à leur place . . . Si le Caprice suffisait de lui-même (de tout seul) pour faire marcher l'homme d'un pas ferme (uniform [sic] et toujours droit) et jamais divergent dans le sentier du bonheur, l'utilité n'auroit qu'à se taire . . . *Il faut démontrer les vérités palpables pour faire recevoir cells qui ne le sont pas: c'est par elles qu'on parvient* (parviendra) *à faire recevoir le vrai principe, qui une fois reçu servira a* (sic) *faire recevoir les autres vérités.*"

The italics in all four texts emphasizing the variations of the four versions are mine, and I readily admit that at first glance these differences may be thought to be negligible so far as the essence of Bentham's doctrine is concerned. But I think I do not exaggerate in believing that a closer analysis reveals that Dumont's, and even more Bowring's and Mill's texts, contain a considerable alteration of Bentham's theses.

First, apart from minor points, where Dumont speaks of "d'autres vérités qui en dépendent," there these words "qui en dépendent" are a mere *addition* of Dumont. Further, all the radical utterances about "briser le sceptre de l'instinct" et du "préjugé" et du "caprice" and the reference to the principle of utility are *omitted* by Dumont. Third, it is *omitted* that "il faut s'attacher a faire voir la mauvaise *qualité* de l'assassinat"; and this phrase is replaced by a reference *not* to the *quality* of assassination (which should be proved as morally bad on the ground of its consequences), but by a reference to the mischievous *consequences* *themselves* ("funestes effets"); and there are only different degrees of badness distinguished within these consequences; but as to demonstrating the bad quality of the action on the ground of its consequences, all attempts of this kind are completely abandoned. Fourth, and this seems to me the decisive point, Bowring and Mill change simply the words "le vrai principe," that is obviously the principle of utility, into the words "first principles," that is obviously such principles as the wrongness of assassination, maxims which are uncritically, wrongly supposed to be "first principles."

Taking all these alterations together, I think the emphasis which Bentham laid on certain statements has been shifted over to quite different points. Bentham

27

The difference of meaning between this quotation by Mill and Bentham's MS seems to me, briefly speaking, this: Dumont's and even more Bowring's and Mill's texts say that there are in ethics "first principles," such as the wrongness of assassination, whose validity needs no proof. If, all the same, proofs are given for them, then it is only done in order to ground other truths "which depend upon them," and, as Mill adds, in order to "discipline the mind." Bentham, however, declared here—as he always does—that even conventionally accepted "truths" ("tout le monde en convient") or so-called "acknowledged truths," such as the moral wrongness of assassination, may be wrong (compare e.g. Bentham's *Introduction*, 1789, chap. x sect. I, chap. II sect. IV), and that they *cannot* form first principles in ethics. Therefore, Bentham demands proofs even of the validity of these "acknowledged truths," proofs which are based on the sole "vrai principe," the principle of utility, though practically such proofs are of minor importance. In a *theory* of ethics, however, such proofs are as fundamentally required as the proofs of the validity of truths which depend upon acknowledged truths. For these reasons, I think that here again Bentham has shown himself a far more critical mind than the editions of his works by Dumont and Bowring have hitherto enabled us to perceive.

But even if one finds the text of Mill's quotation correct, then it is still worth stressing that John Stuart Mill's quotation is a least ill-chosen. For these references of Mill's by no means show Bentham's "questioning spirit" at its height. They can only show that, according to Bentham, such truths as the moral wrongness of assassination *can*

---

wishes, above all, to lead back from conventionally acknowledged truth to the principle of utility, as only thus both the moral conventions and the open moral questions can be analyzed in a satisfactory way. Dumont, Bowring and Mill, however, are far less interested in the examination of acknowledged moral conventions than Bentham is.

In other words, the drift of Bentham has to be indicated more explicitly somewhat as follows: the proof of the validity of an acknowledged moral truth is of no immediate practical value. It is only of theoretical importance, and it gains indirect practical value with regard to more complicated, unsolved moral questions which are connected with the acknowledged ones. Bowring and Mill, however, neglect along with the practical importance the theoretical necessity for finding proofs of acknowledged moral truth.

But even if the interpretation I give of the different texts should not be approved, it seems to me at least misleading in Mill that he quoted just these Bentham passages for the sake of illustrating Bentham's radical questioning spirit. For, in the interpretation of Mill, this passage must be understood as a marked weakening, not as a strengthening, of Bentham's ethical radicalism.

be proved, but *not* that they need be proved. They show only that proofs given for the wrongness of assassination and the like are a kind of *theoretical luxury*. In his main line of thought, however, Bentham insists everywhere that such proofs are *theoretically indispensable*. According to the gist of Bentham's teaching, every acknowledged truth in ethics, even the wrongness of murder, has to be examined first for its own sake, and not for the sake of training the mind. In consequence of this, Bentham actually examined the philosophic *basis* of moral and juristic laws as well as accepted moral and juristic laws themselves.

It is in this spirit that the young thinker announces in the preface of his first work that "the interests" of moral "reformation and through them the welfare of mankind" demand the complete "downfall" of the work of every author who "avows himself a determined and persevering enemy" of moral criticism and improvement.[29] In fact, there is scarcely any one of Blackstone's moral and juristic valuations analyzed by Bentham—whether in the *Fragment*, or in the much larger discussions of the *Comment on the Commentaries*—which was not vehemently assailed by him either in itself or at its root. In all these polemics, Bentham is most careful to draw one distinction which, even to-day, is usually neglected, namely, the distinction between the description of acknowledged laws and the discussion of the reasons for their acknowledgment; that is, the distinction between the mere fact of existing laws and the reasons given for the validity of such laws.

But perhaps even Bentham has explained the difference between these problems nowhere better than here. He says: "In practice, the question of law has commonly been spoken of as opposed to that of *fact*: but this distinction is an accidental one. That a law commanding or prohibiting such a *sort* of action, has been established, is as much a *fact*, as that an *individual* action of that sort has been committed. The establishment of a Law" has to be "spoken of as a *fact* at least for the purpose of distinguishing it from any consideration that may be offered as a *reason* for such Law."[30] This, and the few reflections to

---

[29] Bentham, *A Fragment on Government*, ed. by Montague, 1891, p. 94, (*Works*, 1843, vol. 1, p. 227b, a). It was not without reason that Bentham chose as motto of his onslaught upon Blackstone a specially aggressive saying of Montesquieu's *De l'esprit des lois*, livre 30, chap. 15, 1749, p. 526: "Rien ne recule plus le progrès des connoissances qu'un mauvais Ouvrage d'un Auteur célèbre, parce qu'avant d'instruire il faut commencer par détromper." (Bentham, *A Fragment on Government*, ed. by Montague, 1891, p. 91, *Works*, 1843, part 1, p. 221.)

[30] Bentham, *A Fragment on Government*, ed. by Montague, 1891, p. 98 (*Works*, 1843, vol. 1, p. 229a).

follow, remove in my opinion certain dangerous confusions and mis-
understandings in regard to the basis of any theory of law and ethics;
and to have done this is one of Bentham's greatest services. For it is
surely a main defect of all ancient and of most modern systems of
morals that, according to them, the philosophic validity of moral laws
means nothing but the mere actuality of existing laws.

Not only the public, but moralists, too, often make such disastrous
identifications (particularly in cases which seem to them simple, though
they are by no means a matter of course): It is argued that, because
such or such a law is actually established, or because people believe
that such and such a valuation is ethical, therefore these valuations or
laws are sound.[31] And other ethical theories even declare explicitly that
there is no justification to be found for moral valuations beyond the
fact that they are valuations of a community itself, and that, therefore,
the identification of the actuality and validity of moral laws is legitimate.

But from the very beginning, Bentham makes this distinction perfectly clear: "There are two characters, one or other of which every
man who finds anything to say on the subject of law, may be said to
take upon him; that of the *Expositor*, and that of the *Censor*. To the
province of the *Expositor* it belongs to explain to us what, as he supposes, the Law *is*: to that of the *Censor*, to observe to us what he thinks
it *ought to be*. The former, therefore, is principally occupied in stating,
or in enquiring after *facts*: the latter, in discussing *reasons*."[32] "That
which *is* Law, is, in different countries, widely different: while that
which *ought to be*, is in all countries to a great degree the same. The
Expositor, therefore, is always the citizen of this or that particular
country: the *Censor* is, or ought to be, the citizen of the world. To the
Expositor it belongs to shew what the *Legislator* and his underwork-
man the *Judge* have done *already*: to the *Censor* it belongs to suggest
what the *Legislator ought* to do *in future*."[33] So wherever "the word

---

[31] Compare for instance G. E. Moore's criticism of the belief that *this is good*
means *someone approves of it* in his *Ethics*, 1912, pp. 122 ff. In his *Ethics and
Language*, 1944, pp. 272, 21 ff, 26, C. L. Stevenson—contrary to Bentham and
G. E. Moore—takes the belief that *X is good* means *someone approves of X* as
an analytic judgment. But he, too, admits that it is "a distressingly meager conclusion" to state only: "If a man says 'X is good,' and if he can prove that he
really approves of X, then he has all the proof that can be demanded of him"
in ethics.

[32] Bentham, *A Fragment on Government*, ed. by Montague, 1891, p. 98 f
(*Works*, 1843, vol. 1, p. 229a).

[33] *Ibid.*, p. 99 (*Works*, 1843, vol. 1, p. 229a).

'*duty*' is in anyone's mouth," there "a *Censor* . . . begins talking to us of what ought to be." And this "ought to be" and "the is" are two quite "opposite . . . points."[34]

A quite similar distinction of problems in the general theory of knowledge was drawn by Kant, about the same time, in his classical distinction between "quaesto facti" and "quaesto juris" in the *Critique of Pure Reason*.[35] And it is worth noting that Kant and Bentham even use the same terminology: Kant speaks of the contrast between the pure "*exposition*" of laws[36] and the "*critical*" inquiry into their validity, their eventual "deduction"; while Bentham, too, sometimes styled his "censorial" method "criticism."[37]

In his theory of morals, Kant unfortunately did not maintain clearly enough this fundamental distinction between "censorial" and "expository" inquiries.[38] In the whole literature of ethics, however, there is perhaps no clearer account of this distinction than that given by Bentham.

Notwithstanding these emphatic statements concerning the importance of the moral *ought*, statements which are to be found on the first pages of Bentham's first book, A. E. Taylor assured us as recently as in 1940: "Bentham's doctrine is . . . from the strictly ethical point of view an inferior type of ethic. . . . I am thinking, of course, of Bentham's known and violent animosity against the very use of

[34] Bentham, *A Fragment on Government*, chapter v, §10 (*Works*, 1843, vol. I, p. 294b), compare chap. IV, §10, the stress laid upon the discrimination between "what they intend" and "what they ought to intend"; or chap. III, §11, the difference between "it . . . was" and "it . . . should be."

[35] I. Kant, *Critique of Pure Reason*, translated by Norman Kemp Smith, 1934, p. 75: "Jurists when speaking of rights and claims distinguish in a legal action the question of right (quid juris) from the question of fact (quid facti). . . . Proof of the former, which has to state the right or the legal claim" of a concept or a law, is entitled "the deduction" of it (*Analytic of Concepts*, chap. II, sect. I, §13).

[36] I. Kant, *Critique of Pure Reason*, 2nd German edition, p. 38 and I. Kant, *Critique of Practical Reason*, translated by Th. K. Abbott, 1883, p. 135 f: "The *Exposition* of the supreme principle of practical reason is now finished; that is to say it has been shown first, what it contains . . . and next in what it is distinguished from all other practical principles. With the *deduction* that is the justification of its objective and universal validity . . . we cannot expect to succeed as well as in the case of the principles of pure theoretical reason. . . . Yet . . . the objective reality of the law . . . is firmly established of itself."

[37] Bentham, *A Fragment on Government*, ed. by Montague, 1891, p. 99 (*Works*, 1843, vol. I, p. 229b).

[38] See this terminology in Bentham, *A Fragment on Government*, ed. by Montague, 1891, pp. 106, 120 (*Works*, 1843, vol. I, pp. 232a, 238a).

31

the word *ought* in moral and political reasoning."[39] If any proof were needed to demonstrate the desirability of a new and more detailed analysis of Bentham's theory of morals, I think this strange declaration of one of the most learned contemporary historians of philosophy may be considered as sufficient evidence of this need.

Of course, there are moralists who, in contrast to Bentham, deny that there exists a universally valid *ought*, that there are any ethical laws which can be proved to be valid at all times and in all countries. It is possible even to go so far as to state that there exist only positive laws, whose ethical validity is not susceptible of proof, and that such laws alone can be meant in speaking of valid laws. But even then it would by no means be superfluous to distinguish between the tasks of an Expositor and a Censor as Bentham did, i.e. to distinguish between the conservative interpretation of actual laws, and the critical analysis of their moral validity, or better, their lack of absolute ethical validity.

Even if morally valid laws are deliberately identified with actually existing laws, this identification implies at least a conscious ideal distinction between pure actuality and the moral validity of this actuality. And this conscious identification of existing and valid laws (found partly in Hobbes or in Lévy-Bruhl) ranks in any case scientifically much higher than the unnoticed confusion of the two fields of ethical inquiry. For the deliberate identification of these two branches of analysis shows a clearer insight into the essence of the moral problem than the common intermixing of the spheres of an Expositor and of a Censor—an intermixture which takes place even in very famous systems of ethics both before Bentham and in more recent times.

If we had to find a criterion differentiating between critical ethics and conventional ones, I believe that we could hardly name a more characteristic standard than the clear separation of "censorial" from "expository" problems.

Seen from this angle, it seems to me especially misleading of James Seth to plead for the thesis that "Bentham's interest is purely practical; he preaches utilitarianism as an ideal of social and political conduct. J. S. Mill is the philosopher of the school, he alone attempts the 'proof' of the principle of utility, he alone investigates the nature of evidence generally."[40] In truth, such a judgment contradicts not

[39] A. E. Taylor, "The Right and the Good," in *Mind*, vol. XLIX, No. 194, April 1940, pp. 222, 220.
[40] James Seth, *English Philosophers and Schools of Philosophy*, 1925, p. 240 f.

only the conviction of J. S. Mill himself;[41] it overlooks precisely one of Bentham's greatest merits, his lifelong rejection of any moral sermon and argument advanced without sufficient evidence or proof. Bentham saw in the principle of utility the only fundamental axiom of a consistent theory of ethics, but he arrived at this conclusion as a "Censor," after a deliberate examination of other moral principles. For no other principle could give, in his view, a consistent basis for moral valuations; all other so-called axioms of ethics lead, as he tried to show, either to vagueness and inconsistencies, or back in a circle to the principle of utility.[42] Thus Bentham never preached a moral or social ideal as something which simply ought to be; as a "Censor," he tried to give evidence of the validity of his concrete ideals by founding them on an axiom which, according to his analysis, was the only possible presupposition of any proof whatever.

As to mere terminology, of course, a certain distinction between "is" and "ought" is only too familiar to everyday language and to the moralists. But this common way of discriminating between such questions has a merely superficial similarity to Bentham's distinction between the problems of the moral "Censor" and the moral "Expositor"; Bentham demands conclusive reasons for the *ought* of the moral "Censor"; usually, however, this *ought* is opposed to the empirical *is* without any further explanation of the reasons for the *ought*, the reasons for the duty. The *ought* is considered as highest reason in itself and said to be even less in need of any explanation by cause or reason than the metaphysical *is*.

Bentham, however, demands a *reasoned ought*; and in this way he distinguishes himself from both the naturalistic empiricists who wrongly deny the assumption of any meaningful moral *ought* (however carefully described and empirically justified) and from the dogmatic deontologists who wrongly deny the possibility and necessity of giving reasons for the ethical *ought*.

The Principle of Utility and Bentham's Place in Its History

Only after these prolegomena can we turn to that principle of

[41] J. S. Mill, *Works*, vol. IV (The New Universal Library; essay on Bentham), e.g. p. 271: "Bentham has been in this age and country the great questioner of things established . . . to Bentham more than to any other source might be traced . . . the disposition to demand the *why* of everything."

[42] See e.g. Bentham, *Introduction to the Principles of Morals and Legislation*, chap. I and II.

Bentham's ethics which is often erroneously considered his most original conception, the principle of utility. In truth, this principle is not an original idea of Bentham's, any more than the principle of the idealistic character of space and time is an original discovery of Kant. (It was Schopenhauer and a few other influential thinkers who misjudged the *Critique of Pure Reason* in this way while the similar misjudgment on Bentham is even more widespread.) At any rate, the principle of utility appears at the very beginning of Bentham's first book as a well known axiom, not as an innovation. In the very first sentences of the preface of his *Fragment on Government*, Bentham explicitly states that it is only "the consequences" of the utility principle which have "been as yet developed . . . with so little method and precision."[43] But that "this fundamental axiom . . . the greatest happiness of the greatest number" has already been called "the measure of right and wrong"[44] by his predecessors is unmistakably granted by Bentham right at the beginning of his career as a philosophical writer.

In the preface, as well as in his first book itself, the principle of the greatest happiness of the greatest number appears frequently under the name of the principle of utility.[45] It was probably only *before* the publication of the *Fragment on Government* that Bentham used other formulas for the utility principle. Thus we find in an unpublished manuscript the formulation, "the greatest possible welfare," and in the margin is added: "It was not till about 25 years ago that it revealed itself to the philosopher in his closet."[46] (This could be a reference to

[43] Bentham, *A Fragment on Government*, ed. by Montague, 1891, p. 93 (*Works*, 1843, vol. 1, p. 227a).

[44] *Ibid.*, p. 93. H. Rashdall in his *The Theory of Good and Evil*, 1907, vol. 1, p. 12, obviously implies that in Bentham's writings not what ought to be desired but "what is desired is always the greatest prospective sum of pleasures." As Bentham states at the very beginning of his first book that the utility principle is the "measure of right and wrong," Rashdall's criticism on this point is evidently unwarranted. Even J. S. Mill's "Utilitarianism" considers the greatest happiness principle not only as the principle of what is desired but also as that which ought to be desired. Bentham, however, understood the relation between *ought* and *is* to be far more complex and intricate than did Mill, as we shall see later in more detail. Both, however, clearly distinguish between "the greatest prospective sum of pleasures" which every individual desires for himself and the greatest prospective sum of pleasures of the greatest number which everyone ought to desire.

[45] Bentham, *A Fragment on Government*, ed. by Montague, 1891, pp. 118 f, 120, note 3, 154 f, 163, 214, 219, 226 f, 233 ff (*Works*, 1843, vol. 1, p. 257a, b, 238a note, chap. IV, §xx, chap. IV, §xxviii, chap. IV, §xxxix, chap. v, §vi, notes).

[46] Bentham MSS, University College, London, Portfolio 32, Folder 13, p. 148, *unpublished*.

the use of the formula by Helvétius and Hume about fifteen to thirty years before Bentham.) Also, the version "the happiness the greatest possible," or "the greatest possible happiness," appears in this unpublished manuscript.[47] Only in the published works do we find "the principle of the greatest happiness of the greatest number" and "the principle of utility" as the most common expressions.

But there can be no doubt that, as early as in the *Fragment on Government*, Bentham wished to make clear that he had not discovered the principle of utility. It is superfluous criticism when Théodore Simon Jouffroy exclaims in an analysis of Bentham's work: "La doctrine de l'utilité nouvelle! elle que nous trouvons en Grèce avant les sophistes qui étaient avant Socrate."[48] Indeed, the principle of utility is probably as old as human thought itself.

As the present study tries to protect Bentham from the undeserved discredit brought upon him as well as from mistaken credit given him, it can hardly be emphasized enough that it is historically absurd to see in him the discoverer of the greatest happiness principle. It comes much nearer the truth to realize that the importance of Bentham's ethics consists in all those numerous careful epistemological analyses he carried through *despite* his espousal of the very common and easily misinterpretable utility principle which he took over from other moralists of ancient and modern times. In any case, it seems to me appropriate to show in greater detail than has hitherto been done why it is impossible to praise or condemn Bentham for having coined[49] the formula of the greatest happiness of the greatest number.

Allusions to the principle of utility are not only to be found among the pre-Socratics, in the eudaemonistic ethics of Democritus, but also in Indian philosophy about 500 B.C.[50] and, most likely, in every phase of human history.

Bentham himself and Bowring, his biographer, often commented on a number of earlier advocates of the utility principle to whom Bentham felt himself indebted. Already "at the age of six or seven," by reading Fénelon's

[47] *Ibid.*, Portfolio 32, Folder 13, p. 147, *unpublished.*
[48] Th. S. Jouffroy, *Cours de droit naturel*, 1843, tome I, p. 380.
[49] Even William L. Davidson in his *Political Thought in England; the Utilitarians from Bentham to J. S. Mill*, as late as in 1916, states: Bentham "substituted for 'the principle of utility' the more significant phrase 'the greatest happiness principle,' or (as he first expressed it) 'the greatest happiness of the greatest number' principle."
[50] See e.g. P. Deussen, *Vier philosophische Texte des Mahabharatam*, 1906, S. 985: "Jeder schätzt jedesmal dasjenige als Pflicht, woran er gerade sein Gefallen findet."

35

"Télémaque," the "first embers" of the principle of utility were "kindled" in Bentham, according to several communications made by him to Bowring.[51] And still more detailed, even dramatic, is the long report given by Bentham of his first acquaintance with the greatest happiness principle in Priestley's *An Essay on the First Principles of Government and on the Nature of Political, Civil and Religious Liberty*, 1768.[52] The phrase which may have impressed Bentham most in the *Essay on Government* reads as follows: "The good and happiness of the members, that is of the majority of the members of any state is the great standard by which everything relating to that state must finally be determined."[53] And similar formulas of the principle of utility are rather frequently repeated in Priestley, such as "promote the public

[51] Bentham, *Works*, 1843, part XIX, pp. 10b, 79b.

[52] See Bentham MSS, University College, London, Portfolio 14, Folder 47, pp. 422, 423, 11-12, first printed in Bowring's Appendix to Bentham's *Deontology*, 1834, vol. I, pp. 298-300, and compare *Works*, 1843, part XIX, pp. 46a, b, 79b, 142b, part XX, p. 567. Unfortunately these different reports of Bentham's first acquaintance with the principle of utility do not fully agree with each other. The longest of them, first printed in *Deontology*, vol. I, pp. 298 ff even describes in detail the library belonging to a coffee-house attached to Queens College in Oxford where Bentham found Priestley's "Essay on Government" in 1768. And then it goes on to narrate emphatically: "It was by that pamphlet and that phrase in it, that my principles on the subject of morality, public and private together were determined." "It was from that pamphlet and that page of it that I drew the phrase, the words and import of which have been so widely diffused over the civilized world. At the sight of it I cried out, as it were in an inward ecstasy, like Archimedes . . . Ευρηκα." But another passage extracted by Bowring from Bentham's "Commonplace Book," written about 1783, says in some contrast to this: "Priestley was the first (unless it was Beccaria) who taught my lips to pronounce this sacred truth: that the greatest happiness of the greatest number is the foundation of morals and legislation" (Bentham, *Works*, 1843, part XIX, p. 142b). Here it is certainly astonishing to see that the ecstatic Ευρηκα of the first mentioned report was so little remembered by Bentham that he even did not distinctly know what author had given him his first acquaintance with the fundamental axiom of his ethics. Another version reported by Bowring narrates only: "By an early pamphlet of Priestley's the date of which has fled from my recollection, light was added to the warmth. In the phrase 'the greatest happiness of the greatest number' I then saw delineated for the first time, a plain as well as a true standard for whatever is right or wrong . . . whether in the field of morals or of politics" (Bentham, *Works*, 1843, part XIX, p. 79b). Compare a "Recollection of Bentham's own words," mentioned by Bowring, *Works*, 1843, part XIX, p. 46b. Or cf. a "Document" printed *ibid.*, part XX, p. 561. Finally see Bowring's "verbatim" reproduction of a conversation of Bentham in 1822 which says much the same, adding however that Priestley "knew nothing" of the value of the principle of utility and "did not turn it into a system" (*Works*, 1843, part XX, p. 567b).

[53] Priestley, *An Essay on the First Principles of Government and on the Nature of Political, Civil and Religious Liberty*, 1768, p. 17, part I, of liberty.

good,"[54] "consult the good of the whole."[55] "The divine being appears to be actuated by no other views than . . . the happiness of his creatures. Virtue and right conduct consist in those affections and actions which terminate to the public good; justice and veracity . . . having nothing intrinsically excellent in them separate from their relation to the happiness of mankind . . . the decisive question when any of these subjects are examined being: what is it that the good of the community requires?"[56] "The interest . . . of the people,"[57] "the happiness of the whole community is the ultimate end of government."[58] Also other writings of Priestley contain hints of the principle of utility, as for instance his "lectures on history": "the only proper object of Government, *the happiness of the people*, is now almost universally seen and alone attended to."[59] Thus, even the manner in which the principle of utility is introduced by Priestley shows that it was only by chance that Bentham first met the principle of utility in a writing of the discoverer of oxygen. For, as Priestley himself indicates, this principle plays no greater part in his work than in other moral, juristic, and political theorists of the eighteenth century.

How fully Bentham himself was aware of this fact becomes evident in an unpublished manuscript, where it is stated "Before it [the principle of utility] was mine it was M. Beccaria's. Before it was his [Beccaria's] it was Helvétius', before it was Helvétius' it was in some sort anybody's. Enough? Helvétius for placing it in full light was persecuted. The light shone in the darkness, but the darkness comprehended it not."[60] Certainly such emphatic words are sufficient evidence of how little Bentham believed that the major principle of his ethics and jurisprudence was exclusively his own.

Elie Halévy could, therefore, justly maintain that "nul penseur n'a été moins soucieux que Bentham de dissimuler ce qu'il emprunte à ses devanciers, à ses contemporains."[61] Yet Bentham was so little interested in the merely "historical" question as to who had stumbled on the principle of utility before him that he has sometimes forgotten to mention in this connection even the name of the thinker to whom in general he felt most indebted; and on the whole, he is very careless in his accounts of the way in which he first became acquainted with the principle of utility. Most

[54] *Ibid.*, p. 18.
[55] *Ibid.*, p. 11 (introduction), compare p. 17.
[56] *Ibid.*, p. 18.   [57] *Ibid.*, p. 44.
[58] *Ibid.*, p. 59; and see H. J. Laski, *Political Thought in England from Locke to Bentham*, 1920, p. 151: "In substance . . . if not completely in theory, we pass with Priestley from arguments of right to those of expediency."
[59] J. Priestley, *The Theological and Miscellaneous Works*, vol. 24, ed. by J. T. Rutt, 1826, p. 35 f.
[60] Bentham MSS, University College, London, Portfolio 27, Folder 16, sheet 100, p. 23, written about 1776.
[61] E. Halévy, *La formation du radicalisme philosophique*, 1901, tome I, p. 30.

likely, he was first influenced on this point by Priestley. But occasionally, he attributed much greater importance to Beccaria,[62] Helvétius,[63] and Hume[64] in this connection; and he even entirely omits the name of Priestley, as for instance in a remark in a diary written about 1769: "Montesquieu, Barrington, Beccaria and Helvetius, but most of all Helvetius set me on the principle of utility."[65] Beccaria and Helvétius certainly have influenced him much more in detail by their use of the principle of utility than either Priestley or Hume.

Beccaria, in the introduction of his famous *Trattato dei delitti e delle pene,* (1764), speaks explicitly of the principle of "la massima felicità divisa nel maggior numero" as the main end of all social institutions; and in the first sentence of the first chapter of his work, special stress is laid upon the "utile alla società." Moreover, in practically all the discussion of the various crimes and punishments which fills the different chapters of Beccaria's work, the estimate of the utility of the punishment in question appears as the most important issue.[66] Even the well-known passage of the utility principle with which Bentham opens his *Introduction to the Principles of Morals and Legislation* has its model in similar formulations of Helvétius (as Halévy has shown), and is also stated in almost the same words by Beccaria: "Il piacere e il dolore sono i motori degli esseri sensibili . . . tra i motivi che spingono gli uomini anche alle più sublimi operazioni, furono destinati dall'invisibile Legislatore il premio e la pena."[67] It is true that occasionally for Beccaria the just in conduct is to be discriminated from the useful,[68]

---

[62] See Bentham, *Works,* 1843, vol. III, p. 286b (Appendix to Bentham's "Nomography," written between 1811 and 1831): "It was from Beccaria's little treatise on crimes and punishments that I drew, as I well remember, the first hint of this principle" ("Elements or dimensions of value in regard to pleasures and pains"); *Works,* 1843, vol. X, p. 142b: "Priestley was the first (unless it was Beccaria) who taught my lips" the principle of utility.

[63] See Bentham, *Works,* 1843, vol. X, p. 54a: "most of all Helvetius set me on the principle of utility"; compare *ibid.,* vol. IV, p. 447b, where only the influence of Helvétius and David Hume is mentioned. ("Jeremy Bentham to his Fellow-Citizens of France on Houses of Peers and Senates," 1830.)

[64] See Bentham, *A Fragment on Government,* chap. I, §xxxvi, note.

[65] Bentham, *Works,* 1843, part XIX, p. 54a.

[66] See Beccaria, *Dei delitti e delle pene,* e.g. the beginning of §16: "Questa inutile prodigalità di supplizii, che non ha mai resi migliori gli uomini, mi ha spinto ad esaminare se la (pena di morte) sia veramente utile e giusta in un governo bene organizzato." Or §19: "Ho detto che la prontezza della pena è più utile"; §20 no "separare ad ogni momento il ben pubblico dal bene de' particolari"; §21: "Mi restano ancora due questioni da esaminare; l'una, se gli asili sieno giusti, e se il patto di rendersi fra le nazioni reciprocamente i rei, sia utile o no"; §22: "L'altra questione è, se sia utile il mettere a prezzo la testa di un uomo conosciuto reo."

[67] Beccaria, *Dei Delitti e delle Pene,* §23.

[68] E.g. *ibid.,* §21.

38

while they are identified by Bentham. Yet there can be no doubt that in Beccaria, too, the utility of the greatest number is a leading term.

Even more than by Beccaria or Priestley, Bentham was, probably, influenced by the use of the principle of utility in his "favourite book,"[69] in Claude-Adrien *Helvétius' De l'esprit*, first published in 1758. In the preface to this book, the principle of the greatest happiness of the greatest number is mentioned in the following way: "La morale commune aux hommes de toutes les nations ... ne peut avoir ... pour objet ... que le bien public ... l'intérêt générale."[70] And certainly still more instructive for Bentham were many other formulations of the principle of utility in Helvétius' most influential work, for example, the following: "Il faut pouvoir, rapporter toutes ... les lois ... à un principe simple, tel que celui de l'utilité du public, c'est-à-dire du plus grand nombre d'hommes."[71] "Les principes d'une bonne morale ... doivent toujours être appuyés ... sur ... l'intérêt public, c'est à dire celui du plus grand nombre."[72] "La justice ... consiste ... dans la pratique des actions utiles au plus grand nombre."[73] "La conclusion générale de tout ce que je viens de dire, c'est que la vertu n'est que le désir du bonheur des hommes."[74] "Un homme est juste, lorsque toutes ses actions tendent au bien public."[75] "Les passions, dont l'arbre défendu n'est selon quelques Rabbins, qu'une ingénieuse image, portent également sur leur tige les fruits du bien et du mal."[76] Or, in an apology for La Rochefoucauld: "s'irriter contre les effets de leur amour-propre (l'amour propre des hommes), c'est ce plaindre des giboulées du printemps, des ardeurs de l'été ... et des glaces de l'hiver."[77] "La justice ... de nos actions n'est jamais que la rencontre heureuse de notre intérêt avec l'intérêt publique."[78] "Tous les hommes ne tendent qu'à leur bonheur ... on ne peut les rendre vertueux qu'en unissant l'intérêt personel à l'intérêt général."[79] "Par ce mot de vertue,

[69] See Bentham, *Works*, 1843, part XIX, p. 54b; compare MSS, University College, London, Portfolio 27, p. 109, quoted by E. Halévy, *La formation du radicalisme philosophique*, tome I, 1901, p. 291: "To Helvetius I owe the principle of utility, the foundation of the work, to M. Beccaria the consideration of the ingredients in the value of a punishment which put me upon extending the application of it to pain and pleasure."

[70] C. A. Helvétius, *Oeuvres complètes*, 1818, tome I, p. vii (preface of "De l'esprit").

[71] *Ibid.*, p. 159 ("De l'esprit," discours II, chap. 17).

[72] *Ibid.*, p. 203 ("De l'esprit," discours II, chap. 23).

[73] *Ibid.*, p. 209 ("De l'esprit," discours II, chap. 24).

[74] *Ibid.*, p. 127 ("De l'esprit," discours II, chap. 13).

[75] *Ibid.*, p. 71 ("De l'esprit," discours II, chap. 6).

[76] C. A. Helvétius, *Oeuvres complètes*, 1818, tome I, p. 218 ("De l'esprit," discours II, chap. 24).

[77] *Ibid.*, p. 33 f ("De l'esprit," discours I, chap. 4).

[78] *Ibid.*, p. 83 ("De l'esprit," discours II, chap. 7).

[79] *Ibid.*, p. 147 ("De l'esprit," discours II, chap. 15).

l'on ne peut entendre que le désir du bonheur général; . . . par conséquent le bien publique est l'objet de la vertue."[80] "La douleur et le plaisir sont les seuls moteurs de l'univers moral; et . . . le sentiment de l'amour de soi est la seule base sur laquelle on puisse jeter les fondemens d'une morale utile."[81] "L'utilité est le principe de toutes vertus humaines, et le fondement de toutes les législations."[82] For these and for other reasons as well,[83] it becomes comprehensible why Bentham could occasionally rate the importance of Helvétius inordinately high, as in the following remark of his "Sundry Memoranda," made in 1773-74 and quoted by Bowring: "A digest of the Laws is a work that could not have been executed with advantage before Locke and Helvetius had written."[84] (But as he later, in 1830, declared rightly: "Locke had no clear view . . . of the greatest happiness principle.")[85] "From Locke . . . the Law must" only "receive the ruling principles of its form—from Helvetius of its matter. . . . The matter of the Law is to be governed by Helvetius."[84] In a draft-letter to Voltaire, written before 1778, Bentham speaks only of Helvétius as his inspirer in matters of the principle of utility: "I have built up wholly on the foundation of utility laid as it is by Helvetius."[86] Though in this letter the exclusive mention of the Frenchman Helvétius as predecessor may have been partly prompted by Bentham's sense of politeness, it is not substantially exaggerated.

In comparison with Priestley, Beccaria, and Helvétius, other advocates of the principle of utility mentioned by Bentham have unquestionably influenced him far less on this main point. As we saw, Bentham also refers in this connection to the lawyer Daines *Barrington*, whom he praises in his *Fragment on Government*, and whose work for the cause of reformation he recommends there as an "antidote" to Blackstone's "poisons."[87] Barrington's

[80] *Ibid.*, p. 121 ("De l'esprit," discours II, chap. 13).
[81] *Ibid.*, p. 210 ("De l'esprit," discours II, chap. 24).
[82] *Ibid.*, p. 74 ("De l'esprit," discours II, chap. 6).
[83] Compare for instance the first and the last sentences of Bentham's *Introduction to the Principles of Morals and Legislation* which deliberately imitate formulations of Helvétius.
[84] Bentham, *Works*, 1843, part XIX, pp. 70b, 71a.
[85] *Ibid.*, part VIII, pp. 447a, b ("Bentham to his Fellow-Citizens of France," 1830).
[86] Bentham MSS, University College, London, Portfolio 169, Folder 3, sheet 13, pp. 1 f, published by C. W. Everett, *The Education of Jeremy Bentham*, 1931, pp. 110 ff. This letter is very characteristic of the mixture of self-confidence and timidity in the young Bentham, a condition of the soul which he himself has later fascinatingly described as typical of great discoverers (see *Works*, 1843, part V, pp. 49b, 50, "A Manual of Political Economy").
I reprint this letter as Appendix II of the present volume with the addition of an *unpublished* draft-letter addressed to the Empress Catherine II of Russia and connected with the letter to Voltaire on the same sheet.
[87] Bentham, *A Fragment on Government*, ed. by Montague, 1891, p. 123 f (*Works*, 1843, vol. I, pp. 239a, b).

only juristic work which can come into question here, his *Observations upon the Statutes*, 1766, has, indeed, something of the spirit of a philosophy of the greatest happiness principle; yet it shows scarcely a trace of the direct formulation of this principle. I could at best quote the following phrase: "The time will come when a king revered by Europe, adored by his subjects . . . will show that a steady attention to the true welfare of his people will form the most amiable and respectable character in history without his having become the general of his army."[88] For the most part, however, Barrington's utilitarianism is to be seen rather in the "humane"[89] line he pursues in the details of his criticism of ancient laws, for instance, in his protest against "the most horrid practice" of torture,[90] against slavery as "contrary to . . . Christian religion . . . and . . . common law,"[91] in his protest against other "unintelligible trumpery" of ancient laws which contradict the spirit of "this enlightened age,"[92] in his pressing forward the abolition of the "shameful prejudices" against the "defenceless" and "most extraordinary" people of the Jews,[93] and in his fight for the repeal of the laws against "forestallers" and "regraters."[94]

Little, however, as Bentham's philosophy of utility was derived from Barrington, it owed still less to Montesquieu. As a matter of fact, Bentham once mentioned the name Montesquieu in this connection;[95] and there are to be found in Montesquieu statements such as these: "[La vertu] demandant une préférence continuelle de l'intérêt publique au sien propre, donne toutes les vertues particulières; elles ne sont que cette préférence."[96] But how little such moral ideas have to do with the principle of utility becomes clear at once from the following supplementary remark of Montesquieu: "La vertu est un renoncement à soi-même qui est toujours une chose très pénible";[96] and thus the author of *De l'esprit des lois* can hardly be regarded as a utilitarian of the type of Bentham or Helvétius.

[88] Daines Barrington, *Observations upon the statutes, chiefly the more ancient from Magna Charta to the Twenty-first of James the First Ch. XXVII, the second edition with corrections and additions*, 1766, p. 57, compare p. 428.

[89] *Ibid.*, p. 418 f and see for instance the following remark on the Elizabethan statute with regard to the maintenance of the poor, p. 419: "England hath to its peculiar honour not only made their poor free but has provided a certain and solid establishment to prevent their necessities and indigence . . . and are not these beneficent and humane attentions to the miseries of our fellow-creatures the first of those poor pleas which we are capable of offering in behalf of our imperfections to an all-wise and merciful Creator?"

[90] *Ibid.*, p. 70.　　　　　　　　　[91] *Ibid.*, p. 253.

[92] *Ibid.*, p. 101.　　　　　　　　[93] *Ibid.*, pp. 89, 180.

[94] *Ibid.*, p. 172. Forestalling, the buying of goods before they reach the public market, and certain practices of regrating, *i.e.* retailing, were in Barrington's time indictable offenses.

[95] Bentham, *Works*, 1843, part XIX, p. 54a.

[96] Montesquieu, *De l'esprit des loix*, 1749, p. 30, livre IV, chap. v.

41

Moreover, with his great interest in history, Montesquieu was certainly—as Bentham termed him later—far more an "antiquarian" than a systematic thinker;[97] and so it is not astonishing to see that, a few years after Bentham's first mention of Montesquieu, he no longer finds much in common with this "brilliant . . . rapid . . . writer"[98]—an attitude which Bentham maintained without any essential variation during the remainder of his lifetime,[99] despite the revolutionary motto he had once quoted from Montesquieu on the front page of his first published book.

Finally, among the Utilitarians who are explicitly noticed by Bentham as his forerunners, only one name of major importance remains to be considered: that of David Hume. When, in the *Fragment on Government*, he tells us of his first reading of Hume, it is with the same enthusiasm with which he wrote of his first acquaintance with Priestley and Helvétius. Concerning the third volume of Hume's *"Treatise of Human Nature,"* he assures us in the *Fragment on Government*: "No sooner had I read that part of the work which touches on this subject [the principle of utility] than I felt as if scales had fallen from my eyes";[100] and so late as in 1828, in the preface intended for the second edition of *A Fragment on Government*, he repeats: "the name of the principle of utility . . . was . . . adopted from David Hume."[101] This, however, is somewhat surprising to say the least if, as Bentham does, we think of Hume's *Treatise of Human Nature* and not of his

[97] See Bentham, *An Introduction to the Principles of Morals and Legislation*, Oxford, 1879, chap. xvii, §27, note: "Montesquieu sets out upon the censorial plan" for a critical, systematic ethics, "but long before the conclusion, as if he had forgot his first design, he throws off the censor, and puts on the antiquarian" (Bentham, *Works*, 1843, vol. i, p. 150b); and compare 1776, *A Fragment on Government*, ed. by Montague, p. 105: "Montesquieu's was a work of the mixed kind" that is to say of the expository and partly of the censorial class (*Works*, 1843, vol. i, p. 231b); or see even *A Fragment on Government*, chap. i, §42, and compare other criticism concerning Montesquieu in the *Comment on the Commentaries*, ed. Everett, 1928, p. 33 f.

[98] See Bentham's "Commonplace Book" written about 1782, *Works*, 1843, part xix, p. 143b.

[99] See for instance Bentham, "A General View of a Complete Code of Laws" (*Works*, 1843, part v, p. 158b) first published by Dumont, 1802; see *Traités de législation civile et pénale*, 1820, tome iii, p. 191: "dans les derniers livres de *L'esprit des lois*, . . . Montesquieu . . . le législateur est devenu antiquaire et historien, et on a pu comparer son ouvrage à ce fleuve qui, après avoir parcouru et fertilisé de superbes contrées n'arrive pas jusqu'à la mer, et se perd dans les sables."

[100] *A Fragment on Government*, ed. by Montague, 1891, p. 154 (chap. i, §36, note).

[101] Bentham, *Works*, 1843, part i, p. 242b. Compare part viii, p. 447b ("Jeremy Bentham to his Fellow-Citizens of France on Houses of Peers and Senates," 1830, §xii, 19, note): "see . . . the greatest-happiness principle at that time, in compliance with custom denominated the *principle of utility*, from *David Hume* and *Helvetius*."

An Enquiry concerning the Principles of Morals, 1751. In his *Treatise,* it is true, Hume frequently speaks of "the good of mankind,"[102] "the interest of Society,"[103] "the public good";[104] and he points out that "the interest on which justice is founded is the greatest imaginable and extends to all times and places"; "most people will readily allow that the useful qualities of the mind are virtuous, because of their utility";[105] but he adds: "Now this being once admitted the force of sympathy must necessarily be acknowledged . . . the public good is indifferent to us except so far as sympathy interests us in it."[106] Therefore, it is comprehensible that in as early a work as *A Fragment on Government,* a decisive alteration of this praise of Hume's ethics appears immediately after Bentham mentions its great influence on himself. The passage reads: "That the foundations of all *virtue* are laid in *utility* is there [in Hume's *Treatise*] demonstrated . . . with the strongest force of evidence"; but "a few exceptions" are "made," and "I see not, any more than Helvetius saw, what need there was for the exceptions."[107] And even sharper criticism of Hume's ethics appears in an *unpublished* remark: "Utility ill understood for instance by Hume."[108] Clearly, though Bentham borrowed the term of the principle of utility from Hume, he did not agree with the sort of application of it made there; he wanted to apply it more fundamentally and consistently.

In Hume's *Enquiry concerning the Principles of Morals,* it is true the principle of utility plays a far greater part than in his *Treatise;* but as far as I can ascertain, Bentham nowhere refers to Hume's *Inquiry* itself, and he mentions Hume's Essays very seldom.[109] He speaks of Hume's *Treatise of Human Nature* far more frequently;[110] and in reference to it, he usually

[102] David Hume, *Treatise of Human Nature,* 1740, vol. III, p. 207 (ed. Green and Grose, 1898, vol. II, p. 337).

[103] *Ibid.,* p. 207.

[104] *Ibid.,* p. 279 (ed. Green and Grose, 1898, vol. II, p. 372).

[105] *Ibid.,* p. 279 (ed. Green and Grose, 1898, vol. II, pp. 373, 372).

[106] David Hume, *Treatise of Human Nature,* 1740, vol. III, p. 277 (ed. Green and Grose, 1898, vol. II, p. 372).

[107] Bentham, *A Fragment on Government,* chap. I, §36, note.

[108] Bentham MSS, University College, London, Portfolio 27, Folder 12, sheet 100, pp. 24 f, *hitherto unpublished.*

[109] See e.g. *Deontology,* 1834, ed. Bowring, vol. II, p. 69 f; *Works,* 1843, part XX, p. 562b, and see a MS, *hitherto unpublished,* University College, London, Portfolio 27, Folder 5, sheet 35, p. 2, Appendix IV of the present work, vol. II, p. 272.

[110] See e.g. Bentham, *Chrestomathia,* 1816, p. 346 (*Works,* 1843, part XV, p. 128, note) where Hume's *Treatise of Human Nature* is praised on account of its censorial attitude in ethics, but blamed because "in proportion to the bulk of it no great quantity of useful instruction seemed derivable." Or see particularly Bentham, "Rationale of Judicial Evidence" (*Works,* 1843, part XI, p. 240a, note) where Hume's *Treatise* is criticized because "on some occasions the principle of utility was recognized by him as a criterion of right and wrong, and in this

complains about Hume's inconsistent application of the utility principle.

Aside from mentioning such contemporaries as Hume, Helvétius, Beccaria, or Priestley, however, Bentham had no interest in clearing up more carefully any historical question concerning his relation to other utilitarians. As he said with special emphasis in an *unpublished manuscript*, "It seemed to me that greater advances might be made and sooner by diving at once into the recesses of the human understanding, with Locke and with Helvetius, of the human heart than by wandering about in the maze of history."[111]

The further pursuit of these historical questions was left to Bowring and to later historians such as Leslie Stephen and Halévy. Bowring finds the first formulation of an ethical principle of utility in *Horace*,[112] strange as this is in view of *Epicurus*, or even *Aristippus* and *Democritus*, and in view of the fact that the names of Epicurus, of Aristotle, and Carneades were casually noticed in this connection by Bentham himself.[113] Apart from Horace, Bowring mentions as the only other ancient utilitarian the Roman fabulist *Phaedrus*,[114] the younger contemporary of Horace. After Phaedrus, he passes immediately to David Hume, leaving unnoticed seventeen centuries

sense the efficient cause of obligation. But on other occasions the *ipse dixit* principle, under the name of the moral sense, was, with the most inconsistent oscitancy, seated by his own hands on the same throne."

[111] Bentham MSS, University College, London, Portfolio 27, Folder 16, sheet 95, p. 1, or compare Bentham, *Deontology*, ed. Bowring, 1834, vol. I, p. 280 f, and compare Bentham's continuous denial of any intrinsic value in the history of philosophy and the history of law beginning with his letters in the *Gazetteer* up to the end of his life.

[112] Bentham, *Deontology*, ed. by Bowring, 1834, vol. I, p. 290, and Horatius, *Sermones*, liber I, 3, 98: "Atque ipsa utilitas, justi prope mater et aequi"; compare Bentham on the utilitarianism of Horace in his *Deontology*, 1834, vol. II, p. 84 f and especially *The Limits of Jurisprudence Defined*, ed. by Everett, 1945, p. 116 f.

[113] See Bentham, *Introduction to the Principles of Morals and Legislation*, chap. II, §7 (*Works*, part I, p. 5a). Or compare Bentham, *Traités de législation*, 1820, ed. Dumont, tome I, pp. 27 ff and see *A Fragment on Government*, ed. Montague, p. 118 (Preface): "The end . . . is *Happiness*. . . . Let this be taken for a truth upon the authority of Aristotle: I mean by those, who like the authority of Aristotle better than that of their own experience. Πᾶσα τέχνη, says that philosopher καὶ πᾶσα μέθοδος ὁμοίως δὲ πρᾶξίς τε καὶ προαίρεσις ἀγαθοῦ τινος ἐφίεσθαι δοκεῖ. διὸ καλῶς ἀπεφήναντο τἀγαθὸν οὗ πάντα ἐφίεται. Διαφορὰ δέ τις φαίνεται τῶν (understand τοιούτων) ΤΕΛΩΝ.—Arist. Eth. ad Nic. L. I c. 1." On Carneades see *The Limits of Jurisprudence Defined*, ed. by Everett, 1945, pp. 116, 117.

[114] See Bentham, *Deontology*, ed. Bowring, 1834, vol. I, p. 290, quoting the rather vague verse: "Nisi utile est quod faceris, stulta est gloria." And apart from the strangeness of counting Phaedrus among the philosophical utilitarians, the quotation is only a repetition of a quotation to be found in Hume's *Inquiry Concerning the Principles of Morals*, 1751, sect. IV, see Hume, *Essays*, ed. Green and Grose, 1898, vol. II, p. 198.

44

and proving thus that a deeper understanding of the history of philosophy was certainly not one of the characteristic fruits of Bentham's personal instruction in philosophy, as it was, in truth, no virtue of the whole Benthamite school.

The very date of the appearance of Hume's *Treatise* is not correctly given by Bowring (1742 instead of 1740). But Bowring's short analysis of Hume's utilitarianism shows again how much more Bentham found to criticize in the moralist Hume than in Helvétius or Priestley.[115] Even Beccaria is not mentioned by Bowring, and apart from the three indispensable names among the predecessors of Bentham—Hume, Helvétius, Priestley—he merely glances at Hartley and[116] concludes with William Paley, drawing a very unfavorable picture of his character and of his use of the utility principle in his *Principles of Moral and Political Philosophy*[117] (published in 1785, before Bentham's *Introduction*, yet most probably written after Bentham's book); and here again Bowring is inaccurate: he reproduces the title page of Paley's work incorrectly; he speaks of Paley's "elements" instead of Paley's "principles of moral and political philosophy."

It was not until the beginning of the twentieth century that historians of philosophy gave a richer and more careful account of the history of the greatest happiness principle than Bentham's favorite was able to do. W. R. Scott, in his book on Hutcheson, draws attention even to Cicero—in whose writings formulas of the utility principle were foreshadowed—[118]and to the Stoics of the Roman Empire, though by them, of course, stress was laid upon the altruistic side of the greatest happiness principle.[119] As a "Commoner of Queen's College," the young Bentham had once written to his father from Oxford with the exaggeration of a boy: "I am deeply immersed in philosophy."[120] For, at the age of 14, he had had to study Cicero and, as a fruit of these studies, he once sent to the old Jeremiah Bentham his "translation of the first Book of Tully's Tusculan questions" in a most excellent

[115] See Bentham, *Deontology*, ed. Bowring, 1834, vol. I, pp. 291 ff, 295 ff, 298 ff. And compare the detailed criticism of Hume's list of virtues, *ibid.*, pp. 232-258.

[116] *Ibid.*, p. 295.

[117] *Ibid.*, p. 310 f.

[118] See W. R. Scott, *Francis Hutcheson*, 1900, pp. 274 ff and see for instance Cicero, *De finibus boni et mali*, 3, 20: "Impellimur autem natura, ut prodesse velimus quam plurimis"; *De divinatione*, II, I: "prodesse quam plurimis"; *De officiis*, I, 16: the ideal condition of society would be found—"si, ut quisquis erit coniunctissimus, ita in eum *benignitatis plurimum* conferetur."

[119] See W. R. Scott, *Francis Hutcheson*, 1900, pp. 276 ff and see for instance Seneca, *De clementia*, II, 5: sapiens est "natus . . . in . . . publicum bonum"; Seneca, *De vita beata*, 24: "Ubicunque homo est ibi beneficii locus est"; Marcus Aurelius Antoninus, Τὰ εἰς ἑαυτόν XII 23: καλὸν δὲ ἀεὶ πᾶν τὸ συμφέρον τῷ ὅλῳ.

[120] Bentham MSS, British Museum Library, 33, 537, p. 83. A letter of Jeremy Bentham to his father written on March 29, 1761, *unpublished*.

calligraphic handwriting.[121] But naturally, with his ever-increasing antipathy for the eclectic Stoic Cicero,[122] Bentham did not become aware of the similarity between a few formulas quoted by Cicero and his own utility principle.

Oskar Kraus even linked Bentham's utility principle with Thomas Aquinas' saying: "Finis humane legis est utilitas hominum."[123] Of course, there is no evidence that Bentham was ever aware of the statement of Aquinas. That, however, neither Bentham nor Bowring ever took notice of Hutcheson's formula of the greatest happiness principle is indeed difficult to understand. The first writers to draw attention to Hutcheson in this connection were modern historians of philosophy such as Leslie Stephen, W. R. Scott, E. Halévy, E. Albee;[124] and it is to them, rather than to Bowring, that we must go for useful hints for a brief history of the utility principle. These hints need, however, considerable addition and correction.

E. Albee believes "it might very well seem" as if *Henry More* were already an exponent of the utilitarian principle.[125] For, in More's view, a certain amount even of external goods is necessary for the perfect life. "Nemo potest esse vita perfectus sine bonis Fortunae."[126] But More's strict distinction between "appetitus animales" and "facultas boniformis,"[127] between "bene" and "beate" vivere,[128] and his assumption of the obedience to God as the only "summum bonum"[129] do not allow us to see in his ethics more than a rather vague "theological" hedonism.

Perhaps with a little more right *Richard Cumberland* could be termed a utilitarian, in Albee's view the first English moralist of this type.[130] In his voluminous work *De legibus naturae*, 1672, English 1727, may be read: "*No action* of the will is enjoin'd or recommended by the Law of Nature, and, consequently, *Morally Good*, which does *not*, in its own nature, *contribute*

---

[121] See Bentham MSS, British Museum, 33, 537, pp. 83-120, *unpublished*; on p. 121 Bentham notes there: Sperne voluptates, nocet empta dolore voluptas.

[122] See Bentham, *Deontology*, ed. Bowring, 1834, vol. I, pp. 300 ff.

[123] See O. Kraus, *Zur Theorie des Wertes, Eine Bentham-Studie*, 1902, p. 6.

[124] See Leslie Stephen, *The English Utilitarians*, 1900, vol. I, p. 178 f; W. R. Scott, *Francis Hutcheson*, 1900, pp. 272 ff; E. Halévy, *La formation du radicalisme philosophique*, vol. I, pp. 16 f, 283 f; E. Albee, *A History of English Utilitarianism*, 1902, pp. 60 ff.

[125] E. Albee, *A History of English Utilitarianism*, 1902, p. 12.

[126] Henricus Morus, *Enchiridion Ethicum praecipua moralis philosophiae rudimenta complectens* (1667), 1669, lib. I, cap. I, §2, and compare *ibid.*, lib. II, cap. x, §1 "De bonis externis."

[127] *Ibid.*, lib. I, cap. II, §7, cap. IV, §5.

[128] *Ibid.*, lib. I, cap. I, §1.

[129] *Ibid.*, lib. I, cap. v, §1: "Divina . . . sapere summa hominis sapentia est, summaque felicitas" or compare lib. I, cap. IV, Noema XXI: "Melius est Deo parere quam hominibus propriisque nostris cupiditatibus."

[130] E. Albee, *A History of English Utilitarianism*, 1902, p. 14.

somewhat to the Happiness of Men."[131] "*Our own* Advantages can afford but *small matter of Joy*; the Subject will be exceedingly *inlarged*, if we are delighted with the Happiness of *every other person*."[132] This also may be styled a formula of the greatest happiness principle. But here too, in the end, the happiness of any single person and of rational beings in general is rather persistently subordinated to "the Honour of God,"[133] "the Glory of God"[134] as "the superior End," as the "Chief End" of every moral agent,[135] and apart from this there is introduced alongside the "Happiness of all" a further ideal: the "perfection" of mankind.[136] So that taking both these points into account, it is certainly difficult to put Cumberland's ethics beside the far more consistent and secular utilitarianism of Bentham.

A similar precaution has to be observed and generally has been observed in stating *John Locke's* utilitarianism, though in his *Essay concerning Human Understanding* (1690) it is actually said that "good and evil . . . are nothing but pleasure or pain," or that which "occasions or procures pleasure or pain to us."[137] Yet, despite his general esteem for Locke, Bentham himself pertinently declared: "Of the greatest happiness principle . . . Locke had no clear view."[138] In fact, Locke draws no consequences from his occasional assent to the utilitarian standpoint.

The first writer in the history of English ethics who fully achieved the exact utilitarian formula of the greatest happiness principle was Francis Hutcheson. In his *Inquiry into the Original of Our Ideas of Beauty and Virtue*, 1725, he explicitly states: "That *action* is *best*, which procures the *greatest Happiness* for the *greatest Numbers*; and *that, worst*, which, in *like*

[131] Richard Cumberland, *A Treatise of the Laws of Nature*, 1727, chap. v, §IX, p. 204.

[132] *Ibid.*, chap. v, §xv, p. 213; compare chap. VII, §II, p. 314: "the Common Happiness of All" or compare the apology of Epicurus and the Epicureans, chap. v, §41, p. 262.

[133] *Ibid.*, chap. v, §47, p. 275, §45, p. 248, chap. VI, §1, p. 305.

[134] *Ibid.*, chap. v, §49, p. 280: "The *Glory of God* is *Chief*, then follows the *Happiness of Many Good Men*, and *Inferior* to this is the *Happiness of any Particular Person*," compare chap. VI, §1, p. 305.

[135] *Ibid.*, chap. v, §45, pp. 270 ff.

[136] *Ibid.*, chap. VI, §1, p. 305.

[137] Locke, *An Essay concerning Human Understanding*, 1690, book II, chap. 28, sect. 5; compare chap. 20, sect. 2, chap. 21, sect. 42.

[138] Bentham, *Works*, 1843, vol. IV, pp. 447a, b. Bertrand Russell in his *A History of Western Philosophy*, 1945, p. 775, blames Bentham for "attributing . . . utilitarianism . . . to Priestley who, however, had no special claim to it." Russell rightly mentions Francis Hutcheson as an early advocate of utilitarianism in English ethics of the eighteenth century. But, without sufficient justification, Russell names Locke as an even earlier representative of the doctrine and he overlooks the fact that Bentham himself had strongly emphasized the influence which Helvétius, Beccaria and Hume exercised on him along with Priestley.

manner, occasions *Misery*."[139] "We must . . . observe that every *moral Agent* justly considers himself as a Part of this *rational System*, which may be useful to the *Whole*; so that he may be, in part, an Object of his own Benevolence."[140] "Our Reason can indeed discover certain Bounds, within which we may not only act from *Self-Love*, consistently with the *Good* of the *Whole*, but every Mortal's acting thus within these Bounds for his own *Good*, is absolutely necessary for the *Good* of the *Whole*; and the Want of such *Self-Love* would be *universally pernicious*."[141] Notwithstanding this, Hutcheson is no radical utilitarian. Tendencies such as those just illustrated are always thwarted in his doctrine by opposite tendencies combined with his teaching on the moral sense, so that Albee[142] even goes so far as to deny that Hutcheson was "a proper utilitarian."

Considerably more weight has been laid—and should be laid—on the consistency of the utilitarianism of *John Gay*, developed in an anonymously published dissertation on "the fundamental principle of virtue or morality" (1730), which was first taken into account by Halévy.[143] Actually, Gay also takes it for granted in his *Preliminary Dissertation concerning the Fundamental Principle of Virtue or Morality* that "the Happiness of Mankind may be said to be the Criterion of Virtue."[144] Moreover, he ventures the radical statement: "To ask why I pursue Happiness, will admit of no other Answer than an Explanation of the Terms."[145] But, as Halévy has already implied, like Berkeley and others Gay can at best be called a "theological utilitarian"; for, in Gay's doctrine, though the conception of moral obligation is certainly founded upon the notion of the "happiness of mankind," yet this happiness has itself been based originally on the "Will of God."[146] It is true, as Albee points out, that Gay did not think of the will of God as being arbitrary[147] but urged, on the contrary, that "The Happiness of Mankind" is

---

[139] F. Hutcheson, *An Inquiry into the Original of Our Ideas of Beauty and Virtue*, II, treatise: "An inquiry concerning moral good and evil," sect. 3, §8, 1729, p. 180.

[140] *Ibid.*, sect. 3, §6, p. 176.

[141] *Ibid.*, sect. 3, §5, p. 174 f

[142] See E. Albee, *A History of English Utilitarianism*, 1902, p. 62.

[143] See E. Halévy, *La formation du radicalisme philosophique*, 1901, vol. I, pp. 4, 278 f, and E. Albee, *A History of English Utilitarianism*, 1902, pp. 69-83, e.g. p. 83: "The whole outline of Utilitarianism in its first complete and unencumbered form, is to be found in Gay's Preliminary Dissertation."

[144] John Gay, *Preliminary Dissertation concerning the Fundamental Principle of Virtue or Morality*, prefixed to Edmund Law's translation of Archbishop William King's *An Essay on the Origin of Evil*, 4th edition, 1758, sect. II, "concerning obligation," p. xxix.

[145] *Ibid.*, sect. IV, "Approbation and Affection consider'd with Regard to Merit, or the Law of Esteem," p. xxxiv.

[146] *Ibid.*, sect. II, p. xxix.

[147] See E. Albee, *A History of English Utilitarianism*, 1902, p. 82.

"the Criterion of the Will of God."[148] Nevertheless, he insists also that "the Good of Mankind" is not "a sufficient Obligation."[149] "A full and complete Obligation which will extend to all Cases, can only be that arising from the Authority of God; because God alone can in all Cases make a Man happy or miserable."[150] And so "the Happiness of Mankind" can never be "the immediate Criterion of Virtue."[151] Moreover, a special "Moral sense" (besides the valuation of the happiness of mankind) is supposed by Gay to be "necessary in order to solve"[152] all ethical questions, although he denies that this "Moral Sense" is "innate, or *implanted*"[152] in us. He thinks it is "acquired either from our own *Observation* or the *Imitation* of others."[152] But the consistency of John Gay's secular hedonism must by no means be overrated.

In the class of "theological Utilitarians" should also be mentioned *John Brown*, the Vicar of Newcastle upon Tyne. His *Thoughts on Civil Liberty* (1765) were so extensively discussed in Priestley's "Essay on Government" that Bentham, without going further, could have met with Brown's ideals of the great end of "public happiness" and of "the general welfare" as "first and leading object" in Priestley's quotations.[153] Apart from this, the principle of utility emerges *expressis verbis* in John Brown's *Essays on the Characteristics*, 1751. Virtue is defined there as the "conformity of our affections with the public good: or the voluntary production of the greatest happiness."[154] But he adds that only an "all-powerful God" will make men "happy or miserable as they designedly promote or violate the happiness of their fellow-creatures."[155] Therefore, the "belief in an all-seeing and all-powerful God"[155] is said to be indispensable for the moralist. This belief is thought to be the basis for any ethical doctrine; and so here again a radical, secular utilitarianism has deliberately been avoided.

An even more "theological" and less consistent utilitarian than either John Brown or Gay is *David Hartley*. Bentham acknowledged that he felt him-

---

[148] John Gay, *Preliminary Dissertation concerning the Fundamental Principle of Virtue or Morality*, prefixed to Edmund Law's translation of Archbishop William King's *An Essay on the Origin of Evil*, 4th edition, 1758, sect. II, p. xxix.

[149] *Ibid.*, p. xxx.   [150] *Ibid.*, sect. II, p. xxviii.

[151] *Ibid.*, sect. II, p. xxix.   [152] *Ibid.*, sect. IV, p. xlii.

[153] John Brown, *Thoughts on Civil Liberty, Licentiousness, and Faction*, by the Author of Essays on the Characteristics, 1765, p. 10: "The public Happiness of Mankind," p. 15: "The Welfare of the Public," p. 39: "public Liberty and Happiness," p. 28: "The Happiness of the Community," the *general Welfare*, p. 29: The Welfare of the *whole* Country, p. 161: public Utility, compare p. 46 and see J. Priestley, *An Essay on the First Principles of Government and the Nature of Political, Civil and Religious Liberty*, 1768, pp. 64 f, 66.

[154] John Brown, *Essays on the Characteristics*, 1751, §III, p. 136. Cf. p. 180 on the "Happiness of Mankind," p. 272: "The Goodness of the Deity is seen in the designed end of Purpose of Creation which is 'The Happiness of all his Creatures.'"

[155] *Ibid.*, §VIII, p. 198.

self indebted to Hartley for the extensive and persistent manner in which Hartley applied the principle of association not only to psychology but also to ethics[156] (in the chapter "Of the Rule of Life" in his *Observations on Man*, 1749). But as a matter of fact, the principle of utility also plays a certain part in Hartley's moral philosophy. There are such formulas as these: "We are to direct every action so as to produce the greatest happiness and the least misery, in our power."[157] "The sum total shall always be the best direction in our power for promoting the happiness, and lessening the misery, of others."[158] "We are . . . sent hither to promote . . . convenience and utility . . . publicly and privately."[159] "All the pleasures of malevolence are forbidden, as being so many direct hindrances and bars to our happiness."[160] Yet even "Gross-self-interest" is "sometimes" not quite "condemned."[161] In different sections, the different possible "pleasures" are estimated one after the other in their different moral value: in section II, the pleasures of sensation (eating, drinking, diet, commerce between the sexes); in section III, the pleasures of imagination; in section IV, the pleasures of honor and the pains of shame; in section V, the pleasures of self interest; in section VI, the pleasures of sympathy; in section VII, the pleasures and pains of theopathy.[162] But how far this utilitarianism remains from any consistent secular application of the greatest happiness principle may be seen from some of the major results of this ethical analysis of the different pleasures and pains, for example, by the demand that "we ought never to be satisfied

---

[156] See Bentham, *Works*, 1843, part xx, p. 561b, *Introduction to the Principles of Morals and Legislation*, chap. x, §38 (*Works*, vol. I, p. 57b, Oxford edition 1879, p. 124), and see *Works*, 1843, vol. III, p. 286b: "Whether there ever were a time at which the word happiness failed of presenting to my mind the character of an aggregate, or compound, of which pleasures, and the exemption from corresponding pains, were the sole elements, is more that at present I can recollect. The satisfaction I remember to have experienced at the observation of this interpretation, as given to it in the first place by Helvetius, . . . and afterwards by Hartley, . . . affords some presumption of its being at the first of these times new to me. But perhaps the cause of that satisfaction was not the novelty of the notion in relation to my own conceptions, but the circumstance of seeing the confirmation given to them in these works." "Logical arrangements of instruments of invention and discovery" (written between 1811 and 1831). Hence even here in the question concerning the use of the principle of association Bentham rates the merits of Helvétius peculiarly high and considers him to be more original than Hartley in this respect also.

[157] D. Hartley, *Observations on Man, His Frame, His Duty and His Expectations*, 5th edition, 1810, part II, chap. III, sect. VI, prop. LXX, p. 303.

[158] *Ibid.*, p. 304.

[159] *Ibid.*, chap. III, sect. III, prop. LVII, p. 259.

[160] *Ibid.*, sect. VI, prop. LXVIII, p. 299.

[161] *Ibid.*, sect. V, prop. LXVII, p. 292.

[162] *Ibid.*, pp. 219-250; pp. 251-268; pp. 269-280, pp. 281-293, pp. 294-319; pp. 320-348.

with ourselves till we arrive at perfect self-annihilation and the pure love of God,"[163] or "the love of God regulates, improves, and perfects all the other parts of our nature and affords a pleasure superior in kind and degree to all the rest: it is therefore our primary pursuit."[164] "The moral sense ought to be made the immediate guide of our actions on all sudden emergencies; and therefore its pleasures may be considered as making part of our primary pursuit."[165] Finally, in agreement with the Scripture, even Zionism—that is, "the restoration of the Jews" to Palestine—and "the universal establishment of the true religion" are considered to be necessary causes of greater moral "happiness" which will "change" the face of this world much for the better.[166]

Abraham Tucker may also be counted among the Utilitarian predecessors of Bentham both by reason of a certain number of well observed details and on account of the general tendencies of his somewhat garrulous work *The Light of Nature Pursued*, first published in 1768 under the pseudonym of Edward Search Esq. Here also we meet with the conviction that "the rules of morality stand on the foundation of happiness," that all notions of them which have not this basis to rest upon are "fantastic and unstable."[167] The "summum bonum" is happiness, which is "the aggregate of satisfaction" that is to say, "pleasure taken in the largest sense, as comprising every complacence of mind together with the avoidance of pain or uneasiness."[168] And "why is satisfaction good? Here you must stop, for there lies nothing beyond to furnish materials for an answer: But if anybody denies it you can only refer him to his own common sence by asking how he finds himself, when in state of satisfaction or disquietude" and which of them "he would prefer to the other."[169] "The value of existence depends upon the quantity of happiness received therein."[170] Tucker does not hesitate to confess that he would not be "ashamed of joining with . . . Epicurus";[171] except in as far as Epicurus may have confined pleasure "to gross sensual delights" or to other "pleasure in the vulgar acceptation" which "will not always please."[172] "I can not consent to shut myself up within such narrow limits";[173] but

---

[163] D. Hartley, *Observations on Man, His Frame, His Duty, and His Expectations*, 5th ed., 1810, chap. III, sect. V, prop. LXVII, p. 293.

[164] *Ibid.*, chap. III, sect. VII, prop. LXXI, p. 320.

[165] *Ibid.*, chap. III, sect. VIII, prop. LXXIV, p. 349.

[166] *Ibid.*, chap. IV, sect. II, prop. LXXXV, p. 392, prop. LXXXIII, p. 386 f.

[167] Edward Search, Esq., *The Light of Nature Pursued*, 1768, vol. I, part II, chap. 36, §9, p. 380, "Limitation of Virtue." This first edition of Tucker's work is rare today. There is no copy in the British Museum.

[168] A. Tucker, *The Light of Nature Pursued*, 1st edition, 1768, vol. I, part II, chap. 27, §5, §2, pp. 188, 182.

[169] *Ibid.*, chap. 27, §4, p. 186.

[170] *Ibid.*, vol. II, part I, chap. 16, §16, p. 251.

[171] See for example *ibid.*, vol. I, part 2, chap. 27, §2, p. 182, §3, p. 185.

[172] *Ibid.*, chap. 27, §3, p. 185.

[173] *Ibid.*, chap. 27, §2, p. 182.

apart from that "I can not refuse him my assistance against all opponents."[172] Benevolence with its care for "the good of the public,"[174] is considered by Tucker a cardinal virtue. For "our own good is contained in the good of others."[175] Whatever promotes the general good of the Universe, or of any community comprehended therein, must promote that of every particular."[176] The perfection of our nature lies in entire subjection of the sensitive faculties to the rational; ... the rational faculty constantly prompts to pursue the ... greater good ... in preference to any particular pleasure."[177] And as Bentham did later on, Tucker protests against any "tissue of unmeaning words filling the ear and raising whirlwinds in the imagination but never touching the understanding,"[178] against the "mystery throughout" into which religion and philosophy have sometimes been turned.[178] Nevertheless Tucker also takes great pains to show the "absolute necessity" of true religion "to make the system of morality compleat" [179]—the whole second volume of his work with its bulky three parts has the title "Theology"—and again the assumption of a special "moral sense" (apart from the use of the principle of utility) is not altogether absent. While, therefore, the author seems at times to have the intention of applying the greatest-happiness principle exclusively and with a consistency that would have anticipated Bentham, he has by no means carried out this intention.

In the second volume of Henry Grove's *A System of Moral Philosophy*, written in large part by *Thomas Amory*, the utility principle appears as the principle of the "greatest happiness" of God's creatures. But Amory adds to the phrase "God's creatures" "especially . . . the virtuous and well deserved."[180] This limitation, of course, makes it impossible to carry out a consistent ethical employment of the utility principle. The criterion of morality is here, as generally elsewhere, presupposed to be independent of the utility principle. The standard of morality is, clearly, something other than the utility principle itself.

Adam Smith, too, discusses in his *The Theory of Moral Sentiments* (1759) the problem of the "universal happiness of all rational and sensible beings."[181] He adds, however: "The care of the universal happiness" is only "the busi-

---

[174] *Ibid.*, chap. 34, §2, p. 311 f and chap. 36, 11, p. 384.

[175] *Ibid.*, chap. 34, §2, p. 312.

[176] *Ibid.*, vol. 2, part 3, chap. 29, §2, p. 384.

[177] A. Tucker, *The Light of Nature Pursued*, first pseudonymously published under the name of Edward Search, 1768, vol. ii, part 3, chap. 31, §15, p. 535.

[178] *Ibid.*, vol. i, part 2, chap. 36, §10, p. 382.

[179] *Ibid.*, vol. i, part 2, chap. 36, §10, p. 382.

[180] Henry Grove, *A System of Moral Philosophy*, 1749, vol. ii, p. 556 f. That Amory is the author of chapters xiii-xx of this volume including this passage, Amory says himself, *ibid.*, p. A 2, "Advertisement."

[181] Adam Smith, *The Theory of Moral Sentiments*, vol. ii, part vi, sect. 2, 1790, p. 118.

ness of God and not of man."[182] And how clearly the whole of his ethics differs from Bentham's utilitarianism may be illustrated by the constant emphasis with which he affirms "that it is not the view of . . . utility or hurtfulness which is either the first or principal source" of our moral "approbation and disapprobation."[183]

Strange as it may seem, even such a leading anti-utilitarian as *Joseph Butler* should not be omitted entirely in an account of the development of the utility principle. In his *Fifteen Sermons*, he declares that "nothing can be of consequence to Mankind, or any creature, but happiness. . . . We can therefore owe no Man any thing, but only to further and promote his happiness, according to our Abilities. And therefore a Disposition and Endeavour to do Good to all with whom we have to do . . . is a Discharge of all the obligations we are under to them." "The End of benevolence" is "the greatest publik Good."[184] "Benevolence in the strictest sense includes in it all that is Good and Worthy; all that is Good which we have any Notion of."[185] Nevertheless, this does not make Butler a utilitarian. For—apart from a number of qualifications made in connection with these theses—virtue, according to Butler, does not consist in bringing about the public good. Virtue is only a *disposition* to do so. At any rate Bentham, as we have seen, knew Butler's "Analogy,"[186] and thus even in Butler's writings he could have found reference to the ethical importance of the public welfare.

The extent to which ethical intuitionists, at least in England, combine their anti-utilitarianism with hedonistic tendencies may be further illustrated by the example of *Samuel Clarke*, who lays down as "the Second Branch of the Rule of Righteousness" with respect to our "Fellow-creatures . . . a constant indeavouring to promote in general to the utmost of our power the welfare and happiness of all men."[187] "The exact Observance of all those moral Obligations which have been proved to arise necessarily from the Nature and Relations of Things . . . is the certainest and directest means to promote the Welfare and Happiness, as well of Every man in particular . . . as of all men in general considered."[188] For an avowed intuitionist, it is certainly difficult to give more room to the principle of utility.

---

[182] *Ibid.*, pp. 118 f.

[183] *Ibid.*, vol. I, part IV, chap. 2, p. 476.

[184] Joseph Butler, *Fifteen Sermons, Preached at the Rolls Chapel in London*, 1736, pp. 248 f.

[185] Joseph Butler, *Fifteen Sermons*, 1736, Sermon XII, p. 252.

[186] See Bentham's translation of Voltaire's *Taureau Blanc*, entitled *The White Bull*, 1774, p. xl.

[187] Samuel Clarke, *A Discourse concerning the Unchangeable Obligations of Natural Religion and the Truth and Certainty of the Christian Revelation*, 1724, p. 57.

[188] *Ibid.*, p. 96, compare A. Clarke, *A Demonstration of the Being and Attributes of God*, 1705, p. 116.

Leslie Stephen reminds us of *Le Mercier de la Rivière* and his formula "le plus grand bonheur possible à la plus grande population possible."[189] But there is no evidence that Bentham knew anything of Le Mercier's anonymously published chief work, though Adam Smith appreciated it as the clearest and most detailed exposition of the physiocratic doctrine. In any case, there occur formulas of the utility principle such as these: "L'ordre essentiel à toutes les sociétés particulières est donc l'ordre des devoirs et des droits réciproques dont l'établissement est essentiellement nécessaire à la plus grande multiplication possible des productions, afin de procurer au genre humain la plus grande somme possible de bonheur et la plus grande multiplication possible,"[190] "assurer le plus grand bonheur possible à chacun de ceux qui vivent en société,"[191] "assurer le plus grand bonheur possible à la plus grande population possible."[192] Nevertheless, in spite of the common usage of the greatest happiness formula, how greatly the political and religious background of Lemercier's thought differs from that of Bentham may be seen from Lemercier's own expression of his convictions and aspirations: "Il existe un ordre naturel ... qui nous assure nécessairement toute la félicité temporelle à laquelle nous sommes appellés pendant notre séjour sur la terre, toutes les jouissances que nous pourrions raisonnablement y désirer ... un ordre pour la connaissance duquel la nature nous a donné une portion suffisante de lumières et qui n'a besoin que d'être connu pour être observé; un ordre où ... tous les intérêts sont si parfaitement combinés, si inséparablement unis entre eux, que depuis les Souverains jusqu'au dernier de leurs sujets le bonheur des uns ne peut s'accroître que par le bonheur des autres; un ordre enfin dont la sainteté et l'utilité en manifestant aux hommes un Dieu bienfaisant les prépare ... à l'adorer, à chercher par intérêt pour eux mêmes l'état de perfection le plus conforme à ses volontés ... Plût au Ciel que je pusse ... démontrer ... cette evidence ... aux autres comme je la sens. Plût au Ciel qu'elle fût universellement répandue; elle ne pourroit l'être, qu'elle ne changeât nos vices en vertus."[193]

Another forerunner of Bentham briefly touched upon by E. Halévy is *François Jean Marquis de Chastellux*, a correspondent of Thomas Jefferson who served in the war of American independence and wrote one of the best

---

[189] See L. Stephen, *The English Utilitarians*, 1900, vol. i, p. 178. Stephen quotes only a much shortened extract of Lemercier's work in Eugène Daire's *Physiocrates*, 1846. Lemercier's work itself appeared in 1767 and the formula quoted by Stephen is there to be found in chap. xxix, p. 239.

[190] Le Mercier de la Rivière, *L'ordre naturel et essentiel des sociétés politiques*, 1767, anonymously published, chap. iv, p. 28.

[191] *Ibid.*, p. 31.

[192] *Ibid.*, chap. 29, p. 239.

[193] Le Mercier de la Rivière, *L'ordre naturel et essentiel des sociétés politiques*, anonymously published, 1767, p. vi f.

works on American society of his time.[194] Bentham got into personal touch with Chastellux and read his book "De la félicité publique ou considération sur le sort des hommes dans les différentes époques de l'histoire," anonymously published in 1772. There still exists an *unpublished* long draft-letter of Bentham to Chastellux showing that he had noted carefully many passages of the book of this French general and author.[195] Here, indeed, he could find such encouraging utilitarian remarks as these: "quand même la plus grande félicité des hommes auroit été l'unique but de toute société, il ne seroit pas étonnant qu'il n'eut pas encore été atteint. . . . La physique, il est vrai, atteste l'ancienneté du monde, mais l'histoire démontre que les sociétés sont encore très recentes,"[196] views which obviously run parallel to Bentham's own line of thought.

Professor Everett mentions among the English thinkers of the eighteenth century *Matthew Tindal* and his Deistic principal work *Christianity as Old as the Creation* (1730), where again Bentham could read that those actions "that tend to promote human Happiness are always good; and those that have a contrary Tendency are always bad. . . . 'Tis the Circumstances Men are under by which we are to judge of the Tendency of Actions." Even the "killing a Man . . . by the Magistrates, when the publick Good requires it . . . is an Action always good."[197] Bentham himself told the American journalist John Neal, in 1826, how deeply he felt himself influenced by Tindal in his early youth, and that "Tindal made a free thinker out of me before I was thirteen."[198] Professor Everett himself, however, questions the accuracy of Bentham's memory on this point: I think rightly so; and his doubts are strengthened, in my opinion, by the young Bentham's letters home from Oxford.

But perhaps more important than any of the writers last mentioned are Thomas Chubb and Bernard Mandeville, who have hitherto been overlooked in this connection. There is a rather interesting discussion between *Thomas Chubb* and Thomas Morgan, which began about the year 1728, on questions involving the greatest happiness principle. In a treatise, "Some short Re-

---

[194] E. Halévy, *La formation du radicalisme philosophique*, 1901, tome I, pp. 25, 289 and see C. A. Beard, *The Rise of American Civilization*, 1937, vol. II, p. 445.

[195] Bentham MSS, University College, London, Portfolio 169, Folder 7, sheets 1-18.

[196] F. J. Marquis de Chastellux, *De la félicité publique ou consideration sur le sort des hommes dans les différentes époques de l'histoire*, 1772, anonymously published, tome I, Introduction, p. xvi.

[197] M. Tindal, *Christianity as Old as Creation: or the Gospel a Republication of the Religion of Nature*, 1730, chap. XIII, p. 345; see C. W. Everett, *The Education of Jeremy Bentham*, 1931, pp. 19, 199 f.

[198] See John Neal's translation of Bentham-Dumont's *Traités de législation*, entitled *Principles of Legislation*, Boston, 1830, and his "biographical notice" of Bentham there attached, p. 79.

flections on Virtue and Happiness," Chubb had asserted that "Virtue is solely founded in Benevolence. Selfishness and Benevolence are two distinct and independent principles of action."[199] He nevertheless went on to declare: "That pleasure and pain or happiness and misery are really distinct and different in nature . . . that happiness is really delectable . . . misery disagreable is evident from experience to all mankind . . . so that this must be allowed to be a self-evident proposition or a common principle. . . . Then it will unavoidably follow that happiness is *preferable* to misery . . . and . . . the greater . . . happiness . . . preferable to the less."[200] "A more general happiness is preferable to a less general."[201] "Happiness is the *great end* of being to every sensible creature; and therefore the particular happiness of each individual must and will be the object of desire to every such creature; and consequently selfishness is the product of, or is a part of, the *human Constitution*. But though private happiness be the object of desire to every man, yet it is not the *sole* and *only* object of that affection, for as happiness is *desirable* for oneself, so it is desirable for others also . . . so that benevolence as well as selfishness, is the result of . . . our natural constitution."[202] But if "private and public happiness . . . come in competition . . . the good of the whole . . . of the creation in general . . . comes into case,"[203] "the common felicity."[204] "When . . . man . . . pursues his own happiness under a strict regard to the common good, his own happiness in conjunction with the happiness of well-being of the rest of" his "fellow-creatures" then he is virtuous and on "the high road . . . to solid and lasting felicity," not only in "this life but also in another."[205] Chubb was attacked by Thomas Morgan in a "Defence of Natural and Revealed Religion," 1728, on the ground that he "confounded together a virtuous and a vicious selfishness."[206] To this attack Chubb replied in his treatise "Some short Reflections on Virtue and Vice": "Virtue . . . in a larger sense . . . includes all such actions as are

[199] Thomas Chubb, "Some Short Reflections on Virtue and Happiness," reprinted in Th. Chubb, *A Collection of Tracts on Various Subjects*, 1730, treatise XXXII, p. 433, compare p. 437.

[200] Th. Chubb, *A Collection of Tracts on Various Subjects*, 1730, treatise XXXII, p. 434.

[201] *Ibid.*, p. 435.　　[202] *Ibid.*, p. 437.　　[203] *Ibid.*, pp. 438, 436.

[204] *Ibid.*, p. 447.　　[205] *Ibid.*, p. 447 f.

[206] See Th. Morgan, *Defence of Natural and Revealed Religion*, 1728, p. 29 f, where he replies to Chubb that it is "inconsistency" to say "that acting upon the desire of Personal happiness must at least be as reasonable and fit, that is as virtuous as acting upon the other independent principle of benevolence, or the Desire of public Good and to say that *Virtue* is *solely* founded in benevolence." This "is a thing that I cannot possibly conceive." "He confounds all along the rational regular Desire . . . of personal Happiness with a vitious unreasonable selfishness," "a continued Ramble of Absurdity and contradiction." *Ibid.*, p. 9: "This natural necessary Desire of Happiness . . . cannot be the Ground of any moral Distinction at all."

in themselves right and fit and thereby includes" also selfishness. "In a restrained sense it includes only such as are acts of kindness and beneficence unto others."[207] "All virtue is, in reason, approvable; yet all is not . . . rewardable"[208] (that is to say the selfish virtue is not rewardable). And tho all vice is . . . in reason condemnable; yet all is not, in reason, punishable[208] (that is to say, the vice of acting against his own interest). But it is "unreasonable . . . benevolence when a man chooses to undergo great and durable pains himself, merely to procure a very low degree of short-lived pleasure to another";[208] and it is "unfit and unreasonable" selfishness when a man does not "deny himself one hour's pleasure to day that he may enjoy two hours pleasure to morrow."[209] Further, like Bentham, Chubb points out that "effect, . . . result of action" and "motive to action" are to be distinguished.[210] Despite his discussions concerning punishment and reward by God[211] and despite other theological details, Chubb's ethics shows thus considerable analogy with Bentham's doctrine of the greatest-happiness principle. Yet we are unable to prove that Bentham knew Chubb's treatises.

In regard to *Bernard Mandeville*, it is true that his major tendency is to show that all actions which are most subservient to the "grandeur and the worldly happiness of the whole"[212] are in truth "private vices." This seems to be, to judge by the wording, entirely contrary to the greatest-happiness principle. In the matter itself, however, in the spirit of his investigation, Bentham surely has closer relations with Mandeville than with very many of the earlier utilitarians and hedonists. For everywhere in Mandeville's work we meet attempts at showing the "secret Stratagems of Self-Love,"[213] the thoroughgoing strife for happiness in every individual and society and the *"many Discoveries"* which have still to be *"made in the World of Self-Love,"* the "abundance of Terra incognita *left* . . . yet . . . *behind*" there.[213] All such tendencies fit into Bentham's philosophy of utility, apart from the fact that the formula of the "happiness of the whole" appears explicitly in Mandeville.[214] It is, therefore, comprehensible why Bentham himself acknowledged a certain agreement with Mandeville in at least two characteristic remarks. First, in his *Introduction to the Principles of Morals and Legislation*, where he says emphatically: To the "imperfection of language, and nothing more, are to be attributed in great measure the violent clamours that have from

---

[207] Th. Chubb, *A Collection of Tracts on Various Subjects*, 1730, treatise XXXIII, "Some Short Reflections on Virtue and Vice," p. 448 f; cf. *ibid.*, treatise XXVII, "Reflections on Natural Liberty," p. 374.

[208] *Ibid.*, p. 451.　　　　　　　　[209] *Ibid.*, p. 450.

[210] *Ibid.*, p. 452.　　　　　　　　[211] *Ibid.*, p. 448.

[212] See B. Mandeville, *The Fable of the Bees, or Private Vices, Public Benefits*, ed. by Garman, 1934, p. 25, preface, and frequently elsewhere.

[213] B. Mandeville, *The Fable of the Bees* (anonymously published), 6th edition, 1732, vol. I, p. 256 (Remark T.) (ed. by Garman, 1931, p. 178).

[214] B. Mandeville, *The Fable of the Bees*, ed. by Garman, 1931, p. 25 (preface).

time to time been raised against those ingenious moralists, who, travelling out of the beaten track of speculation, have found more or less difficulty in disentangling themselves from the shackles of ordinary language: such as Rochefoucault, Mandeville and Helvetius. To the unsoundness of their opinions, and, with still greater injustice, to the corruption of their hearts, was often imputed, what was most commonly owing either to a want of skill, in matters of language on the part of the author, or a want of discernment, possibly now and then in some instances a want of probity, on the part of the commentator."[215] As early as in his Commonplace Book for 1774-75, Bentham notes: "The paradoxes of Hobbes and Mandeville (at which divines affect to be so much scandalized) were of service: they contain many original and bold truths, mixed with an alloy of falsehood, which succeeding writers, profiting by that share of light which these had cast upon the subject, have been enabled to separate."[216] Indeed, it is especially his paradoxical way of expression and the more destructive, negative attitude of his mind[217] that separate Mandeville from the constructive and systematic thought of Bentham. Only by such attributes was Bentham able to give his ethics a far more positive, sounder, universal basis.

But even these many names which could not be omitted do not exhaust the list of English moralists who touched on the principle of utility before Bentham. E. L. Kayser goes back as far as Milton's saying: "to place everyone his private welfare and happiness in the public peace, liberty and safety," and finds it "perfectly in harmony with the formula of the greatest good for the greatest number."[218] I should like, finally, to make brief mention of Archibald Campbell, Adam Ferguson, Henry Home and the Frenchman Morelly.

Archibald Campbell, Regius Professor of ecclesiastical history in the University of St. Andrews, tells us even in the title of the second edition of his *Enquiry into the Original of Moral Virtue*, 1733, that "Virtue . . . is the great means of private and publick happiness."

[215] Bentham, *An Introduction to the Principles of Morals and Legislation*, chap. x, §13, note (*Works*, 1843, part I, p. 49, Oxford edition, p. 104).

[216] Bentham, *Works*, 1843, part XIX, p. 73b; compare even *Deontology*, 1834, vol. I, p. 105.

[217] See for instance Mandeville's confession which, however, contains deliberate exaggeration: "what good these notions will produce; truly, besides the reader's diversion, I believe none at all"; at best people should "be made ashamed of always railing at what they are more or less guilty of themselves" (Mandeville, *The Fable of the Bees*, ed. by Garman, 1934, p. 25, preface) or see *ibid.*, p. 230: I even "confess, that I have not been half so solicitous to gain the approbation of others, as I have studied to please myself." (A search into the nature of society.)

[218] See E. L. Kayser, *The Grand Social Enterprise*, 1923, p. 17; and see Milton, *The Prose Works*, ed. J. A. St. John, 1844, vol. II, p. 126 ("The Ready and Easy Way to Establish a Free Commonwealth"); cf. *ibid.*, vol. III, p. 145: the "dear affection to the public good" ("An Apology for Smectymnuus").

58

In Morelly's *Code de la Nature* we read: "Il est incontestable que le motif ou la fin de toute action humaine, est le désire d'être heureux. . . . Tout semble . . . crier . . . à . . . l'homme . . . : *Tu veux être heureux, sois bien-faisant.*"[219]

Adam *Ferguson* was quoted[220] by Bentham in his *White Bull* and, indeed, in Ferguson's *Institutes of Moral Philosophy* are to be found statements to the effect that "the definitions of virtue and happiness are the same,"[221] that "probity implies the love of mankind"[222] and that it constitutes "the whole or the most essential part of virtue."[223] Or lastly: "The fact is that the laws of self-preservation and of society, when well understood, coincide in all their tendencies and applications."[224] "Virtue is the respect . . . and esteem of what tends to the good of mankind."[225]

Even *Henry Home*, while presupposing a special moral sense, does not neglect to remark that "justice never fails to advance the happiness of those who obey its dictates."[226] Such statements, however, do not entitle either Ferguson or Home to be regarded as "forerunners" of Bentham. Home limits his thesis at once by adding that the happiness advanced by justice is only "mental satisfaction,"[227] and that justice and the other "primary virtues are . . . more universal . . . than generosity or any secondary virtue."[228] Ferguson also imposes a strict limitation on his greatest-happiness principle by declaring that "pleasure is a term too vague to be substituted for happiness."[229] For "all good is pleasant, but . . . all pleasure is not good."[230] With similar limitations, the greatest happiness principle may be found tacitly or expressly adopted nearly everywhere in English ethical writings of the eighteenth century.

This very rough sketch of a history of the principle of utility may at least bring out one fact: that it was far more difficult for any moralist of Bentham's time to have overlooked the various *formulations of the greatest-happiness principle than to have become acquainted with it.* Bentham was by no means the first to coin the formula of this principle of utility: it was common currency *before* him. In fact, he con-

---

[219] Morelly, *Code de la nature ou le véritable esprit de ses loix*, 1755, p. 156 f.

[220] See Bentham, *The White Bull, an oriental history, from an ancient Syrian manuscript communicated by Mr. Voltaire cum notis editoris et variorum: sc., the whole faithfully done into English*, 1774, p. xlviii.

[221] A. Ferguson, *Institutes of Moral Philosophy*, 1769, p. 159.

[222] *Ibid.*, p. 106. [223] *Ibid.*, p. 111.

[224] *Ibid.*, p. 115. [225] *Ibid.*, p. 104.

[226] H. Home, *Essays on the Principles of Morality and Natural Religion*, 1758, p. 54.

[227] *Ibid.*, p. 54. [228] *Ibid.*, p. 46.

[229] A. Ferguson, *Institutes of Moral Philosophy*, 1769, p. 160.

[230] *Ibid.*, p. 161.

ceded this frankly and clearly in the following *unpublished* notice: "The principle which I have taken for the ground work of the whole is so far from being (in itself a new one) a new principle that it is no other than the same which men have had and actually have almost for ever in their mouths. What was wanting was not sagacity to discover it, but only resolution to pursue it. A work . . . built (grounded) altogether upon a single principle and that so far from being new that it may be surely deemed as old as the creation."[231] Yet such confessions are to be found not only in unpublished or later published memoranda but in the very beginning of Bentham's first published work, on the very first page of his first book.

The whole tenor of Bentham's *Fragment on Government* shows that he by no means pretended to be the discoverer of the greatest happiness principle. All he wished to do was to say that "the consequences of this fundamental axiom have" not "been as yet . . . developed . . . with sufficient method and precision."[232] That the utility principle ought to be applied to the largest possible extent had already been demanded by Helvétius.[233] Bentham acted in conformity with this postulate of Helvétius. Both in ethics and jurisprudence, he made use of the greatest happiness principle with much greater consistency and circumspection than any of his predecessors. It is this, not the discovery of that axiom, which constitutes the essence of his ethical "reformation."

Strangely enough, however, not only men of the world but also professional philosophers have often ridiculed any attempt to establish a single consistent criterion of morality. In the opinion of these opponents of consistent hedonism, it is evidence of superior wisdom to acknowledge the validity of more than one fundamental moral prin-

[231] Bentham MSS, University College, London, Portfolio 27, Folder 6, sheet 100, p. 21, *unpublished*.

[232] Bentham, *A Fragment on Government*, ed. Montague, 1891, p. 93 (*Works*, 1843, part I, p. 227a). But see in contradiction to this the astonishingly unjustified reproach raised by Albee (*A History of English Utilitarianism*, 1902, p. 166) against Bentham that he "always writes as if he were the first propounder of the Utilitarian principle." Or compare a similar reproach in C. Phillipson, *Three Criminal Law Reformers*, 1923, p. 180. As a matter of fact, Bentham praises even in his first work at least two of his predecessors on this ground: Hume and Helvétius (see *A Fragment on Government*, ed. Montague, 1891, p. 154, chap. I, §36, note).

[233] See C. A. Helvétius, *Oeuvres complètes*, 1818, tome I, discours II, chap. XVII, p. 159: "Le principe . . . de l'utilité du publique, c'est-à-dire du plus grand nombre d'hommes: principe dont personne ne connaît toute l'étendue ni la fécondité; principe qui renferme toute la morale et la législation." ("De l'esprit," discours II, chap. 17.)

ciple, even of a multitude of such principles independent of each other. This pluralism has, of course, to be taken seriously, if it aspires to clarify precisely how these various principles can be applied in order to arrive at trustworthy moral evaluation. But as we shall see later, even C. D. Broad's most acute effort in this direction could not succeed.

If, however, this task of clarification is loftily neglected, these ethical inconsistencies are just as much evidence of intellectual irresponsibility and impotence as, for example, the introduction of different laws of addition in a bank account. Nor is this inconsistency in ethics any less disastrous than it would be in mathematics.

INCONSISTENCIES OF BENTHAM'S UTILITARIAN PREDECESSORS

As we have seen, even the most consistent among the secular utilitarians prior to Bentham were neither able nor willing to avoid some mixture of their leading principle with other not sufficiently definable and not sufficiently fundamental axioms. Even Helvétius (whom Bentham himself appreciates as the most consistent utilitarian amongst his predecessors)[234] likes to introduce the notion of "la grandeur . . . des peuples" without any further explanation alongside the idea of "la félicité temporelle des peuples."[235] He has given the name of "vertus" even to "la chasteté des vestales et les austérités de ces fakirs insensés dont l'Inde est peuplée; vertus . . . dont l'observation exacte ne contribue en rien au bonheur publique . . .; vertus . . . souvent indifférentes et mêmes nuisibles à l'état." He calls them "de vertus de préjugé."[236] At any rate, in comparison with that of Bentham, the framework and design of Helvétius' investigation is far less systematic, and he is much less interested in any exhaustive exposition of the consequences of his principles. Bentham himself implies that much but, at the same time, he acknowledges honestly his obligation to his forerunners in a notice first published by Halévy: "Oh, my master" (Beccaria) and Helvétius who "had already assisted you," "you who have made so many useful excursions into the path of utility, what is there left for us to do?— never to turn aside from the path."[237]

A similar reservation holds good for *Mandeville*. For in Mandeville,

---

[234] See Bentham, *A Fragment on Government*, chap. I, §36, note.

[235] C. A. Helvétius, *Oeuvres complètes*, 1818, tome I, p. 143 f ("De l'esprit," discours II, chap. 15).

[236] *Ibid.*, p. 128 ("De l'esprit," discours II, chap. 14).

[237] E. Halévy, *The Growth of Philosophic Radicalism*, 1928, p. 21 (the English original of this manuscript was published by Halévy first in the English translation of his works).

the "grandeur," the "strength" and "wealth" of "Kingdoms and States"[238] and even of smaller social groups of society plays an even more important part than in Helvétius, or in the much more democratic Bentham. Moreover, some regard for eternal welfare in distinction from "temporal happiness,"[239] or some hints on "the fall of our first parents" and the greater "state of innocence" of man before it,[240] certainly cause some breach in the unity of Mandeville's extremely worldly utilitarianism.

Finally, in Beccaria too, Bentham might well feel disturbed by the inconsistency of the argument concerning the assumption of a special "patto sociale"[241] as a "leading term"[241] in ethics and law in addition to the principle of utility. For Bentham, however, right from the beginning it was impossible to admit any other notion or axiom as equal in rank with the principle of utility, with the reference to happiness, pleasure and pain. And so, as we shall soon see, he launched heavy attacks against many of the ideas which played so influential a part in the ethics and jurisprudence of the time, such as those of an original contract, of the rights of men[242] or the law of nature.

On all these grounds it becomes, I think, comprehensible that Bentham should feel himself the "Newton" of ethics, coming after all his narrower and less consistent predecessors in matters of utilitarianism. "What Bacon was to the physical world, Helvetius was to the moral. The moral world has therefore had its Bacon, but its Newton is yet to come."[243] "What Bacon did was to proclaim—'Fiat experimentum'; but his own knowledge of Natural Philosophy was ignorance . . . what Newton did, was to throw light on one branch of science. But I have planted the tree of utility—I have planted it deep, and spread it

---

[238] B. Mandeville, *The Fable of the Bees*, 1931, ed. by Garman, p. 25 (preface).

[239] *Ibid.*, p. 53 (An enquiry into the origin of moral virtue).

[240] B. Mandeville, *The Fable of the Bees*, 1732, vol. I, p. 398 (A search into the nature of society).

[241] C. Beccaria, *Dei delitti e delle pene*, §xxxvii; and see Bentham, *A Fragment on Government*, chap. I, §3; further cf. Bentham, *Traités de législation*, ed. by Dumont, 1820, tome I, principes de législation, chap. xiii, p. 104, where it is mentioned too that "il y a encore dans son (Beccaria's) ouvrage quelques raisonnements tirés des fausses sources." But it is not clearly stated what this reasoning drawn from false sources is, not even on p. 69, p. 114.

[242] See for instance Adam Ferguson, *Institutes of Moral Philosophy*, 1769, p. 104: "Virtue is a respect of the rights of men, and esteem for what tends to the good of mankind."

[243] See E. Halévy, *La formation du radicalisme philosophique*, tome I, 1901, p. 290 (quoted from Bentham MSS, University College, London, Portfolio 32).

wide."[244] We have seen to some extent, and shall show more fully later, that there are reasons enough for accepting this self-estimation, at least in a circumscribed sense; and the *Fragment on Government* already throws valuable light both on this point and on the problem of a "censorial" moral philosophy in general.

Loyalty to Promises (The Original Contract) and Other *Leitmotifs* of the *Fragment*

The "formation of Government," the "right" and the "duty of the supreme power to make laws," are based, according to Blackstone, on an original contract. Commenting on Blackstone's argument,[245] Bentham tries to demonstrate in different chapters of his *Fragment* why the "original contract," the *contrat social*, can never take the place of a fundamental concept in a "censorial" ethics and jurisprudence, and why it can never replace the principle of utility.

Blackstone himself did not suppose "that there ever was a time when . . . individuals met together in a large plain, entered into an *original contract*, and chose the tallest man present to be their governor. This notion of an actually existing" original contract is not "to be seriously admitted."[246] Yet, "though perhaps in no instance" has any such "*original contract of society* . . . ever been formally expressed at the first institution of a state," according to Blackstone it "must always be understood and implied . . . in nature and reason . . . in the very act of associating together." Certainly, this is an appropriate comment on the extremely influential theory of an original contract. In the most important systems of the law of nature,[247] the original contract is *not*

[244] Bentham, *Works*, 1843, part xx, p. 587 f (Memoranda from Bentham's conversation in the years 1827/28).

[245] The first and longest chapter of Bentham's *Fragment on Government* is entitled "Formation of Government." Here, but also in the fourth chapter on "Right of the Supreme Power to Make Laws" and in the fifth chapter on "Duty of the Supreme Power to Make Laws" Bentham discusses the *contrat social*.

[246] See W. Blackstone, *Commentaries on the Laws of England*, 1773, and Bentham, *A Fragment on Government*, chap. 1, §2.

[247] See e.g. Kant, *Werke*, ed. by E. Cassirer, 1912 ff, Band vi, S. 380 f: "Der ursprüngliche Vertrag" ist "keineswegs als ein *Faktum* vorauszusetzen nötig, ja als ein solches gar nicht möglich, gleichsam als ob allererst aus der Geschichte vorher bewiesen werden müsste, dass ein Volk, in dessen Rechte und Verbindlichkeit wir als Nachkommen getreten sind, einmal wirklich einen solchen Aktus . . . verrichtet haben müsse, um sich an eine schon bestehende bürgerliche Verfassung für gebunden zu achten. Sondern es ist eine *blosse Idee* der Vernunft, die aber ihre unbezweifelte (praktische) Realität hat: nämlich jeden Gesetzgeber

63

thought to be an *actual fact of history*, but a presupposition a priori for the understanding of all moral and juristic relations of human society; it is not a historical fact at the inauguration of political societies but merely a logical condition for explaining the moral facts acknowledged in every possible human community.

Bentham, however, tries to prove that even the presupposition of such "an implied" original contract is in truth a mere "fiction."[248] According to him, from the point of view of the justification of good and evil, the original contract is a "chimera"[249] as useless as it is injurious; and "the indestructible prerogatives of mankind have no need to be supported upon the sandy foundation of a fiction."[250] The season of "Fiction is now over."[251] Only utility can be "the test and measure of all virtue";[252] and no presupposition of any original contract is needed in addition to it. For the obligation of a "contrat social" can never stand against that of utility, while that of utility can and must stand against all obligations of a "contrat social." "Suppose the King to promise that he would govern his subjects . . . not in the view to promote their happiness: would this be binding upon *him*? Suppose the people to promise they would obey him *at all events* . . . let him govern to their destruction. Would this be binding upon *them*?"[253] Solely "the obligation to minister to general happiness" is "an obligation paramount to and inclusive of every other."[252] So any use of the original contract for finding a criterion of virtue is not only superfluous, it is even detrimental in itself and prejudicial to the consistency of any theory of morals. The principle of utility alone in ethics and in law "depends not upon any higher reason, it is itself the sole and all-sufficient reason for every point of practice whatsoever."[254]

---

zu verbinden, dass er seine Gesetze so gebe, als sie aus dem vereinigten Willen eines ganzen Volkes haben entspringen *können*."

[248] Bentham, *A Fragment on Government*, chap. I, §36, §37. It is to be observed as resulting from the next three quotations that Bentham in the *Fragment on Government* had not yet reached the views concerning fictions which he laid down in "A Fragment on Ontology," in his "Chrestomathia" and his "Essay on Logic" (see *Works*, vol. viii, pp. 198b, 199a; vol. viii, p. 119b; vol. viii, p. 262b). At this later time Bentham carefully distinguished fictitious entities from "unreal" or "fabulous" ones, and even justified the usage of fictions, if exercised in a critical way. For without employing fictions "the language of *man* could not have risen above the language of *brutes*" (see *Works*, 1843, vol. vii, p. 119).

[249] *Ibid.*, chap. i, §36 (ed. Montague, 1891, p. 153).

[250] *Ibid.*, chap. i, §36 (ed. Montague, p. 153).

[251] *Ibid.*, chap. i, §37.   [252] *Ibid.*, §36, note.

[253] *Ibid.*, chap. i, §45.

[254] Bentham, *A Fragment on Government*, chap. i, §48.

To approach the same problem from another angle, Bentham has interrupted his theoretical inquiries and has inserted in his *Fragment on Government* some brief autobiographic notes, because, he adds as an excuse, "perhaps a short sketch of the wanderings of a raw but well intentioned mind in its researches after moral truth, may, on this occasion, be not unuseful: for the history of one mind is the history of many."[255] He tells us how he grew up in his first youth in "a monkish atmosphere" and was penetrated by the moral ideals of this atmosphere. (As a matter of fact, Bowring reported that at least the females of Bentham's race were "devoutly believers."[256]) "The Genius of the place I dwelled in, the authority of the state, the voice of the Church in her solemn offices; all these taught me to call Charles a Martyr and his opponents rebels."[255] In short, even for the great radical Bentham, at first only "the Christian Virtues" of "passive obedience, . . . humility and self-denial" were "stamped with the seal"[257] of morality. And what he later on recognized as "the efforts of the oppressed to rescue themselves from Oppression" seemed to him at first to be mere "selfishness and an obedience to the call of passion."[255] Then, "conversing with lawyers," he "found them full of the virtues of their original contract."[255] But they had to confess to him the whole to be a fiction."[258] Therefore, he answered them: Is not "the characteristic of truth to meet no proof but truth?" Only "to prove fiction" there may be "need of fiction." Obviously, you "indulge yourselves in the licence of supposing that to be true which is not, and as well . . . you . . . may suppose that proposition itself to be true, which you wish to prove, as that other whereby you hope to prove it."[258] "Thus continued I unsatisfying and unsatisfied till I learned to see that *utility* was the test and the measure of all virtue; of loyalty as much as any. . . . Having thus got the instruction I stood in need of, I sat down to make my profit of it . . . I bid adieu to the original contract."[258] Here again, Bentham has thus indicated distinctly enough that he did not regard the discovery of the utility principle as his own, but only its consistent and critical application.

Not only Blackstone, but even Beccaria had used the return to the "fiction" of a "contrat social"[259] as a basic, independent title for the derivation of political and moral duties. Bentham, however, emphati-

[255] *Ibid.*, chap. i, §36, note.
[256] Bentham, *Works*, 1843, part XIX, p. 11b.
[257] Bentham, *A Fragment on Government*, chap. i, §36, note.
[258] *Ibid.*, chap. i, §36, note.
[259] See W. Blackstone, *Commentaries on the Laws of England*, 1773, book I, p. 47 f (Introduction, §2) and Beccaria, *Dei delitti e delle pene*, §XXXVII.

cally refuses to follow this line of argument. In the first thirty-five sections of the *Fragment on Government*, he primarily tries to show the unsubstantiality of the alleged differences between "state of nature" and "government." According to him, there never was a state of nature out of which government was formed, and there never was an original contract by which government was created. Yet these discussions need be mentioned here only incidentally. For the contradictions which Bentham found in Blackstone's statements are primarily due to Bentham's interpretation of these different states of society as actual facts. Blackstone, however, does not regard "the state of nature" and the original contract merely as historical facts. Both are to him essentially logical conditions for explaining the moral "nature and reason"[260] of any possible political body. Bentham himself grants that there is a decisive difference between the problems of logical or moral validity on the one hand, and those of factual character on the other; yet, in his view, Blackstone's discussion of the original contract lacks any clear distinction between those questions of a logical or moral Censor and those of an Expositor of facts.[261] But whatever may be the political interest of these discussions, with their details regarding the Spanish, Dutch, Venetian, Neapolitan, Hindustan and Hottentot governments,[262] they are of far less ethical interest. There are, however, some other chains of reasoning in the *Fragment on Government* concerning the original contract; and they do have a definitely ethical relevance.

Bentham's line of argument in these later sections of the *Fragment* is as follows: First, even if it could be granted that a promise, a contract, creates strict moral obligation, "that men are bound by compacts,"[263] this can only be so on the additional tacit presupposition that the promise concerned is valid. And "what is it then that . . . being present makes . . . the promise . . . valid? What is it that being *wanting* makes it *void*? . . . That circumstance . . . , whatever it be on which the validity of a promise depends, that circumstance, I say, and not the promise itself must, it is plain, be the cause of the obligation which a promise is apt in general to carry with it"[264] or to become void. Such circumstances are nothing but the beneficence or the mischievousness of a promise to both parties of the contract. However, as Bentham adds, "if this . . . be the result of the argument, why not come to it at once?

[260] *Ibid.*, book I, p. 47 f.
[261] Bentham, *A Fragment on Government*, chap. I, §30.
[262] *Ibid.*, chap. I, §23, §24, §15, §23 note, §29.
[263] *Ibid.*, chap. I, §36.   [264] *Ibid.*, chap. I, §46.

Why turn aside into a wilderness of sophistry, when the path of plain reason is straight before us?"[265] It is in any case practically speaking dangerous and, theoretically speaking, unscientific, to do this.

As a matter of fact, "that men are bound by compacts is a proposition which men, without knowing or enquiring why, were disposed universally to accede to."[266] "But, after all, for what *reason* is it, that men ought to keep their promises? The moment any intelligible reason is given, it is this: that it is for the *advantage* of society they should keep them."[267] It is the *"duty"* of the subjects "to obey, just so long as it is their *interest*, and no longer. This being the case what need of saying of the one, that he promised so to govern; of the other that they promised so to obey, when the fact is otherwise?"[268] So "it is manifest, on a very little consideration" that no difficulty is "removed"[269] by substituting in place of the principle of utility the assumption of an original contract.

If there are certain bounds which no moral conduct and even no authority of the legislator ought to transgress "of what use is it to say so when these bounds are what no body has ever attempted to mark out to any useful purpose; that is, in any such manner whereby it might be known beforehand what description a law must be of to fall *within*, and what to fall *beyond* them? . . . what rule does this sort of discourse furnish us for determining whether any one that is in question is, or is not of the number? As far as I can discover, none. Either the discourse goes on in the confusion it began . . . and no intelligible argument at all is offered; or if any, such arguments are drawn from the principle of *utility*: arguments which, in whatever variety of words expressed, come at last to neither more nor less than this; that the tendency of the law is, to a greater or less degree, pernicious."[270] Therefore, Bentham always comes to the conclusion that "it is the principle of *utility*, accurately apprehended and steadily applied, that affords the only clue to guide a man through these straits."[271] Only utility can be the "standard to which . . . men . . . refer . . . in judging" of moral and juristic "approbation or disapprobation."[272] This is, in any case, in itself a consistent "censorial" argumentation,[273] leading beyond the surface of common ethical reasoning.

[265] *Ibid.*, chap. IV, §28.   [266] *Ibid.*, chap. I, §38.   [267] *Ibid.*, §42.
[268] *Ibid.*, §43.   [269] *Ibid.*, §40.   [270] *Ibid.*, chap. IV, §28.
[271] *Ibid.*, chap. IV, §20.
[272] Bentham, *A Fragment on Government*, ed. Montague, 1891, p. 120, preface (*Works*, 1843, vol. I, p. 238a.)
[273] It would be out of place to discuss here at full length why Bentham's anal-

Second, Bentham argues: "Allow for argument's sake, what we have disproved: allow that the obligation of a promise" of an original contract "is independent of every other: allow that a promise is binding

ysis of the duty of fulfilling promises is, at least in my view, more conclusive than the most acute inquiries into the same question made by contemporary anti-hedonists. I wish, however, to mention briefly Sir David Ross's analysis of the duty of fulfilling promises. He says in his *The Right and the Good*, 1930, p. 17 (cf. W. D. Ross, *Foundations of Ethics*, 1939, pp. 19 ff): "When a plain man fulfills a promise because he thinks he ought to do so, it seems clear that he does so with no thought of its total consequences, still less with any opinion that these are likely to be the best possible. He thinks in fact much more of the past than of the future. What makes him think it right to act in a certain way is the fact that he has promised to do so—that and, usually, nothing more. That his act will produce the best possible consequences is not his reason for calling it right. . . . It must of course be admitted that . . . exceptional cases . . . exist. If I have promised to meet a friend at a particular time for some trivial purpose, I should certainly think myself justified in breaking my engagement if by doing so I could prevent a serious accident or bring relief to the victims of one. And the supporters of the view we are examining hold that my thinking so is due to my thinking that I shall bring more good into existence by the one action than by the other. A different account may, however, be given of the matter, an account which will, I believe, show itself to be the true one. It may be said that besides the duty of fulfilling promises I have and recognize a duty of relieving distress, and that when I think it right to do the latter at the cost of not doing the former, it is not because I think I shall produce more good thereby but because I think it the duty which is in the circumstances more a duty. This account surely corresponds much more closely with what we really think in such a situation. If, so far as I can see, I could bring equal amounts of good into being by fulfilling my promise and by helping some one to whom I had made no promise, I should not hesitate to regard the former as my duty. Yet on the view that what is right is right because it is productive of the most good I should not so regard it." On this the utilitarian has to remark, first, that Bentham does not deny that the plain man thinks generally in the way characterized by Sir David. As to this point, Bentham cannot be refuted because he does not draw this point into debate. But Sir David, I think, is mistaken in introducing it in support of his thesis.

Anti-hedonism commonly becomes guilty of the same fallacy for which, without reason, it blames consistent hedonism, namely, the illicit identification of what people *actually* think or desire with what they rightly ought to think or ought to desire. It is true that in Sir David's argument this fallacy is hidden by the fact that he speaks of people actually thinking that this or that is *right*, and not thinking that this or that feeling *exists*. Nevertheless, there is an obvious paralogism implied.

It is a paralogism to imply that all *is* right that people think right. Hedonists are certainly wrong if they (as perhaps John S. Mill, but not Bentham, does) conclude that all is morally right that is actually desired as useful. But anti-hedonists commit a fallacy of the same type if they argue, as they often do, that all is morally right of whose rightness people are actually convinced. (Cf. G. E. Moore, *Ethics*, 1912, p. 124: "It is totally impossible . . . that to believe an action to be right can be the same thing as believing that we ourselves or some-

propria vi." There occurs a second difficulty: on whom is this promise binding? "on him certainly who makes it. Admit this: For what reason is the same individual promise to be binding on those who *never* made

---

body else believe it to be right.") Again, this paralogism is not committed by Bentham.

Second, as to the problem of moral conflicts, Sir David Ross admits that in certain circumstances promises must not be kept if they force us to neglect an act which is more a duty. But this is no refutation of Bentham either. For Bentham says precisely the same. The difference is only this: Bentham adds that the higher duty is that whose fulfillment produces more general happiness, while the anti-hedonist insists upon the statement that the higher duty is simply that which we actually think to be the higher duty, and that it is incorrect to define duty or morally "right" by reference to anything else. Also, in his lecture on "The Meanings of Good" (*Travaux du IXe Congrès International de Philosophie*, fascicule XI, 1937, p. 80) Sir David refers explicitly to the actual thought of the plain man as the ultimate instance in matters of duty. But this pronouncement of the anti-hedonist is by no means more satisfactory or even more correct than that of his opponent. It is at best as wrong as that of the hedonist. For granted even that consistent hedonism were wrong in basing duty on the greatest happiness of the greatest number, then the argument of the anti-hedonist leads to a not less untenable conclusion in the case of a conflict of duties.

For who decides what *is* the higher duty? As to the example of Sir David Ross, I too think that it is the higher duty to help the victims of an accident. But there are hundreds of thousands of people who do *not* think that it is their duty to help victims of an accident, but to keep appointments for some "trivial purpose." At best, without noticing it, they confirm a general observation made by Bentham, namely, they distribute eulogistic and dyslogistic terms in a different way than we do, calling their appointments diplomatic duties, social obligations, non-intervention committees and the like, and the victims of "serious" accidents red mischief-makers or capitalistic criminals. Therefore, in this and in hundreds of perhaps even more important examples, the consistent anti-hedonist, excluding the reference to happiness or other "good things" can give only one instruction, namely, that the higher duty is whatever men actually think it to be. That is to say, A.'s statement that this is the higher duty and B.'s statement that this is not the higher duty are both right. I cannot admit that an ethical analysis leading to a conclusion such as this is less unsatisfactory than the argument of hedonism, even if it were wrong.

Third, it is again no refutation of hedonism to assume that a hedonist would not regard it as my duty to fulfill a promise, "if, so far as I can see, I could bring equal amounts of good into being by fulfilling my promise and by helping someone to whom I had made no promise" (*ibid.*, p. 18). In contrast to this, it seems to me obvious that on this point again hedonism comes to the same result as its adversary. That Sir David questions this is, I assume, due to the fact that he neglects a sufficiently careful application of the moral calculus. In his examples, reckoning with equal amounts of happiness or with a preponderance of 1/1000 unit of happiness on the side of the duty of the philanthropist (*ibid.*, pp. 34 f and even pp. 38 f) he obviously does not take into consideration that, at all events, the amount of happiness produced by the fulfillment of promises or the corresponding loss of happiness in the case of their nonfulfillment must form a

it? The King, *fifty years ago*, promised my *Great-Grandfather* to govern him according to Law: my Great-Grandfather, *fifty years ago*, promised the King to obey him according to Law. The King, *just now*, promised my *neighbour* to govern him according to Law; my neighbour, *just now*, promised the King to obey him according to Law.—Be it so—What are these promises, all or any of them, to me?"[274] So if political duties are interpreted ethically as promises made by those persons to whom these duties are obligatory then these promises cannot be proved to be binding; for these promises have not been made by the persons in question, but only by their ancestors.

Third, according to Bentham, nothing makes an impression of greater unreality amid the exciting events of history than do the arguments from the conception of an original contract. "Armed and full of indignation . . . malcontents are making their way to the royal palace."[275] But, adds Bentham sarcastically: "In vain." Every adherent of the theory of the original contract has always the power to disarm malcontents by a kind of "enchantment." Every adherent of the doctrine of the original contract has always a certain magic to "put his hook into the nose" of rebels; he can tell them: "to disagree, to clamour, to take back . . . their wills again, is now . . . too late: . . . their wills have been put in hotchpot along with the rest: they *have* 'united'— they *have* "consented'—they *have* 'submitted.' "[275] And, therefore, they will "go back as they came, and all is peace"! It is true, so Bentham concludes these reflections, "now and then . . . one error may be driven out, for a time, by an opposite error: one piece of nonsense by another piece of nonsense. But for barring the door effectually and for ever against all error and all nonsense, there is nothing like the simple

---

considerable part of the sum of the total happiness at issue. If, nevertheless, the balance in favor of the fulfillment of the promise is only 1/1000 unit, or if there is even a number of units in favor of the duty contrary to the fulfillment of the promise, then the promise must necessarily concern a relatively trivial purpose in comparison with the other duty. With regard to promises of this type, however, Sir David *allows* breach of a bond, just as the utilitarian does, with one single difference in favor of the utilitarian, namely this: The consistent hedonist tries to understand why certain purposes in our examples should be called trivial, while the anti-hedonist cannot tell us in any way which purposes should be called trivial and which accidents serious. He must finally leave such decisive ethical questions to arbitrary, capricious discretion; and the ethical judgment of the anti-hedonistic fascist will on all essential points be contradictory to that of the Quaker democrat.

[274] Bentham, *A Fragment on Government*, chap. I, §47.
[275] *Ibid.*, chap. IV, §16.

truth."[276] This simple truth is here always the principle of utility, the utility "of all the individuals . . . that compose . . . a state . . . without distinction."[277] Certainly, the second and the third of these arguments are much less convincing than the first. This first one, however, is I think, of vital importance.

Further, the *Fragment on Government* laid down some basic ethical definitions, the list of which has been but little enlarged in Bentham's *Introduction to the Principles of Morals and Legislation* and in his later publications. Already, at the end of the *Fragment on Government*, he states: "For expounding the words *duty, right* . . . and . . . other terms of the same stamp that abound so much in ethics and jurisprudence . . . the only method by which any instruction can be conveyed" is the reference to happiness and pain, the principle of utility.[278] "Political duties created by punishment" (causing pain): "or at least by the will of persons who have punishment in their hands. Religious duty is also created by punishment: by punishment expected at the hands of a person *certain*—the Supreme Being. Moral duty is created by a kind of motive, which from the *un*certainty of the *persons* to apply it, and of the species and degree in which it will be applied, has hardly yet got the name of punishment: by various mortifications resulting from the ill-will of persons *un*certain and variable—the community in general: that is such individuals of that community as he, whose duty is in question, shall happen to be connected with."[279] In similar definitions, Bentham has always broken down the notions of political, religious and moral duty and has expressed their meaning in terms of pleasure and pain alone, thus evading the original contract as well as all other less palpable and elementary concepts.

It is this elementary and palpable character of pleasure and pain,

[276] Bentham, *A Fragment on Government*, chap. iv, §16.
[277] *Ibid.*, chap. ii, §34, note iii. A historically interesting view of Bentham formulated on this occasion may be added. Bentham mentions that for good reasons he never could call the Athenian Commonwealth a true democracy. For "in the Athenian Commonwealth, upon the moderate computation, it is not one tenth part of the inhabitants of the Athenian state that ever at a time partook of the supreme power: women, children, and slaves, being taken into the account. Civil lawyers, indeed tell you with a grave face, that a slave is *nobody*." But, for the radical democrat Bentham, a democratic state which neglects the interests of so many of its members is as much a caricature of a democracy as a fool who has stuck himself up one day on the throne "with a stick, by way of a sceptre," is a caricature of a reigning king (see chap. ii, §34, note i and 3).
[278] *Ibid.*, chap. v, §6, note 5.
[279] *Ibid.*, chap. v, §6, note 9, 2-4.

which is, I think, rightly emphasized by Bentham as being of primary importance; and it is from this fact that he infers a main reason for the superiority of the greatest happiness principle over all other ethical axioms. For, as he says in the preface of his work, "the only consequences that men are at all interested in, what are they but pain and pleasure?"[280] These terms, indeed, "if they can be said to belong to any science, belong rather to Ethics than to Jurisprudence"; or as Bentham humorously puts it, "*pain* and *pleasure* at least, are words which a man has no need, we may hope, to go to a Lawyer to know the meaning of."[280] Therefore only by such words as pain and pleasure should ethical principles be expressed.

This vital point of consistent hedonism, the recognition of the "indubitable fact" that no "direct experience" of pleasure or pain can be "illusory"[281] is, as far as I can see, nowhere more impressively and graphically expressed than in a most recent work by Clarence Irving Lewis. Chapter XIII of Professor Lewis' *An Analysis of Knowledge and Valuation* is entitled "The Immediately Valuable" and in this chapter it is expounded over and over again why "pleasure is a kind of good which is immediate, and concerning which finding or not finding is conclusive."[282] And "the illusion of a painful state of affairs" can be illusory only "as regards the state of affairs"[283] but never as regards the immediately felt pain. Value can and should be defined only "in a way which brings it home in the end to a quality directly disclosed or disclosable in experience, and a quality which *when* disclosed is unmistakable" such as pleasure and pain.[284] "Any deed done is permeated with an immediately felt good or ill."[285] As to pleasure and pain immediately experienced "*esse* is *percipi*."[286] For, "if our direct value-apprehensions should have *no* correlation with the objective value-properties of things, then it would be totally impossible for us to learn from experience how to improve our lot in life; because our pleasures and displeasures on earlier occasions must then utterly fail to teach us what gratifications or what pains we are to expect on later occasions."[287]

Giovanni Gentile and Salomon Friedlaender[288]—following an old speculative tradition which culminated in the metaphysical teachings

---

[280] *Ibid.*, p. 121 (*Works*, 1843, vol. I, p. 238a).
[281] C. I. Lewis, *An Analysis of Knowledge and Valuation*, 1946, pp. 407, 409.
[282] *Ibid.*, p. 397.   [283] *Ibid.*, p. 407.   [284] *Ibid.*, p. 398.
[285] *Ibid.*, p. 502.   [286] *Ibid.*, p. 407.   [287] *Ibid.*, p. 423.
[288] See S. Friedlaender, *Schöpferische Indifferenz*, 1918.

of Jacob Böhme, Fichte, and Hegel—tried to deny completely that pain is a non-value. They insist that pain is "providentially" as vital for us as pleasure to "spur us from task to task."[289] It is pain which has to be recognized "as the inner spring by which the mind progresses and lives on condition of progressing."[289]

But despite this recognition of the value of pain, these "polaristic" philosophies, too, admit in the end that the ultimate value can be only the perpetual overcoming of pain, the conquest of the "painful . . . not being of the mind" by the supremely joyous life and being of the mind, by the blissful superiority over pleasure and pain in the state of an elated "creative indifference."

Georges Sorel obviously tries to go even further than the philosophical polarists and insists that pain is more valuable for the development of mankind than pleasure.[290] Yet he, too, must admit that, in the end, it is not pleasure itself which is to be rejected; the rejection concerns only the dilapidating effects of those pleasures which lead to the greater pain of decay—a pain which is certainly greater than the pain connected with the hard work of bodily and mentally healthy men.

Even Alfred N. Whitehead agrees that his formalistic philosophy of the good stands in need of supplementary analyses of "emotional . . . experience,"[291] i.e. unavoidably analyses of pleasure and pain.

A second (practically the same) important reason for the preference of the utility-principle above other ethical axioms is, according to Bentham, its reference to what he rather inaptly calls "external events,"[292] to pain and punishment in contrast to uncontrollable subjective convictions. It is with deliberation that Bentham, in his definitions of political, religious and moral duties, referred to nothing but three sorts of punishment. For, as he explains in the *Fragment*, it is exclusively by reference to such "extrinsic . . . events" as the pain of punishment

[289] G. Gentile, *Teoria Generale dello Spirito come Atto Puro*, 1944, pp. 234, 233 ff: "Ecco il dolore provvidenziale che ci spinge di collo in collo e che è stato sempre riconosciuto la molla interna per cui lo spirito progredisce, e vive a patto di progredire."

[290] G. Sorel, *Introduction à l'économie moderne*, 2nd ed., 1922, pp. 403 ff. Compare Louis de Bonald, "Pensées sur divers sujets et discours politiques" in *Oeuvres*, 1845, tome VI, p. 203: "Le bonheur est vulgaire et familier. . . . Il n'y a de noble que le malheur."

[291] See A. N. Whitehead, "Mathematics and the Good," in *Essays in Science and Philosophy*, 1948, p. 85.

[292] Bentham, *A Fragment on Government*, ed. by Montague, 1891, chap. v, §6, note 9, 5.

that a man who speaks of duty can distinguish duty proper from "his own internal sentiment" as well as from the conduct of the party spoken of. If however a man persists in asserting something "to be a duty, but without meaning it should be understood that it is on any of these three accounts; . . . all he then asserts is his own internal *sentiment*: all he means then is, that he feels himself *pleased* or *displeased* at the thoughts of the point of conduct in question, but without being able to tell *why*. In this case, he should e'en say so: and not seek to give an undue influence to his own single suffrage, by delivering it in terms that purport to declare the voice either of God, or of the law, or of the people."[293] Hence it is just by its reference to such "extrinsic events" as constitute punishment that the principle of utility makes it possible to get rid of the common definitions of duty which move in a circle of vague "internal" sentiments. Physical pain, too, has later been characterized by Bentham as punishment by nature.

Third, in Bentham's view the consistent use of the utility-principle gives a real chance of adjustment between contending parties in difficult cases of moral disputes. If, however—neglecting the "censorial" use of the utility principle—everyone could call his unfounded internal approbation of a moral rule a proof of this rule, then the chances of ever coming to an agreement would be very slight. "A pair of disputants . . . may go on irritating and perplexing one another for everlasting."[294] For then their argument "is no more than announcing, and that in an obscure . . . manner, their opposite persuasions, or rather affections, on a question of which neither of them sets himself to discuss the grounds";[294] and "it is the perplexity of ambiguous and sophistical discourse that, while it distracts and eludes the apprehension, stimulates and inflames the passions."[295]

By reference to the principle of utility, however, "the door to reconcilement" of morally contending parties "would be much more open," because they then might see that their dispute does not concern "a mere affair of passion" and of "warped and clouded . . . language,"[296] but a difference of sincere judgment based on observation of facts. If the debate "is instituted on the footing of utility, the parties might at length . . . come to an agreement or at least to a visible and explicit issue" comparing the amounts of future beneficial and mischievous contingencies of the problematic measure.[297] At any rate, after having

[293] *Ibid.*, chap. v, §6, note 9, 5. [294] *Ibid.*, chap. iv, §40.
[295] *Ibid.*, chap. iv, §41. [296] *Ibid.*, chap. iv, §39 f.
[297] *Ibid.*, chap. iv, §41, §39.

reduced moral discussions to a debate on the different amounts of happiness which are involved, we are in our disputes on far more objective and firmer ground than in opposing each other with so-called moral intuitions. For between different ethical intuitions no understanding can be reached. Every common basis of argument is missing, and all reasoning must stop. In matters of pain and pleasure, however, there may be differences of opinion; but there is a common and objective ground for discussion.

Further, we find in the *Fragment* the first indications of the consistent employment of a moral calculus combined with the consistent use of the principle of utility. Bentham urges that not only the production of mischief is immoral, but even the omission of an act which would have increased a certain state of well-being if it had been performed.[298] But he by no means underrates the difficulties to be overcome in a moral arithmetic, as may be seen in the following reflection: "A natural question here is—by what sign" the probability of mischievous consequences of a planned action shall be "conspicuous and perceptible to all . . . *Common* sign for such a purpose, I for my part, know of none: he must be more than a prophet, . . . that can show us one. For that which shall serve as a particular sign to each particular person, I have already given one—his own internal persuasion of a balance of *utility*."[299] It is clear that the necessary risk which has to be undertaken in judging the extent of the beneficent or mischievous consequences of an act is here not underestimated by Bentham.

Yet the extremely superficial kind of moral calculus casually suggested by Blackstone is energetically rejected by Bentham—in spite of his own inclination for a moral arithmetic. Blackstone had worked out "without hesitation" in a strange "piece of intelligence" that, by its very nature, a democratic government possesses a greater quantity of honesty than a monarchic or an aristocratic one, while the most characteristic attribute of an aristocracy is more wisdom, of a monarchy more strength; the British Constitution, however, representing a union of the three possible sorts of government and combining, therefore, their "three great qualities," is the most excellent of all imaginable ones.[300] Bentham, in "plain English," in his chapters on "Forms of

[298] Bentham, *A Fragment on Government*, ed. by Montague, 1891, p. 101 (preface), *Works*, 1843, vol. I, p. 230a.
[299] Bentham, *A Fragment on Government*, chap. IV, §22.
[300] See W. Blackstone, *Commentaries on the Laws of England*, 1773, book I,

Government" and on "British Constitution," only makes fun of such "sycophantical . . . songs of eulogy."[301] In contrast to them he stresses both the desirability and the difficulties of a systematic moral calculus; and it is just at this point that the motives leading to the erection of a moral arithmetic become apparent in some of their most attractive features.

Thus, from every vantage point, Bentham reaches the conclusion that only on the basis of the principle of utility can a consistent "censorial" and, as far as possible, an exact theory of morals be erected. Bentham never overlooked the notable fact that "the consideration of utility" may often govern the judgment upon moral matters "*secretly*," not consciously; but he insists that, *at least* unconsciously, it governs the judgment of "every reflecting man . . . unavoidably."[302] "The *reason* of a Law" can be no other than "*pain* or pleasure."[303] Subjectively the lawgiver or any moral agent may be entirely unaware that he is directed by weighing degrees of pleasure and pain in his activities. But no human being can refrain from being subject to the necessity of these "calculations." Moreover, what is far more important, even if the moral agent denies that the weighing of pleasure and pain has any bearing on his actual behavior, the objective criterion of the moral value of his action can be judged only by reference to the greatest happiness principle. Georg Simmel expressed this difference between "psychological hedonism" and "ethical hedonism" most radically by stating: "Der kategorische Imperativ des Utilitarismus . . . wird . . . in keiner Weise von der Wahrheit oder Falschheit des tatsächlichen Eudämonismus berührt."[304] Ethical hedonism and the validity of its utility principle certainly does not presuppose the acceptance of the belief that all behavior of men is, in some way, determined by hedonistic reflections.

However, before actually building a consistent utilitarian ethics on

---

pp. 49 f, 51 and Bentham, *A Fragment on Government*, chap. II on "Forms of Government" and chap. III on "British Constitution."

[301] Bentham, *A Fragment on Government*, chap. III, §21, and chap. II, III in general.

[302] *Ibid.*, chap. I, §45.

[303] Bentham, *A Fragment on Government*, ed. by Montague, 1891, p. 121, note 1 (*Works*, 1843, part I, p. 238a): "The *reason* of a Law . . . is no other than the *good* produced by the mode of conduct which it enjoins . . . the mischief produced by the mode of conduct which it prohibits. This mischief or this good—can not but shew themselves somewhere or other in the shape of *pain* or *pleasure*."

[304] G. Simmel, *Einleitung in die Moralwissenschaft*, vol. I, 1892, p. 312.

this ground, Bentham found it necessary first to justify not only the theoretical indispensability, but also the practical importance of his new critical attitude toward existing morality. So, with great fairness and ripe impartiality, he finds: "If, on the one hand, a hasty and undiscriminating condemner of what is established, may expose himself to contempt; on the other hand, a bigoted or corrupt defender of the works of power becomes" not less "guilty of the abuses which he supports."[305] Or if "there be some institutions which it is 'arrogance' to attack, there may be others which it is effrontery to defend. Tourrell has defended torture: torture established by the 'public judgment' of so many enlightened nations. Beccaria ('indecent' and 'arrogant' Beccaria!) has condemned it. Of these two, whose lot among men would one choose rather—the Apologist's or the Censor's?"[306] Moreover—and this judgment likewise is not too sweeping—Bentham finds no lawyer and no moralist "guiltless" who, even as an Expositor of existing moral valuations, contributes to circulate any "faults and sophistical . . . reasons" on behalf of an institution or a moral conviction, even when he only delivers such reasons "as from other writers without censure."[307] For "a man will scarcely . . . without some note of disapprobation be the instrument of introducing in the guise of a reason, an argument which he does not really wish to see approved. Some method or other he will take to wash his hands of it . . . if he omits to do this, the most favourable cause that can be assigned to the omission is indifference: indifference to the public welfare—that indifference which is itself a crime."[308] So far does Bentham wish to extend the necessity of moral criticism.

On the other hand, he admits that the "humbler function" of a mere "Expositor of existing morality is a quite legitimate one."[309] Yet the "professed object" of such an expositor has merely to be to explain what the present laws are; "ita lex scripta est" is "the only motto" which he stands "engaged to keep in view."[310] As soon as any author wants to superadd to his work as an expositor anything of the business of a censor, of a moral critic, quite "new duties, . . . additional obligations" are imposed on him; and in any case this function of a Censor ought

[305] *Ibid.*, p. 100 (*Works*, 1843, vol. 1, p. 229b).
[306] *Ibid.*, p. 105 f (*Works*, 1843, vol. 1, pp. 231b, 232a).
[307] *Ibid.*, p. 100, preface (*Works*, 1843, vol. 1, p. 229b).
[308] *Ibid.*, p. 100 f (*Works*, 1843, vol. 1, pp. 229b, 230a).
[309] *Ibid.*, p. 100 (*Works*, 1843, vol. 1, p. 229b).
[310] *Ibid.*, p. 99 (*Works*, 1843, vol. 1, pp. 229a, b).

to be executed with strictest "impartiality, or not at all."[309] But every uncontrolled mixture of "censorial" and "expository"[311] methods, every confused combination of occasional moral criticism with the work of an out and out Expositor, is detrimental. It is contrary to the very task of ethics to blunt criticism of existing laws in this way.

In the eyes of Bentham, in sharp contrast to Blackstone, it remains ridiculous "to look upon it as a kind of presumption and ingratitude" or even "rebellion and cruelty . . . to imagine" that old-established laws could be to a large extent "a fit object of condemnation."[312] Why should "the merit of justifying a law when right . . . be thought greater than that of censuring it when wrong"?[312] "The motto of a good citizen" has to be not only "*to obey punctually*," but also "to censure freely."[312] "A system that is never to be censured, will never be improved."[312] The "disposition to find everything as it should be" is, in Bentham's view, not only "at variance . . . with utility" it is at variance even "with itself . . . ; since whatever *now* is established, *once* was innovation."[313] All these are certainly well-chosen and persuasive arguments in favor of freedom of moral criticism.

Again, in addition to showing the theoretical necessity of the censorial attitude in morals, Bentham tries to demonstrate its practical innocuousness. He argues that "precipitate censure, cast on an . . . institution, does but recoil on the head of him who casts it. From such an attack it is not the institution itself, if well grounded, that can suffer. What a man says against it either makes impression or makes none. If none, it is just as if nothing had been said about the matter: if it does make an impression, it naturally calls up some one or other in defence. For if the institution is in truth a beneficial one to the community in general, it cannot but have given an interest in its preservation to a number of individuals. By their industry, then, the reasons on which it is grounded are brought to light: from the observation of which those who acquiesced in it before upon trust now embrace it for conviction. Censure therefore, though ill-founded, has no other effect upon

[311] *Ibid.*, pp. 106, 120, preface (*Works*, 1843, vol. i, pp. 232a, 238a).

[312] *Ibid.*, p. 101 (*Works*, 1843, vol. i, p. 230a).

[313] *Ibid.*, p. 101, preface (*Works*, 1843, p. 230a); compare Bentham, *Defence of Usury*, 1818, p. 145 (*Works*, 1843, part v, p. 22b). This "disposition to find everything as it should be," the avowed "hostility to every . . . liberal plan of . . . discussion" (p. 103) is also elsewhere especially attacked by Bentham, see for instance p. 110 or chap. iv, §9, where he assumes that Blackstone wished perhaps to defend the point of view that "whatever persons do actually exercise supreme power . . . those persons have the right to exercise it."

an institution than to bring it to that test, by which the value of those, indeed, on which prejudice alone has stamped a currency, is cried down, but by which the credit of those of sterling utility is confirmed."[314] This line of argument is, it is true, rather optimistic, but on the whole it is not unsound; without giving way to youthful exaltation it certainly reveals a sincere recognition of the dangers of super-radicalism.

THE RESISTANCE AGAINST CONSISTENT "CENSORIAL" ETHICS.
SOME PSYCHOLOGICAL CAUSES AND EFFECTS OF THIS RESISTANCE.

Similarly, Bentham's psychological analysis of the motives of ultra-conservative anti-Reformers is to a large extent fair and well balanced. Not without reason, Bentham mentions as a specially common prejudice "mechanical veneration for antiquity" or "a kind of *personification* . . . as if the Law were a living creature."[315] Blackstone had characterized it as *"the utmost arrogance . . .* to censure what has, at least a better chance to be right, than the singular notions of any particular man."[316] But Bentham brings to light the confusion produced by such feelings of "holy zeal" by pointing out that "not laws" but only men can ever be "the butt of arrogance."[317] "When it is from passion and ill-humour that men speak, it is with *men* that they are in ill-humour, not with laws"[317] or moral principles. "The Law is no man's enemy: the Law is no man's rival."[318] Modern inquiries could perhaps add that the provisions of old laws are frequently interpreted or unconsciously felt as commandments of dead ancestors who are supposed still to have the power to impose respect. Be this as it may, in a "science of ethics" the personification of moral laws is certainly a very misleading metaphor.

This is not the only way, however, in which Bentham tries to unmask the mentality of decided "anticensorial" moralists. He also shows —as he did later very often with special success—how only too many

[314] *Ibid.*, p. 101 f (*Works*, 1843, vol. 1, pp. 230a, b).

[315] *Ibid.*, p. 101 and see e.g. the following phrases of Blackstone: "The Law will not suffer itself to be trifled with" (*ibid.*, p. 109), "The Law has to be justified of her children" (*ibid.*, p. 111).

[316] W. Blackstone, *Commentaries on the Laws of England*, 1773, vol. IV, p. 50, meaning thereby certain ecclesiastical institutions.

[317] Bentham, *A Fragment on Government*, ed. Montague, 1891, p. 102 (*Works*, 1843, vol. 1, p. 230b).

[318] *Ibid.*, p. 103 (*Works*, 1843, vol. 1, p. 231a).

lawyers in all ages are fond of covering their unfounded resistance against moral reforms by arguments which prove, on close scrutiny, to be mere tautologies.

Thus, Bentham here compares the text of the first edition of Blackstone's *Commentaries* with the later one and finds that it was only "in the first transport of holy zeal, before discretion had come in to his assistance" that Blackstone wrote the sentence: It is "indecency to set up private judgment in opposition to public."[319] In the later edition—after Priestley and Furneaux had protested against this passage—Blackstone radically toned down his sentence by adding "in virulent and factious opposition to public *authority*." Similarly, in the earlier edition, he had been cautious enough to restrict himself to the statement that it is arrogance to censure institutions "with contempt and rudeness."[319] Bentham rightly exposes this kind of tautological "rhetorical lumber"[320] by the witty remark: "as if there needed a professor to inform us that to treat anything with contempt and rudeness is arrogance."[321] Naturally, such tautological arguments cannot solve a single one of the "censorial" problems of ethics. They are only conscious or instinctive means by which adversaries of ethical criticism try to cloak their practical resistance against the censorial problems of morals.

Similar examples of flagrant question-begging are detected by Bentham in the frequent use of poetical, hyperbolic and obscure or even "childish paradoxical" phrases in ethics. Blackstone, for example, attributes the characteristics of "ubiquity," "all-perfection" and "immortality"[322] to the King, and then tries to draw consequences from

[319] *Ibid.*, p. 102 f, preface (*Works*, 1843, vol. I, p. 230b).

[320] *Ibid.*, p. 103 (*Works*, 1843, vol. I, p. 230b).

[321] *Ibid.*, p. 102 (*Works*, 1843, vol. I, p. 230b); or compare *ibid.*, p. 111 f, and the same argumentation in Bentham, *A Comment on the Commentaries*, ed. by Everett, 1928, p. 194, the exposure of the tautology in the following passage of Blackstone: "Whenever a . . . Law of which the reason, perhaps, could not be remembered or discerned, hath been *wantonly* broken in upon by . . . *new resolutions*, the wisdom of the rule has in the end appeared from the inconveniences that have followed the innovation" (W. Blackstone, *Commentaries on the Laws of England*, book 1, 1773, p. 70); by the addition of the word *wantonly* Blackstone's whole sentence becomes of course tautological. Or compare Bentham, *A Fragment on Government*, chap. IV, §8, where again "the consequent" in an enthymeme of Blackstone "is but a repetition of the antecedent."

[322] Bentham, *A Fragment on Government*, ed. Montague, 1891, p. 114 f (*Works*, 1843, vol. I, p. 235b), compare Bentham, *A Comment on the Commentaries*, ed. by Everett, 1928, pp. 128, 132, and cf. Bentham, *Traités de*

such "flashes of ornament" which "are not more adverse to manly sentiment, than to accurate apprehension."[323] Yet, as Bentham is fond of emphasizing, unfortunately "under the sanction of a great name every string of words however unmeaning, every opinion however erroneous, will have a certain currency . . . which had they stood alone might have drawn nothing, perhaps, but contempt. Popular fame enters not into nice distinctions. . . . Wonderful, in particular, is that influence which is gained over young minds, by the man who on account of whatever class of merit is esteemed in the character of a preceptor."[324] Indeed, there can be no doubt that by the hyperbolic pictures, the "showy language,"[325] "the artillery of the tongue"[326] of such preceptors, no exact proof of any moral or juristic obligation can be given. On the contrary, vague, metaphoric and hyperbolic language on the part of scientists must lower our opinion of the sincerity of such thinkers, just as it impairs the stringency of their arguments.

Even more important, though still bordering on tautology, are other kinds of sophistical proofs against which Bentham argues. These are the common references to "justice in general," "right reason," the "law of nature"—vague attempts at demonstrations by which moralists wish to evade their obligations to moral criticism. All such phrases as "Justice, Right Reason requires it," "The Law of Nature commands it," such "common place retinue" of versions of the so-called doctrine of the law of nature are "rather . . . the way of memento or instruction to acquiescing auditors, than . . . the way of proof against opponents."[327] They are obviously no more than "ways of intimating that a man is firmly persuaded of the truth of this or that moral proposition, though he either thinks he *need not*, or finds he can't, tell *why*."[327] But there is commonly some concrete interest behind such moral com-

---

législation civile et pénale, ed. Dumont, 1820, tome I, "Principes de législation," chap. XIII, §6, p. 71 where the same metaphors are criticized.

[323] Bentham, *A Fragment on Government*, ed. by Montague, 1891, p. 115 (*Works*, 1843, vol. I, pp. 235b, 236a). It is in connection with this line of criticism that Bentham protests against the use of Latin as the language of the laws, and that he mocks at Blackstone who found that even after "the Proceedings at Law" were "done into English . . . the people are now as ignorant in matters of law as before" (*Ibid.*, p. 113); that is to say, as Bentham ironically adds, "our author instead of calling for . . . clouds to be removed, deprecates all light, and pleads for total darkness" (*ibid.*, p. 114).

[324] *Ibid.*, p. 107 (*Works*, 1843, vol. I, pp. 232a, b).

[325] *Ibid.*, chap. V, §13 and compare this whole section.

[326] *Ibid.*, chap. IV, §33.   [327] *Ibid.*, chap. I, §38.

mands of reason, such requirements of justice. For it is interest which always "smooths the road to Faith."[327] Indeed, if it be true that an appeal to the Law of Nature is insufficient to justify any of the concrete laws which are supposed to be dictated by it,[328] then it becomes appropriate to raise the question: what particular interests have dictated the various concrete formulations of the law of nature? And the urgency of this question is increased by the fact that these various formulations of the law of nature often flatly contradict one another.

Bentham, perhaps, does not go too far in saying that a great many of the appeals to the demand of reason or the law of nature are consciously made "rather for form's sake than for anything else."[329] Surely, by the mere statement that this or that is a command of pure reason, nothing as to the validity of such a command can ever be proved, in Kant or Blackstone any more than elsewhere.[330] As we shall see in greater detail in the analysis of Bentham's *Comment on the Commentaries*, it is impossible to evade the censorial problems of ethics by taking refuge in dogmatic dictates of Right Reason.

Again, exclusive recourse to the authority of divine commandments cannot provide an adequate solution of the censorial problems of morals. Blackstone had argued with "overawing . . . theological flourish"[331] that for every government, for all ethics and law, the highest model of human goodness has to be seen in the goodness of the "Supreme Being."[332] But Bentham finds, in strict opposition to this, that "beginning thus is beginning at the wrong end: it is explaining *ignotum per ignotius*."[333] For in the view of the consistent empiricist Bentham, it can never be "from the attributes of the Deity, that an idea is to be had of any qualities in men: on the contrary, it is from what we see of the qualities of men, that we obtain the feeble idea we can frame to ourselves, of the attributes of the Deity. . . . Every thing in its place. Theology in a sermon, or a catechism. But in this place, the flourish we have seen, might, for every purpose of instruction,

[328] Bentham tries to prove this in greater detail in his *Comment on the Commentaries*.

[329] Bentham, *A Fragment on Government*, chap. I, §38.

[330] Compare D. Baumgardt, *Der Kampf um den Lebenssinn unter den Vorläufern der modernen Ethik*, 1933, Teil I.

[331] Bentham, *A Fragment on Government*, chap. II, §2.

[332] W. Blackstone, *Commentaries on the Law of England*, 1773, vol. I, p. 48.

[333] Bentham, *A Fragment on Government*, chap. II, §5.

have much better . . . been spared."[334] Any uncritical mixture of theology and morals is for Bentham not only unscientific, but also dangerous politically and ethically.

To infer that the law of "revelation" should bind us to transgress every human law is to him a most "mischievous tendency."[335] For there will be "scarce any law whatever but what those who have not liked it have found, on some account or another, to be repugnant to some text of scripture"; and then "I see no remedy but that the natural tendency of such doctrine is to impel a man . . . to rise up in arms against any law whatever he happens not to like."[335] The best that can be hoped for such "frivolous pretences"[336] is that they may be mitigated in practice by their hyperbolic vagueness, and by the determined resistance of worldly governments. Indeed, it happens not seldom that very revolutionary moral consequences are drawn from religious presuppositions only because the proclaimers of such radical principles know that their application is sufficiently checked by mundane conservative powers.

In any case, Bentham excludes every "theonomic" foundation of morals from his scientific theory of ethics, just as Kant did at about the same time; and as we shall see, in his *Comment on the Commentaries* he justifies even more fully his exclusion of all uncritical theological argumentation, of disguised tautological reasoning, mere poetical metaphors and unprovable commands of justice and right reason. Certain philosophic, aesthetic and religious convictions have indeed, throughout history, been not much more than a pretext for a suspicious dislike of moral improvement and of free secular criticism; and it is one of the main tendencies of Bentham's earliest writings to provide a critical analysis of the contents as well as the religious and psychological background of older, reactionary ethics.

To clear the way for a frank censure of established morality, Bentham resorts occasionally even to more personal means. He draws a picture of the character of the average lawyer, politician and moralist which is certainly not very flattering, though unfortunately not entirely false; and if we are to give a full account of the temper of Bentham's psychological analyses, even these least reserved of his utterances should not be omitted. According to Bentham, the men "who

[334] *Ibid.*, chap. ii, §5.
[335] *Ibid.*, chap. iv, §19 and compare §18.
[336] *Ibid.*, §17.

have always occupied too large a space in the circle" of this profession are only "a passive and enervate race, ready to swallow any thing, and to acquiesce in any thing . . . shortsighted, obstinate: lethargic, yet liable to be driven into convulsions by false terrors . . . obsequious only to the whisper of interest, and to the beck of power."[337] As "it is the nature of owls to hate the light . . . it is the nature of those politicians who are wise by rote, to detest everything that forces them either to find (what, perhaps, is impossible) reasons for a favourite persuasion, or (what is not endurable) to discard it."[338] As Bentham often emphasizes, there exists a most "intimate connexion between some of the gifts of the understanding and some of the *affections* of the heart."[339] It is not only want of sound reasoning, but also moral weakness and frequently "sinister bias of the *affections*"[340] which, according to him, form the characteristics of the average politician, jurist and moralist. In comparison with the majority of ethicists, governed by "propensities" of "the multitude of men,"[341] Bentham finds only a much smaller number of moralists gifted with "the discernment which enables a man to perceive and with the courage which enables him to avow the defect of a system of institutions"[342]—people who, like Bentham himself, are "resolved to persevere without deviation in the line of truth and utility," and who "prefer the still whisper of an enduring approbation, to the short-lived bustle of tumultuous applause."[343] "Those who . . . consider upon what slight trivial circumstances, even in the happiest times, the adoption . . . of a Law so often turns . . . the desolate . . . state of the human intellect, during the periods in which so great a part of the still subsisting mass of institutions had their birth—those who consider the backwardness there is in most men, unless when spurred by personal interests or resentments to run a-tilt against the colossus of authority— those . . . who give these considerations their due weight" will certainly not be "so zealous . . . to terrify men from setting up what is now 'private judgment' against what once was public."[344] As one of such rare, truly censorial moralists Bentham especially praises Beccaria,

[337] Bentham, *A Fragment on Government*, ed. Montague, p. 104, preface (*Works*, 1843, vol. I, p. 231a).

[338] *Ibid.*, p. 112 (*Works*, 1843, vol. I, p. 234b).

[339] *Ibid.*, p. 95 (*Works*, 1843, vol. I, p. 232a).

[340] *Ibid.*, p. 107 (*Works*, 1843, vol. I, p. 232a).

[341] *Ibid.*, p. 105 (*Works*, 1843, vol. I, p. 231b).

[342] *Ibid.*, p. 106 (*Works*, 1843, vol. I, p. 232a).

[343] *Ibid.*, p. 125 (*Works*, 1843, vol. I, p. 239b).

[344] *Ibid.*, p. 104 f (*Works*, 1843, vol. I, p. 231b).

whom he likes even to "style the father of *Censorial Jurisprudence*," and whom here already he prefers to the "antiquarian" Montesquieu. For Montesquieu's "Esprit des Lois" is only "a work of the mixed kind," a mixture of expository and censorial inquiry,[344] while Grotius and Puffendorf are, in Bentham's view, nothing more to censorial jurisprudence than "the schoolmen were to Natural Philosophy"[344]— an estimate which certainly comes nearer to truth than the common overrating of the radicalism of both those seventeenth-century jurists.

To sum up, in his *Fragment* Bentham has ingeniously contrived, in the course of what is ostensibly only a criticism of Blackstone, to discuss a fair number of fundamental points of ethics and law in their epistemological, psychological and, to a certain extent, historical aspects. And broadly speaking, though Bentham in the last sentences of the *Fragment* does not flatter himself with the hope of being the Messiah, the coming renovator of jurisprudence and ethics (but only the John the Baptist, to prepare the way before him), it is easy to trace certain well considered constructive, reformatory tendencies throughout this first published work. Notwithstanding the aggressive tenor of the treatise,[345] caused by its topic, and despite his caustic attacks on Blackstone, Bentham has not forgotten to speak of his opponent on various occasions as perhaps the most able expositor of English law of his epoch.[346] The purity of Bentham's intentions, his impersonal and sincere eagerness for moral improvement and for a more fundamental, scientific basis of morals, appear here already in the best light. It is a mental attitude which is as far from blind and reckless criticism as it is from a merely dry utilitarian dogmatism and rationalism, as far from an idealizing tolerance of existing morality as it is from the narrow-minded intoxication of a reforming fanatic. Any estimate of Bentham which sees in him only the biased radical fails to do justice either to his general attitude of mind, or to the rich details of the psychological and ethical analyses of the very first published work of his youth.

[345] See for instance such cutting remarks as the following: "The fortunes of . . . the members of the House of Commons are yet to make. The fortunes of those of the House of Lords (I speak in general) are made already" (*A Fragment on Government*, chap. III, §16). But even such passages did not weaken the strong impression made by the *Fragment* on contemporary readers such as Lord Shelburne or Lord Mansfield (see Bentham's preface intended for the second edition of his *Fragment on Government*, 1828, *Works*, 1843, vol. I, pp. 248b, 246b).

[346] See *A Fragment on Government*, ed. by Montague, 1891, pp. 116 f, 122 (*Works*, 1843, vol. I, pp. 236a, b, 238).

A COMMENT ON THE COMMENTARIES

In comparison with the miniature-painting of the *Fragment on Government*, Bentham's *Comment on the Commentaries*, containing his further criticism of Blackstone, appears at first sight as a rough charcoal-drawing or a rough pencil-sketch; and it is, I think, less balanced in its emotional outbursts. We know that it was written during a period which, for the young Bentham, was one of high-pitched emotion: during the years 1774-75 he had seriously fallen in love. He never gave his consent to the publication of this work, and it was not published until 150 years after its composition. Nevertheless, in contrast to the carefully worked out miniature of the *Fragment* it is an impressive *alfresco*, and its merit is enhanced by Bentham's freshness of temperament and of thought.

While the *Fragment* is concerned with only seven pages of Blackstone's *Commentaries on the Laws of England* (from pages 47-53 of volume I), the material treated in Bentham's *Comment* covers two full sections of Blackstone's work, the second and third sections of the introduction of the first volume containing 54 pages. Yet here again, as in the *Fragment*, the whole ethical discussion is centered essentially round the two points we have already noticed: the importance of raising the censorial problems in opposition to the expository treatment of the same questions; and, secondly, the value of the principle of utility for the solution of these censorial problems in ethics.

But, in passing, the parallel between natural sciences and moral philosophy is also touched upon in a new way. Bentham asks the moralists to think of the beginning of the history of natural philosophy when—as D'Alembert had already observed—"contradictory propositions" had been proved "with equal fluency"[347]; and statements just as crude have yet to be overcome in the science of morals. Moreover, other fundamental characteristics of Bentham's ethics, such as the thoroughgoing *inductive* character of his method and his rejection of all morality of pure reason, are brought out here more clearly than perhaps anywhere else in his writings; and we find in this *Comment* a problem

[347] Bentham, *A Comment on the Commentaries*, a criticism of William Blackstone's *Commentaries on the Laws of England*, now first printed from the Author's Manuscript, ed. by Ch. W. Everett, 1928, p. 234 f, note.

which elsewhere, by a striking omission, he has almost entirely passed over: the question of Free Will.

Free-Will. "L'abus des Mots"

Concerning the problem of free-will, Bentham begins with the rejection of the often used parallel between laws of nature and laws for men—"Laws of Nature," "Laws of Mechanics," even "Laws for Clocks" on the one hand and "Laws for Men"[348] on the other. According to Blackstone, both kinds of law are invariably and inevitably binding; yet man is said to have free will.

Bentham, in the manner of a great satirist, shows in but a few strokes how superficial and contradictory such explanations are; and special ridicule is poured on the complicating and misleading inclusion of laws of clocks. "A Clock . . . , one of those 'creatures that' . . . 'have neither the power to think nor to will,' . . . is governed by . . . Laws" which are binding . . . and must 'be *invariably* obey'd' . . . (whether the clock go true or no)."[349] "A Man, being a creature endow'd with both reason and Free Will is 'necessarily subject' to the laws that belong to *him,* . . . '*inevitably* obliged'" and "bound" by them.[350] Such laws are the "Will of his maker" and the laws of human legislators; "this being the case, he may '*choose*' . . . whether he will do or no what they bid him. Now it is to be hoped you understand completely the difference between the way a clock is *bound* and the way a man is bound? A clock does what it is bound to do '*invariably*' while it varies: a man does it '*necessarily*' and '*inevitably*': that is he takes his '*choice*' and does no such thing. Lord help you if you don't know what the word *bound* means now."[351] It might perhaps be supposed that Bentham refrained here from any detailed discussion of the problem of free-will only on account of the polemic and satirical character of his work. But as we learn from his later work, and particularly from a short remark in one of his letters in 1789, he never felt inclined to embark on a detailed analysis of this old and complicated problem.

"*Entre nous*"—he writes in 1789 to his friend Wilson—"I don't care two straws about liberty and necessity at any time. I do not expect any new truths on the subject: and were I to see any lying at my feet, I should hardly think it worth while to stoop to pick them up."[352] He

[348] Bentham, *A Comment on the Commentaries,* ed. by Everett, 1928, p. 31 f.
[349] *Ibid.*, p. 32.   [350] *Ibid.*, p. 33.   [351] *Ibid.*, p. 33.
[352] Bentham, *Works,* 1843, part xix, p. 216a (a letter to George Wilson, July 8, 1789); compare Bentham's similar attitude towards the problem of free-will in

felt certain that debates on free-will can only show "how excusable error is, and how many illustrious names a man will find to countenance him in it."[352] In short, he confessed that he had no interest in subjects "so purely speculative."[353] In Bentham's whole life-work, refinements of metaphysical speculation play no part.

But it would be rash to conclude from his neglect of the problem of free-will that his general attitude was unphilosophical. For I do not think, as is generally assumed, that the belief in free-will must form a fundamental and indispensable article of faith in every sort of ethics. On the contrary, not only can the inquiry into the problem of free-will be relegated to the sphere of pure metaphysics or the theory of nature, but a consistently descriptive ethics (which eschews all normative expression) may omit even the *reference* to such problems.

There is no doubt that Bentham always deliberately avoided any detailed examination of the problem of free-will in his ethics. In his *Introduction*,[354] too, he speaks only of the ambiguity characteristic of the concepts of *free* and *voluntary* conduct.

After having adumbrated this characteristic attitude toward the problem of moral freedom, Bentham extends the heavy assaults on abuses of language in ethics begun in his *Fragment on Government*. In the *Fragment*, he had only occasionally criticized some "flashes" of poetical ornament, with the confession that he found such poetical figures of speech in morals "not more adverse to manly sentiment than to accurate apprehension."[355] But now he goes much further and insists, with an energy very rare in the history of ethics, that all uncritical use of poetical and rhetorical language has strictly to be avoided in moral science; for in his opinion it inevitably obscures the accuracy required in scientific thought. It is never permissible to "pay . . . with declamation," when we "owe . . . a definition."[356] Only "those who dare not *judge*, may venture to imagine. But the firm beauties of precision love a purer air."[357] The distinction between poetry and moral science must, in his view, be most scrupulously observed.

---

his *Table of the Springs of Action*, 1815, Observations, §7, *Works*, 1843, vol. I, p. 218a.

[353] *Ibid.*, part XIX, p. 216b.

[354] See Bentham, *An Introduction to the Principles of Morals and Legislation*, chap. XVII, sect. 19, 1823, vol. II, p. 254.

[355] Bentham, *A Fragment on Government*, ed. by Montague, 1891, p. 115 (*Works*, 1843, vol. I, p. 235 f).

[356] Bentham, *A Comment on the Commentaries*, ed. by Everett, 1928, p. 85.

[357] *Ibid.*, p. 36, note.

Every careless transition from one province to the other should be definitely forbidden. In Blackstone, Bentham finds constant trespassing from one intellectual field to the other. Blackstone too, he assumes, must obviously have recognized "the accuracy which is to instruct . . . as incompatible with the ornament which is to allure."[357] Yet "neither daring nor knowing how to possess himself of the former," he always liked to "turn aside" after the other.[357] So Bentham, in the full vigour of his youthful spirits, raises the question: why did Blackstone not write in verse?[358] Or why did not some of "his admiring pupils" turn his books into rhymes?[359] For if his books were written in verse, they would be something; now they are "nothing"[360] because they are, in the eyes of Bentham, neither poetry nor science. In a "science," however, only "precision" can be "the very life and soul."[361] But such precision, continues Bentham, "the firm beauties of precision . . . grow not in those torpid and pestilential regions where the grim spectre of superstition" and where empty rhetorical flourishes "sit sentinel over the foundations of moral science. Vain are his hopes who thinks to learn to see clearly in that gloomy circle in which the first vow he makes at entering is to shut his eyes."[362] With his customary sharp wit, Bentham never tires in his warnings to moralists and lawyers who can "no more speak . . . without a fiction in their mouth, than Demosthenes without his pebbles,"[363] people who are afraid of "the danger of being intel-

[358] *Ibid.*, p. 35.   [359] *Ibid.*, p. 36 and compare p. 127.

[360] *Ibid.*, p. 35 f. That it is not poetry in itself, but the uncritical mixture of poetry and science which is objectionable to the scientific moralist is today especially emphasized by Professor R. B. Perry, see *Contemporary American Philosophy*, 1930, vol. II, p. 202: "It is confusion, and not feeling, imagination or conviction, which the knowing mind has most to fear. . . . The man who can best afford to indulge in 'over-beliefs,' or in a faith supported by love and hope, is the man who is aware of the difference between cash and credit or between science and poetry."

[361] Bentham, *A Comment on the Commentaries*, ed. by Everett, 1928, p. 35.

[362] *Ibid.*, p. 36, compare p. 113 f, note, Bentham's making fun of the relation of Blackstone to precision: "*Precision* (if we may be allowed to make a grace, or a virtue of her) is in general no great favourite of our Authors, and it happens whimsically enough while in a sudden fire of gallantry, he is throwing his arms about to catch her, he stumbles into ambiguity and contradiction . . . he saves himself from obscurity by stumbling on contradiction."

[363] *Ibid.*, p. 75. Here again as in his *Fragment on Government* Bentham obviously still accepted the common usage of the word fiction as signifying a non-entity, while later on, at least from about 1813, he insisted upon a careful distinction being made between "real entities" and justifiable "fictitious entities" on the one hand and non-entities on the other. Fictitious entities have then in his eyes a sort of verbal reality and have to perform a valuable and even indispensable

ligible,"[364] such as "Blackstone and his fellow dealers in fiction."[365] Bentham is certain that the unchecked use of such poetical metaphors must lead to "prejudices" which "deprive the understanding."[363] Even if people, then, are in their moral discussion "chin deep . . . in nubibus . . . seeing no other words than what they are used to . . . they take for granted, they understand the sense."[364] Lawyers and moralists "feed upon" rhetorical pictures and "untruth, as the Turks do upon opium, at first from choice and with their eyes open, afterwards by habit till at length they lose all shame, avow it for what it is, and swallow it with greediness, not bearing to be without it."[366] There are two sorts "of policy in the moral department of Science: . . . speaking unintelligibly," a teacher of morals "may all along keep fair with the prejudices that are in fashion" speaking, however, "all along the plain truth, he may be obliged ever and anon to strike out light very offensive to the eyes of those, who have the distribution of those things which are pleasing in his own."[367] For himself, Bentham preferred the second way. He always felt himself called upon to fight against "well polished confusion"[368] and fictions in moral sciences wherever he found them. Fortunately, however, he did not conduct this fight in the manner of a dry pedant, but in that of a gifted satirist, with a diction trenchant, fresh and even poetical in its polemic against poetry.

It may be granted, however, that Bentham never faced the problem "poetry and philosophy" in all its intricacies. The use of poetical language is sanctioned by the authority of Plato and more ancient thinkers, as well as by great names of the last two centuries. Again and again it happens that, after periods of exclusion, poetical language is employed anew in ethics and even in the metaphysics of nature. Where this has been done for the sake of edification, and not to provide a substitute for consistent reasoning, the employment of poetry seems to me fully justifiable. It is the uncritical mixture of science and poetry which is harmful to both poetry and science; and it is a notable merit of Bentham that he insistently warned against this misuse of poetry.

In the philosophy of nature, an exact basis of inquiry is safeguarded by the existence of mathematical physics. But as there is no sufficient

---

function in thought and language (see "A Fragment on Ontology," Bentham, *Works*, vol. VIII, pp. 198, 199, "Essay on Logic," vol. VIII, p. 262b). Leslie Stephen, *The English Utilitarians*, 1900, p. 247 f and C. K. Ogden, *Bentham's Theory of Fictions*, 1932, only refer to this later evolved theory of fictions in Bentham.

[364] Bentham, *A Comment on the Commentaries*, ed. by Everett, 1928, p. 133.
[365] *Ibid.*, p. 67.   [366] *Ibid.*, p. 75.
[367] *Ibid.*, p. 111.   [368] *Ibid.*, p. 61.

safeguard in anti-hedonistic ethics, despite all uncritical assurances to the contrary, the confusion caused by the uncritical use of poetic language in ethics is even greater than in any metaphysics of nature.

Bentham, however, did not restrict himself to warring against an allegorizing, poetical terminology in ethics; he extended this criticism to all those careless usages of language so common in moral discussion. "The age of Locke forms an epoch since which it is no longer so excusable to use words loosely as it might have been before."[369] After Helvétius had declaimed against "l'abus des mots" in a particular chapter of his *De l'Esprit*, Bentham stresses the same point in his *Comment* and to an even greater extent in his later writings: "to be fortified" not only "against the fascinations of tinsel rhetoric," but even "to stand apprized of the improprieties of the current language" although "custom obliges . . . to adopt it."[370] Helvétius had already illustrated by some stories the disastrous or amusing effects which ambiguous language may cause in morals and jurisprudence—either the use of misleading synonyms for different things, or the use of different terms for exactly the same thing. So Helvétius tells the story of a Swiss: "on lui avait consigné une porte des Tuileries, avec défense d'y laisser entrer personne. Un bourgeois s'y présente: 'On n'entre point,' lui dit le Suisse. 'Aussi,' répond le bourgeois, 'je ne veux point entrer, mais sortir,' reprend le Suisse, 'monsieur, vous pouvez passer.' Qui le croirait? ce conte est l'histoire du peuple romain; . . . les Romains, faute d'attacher des idées précises au mot de royauté," accordaient à César "sous le nom d'*imperator*, la puissance qu'ils lui refusent sous le nom de *rex*."[371] Similarly, Bentham tries to illustrate the magic power of mere termi-

---

[369] *Ibid.*, p. 242.

[370] *Ibid.*, p. 198. In his *The Limits of Jurisprudence Defined*, ed. by Everett, 1945, p. 57, Bentham states in a similar vein: Words "are a sort of paper currency: if we know how at any time to change them and get sterling in their room, it is well: if not, we are deceived, and instead of being masters of so much real knowledge as by the help of them we mean to supply ourselves with, we possess nothing but nonsense." Compare *ibid.*, p. 324, the even more far-reaching statement: "abstract phraseology must on many occasions be tolerated . . . but on no occasion can it be clearly understood unless it can be translated into such expressions as have a direct reference to the sensible objects that are in question." See further, *ibid.*, p. 125, note 12: "In *audio te*, I hear you, the course taken by the act is the reverse of that which is attributed to it by the grammarian. If I *beat* you, the act proceeds from me and the impression which is a physical one terminates in you: . . . but if I *hear* you, the act which is a physical one proceeds from you, and the impression terminates in me."

[371] C. A. Helvétius, *Oeuvres complètes*, 1818, tome I, p. 37 ("De l'esprit," discours I, chap. IV).

nology in morals and legislation by the not uncommon attitude of people who prefer the payment of five thousand pounds to the payment of five, when the payment of five thousand pounds is not "called a penalty";[372] and he mentions a case in point of a Jew who "happen'd by misfortune to have a Christian relish for Westphalia Hams: at the same time that he was a devout observer of the Law. To reconcile his conscience with his palate" he tried to "cheat of the Devil . . . he took a method with those Hams. He called them stock-fish; and with the said stock-fish (retaining always his aversion for the flesh of swine) did he fill his belly."[373] No less strange is the attitude of those many gentile judges who are much less interested in their proceedings themselves than in the name they give them,[373] so that "to strain at a gnat, and swallow a camel" is by no means "a character peculiar to the Jewish Lawyers."[374] Bentham everywhere tries to unmask this tyranny of mere words and the worship of "legal astutia" which tries to deviate at any price from plain sense for the purpose of making its "notions respectable."[375] All such "verbal arguments" in morals and legislation, "sound . . . rather than substance,"[376] all such "pompous nothingness of half-learned pedants"[377] is constantly attacked here, both in the polemics against the conservative, historical school of jurisprudence[378] and in those against the liberal defenders of "natural rights."

Criticism of the Law of Nature

As he did in the *Fragment*, Bentham seeks in his *Comment* to bring to light especially the hidden use of tautologies in moral reasoning; and this leads him directly to questions that are substantial and not merely formal, namely, to his fundamental criticism of the "Law of Nature" and the laws of universal reason in general. Primarily, this old doctrine of a special "Law of Nature" or "Natural Right" has always been maintained for the purpose of solving the "censorial problems" of morals, for providing the foundations of existing morality. But as Bentham tries to show, this ethical law of nature merely consists of tautological statements repeating the valueless assertion that only the right moral law is the morally valid law.

[372] Bentham, *A Comment on the Commentaries*, ed. by Everett, 1928, p. 183.
[373] *Ibid.*, p. 193. Cf. the story of the "good Mussulman who abhors the very name of wine, finds means to amuse himself with brown water."
[374] *Ibid.*, p. 231.   [375] *Ibid.*, p. 168.   [376] *Ibid.*, p. 184.
[377] *Ibid.*, p. 162; or compare p. 143 on prolixity as adverse to precision.
[378] Such jurists as Lord Coke who was, like Blackstone, "impregnated with" legal astutia "to the very marrow"; see *Comment*, p. 168.

There is no doubt that historically progressive moralists have very often fought under the banner of the law of nature. For centuries, existing traditional law has been attacked by champions of natural rights. But in itself, the ethical theory of natural law is so ambiguous that its teaching has often proved compatible with the maintenance of reactionary law as well.

At any rate, in comparison with consistent hedonism as seen from the standpoint of the critical moralist, the ethical theory of the law of nature is, philosophically speaking, extremely vague and open to basic objections. It is, in my opinion, one of Bentham's special merits that he tried to unearth the roots of the fallacies which are at least implicitly coupled with any possible application of this theory.

Blackstone, as an adherent of the old doctrine of the law of nature, assumed that there exist "eternal immutable laws of good and evil" which "human reason" is able "to discover,"[379] and which form the so-called "law of nature" in contrast to the changing laws or moral codes of different communities and different times. Among such laws of nature, Blackstone especially pointed to the "three general precepts . . . to which Justinian had reduced the whole doctrine of law," namely, "that we should live honestly, should hurt nobody, and should render to everyone his due."[380] Bentham, however, shows in a short but instructive analysis how meaningless these pronouncements are and how little demonstrable is the moral validity of these laws.

First of all, as Bentham does not forget to mention, it is not correct to translate Justinian's "honeste vivere" by "live honestly," as Blackstone did, though neither the Latin nor the English phrase has a precise meaning. If this precept "will admit of any explanation that is at all precise," it may perhaps be this: "According to *what Justinian meant* by it, it signifies to act right . . . in matters wherein other men's interests *are not* directly concerned: as by abstaining from drunkenness, obscenities, and so forth. According to what *our author has made* of it it signifies to act *right* in matters wherein other men's interests *are* directly concerned."[381] But no matter whether we understand this moral or legal rule of Justinian in the first or in the second sense, in both these cases the "honeste vivere" merely expresses in another word, in a common

[379] See W. Blackstone, *Commentaries on the Laws of England*, 1773, vol. I, p. 40; Bentham, *A Comment on the Commentaries*, ed. by Everett, 1928, p. 38.
[380] W. Blackstone, *Commentaries on the Laws of England*, 1773, vol. I, p. 40; and see Bentham, *A Comment on the Commentaries*, 1928, p. 38 f.
[381] Bentham, *A Comment on the Commentaries*, ed. by Everett, 1928, p. 39 f.

name, what is already expressed in the detailed prescripts concerning the "honestum" or living honestly.

To begin with Justinian's meaning of honestum, it is obvious that Justinian, in his alleged law of nature concerning the honestum, has by no means given a moral justification of his concrete rules respecting this honestum. His general law of nature about the honestum contains, summarized by a general term, only what he (Justinian) thought to be honestum in particular. That is to say: we are here moving in a circle. If we want to know what is honestum in itself, honestum in general, we only hear what Justinian decrees to be honestum in his different concrete prescripts, namely, abstaining from drunkenness and the like. And if we want to know why precisely abstaining from drunkenness, etc., is commanded by the general law, we are answered that it is because only these and no other concrete prescripts constitute the proper content of the general law of nature in question.

Actually, we deal here with certain concrete precepts given by a human legislator. The assumption that, besides these concrete laws, a superior law of nature exists, and that those concrete prescripts follow from that higher law, leads only to the introduction of a new term for the very same precepts. This new term looks as if it were being qualified to give a valid foundation to the concrete rules in question. But it is only a new name for the old contents.

In the end, the same applies to Blackstone's general law to live honestly. This law of nature cannot tell us in the least what honesty is in the concrete sense. As Bentham briefly states, if "any sense . . . is" in it, then this moral law means nothing but that "we should do as we ought to do" which "brings the precept . . . to this incontestable" tautology: "what we ought to do, we ought to do."[382] Though formulated in a rough and summary way, these reflections of Bentham contain, I think, some of the most important arguments against the doctrine of the law of nature and its enormous influence on morals and jurisprudence. At any rate, we are dealing here with much more than a mere criticism of Blackstone. Certain arguments of the *Comment on the Commentaries* have been used, completely independently of Bentham, by Hegel and by thinkers of extremely different philosophical schools against the most acute representative of the ethical theory of the law of nature, Immanuel Kant.[383]

[382] *Ibid.*, p. 39.
[383] See D. Baumgardt, *Der Kampf um den Lebenssinn unter den Vorläufern der modernen Ethik*, 1933, especially pp. 101 ff, 111 ff, 114 ff.

94

Bentham has indicated very well that either the so-called general laws of nature are quite formal tautologies having no concrete content at all, and saying only that we ought to do what we ought to do without telling us anything about what concretely ought to be done, or, if such laws of nature are thought to embrace a concrete content, then they are again of no value in ethics. For in this case, the general law of nature concerning the honestum and the justum merely signifies a general term for empirical rules concerning the honestum and the justum; and it is an obvious fallacy to infer from the introduction of such a general term the ethical validity of any concrete rules, unless it is proved first that precisely these and no other rules deserve that general ethical name. This condition, however, is not fulfilled by the *dogmatic assumption* that only certain rules comply with the general law of nature and others not. The mere assumption of a general law of nature is of as little value in ethics as the assumption of a general term in a syllogism, unless in both cases the relations between the general and the particular terms are satisfactorily determined.

No less justifiable is Bentham's criticism of the second law of nature mentioned by Justinian: "We should hurt nobody." This moral rule could, as a law of nature, first have a quite formal tautological meaning, namely, that "we should not i.e. ought not to give pain to anyone but when we ought."[384] And this is certainly such a "sagacious precept,"[384] that nobody can contradict it, while it is equally clear that nobody can gain any insight by it.

But if we understand this moral law "we should hurt nobody" in the strictest sense, if we think it means "that we should not give pain to anyone at all" (without the restriction: except in so far as we ought to do so) then, indeed, this concrete rule no longer is an empty tautology; but it also no longer represents a universally valid law of ethics. On the contrary, its moral validity becomes rather doubtful. For, as Bentham ironically adds, if it is forbidden to hurt anyone (not only those we ought not to hurt), then it makes it "rather puzzling to us what to think of several professions hitherto thought useful ones: for example, those of the Judge, the Surgeon, the Soldier, not forgetting the Hangman."[385] Certainly, neither Justinian nor Blackstone admit that the profession of the judge or the surgeon is an immoral one.

With regard to this second law of nature, as with regard to the first, either this kind of "sagacious precept" expresses a mere tautology and

---

[384] Bentham, *A Comment on the Commentaries*, ed. by Everett, 1928, p. 40.
[385] *Ibid.*, p. 40.

can, therefore, not serve as a concrete rule at all, or, if it is understood as a concrete rule, this concrete rule does not represent a law of nature. It is not a universal law of morals whose validity is so clear in itself that other moral rules can be derived from it. On the contrary, this so-called law of nature is, concretely understood, morally of rather questionable value.

Again, the third law of nature mentioned by Justinian and Blackstone, "We should render to everyone his due," is subject to similar criticism. This third law of nature may have the meaning of the merely analytic judgment that "we ought to render every man what we ought to render him"; and then it is an evident tautology. It only says "once more" that "we ought to do what we ought to do." In this case, this so-called law of nature cannot be found to be wrong; but it is empty of all meaning with regard to reality. It cannot tell us what we ought to do to anyone and what we ought not to do to him.

Another meaning of this third law of Justinian could be "that we should forbear to violate" anyone's "property: that is, should forbear to deal with anything which . . . the *municipal Law* as our author calls it shall have declared to belong to him, in a manner which the law shall have commanded us not to deal with it."[386] If we suppose in this way that, parallel to those concrete rules of the municipal law, of the official legislator, there exist certain laws of nature, then these laws of nature can stand only in the relation of identity to those concrete municipal laws. In this case, the law of nature is only a superfluous reduplication of the existing law, but it cannot give reasons for the moral validity of any concrete existing ethics or jurisprudence. Thus, with respect to all concrete moral questions, the law of nature is either completely ambiguous, has every and no meaning, and is identical with the analytic judgment that we ought to do what we ought to do; or, if it is not merely an analytic judgment, then it is completely identical with the existing municipal law and has, therefore, no original meaning either.

Bentham also arrives at the same result in the following way: "Since nothing will serve . . . but a Law for the measure of right and wrong, the measure of this right . . . must either be that Law itself or some other Law: if some other" as for instance "the pretended Law of Nature . . . then what we learn of it . . . is that what it (the municipal law) does in the way of commanding and prohibiting is just nothing; if that law itself, then what we are informed . . . is that it prohibits

386 *Ibid.,* p. 40.

what it prohibits and commands what it commands" (without being able to be proved as morally valid) and that it is "prescribed by those who prescribe it."[387] Bentham, therefore, summarizes his judgment on Justinian's three laws of nature by saying sarcastically that their most characteristic feature is their "edifying and instructive sense"[388] of mere tautology, a tautology by which either the mere form of ethical judgments is identified with itself, or the laws of nature are identified with the existing municipal law.

As the *Fragment on Government* had already declared, the law of nature is "nothing but a phrase,"[389] and as he found it possible to "shew . . . at large" in further "examining,"[389] in spite of all "the pompous declarations" on natural law, the law of nature remains for Bentham a "formidable nonentity."[390] "Indeed, from the whole of what appears, as well from what has been said by others, as from what has been said by our author concerning the . . . Law of Nature . . . it appears . . . to be incontestably of the same genus with a certain production called 'zeal' which according to the history given of it in the Tale of a Tub, 'proceeded at first from a *notion* into a *word*, and from thence, in a hot summer ripen'd into a tangible substance.' "[391] The "censorial" problems of ethics and jurisprudence cannot be solved by the mere assumption of a Law of Nature as "superior" to existing morals and legislation. For, as we have seen, this seemingly superior Law of Nature does not lead beyond the circle of tautologies in its relation to the empirical, municipal law. In view of the exceedingly large part which such tautologies[392] have played in morals and in the philosophy of law down to the present time, I believe it would be unfair to underrate the service which Bentham has done to a critical theory of ethics on that point.

As he rightly remarks in this and in another connection, those assertions are by no means "innocent, the tendency of which is to betray men into a notion that something is said when it is just as much as comes to

---

[387] *Ibid.*, p. 73.   [388] *Ibid.*, p. 40.

[389] Bentham, *A Fragment on Government*, chap. IV, §19.

[390] Bentham, *A Comment on the Commentaries*, ed. by Everett, 1928, p. 44.

[391] *Ibid.*, p. 44.

[392] Cf. *ibid.*, p. 143, Bentham's mockery at all such "lovers of tautology," or pp. 64, 193, on the "sublime discovery" of tautologies; or p. 135 where Bentham quotes Blackstone's amusingly tautological statement that a statute which restrains does not enlarge any more than a statute which enlarges does restrain. Certainly *per definitionem* an enlarging statute *qua* enlarging does not restrain. But, as Bentham adds, in fact, in reality there is never an enlarging statute which does not at the same time restrain in another respect. "To enlarge the power of one man, there is but one way, and that is, to restrain the conduct of another."

nothing: to habituate them to pay themselves with sound instead of sense."[393] As Bentham sees it, the ethical law of nature does nothing but give the misleading impression that it provides the justification of the validity of all other moral laws. In truth, the law of nature adds only another set of dogmatic general statements to the dogmatic, concrete demands of existing morality.

The representatives of the doctrine of natural rights are convinced that there exists a law of nature independently of all concrete dictates given by human legislators, and that those laws of nature can determine which prescripts of human rulers are valid. In this reasoning, however, the wish alone is father to the thought—the wish to find a fundamental basis of morals. Bentham has here, and in further chapters of his *Comment on the Commentaries*, acutely explained why these wishes cannot be fulfilled by the doctrine of natural rights.

Though Bentham's analysis of all these questions is not exhaustive, it seems to me more lucid and pregnant here than in his "Anarchical Fallacies," first published in full by Bowring in 1843, and in the very short remarks of his *Introduction*, 1789. At any rate, in the intricate polemics of the last centuries against the law of nature, Bentham's argument deserves much more attention than it has found hitherto.

Criticism of Theonomic Ethics

No less forceful than his repudiation of the law of nature is Bentham's polemic against the divine law, the law of revelation. Again, the discussion of the *Comment on the Commentaries* is fuller and more systematized than the corresponding remarks in the *Fragment on Government* or in the *Introduction*. Throughout the centuries, the divine law was thought to answer the "censorial" problems of ethics and jurisprudence, and to give them their ultimate basis. Bentham, therefore, rightly felt that not only Blackstone's defense of the law of nature but also his assumption of a law of God had to be examined. For only by such a criticism of the most influential older theories could the way be cleared for new solutions of these fundamental censorial problems.

Bentham distinguishes between moral or juristic laws dictated by "natural theology" and laws dictated by revelation. But he is convinced right from the beginning of "the impropriety of mixing theology either natural or revealed ... with either Jurisprudence or Morality," and even of "the absurdity of jumbling" these "things sacred with profane."[394]

[393] *Ibid.*, p. 75.   [394] *Ibid.*, p. 46.

"Those . . . who think to blend together things so dissevered . . . involve themselves . . . in . . . inextricable difficulties; . . . to act consistently they . . . must be either Legislators altogether or Divines altogether . . . they must either shut up their Bible or their Statute Book."[395] The idea of God remains for Bentham "absolutely unserviceable and indeed disserviceable . . . for the purpose of solving any political" or moral "problem."[394] "If it is difficult, as it may be, to say what is the human Common Law, it is a thousand times more difficult to say what is the Divine Law. So that if it be but too easy for a man to find an inlet for his own caprice under shelter of the first mentioned exception, it is a thousand times more easy under shelter of this last. Farewell Law and Common Sense: Welcome Fanaticism!"[396] Certainly, by these warnings against an *uncritical* transition from science to religion, Bentham has done meritorious work—work of much greater philosophic relevance than his criticism of sanctimonious pretense.

NATURAL THEOLOGY

To begin with his analysis of the function of natural theology, Bentham admits that natural theology "may furnish . . . a *sanction*"[397] for laws already established by human legislators. But such a sanction is not a scientific vindication of the moral validity of any earthly law. Moreover, natural theology is not capable of finding out which human laws do or do not deserve religious sanction. This Bentham briefly explains as follows: Natural theology "sets out with the supposition that there is no positive command, no will of God expressed by any ostensible instrument in the case"; it "supposes however the will of God to be collected or at least collectible from inference."[398] In truth, all these inferences can never determine in a scientific ethics what is right or wrong according to the will of God. They are much too indeterminate for this purpose.

[395] *Ibid.*, p. 51.

[396] *Ibid.*, p. 192. Besides this Bentham in his polemics against subaltern religiousness derides particularly the absurd exaggerations in the compliments of many theologians to the Deity, giving God even the ridiculous "power of altering all events" (*ibid.*, p. 243). Or he scoffs at the childish anthropomorphisms that seek to glorify the Deity by adopting the style of sentiment of the American savage who summing up his panegyric of his friend the Frenchman recommended him to the other savages with the words: "in short . . . he is one of us" (*ibid.*, p. 40 f), and compare a similar story told in Helvétius, *Oeuvres complètes*, 1818, tome I, "De l'esprit," discours II, chap. 3, p. 55.

[397] Bentham, *A Comment on the Commentaries*, ed. by Everett, 1928, p. 47.

[398] *Ibid.*, p. 46.

No more than the law of nature, can natural theology give us any-thing but a duplicate of the existing empirical law of human moralists. It is not on the basis of natural theology that human legislation has always been established. On the contrary, laws established by human beings receive a special sanction by the unwarranted belief that natural theology commands, rewards or punishes the same kinds of conduct as human rulers or human revolutionists command, reward or punish. What is concretely the moral right or wrong can be, and always has been, determined exclusively by earthly authorities. Direct, immediate commands of God are not found in natural religion, but only in the revealed law. Therefore, natural theology can collect the will of God from nothing but the decisions of human moralists whose decisions, *qua* dogmatic decisions, can never give a guarantee either of their moral or of their religious validity. Since we have seen that even the law of nature could not supply the ground for the validity of concrete moral laws, it is not astonishing that natural theology which has no other sources is no more successful.

The divine law in the field of natural theology provides, at best, the so-called religious sanction. As Bentham explains even in this early work, "Reward or Punishment, at the hand of God, forms the Religious Sanction. . . . Reward or Punishment at the hands of men, liquidated by Law, forms the Political Sanction. Reward or Punishment at the hands of men, unliquidated by Law, forms the Moral Sanction."[399] In about the same way Bentham always defined the different types of sanctions, and he considered religion exclusively in this connection.

From this time onward, Bentham ascribes to religious motives only this very modest part: to furnish a sanction, that is, to "afford . . . a help . . . to suggest motives to governors to adopt and to people to sub-mit to such regulations as by other considerations shall have been de-termined to be proper."[400] But he rightly denied that natural theology has any means of deciding whether a certain precept or rule is moral or immoral. Granted that the command of God has an absolutely bind-ing force in morals, natural theology is not capable of demonstrating sufficiently what the command of God is. Bentham denies that re-ligion can theoretically determine anything in ethics without denying

[399] *Ibid.*, p. 95; and compare the corresponding definitions of religious, political, and moral duty in the *Fragment on Government*, chap. v, §6, note 9, 2-4, formu-lated about the same time, 1775.
[400] *Ibid.*, p. 47.

that religion may play a very subordinate part in morals by furnishing an additional sanction to the political and moral one.

LAW OF REVELATION

Even more chimerical than the role of natural theology is that of revealed religion in scientific ethics and jurisprudence, as Bentham tries to show further on. To him, it is merely a phantom creating confusion. This "Law of Revelation, among Christians, is divided into two parts: the one containing the Law delivered by Moses; the other containing the so-called Law delivered by Jesus and his Apostles."[401] But as Bentham shows in detail, there are, unfortunately, insurmountable difficulties involved with regard to the obligatory character of both these parts of the Law of Revelation.

First, it is altogether obscure as to what extent the Mosaic Law "still has binding force, and that over all nations: for example over our own."[402] For, though the Mosaic Law is said to be the "expression of the . . . explicit Will of God," it is likewise the work of the "human Legislator Moses";[401] and certainly, the binding force of the precepts of the Old Testament extends "no further than as it may have been tacitly adopted by Jesus, himself a part of God, the most recent and authoritative announcer of the will of himself . . . , and by the Apostles, interpreters of the will of Jesus."[403] But how much of the Law of Moses is actually adopted by Jesus and the Apostles is altogether undetermined and undeterminable.

To minimize this indeterminateness as far as possible, the Mosaic Law is commonly divided into two parts, "the Ceremonial Law containing what is supposed to have been abolished by Jesus; and the Moral Law, containing what is supposed to have been adopted and retained."[404] Yet despite this, we are "left in the dark"; for "neither by Jesus nor by any Apostle have respective parcels" of the Mosaic Law "been anywhere ascertained."[404] On the contrary, "the general aspect of their discourse toward the whole Law of Moses" is that they now are "speaking in favour of it, . . . now in derogation."[404] We find Jesus "treating the Law itself with contempt. . . . This they say is the ceremonial part, . . . not the moral. . . . At another time, we find the same Jesus declaring of the whole Law that he came not to destroy but to fulfill it."[405] Even against the ceremony of "circumcision Jesus had said nothing; and he himself was circumcised."[406] But, as Bentham adds

[401] *Ibid.*, p. 47.
[402] *Ibid.*, p. 47 f.
[403] *Ibid.*, p. 48.
[404] *Ibid.*, p. 48.
[405] *Ibid.*, p. 48 f.
[406] *Ibid.*, p. 49.

with the air of an examining magistrate, "to speak now in favour, now in derogation of the same whole . . . seems to . . . savour . . . of levity and inconsistency"; and this is certainly not the right model of the "discourse of a Legislator, much less of a divine one."[404] At any rate, the extent to which the Mosaic Law is binding is so uncertain that this precludes the general validity of any moral rule deducible from the Pentateuch.

But even if, under given circumstances, people have chosen a way out of these difficulties in adopting the Mosaic law "in its whole extent,"[407] then again difficulties arise at once. On the one hand, "persons of all sects," and "orthodox . . . writers of our own Church" had of late to "explode . . . universally" such attempts at retaining the whole moral and legal precepts of Moses in the "European settlements in America," for many of these laws were "very ill suited to the customs, genius or circumstances of that country and of those times; for which reason they have since fallen in disuse."[408] On the other hand, if nevertheless some "sticklers for the universal and perpetual authority of that law . . . of Moses oppose" this by the "rather . . . perplexing . . . argument" that the whole biblical law is appropriate to every country and to every epoch of history, what would be then the condition of society, if, as Blackstone requires, such people were allowed to obey the higher religious biblical commandments and, in the case of a conflict, not to obey the existing secular, moral and legal precepts of their state? No political society could then any longer exist.

Thus, inextricable complications result from the subordination of scientific ethics to "the more ancient part of the Law of Revelation."[409] And "the same observations . . . may be equally applied to the more modern."[409] In the New Testament we meet at best with new, but again with insurmountable difficulties. In the New Testament it is necessary to deduce moral rules from a mere report of the life of Christ and the Apostles. The Mosaic Law "alone was once a Law . . . in the strict and proper sense of the word. . . . It was a collection of specific

[407] *Ibid.*, p. 49 f.

[408] *Ibid.*, p. 50, and compare E. Burke, *An Account of the European Settlements in America*, the 4th edition, 1765, vol. II, p. 147. Edmund Burke had added that those colonists in his view "were generally persons of a contracted way of thinking." But Bentham goes even further in being convinced that these people of Massachusetts were completely deluded in "tainting the air with the pestilence of murdering perjury . . . according to the law of Moses" and assuming that since "Witchcraft had been common" in the epoch of the Bible it must be common also now (*A Comment on the Commentaries*, 1928, p. 193).

[409] *Ibid.*, p. 51.

commands delivered to a certain people . . . called the Jews."[410] The
New Testament, however, contains "rather a history of transactions"
from which moral rules "may only be deduced";[410] and it is indeed
possible to interpret a fair number of "transactions" of the New Testament in different ways and to draw from them different conclusions in
the field of morals, as so many discussions between different Christian
sects may illustrate. Thus, genuine moral laws cannot be derived from
either part of the Law of Revelation: neither from the Old Testament,
primarily because it is not clear to what extent its law still has binding
force; nor yet from the New Testament, because there is no definite
law therein formulated. In other words, in the former case there exists
a Law, but it is not strictly obligatory; in the latter case there exists
binding force, but not a sufficient number of explicit moral laws.

In these unavoidable embarrassments theologians, as Bentham thinks,
had necessarily to adopt a desperate measure, namely, to "frame their
own mark for distinguishing" between those divine moral and legal
laws which should be valid and those which are not or should not be
valid any longer; and they found that "this mark is a particular utility
of the . . . regulation in question!"[411] But at this point, it naturally becomes evident that the principle of utility alone is the supreme, decisive
criterion in all questions of morals and legislation and no longer the
Divine Law. On historical and philosophic grounds, the divine law
itself is, thus, not capable of giving any satisfactory answer to the fundamental questions of the critical moralist.

Theologians tried, as Bentham adds, to obscure these facts by arguing
that there is at least an a priori identity between the dictates of the
Divine Law and those of utility, not a primacy of the utility principle.
And to this end the advocates of the Law of God interpret Scripture
too often even "against the most obvious import of the words so as to
bring it to a conformity with the dictate of utility in that behalf."[412] Or
they make efforts to persuade us of the utility of a law in spite of our
perception of its mischievous character, or they declare as regards the
Mosaic Law that if only it can be shown that one of its provisions is
"generally useful to all who should observe it, of any other nation as
well as of the Jewish," this provision "is an article of the moral Law. . . .
If no utility can be found or supposed in our observing it, its utility is
then of the special kind, and it belongs . . . only . . . to the Jews to whom
it was delivered."[413] However, if the principle of utility is considered in

[410] *Ibid.*, p. 47.
[412] *Ibid.*, p. 51.
[411] *Ibid.*, p. 49.
[413] *Ibid.*, p. 49.

this way to be the decisive criterion of the morality of laws even in a conflict with divine prescripts, how much more so in other cases on which the Bible is silent!

The logical conclusion which Bentham draws from all these reflections is that only the principle of utility, not any divine law, decides what is morally right or wrong, and that it is hopeless to test the propriety of a moral or political regulation "by any other test than by that plain and luminous one, the principle of utility" which "admits of no rival, admits not even of an associate."[414] The principle of utility alone can show "at once the readiest" and the surest "way of knowing . . . whether a measure is conformable to the . . . law of revelation"; the law of revelation is by no means able to do the same with regard to the principle of utility. The principle of utility is not only capable of being a definite guide in morals, but even theologians themselves need it to determine what is actually divine law.

Taking all in all, Bentham's reflections on theology and morals certainly belong to the most summary, but also to the most coherent and concise among the very numerous disquisitions of this kind in the epoch of enlightenment. Bentham's argument is instructive and, to a very large extent, sound, in so far as it is directed against a theology claiming to be a substitute for scientific morals or legislation. But wherever he touches religion in its more sublime and subtle aspects, his criticism is unsatisfactory. It is, for instance, characteristic that as regards the ancient and profound religious belief in the fall of man (and in the consequently corrupt condition of our reason) Bentham is only able to confess that such religious ideas are "far above" his "comprehension."[415] He was not able to grasp that such religious teachings can be and have often been clearly separated from the establishment of rational science and held as admittedly mystic, religious convictions beyond the realm of rational reasoning. And as such "truths" of symbolic, "expressive" (not of simply "representative") character, religious teachings are not exposed to the criticism of scientific reasoning.

For Bentham, however, all such religious creeds remain a sheer "theological galimatias,"[416] or a hypocritical "grasping the horns of the altar" by moralists when they are "hard pressed" scientifically; and here his intellectual limitations are only too visible. But in drawing lines of demarcation between theology and moral sciences he has doubtless done useful work. He certainly is right in insisting that it is no substitute for scientific thought to give a "decent sermon," and to

[414] *Ibid.*, p. 51.   [415] *Ibid.*, p. 45.   [416] *Ibid.*, p. 46.

"atone by the exuberance of . . . piety for the defects of . . . penetration."[417] For the fusion of non-rational religion and rational argument destroys the integrity of rational analysis, as well as the primal right of mystical, religious thought.

The Connection of Natural, Divine and Municipal Laws. Law of Nations

Seen from the point of view of Bentham's censorial ethics, the law of nature and the law of God are mere "non-entities."[418] He further illustrates this in a special chapter on the "connection of Laws, Natural, Divine, and Municipal." As Bentham wittily points out, between natural and divine law "and their old crony human or Municipal Law . . . there subsists . . . as it is natural to suppose . . . a very strict sort of intimacy . . . , a strict intimacy indeed, and so strong a likeness . . . that when Municipal Law has got their livery on his back, as he commonly has when he is about his business, you would hardly know one from t'other."[419] What Municipal Law has to do for natural and divine law "seems to be much the same as Mr. *Andrew* in the *Puppet-shew* does for Mr. *Punch*: say his good things over again for him, for fear any of them should escape the company: a good office which, as this last-mentioned facetious gentleman is apt now and then like those we have been speaking of, to be troubled with a huskiness in his throat, is something not much more than necessary."[420] In the company of the Natural and Divine Law "that poor Municipal Law makes . . . not . . . any great figure in the group: the connection being altogether of the unequal kind, such as between Patron and Toadeater of the lowest form: the amicitia inaequalitatis, as it is somewhere called, this humble understrapper feeding upon the scraps of obedience the others leave."[421] As a matter of fact, according to Blackstone as well as to many leading theorists of the seventeenth and eighteenth centuries, the empirical, municipal, human laws can or ought to be solely "declaratory" of the law of nature and the law of God (at least "with regard to such points that *are not* indifferent"); and so all human laws depend entirely "upon these two foundations," they can act only "in subordination" to them.[422] This belief in the primacy of the divine and the natural law is certainly one of the cardinal points in all theories concerned with them.

[417] *Ibid.*, p. 40.   [418] *Ibid.*, pp. 44, 78.   [419] *Ibid.*, p. 53.
[420] *Ibid.*, p. 53 f.   [421] *Ibid.*, p. 53.
[422] W. Blackstone, *Commentaries on the Laws of England*, book I, Introduction, 1773, p. 42.

One of Bentham's main intentions, however, is to release human law from this domination by superior divine and "pretended"[423] natural laws. Accordingly, he continues caricaturing the doctrine of the alleged inferiority of human law, asking "the gentle Reader" a most puzzling conundrum. It is the question: how to make murder lawful, in consequence of the widely assumed subordination of human law under the divine and natural laws? The answer is in brief: "Suppose ... in human laws there is an article against murder," in the other two sorts of law "there is (suppose) no such article. This being the case, murder you are to understand is not unlawful,"[424] since according to the presuppositions "human laws must act in subordination" to the others with regard to all "such points as *are not* indifferent" like murder.[425] And what about the "indifferent actions," that is to say, actions that do "neither good nor harm"[426] in society? Herein human laws are said to "have their greatest . . . efficacy";[427] with regard to these indifferent actions the answer must be that in this field of moral "adiaphora" the lawgiver is free to make any stipulation whatsoever. So that paradoxically "what it does no harm to do" the human laws "would make us *not* do: what it does no harm *not* to do" they "would make us *do*."[426] For example "exporting Wool to *foreign* countries . . . would do no harm to *this*; in consideration whereof" it "should be forbidden" according to Blackstone.[426] Such are the paradoxical and ridiculous consequences of theories in which all human laws depend upon the law of God and Nature. "To find them placed on foundations thus solid and conspicuous cannot but be matter of singular comfort and satisfaction,"[425] as Bentham caustically adds. "Certainly," he continues, "it is not easy to tell what meaning" theories have which have none.[428] This is doubtless a drastic, audacious method of bringing out some of the incongruities with which the doctrines of natural and divine law are afflicted. With all due respect to Bentham, the assumption will not generally be granted, even by way of supposition, that the law of nature and that of God would have no article against the most important crimes such as murder. Nevertheless, Bentham's conundrum illustrates, I think not inaptly, at least part of the inconcinnities existing here. Unfortunately, these difficulties are, even today, more frequently circumvented than carefully debated.

[423] Bentham, *A Comment on the Commentaries*, ed. by Everett, 1928, pp. 73, 38.
[424] *Ibid.*, p. 54.   [425] *Ibid.*, p. 53.   [426] *Ibid.*, p. 56.
[427] W. Blackstone, *Commentaries on the Laws of England*, book I, introduction, 1773, p. 42.
[428] Bentham, *A Comment on the Commentaries*, 1928, pp. 53, 56.

In a very brief chapter, Bentham goes on from the dethronement of the natural and divine law to the overthrow of a third law which is "no law at all,"[429] namely, the law of nations. At least a part of the law of nations (in Blackstone and elsewhere) is provided by the law of nature; and so Bentham tries here again to show what nebulous conceptions or even contradictions we fall into if we presuppose the metaphysical existence of a law of nature, independent of positive law and morality.

Justinian had stated that "the Law of Nations is what Natural Reason has established among the Nations"; and, as Bentham ironically adds, since it is such "a rare thing to be a Roman Emperor and to write in Latin ... either of them" is "an incontestable title ... to our Author's worship."[430] But if we now ask what are the moral precepts or compacts of which the law of nations consists, there is nothing said. We only are bid again to go to the law of nature, "and that will do our business." Instead of telling us forthrightly what the law of nations is, Blackstone informs us of something quite different, viz. that it is impossible the world should be all in one nation or state.[431]

On this Bentham remarks in good humour: it is "improbable enough ... I should suppose" that we all live in one state, "but ... impossible?" At any rate, to hear that one thing is impossible can surely be no substitute for knowing whether another thing *is* and *what* another thing is.[432] Blackstone and other jurists assume that the law of nature, of which the law of nations is part, is bound to "a State of Nature" where there are "no such things" as true laws at all. So here again, in Bentham's view, we arrive at a most embarrassing result; for we find that the law of nations "consists partly of another law and partly of a thing that isn't Law at all."[433] For this reason Bentham claims the right to consider the law of nations as a phantom and fiction causing only confusion.

Empirical, Municipal Law

Only after these discussions of the three kinds of laws which, according to Bentham, do *not* exist, do we come to the analysis of that

---

[429] *Ibid.*, p. 58. Compare *Works*, 1843, part VII, p. 160, where the law of nature and the law of nations are termed "chimerical laws" ("View of a Complete Code of Laws").

[430] Bentham, *A Comment on the Commentaries*, 1928, p. 59.

[431] *Ibid.*, p. 57.

[432] *Ibid.*, p. 57.

[433] *Ibid.*, p. 58. Cf. *ibid.*, p. 162, where such concepts in a slightly different connection are described as "pompous nothingness."

kind of law which alone he recognizes as existing, namely, the empirically given law, the municipal law containing especially the written "Statute Law," in contrast to the unwritten "Common Law" which consists to a considerable extent of ancient moral and legal customs.[434] Only when we speak of this Municipal and Statute Law do we descend, as Bentham merrily remarks, "from the craggy region of unintelligibles; and . . . get footing in the champaign territory of real and ostensible existence"[434] (a simile strongly reminiscent of Kant's remark about theoretical metaphysics with its lofty, wind-blown towers; Kant also preferred the fertile "bathos" of experience to those rocky regions of metaphysical idealism).[435] According to Bentham, we should tolerantly excuse the metaphysical and theological moralists "from describing what exists not to be described"[436] (to wit, their "superior laws" of God and nature),[437] if only they would properly describe the essence of the empirical, existing law. But even this is not the case, in his view, at least not in Blackstone.

Analyzing Blackstone's definition of the municipal law, and some other definitions connected therewith, Bentham continually observes that all these defenders of natural and divine law and their "fellow dealers in fiction"[438] do not think concretely or empirically enough even in speaking of empirical laws; and thus every explanation they give "wants another," and if they "were to give another that would want a third: and if a third that would want a fourth: and the more explanation" they "gave it, one might venture to say the more would still be wanting."[439] Blackstone's definition of the municipal law which is, according to his own statement, an actually "proper definition" reads: "Municipal Law is a rule of civil conduct prescribed by the su-

[434] *Ibid.*, p. 124. As Bentham mentions explicitly in his *Introduction to the Principles of Morals and Legislation*, chap. XVII, sect. 26, note, the term *municipal law* first signified local, particular jurisprudence, "till it was taken by an English author of the first eminence, to signify internal law in general, in contradistinction to international law and the imaginary law of nature." Of the Common Law, however, "a considerable proportion" is in the "oral and unwritten state," see *The Book of Fallacies*, 1824, chap. II, sect. 2, p. 59 note.

[435] I. Kant, *Sämtliche Werke*, ed. by Hartenstein, 1867 ff, Band IV, p. 121 ("Prolegomena zu einer jeden künftigen Metaphysik, die als Wissenschaft wird auftreten können").

[436] Bentham, *A Comment on the Commentaries*, ed. by Everett, 1928, p. 60.

[437] *Ibid.*, pp. 79, 95.

[438] *Ibid.*, p. 67.

[439] *Ibid.*, p. 60. Compare p. 124: Commentaries of Blackstone need further comment, his introduction a further introduction, his interpretation further interpretation.

preme power in a state commanding what is right and prohibiting what is wrong."[440] But Bentham, analyzing this definition piece by piece, finally comes to the conclusion that it explains nothing and is quite empty; for it is built up on the unexplained and unexplainable concepts of divine and natural law.

As in our analysis of the *Fragment on Government*, we must disregard here all questions of a purely juristic and political nature. However, there are some important ethical points left for consideration, particularly the characteristic, short analysis of conscience, and further analyses of the relation between municipal law and the other "superior" types of law.

CONSCIENCE

What is for Bentham "the signification of the word conscience: that ill-fated word which scarce ever appears but it brings confusion in train"?[441] Conscience represents one of the most fundamental concepts in practically all moral theories which are linked with natural or divine law, moral ideas a priori, moral sense or ethical intuition. Obviously, for precisely this reason, the concept of conscience is almost non-existent in Bentham.

Very seldom in the history of ethics has so low an estimate of the moral importance of conscience been given. Bentham finds that "only ... the expectation ... of a pain ... from the displeasure of the deity" can be "said ... according to common speech ... to touch the conscience."[442] Bentham, that is, attributes conscience only to religious people as a kind of superstition; even such an ethical radical as Nietzsche did not go so far, for he denied only that criminals had *ordinary* conscience, and found even among them a kind of substitute for moral conscience.[443] To Bentham, however, the "*Forum Conscientiae* is a Latin phrase" which "shews a man's learning, and comes in very prettily, when he knows what he means by it."[444] But until this clearness of knowledge is achieved, the word *conscience* is an especially dangerous "source of confusion and error."[445] Originally and correctly, according

[440] *Ibid.*, p. 60. Cf. W. Blackstone, *Commentaries on the Laws of England*, 1773, book I, p. 44 (not p. 47 as Bentham says).
[441] Bentham, *A Comment on the Commentaries*, ed. by Everett, 1928, p. 64.
[442] *Ibid.*, p. 64. Cf. p. 95 f.
[443] See F. Nietzsche, *Zur Genealogie der Moral*, II. Abhandlung, §15 (Taschenausgabe, Bd. VIII, S. 377).
[444] Bentham, *A Comment on the Commentaries*, ed. by Everett, 1928, p. 55.
[445] *Ibid.* p. 96.

to Bentham, the term *conscience* can mean only the "Will . . . as being acted on by pain or pleasure expected from causes that are invisible"[446] —invisible causes which are, in Bentham's view, imaginary ones.

Bentham admits that often not only religious fears but a combination of religious, political and moral motives are thought to be obligations *"in foro conscientiae."*[444] Once he even adds: I shall leave this "for those to consider further who think it worth their while."[444] In another connection, he grants that there is no harm in using the term conscience, "when it is known to be a question but of words."[445] At any rate, the concept of conscience, according to Bentham, has to be related specifically to religious and never to moral or political concerns, unless those secular concerns are linked up with religion.

Bentham, thus, does not concede any importance to conscience in the sphere of a secular science of morals and legislation. He even denies its existence as a non-religious, moral phenomenon. This, however, seems to me a kind of superradicalism. It is obviously an evidence of intellectual short-sightedness and insufficiency even as regards the observation of moral phenomena.

Though Bentham is, I think, by no means mistaken in rejecting conscience as a basic concept of ethics, he obviously goes too far in denying that there exists any kind of moral conscience independently of religious ideas. Even if bad conscience is understood only as the effect of fear of punishment, bad conscience evidently exists not only as a fear of being punished by the deity, but also of being punished by men; and so it has no necessary relation to religious motives.

As in the *Fragment*, Bentham distinguishes in the *Comment* three of the four sanctions he later enumerates in his *Introduction*: the political or legal sanction inflicting penalties through the judge and the state, the moral or popular sanction inflicting "displeasure . . . through uncertain persons"[447] of the community, the religious sanction or infliction of punishment by a superior invisible being; and to these three sanctions three kinds of pain correspond: "the fear of being hanged . . . , the fear of being hated, the fear of being damned."[448] In this connection, conscience is, according to Bentham, related exclusively to the superstitious "fear of being damned," to the religious sanction. But I think facts contradict Bentham's statement. Bad conscience is unquestionably often connected only with the fear of political or popular sanctions without relation to religious fears. There are many reasons

[446] *Ibid.*, p. 95. [447] *Ibid.*, p. 64.
[448] *Ibid.*, p. 55. Compare p. 95.

why the concept of conscience has to be ruled out from the fundamental concepts of a critical ethics; but from this it does not follow
that it is justifiable to exclude conscience as, so to speak, a theological
concept, from the whole of secular ethics and jurisprudence.

ETHICS AND JURISPRUDENCE IN THE *COMMENT*

Between the two secular sciences, jurisprudence and moral philosophy, Bentham never wished to draw strict lines of demarcation. As in
the *Fragment* and later in the *Introduction*, he denied in the *Comment* that there are any fundamental differences between moral and
legislative problems and between "civil" conduct, between the conduct
of a citizen on the one hand and "moral conduct" on the other. In contrast to Blackstone, he explicitly terms "civil conduct" also a kind of
moral conduct. "As if the conduct which men are made to observe by
force of Municipal Laws were not a *moral* conduct!"[449] The same attitude, we shall see, is always taken by Bentham.

This denial of any fundamental difference between the sphere of
jurisprudence and ethics is again connected to a large extent with Bentham's rejection of the "pretended"[450] natural law as a "superior"[451]
source of morals—a thesis to which he frequently returns as one of his
central convictions. There exists no law of nature, no separate body of
a higher metaphysical law which can serve as a criterion to ascertain
or nullify the moral validity of empirical laws. Bentham here tries to
demonstrate this by a fresh argument.

Blackstone, like every jurist, has to admit in the definition of existing law that the rules prescribed by it have to be "notified; . . . a bare
resolution . . . without manifesting itself by some external sign can
never be properly a law. It is requisite that this resolution be notified
to the people who are to obey it."[452] But if this is the case, Bentham
justifiably asks "once more, what sort of Law . . . is the Law of Nature
and one half of the Law of Nations?"[453] Who has notified or who can
notify them legitimately? Nobody. Therefore, once more, they are no
proper laws. As a matter of fact, Blackstone went so far as to declare
roundly that the *manner* in which the notification of a law "is to be
made, is matter of very great indifference."[452] But Bentham adds,
rather: "In this, it is my ill fortune to be obliged to think differently:

[449] *Ibid.*, p. 64.   [450] *Ibid.*, p. 73.   [451] *Ibid.*, pp. 79, 95.
[452] W. Blackstone, *Commentaries on the Laws of England*, 1773, book 1, introduction, p. 45.
[453] Bentham, *A Comment on the Commentaries*, ed. by Everett, 1928, p. 66.

to me, I must confess it seems a matter of very great importance."[454] Blackstone tells us of Caligula, who hung up his laws "in a small character" and upon high pillars; but Bentham, with full emphasis, wishes to stress precisely the other side of this fact: despite the small characters and the high pillars, even the Roman tyrant Caligula hung up his laws.[455] As, however, the law of nature *qua* law of nature cannot be properly promulgated, Bentham concludes again that the law of nature is no law at all.

Here, too, the cardinal point in Bentham's argument is that the law of nature is only an artificial reduplication of the existing municipal law. In Blackstone the right, the moral municipal law is only that which "our old friend the Law of Nature" and perhaps "in a masquerade . . . the Law of Revelation have . . . already . . . commanded"; the true commands and prohibitions of municipal law are, according to Blackstone, only those which "are already issued by the Law of Nature."[456] The only distinction between the two kinds of law which Blackstone can give is this: the municipal law "takes its instructions from the supreme power in the state," the natural one "from God himself." But, as Bentham correctly observes, the operations of both "spirits," the state and God, are so suspiciously identical[456] that it would be futile to expect the law of God to prescribe to the state anything different from the law of the state.

As a matter of course, Blackstone as well as Bentham feels himself obliged to find a criterion for distinguishing between bad and good empirical laws, between right and wrong in municipal law; and therefore, as Bentham notes, besides the reference to the law of nature and the law of God, Blackstone occasionally uses another common means to get rid of wrong municipal law. He simply declares that bad laws are in truth no laws at all.[457] This old, well-known "recipe" of judges which they "learnt of the brethren of the trade"[456] is also rightly attacked by Bentham. It is, indeed, extremely simple to use this recipe but for all that, it is as "pernicious as it is common."[458] For it opens all doors to arbitrary decisions of judges or "popular impatience"; and "nothing is more apt to confound men's understandings," as well as to "inflame their passions."[459] It is evident that bad laws are laws by

---

[454] *Ibid.*, p. 67.

[455] *Ibid.*, p. 69. Compare Bentham's *The Limits of Jurisprudence Defined*, ed. by Everett, 1945, pp. 155, 282.

[456] *Ibid.*, p. 71.

[457] *Ibid.*, p. 71. Compare pp. 197, 193.

[458] *Ibid.*, p. 72.

[459] *Ibid.*, p. 72.

definition. To deny this is very improper as well as misleading. But even if we could be permitted to deny it, we should be no further forward. Even after having characterized immoral laws as no laws at all, we have not found thereby what we went to search for—the criterion which would enable us to distinguish between moral laws and immoral non-laws.

Neither the degradation of moral laws to be "no laws at all," nor the assumption of a "pretended"[460] natural law, can give us the fundamental criterion of morals which we need in critical ethics and jurisprudence. Blackstone, with his perpetual reference to that "nonentity,"[461] the natural law, or to similar question-begging terms, must continually relapse into mere tautologies even in his analysis of the empirical, municipal law. The final result which his work achieves in his "elaborate definition"[462] of municipal law is the merely tautological statement that "(contradictions apart) . . . Municipal Law . . . is a rule of conduct for those who are to observe it, prescribed by those who prescribe it, commanding what it commands and forbidding what it forbids."[462] Seen from the viewpoint of censorial ethics and jurisprudence, this is in truth a complete caricature of a definition.

Not only as regards this general definition of the municipal empirical law, but also with regard to a good number of its further details, Bentham shows in the subsequent chapters of his work how often Blackstone and similar moralists move in an "unamusing kind of blind man's buff that consists in playing with words whose meaning . . . is not visible."[463] About Blackstone's discussion "on Government," Bentham is exceedingly brief in section VII of his *Comment*. For this topic is developed at length in his *Fragment on Government*, published in 1776. In his *Comment* he criticizes only one point of this topic, viz. Blackstone's most inadequate answer to the cardinal question: what is the ethical essence of legislative power?

Blackstone simply said "that the natural, inherent right . . . of making and enforcing laws . . . belongs to the sovereignty of a state, wherever that sovereignty be lodged."[464] Bentham, however, acutely detects why this attribution likewise is only tautological—an analytic judgment, as Kant some years later termed such judgments in distinction from synthetic judgments which alone are pertinent to this

---

[460] *Ibid.*, pp. 73, 81.
[462] *Ibid.*, p. 73.
[461] *Ibid.*, pp. 44, 78.
[463] *Ibid.*, p. 96.
[464] W. Blackstone, *Commentaries on the Laws of England*, 1773, book I, introduction, p. 47.

question. In Blackstone's answer, it is clear, the predicate is already immanent in the subject; and by such analytic judgments no questions concerning reality can ever be answered.

If we are asked who is ethically entitled to make laws, it would be quite preposterous to answer that, logically, the mere definitions of sovereignty and legislature can be regarded as "convertible terms."[465] For it is not this analytic judgment which is in debate but an entirely different problem, namely, the question: who has the moral and juristic right to make laws in reality, independently of all reasoning based on mere definitions?

In answer to this second question, Bentham points out clearly and convincingly: had Blackstone "had any ideas in his mind before he could have thought of making a question of it: this is what he must have done. In the first place he must have formed to himself a notion of sovereignty, a sovereign body in a state, without any notion of the power of making Laws, which I should suppose to be no easy matter. This however he must have begun with: in order to have a notion of the subject to which the attribute in question might or might be not conceived to belong: and then and not till then would he have set about enquiring whether the attribute did in fact belong to it."[466] Blackstone's definitions refer only to the realm of words, not to that of facts, by which alone words acquire a meaning pertinent to reality. Therefore, Blackstone's verbalisms are not of the slightest avail in the sphere of critical ethics. They can only lead the uncritical inquirer to lose sight of the ethical problem in question: i.e. the question to whom ought to be attributed legislative power "in fact,"[466] who is ethically entitled to be sovereign in reality?

In his treatment of the different "parts of a law," Blackstone distinguished four such parts: the declaratory, the directory, the remedial and the vindicatory;[467] and Bentham, even in his analysis of these specifically juristic discussions in section VIII of his *Comment*, again takes the opportunity of broaching some ethically relevant questions combined therewith.

So once more the natural and the divine law appear in the debate. In the view of Blackstone and of other adherents of "superior laws,"

---

[465] See Bentham, *A Comment on the Commentaries*, 1928, p. 75.

[466] *Ibid.*, p. 75.

[467] W. Blackstone, *Commentaries on the Laws of England*, 1773, book I, introduction, p. 53 f.

the so-called "natural rights . . . such as . . . life and liberty need not be declared" by human, municipal laws, since those rights are already established by "God and Nature" and cannot, therefore, receive "any additional strength . . . by the . . . declaratory part" of human laws.[468] To this, Bentham again objects that it is necessary to ascertain, first, on what part of divine law the municipal law depends; and even then, it remains uncertain in what sense it could depend on that part, whatever it is; secondly, "of the Law of Nature, as I have often said, I know nothing, since it is a non-entity."[469] Therefore, as Bentham wittily continues, "I am heartily glad of the aid of the human Laws to invest in me my life and liberty, needless as he [Blackstone] may think it: that I do conceive my right to them at least very much strengthened by these same human Laws: and that were it not for the said Laws, I should be much puzzled to say what right I had to them at all."[470] But if, nevertheless, "the municipal Law must at all events, come what will of it, depend . . . upon" the natural and divine Law, "it must require no small share of wisdom, I should conceive, to find out what they have to do in the affair."[469] In fact, it remains "utterly" impossible to understand precisely which moral rights "God and Nature have established" and what power is left to the human legislator under the assumption of superior natural and divine laws. "Has the legislator or has he not *power* to declare what act *shall* amount to a forfeiture" of life and liberty? "If he has, what is the subject the better for this want of power in the legislator that so much stress is laid on? If not, what is to become of those laws that inflict loss of life or liberty for their sanction? That is what is to become of the greatest part of all our Laws?"[471] Whatever one may think of the extent of moral and legislative power invested in municipal law, under the presupposition of natural rights there are inextricable difficulties involved as to the degree of this extent.

These dilemmas can, perhaps, best be characterized in the following way: The doctrine of natural rights, such as life and liberty, either teaches nothing with regard to what is moral or immoral in reality, leads to the nullification of municipal law, or leads to flat contradictions.

First, the law of nature contains flat contradictions if it declares, on the one hand, that the life and liberty of men should be inviolable for

[468] *Ibid.*, book 1, introduction, §2, p. 54.
[469] Bentham, *A Comment on the Commentaries*, 1928, p. 78.
[470] *Ibid.*, p. 79.   [471] *Ibid.*, p. 79.

the legislator, and on the other hand that they should be not inviolable, "if some act is committed that amounts to a forfeiture."

Second, if the first part of the former declaration alone were maintained, if the life and liberty of men were inviolable for the legislator under all circumstances, this would deny the concurrent validity of natural and municipal law. For then all municipal law with regard to life and liberty must disappear. The human legislator would then have no power at all with regard to these natural rights; and such a fargoing invalidation of municipal law is, of course, rejected by Blackstone.

Third, if only the latter part of the original declaration is maintained, if the life and liberty of men are not inviolable, then the law of nature teaches nothing at all concerning actual moral decisions. It neither says that life and liberty are inviolable nor under which circumstances they are violable. Instead of this, the law of nature exhausts itself in the merely analytic judgment that "no human legislator has power to abridge or destroy them (the natural rights, such as life and liberty), unless the owner shall himself commit some act that amounts to a forfeiture";[472] or more simply expressed: life and liberty are inviolable, unless they are under certain conditions violable.

Therefore, no moral question concerning life and liberty can be answered by reference to the law of nature. Within the boundaries of municipal law, the legislator can and must search for criteria to determine in which circumstances it is morally right to violate life and liberty, and in which circumstances it is wrong. It is useless or even detrimental for the legislator to refer to natural rights or to the law of God; both he and the moralist must confine themselves to municipal law and empirical ethics.

"Intrinsically" Right Actions, *mala in se* and the Law of Nature

All this becomes even clearer in the annexed discussion on *mala in se* (in contrast to *mala prohibita*),[473] on "naturally and intrinsically"[474] wrong or right actions and "the thing itself," in contrast to the "particular circumstances and mode of doing it."[475] All these interesting

[472] W. Blackstone, *Commentaries on the Laws of England*, 1773, book i, introduction, §2, p. 54.
[473] W. Blackstone, *Commentaries on the Laws of England*, 1773, book i, introduction, §2, p. 54; Bentham, *A Comment on the Commentaries*, p. 79 f.
[474] Blackstone, *ibid.*, p. 54; Bentham, *ibid.*, p. 81.
[475] Blackstone, *ibid.*, p. 55; Bentham, *ibid.*, p. 82.

ethical concepts belong closely together. They are, in Blackstone and generally, linked up with metaphysical ethics, or at least with some kind of intuitionistic absolutism.[476]

Blackstone explicitly assigned all these concepts to the metaphysical law of nature or the law of revelation. "Crimes and misdemeanours" that are "stiled *mala in se*" are "forbidden by the superior laws" (the divine and natural law),[473] as he emphasizes with special stress. Only as regards "*mala in se* . . . are we bound in conscience, because we are bound by superior . . . not . . . human laws before those human laws were in being,"[477] which also indicates distinctly the a priori character of those notions and their relation to a conscience a priori. On the other hand, in cases of "*mala prohibita* . . .[prohibited by empirical laws] annexing a penalty to non-compliance, here . . . conscience is no further concerned, than by directing a submission to the penalty in case of our breach of those laws: for otherwise the multitude of penal laws in a state would . . . be a very wicked thing, if every such law were a snare for the conscience of the subject."[478] In short, Blackstone makes full use of the large apparatus of terminology which commonly is employed in dualistic metaphysical ethics. There are, on the one hand, metaphysical laws, the metaphysical "nature" of things, things in themselves, the intrinsically moral character of actions, *conscience a priori, mala in se*; on the other hand there are merely empirical laws, the empirical character of things, phenomena, the accidental, peculiar circumstances of actions, the mode of doing them, the empirical judgment on actions, *mala prohibita*.

Aside from this, as we shall see later, the theories of the law of nature in the seventeenth and eighteenth centuries still commonly introduced the central concepts of reason and of rational characteristics in contrast to experience and empirical attributes. This is much less prevalent in modern ethics. But even in modern ethics (foregoing any explicit metaphysics) similar schemes of thought are to be found. Contemporary ethics still operate with "productions right in themselves," with "intrinsic values," values in themselves, values a priori and with their con-

---

[476] Compare my essay "Ernst Cassirer and the Chaos in Modern Ethics," *The Library of Living Philosophers*, ed. by P. A. Schilpp, 1949, vol. VI, especially pp. 582-598 and compare C. L. Stevenson, *Ethics and Language*, 1944, chap. VIII on "Intrinsic and extrinsic value," pp. 174 ff.

[477] W. Blackstone, *Commentaries on the Laws of England*, 1773, book I, introduction, §2, p. 57; Bentham, *A Comment on the Commentaries*, p. 95.

[478] W. Blackstone, *Commentaries on the Laws of England*, 1773, book I, introduction, §2, p. 58; Bentham, *A Comment on the Commentaries*, 1928, p. 95.

trast, namely, empirically, accidentally valuable actions, modes of doing which put into practice the values a priori.[479] Therefore the question still arises for us, as it did for Bentham: can the censorial problems of ethics be answered by means of these old schemes of argument?

Bentham denies this completely. As he points out, Blackstone himself was not able to use the terms *mala in se* and *mala prohibita* consistently. Blackstone himself at first declares that theft is a "malum in se," forbidden by the law of nature and of God; yet in the fourth volume of his "Commentaries" he grants that theft is only a "malum prohibitum," solely forbidden by municipal, not by natural law.[480] But if, on a vital point, a radically different classification of the same action is possible in the thought of the same author, how much less unity of judgment can be expected in different authors! How ambiguous and valueless is, then, the distinction between *mala in se* and *mala prohibita*, between the pretended superior laws and the empirical law!

There are, it is true, defenders of such ethical notions as *mala in se* or actions in themselves, intrinsically moral and immoral actions, who admit that their theories do not enable us to make concrete ethical decisions. But as they claim, this is by no means a defect of their doctrines and terminology. Blackstone grants, for instance, that only obedience to superiors in general is ordered by the revealed as well as by the natural law.[481] This obedience is a prescribed order in itself, an intrinsically right doing; yet "who those superiors shall be," and in what particular, concrete "circumstances or to what degrees" and in what "mode of doing . . . they shall be obeyed, is the province of human laws to determine."[481] What does that mean? Surely, if the law of nature in this and similar cases can teach us no more than that some superiors have to be obeyed, and if only the municipal law can tell us which superiors and in which way they have to be obeyed, then the law of nature does not give us the slightest ethical knowledge and we can perfectly well do without it.

[479] See W. D. Ross, *The Right and the Good*, 1930, p. 47: "Such production is right in itself apart from any consequence"; and see p. 14: "The human mind . . . has in fact an *a priori* insight into certain broad principles of morality." Values a priori (in their contrast to empirical valuable actions) and intrinsic values are the basic concepts of M. Scheler's, N. Hartmann's and G. E. Moore's ethics. See my criticism of this type of modern ethics in "Philosophy," April 1938, pp. 183-195 and in *The Library of Living Philosophers*, vol. vi, 1949, pp. 575-603.

[480] See W. Blackstone, *Commentaries an the Laws of England*, 1773, book i, introduction, §2, p. 54 and book iv, p. 28 f; Bentham, *A Comment on the Commentaries*, 1928, p. 80.

[481] W. Blackstone, *ibid.*, p. 55; Bentham, *ibid.*, p. 82.

The same formulated more succinctly: if we have to consult the municipal law in all concrete questions of morals and jurisprudence, then, to come to some general conclusions relating to these concrete cases, we only need the help of formal logic; we by no means need the help of a special branch of morals aside from the municipal law and concrete empirical ethics.

Thus, Bentham could reply to Blackstone simply: "As to this matter what I conceive is this . . . that as to a Law commanding men to do the act of paying obedience to superiors, unless it declares who those superiors are, it is a law that says just as much as comes to nothing." If all decisions on concrete moral questions must be "left" to the empirical legislature and to empirical ethics to decide, "what others must it not?"[482] Or at least, what other decisions are left which have anything to do with problems of reality and not merely with formal logic? It is beyond doubt that Bentham's argument has to be polished and improved in many details before it can be said to be completely satisfactory; but its fundamental point of view seems to me sound and not shakable by its opponents.

THE RATIONAL NATURE OF MAN AND THE LAW OF PURE REASON

In section IX of his *Comment* dealing with "Interpretation of Laws" Bentham again treats detailed juristic questions. But here too he goes back to his criticism of the assumption of a general, metaphysical "nature of things" and "nature of actions"; and in doing so he throws light on another concept of central significance which, throughout the centuries, has been intertwined with the theories of an ethical law of nature.

Blackstone speaks occasionally of "rational civilians"; this is genuinely in accordance with the dualistic character of the law of nature. The law of nature generally distinguishes the rational, essential part of things and actions from their empirical, accidental side; the rational characteristics of moral agents (which belong to the "nature of things in themselves") from their purely empirical, phenomenal attributes. To these assumptions Bentham summarily objects as follows: "As to 'the *nature of things*' so glibly spoken of, he must be more than a 'rational civilian'[483] who can tell what sort of 'constitutions' those are of, that in contradistinction to others, have *that* only for their guide. . . . What sort of a 'guide' 'the nature of *things*' is to make for 'a constitu-

---

[482] Bentham, *A Comment on the Commentaries*, ed. by Everett, 1928, p. 83.
[483] W. Blackstone, *Commentaries on the Laws of England*, 1773, book I, introduction, §2, p. 58.

tion,' or what meaning the phrase, smooth as it is, has here, is what I must confess myself unable to conceive. When he speaks of 'general constitutions,' he speaks to be understood . . . but when he goes on and talks of 'the nature of things,' I see him wrapt in clouds."[484] As a matter of fact, I believe that even the most developed and most acute theories of a rational law of nature (as for instance, the ethics and jurisprudence of Kant) remain on this decisive point in the clouds and must remain so.[485] To summarize the complicated argument involved here: since all "synthetic" knowledge can concern only combinations of rational and empirical elements, the rational purity of moral laws must remain merely formal without any content; or the alleged rational purity must be abandoned and the same content must be adopted as is contained in the empirical side of these laws. Therefore, all attempts at distinguishing clearly between the rational and empirical nature of actions must be hopeless.

The law of nature is also called, by many of its advocates, the law of pure reason. And since, for Blackstone and all his "brother adepts," the empirical law has to be based on the more fundamental law of nature and reason, those moralists and jurists "are fond of proclaiming in their moments of enthusiasm" that "*reason* . . . is the life"[486] of every moral and juristic law. "The Law is the perfection of reason, it always intends to conform thereto, and . . . what is no reason is not law."[487] Combining these last two pronouncements, we obtain what Bentham effectively ridicules as "a definition of the Law, by which we may learn that it is a sort of a thing which is a perfection of its own life."[487]

But, apart from this obvious mockery, Bentham on various occasions in his *Comment* tries to take up the problem of pure reason in a very serious and essential way—asking, for instance: what is the fallacy which everywhere "lurks in the words 'reason' and 'unreasonable' "?[488] "It consists," as he points out in the chapter on the "Construction of Statutes," in "supposing . . . the words 'reason' and 'unreasonable' . . . to stand for something that is fixed and certain. . . . This is not the case. A regulation lies before me. I look at it and pronounce that it is 'un-

---

[484] Bentham, *A Comment on the Commentaries*, ed. by Everett, 1928, p. 104 f.
[485] See D. Baumgardt, *Der Kampf um den Lebenssinn unter den Vorläufern der modernen Ethik*, 1933, Teil 1. In this book, I analyze at full length the numerous modern attempts to revive Kant's formalistic rationalism in ethics and try to show why none of these attempts could possibly succeed.
[486] Bentham, *A Comment on the Commentaries*, ed. by Everett, 1928, p. 119
[487] *Ibid.*, p. 194.   [488] *Ibid.*, p. 153.

reasonable': what is it that I mean by this? just this much and no more; that my reason, i.e. I myself, applying to it that faculty in me which is called reason, do not approve of it. I go farther. I cry out that it is 'manifestly contrary to common reason'—what mean I here? still no more than that it is what I readily and strongly disapprove of, conceiving at the same time that it will be equally disapproved of by most others. . . . This being the case . . . when all comes to all, reasonableness or unreasonableness is nothing but conformity or nonconformity to, at least can be decided by nothing but, opinion."[489] Though these are certainly the declarations of a radical empiricist, it is, I think, worth noting that Bentham has not simply laid them down dogmatically. He tried to ground them epistemologically. He attempted to show why decisions on the basis of so-called common reason cannot claim any universal validity by their mere dogmatic reference to so-called reason.

To these epistemological arguments, Bentham has added a well observed psychological reason to explain why philosophers, jurists and mankind in general are not willing to give up the belief in "common,"[490] universal reason. He finds: "To confess that as against other men's opinion" a man has no other "warrant for his own opinion than itself, is what few men indeed will bring themselves to admit so long as they can help it. Nothing is more shocking to man's pride, nor galling to his impatience. Yet this being the case it were fit it should be understood."[490] Psychological analyses of this type seem to me very much to the point, at least as far as such defenders of pure reason as Christian Wolff or Fichte are concerned. Recently, similar psychological interpretations have been applied even to Kant.[491]

Bentham describes his attitude toward an alleged universal moral reason even more vividly in the chapters on "Judicial Decisions" and on "Particular Customs-Rules." The question is here: whose opinion shall be the standard? "Whose reason? . . . Everybody's? No, that can not be. . . . In truth it must be the reason, of you, of me, of any one before whom the determination is supposed to be proposed to judge of. It is easy to say, but very fruitless, not so, but the general reason of mankind. Good, but how am I to come at this general reason, in a case too that not above

[489] *Ibid.*, p. 153 f.   [490] *Ibid.*, p. 154.

[491] See K. Breysig, *Der Aufbau der Persönlichkeit von Kant*, 1931, where also the "Denkerstolz" and the "Herrschaftswille" is stressed, which may be discovered in Kant's declaration of strictly universal laws of reason, see e.g. *ibid.*, p. 86: "Kant's Apriori . . . zeugt . . . von . . . höchster Erfülltheit . . . von der eigenen Unwiderlegbarkeit, . . . von herrscherlicher Verkündigung . . . und . . . von . . . einer jeden Widerspruch im Voraus zu Boden schmetternden Stosskraft."

twenty people ever thought of? I cannot go round the world and count suffrages. I must guess at it by my own. Unhappy necessity!"[492]

An equally "unhappy necessity" however, becomes transparent when we turn from the subjects who should have reason to the objects, to the content of the maxims which should have it, i.e. which should be called reasonable. "Now then what are the circumstances in the character of a custom"[493] or of any moral rule which can demonstrate its reasonableness? "To ascertain them would be a work of great instruction, but of no small difficulty. Accordingly our Author washes his hands. On this, as on so many other occasions our Author puts us in mind of those sage parents, who are incessantly recommending it to young people to be prudent. This is mighty well; but what is prudence, that is the question."[493] In fact, it is as hopeless to try to decide merely a priori which concrete moral rules are reasonable, as it is impossible to decide a priori which concrete actions are prudent, or which concrete natural laws are valid in physics or chemistry.

Arguments of this kind have, of course, frequently been used against judgments of pure reason in the theory of knowledge, but hardly ever have they been employed with the same plainness and lucidity in morals. Certainly, Bentham's criticism does not hit merely formal or merely analytic judgments of pure reason. His objections apply essentially to concrete, "material" moral judgments which claim to be a priori, of universal validity. But it is just these concrete a priori judgments which the contemporary theories of "material values" have in view, and only these concrete valuations are of decisive importance in ethics.[494] Therefore, at least so it seems to me, Bentham's censure is, in the main, not out of place nor is it yet out of date.

No matter whether dressed up as universally valid valuations of pure reason, or presented as non-rational valuations of a universal "ordre du coeur,"[495] no concrete moral principles can be proved to be a priori of universal validity. As Bentham formulates this tartly and pointedly, a universal "natural reason" exists only as much or as little with regard to the law of nations as with regard to "a Mouse-trap."[496] The problems

---

[492] Bentham, *A Comment on the Commentaries*, ed. by Everett, 1928, p. 191.

[493] *Ibid.*, p. 227.

[494] See the present writer's *Der Kampf um den Lebenssinn unter den Vorläufern der modernen Ethik*, 1933, pp. 59-72, 101 ff.

[495] See M. Scheler, *Der Formalismus in der Ethik und die materiale Wertethik*, 1921, p. 59; N. Hartmann, *Ethics*, 1932, vol. II, p. 177; and both authors' reference to Pascal's principle of an "ordre du coeur."

[496] Bentham, *A Comment on the Commentaries*, ed. by Everett, 1928, p. 59.

of a critical concrete ethics can never be solved by simple recourse to any pretended moral laws of universal reason, or of non-rational values a priori. On this point ethical empiricism is in the right, in my opinion, though today it certainly needs a much broader substructure than Bentham gave it.

Criticism of Customary Morality (Common Law, the "Historical School" of Jurisprudence and Ethics)

Bentham rejects the belief in any universal moral reason and in the ethical law of nature. But all the same, he is no less an adversary of the so-called historical school of jurisprudence and morals, which tries to justify the validity of moral laws by the antiquity of historical customs.

As Professor Everett points out, it seems "curious . . . that the conservative Blackstone talks of natural rights almost in the tone which the American Declaration of Independence was to use later, and that Bentham, the champion of reform, denies their existence."[497] Certainly, the political scientist is entitled to presuppose that, in great measure, the belief in natural rights is historically tied up with political progress. That nevertheless Bentham, the champion of reform, rejects the law of nature is, I think, mainly due to epistemological rather than political reasons. It is only his fight against the conservative historical school which is determined by political as well as philosophic considerations.

In his opposition to the liberal theory of natural rights Bentham is, I believe, essentially motivated by philosophic interests, far more than by the political "demand . . . for a . . . British road to democracy" of which Professors Carl Becker, Paul A. Palmer and A. V. Dicey have spoken.[498] It is a fundamental lack of philosophic precision which Bentham observes in both the historical conservative and the liberal democratic school of jurisprudence. Therefore, he filled his *Comment* with a detailed criticism of the conservative common law as well as of the liberal law of nature. Independently of the antagonistic political trends of his time, he tried right from the beginning to ground his own political and moral thought on a philosophically sounder, critical basis.

[497] Ch. W. Everett in the introduction to his edition of Bentham's *Comment on the Commentaries*, 1928, p. 17.

[498] See C. Becker, *Declaration of Independence*, 1922, p. 236; P. A. Palmer, "Benthamism in England and America," *The American Political Science Review*, October 1941, vol. xxxv, p. 868; A. V. Dicey, *Lectures on the Relation between Law and Public Opinion in England*, 1924, pp. 171 ff.

Before Bentham, perhaps the most notable opponent of the conservative historical school was Hobbes with his "analytical position"; and as Everett remarks, this kind of "quarrel was to descend to the nineteenth century with Austin and Maine."[499] In Germany, a similar struggle went on between the historical school of Savigny and Gustav Hugo, on the one hand, and philosophically very heterogeneous theories on the other. In the main, there are on the conservative side the "theological" school, influenced by De Maistre and De Bonald, as well as the historical school. On the side of political progress, however, manifold philosophical tendencies have been active; not only social utilitarianism, but also Kantianism and such philosophically conservative ideologies as Hegelianism, appearing there in the guise of Marxism.

On the whole, neither in England, France or Germany is there any philosophical attitude or method which is definitely bound up with only one political trend and not also, occasionally, with its political opposite. Dicey thinks it was Bentham's "failure to perceive" that "towards the close of the eighteenth century appeals to the doctrine of utility and appeals to the law of nature were often in reality, though not in words, appeals to one and the same principle."[500] Professor P. A. Palmer seems to imply that the rejection of the law of nature by the legal reformer, Bentham, can best be explained as an illogical hangover from the earliest days of Bentham's loyalty to political Toryism.[501] However, I hope our analysis will show why the ethicist Bentham had ample philosophic reason to object with equal energy to the conservative and the liberal thought of his time. After having, therefore, dedicated the first part of his *Comment* to an extensive criticism of the law of nature, he subjects the conservative common law to an equally strict censure in the later part of his work.

Here again he adheres primarily to that basic conviction which he had already expressed in another form in his *Fragment on Government*: "To prove the existence of a practise is one thing, to prove the expediency of establishing it by force of law," or to justify it as a maxim that ought to be morally and legally binding, to prove the right of "making such a custom obligatory . . . is another" thing.[502] The eclectic

[499] Ch. W. Everett in the introduction to his edition of Bentham's *A Comment on the Commentaries*, 1928, p. 16.

[500] A. V. Dicey, *Lectures on the Relation between Law and Public Opinion in England during the Nineteenth Century*, 1924, p. 145.

[501] See P. A. Palmer, "Benthamism in England and America," *The American Political Science Review*, vol. xxxv, October 1941, pp. 856 ff.

[502] Bentham, *A Comment on the Commentaries*, ed. by Everett, 1928, p. 218.

Blackstone had tried to use for his purposes both the argument of the more liberal law of nature and that of the more conservative historical school. But being, in truth, far more a conservative, and applying the law of nature in close connection with divine law, Blackstone is inclined to rely to the largest extent on the common law and on authorities of the conservative historical school, such as Glanville and Bracton, Fleta and Britton, Littleton, Statham, Broke, Fitzherbert, Staunford and Edward Coke.[503] Bentham did not make the attempt to analyze every detail presented by Blackstone's usage of the common law; and for this he repeatedly apologizes.[504] We too, therefore, must forego the numerous specifically juristic discussions involved here, and confine ourselves to those issues which are of ethical relevance.

Blackstone, as well as the historical school and traditional moralists, consider the mere antiquity of their national customs as the main guarantee for the ethical value of these customs. It is true, of course, that all written law originated from unwritten traditional customs which grew up organically in a community, were kept in its memory, executed in its life and practice and then, though unwritten, were morally sanctioned by decisions of its courts of justice or the convictions of moral leaders of the group. Therefore, Blackstone had urged that this "general immemorial custom, or common law . . . digested . . . in the authoritative writings of the venerable sages of the law" is rightly thought to be "the first ground and chief corner stone of the laws of England."[505] That is, surely, a decided assertion of the lasting value of ancient law.

Bentham, however, demonstrates in ever new ways the "glorious uncertainty,"[506] the difficulty of applying those principles and the hidden fallacies which are generally committed in the utilization of the unwritten common law. In the section on "Reports and Treatises" of the common law, he asks, for instance: where is the "line . . . to be drawn" between treatises that "are, and such as are not of authority"? This Blackstone "with very good reason has not taken upon him, any otherwise than by approximation to determine."[507] All he does is to give the assurance that Edward Coke is "one of the last" whose treatises

[503] See W. Blackstone, *Commentaries on the Laws of England*, 1830, book 1, p. 72 f.
[504] See, for instance, Bentham, *A Comment on the Commentaries*, 1928, p. 156.
[505] W. Blackstone, *Commentaries on the Laws of England*, 1830, book 1, introduction, §3, p. 73.
[506] Bentham, *A Comment on the Commentaries*, 1928, pp. 204, 237.
[507] *Ibid.*, p. 202.

125

on common law are "of authority."[508] But in view of the vital issues which are here at stake, this is certainly a vague and unsatisfactory answer.

Bentham, therefore, goes on to inquire: is Coke, whose last treatise was written in 1628, "the very last" authority? It is hardly possible to maintain this. The authority of Matthew Hale, for example, who died in 1676 is generally believed to be by no means "inferior . . . to that of Coke."[509] At least, Hale's impartiality of judgment is considered to be far superior to that of the more stubborn Coke; and the comparative estimate of the two lawyers which Bentham gives is even today still maintained.[510]

Even if one allows "the line to be drawn anywhere through a certain point" of history for the sake of distinction between old authorities and modern unauthoritative moralists—"the misfortune is"[509] that even then new difficulties and new uncertainty arise. For in the frequent cases of difference of opinion between two acknowledged authorities, there is no common measure to weigh their specific gravity. Neither the greater antiquity[511] nor the difference between "licensed" and "not-licensed" reports is such a measure. Though, for instance, "the Reports of Siderfin are licensed: those of Shower are not," there is "perhaps none, either on the Bench or at the Bar, who would not be ready to give more weight to the latter than to the former."[512] In short, as there is no criterion to decide on the moral validity of any ancient customs, it is natural that in this "dark chaos of common law . . . different Judges have drawn . . . not unfrequently . . . opposite conclusions," either "from the same data" or "because the data that one Judge has had before him to another have been unknown."[513] All this shows how much that is arbitrary and fortuitous has gone to the building up of moral laws on ancient custom.

The common law is generally based on the strange assumption "that the weight of a writer's authority is in the conjunct ratio of his supposed intrinsic merit and his antiquity: but a certain degree of antiquity is a requisite not to be dispensed with. In treatises considered as aids

---

[508] W. Blackstone, *Commentaries on the Laws of England*, 1830, book 1, introduction, §3, p. 72.

[509] Bentham, *A Comment on the Commentaries*, 1928, p. 203.

[510] See H. Potter, *An Introduction to the History of English Law*, 1926, p. 38; W. S. Holdsworth, *A History of English Law*, 1924, vol. VI, pp. 595, 594, 580; R. M. Jones, *George Fox*, 1930, p. 109 f.

[511] Bentham, *A Comment on the Commentaries*, ed. by Everett, 1928, p. 203.

[512] *Ibid.*, p. 204.   [513] *Ibid.*, p. 191.

to conjecture, it is not *any* degree perhaps, of merit that would give the authority of a living writer the *preponderance* over that of a dead one."[514] All these criteria of valuation are certainly so vague or absurd that Bentham winds up these reflections in the following sarcastic way: lawyers, with respect to their sages, always "have done by tacit agreement what Popes in respect of their *saints* have done by an express rule; deferred their canonization till those who could give testimony of their frailties shall be no more";[515] and on top of that they refashioned their authorities in their own images. Thus, even if we were to grant the general criterion of antiquity in common law, insuperable difficulties arise in applying this principle.

However, the major emphasis of Bentham's argument against common law remains concentrated on the demonstration that antiquity itself, the antiquity of a moral custom equally with that of a moralist or a lawyer, can never serve as a criterion of moral value. Moral merit and moral value can never "grow out of antiquity."[516] In jurisprudence and in ethics there must be a clear discrimination between the *questio facti* and the *questio juris*; and it is the $\pi\rho\hat{\omega}\tau\text{o}\nu$ $\psi\epsilon\hat{\upsilon}\delta\text{o}\varsigma$ of the common law that it consciously ignores or unconsciously loses sight of the cardinal difference between these two questions.

Bentham, however, was not likely to commit this basic methodological error into which representatives of the common law generally fall. He obviously did not feel the slightest temptation to substitute historical research for systematic inquiry. He had even less reverence for the past than the average thinker of the 18th century. He roundly stated: "I know not that we owe any deference to former times that we owe not to our own."[517] On the contrary, "I would give very little to know the period when Tithes were instituted: I would give more to see the day when they shall be abolished."[518]

Blackstone, the avowed defender of common law-principles, went so far as to declare: "Though the reason . . . of precedents and rules be not obvious at first view, yet we owe such a deference to former times as not to suppose they acted wholly without consideration."[519] To this, Bentham replies by again distinguishing clearly between historical and systematic interests: whether an ancient rule "never had a reason, or whether having once had a reason, that reason is now ceased makes no

[514] *Ibid.*, p. 205.   [515] *Ibid.*, p. 205.   [516] *Ibid.*, p. 204.

[517] *Ibid.*, p. 195.   [518] *Ibid.*, p. 136.

[519] Blackstone, *Commentaries on the Laws of England*, 1773, book 1, introduction, §3, p. 70.

127

difference with respect to the reason we now have for adhering to it."[520] Likewise, the demand for stability of customs mentioned by Blackstone is for the reformer Bentham such a weak argument that it never can give ethical validity to morally questionable customs.[520] And the same applies to that reasoning of the historical school which may be thought its most persuasive argument, namely, the contention that in its early customs a community reveals its most original tendencies of life in the fullest vigor. Such a view probably never crossed Bentham's intellectual horizon. Yet, even if he had met it, he could not have approved of it; for it could not satisfy his censorial requirements either.

In Bentham's eyes, it is nothing but reactionary sloth and narrow-mindedness to allow somebody's moral notion to pass with us for valid simply because the author of this notion "lived a long while ago," or belonged to the nation of classical lawyers and "talked in Latin."[521] "To sanctify all that doting pedants have drivelled . . . in the way of . . . their encomiums on the common law" is, for Bentham, nothing but "miserable sophistry."[522] And besides this Bentham, as a rather well-informed historian of law, does not forget to mention that many of the so-called ancient maxims concerning property (lease and release, bargain and sale, fine and recovery) are by no means as ancient as they are thought to be. They are, in truth, of comparatively recent date; at least "our Saxon Ancestors with all their misfortunes were not so unfortunate as to have been tormented with these engines of chicane."[523] Indeed, the antiquity of traditions is often overrated in nearly all communities. For the most part, these traditional moral rules only survived with considerable alterations and this, too, tells against the ethical authority of the ancient common law.

Further, as the unwritten common law is "pretty apparently . . . made not by the people but by Judges," it is for Bentham nonsense to assure the public, as Blackstone did, that the authority of old moral and legal customs carries along with it any evidence of the freedom of a nation.[524] This is only a prejudice of lawyers of the historical school, and a prejudice which is "by no means unfavorable to their passions."[525] Yet, if lawyers were right on this point, then France in the middle of the eighteenth century must have been the freest country; for "nowhere else does Custom make a greater figure."[525] According to Ben-

---

[520] Bentham, *A Comment on the Commentaries*, 1928, p. 196.
[521] *Ibid.*, p. 145.   [522] *Ibid.*, pp. 193 ff.   [523] *Ibid.*, p. 160 f.
[524] W. Blackstone, *Commentaries on the Laws of England*, 1773, book I, introduction, §3, p. 74.
[525] Bentham, *A Comment on the Commentaries*, 1928, p. 213.

tham, however, precisely the contrary is true, namely, that ancient moral and legal customs are generally "still tainted with the breath of ancient despotism"; and it is a fallacy of lawyers to speak of general assent given to an ancient maxim by the people, thus identifying the assent given by a community *after* the threat of punishment with the assent given *before* this threat.[526] Only by means of such a fallacy and "logical anachronisms"[527] could lawyers venture to praise the tyranny of the unwritten law as the symbol of the freedom of a nation; and, cunningly, this ancient law has been hidden in so many volumes that, like certain ancient tyrants, it was completely "turned into an abstruse and invisible quiddity . . . which . . . was never to shew itself in public: like them it was to make its existence perceivable only by means of its delegates. . . . Thus . . . these judicial decisions" of the unwritten ancient law "were . . . to use our Author's own apposite similitude, Oracles," and they were "not the words of the Pythia . . . , but . . . the evidence of an Apollo whose oracles they were."[528] Summarizing all these reflections on the common law, then, the principle on which it is based is, according to Bentham, neither clear in itself, nor methodologically sound, nor consistently applicable, nor derivable from adequate sources, nor conducive of politically desirable results.

Moreover, as one of the most anti-historical minds of the unhistorical eighteenth century, Bentham goes so far in his polemics against ancient law as to declare that ancient common law in itself is practically of no interest at all. "The past is of no value but by the influence it preserves over the present and the future";[529] at least "let us accustom ourselves to appreciate and settle the precedency among the objects of our attention. Let us reflect that our first concern is to learn how the things that are in our power *ought to be*: that the knowledge of what they have been is of no further use, than as by pointing out the causes by the influence of which they have been brought to what they ought to be, in the few articles of ancient date in which they have been what they ought to be, and by which they have failed of being what they ought to be in the many instances in which they have *not* been what they ought to be, they lead us to the knowledge of the means by which they may be brought to what they ought to be in future." Our first business should not be "with antiquities but with Jurisprudence."[529] This is certainly a very radical utilization of history for systematic purposes. But Bentham justifies his resolute polemics against historicism

[526] *Ibid.*, p. 212.
[528] *Ibid.*, p. 189.
[527] *Ibid.*, p. 168.
[529] *Ibid.*, p. 136.

by adding that, in referring merely to antiquities, we should most dangerously "smooth the approaches of those who mean to travel" on "the most arduous and noblest road"[529] of systematic research, but who with their "weak minds and cold bosoms," with their "envy . . . timidity and ignorance" are greatly to be suspected of suffering from that "malady for which no certain name has yet been found by our pathologists, but which might perhaps be termed, the hydrophobia of innovation."[530] So we are led again by these reflections to what we have already found to be Bentham's most pragmatic objection to the common law, namely, that it is full of "obstinacy"[531] toward reform in morals, an obstinacy caused by blindness toward the censorial problems of ethics and jurisprudence, by the untenable identification of historical with systematic inquiry, and by the confusion between what is and what ought to be. The common law forms a specially characteristic part of those manifestations of law which embody the pernicious creed that "everything is as it should be,"[532] and that the question of what ought to be is superfluous.

That the problems of what law ought to be are already solved, would be, in fact, "much better news than one could have imagined to be true"; only "devoted adorers . . . of the works of the powers that be and still more of those that have been"[533] can announce such an "indiscriminate panegyric" and stick to this attitude as revoltingly "tranquil copyists"[534] of what is and what has been in ancient times. Nowhere in the common law is there a clear discrimination between historical "reports" concerning ancient customs, on the one hand, and "argumentative treatises" concerning these rules on the other hand. On the contrary, there exists everywhere a complete confusion between "true *representations* of . . . matters of fact" and "just *conclusions* in matter of *opinion*."[535] " 'Ita lex scripta est' is . . . enough for . . . practical lawyers";[536] written and even unwritten ancient rules find their approval, simply because they existed in ancient times. And in a similar way are identified the "two very different questions . . . 'how are . . . Customs or Maxims to be known, and by whom is their validity determined?' "[537] questions again closely connected with the two main problems: what laws exist, and what are the reasons why these and not

[530] *Ibid.*, p. 194 f.   [531] *Ibid.*, p. 194.   [532] *Ibid.*, p. 77.
[533] *Ibid.*, p. 76 f.   [534] *Ibid.*, p. 174.
[535] *Ibid.*, p. 200 f, and see the whole section xvi under the title "Common Law: Reports and Treatises."
[536] *Ibid.*, p. 131.   [537] *Ibid.*, p. 186.

other laws should exist. That all these different issues are so frequently confounded truly mirrors the general error committed in the usage of ancient common law. This error consists in approving ancient rules without sufficient ethical examination, in identifying antiquity with morality.

Moreover, according to Bentham, the "hydrophobia of innovation" from which the average lawyer suffers, leads these lawyers even one step further: not only to the dangerous identification of what is with what ought to be, but even to the invention of so-called facts which are no facts. "These defenders à outrance of the Laws that are (because they are) . . . suppose" even "a fact . . . to exist . . . when they speak of" this fact "as being necessary for any purpose (for instance to justify a law) . . . although . . . the fact . . . does not . . . exist"; they "need not a medium less efficacious than one by which any one thing may be proved right as well as any other."[538] Thus Bentham, from all sides, reaches the same conclusion that none of the leading traditional theories of ethics and jurisprudence can solve the censorial problems of morals: neither the metaphysical law of nature, because it only duplicates existing concrete laws, nor the divine law, because this also is existing law without sufficient ethical justification and clearness, nor the common law which is, at best, "the Shadow"[539] of the municipal law, nor this municipal law itself, because it, too, speaks traditionally of existing laws and not of the justification of their validity.

Bentham's Ethical Empiricism

Neither the natural law, with its notion of a universal reason, nor the divine law, with its notion of revelation, nor the common law, with its notion of antiquity, nor the empirical municipal law can offer a satisfactory answer to the questions of critical ethics. Only an entirely different notion, according to Bentham, can show the way out of these difficulties: this is the notion of utility. "My notion of man is, that, successfully or unsuccessfully, he aims at happiness, and so will continue to aim as long as he continues to be man, in everything he

[538] *Ibid.*, pp. 195, 67.
[539] *Ibid.*, p. 125. Compare *ibid.*, p. 99: "The Law in general" and the law of nature are "Law in nubibus; . . . with the Law of Revelation" we have "nothing to do"; the common law is "no Law," ancient lawyers "saw their way through it, but dimly," yet if "our author speaks the word . . . all is darkness" (pp. 104, 174); and even with the municipal law Blackstone, like the majority of moralists, knows "not what to make of it" (p. 99).

does."[540] Therefore, the principle of utility, based on this empirical "notion of man," is for Bentham the only right principle of ethics and legislation as well as of the psychology of moral conduct.

"The end" of any moral and juristic law is, in Bentham's view, nothing more than "the suppression of the supposed mischief that gave occasion to it, when it is a mischief; or the procurement or advancement of the benefit, when it is a benefit."[541] As we have seen, all attempts at establishing reasonableness as the criterion of morality must be vain; but utility as the end of moral laws is a "much more explicit term."[542] For here we do not move about in the "craggy region of unintelligibles," but "get footing in the champaign territory"[543] of the empirical world. Everyone knows sufficiently by his own experience what happiness and utility are.

Whenever the "reason and spirit of laws" are invoked, Bentham says, actually only their utility can be meant; or, as he formulates this frequently throughout his work, "reasonable" laws are "such as a man would *like*."[544] "Repugnant to natural justice" means "repugnant to utility."[545] "The most prompt . . . translation of the phrase 'contrary to reason' is 'contrary to what I like'; I will speak plainly, and confess that with me to be most evidently contrary to reason is to be most evidently contrary to my reason, i.e. to what I like; perhaps I might go farther and add, apprehending it at the same time to be contrary to what would be liked by others, being in a situation to be apprized of the circumstances that are in the case."[546] Had Blackstone "instead of reason said utility, he would have said something. He would have referred us for a foundation for our judgment, to something distinct from that judgment itself. . . . How have stood the stocks of Pain and Pleasure upon such a disposition of things as the determination in question is calculated to bring on? This is the question, stated indeed in the most general and comprehensive terms, which a judge ought to put to him upon the occasion of every fresh case. . . . Let it suffice just to hint that the answer ought to be the summing up the several pains and pleasures that are certain or probable to happen upon each side of the alternative that is proposed."[547] The utility of a moral law, therefore, is not dependent on its reasonableness; its reasonableness is dependent on its utility.

"What is not reason is not law. This latter proposition is easily made

[540] *Ibid.*, p. 84.   [541] *Ibid.*, p. 107.   [542] *Ibid.*, p. 107.
[543] *Ibid.*, p. 124.   [544] *Ibid.*, p. 227.   [545] *Ibid.*, p. 196 f.
[546] *Ibid.*, p. 190.   [547] *Ibid.*, p. 192.

good when one knows the key of the conundrum. The trick is, when you are satisfied the thing is not Law"—when a law is of no utility—"say it is not reason."[548] In truth the term *utility* is the only essential one; the term *reason* serves merely to conceal the issue.

If the term "reason" or "reasons" of a law or "right law" are to be of any use in this connection, it can be only secondarily, in subordination to utility. "The only reason that could belong" to a law is its "utility, derived from expectation"; "by a fundamental principle of utility recognized by all Laws, no man is to have his hands bound or to be compelled to do a thing without some reason can be given for it."[549] "Instead of the unintelligible words, unintelligible as he (Blackstone) uses them, right and wrong, just and unjust," we are to "put the words beneficial and mischievous which are intelligible, and bear a meaning nearest to what the first mentioned set of words appear to point to"; and "by a beneficial sort of an action I mean a sort of action that is more apt to produce pleasure than it is pain: by a mischievous, more apt to produce pain than it is pleasure"[550] or "the expectation"[551] of pleasure. "Motives are the idea of pain or pleasure"; and whether the motive "acts upon being called will at one time and conscience at another . . . , it is still but pain or pleasure."[552] Acts are condemned by conscience, acts are contradictory to moral reason, "acts . . . are wrong: that is" they "are mischievous."[553] If, in the judgment on a moral question, "equal opposite reasons leave the scale in *equilibrio*," the moral theorist has "to resort to the dictates of original utility for arguments to turn it."[554] Only general utility can provide us with an adequate moral criterion in cases of moral conflict.

Even concerning the moral right to rebel against bad laws, there is no other criterion than utility, the "prospect of success."[555] "Many are the Laws I could conceive, against any of which I should think it right to rebel as soon as I could get enough to join with me to give me a prospect of success. . . . I would rebel, in short, whenever the probable mischiefs of rebellion seemed less to me than the probable mischiefs of submission. This is the only rule I can think of for submission and resistance. Does it fail of being explicit? I know of none that's more so. At the worst there is nothing in it to favour the pretensions of fanaticism either political or religious. It places a question difficult to solve

---

[548] *Ibid.*, p. 194.   [549] *Ibid.*, p. 222.   [550] *Ibid.*, p. 83 f.
[551] Compare *ibid.*, pp. 238, 233 f.
[552] *Ibid.*, p. 96.   [553] *Ibid.*, p. 179.   [554] *Ibid.*, p. 191.
[555] *Ibid.*, pp. 72, 72 f; cf. *A Fragment on Government*, chap. IV, §21 ff.

133

in its natural light of difficulty, without deluding men with a false solution."[555] "I would then leave our Author to pour forth his lamentations at his leisure; in peace might he adore the exploded divinity of the institution, and stigmatize with irreligion those who should cease paying . . . Tithes . . . after the Laws shall have ceased demanding them, as he has done those who omitted to begin: fit employment for a pious and enlightened jurist—passionate follower after any standard of right and wrong that will set him free from that odious and profane one of the public good."[556] The ideal of the public good, the greatest happiness principle alone, provides an applicable measure for deciding on the morality or immorality of a revolution. Bentham frankly admits that special difficulties are here involved; but he is confident that other criteria are far less adapted to their solution, because these other criteria are far more lacking in precision.

The formula of the greatest happiness of the greatest number is nowhere explicitly mentioned in the *Comment on the Commentaries*, but it is implied in the phrase "the public good" or the "happiness of the Society"; and everywhere, after all criticism of older theories, this remains the last positive constructive aim: to replace the complicated, inconsistent and unsatisfactory argumentation of the law of nature, the law of God and the common law, by a new, thoroughgoing empirical theory of morals based exclusively on the principle of utility, of the happiness of society. "To provide according to the best . . . for the happiness of the Society," this is "the course . . . that will cost . . . infinitely less painstaking and deliberation" than to consult "at all events" the "non-entities"[557] of superior laws "in nubibus."[558] The title of this work of Bentham's youth, it is true, shows that he intended in it to give no more than a criticism of Blackstone. I hope the long list of my quotations has shown how many hints of his new constructive ideas he has already given in this rather unknown early work.

INDUCTION AND DEDUCTION IN BENTHAM'S EMPIRICAL ETHICS

The metaphysical law of nature, the theological law of God and the historical common law are, in Bentham's opinion, built up on "unintelligible" or ambiguous principles. He himself seeks to base his whole doctrine on strictly empirical grounds by means of his principle of utility; and perhaps nowhere in his writings has he more clearly emphasized the importance he attributes to a consistently empirical

[556] Bentham, *A Comment on the Commentaries*, ed. by Everett, 1928, p. 136 f.
[557] *Ibid.*, p. 78.   [558] *Ibid.*, p. 99.

method than in his *Comment on the Commentaries*. Empirical observation and induction which proceeds from particular observation to general rules—this he thinks to be the principal form of inquiry in all concrete questions of morals.

"The question concerning the utility of a measure of government, of an article of conduct in the subject . . . depends upon experience, and is to be collected by observation"[559] and induction. "The only form of reasoning by which instruction is to be acquired, by which Bacon, for example, and Locke and Newton learnt what they have taught us, is that which proceeds from 'particulars to generals.' Induction is that form."[560] In strict contrast to this, true to the whole trend of his thought, Blackstone had supposed that deduction and syllogisms are the only proper forms of reasoning. Bentham, therefore, holds him up to ridicule, because obviously "the good old verse our author used to con over to his tutor 'Syllogizari non est ex particulari' was . . . still jingling in his ears"; yet "even his own Saunderson might have informed him that there is such a form of reasoning as induction: that the nature of it is to argue from particulars to generals, and that notwithstanding this, it is a 'true' one"; as a matter of fact "how much is to be learned by *induction* and how little by any other 'form of reasoning.'"[561] This last, more moderate and cautious, recommendation given the principle of induction is, I think, truly original and of high value in the province of morals.

For it should be remembered that Newton, one of the examples cited by Bentham, lays as much weight on the method of induction as on that of deduction. He, like Bentham, repudiated any hypotheses which depend on entities entirely separate from the world of empirical, observable phenomena. But Newton never rejected deduction altogether. In Bacon, on the other hand, we see the dangers which follow from uncritical observation, precipitate induction, and the neglect of deduction.

The out and out disdain of all deduction proclaimed in one of Bentham's sentences certainly represents a program of questionable value. Moreover, such a program would by no means be consonant with the well-elaborated scheme of combined deduction and induction which has been developed in Newton's and Galileo's classical physics; and it is this elaborate scheme of scientific method which Bentham wished to make fruitful for ethics.

Understood with the circumspection implied in his appeal to Newton, Bentham's methodological remarks seem to me of fundamental

[559] *Ibid.*, p. 52.   [560] *Ibid.*, p. 105.   [561] *Ibid.*, p. 106.

value, particularly because they put aside the "syllogizari" from simple generic names and because they insist on verification by induction.

It should not be overlooked that, in the method of consistent hedonism, induction by itself does not constitute the whole process. The moral validity of the utility principle cannot be justified by induction. The utility principle serves only as the basis for deduction in ethics. But the salient point is that all the deductive inferences drawn from this fundamental axiom have to be verified by matters of fact concerning pain and pleasure.

If the hypothesis is correct that the maximization of felicity is the only fundamental principle of ethics, then it is, of course, not sufficient to say that a certain act (e.g. telling the truth) is ethical because this act is generally thought to be ethical, or is supposed to produce the greatest possible happiness. One must verify by observation whether this act actually serves the greatest interest of the greatest number in a concrete case, after all the relevant elements of this complicated calculation have been taken into consideration.

Bentham's contention is that, if observation of concrete feelings and induction have been taken into account in this way, the very meaning and aim of ethics can be understood far more adequately than by the uncritical belief in any existing concrete moral laws. He rightly demands a recurrence to concrete cases, empirical examples in morals, and hates "pitching and tossing among generals" where "we can feel no ground."[562] "I rejoice always when I get hold of an example"; for only "by examples we are enabled to feel our way," when the general "rules . . . delude our grasp."[563] In any case the inferences drawn from general moral rules have to be verified by observation, by given and "collected . . . matters of fact."[564] This emphasis laid upon experience and the concrete case, upon matters of fact, remains characteristic of Bentham's whole system of ethics; and it by no means contradicts his criticism of existing normative laws.

Bentham insists on proofs of the validity of concrete ethical norms; and these proofs have to refer to matters of fact. Yet the decisive point is that these matters of fact must be, not existing conventional norms or values, but psychological facts of pain and pleasure which are commonly considered to be neutral as regards ethical values, and independent of them.

[562] *Ibid.*, p. 236.

[563] *Ibid.*, p. 196; cf. to a certain extent p. 215: only "examples may afford light when the text" of laws and rules "is darkness."

[564] *Ibid.*, p. 52.

In this way, the two different parts of Bentham's method hang together: his critical demand for the legitimation of existing moral laws on the one hand and, on the other hand, his insistence on induction of ethical laws by means of concrete psychological observation. These two different sides of Bentham's inquiries are brought together by his demonstration that existing moral norms cannot be justified by other concrete existing norms or by themselves; they need reference to observable psychological facts concerning pleasure and pain.

Bentham and Contemporary Positivism

It is in this sense that censorial ethics forbids the uncritical acknowledgment of existing norms of morality or moral reason; but it allows the reference to mankind's general "aiming at happiness," at pleasure, at utility. If we want to judge the morality or the moral reasonableness of a human action, we have to refer "for a foundation for our judgment, to something distinct from that judgment itself"; we have to refer "to calculation founded upon matter of fact: future contingent utility founded upon past utility experienced. How have stood the stocks of Pain and Pleasure upon such a disposition of things as the determination in question is calculated to bring on?"[565] By these and similar declarations, Bentham's theory of morals comes comparatively near to contemporary "logical positivism."[566] On the negative side, logical positivism also rejects concrete normative or value statements

[565] Bentham, *A Comment on the Commentaries*, ed. by Everett, 1928, p. 192.

[566] See R. Carnap, *Philosophy and Logical Syntax*, 1935, p. 25: Propositions on moral questions are "deducible only from psychological propositions about . . . emotional reactions. . . . These propositions are indeed verifiable and not without sense. They belong to psychology, not to philosophy; to psychological ethics . . . not to philosophical or normative ethics. The propositions of normative ethics, whether they have the form of rules or the form of value statements, have no theoretical sense, are not scientific propositions." Compare A. J. Ayer, *Language, Truth and Logic*, 1938, pp. 152 f, 161: Moral judgments as "a sub-class of psychological or sociological judgments . . . are very attractive to us." But "moral judgments" as "pure expressions of feeling . . . do not come under the category of truth and falsehood." Compare Bertrand Russell, *Religion and Science*, 1935, p. 250: "Since no way can be even imagined for deciding a difference as to values, the conclusion is forced upon us that the difference is one of tastes, not one as to any objective truth"; and see *ibid.*, pp. 248 f, 255. In his *Human Knowledge*, 1948, p. 398 f, Russell made his few remarks on "Probability and Conduct" sound somewhat less aggressive but, as to the matter itself, no concessions are made. If one isolated one of his observations, it would be even more radical than all he said in his earlier works. On p. 398 of his *Human Knowledge* he goes so far as to say: "So far as the relation to probability is concerned it makes very little difference what end is chosen" [in ethics].

because they are not justifiable by themselves; and on the positive side, this contemporary positivism, too, demands the verification of "all assertive propositions"[567] in morals by connecting them with psychological facts. It is, therefore, comprehensible why Mr. Ayer, for instance, finds utilitarianism "attractive,"[568] because he, like the utilitarian, rejects the "mysterious intellectual intuition"[569] of ethics of values; he insists upon basing all scientific statement on observation of facts.

Despite this declaration of sympathy there is, however, one reason left why Mr. Ayer rejects utilitarianism: it is because he thinks the utilitarians give no "analyses of our existing ethical notions"; "our contention is simply that, in our language, sentences which contain normative ethical symbols are not equivalent to sentences which express psychological propositions, or indeed empirical propositions of any kind."[570] But if this is the only objection that can be raised against utilitarianism, then it seems to me that modern physics is open to precisely the same criticism as consistent hedonism.

Without entering into the details of this very intricate problem, I think it has to be said that not only ethical laws but also "laws" of physics are at least "in our language" nearer to normative symbols than to merely psychological propositions or observations. For the laws of nature themselves are not simply generalizations of "given facts"; they, too, are normative statements about "true" reality. True reality has to be distinguished from appearance by hypotheses which are based on the assumption that the truth value of our observations of nature can be ascertained only in so far as these observations are understood by those hypotheses and the hypotheses verified by the observations.

Take the statements "the physicist should not regard a stick as broken whose lower part is dipped into water" or "this stick is, in truth, not broken" or the statement "we should never believe that the sun is really rising or setting." These statements which represent, I think, quite legitimate expressions of laws of applied physics are certainly as near to normative symbols as the ethical proposition "this action is good in so far as it does not violate the highest hypothetical principle of moral judgments, the maximization of happiness."

Nature as the object of scientific analysis has successfully been deprived of its "mysterious" character by logical positivists. Nature as

[567] See R. Carnap, *Philosophy and Logical Syntax*, 1935, p. 25.
[568] A. J. Ayer, *Language, Truth and Logic*, 1938, p. 152 f.
[569] *Ibid.*, p. 156.　　　　　　　　　　[570] *Ibid.*, p. 155.

object of the physicist is rightly conceived by them as nothing but a certain context of observations on nature. Why should it be precisely the logical positivist who insists that a recast of the concept of moral goodness quite similar to that of "true" nature should not be permitted? Such a recast of normative ethical statements seems to be prepared by Ray Lepley's[571] thesis of the "translatability" of ethical propositions into descriptive ones, although Lepley has followed up these suggestions hardly far enough. On this point, obviously a strict parallel can be drawn between physics and ethics.

In physics, too, not all observations can be regarded as true but only those which do justice to hypotheses creating coherence between all the observations concerned; and in ethics not all feelings of happiness or all feelings of suffering can be regarded as moral but only those which do justice to the hypothesis of the maximization of happiness— a hypothesis harmonizing pleasure and pain.

Both the moralist and the physicist are, of course, powerless if confronted with "scientists" who prefer an incoherent interpretation of nature or capricious distribution of happiness as their fundamental hypotheses. But after a confession of this kind of powerlessness, it seems to me, the physicist and the moralist find themselves in an equally strong position; and the logical positivist should be invited to use the same revolutionary method of interpreting reality in ethics that he uses in his theory of physics.

Logical positivism allows us to replace our existing primitive notions concerning nature by new scientific concepts; therefore, I cannot see any reason why the same "concession" should or could be denied to utilitarian ethics. Surely, Mr. Ayer is a greater radical than Bentham. But unfortunately, this radicalism carried through consistently would lead not only to the nullification of ethics but also to that of physics; and this, I think, makes it manifest that Mr. Ayer's radicalism in ethics is excessive.

Professor Carnap does not go so far as Mr. Ayer; he does not nullify ethics altogether. He denies that normative or philosophic ethics makes any sense; but he admits that it is perfectly legitimate to build up a so-called "psychological ethics"[572] which consists of nothing but psychological statements concerning emotions. Yet, I think, this again is

[571] R. Lepley, *Verifiability of Value*, 1944, e.g. pp. viii, 137 ff, 225. Compare similar tendencies in Stephen C. Pepper's essay "Values and Value Judgments," *The Journal of Philosophy*, July 7, 1949, pp. 429-434.
[572] See R. Carnap, *Philosophy and Logical Syntax*, 1935, p. 25.

no way out of the difficulties here involved. For certainly, it is no more permissible to speak of *psychological ethics* than of *psychological physics*. It is not admissible to identify ethical statements with mere psychological statements, any more than to identify statements of the physicist with psychological statements concerning perceptions. What is relevant here is that laws of physics need to be verified ultimately by reference to data of the senses in the same way that laws of ethics need to be verified by reference to feelings.

Both Carnap and Ayer suppose that the only possible alternatives in ethics are dogmatic normative ethics, on the one hand, and "psychological ethics" or non-ethical psychology on the other. But they overlook the fact that there is still consistent hedonism, grounding ethical laws on feelings and on the hypothesis of the utility principle,[573] as in physics laws are grounded on hypotheses and sense data. That is to say, both normative and "psychological" ethics are more truly opposed to logical positivism than is utilitarianism. Indeed, positivistic methods consistently applied to ethical questions do not lead to "psychological ethics" or to the nullification of ethics but to a kind of Benthamism.

In jurisprudence, Bentham found an overwhelming agreement with his criticism of the existing law, as well as with his constructive reform of the law of England based on the consistent application of the utility principle. But his parallel efforts in the field of ethics are partly disapproved even by his own school. Yet at least one point is generally forgotten in this connection. Attention is paid only to the fact that Bentham referred from judgments on moral values to judgments on observable emotions, pleasure and pain; and it is wrongly assumed that Bentham simply identified or confused the sphere of moral valuation with the sphere of experience of pain and happiness. The truth is that Bentham referred from the former to the latter *despite* his clear distinction between moral laws and psychological feelings. For he made it clear why the validity of moral values cannot be legitimated by other or by the same valuations, i.e. intrinsic values or alleged moral principles; but the validity of ethical valuations can be certified by a certain type of reference to such psychological data as pleasure and pain the character of which is undeniably self-evident.

Logical positivists and other critics of Bentham speak only of an alternative between uncritical normative ethics and ethical or non-ethical psychology. But Bentham shows how to base ethics critically on

[573] See Bentham MS, *hitherto unpublished*, University College, London, Portfolio 27, Folder 2, sheet 15, written about 1776.

psychological observations. He leads from the sphere of normative and implied normative judgments to another sphere for legitimating them.

BENTHAM AND "EMOTIVE ETHICS"

The method of "emotive ethics" suggested by Professor Charles L. Stevenson, recently defended by A. I. Melden[574] and, on occasion, accepted in part by G. E. Moore[575] has much in common with logical positivism. Stevenson emphasized in his *Ethics and Language* that he "finds much more to defend in the analyses of Carnap, Ayer, and the others, than [he] finds to attack."[576] He fully maintains the validity of the critical standard by which logical positivism unmasks traditional ethics as scientifically meaningless; but he tries to justify ethical statements as meaningful in a sense rather different from that explored by Ayer and Carnap.

To this end he stresses at the outset what he calls the *"dual* nature"[577] of any ethical agreement or disagreement. Ethical opinion, as it presents itself in common expression, reveals partly an attitude and partly a belief.[578] Agreement in belief concerns theoretical states of affairs and can, therefore, be reached by rational discussion; agreement in attitude, however, concerns "purposes, aspirations, wants, preferences, desires"—in brief, "interests"[579]—and is, therefore, quite independent of agreement in belief.

As far as agreement in belief goes, we are dealing with cognitive meaning exclusively or, as Stevenson often prefers to put it, "descriptive" meaning.[580] As far as agreement in attitude goes, we are confronted essentially with emotive meaning, i.e. "a meaning in which the response (from the hearer's point of view) or the stimulus (from the speaker's point of view) is a range of emotions."[581] Agreement in belief "is concerned with how matters are truthfully to be described and explained"; agreement in attitude is "concerned with how they are

---

[574] See A. I. Melden, "On the Method of Ethics," in *The Journal of Philosophy*, vol. XLV, No. 7, 1948, pp. 169 ff.

[575] See *The Philosophy of G. E. Moore*, ed. by P. A. Schilpp, (*The Library of Living Philosophers*), vol. IV, 1942, G. E. Moore's "Reply to My Critics," p. 554 f; and see my comment on Moore's statements in my essay "Cassirer and the Chaos in Modern Ethics," in *The Philosophy of Ernst Cassirer*, ed. P. A. Schilpp, 1949, especially pp. 592 f.

[576] C. L. Stevenson, *Ethics and Language*, 1944, p. 267.

[577] *Ibid.*, p. 19. [578] *Ibid.*, e.g. p. 41.

[579] *Ibid.*, pp. 3, 268. [580] See *ibid.*, e.g. pp. 4, 21, 36, 70 ff.

[581] *Ibid.*, p. 59.

to be favored . . . , and hence with how they are to be shaped by human efforts."[582]

"The model for 'this is good' consists of the conjunction of (a) 'I approve of this,' and (b) 'Do so as well.' . . . Sentence (a) . . . makes an assertion about the speaker's state of mind, and like any psychological statement, is open to empirical confirmation or disconfirmation, whether introspective or behavioristic."[583] Sentence (b), however, being "an imperative . . . is not open to proof at all. . . . If we told a person to close the door and received the reply, 'Prove it!' should we not, to speak mildly, grow somewhat impatient? . . . The very request for a proof" of a command is "nonsensical."[583]

Nevertheless, unlike Professor Carnap, Professor Stevenson does not restrict the proof of "this is good" to the "distressingly meager conclusion" of ethical skepticism that "if a man says 'X is good,' and if he can prove that he really approves of X, then he has all the proof that can be demanded of him."[583] Stevenson agrees with logical positivism that something similar to an imperative,[584] to "exhortatory aims,"[585] to a "quasi imperative function"[586] is implied in every ethical judgment; and he, too, rightly insists that imperatives cannot be proved or verified like scientific statements. But despite all these concessions to logical positivism, Stevenson stresses the fact that imperatives and attitudes can be "supported" by some "substitute for a proof," by some "reasoned argument."[587]

Reasoned arguments containing "descriptive meaning" can decisively support or may decisively alter attitudes and imperatives which have merely emotive meaning. My command "Shut the door!" may be supported by the observation that "it is too drafty,"[587] or if reasons can be given why the draft will soon disappear, I may no longer think that it is good to shut the door. I may disapprove of closing the door and alter my command by now ordering the opposite: "Leave the door open!" After the beliefs which supported the issue of the imperative have changed, my attitude and my order may change correspondingly. "The central problem" of ethical methodology is, therefore, according to Stevenson, "one of showing in detail how beliefs and attitudes are related";[588] and he deals with this problem ingeniously and illuminatingly.

He analyzes long, though "incomplete,"[589] lists of illustrations in which he shows how ethical judgments are supported or attacked by

[582] *Ibid.*, p. 4.   [583] *Ibid.*, p. 26.   [584] *Ibid.*, pp. 33, 36.
[585] *Ibid.*, p. 231.   [586] *Ibid.*, pp. 257, 256, 258.   [587] *Ibid.*, p. 27.
[588] *Ibid.*, pp. 11, 174.   [589] *Ibid.*, p. 129.

beliefs related to them logically or—what is far more often the case—psychologically,[590] how moral attitudes are influenced by beliefs directly attacking them or only counterattacking them, as in a procedure characterized by the saying "People in glass houses should not throw stones."[591] Further, there are illustrations of the influence of beliefs on interpersonal as well as on personal moral conflicts.[592] And beliefs—not only in the shape of reasoning but also in that of "nonrational . . . persuasion," in the shape of "persuasive" definitions[593] and "persuasive quasi-definitions"[594]—are taken into account; and, finally, "detached definitions"[595] are analyzed which directly concern only knowledge but indirectly have important emotive consequences as far as our *interest* in knowledge has a fundamental emotive impact on our moral attitudes.

Bentham's consistent hedonism has certainly more in common with this type of emotive ethics than with the dogmatic "old school" systems[596] under which Professor Stevenson, unfortunately, seems to classify every kind of utilitarianism. As the present work tries to explain in detail, Bentham, too, primarily wants to "free ethics from the confusions that are most prevalent and central,"[597] from the belief "that a moralist must be irrational or dogmatic."[598] Bentham, too, especially "stresses the distinction between verifiable and nonverifiable statements."[599] He, too, rejects the assumption of intrinsic values as subject matters of an absolute moral knowledge,[600] the belief in "nonnatural" moral qualities or in self-evident principles of moral rightness as a "peculiar and occult subject matter of ethics."[601] Bentham, too, like every consistent empiricist, refuses to base his theory of morals on any "higher things";[602] in presenting his utility principle as a mere "hypothesis";[603] he, too, maintains that any "ultimate principles" and[604] "ultimate proof" in the sense of absolute knowledge are "beyond possibility"[605] in morals. Bentham, too, fought against "the unfounded fears" of the "chaotic implications! . . . of science . . . which make a retreat to the past seem necessary";[606] and in the parallel which Stevenson draws between some "aspect of ethical analysis and theories of pun-

---

[590] *Ibid.*, pp. 115 ff.   [591] *Ibid.*, pp. 127 ff.   [592] See *ibid.*, pp. 130 ff.
[593] See *ibid.*, pp. 139 ff.   [594] See *ibid.*, pp. 278 ff.   [595] See *ibid.*, pp. 283 ff.
[596] *Ibid.*, pp. 247, 265.   [597] See *ibid.*, p. 221.   [598] See *ibid.*, p. 268.
[599] See *ibid.*, p. 294.   [600] See *ibid.*, pp. 174 ff.
[601] See *ibid.*, pp. 108 f, 97.   [602] *Ibid.*, p. 246.
[603] See the present work, p. 140, note 573.
[604] C. L. Stevenson, *Ethics and Language*, 1944, p. 336.
[605] *Ibid.*, p. 242.   [606] *Ibid.*, p. 320 f.

ishment,"[607] he reveals a special kinship to Bentham's theory of morals.

Nevertheless, for quite a number of reasons, Bentham's consistent hedonism seems to me superior to contemporary emotive ethics. Even if one fully subscribes to Professor Stevenson's maxim that a critical study in ethical methodology should cut through the "pretentiousness" of traditional theories and "enable ethics to accomplish more by attempting less,"[608] his work gives us, in my opinion, too little and unduly so.

All his many subtle and searching investigations can lead him only to the frequently repeated conclusion that "if any ethical dispute *is* rooted in disagreement in belief, it may be settled by reasoning and inquiry to whatever extent the beliefs may be so settled. But if any ethical dispute is *not* rooted in disagreement in belief, then no *reasoned* solution of any sort is possible."[609] Rational methods can resolve ethical disagreement if, and only if, it is rooted in disagreement in belief.[610] Moreover, to this we must add: even ethical agreement in attitude reached by agreement in belief does not give the slightest guarantee of agreement as to the "qualities that moralists have upheld as the virtues," namely "altruism, benevolence, temperance, courage, sympathy"[611] and all the many other virtues of the Judaeo-Christian world of democratic values.

Ethical agreement in attitude rooted in agreement in belief may also mean, and has meant for millions of men, ethical preference for cruelty, ruthlessness, fanaticism and hatred rooted in the "factual conclusion"[612] that sympathy with the weak often endangers the physical and mental health of the race, while fanaticism frequently strengthens nations and individuals; or ethical agreement in attitude may mean preference for monkish asceticism or asocial self-concern or misanthropy rooted in the belief that cultural creators are generally great egotists.

If this is properly taken into account, as it must be in a critical empiristic ethics, we shall, unfortunately, be unable to share even the moderate optimism of Professor Stevenson as to the beneficent results of his methodological views. There will be no hope left that, after the adoption of his ethical methodology, "enlightened norms," such as those of altruism, sympathy with one's fellowmen and benevolence, do not "lie permanently beyond human attainment";[612] and there will be no reason left for assuming that the "slow results" of emotive ethics "will be cumulative, contributing to an ethics that will pro-

[607] *Ibid.*, p. 307.   [608] *Ibid.*, p. 319.   [609] *Ibid.*, p. 138.
[610] *Ibid.*, p. 237.   [611] *Ibid.*, p. 322.   [612] *Ibid.*, p. 332.

gressively come to grips with the issues of practical life"[612] in the sense of a morality of benevolence and not a morality of extreme selfishness. Agreement in attitude rooted in agreement in belief can be obtained by bands of gangsters as well as by devout adherents of Gandhi. I.e. contrary to Professor Stevenson's hopes, under *no* circumstances can "ethical arguments . . . be resolved by scientific means"[613] within emotive ethics. Wherever they *seem* to be resolved by scientific means, some agreement in attitude must be *presupposed* besides any agreement in belief by scientific "persuasion." And where are the criteria for settling the main ethical issue, namely the question as to which "persuasion" by scientific means should be "accepted" and which "avoided"?[614]

G. E. Moore seems to have indicated the impossibility of answering this principal ethical question in his latest reference to the emotive meaning of ethical judgments;[615] and C. I. Lewis has gone further in stating that emotive ethics means, in fact, ethical skepticism.[616] The true extent of Stevenson's skepticism may, however, be veiled to many avowed equalitarians, for Stevenson obviously shares the widespread erroneous belief of democrats that "the norms which are generally accepted and embodied in the mores of any given society, are undoubtedly more numerous than the controversial ones."[617]

It is evidently for this reason only that he could dismiss as irrelevant the question of "the possibility of rival moral codes, each equally well supported by reasons" and could leave the settlement of this question exclusively to the extravagant ambitions of believers in "an absolutely definite method for normative ethics."[618] In fact, unfortunately and I think illegitimately, he refers in his illustrations, practically without exception, to disagreement of attitudes *within* the field of democratic ethics. He refers to fascism[619] only to refute a sort of dogmatic utilitarianism *not* advocated by Bentham and he does not take into account Bentham's warnings against any dogmatic use of eulogistic and dyslogistic predicates of motives.[620] Only in this way do his analyses gain a far less skeptical appearance than his theses warrant.

[613] *Ibid.*, p. 268.   [614] *Ibid.*, p. 250.

[615] See *The Library of Living Philosophers*, ed. by P. A. Schilpp, vol. IV, p. 554 f, and see my essay, "Cassirer and the Chaos in modern Ethics," *ibid.*, vol. VI, 1949, pp. 592 ff.

[616] C. I. Lewis, *An Analysis of Knowledge and Valuation*, 1946, pp. viii, 365 f; p. 413: emotive ethics "destroys the basis for any valid imperative."

[617] C. L. Stevenson, *Ethics and Language*, 1944, p. 5.

[618] *Ibid.*, p. 31.   [619] *Ibid.*, p. 218.

[620] *Ibid.*, p. 121. Stevenson seems to subscribe to the opinion (confuted in detail

The difference between the ethics of logical positivism and that of emotive ethics is only this: Bertrand Russell and A. J. Ayer state that ethical judgments possess neither truth nor falsehood;[621] and emotive ethics states that "an ethical judgment *can* be true or false" but it should be pointed out in any case that "its descriptive truth may be insufficient to support its emotive repercussions."[622] If, then, the term "ethical skepticism" is best reserved for the characterization of Ayer's and Russell's ethical views, the term "semi-skepticism" may not be too harsh for the characterization of emotive ethics.

Bentham's consistent hedonism offers, in my opinion, several advantages in comparison with emotive ethics at no sacrifice of the critical empiristic approach which these two theories have in common. If—to speak in Professor Stevenson's language—one would try to point out "persuasively" these advantages "by altering attention," rather than by any "emotive pressure,"[623] one could, perhaps, briefly do so as follows: Professor Stevenson *underrates* the value of general hypotheses in ethics and, apparently, even in science when he states that hypotheses ordinarily designate "only those empirical statements which lack a high degree of confirmation."[624] He distrusts "all embracing aims," and "broad principles"[625]—at least at the beginning of an inquiry—and is especially diffident of settling issues concerning "broader ranges of attitudes."[626] On the other hand, he has too much trust in the efficiency of a slow ascent from specific judgments[627] to broader conclusions, from "modest" beginnings, from "focal aims . . . valued partly as an end"[628] to broader and general ends.

But this distrust in general hypotheses does not seem to me justified either in science or in ethics. This distrust would make us prefer Tycho

---

especially in Bentham's *A Table of the Springs of Action*) that even the uncritical eulogistic and dyslogistic appellations of "motives are clues to much else."

[621] See Bertrand Russell, *Religion and Science*, 1935, e.g. p. 249: "If two men differ about values, there is not a disagreement as to any kind of truth but a difference of taste"; p. 255: "Questions of value . . . lie outside the realm of truth and falsehood"; and see A. J. Ayer, *Language, Truth and Logic*, 1938, pp. 152 f, 161. In his essay "The Principle of Utility" in *Jeremy Bentham and the Law*, ed. by G. W. Keeton and G. Schwarzenberger, 1948, p. 254, Ayer seems to adopt the attitude of emotive ethics by stating: "The principle of utility is not a true, or even a false proposition; it is a recommendation." Its definitions "are not so much descriptive as persuasive."

[622] C. L. Stevenson, *Ethics and Language*, 1944, p. 267.

[623] *Ibid.*, p. 290.   [624] *Ibid.*, p. 291.   [625] *Ibid.*, p. 330.
[626] *Ibid.*, p. 290.   [627] See *ibid.*, pp. 331, 165.   [628] *Ibid.*, p. 329 f.

Brahe's astronomical theses to those of Copernicus and Kepler, Aristotle's observations on the free fall of bodies to Galileo's law, H. A. Lorentz's description of the Michelson experiment to Einstein's "general hypotheses" on time-measurements, certainly to the definite detriment of a consistent objective understanding of all the phenomena in question. Of course, nothing should be called a scientific hypothesis which cannot be confirmed in every respect. But if this is duly admitted, then, contrary to Stevenson's assumptions,[629] particular phenomena in science are better understood by means of a confirmed hypothesis; and agreement on focal aims in ethics does not methodologically precede a general hypothesis but it presupposes, at least, a transformation of the uncritical evaluation of the focal aim into a critical one by means of a fundamental hypothetical principle of morals comparable to the principle of verification in science.

Professor Stevenson tried hard to eliminate any general hypothesis of this kind and to impose the burden of moral decisions exclusively on concrete beliefs and attitudes.[630] Nevertheless, the presupposition of some such hypothesis appears even with him in the observation that the "practical problem is not to avoid all persuasion, but to decide which to avoid and which to accept,"[631] and for this decision obviously some presupposed criterion is needed.

As we shall see later, in his maturest thought Bentham presents his greatest happiness principle as a general "hypothesis" which does not dogmatically settle all concrete ethical issues but opens a critical discussion of them. Bentham explicitly invites a discussion even of what he calls the "wolf's Bible";[632] he does not, as Stevenson implies,[633] present the utility principle as an ethical law which dogmatically excludes the discussion of master-morality in favor of a one-sided "shepherd's Bible."[632] Bentham, further, does not "exalt some one factor as *the* end,"[634] namely, pleasure; but, like Stevenson,[635] he insists that all the many different pleasures and pleasant activities involved in an issue be taken into account. Can emotive ethics do better than Bentham?

I fail to see how it can. In emotive ethics, too, all the persuasion

[629] See *ibid.*, pp. 165, 331.

[630] Compare my discussion of similar contemporary theories in my essay "Cassirer and the Chaos in Modern Ethics," *The Library of Living Philosophers*, ed. by P. A. Schilpp, vol. v, 1949, pp. 575 ff.

[631] C. L. Stevenson, *Ethics and Language*, 1944, p. 250.

[632] See J. Bentham, *Defence of Economy against the Late Mr. Burke*, 1817, p. 28.

[633] See C. L. Stevenson, *Ethics and Language*, 1944, p. 218.

[634] *Ibid.*, p. 329.   [635] See *ibid.*, p. 190.

which is to be used for the conversion of Machiavellians and criminals can be elevated to an "acceptable," i.e. to a morally valuable, "persuasion" only if the interests and pleasures of all, even of the most wicked criminals, are fully respected—but respected *along* with the interests of all their opponents and, if necessary, negated in the face of the greater pleasures of these opponents. And the most rational and least capricious hypothesis requiring and allowing this kind of "verification" by pleasures and interests is the greatest happiness principle, provided that the meaning of the principle is given that epistemological refinement which Bentham (though not J. S. Mill)[636] wished to give it. Emotive ethics, however, it seems to me, manifests an unnecessary and injurious fear of hypotheses by identifying them with dogmatic statements of a pretended absolute validity.

Closely connected with these unwarranted fears and presuppositions of emotive ethics is an overestimation of the validity of scientific theories, belief theories, and the negation of any possible validity of attitude theories in the strict sense of the term validity.[637] Even the most fundamental principle of science, the principle of the final verification of truth by sense data, is not valid in the strictest sense of the logical principle of identity. Older theories of nature held by great scientists such as Descartes and Leibniz insisted on including statements as "true" which cannot be verified by empirical observation; and no logical refutation of the fundamental principles of these theories is possible on this account. But this has rightly not prevented modern science from

---

[636] Just as the present book goes to press, Professor Everett W. Hall kindly calls my attention to his essay "The 'Proof' of Utility in Bentham and Mill," in *Ethics*, vol. LX, No. 1, October 1949, pp. 1-18; and I take his argument as welcome strengthening of my position. In a penetrating scrutiny of the main argument of J. S. Mill's *Utilitarianism*, Professor Hall shows in his essay why Mill's reflections cannot be held accountable for the gross blunders which G. E. Moore imputes to Mill.

On p. 14 of his essay, Hall gives the impression that he has exhaustively treated the "devices" of justification of the utility principle in Bentham while, in my opinion, the most important of these devices are to be found in the critical analyses of the relevance of motives and consequences of acts which fill the central parts of Bentham's *Introduction*. Unfortunately, Professor Hall did not take into account these extended analyses of Bentham. But Hall's principal lines of defense of utilitarianism against Moore's early ethical intuitionism is evidently similar to my own, although he illustrates his theses in a different way.

[637] *Ibid.*, chap. VII on "Validity," pp. 152 ff. In this respect, there is obviously partial, though no complete, agreement between my criticism of Stevenson and the views sketched by Professors Asher Moore and Vincent Tomas in *Bulletin of the Eastern Division of the American Philosophical Association* published for its Forty-sixth Annual Meeting, December 1949.

excluding the reference to anything which cannot ultimately be verified by data of the senses.

Immediately experienced attitudes, interests, satisfactions, pleasures and pains are no less fit for serving as elements of a coherent theory of morals than sense data are for a coherent theory of nature. Science is concerned with what upholds the limited validity of every experienced sense datum; and ethics is concerned with what upholds the limited validity of every experienced attitude or pleasure. Truth in science has, therefore, far *less* merely descriptive meaning, and validity in ethics has far *more* descriptive meaning than emotive ethics presupposes.

The lack of merely descriptive meaning in science is only kept out of sight by the "common-sense" opinion that our senses describe, i.e. copy nature "truly," while, in fact, science has always to "evaluate" the data of the senses until each datum has been assigned its proper place in a coherent and consistent "interpretation" of nature. The descriptive meaning of ethical judgments, however, has been lost sight of because it is not generally realized that by means of a fundamental hypothesis the "imperative" character of moral evaluations can be dropped and ethical judgments can be presented as merely descriptive statements as to what the most coherent and consistent safeguard of all interests in question would be.

A. I. Melden invoked the authority of Kant in favor of emotive ethics —an attempt which Stevenson wisely eschewed. For Melden is certainly mistaken in stating that "Kant never entertains the suggestion ... that the imperative form may be dispensed with"[638] in ethics. Kant now and then explicitly speaks of his categorical imperative in non-hortatory terms.[639]

The transformation of an ethical judgment into a descriptive statement implies no greater distortion or protection of its meaning than the transformation of a description of nature into a theory of nature. In science as well as in ethics the main emphasis lies on the effectuation

[638] A. I. Melden, "On the Method of Ethics" in *The Journal of Philosophy*, 1948, p. 172.

[639] See e.g. *Lose Blätter aus Kants Nachlass*, ed. by R. Reicke, 1899, Heft 1, p. 14: Der kategorische Imperativ "ist das Prinzip . . . der formalen Bedingung aller Glückseligkeit (parallel mit der Apperception)"; *Kritik der Praktischen Vernunft*, ed. by K. Vorländer, 1929, p. 34: Der kategorische Imperativ ist das "Selbstbewusstsein einer reinen praktischen Vernunft"; Kant, *Werke*, ed. by E. Cassirer, vol. vii, p. 184: "Der Probierstein einer Tugendpflicht" ist es: "wie, wenn nun ein jeder in jedem Fall seine Maxime zum allgemeinen Gesetz machte, würde eine solche wohl mit sich selbst zusammenstimmen können?"

149

of a coherent and consistent rational connection between all relevant given phenomena, i.e. data of the senses in science and interests in ethics. On this account there seems to me no reason why Professor Stevenson should insist on the correctness of the popular idea of a specific hortative, non-cognitive character of ethical judgments; and there seems to me no reason why—contrary to Bentham—he resists the idea of any transformation of ethical statements into descriptive judgments and why he, thus,[640] deprives the moral judgment of any possible validity, in the sense of empirically well grounded, though of course not "absolute," truth. The fact that Bentham's ethics, on account of the difficulties of the felicific calculus, cannot claim to be an exact science such as physics does not make it necessary to maintain a strict contradistinction between the methods of science and ethics any more than between those of physics and biology.[640]

BENTHAM'S "APRIORISM"

The consistent empiricism of Bentham has occasionally been styled "apriorism" by Macaulay,[641] by C. B. R. Kent[642] and by Graham Wallas.[643] But certainly, applied in this way, the term "apriorism" does not have a strictly philosophical meaning. Bentham makes use exclusively of a conditioned a priori, not of the "unwarranted generalisation" a priori for which Kent blames him.[642] He employs generalizations which are referred methodologically to facts a posteriori.

How relative, how dependent on facts Bentham's apriorism is, a single one of his "reflections a priori" may demonstrate. By a "consideration a priori" he understands, in his *Comment*, a consideration concerning relatively general but by no means universal facts; and under a consideration a posteriori, he understands a consideration concerning more particular facts.[644] Or we may infer the same from his polemics against

---

[640] Stevenson emphasizes this principal contradistinction between the methods of science and ethics in his *Ethics and Language*, 1944, e.g. pp. 173, 275 and perhaps even 248.

[641] See Macaulay, *The Miscellaneous Writings and Speeches*, 1889, p. 197 f, where Macaulay reproaches James Mill and Bentham, because they try to "deduce syllogistically from pretended principles" "being prior in order" and neglect "inductive . . . reasoning."

[642] C. B. R. Kent, *The English Radicals*, 1899, p. 233: Bentham and his followers "reasoned solely on the geometrical or *apriori* method."

[643] G. Wallas, *The Art of Thought*, 1927, p. 172: "Bentham's *apriori* deduction of social machinery."

[644] Bentham, *A Comment on the Commentaries*, ed. by Everett, 1928, p. 182.

ethical theses which speak of different "degrees . . . in validity."[645] Apriorism proper strictly distinguishes at least between two different degrees in validity of judgments, namely, between statements of absolutely universal validity, statements of "pure reason" independent of all experience on the one hand, and on the other hand, statements based on the empirical observation of a large number of facts. Bentham nowhere adopts principles of universal validity a priori, independent of all experience; and therefore it is comprehensible why for him this distinction between degrees of validity is entirely out of place. For him, as for contemporary empiricism, the validity of concrete ethical judgments has to be based on matters of fact and cannot be grounded on purely formal reason a priori.

Lastly, on another cardinal point, the *Comment* hints at the importance of facts in morals. Throughout his life, Bentham laid the utmost stress on the actual consequences of human acts, in contrast to the ethical "apriorist" Kant who placed all his emphasis on the pure and even unrealized intentions of the moral will. While for Kant "nothing can be called morally good, except the good will,"[646] i.e. good motives, Bentham characteristically says: "Will without power to back it is just nothing."[647] This sweeping remark, it is true, is to be found in Bentham's *Comment* only in connection with juristic topics, with regard to the will of legislators. All the same, there is no room for doubt that Bentham has implicitly extended the meaning of this statement to morals in general; he later did so explicitly. But perhaps nowhere is his thought on this point expressed with such striking brevity. Why he rejected all ethics of mere good will, why he built up a coherent "ethics of success," is explained at length, however, only in his later and more definite teaching.

Bentham made no attempt to publish his *Comment*. I believe, however, that this work of Bentham's youth, much more than the *Fragment*,

[645] *Ibid.*, p. 218.
[646] See I. Kant, *Grundlegung zur Metaphysik der Sitten*, 1785, §1, or see J. W. Scott, *Kant on the Moral Life*, 1924, p. 43: "There is nothing either in the world or out of it which is good without qualification except a good will." And see even more distinctly Kant, *Grundlegung zur Metaphysik der Sitten*, §3 (Scott, p. 44): "even if . . . a good will should wholly lack power to accomplish its purpose, if with its greatest efforts it should yet achieve nothing, there should remain only the good will . . . it would still shine by its own light as a thing which has its whole value in itself."
[647] Bentham, *A Comment on the Commentaries*, ed. by Everett, 1928, p. 110.

shows how far his criticism of Blackstone had developed into a fascinating criticism of all leading ethics of his epoch, and how carefully the basis of his own system had been laid there in constant touch with the opposite teachings of his time. The trouble which Professor Everett took in deciphering this manuscript was certainly not wasted on an unworthy object. Bentham's criticism of Blackstone's *Commentaries on the Laws of England* is not merely of historical or of purely national interest within English thought; it is of general systematic value even today, as one of the profoundest attempts to examine dogmatic, uncritical ethics. Beyond all doubt, the *Comment* considerably enhances the vigor and stringency of Bentham's later systematic work. It is a most instructive and invaluable introduction to his *Introduction to the Principles of Morals and Legislation*.

"HARD-LABOUR BILL," "RHYME AND REASON," *DEFENCE OF USURY*

IN ALL probability, it was soon after he had completed his first critical studies in the existing law that Bentham worked out the positive basis of his own theory of morals in the *Introduction to the Principles of Morals and Legislation*. Before, however, this main work appeared, he published two pamphlets concerning problems which, in themselves, have very little to do with ethics. Nevertheless, in at least one of these polemic treatises, the *Defence of Usury*, Bentham's philosophical mind often breaks through despite his rather unphilosophical topic.

On the other hand, the short pamphlet *A View of the Hard-Labour Bill* (1778) is so much concerned with concrete questions of the housing and guarding of prisoners, and is written so specifically for the practical use of the lawyer and politician, that there is hardly any room for philosophical reflections. Only occasionally are to be found some protests against "tautologies and superfluities,"[648] against "the usual complement of tautologies and redundancies"[649] in morals.

A similar absence of ethical discussions is apparent in a queer poem "Rhyme and Reason," 1780. In the catalogue of the British Museum Library it is assumed that Bentham may be the author of this satire.

[648] Bentham, *A View of the Hard-Labour Bill*, 1778, p. vii (Bentham, *Works*, 1843, part VII, p. 4b).
[649] *Ibid.*, p. 6 (*Works*, part VII, p. 4a).

But though it is probable that Bentham, the later resident of Queen's Square, wrote these verses, it is by no means certain. The full title of this pamphlet is: *Rhyme and Reason: or a Fresh Stating of the Arguments against an opening through the wall of Queen's Square, Westminster*, 1780, anonymously published. At any rate the humorous verses of this poem contain no philosophical remarks whatever.

Bentham's "*Defence of Usury*," however, which appeared in 1787, makes at least a few characteristic contributions to his ethical teaching.

In the course of his discussion, he raises the old question as to whether moral and intellectual progress can be found in the history of mankind; and with the typical optimism of the eighteenth century, he shows himself an ardent believer in a constant advance of the human race. There is an "uninterrupted progress of mankind, in our island at least"; among all the different periods of English history there is not one "at which the condition of the country was not more prosperous than at the period immediately preceding it: spite of so many wars, and fires, and plagues, and all other public calamities, with which it has been . . . afflicted, whether by the hand of God or by the misconduct of the sovereign."[650] Hence, for the realization of moral and intellectual ideals, we must look neither to antiquity nor to the present, but to the future. "The golden age, it is but too true, is not the lot of the generation in which we live: but, if it is to be found in any part of the track marked out for human existence, it will be found, I trust, not in any part which is past, but in some part which is to come. . . . In the war which industry and ingenuity maintain with fortune, past ages of ignorance and barbarism form the forlorn hope, which has been detached in advance and made a sacrifice of for the sake of future."[651] With this increase of prosperity, of freedom and prudence, with the growth of organized happiness, Bentham's optimism sees combined a higher moral standard.

Only a very slight shade of tragedy enters into this rather shallow vision of a coming Messianic age of prosperity. Bentham admits that "the career of art, the great road which receives the footsteps of projectors, may be considered as a vast, and perhaps unbounded, plain, bestrewed with gulphs, such as Curtius was swallowed up in. Each re-

[650] Bentham, *Defence of Usury; shewing the impolicy of the present legal restraints of the terms of pecuniary bargains in letters to a friend to which is added a letter to Adam Smith, Esq. LL.D. on the discouragements opposed by the above restraints to the progress of inventive industry*, 1787, p. 150 f (Bentham. *Works*, 1843, part v, p. 23b).

[651] *Ibid*., p. 171 (*Works*, part v, p. 26b). Letter XIII to Dr. Smith.

quires a human victim to fall into it ere it can close."[652] But he adds: "when it once closes, it closes to open no more, and so much of the path is safe to those who follow."[653] All this reveals a credulously hopeful, but rather simplified picture of history; and the whole of this creed, by a prophet of Europe's industrial era, can hardly be counted among the specially valuable parts of his doctrine.

So much the more remarkable seems to me the stress which, here again, is laid upon the necessity of a critical, censorial attitude in ethics and jurisprudence. "It is one thing, to find reasons why it is *fit* a law *should* have been made: it is another to find the reasons why it *was* made: in other words, it is one thing to justify a law: it is another thing to account for its existence."[654] "Custom . . . is the sole basis, which, either the moralist in his rules and precepts, or the legislator in his injunctions, can have to build upon. But what basis can be more weak or unwarrantable?"[655] "It is impossible the bulk of mankind should find leisure, had they the ability, to examine into the grounds of an hundredth part of the rules and maxims, which they find themselves obliged to act upon. Very good apology this for John Trod: but a little more inquisitiveness may be required of legislators."[656] In this way, Bentham insists once more on the indispensability of censorial ethics.

The concrete moral and legal problem with which Bentham's whole pamphlet on usury deals is thoroughly scrutinized from this point of view of critical ethics. In contrast to the common ethical condemnation of usury, Bentham defends it even against Adam Smith, whom he otherwise most sincerely admired and to whom, in the field of economics, he felt largely indebted. "You know," Bentham writes to his friend George Wilson in December 1786 from Russia, "it is an old maxim of mine, that interest, as love and religion, and so many other pretty things, should be free."[657] And thus, more consistent than Smith himself, Bentham applies Adam Smith's principles of economic liberalism even to free trade in money, by showing that there is neither a moral nor an economic reason for Smith's objection to usury.

He enters into a discussion even of the religious, the philosophic-historical, and the literary-historical grounds for the rise of the inveterate prejudice against free trade in money. He mentions, for instance, that

[652] *Ibid.*, p. 169 f (*Works*, part v, pp. 26a, b).
[653] *Ibid.*, p. 170 (*Works*, part v, p. 26b).
[654] *Ibid.*, p. 94 (*Works*, part iii, p. 15b). Letter x.
[655] *Ibid.*, p. 9 f (*Works*, part v, p. 4a). Letter ii.
[656] *Ibid.*, p. 7 (*Works*, part v, p. 3b). Letter ii.
[657] Bentham, *Works*, 1843, part xix, p. 167b.

on the religious side lending money at high price was obviously considered to be "acting like a Jew";[658] and though "all Christians at first were Jews, and continued to do as Jews did, after they had become Christians, yet, in process of time, it came to be discovered, that the distance between the mother and the daughter church could not be too wide."[658] "Indeed the easier method" of getting money as a Christian, "and a method pretty much in vogue, was to let the Jews get the money any way they could, and then squeeze it out of them as it was wanted."[659] Certainly, such "religious" reasons often given for the objection to usury provide no basis for the Christian accusations against usurers.

Within the history of philosophy, Bentham regards Aristotle as especially responsible for the defamation of usury. For Aristotle had stated that all money is in its nature barren.[660] In defiance of the old "despotic empire . . . of Aristotle . . . over the Christian world"[661] Bentham "dares to say . . . that the practical inference from this shrewd observation, if it afforded any, should have been, that it would be to no purpose for a man to try to get five per cent out of money—not, that if he could contrive to get so much, there would be any harm in it"; but would not "two sheep or other useful animals a man could buy for borrowed money . . . probably not be barren?"[662] At any rate, Aristotle's reference to barrenness as an intrinsic "quidditas" of money is in no way more conclusive than any reference to other seemingly fixed, intrinsic qualities of things.

Lastly, Bentham observes that in the history of literature "from the days of Thespis"[663] "selfish affections conspiring with the social" prevent justice from being done to "the man of thrift," the money-lender, and "treasure up" all favor for the borrower of money and even the man of dissipation.[664] This precisely mirrors the feelings of the "inconsiderate that is . . . the great mass of mankind." All "children who have eaten their cake are the natural enemies of the children who have theirs";[665] and the former benefactor of mankind who lent money changes his nature inevitably in the eyes of the inconsiderate crowd and becomes,

[658] Bentham, *Defence of Usury*, 1787, p. 98 (*Works*, 1843, part v, p. 16a). Letter x.
[659] *Ibid.*, p. 99 f (*Works*, 1843, part v, p. 16b). Letter x.
[660] *Ibid.*, p. 100 (*Works*, 1843, part v, p. 16b). Letter x.
[661] *Ibid.*, p. 99 (*Works*, 1843, part v, p. 16b).
[662] *Ibid.*, p. 101 (*Works*, 1843, part v, p. 16b).
[663] *Ibid.*, p. 107 (*Works*, 1843, part v, p. 17b). Letter x.
[664] *Ibid.*, pp. 107, 102 f (*Works*, 1843, part v, pp. 17b, a). Letter x.
[665] *Ibid.*, p. 102 (*Works*, 1843, part v, p. 17a). Letter x.

instead of a benefactor, a "tyrant and . . . oppressor."[666] Therefore, in literature, "from the days of Thespis to the present, . . . the borrower of money . . . was . . . recommended to favour in some shape or other, either to admiration or to love, or to pity, or to all three; and . . . the man of thrift consigned to infamy."[667] Here again, it is Bentham's major aim to dissect such moral prejudices as these, and to carry through his ethical reform, unchecked by religious, philosophical or poetical authorities.

As he repeats here, "whatever is now establishment, was . . . at one time, innovation."[668] Led by this conviction, he does not refrain from moral criticism even in reference to much more harmless types of conduct than usury. He even attacks obtrusiveness in giving moral advice and points out that "the folly of those who persist, . . . without reason, in not taking advice has been much expatiated upon. But the folly of those who persist, without reason, in forcing their advice upon others, has been little dwelt upon, though it is perhaps the more flagrant of the two. It is not often that one man is a better judge for another, than that other is for himself, even in cases where the adviser will take the trouble to make himself master of as many of the materials for judging, as are within the reach of the person to be advised. But the legislator is not, cannot be in the possession of any of those materials. What private can be equal to such public folly?"[669] "There may be worse cruelty: but can there be greater folly?"[670] Bentham applies these general reflections to his concrete moral problem in the following way: Why should the legislator "come and say . . . : you shall not have the money: for it would be doing you a mischief to let you borrow it upon such terms."[671] To prevent our doing mischief to one another, it is but too necessary to put bridles into all our mouths: it is necessary to the tranquillity and very being of society: but that the tacking of leading-strings upon the backs of grown persons, in order to prevent their doing themselves a mischief, is not necessary either to the being or tranquillity of society, however conducive to its well-being, I think cannot be disputed. Such paternal, or, if you please, maternal care . . . certainly is but a work of supererogation."[672]

[666] *Ibid.*, p. 103 (*Works*, 1843, part v, p. 17a). Letter x.
[667] *Ibid.*, p. 107 (*Works*, 1843, part v, p. 17b). Letter x.
[668] *Ibid.*, p. 145 (*Works*, 1843, part v, p. 22b). Letter x.
[669] *Ibid.*, p. 37 (*Works*, 1843, part v, p. 8a). Letter iv.
[670] *Ibid.*, p. 37 (*Works*, 1843, part v, p. 8a). Letter iv.
[671] *Ibid.*, p. 36 (*Works*, 1843, part v, p. 8a).
[672] *Ibid.*, p. 17 f (*Works*, 1843, part v, p. 5a). Letter iii.

All these moral arguments, and similar economic ones, finally lead to the conclusion that one of the fundamental reasons for the slander of usury lies "in the sound of the word *usury*."[673] In the connotations of its words, human language often expresses moral valuations which are without justification, since they have no hold but on common "imaginations" and blind "passions of mankind." Against this tyranny of language, the moralist Bentham states the case here as well as in his *Introduction*, and later in his *Table of the Springs of Action* and his *Deontology*.

Adam Smith had already defended the occupation of middlemen and forestallers against moral obloquy. Bentham wished to extend this moral rehabilitation even to the "highly useful"[674] professions of usurers and projectors; and all these moral, as well as the corresponding economic, arguments of Bentham impressed even Adam Smith.[675] After the appearance of Bentham's polemic, Smith admitted that his support of the Usury Laws[676] was incompatible with his own general principles of free trade. Moreover, this second small publication of Bentham attracted even more public attention than his first one, as several editions and translations in the eighteenth and the beginning of the nineteenth centuries show;[677] and as late as 1848, J. S. Mill maintained that Bentham's *Defence of Usury*, "this triumphant onslaught" made upon usury laws, "may still be referred to as the best extant writing on the subject."[678] We may doubt today whether Bentham's apology of usury is not as questionable as the axioms of radical economic liberalism in general, or even more open to criticism than those axioms. But, entirely apart from this economic question, the fundamental principles of Ben-

---

[673] *Ibid.*, p. 6 (*Works*, 1843, part v, p. 3b). Letter II.

[674] *Ibid.*, p. 187 (*Works*, 1843, part v, p. 29a). Letter XIII.

[675] See Bentham, *Works*, 1843, part XIX, p. 176b: "Dr. Adam Smith himself used this expression to Mr. Adam: The work is one of a superior man. He has given me some hard knocks, but in so handsome a manner, that I cannot complain, and he added that he thought the author was right."

[676] See Bentham, *Defence of Usury*, 1787, pp. 45 ff (*Works*, 1843, part v, pp. 9 ff). Letters VI and VII.

[677] The second edition of the *Defence of Usury* appeared as early as in 1790, a French translation in the same year and in 1828 a Spanish one (see C. W. Everett in E. Halévy, *The Growth of Philosophic Radicalism*, 1928, p. 541). American editions appeared in 1796, printed for Mathew Garey by Lang and Ustick, Philadelphia; in 1837, printed by Croswell, van Benthusyen and Burt, Albany; and as late as 1916, Hayworth Publishing House, Washington, D.C.

[678] John Stuart Mill, *Principles of Political Economy*, book v, chap. x, §2, 1852, vol. II, p. 510.

tham's moral criticism laid down here and elsewhere seem to me at least as much in conformity with the needs of the present time as with those of Bentham's day.

PRINCIPLES OF INTERNATIONAL LAW

No LESS pertinent to modern actualities are a few essays written about the same time, at any rate before the appearance of the *Introduction* —that is, in the years between 1786 and 1789. These essays were not published, however, until 1843, in Bowring's edition of Bentham's works under the title "Principles of International Law." Composed several years before Kant's treatise "Zum Ewigen Frieden" (1795), these essays contain a moral condemnation of war which is at least as passionate as that of the German idealist, but more consistent in its argument and more the work of a practical political mind.

As is to be expected from the most consistent advocate of the greatest happiness principle, Bentham thinks it morally unavoidable to consider international problems from the point of view of a "citizen of the world"; and he regards it as ethically unjustifiable to face them from a merely national angle.[679] That is to say, "inclination and . . . duty" should have as ends "the common and equal utility of all nations," not the happiness of one's own nation alone. "Hence . . . a given sovereign has no other means more adapted to attain his own particular end than the setting before his eyes the general end—the most extended welfare of all the nations on the earth—in the same manner as in its approach to the sun, a satellite has no other course to pursue than that which is taken by the planet which governs it."[680] "Why . . . ought . . . not the sovereign of a state to sacrifice the interests of his subjects for the advantage of foreigners . . . in . . . case . . . it would have been praiseworthy in his subjects to make the sacrifice themselves?"[681] Evidently, it is hardly possible to make a stronger plea for international mindedness, and the primacy of the universal utility principle over all national interests.

On the ground of these general convictions, war appears naturally as an evil, as "the complication of all other evils,"[682] as "madness . . . ex-

---

[679] Bentham, *Works*, 1843, part IV, p. 537a (Essay 1).
[680] *Ibid.*, p. 538a (Essay 1).   [681] *Ibid.*, p. 537b (Essay 1).
[682] *Ibid.*, p. 538b (Essay 1).

treme folly,"[683] as "mischief upon the largest scale."[684] Bentham, therefore, with the "press" as his sole "engine,"[685] draws up a "plan for an universal and perpetual peace."[686] In the course of these sketches, he recommends primarily six measures which ought to be pursued: (1) The establishment of a "tribunal of peace,"[687] of "a common court of judicature,"[688] especially in cases of bona fide divergences of opinion.[687] (2) The creation of a "European fraternity" of states.[689] (3) The abolition of all secret political negotiations.[690] (4) "Liberty of the press in each state, in such sort, that the fraternity of states might find no obstacle to its giving in every state ... to every paper whatever which it might think proper to sanction with its signature the most extensive and unlimited circulation."[691] (5) A fargoing disarmament[692] and (6) The emancipation of colonies.[693]

With special vigor, he urges England and France not to hesitate in making all possible efforts to effect a definite pacification of Europe. Since morality and true utility always coincide they both command this. "Whatsoever nation should get the start of the other in making the proposal to reduce and fix the amount of its armed force, would crown itself with everlasting power. The risk would be nothing—the gain certain. This gain would be the giving an incontrovertible demonstration of its own disposition to peace, and of the opposite disposition in the other nation in case of its rejecting the proposal."[694] One may say that in these reflections certain economic interests in armaments which

[683] *Ibid.*, p. 551b (Essay iv).
[684] *Ibid.*, p. 544a (Essay iii).   [685] *Ibid.*, p. 546a (Essay iv).
[686] *Ibid.*, p. 546a (Essay iv); comp. *ibid.* p. 550b.
[687] *Ibid.*, p. 545a (Essay iii).
[688] *Ibid.*, p. 552b (Essay iv). F. W. Hirst, *The Arbiter in Council*, 1906, anonymously published, p. 348, has already hinted at the fact that "The Hague Convention has created the non-coercive arbitral tribunal which was" what Bentham "asked for" in this connection.
[689] Bentham, *Works*, 1843, part iv, pp. 552b, 553a (Essay iv). C. J. Colombos, *Plan for an Universal and Perpetual Peace*, 1927, p. 8, remarks rightly as to this point that "Bentham may be appropriately described as a pioneer of the present League of Nations."
[690] See e.g. Bentham, *Works*, 1843, part iv, p. 554b (Essay iv).
[691] *Ibid.*, part iv, p. 554b (Essay iv).
[692] *Ibid.*, p. 551a (Essay iv).
[693] *Ibid.*, pp. 548a, 551a. Cf. Bentham's essay "Emancipate your colonies! Address to the National Convention of France," written in 1793, first published for sale in 1830, *Works*, 1843, part viii, pp. 407 ff, e.g. p. 407a: "Emancipate your colonies. Justice, consistency, policy, economy, honour, generosity, all demand it of you."
[694] Bentham, *Works*, 1843, part iv, p. 551a (Essay iv).

exist within every nation are underrated. Perhaps Bentham hints at such difficulties in saying that "it must be allowed that the matter would be a delicate one: there might be some difficulty in persuading one lion to cut his claws; but if the lion, or rather the enormous condor which holds him fast by the head should agree to cut his talons also, there would be no disgrace in the stipulation: the advantage or inconvenience would be reciprocal."[695] "All trade is in its essence advantageous—even to that party to whom it is least so. All war is in its essence ruinous."[696] "Whether . . . it . . . be the interest of a king of Great Britain to turn highwayman, is a question I shall waive: but a proposition I shall not flinch from is, that it never can be the interest of the nation to abet him in it; . . . the booty would be his, . . . the privileges of paying for the horse and pistols is all that would be ours. The booty would be employed in corrupting our confidential servants: and this is the full and exact amount of what we should get by it."[697] "Nothing but confirmed blindness and stupidity can prompt us to go on imitating Alexander and Caesar, and the New Zealanders, and Catherine and Frederic, without the profit."[698] "Difficult and complicated conventions have been effectuated: for examples . . . the German diet, . . . the Swiss league: . . . the American confederation. . . . Why should not the European fraternity subsist?"[699] To assume that a victorious war is profitable, is the same as to assume "that the way to make a man run the quicker is to cut off one of his legs"; for "true enough it is, that a man who has had a leg cut off, and the stump healed, may hop faster than a man who lies in bed with both legs broken, can walk."[700]

But at least as original as these arguments is the warm appeal Bentham addresses to his compatriots in relation to war mentality in general: "Oh my countrymen! Purge your eyes from the film of prejudice— extirpate from your hearts the *black specks* of excessive jealousy, false ambition, selfishness and insolence. The operations may be painful; but the rewards are glorious indeed! As the main difficulty, so will the main honour be with you."[701] And perhaps even more impressive are

[695] *Ibid.*, part IV, p. 545a (Essay III).
[696] *Ibid.*, p. 552a (Essay IV).
[697] *Ibid.*, p. 557a, compare 557b (Essay IV).
[698] *Ibid.*, pp. 557a, 557b (Essay IV).
[699] *Ibid.*, pp. 552b, 553a (Essay IV).
[700] Bentham, *Works*, 1843, part IV, p. 560a ("Principles of International Law," Essay IV).
[701] *Ibid.*, p. 553a (Essay IV).

the personal confessions he makes in connection with his elucidation of war psychology: "I feel it in my own experience . . . men have not yet learned to tune their feelings in unison with the voice of morality in these points. They feel more pride in being accounted strong, than resentment at being called unjust: or rather the imputation of injustice appears flattering rather than otherwise, when coupled with the consideration of its cause."[702] Here Bentham certainly touches upon one of the most important secret sources of war mentality: the emotional confusion between sound vitality and insane greed for sheer power.

Nevertheless, in spite of his highly idealistic love for peace, Bentham wishes to be a realist; and therefore he does not deny the possibility of a moral justification of war in certain, very exceptional cases. "In case of *mala fides* . . . if it appear that the injury in question is but a prelude to others, and that it proceeds from a disposition which nothing less than entire destruction can satisfy, and war presents any tolerable chance of success, how small soever, prudence and reason may join with passion in prescribing war as the only remedy in so desperate a disease."[703] Above all "there would be no great evil if, at the close of his career, every conqueror were to end his days upon the rack"; for there are "properly no other criminals" than the chiefs of nations; however criminal the intention of their chiefs may be, "the subjects are always honest."[704] In any case "the Dutch displayed prudence, while they yielded to the suggestions of indignation, in defending themselves against the force of Spain"; and "though the Spartans at Thermopylae perished to a man, yet the defence of Thermopylae was not without its use."[705] Thus, as "the only remedy in a desperate disease," under a considerable number of aggravating circumstances, morality and prudence do not in the eyes of Bentham forbid recourse to war. All the same, he hopes that enlightenment can overcome even the most deeply rooted passions which lead to wars of aggression and to justifiable defense. He stresses the point that "unjust ambition," that the emotional confusion between healthy strength and mad desire for power has the main share "in the generating of the disposition for war"; a further considerable influence he ascribes to "sincere and honest jealousy,"[706] to "diffidence"[707] and to "religious hatred."[708] None the less, he thinks that it is "a vulgar prej-

---

[702] *Ibid.*, p. 552b ("Principles of International Law," Essay iv).
[703] *Ibid.*, p. 545b (Essay iii).   [704] *Ibid.*, p. 539a (Essay i).
[705] *Ibid.*, p. 545b (Essay iii).
[706] *Ibid.*, p. 553a ("Principles of International Law," Essay iv).
[707] *Ibid.*, part iv, p. 553b (Essay iv).   [708] *Ibid.*, part iv, p. 540a (Essay i).

udice, fostered by passion," which "assigns the heart as the seat of all the moral diseases it complains of; . . . the principal and more frequent seat is really the head: it is from ignorance and weakness that men deviate from the path of rectitude, more frequently than from selfishness and malevolence"; and this Bentham thinks "fortunate,—for the power of information and reason over error and ignorance is much greater and much surer than that of exhortation, and all the moods of rhetoric, over selfishness and malevolence."[706] Oskar Kraus, in 1915, published an essay on Bentham's "Principles of International Law" as an introduction to the translation of Bentham's work into German. Certainly, Europe's political development since 1915 makes Bentham's small work no less interesting in 1950 than it was 35 or 160 years ago.

THE MAIN THEME

*An Introduction to the Principles of
Morals and Legislation*

THE MAIN THEME

An Introduction to the Principles of Morals and Legislation

THE question has often been discussed: when was the term *Utilitarian* adopted for the first time by Bentham and his school? E. A. Albee, in his *History of English Utilitarianism*, assumed on J. S. Mill's authority that John Stuart himself was the first utilitarian to use the word.[1] Leslie Stephen and E. Halévy came much nearer the truth when they wrote in 1900 and 1901 (before Albee's work appeared) that Bentham himself had used the term "Utilitarian" in 1781, and had suggested it to Dumont in 1802 as the proper name for the school instead of "Benthamite."[2] I think we must now go even further back to a hitherto unpublished manuscript of Bentham, written at the latest in 1780.

In this, Bentham described a curious dream about the time he was finishing his *Introduction to the Principles of Morals and Legislation* which was printed in 1780 and appeared in 1789.[3] Bentham tells us, in this amusing manuscript, the following "dream: The world is persuaded not without some colour of reason that all reformers and sys-

[1] See E. A. Albee, *A History of English Utilitarianism*, 1902, p. 197 and cf. J. S. Mill, *Autobiography*, published for the first time without alterations or omissions from the original manuscript in the possession of Columbia University, by J. S. Coss, 1924, chap. III, p. 56: "The name I gave to the society I had planned was the Utilitarian Society. It was the first time that any one had taken the title of Utilitarian; and the term made its way into the language from this humble source." Compare J. S. Mill, *Utilitarianism*, ed. by Oskar Piest, 1948, chap. II, p. 7, note: "The author of this essay has reason for believing himself to be the first person who brought the word utilitarian into use. He did not invent it, but adopted it from a passing expression in Mr. Galt's 'Annals of the Parish.'"

[2] See Leslie Stephen, *The English Utilitarians*, 1900, vol. I, p. 178 note and Bentham, *Works*, 1843, part XIX, pp. 92, 390; E. Halévy, *La formation du radicalisme philosophique*, 1901, tome II, p. 300.

[3] There is still considerable confusion as regards the very title and the date of publication of Bentham's classical work. Jean George Théodore Graesse's *Trésor de livres rares et précieux*, 1859, generally giving accurate information, says (tome I, p. 337) that "la première édition de ce célèbre ouvrage (Bentham's *Introduction*) a paru en 1780, la seconde en 1789" while in truth the first edition of the *Introduction* was printed in 1780, published in 1789 and a second edition did not appear until 1822. William Henry Roberts, *The Problem of Choice*, 1941, p. 147, states that Bentham published in 1789 the *Principles of Morals and Legislation*, and an introduction to this work in 1822.

tem-mongers are mad. . . . Formerly they used to live upon grasshoppers in deserts: walk upon golden thighs or sit upon three legged stools in temples: now they live in garrets: from whence in due time they are removed to Bethlehem, I do not mean such of Juda, but of Moorfields."[4]

"My madness has not yet, as far as I can perceive myself, come beyond a dream. I dreamt t'other night, that I was the founder of a sect, of course a personage of great sanctity and importance. It was called the sect of utilitarians."

"As I was musing one night in flew an angel at my window. I forgot his name—but it would be as [sic] easy to learn it in heaven where he is as well known for the implacable enmity he bears to the demon of chicane as S'Michael is by the battles he has had with Satan. He put into my hands a book which he said he had just been writing with the quill of a phoenix. It was lettered on the back Principles of legislation."[5] This candid self-ridicule of the young Bentham certainly shows no blind overestimation of what is, perhaps, his most important work; and the same is true of the title of his work. In fact, his *Introduction* is much more than an introduction to the principles of ethics and jurisprudence; it gives a detailed analysis of these principles themselves. How detailed this analysis is may be inferred, not only from the present writer's work, but also from unknown Bentham material just prepared for publication by Professor Charles Everett.[6]

[4] Bethlehem Royal Hospital ("Bedlam") situated in Moorfields outside the old wall of London, north of the Tower, was from 1675 to 1814 an asylum for the insane.

[5] Bentham MS, University College, London, Portfolio 169, Folder XIII, p. 79, *unpublished*. The whole of this MS is printed as Appendix I of the present volume.

[6] This material has meanwhile been published by Charles Warren Everett in his *The Limits of Jurisprudence Defined Being Part Two of An Introduction to the Principles of Morals and Legislation by Jeremy Bentham*, 1945. This second part of Bentham's *Introduction* is, as its title and table of contents pp. XI-XXII indicate, not concerned with ethics but almost exclusively with jurisprudence. Bentham is fully aware of the paradoxical character of his statement on p. 299 of the *Limits* when he says here that in one respect "this whole work belongs still to Ethics" in the unusually wide sense which he gave the term "ethics" in the last chapter of the first part of his *Introduction*. Only if ethics in this largest meaning of the term is said to include jurisprudence and "private ethics," can the *Limits* be said to belong to ethics in a quite uncommon sense of the word. As my manuscript was practically completed when this most recent Bentham edition by Professor Everett appeared, I could refer to it only in various footnotes and a brief paragraph. I trust however that this will not impair the comparative exhaustiveness of my analysis of Bentham's ethics.

PLEASURE AND PAIN AND
THE UTILITY PRINCIPLE

BENTHAM'S *Introduction* starts with a solemn declaration which, E. Halévy was able to show, was "copied almost word for word from Helvetius."[7] We may add that much the same can be said for the last sentences of Bentham's most original book.[8] Nevertheless, this work, commencing and finishing with such "plagiarisms," is the creation of a highly original mind, and of a much more systematic and more acute thinker than was his predecessor. It is not without significance that even in the first few sentences of Bentham's *Introduction*, which contain the echo of Helvétius, some deviations already appear.

Helvétius was practically an atheist, as was Bentham.[9] Nevertheless, he declared in his *De l'esprit* that he did not wish to be "contraire aux principes de notre religion";[10] and in the passage which influenced Bentham at the beginning of his *Introduction*, Helvétius speaks of God who has endowed man with the sensibility of feeling, pleasure and pain, so that, stirred by these emotions, he may execute God's unknown plans. Bentham, however, resolutely replaces God by Nature, and no longer speaks about unknown ends of world development which have to be attained by means of pain and pleasure. To him, nothing but the great-

---

[7] E. Halévy, *The Growth of Philosophic Radicalism*, 1928, p. 26; compare E. Halévy, *La formation du radicalisme philosophique*, tome I, pp. 38, 298 and see Helvétius, *Oeuvres complètes*, 1818, tome I, p. 293 f. ("De l'esprit," discours III, chap. IX: "Il semble que . . . Dieu . . . ait dit . . . à l'homme: Je te doue de la sensibilité; c'est par elle qu'aveugle instrument de mes volontés, incapable de connaître la profondeur de mes vues, tu dois, sans le savoir, remplir tous mes desseins. Je te mets sous la garde du plaisir et de la douleur: l'un et l'autre veilleront à tes pensées, à tes actions; engendreront tes passions, exciteront tes aversions, tes amitiés, tes tendresses, tes fureurs; allumeront tes désirs, tes craintes, tes espérances; te dévoileront des vérités; te plongeront dans des erreurs; et après t'avoir fait enfanter mille systèmes absurdes et différens de morale et de législation, te découvriront un jour les principes simples, au developpement desquels est attaché l'ordre et le bonheur du monde moral." Halévy gives no exact reference to this passage in Helvétius either in the French or the English edition of his work.

[8] See Helvétius, *Oeuvres complètes*, 1818, tome I, p. 42 ("De l'esprit," discours II, chap. I); and see Bentham, *Works*, 1843, part I, p. 154b.

[9] See John Quincy Adams, *Memoirs*, 1874, vol. III, p. 563, under the date of June 8, 1817: "Walk with Bentham. He says Place is an atheist. I fear he is one himself." Compare C. K. Ogden, *Bentham's Theory of Fictions*, 1932, p. 9.

[10] Helvétius, *Oeuvres complètes*, 1818, tome I, p. 216 ("De l'esprit," discours II, chap. 24).

est amount of happiness is the aim of human life and of history itself, as we have already seen in the *Defence of Usury*. These are again evidences of a secularization of ethics, more thoroughgoing even than that performed by the radical Helvétius—symptoms which should neither be overrated nor entirely overlooked.

Yet, apart from these indications of a consistent secularism, the first paragraph of Bentham's *Introduction* is animated by an even more profound emotion and pathos than Helvétius' corresponding words. There lives in these introductory sentences something of a spirit at once mundane and solemn, and certainly there lives in them more of the "Weltreligion"[11] of Spinoza than in their model Helvétius. Bentham describes the irremovable domination of pain and pleasure, their uninterrupted and omnipresent rule over living mankind. But he does not describe it as a cool observer from the outside. He obviously cannot and does not wish to conceal his personal feelings.

This is even more evident when he tries to show *why* all is "fastened" to the "throne"[12] of pain and pleasure. He does this in assuming the contrary by way of hypothesis. If we made the attempt to throw off our continual subjection to pleasure and pain, we should realize that every effort of this kind serves but to demonstrate and to confirm this subjection. We may try "to abjure" "this empire"; but then we can only succeed in "words"; in "reality," we shall remain subject to pleasure and pain all the while. Bentham, therefore, repeats with traceable passion in his language that pain and pleasure alone "govern us in all we do, in all we say, in all we think. It is for them alone to point out what we ought to do, as well as to determine what we shall do. On the one hand the standard of right and wrong, on the other the chain of causes and effects, are fastened to their throne."[12] Solely "the principle of utility recognises this subjection, and assumes it for the foundation of that system, the object of which is to rear the fabric of felicity by the hands of reason and of law. Systems which attempt to question it, deal in sounds instead of sense, in caprice instead of reason, in darkness instead of light."[12] Remarkable as we may think the elevated language of these first lines in Bentham's main ethical work, in all probability these sentences are responsible for the almost universal criticism of his ethics on the part of utilitarians as well as of anti-hedonists.

[11] On Spinoza's "Weltreligion" see e.g. D. Baumgardt, *Spinoza und Mendelssohn*, 1932.
[12] Bentham, *Introduction to the Principles of Morals and Legislation*, 1789, chap. 1, sect. 1 (*Works*, 1843, part 1, p. 1).

Professor C. I. Lewis, as we have seen, subscribes to the fundamental reference point of Bentham's theory in as much as he, too, insists that this ultimate reference-point of any valuation which has "the significance of empirical cognition" must be the direct experience of an "immediately valuable" such as "pleasure and pain."[13] "The natural bent of the natural man stands in no need of correction in order validly to be the touchstone of *intrinsic* value."[14] "There can be no illusion of present enjoyment or present pain."[15] "There are no data which can be called upon in support of any objective fact except finally the data of appearance. And if what is relative to appearance is thereby subjective, then everything knowable is subjective; and the word loses all significance."[16] "If there were a complete absence of community in our value-findings on given occasions, or if communities of value-apprehension in the presence of the same object should be mere matters of chance, then no one could, with the best will in the world, learn how to do anybody else any good—or for that matter, how to do him harm."[17] But Professor Lewis adds to these and similar observations: "Any name for the character of being immediately valuable suffers from the difficulty" that "we can only explain one such name by others; and unless those to whom we would express ourselves identify what is intended by *some* name we can use, there will be no manner at all in which our intention can be made precisely clear."[18] If therefore " 'pleasure' or any other name is to serve as synonym for the immediately and intrinsically valuable, then it must be adequate to the wider variety of what is found directly good in life. It must cover the active and self-forgetting satisfactions as well as the passive and self-conscious ones; the sense of integrity in firmly fronting the 'unpleasant' as well as 'pleasure'; the gratification in having one's own way, and also the benediction which may come to the defeated in having finished the faith. It must cover innocent satisfactions as well as those of cultivation; that which is found in consistency and also that of perversity and caprice; the enjoyment of sheer good fortune, and that which adds itself to dogged achievement. All this in addition to the whole range of the sensuously pleasing and the emotionally gratifying. And the immediately disvaluable has its equal and corresponding variety."[19] This critical supplement to Bentham's statements on his fundamental starting point is certainly most appropriate.

---

[13] *Ibid.*, p. 405. In his *Science de la morale*, 2nd edition, 1908, tome 1, pp. 119 ff,
[14] *Ibid.*, p. 398.   [15] *Ibid.*, p. 407.   [16] *Ibid.*, p. 409.
[17] *Ibid.*, p. 423.   [18] *Ibid.*, p. 403 f.
[19] *Ibid.*, p. 405. In his *Science de la morale*, 2nd edition, 1908, tome 1, pp. 119ff,

Bentham himself has too often given the impression that his concept of pleasure is far too narrow. But Professor Lewis' critical observations evidently do not question the principal correctness of the ultimate reference-point of Bentham's consistent hedonism.

Anti-hedonists, however, have, of course, taken much graver offense at the onset of the *Introduction*. These emphatic remarks of Bentham's first sentences generally gave the anti-hedonists reason for assuming that their author, an exceedingly shallow moral sermonizer, confused from the beginning what ought to be done with what actually is done, and confused the "right" with the "good." All these differences, however, between "is" and "ought," and between the "right" and the "good," are supposed to concern vital distinctions preliminary to any ethical inquiry, distinctions whose careful restoration is said to be a special merit of contemporary English ethics.

Yet, granted that the first statements of Bentham's *Introduction* lay themselves open to possible misinterpretation, has not he himself followed up these first sentences by a strict limitation of their verbal meaning? Bentham explicitly conceded that, so far, the first paragraph of his first chapter indulges too much in the language of emotion, of poetry. He, therefore, concludes this paragraph with the following admission: "But enough of metaphor and declamation: it is not by such means that moral science is to be improved."[20] Of course, one may say that this very self-correction demonstrates how much of the zealous prophet and poet lives in the apparently dry theorist of the greatest-happiness principle. But certainly, Bentham wished to be more than an enthusiastic propagandist of utilitarianism.

His main emphasis was on exact reasoning; and I think there is no reason to say that he committed at the very beginning of his main work the "worst" fallacy that can be committed in ethics, the so-called naturalistic fallacy. That is, I do not think that the most frequently quoted first and tenth sections of the first chapter of the *Introduction* can be interpreted in such a way as to contain the fallacious naturalistic definition that moral right, moral good and "ought" mean nothing but useful. On the contrary, Bentham carefully distinguishes, here and elsewhere, between the "chain" of pleasant and painful "causes and effects . . . on

---

Charles Renouvier, too, wished to enlarge the common moral meaning of such terms as "bonheur," "utilité" (see *ibid.*, pp. 134 ff) and "plaisir" (see pp. 143 ff). But Renouvier insists that none of these terms can serve as the basic concepts of ethics.

[20] Bentham, *Works*, 1843, part I, p. 1.

the one hand and the standard of right and wrong on the other."[21] All he says is that this standard and that chain of causes and effects are fastened to the same place in *reality*.

Bentham certainly did not wish to start and to conclude the discussion of the meaning of "good" by imposing the simple definition that "good," "right" and "ought" mean nothing but pleasant or useful. H. Sidgwick has already defended Bentham in this regard[22] and it seems to me that, on this point, Professor G. E. Moore has no cogent reason for stronger objections[23] to Bentham than Sidgwick.

Nevertheless, the anti-hedonist may insist that, though Bentham does not start with a simple naturalistic definition of "good," good means to him, in the end, for many reasons, "conducive to the greatest pleasure of the greatest number"; and this represents a naturalistic fallacy which if not a logical fallacy is, to say the least, a "definist fallacy" because ultimately it treats two entirely different properties as one.[24] But to this Professor W. K. Frankena has already given an answer which seems to me conclusive. It is, as he points out, "begging the question" in favor of intuitionistic anti-hedonism to say in advance that the quality goodness is indefinable and that, therefore, all ethical naturalists commit a fallacy.

The reproach that a moralist commits a "naturalistic fallacy" or a "definist fallacy"—i.e. that he is wrong in defining, for example, goodness in terms of pleasantness—can "enter only at the end of the con-

[21] Bentham, *Works*, 1843, part I, p. 1. Frederik Vinding Kruse, *The Foundation of Human Thought, the Problem of Science and Ethics* (translated from the Danish by Annie Fausbøll and Ingeborg Lund), 1949, pp. 53 f, thinks "in the same place in which Bentham . . . states that the two factors, pleasure and pain do in fact guide all our actions, he says, incidentally, that it is these factors alone which decide what we *ought* to . . . do without being conscious of his transition from the psychological to the ethical." But a careful interpretation of Bentham's statements does not bear out anything of Kruse's extreme criticism. Bentham, the champion of a censorial justification of every *ought,* cannot be charged with not having been aware of the decisive difference between *ought* and *is.* All that can be said on this point is that, despite the strict distinction he made between "the psychological and the ethical," he rightly deemed it necessary to base the ethical judgment ultimately on psychological data, on feelings which are generally thought to be merely subjective or even anti-moral but actually are undeniable objective facts of essential ethical relevance.

[22] See H. Sidgwick, *The Methods of Ethics*, 1901, Book I, chapter III, §1, p. 26 note.

[23] See G. E. Moore, *Principia Ethica*, 1903, pp. 17 f.

[24] See the lucid discussion of these questions in W. K. Frankena's essay "The naturalistic Fallacy," *Mind*, vol. XLVIII, 1939, pp. 468, 471.

troversy"[25] between ethical intuitionism and ethical naturalism. Bentham, however, devoted the most careful analysis to the questions of why a non-naturalistic criterion of morality is untenable in a critical theory of morals. He left, for good reasons, the final justification of practically all the earlier statements of his work to the later sections or even to later writings and filled the first chapters of his work mainly with preparatory and polemical reflections. Thus all I wish to say at this point is that, in my view, Bentham in the first chapter of the *Introduction* did not believe in any way that he had solved the problem of goodness by giving a mere definition of good, of ought and of right. But he gave a few other quite different definitions, one of a principle in general, one of the principle of utility and one of community; and after his first sentences he excused himself for his metaphorical, hyperbolic language.

Only after this half involuntary self-admonition does he go on to give a definition of the meaning of his principle of utility. He does this in the following way: "By the principle of utility is meant that principle which approves or disapproves of every action whatsoever, according to the tendency which it appears to have to augment or diminish the happiness of the party whose interest is in question: or what is the same thing in other words, to promote or to oppose that happiness. I say of every action whatsoever, and therefore not only of every action of the private individual, but of every method of government. By utility is meant that property in any object, whereby it tends to produce benefit, advantage, pleasure, good, or happiness (all this in the present case comes to the same thing) or (what comes again to the same thing) to prevent the happening of mischief, pain, evil, or unhappiness to the party whose interest is considered."[26] Not until 1822, in a note to his first paragraph, did Bentham mention his later attempts to substitute for the term *utility* the phrases *greatest happiness* or *greatest felicity*; and he adds two plausible reasons for this modification of his terminology. First, "the word *utility* does not so clearly point to the ideas of *pleasure* and *pain* as the words *happiness* and *felicity* do." Second, the word utility does not "lead us to the consideration of the *number* of the interests affected; to the *number*, as being the circumstance, which contributes, in the largest proportion, to the formation of the standard here in question; the *standard of right and wrong*, by which alone the propriety of human conduct, in every situation, can with propriety be

[25] *Ibid.*, p. 473.
[26] Bentham, *Works*, 1843, part I, pp. 1 f.

tried."[27] But not only the term *utility* has thus been critically commented on by Bentham. In another note, a note to section two, he tries to explain and to justify even his use of the concept *principle*. He admits that the term *principle* has a rather vague meaning. Like the Latin *principium*, principle seems to mean simply something which combines the meaning of "chief" and "take" and in this way the term *principle* "is applied to anything which is conceived to serve as the foundation or beginning to any series of operations: in some cases, of physical operations: but of mental operations in the present case," that is, of all possible data of consciousness. Just such an indeterminate term is, according to Bentham, most serviceable at the beginning of a general discussion.

After these few remarks on pleasure and pain, and on the principle of utility, Bentham proceeds to expound a third "most general expression" occurring "in the phraseology of morals," namely "the interest of the community";[27] and indeed, the definition of community given here is of great significance. It shows Bentham as one of the most radical representatives of the so-called mechanistic theory of the state, or better, as an avowed opponent of any "organological" theory. For Bentham, state and community are not organisms containing more than an aggregate of independent individuals.

There exists an old tradition of thought, most effectively renewed in the romantic theories of the state in the nineteenth century, according to which state and community possess a "higher" organic life than do human individuals. The community is believed to represent a sort of entity apart from the sum of its members. For Bentham, community understood in such a way is an entirely "fictitious body,"[28] for the introduction of which not reality but only language gives occasion. For him state and community are nothing except "the sum . . . of the several members who compose it"; and the interest of the community is nothing but "the sum of the interests . . . of the individual persons who are considered as constituting . . . its members."[28] Thus, for Bentham only the individuals of a community are organisms; the community as such is, according to him, not only less than an organism but even less than a piece of machinery.

All the same, the usual objections against his theory of the state seem to me to have only partial justification. Such objections say very little if they give no argument of their own but only repeat in a contemptuous

[27] *Ibid.*, p. 1.
[28] Bentham, *Introduction*, 1789, chap. I, sect. IV.

terminology the argument to which they object.[29] Among the English Hegelians, F. H. Bradley e.g. "wished . . . to emphasize . . . that" the "metaphysic" of the individualistic theory of the state "is mere dogmatism."[30] However, can it be denied that the organological theory of the state itself represents equally dogmatic metaphysics? The truth seems to be that each of these hostile schools takes account of certain aspects of community life, while it leaves out of sight those features which are at issue with its one-sided view. A musical composition is not fully understood either by the man who hears solely a melody or by him who hears only a sum of single tones. Understood as mutually exclusive theories, both the individualistic and the organological concept of the community are, in my opinion, wrong because they are one-sided. Understood as different aspects of the same object,[31] methodologically separable from each other, they are of equal value and of mutually complementary truth.

Even granted that Bentham was wrong in attributing exclusive scientific value to his own doctrine, we are equally unjustified in denying his theory any relevance whatsoever. Granted that his concept of an individual person is an "abstractum," it is a methodologically defensible abstraction. It is therefore legitimate, I think, to criticize the conclusions drawn from Bentham's view of the community only in so far as these

[29] See e.g. A. Seth Pringle Pattison, *The Philosophical Radicals and Other Essays*, 1907, p. 38, Seth's criticism of Bentham's and Mill's conceptions of a "pulverised" mind and a pulverized society: "Bentham's ethics are the counterpart of this . . . atomism," of a community consisting only of "separate units accidentally combined." Cf. precisely the same criticism of Hobbes and Kant in Scheler's *Der Formalismus in der Ethik und die materiale Wertethik*, 1921, p. 62.

As to the history of the organological theories of the state in their development in Edmund Burke, Schelling, Hegel, Friedrich Schlegel, Novalis, Baader, Adam Müller, Savigny and their criticism of an "État machine," see D. Baumgardt, *Franz von Baader und die philosophische Romantik*, 1927, pp. 371 ff.

[30] F. H. Bradley, *Ethical Studies*, 1876, p. 150. See the opposite view in S. de Beauvoir, *Pour une morale de l'ambiguité*, 1947, p. 148: "Si l'individu n'est rien, la société ne saurait être quelque chose. Qu'on le prive de sa substance, et l'État n'a plus de substance."

[31] A justification of such a view of community life I see e.g. in the following general statements of Professor Morris R. Cohen: "Two statements which, taken abstractly, are contradictory may both be true of concrete existence provided they can be assigned to separate domains or aspects. A plurality of aspects is an essential trait of things in existence. . . . When opposing statements are completed by reference to the domains wherein they are true, there is no logical difficulty in combining them" (see M. R. Cohen in *Contemporary American Philosophy*, vol. I, 1930, p. 231 f).

conclusions do not correspond to the facts. But it is unjustifiable to presuppose that nothing in this view can correspond to facts.

After having given these definitions of *community* and of *the utility principle,* Bentham goes on to explain the relation of these terms to some other fundamental ones, the terms *right* and *wrong* and *ought.* Applying his first statements about the inescapable rule of pleasure and pain over human life, and anticipating the conclusions of later inquiry, he here already adds that it is "impossible . . . and . . . needless"[32] to trace right or wrong actions back to anything but actions "augmenting" or diminishing "the happiness of a community."[33] A right action is an action "conformable to the principle of utility"[34] or the "law" or the "dictate"[35] of utility, that is, an action which "tends to add to the sum total of . . . pleasures or, what comes to the same thing to diminish the sum total of . . . pains."[36] "At least that is not a wrong action" or an action which "ought not to be done."[37] A wrong action is, accordingly, an action not conformable to the principle of utility, an action which ought not to be done, an act whose tendency to diminish the happiness of the community is greater than any it has to augment it.[38] Only "when thus interpreted, do the words *ought* and *right* and *wrong* and others of that stamp," have, according to Bentham, an ethical "meaning: when otherwise, they have none";[37] this can be contested solely "by those who have not known what they have been meaning."[32] Again, despite some linguistic temptations to do so, I cannot think it justifiable to maintain that in the last quoted sentences nothing but a definition is given, namely, the fallacious statement that *ought, right* or *wrong* and *morally good* mean ethically pleasant or painful *per definitionem.*

These sentences, in truth, say something epistemologically very different, something which is recognized especially by Professor G. E. Moore to be a very different thing,[39] namely, that *the* good is in reality general happiness, and that *the* right is realization of general happiness. Even granted that the wording of these quotations from Bentham would not forbid the interpretation that they were mere definitions, the whole of his doctrine (with its strict distinction between *ought* and *is*) would not permit this interpretation.

As Bentham tries to demonstrate later in connection with his analyses

---

[32] Bentham, *Introduction,* 1789, chap. I, sect. 11.

[33] *Ibid.,* sect. 6. [34] *Ibid.,* sect. 10, 6. [35] *Ibid.,* sect. 8.

[36] *Ibid.,* sect. 5. [37] *Ibid.,* sect. 10. [38] *Ibid.,* sect. 6.

[39] See G. E. Moore, *Principia Ethica,* 1903, p. 18: To define "*the* good as general happiness" is "perfectly consistent . . . with the contention that good is indefinable."

of motives and ethical dispositions, we cannot speak in *reality* of right actions and of any ought independently of the pleasant or painful consequences of these actions. On the other hand, we cannot go beyond pleasure and pain in these questions. Whoever tries to retrace ethical concepts beyond the phenomena of pleasure and pain can only "pretend" to do so, can only do so "in words," but not "in reality."[40] For any "chain of proofs must have their commencement somewhere, . . . that which is used to prove everything else, cannot itself be proved";[41] and there is nothing in the emotional and moral world that can be more palpable ground than are pleasure and pain. Only later does Bentham attempt to show more fully why the concepts of moral right or wrong and good are rendered meaningless when these concepts are deprived of all regard to the consequences of acts.

Still to this day, opinions on this subject are rather evenly divided. Among contemporary moralists, Professor G. E. Moore[42] and, partly, Dr. H. W. B. Joseph, agree with Bentham that moral rightness is in some way dependent on the consequences of acts. As Dr. H. W. B. Joseph sums this up, "Professor Moore agrees so far with the Utilitarians as to hold that rightness in actions is always being causally related to some good; the goodness is not intrinsic to a right action."[43] And even more definitely, Dr. H. B. Acton states that questions concerning duties "cannot be answered without reference to what is good."[44]

On the other hand, Professor H. A. Prichard and Sir David Ross insist that all questions concerning moral rightness can and have to be strictly separated from those concerning moral goodness. Professor Prichard points out: "I would suggest as a prominent instance of the fallacy involved the attempt which is often made nowadays (as e.g. I think it is by Professor Moore and Professor Laird) to maintain a view which implies that we deduce the rightness of certain actions from our knowledge of what is *good* taken in conjunction with our knowledge of our powers of action and of existing circumstances."[45] With equal

[40] Bentham, *Introduction*, 1789, chap. i, sect. i.

[41] *Ibid.*, chap. i, sect. ii.

[42] See *The Philosophy of G. E. Moore*, ed. by Paul Arthur Schilpp (*The Library of Living Philosophers*, vol. iv), 1942, pp. 154 ff.

[43] H. W. B. Joseph, *Some Problems in Ethics*, 1931, p. 73; and see the further explanations of Professor Joseph on this point; *ibid.*, p. 83 on "the instrumental view of rightness"; but compare on the other hand e.g. p. 125.

[44] H. B. Acton, *Is Ethical Relativity Necessary?* in *Proceedings of the Aristotelian Society*, supplementary volume xvii, 1938, p. 179.

[45] H. A. Prichard, *Duty and Interest*, 1928, pp. 41 ff.

force, Sir David Ross urges: If acts are "optimific as well as right, that is interesting but not morally important; if not, we still ought to do them . . . , and the question whether they are optimific has no importance for moral theory."[46]

I hope that the following analyses of Bentham's theory of morals will show conclusively why these two opposite views might seem at first glance equally suitable as preliminary hypotheses; but in fact, the deontological hypothesis must of necessity remain dogmatic, while only the teleological, utilitarian hypothesis lends itself to a thorough critical examination of ethical duties as well as of ethical goods and values.

Performance of Acts and Ethical Testing of Acts

Bentham explicitly admits that "men . . . in general" do not think of the principle of utility, although they "embrace" it in practice.[47] He grants that in general, we do not think of the greatest-happiness principle "for the ordering" of our "own actions," but we think of it for the "trying" of them as well as for the trying of the actions "of other men"; and he even admits that "there have been . . . not many, perhaps, even of the most intelligent who have been disposed to embrace it purely and without reserve. There are even few who have not taken some occasion or other to quarrel with it, either on account of their not understanding always how to apply it, or on account of some prejudice or other which they were afraid to examine into, or could not bear to part with. For such is the stuff that man is made of: in principle and in practice, in a right track and in a wrong one, the rarest of all human qualities is consistency."[48] With these statements, obviously, two concessions are made whose importance has often been overlooked.

W. R. Sorley and other critics of Bentham hold the following objections essential: "Bentham always treats . . . men . . . as pursuing . . . pleasure . . . in a deliberate and intelligent way under the guidance of ideas or opinions; he commits the philosopher's fallacy of substituting a reason for a cause; he overlooks the fact that man was an active being before he was a rational being, that he is a creature of impulses, inherited and acquired, that it is only gradually that these impulses come to be organised and directed by reason, and that this rationalising process is never completed."[49] Bentham, however, "assumed that men were con-

---

[46] W. D. Ross: *The Right and the Good*, 1930, p. 37.
[47] Bentham, *Introduction*, 1789, chap. i, sect. 12.
[48] *Ibid.*, sect. 12.
[49] W. R. Sorley: *A History of English Philosophy*, 1920, p. 223.

stantly controlled by intellectual considerations."[50] This is a criticism quite similar to that frequently directed against the rationalism of Kant.[51] Even as to Kant these objections seem to me by no means justified; they are much less so in reference to Bentham.

In his *Fragment on Government*, Bentham had already granted that the consideration of utility often does not govern the acts of men except "secretly";[52] and in the *Introduction* he makes it again sufficiently clear that, in his view, men generally do not "think" of the principle of utility, although even most "stupid or perverse human creatures on many . . . occasions defer to it."[53] That is to say, Bentham does not deny that human actions are in general caused by impulses and by instincts rather than by reason or thought. He does not deny this of mankind at its present stage of development and much less, of course, in reference to earlier phases of this very long process.

But this is not the main question discussed by Bentham. It is not the question: how are the actions of man caused, by mere passion or by reflection on the utility principle? Not this "ordering of their . . . actions" is in debate, but "the trying of their own actions, as well as of those of other men."[53] That is, he is not essentially concerned with the problem: are human actions caused by an instinctive or reflective pursuit of pleasure? His main point is to make out whether human actions are instinctive, subconscious, reflective pursuing of *pleasure* or whether they are reflective, instinctive, subconscious pursuing of *something else* and whether ethics should, therefore, take into account this "something else."

As to this second question, he arrived at the conclusion that even if "most intelligent" people refuse to acknowledge that instinctive or reflective pleasure-seeking was their motive, a thoroughgoing analysis of their conduct shows that in their instinct and thought they could not avoid striving for ends that give pleasure, though they may not call this pleasure or even satisfaction, but may call it a merely painful self-sacrifice. But they could not have performed an act of painful selflessness if self-sacrifice, despite its pain, had not been, in the end, more attractive to them than any lower self-enjoyment coupled with the pain of self-reproach.

[50] *Ibid.*, p. 225.
[51] See e.g. Herder's objections to Kant and their discussion in D. Baumgardt, *Der Kampf um den Lebenssinn unter den Vorläufern der modernen Ethik*, 1933, p. 253.
[52] Bentham, *A Fragment on Government*, 1776, chap. I, sect. 45.
[53] Bentham, *Introduction*, 1789, chap. I, sect. 12.

The aims of human acts are, of course, not special, isolated entities of pleasure; they are activities which have a hedonic tone, a hedonic tinge rather than an abhorrent, exclusively painful color. One can readily agree with Fréderic Rauh that "l'homme sérieux ne s'arrête à son plaisir: il agit, il travaille, il marche sans y penser."[54] In general we are engaged in activities without thinking of any special entities "pleasure" or "pain" as being independent of these activities. But all the same, if these activities did not have a pleasant or painful coloring, we could not engage in them or refrain from them.

The moralist is, therefore, entitled to concentrate exclusively on the analysis of these hedonic tones in setting up his standard for testing human behavior. The criterion of ethical value cannot be a distinction between hedonic tones and something else which does not exist as a human end, but only between different types of hedonic tones, as is presupposed by the principle of utility.

"Dangerousness" of the Utility Principle and Other Common Objections

Criticism of the utility principle, however, has often not shrunk even from flagrant self-contradictions. Bentham drastically illustrates this by an acrimonious analysis of the widespread saying that "the principle of utility is a dangerous principle." This naïve notion of the dangerousness of the utility principle is, as he demonstrates, evidently vitiated by one crucial oversight, namely, that the import of the utility principle is implicitly confirmed by that very criterion which should demonstrate its irrelevance.

To examine the utility principle from the point of view of its dangerousness means nothing but the confession that dangerousness or usefulness are legitimate criteria in this examination. This, however, means an acknowledgment of the value of the utility principle, quite independent of the possibility that this examination may end with the statement that this principle is not useful, but dangerous.

In Bentham's own words "the principle of utility (I have heard it said) is a dangerous principle: it is dangerous on certain occasions to consult it. This is as much as to say, what? that it is not consonant to utility, to consult utility: in short, that it is *not* consulting it, to consult

[54] Fréderic Rauh, *Études de morale*, 1911, p. 125. Compare Professor T. V. Smith, *Constructive Ethics*, 1948, p. 296 f: "The idea of a fixed and single end lying beyond the diversity of human needs and acts rendered utilitarianism incapable of being an adequate representative of the modern spirit."

it."[55] In an enlargement of this note, added in 1822, Bentham attacks the statement of the dangerousness of the utility principle once more, and much less theoretically, by pointing out that the Earl of Rosslyn, Alexander Wedderburn, who was said to have uttered this statement, was perfectly right—with regard to his own interest and the interest of his class; to the "sinister interest" of this small group of functionaries the greatest-happiness principle was in fact dangerous. For "in a government which had for its end in view the greatest happiness of the greatest number, Alexander Wedderburn might have been Attorney General ... but he would not have been Attorney General with £15,000 a year, nor Chancellor with £25,000 a year" etc.[56] As we shall see later on, in his "book of fallacies," Bentham has further sharpened his criticism of Wedderburn's saying from the political, but not from the philosophical, viewpoint.

Apart from the objection of "dangerousness," Bentham briefly enumerates a number of similarly sweeping objections often raised against the utility principle. There is, first, one type of person who thinks the settling of his opinions on such a subject not worth the trouble.[57] With him, of course, no discussion is needed or even possible. A second type does not go so far, but wishes to forego judging by any *principle*. No worth-while debate is possible with him either, as he is not interested in ascertaining a moral principle even if one could be ascertained. Ethical discussion with anti-hedonists can start only when the validity of one or more ethical principles is maintained in contrast to or apart from the utility principle. It has to be made clear, then, whether this other principle "be not a mere principle in words, a kind of phrase which at bottom expresses neither more nor less than the mere averment" of their "own unfounded sentiments"; that is, what in another person they "might be apt to call caprice."[58] Fourth, in the case of an "intelligible principle" independent of the dictate of utility, it has to be made out whether this other principle is "not despotical and hostile to all the rest of the human race," that is to say, whether it does not refer solely to the sentiment of the judging person instead of allowing the same privilege to "every man's sentiment."[59] If this is granted, and if the new principle is indeed not "despotical," we have to examine fifth:

---

[55] Bentham, *Introduction*, 1789, chap. 1, sect. 13, note.
[56] Bentham, *Introduction*, 1823, chap. 1, sect. 13, note.
[57] Bentham, *Introduction*, 1789, chap. 1, sect. 14.
[58] *Ibid.*, sect. 14, no. 3.   [59] *Ibid.*, sect. 14, no. 3-5.

whether it is not "anarchical," anarchical in such a way, that "even to the same man, the same thing, which is right to-day may not (without the least change in its nature) be wrong tomorrow? And whether the same thing is not right and wrong in the same place at the same time?"[60] In both the last cases, all argument would again be at an end. Sixth: if a moral principle adverse to that of utility has nevertheless some connection with the utility principle, it has to be shown that even then the strict opposition to the greatest happiness principle has already been "deserted"[61] in part. Seventh: If this is admitted, it has to be explained why the utility principle should be adopted in part, and why it should be adopted only in part and not any farther.[62] Obviously this survey of Bentham's on the different degrees of vague opposition to the utility principle is rather carelessly given. He speaks even of ten different attitudes, not only of six, though it is, at least in my view, difficult to find more points of distinction than I have tried to characterize. He also speaks of the principle of utility as the only right principle of judging and acting, while, of course, it can be understood at best as the only right principle of moral judging and moral acting. But he obviously felt that these remarks concerning such vague criticism of his doctrine were not of central importance. For in this kind of opposition, at best, misapplications or misinterpretations of the principle of utility are to be found, but no demonstration that this principle is wrong. If a man wishes "to move the earth . . . he must first find out another earth to stand upon."[63] Such another earth has been searched for in all types of moral philosophy built up on seemingly consistent "principles adverse to that of utility"; and therefore the second chapter of Bentham's *Introduction* is devoted to the discussion of the ethical value of such principles.

CRITICISM OF ANTI-HEDONISTIC PRINCIPLES

AT LEAST from one unpublished manuscript, the impression arises that Bentham, during the composition of his *Introduction*, wanted to give a larger analysis of untenable moral principles than he finally decided to give in his work.

[60] *Ibid.*, sect. 14, no. 6.
[62] *Ibid.*, sect. 14, no. 9.
[61] *Ibid.*, sect. 14, no. 7.
[63] *Ibid.*, sect. 13.

He writes about 1778: "Of principles adverse M. Beccaria has given a brief but interesting (recapitulation) catalogue of the false principles that have been set up in competition with the principle of utility: grounds of so many systems of false reasoning in politics and morals."

"A system of reasoning in politics and morals may be false in two ways, either by having nothing to do with the principle of utility or by making an erroneous application of it. By making an erroneous application of it I mean the making up false account of the profit and loss, the happiness and unhappiness which the rule or measure in question tends to introduce into the community" (in the margin: "exaggerating or unduly depreciating the value of this or that article on the one side or the other, in certain articles that have no place in the account or omitting articles that have").

(In red ink:) "Go on and show how those smashed by Beccaria as being false are so: by being practical: others such as Grotius' and Price's (?) by being fundamentally inapplicable."[64]

Obviously, not all the intentions hinted at in this program were carried out by Bentham. The reasons for that may have been various. First, with some of these topics, such as Grotius' inapplicable doctrine of "pretended natural rights," Bentham frequently dealt elsewhere, for example, in his "Pannomial Fragments . . . , written at sundry times,"[65] and, as we have seen in detail, in his *Comment on the Commentaries.*

Further, in the course of that draft-program of about 1778, still other principles adverse to that of utility appear which were soon recognized as not original principles but only subordinate applications of others. So Bentham speaks in that unpublished manuscript explicitly of a special "Principle of Vengeance"; but he himself then crossed out the word *vengeance* and left only the word *antipathy.*[66]

In the development of his thought, Bentham evidently wanted to concentrate more on the foundation and on the practical application of his own system than on polemic against other theories, as we can see from another unpublished manuscript where he says: "If it were not for the sake of laying a foundation for the practical maxims which occupy the latter (sequel) part of the work I should little have thought of

[64] *Bentham MS*, University College, London, Portfolio 27, Folder 8, sheet 48, p. 101, *unpublished.*
[65] Bentham, *Works*, 1843, vol. III, p. 219, 220a, 211a.
[66] Bentham, *Manuscript*, University College, London, Portfolio 27, Folder 8, sheet 49, p. 109, *unpublished.*

traversing a field so much marked with the wanderings of my predecessors."[67]

Moreover, in yet another unpublished manuscript, he put aside all polemics in the following instructive way: "Happiness is the end of every human action, of every human thought, how can it, or why ought [sic] to be otherwise? This is for those to say who sometimes seem to struggle to dispute it. If they are serious we will hear them in another place: at present by way of hypothesis [in the margin: it shall be an hypothesis] let us suppose it without dispute."[68]

This unpublished manuscript contains, in my view, one of the most important contributions made by Bentham to the development of a "science of ethics." It is most regrettable that, as far as I can see, this presentation of the utility principle has remained unknown down to the present day. If it had become known, it might have eliminated many of the stock objections to Benthamite utilitarianism. If the utility principle is presented in this way, as a scientific hypothesis, and by no means as a dogma, its validity, as we shall see later, can be demonstrated far more conclusively than the validity of any other ethical hypothesis or allegedly self-evident principle or value.

In any case, as we see in the *Introduction* itself, Bentham finally decided to classify all moral ends fully opposed to utility under one main head, namely, that of ascetic ends. Principles, however, which are only partly opposed to the greatest-happiness principle are treated collectively as applications of the principle of sympathy and antipathy. Thus we do not find in the *Introduction* an exhaustive discussion of the principles adverse to that of utility. Nevertheless, I think, it is a valuable analysis despite its brevity and inadequacy on minor points.

The Principle of Asceticism

By the principle of asceticism, Bentham means "that principle, which, like the principle of utility, approves or disapproves of any action, according to the tendency which it appears to have to augment or diminish the happiness of the party whose interest is in question; but in an inverse manner: approving of actions in as far as they tend to diminish his happiness; disapproving of them in as far as they tend to augment

---

[67] Bentham, *Manuscript*, University College, London, Portfolio 27, Folder 2, sheet 13, p. 1. Written about 1776, *unpublished*.

[68] Bentham, *Manuscript*, University College, London, Portfolio 27, Folder 2, sheet 15. Written about 1776, *unpublished*.

it";[69] and it is this principle of asceticism alone which can be regarded as "constantly opposed" to that of utility.[70] To this Bentham adds, first, that in truth this asceticism "never was, nor ever can be consistently pursued by any living creature"; for "let but one tenth part of the inhabitants of this earth pursue it consistently, and in a day's time they will have turned it into a hell."[71] This argument, however, is certainly not conclusive, at least not from the view which has to be taken by an immanent criticism of ascetic morality. For it is the avowed end of consistent asceticism (of which Bentham speaks here) to suffer and to endure a life of hell, or to lead to the death, the "mortification," of mankind.

The decisive points against the common use of the principle of asceticism are first: it is generally denied that thoroughgoing misery is morally valuable. The most rigorous Christian asceticism assures us that misery is valuable only if it is brought upon *us*; but it denies that misery is valuable if it is brought upon *others*. Second: on cardinal points asceticism itself thinks, without noticing it, in terms of utility.

Bentham next draws a rather rough distinction between the application of asceticism by moralists and that by religionists, the former usually "animated" by "hope of honour and reputation at the hands of men," by "hope, the aliment of philosophic pride," the latter filled with fear, "the fear of future punishment at the hands of a splenetic and revengeful Deity."[72] Of these two parties he finds the moralists commonly less consistent in practice, but wiser than the religionists are. For "the philosophical party have hardly gone farther than the making pain a matter of indifference. It is no evil they have said"[73] and it can, therefore, be approved, but it need not be approved. And with regard to pleasure "they have discarded only what they called the gross; that is, such as are organical"; yet the "refined" pleasure is even magnified by them; they, however, carefully change its name, trying thus to "cleanse" it "from the sordes of its impure original"[73] and call it anything but pleasure. They call it the honorable, the glorious, the reputable, the becoming, the honestum, the decorum. But, as Bentham in his *Comment on the Commentaries* has already tried to show, the terms *honestum, decorum* and the like are either meaningless words or they mean one or other pleasurable end. Moreover, when ascetic philosophers[74] an-

[69] Bentham, *Introduction*, 1789, chap. II, sect. 3.
[70] *Ibid.*, sect. 2.   [71] *Ibid.*, sect. 10.
[72] *Ibid.*, sect. 5.   [73] *Ibid.*, sect. 6.
[74] Obviously Bentham is thinking here of Stoics and above all of Cicero whom

nounce that pain is neither evil nor good, they once more abandon the strict principle of asceticism. For, again under "blanket terms," this concession opens the way to a practically unlimited application of the greatest-happiness principle. Here, clearly, is no refutation of the utility principle.

Much more consistent adherents of the principle of asceticism are, according to Bentham, the religious ascetics. They indeed "have frequently gone so far as to make it a matter of merit and of duty to court pain."[75] The word *ascetic* itself is derived from the Greek word signifying exercise, and the exercises of Christian monks frequently consisted in "contrivances they had for tormenting themselves."[76] In this philosophy of asceticism Bentham tries to unearth a completely illogical paradox, as Spinoza had once done before him.

Spinoza had already spoken of the idea of an "envious God" who takes offense at human joy and enjoys human misery.[77] Such a "perverse" idea of God is in fact not infrequently dominant in the religious thought of mankind. Even among atheistic pessimists comparatively similar ideas of the "Weltwesen" are to be found, for instance in Schopenhauer's, E. v. Hartmann's, Mainländer's speculations about the "Weltwille" which continually produces the sufferings of individual life and prevents its pleasure. Yet here contradictions are absent in so far as the "Weltwille" is not said to be good and the "Weltverneinung" of this secular asceticism stands in the service of salvation, that is, not of pain but of exemption from pain. This atheistic asceticism does not aspire, therefore, to be consistent asceticism but is latent hedonism. As to theistic ascetics, however, the illogical paradox which Spinoza and Bentham have in mind is this: the God of these ascetics is confessedly a God who "loves to see us torment ourselves" merely for the sake of self-torture and yet is believed to be "a being of infinite benevolence."[78] Such an idea of God certainly contains a notorious contradiction in itself.

---

he disliked from the time of his College life. See Bentham, *Deontology*, 1834, vol. I, p. 311.

[75] Bentham, *Introduction*, 1789, chap. II, sect. 6.

[76] *Ibid.*, chap. II, sect. 2, note.

[77] See Spinoza, *Ethica*, pars IV, propositio 45, corollarium II, scholium: "Nihil profecto nisi torva et tristis superstitio delectari prohibet. Nam qui magis decet famem et sitim extinguere, quam melancholiam expellere? Mea haec est ratio, et sic animum induxi meum. Nullum numen, nec alius, nisi invidus, mea impotentia et incommodo delectatur, nec nobis lacrimas, singultus, metum, et alia hujusmodi quae animi impotentis sunt signa, virtuti ducit." In all probability, however, Bentham never read Spinoza's *Ethica*.

[78] Bentham, *Introduction*, 1789, chap. II, sect. 2, note.

Apart from this there is, according to Bentham, another more common objection to asceticism. Monks themselves have confessed that by their self-tortures they wished "to ingratiate themselves with the Deity"; for they are convinced that "for every grain of pain it costs us now we are to have a hundred grains of pleasure by and by . . . in a life to come."[78] If this is the reason for the adoption of the principle of asceticism, then, of course, this type of asceticism is no consistent asceticism at all. For then, not the love of pain, but the common strife for more happiness is the decisive motive of action. Under these circumstances, however, asceticism fulfills only the command of hedonism: it prefers a greater sum of happiness in the future to a smaller sum in the present life. The principle of asceticism is, in this case, completely surrendered in favor of the utility principle.

UTILITARIANISM AND THE SELF-TORMENTOR

Far more instructive is the third argument which Bentham uses against radical asceticism: this is a line of analysis which, in the middle of the nineteenth century, was particularly pursued by Ludwig Feuerbach,[79] but already clearly marked out by Bentham in one of the accounts he gave of the course of his thought at the time between the publication of his *Fragment on Government* and his *Introduction*. Here we find the principle of asceticism attacked in an even more fundamental way by a psychological analysis of the very prototype of its votaries: the self-tormentor.

As Bentham points out, even the example of Peregrinus Proteus, "the man whom Lucian saw burning himself alive, though not altogether without reluctance, in the eyes of an admiring multitude, and without any anticipation of hereafter"—even this example offers no exception in favor of the possibility of consistent asceticism. "It was interest, self-regarding interest, that set fire to this so extraordinary a funeral pile. Yes; and interest there is in every human breast for every *motive*, for every desire, for every pain and pleasure. Be it ever so feeble, no pain or pleasure but, under favourable circumstances, as Aaron's serpent swallowed up all other serpents, is capable of swallowing up all other pains and pleasures . . . : no pain, no pleasure so weak, but, under fa-

---

[79] See L. Feuerbach, *Sämtliche Werke*, 1903-1911, ed. by W. Bolin and F. Jodl, Band x, 1911, e.g. pp. 244 ff: "Der heilige Xaver . . . trank . . . sogar den Eiter aus . . . venerischen Geschwüren." But he felt: "Ich werde ewig glücklich sein." Cf. *Heiliges Tag-Buch* von P. Joh. St. Grosez S. J., deutsch von P. B. Vogl, 1755, 1. Theil, S. 85.

vourable circumstances, may have magnitude enough in the mind to eclipse all other pains, as well as all other pleasures; strength enough to close the eyelids of the mind against all other pains, as well as all other pleasures. The pleasure of reputation had, for some time, obtained exclusive possession of the mind of Proteus: it had shut the doors, not only against all future contingent pleasures, but against the pain of burning; or to speak more properly, of suffocation."[80] Indeed, if even the phenomenon of the self-tormentor can and must be explained in this way, then the ultimate stronghold of asceticism is in the hands of its opponent, the utility principle, and the impossibility of radical asceticism is best confirmed by this indirect proof.

G. K. Chesterton holds that utilitarianism is talking nonsense and distending the meaning of the word selfishness, when it calls a man self-indulgent who wants to be burned at the stake.[81] According to Chesterton, all moral meanings would cease if even the martyr and the self-tormentor were called pleasure seekers, as is done by consistent utilitarianism.

In fact, from the standpoint of a foreground psychology, it may seem nonsense—and even provocative nonsense—to call the self-tormentor ultimately self-indulgent. For a deeper psychological and ethical analysis this is by no means the case. Unamuno even goes so far as to think not only individuals but the whole Spanish nation feels that "our heaven is martyrdom."[82] And in any case, all our understanding of the human

[80] Bentham, *Works*, 1843, part XIX, p. 80b. That Peregrinus Proteus' motives cannot have been ascetic, is granted also in Friedrich Schiller's "Über das Pathetische," *Werke*, ed. by Ludwig Bellermann, Band VIII, 1895, S. 141 f, although Schiller's moral judgment of Peregrinus Proteus differs completely from that of Bentham.

[81] See W. M. Urban, *Fundamentals of Ethics*, 1930, p. 79 f, where Urban agrees with Chesterton.

[82] See Miguel de Unamuno, "El Cristo Español" in *Ensayos*, 1942, tome II, p. 318: "Nuestro cielo es el martirio mismo." Perhaps the most thorough investigation of Chesterton's thesis has been undertaken by Professor E. S. Brightman in his *Moral Laws*, 1933, pp. 70 f. Brightman admits—in opposition to Chesterton and in line with Bentham's statements—that it is, of course, not required to presuppose in the martyr a striving for a special entity called pleasure. All that is required for the maintenance of Bentham's so-called "psychological hedonism" is the "awareness of pleasure accompanying all our choices" or, perhaps it were better to say, the conscious or subconscious awareness of some hedonically attractive color in our choices, however conditioned and qualified this attraction may be. Professor Brightman also grants that pleasure may be considered as our subconscious motive. But in the end, he holds, like Chesterton, that "some choices are so painful that [it] . . . is questionable" whether "an awareness of pleasure accompanies all our choices" and he asserts that "we cannot be held responsible

soul would cease, if, in any voluntary secular or religious suffering or self-torture, no strife for an ultimately higher pleasure were involved. Bentham obviously had this alone in view; and apart from that, it certainly was his—as well as Unamuno's—intention to alter to a large extent those moral meanings which are commonly regarded as the only intelligible ones.

ASCETICISM IN POLITICS

Applied to the business of government, the principle of asceticism is doubtless "carried to much less length" than when applied in the sphere of private conduct. Thus, it is far easier for Bentham to justify his denial of the possibility of consistent asceticism in the political province than in its proper domain, private life. Where ascetic measures of governments are in use, as in the Spartan regime, they can and should be explained as dictated ultimately by the supreme command of utility, though they have perhaps to be considered as being highly "precipitate and perverse applications" of the utility principle; "whatever merit a man may have thought there would be in making himself miserable, no such notion seems ever to have occurred to any of them, that it may be a merit, much less a duty, to make others miserable."[83] Even in holy wars and the persecutions for religion, it is not the principle of asceticism which has been applied politically; the infliction of misery is in all such cases confined to persons who are thought to be infidels, heretics, or criminals, and it is never extended to fellow-sectarians as long as they are fellow-believers. All this production of misery falls, therefore, within the limits of the application, or better, of the misapplication of the utility principle. But it has nothing to do with asceticism. Again, governmental measures which ultimately lead to the sapping of the sources of national wealth, to emigration of the population can, of course, not be explained as dictates of the principle of asceticism; but in common with

---

for the subconscious, except in so far as it is influenced by conscious choice." Yet neither of these objections seems to me to shatter Bentham's position. Nor is this the case with regard to Professor Brightman's final statement that Bentham's "psychological hedonism" may be said to boil down to the truism that "everyone desires what he desires," as Georg Simmel, F. H. Bradley and others had already argued. If it can be denied or questioned that some of our painful choices are accompanied by the awareness of pleasure, then, it seems to me, Bentham's contradictory statement that all our choices are accompanied by some tone of hedonic attractiveness cannot be termed a truism.

[83] Bentham, *Introduction*, 1789, chap. ii, sect. 8.

the punishment for the breach of celibacy and for similar "crimes," they are obviously misappropriations of the dictate of utility.

Asceticism generally requires that we do harm only to ourselves, but not to others; and this again shows that asceticism is not capable of any all-out application. "For a man to give himself a certain number of stripes" was thought to be "meritorious: but to give the same number of stripes to another man, not consenting, would have been a sin. We read of Saints who . . . have voluntarily yielded themselves a prey to vermin: but though many persons of this class have wielded the reins of Empire, we read of none who have set themselves to work, and made laws on purpose, with the view of stocking the body politic with the breed of highwaymen, housebreakers, or incendiaries"; yet if "misery were a thing so desirable, it would not matter much whether it were brought by each man upon himself, or by one man upon another."[84] This argument also is, I think, conclusive, especially from the standpoint of Bentham's ethics which, for definite reasons, finds the ethical essence of an act inextricably bound up with the consequences of this act, not with its motives. However, Bentham's objections to asceticism are of interest also to the ethics of motives. As a matter of fact, arguments similar to those of Bentham appear, e.g. in Herder's ethics of motives, in his opposition to Kant's ethical rigorism. Certainly, Herder's as well as Bentham's arguments are still in need of much further development and refinement. But, so far, hedonism has perhaps nowhere been supported more thoroughly by a criticism of its opponents than by Bentham.

The Principle of Sympathy and Antipathy

All attempts to follow strictly non-utilitarian principles serve but to point to utility as the sole end of action. The psychological root of asceticism itself is but utility misunderstood or misapplied; or, as Bentham puts this, asceticism is in the main and originally a "reverie of . . . hasty speculators"; there are "hasty speculators, who having perceived, or fancied, that certain pleasures, when reaped in certain circumstances, have, at the long run, been attended with pains more than equivalent to them, took occasion to quarrel with every thing that offered itself under the name of pleasure. Having then got thus far, and having forgot the point which they set out on, they pushed on, and went so much further as to think it meritorious to fall in love with pain."[85] But to fall constantly in love with pain without having as counterbalance a greater

[84] *Ibid.*, sect. 8.   [85] *Ibid.*, sect. 9.

love of pleasure is impossible, even if the man experiencing such a mixture of feelings should never become aware of the complications of his emotional make up.

Thus, from whatever angle the analysis of asceticism is approached, it leads to the justification of hedonism and, naturally, we cannot expect a different result from an analysis of theories far less adverse to utilitarianism. All the principles of such theories not strictly opposed to hedonism are comprised by Bentham under the title "principle of sympathy and antipathy." "By the principle of sympathy and antipathy I mean that principle which approves or disapproves of certain actions, not on account of their tending to augment the happiness, nor yet on account of their tending to diminish the happiness of the party whose interest is in question, but merely because a man finds himself disposed to approve or disapprove of them: holding up that approbation or disapprobation as a sufficient reason for itself, and disclaiming the necessity of looking out for any extrinsic ground."[86] In a note first printed in 1789, Bentham adds that on the ground of some of its applications the principle of sympathy and antipathy should rather have been styled "the principle of caprice," especially when it is occupied with rights and not with obligations of men. Also, the name "phantastic principle" is here suggested, since sympathy and antipathy are solely "affections of the *sensible* faculty," and affections of imagination, phantastic affections, also play their part in the application of the general principle in question.

Further, as to imagination, Bentham adds that indeed "the goddess" of the imaginative "faculty of harmony has exercised more influence, however latent, over the dispensations of Themis, than her most diligent historiographers, or even her most passionate panegyrists, seem to have been aware of. . . . Every one knows, that measured numbers were the language of the infancy of law: none seem to have observed with what imperious sway they have governed her maturer age. In English jurisprudence in particular, the connection betwixt law and music, however less perceived than in Spartan legislation, is not perhaps less real nor less close. The music of the Office, though not of the same kind, is not less musical in its kind, than the music of the theatre; that which hardens the heart, than that which softens it."[87] In order to illustrate

[86] *Ibid.*, sect. 11.

[87] *Ibid.*, chap. 11, sect. 11, note of January 1789. As to the decisive influence which poetry has had on the development of moral and juristic ideas see, in contemporary literature e.g. E. Cassirer's *Axel Hägerström*, Göteborgs Högskolas Arsskrift, XLV, 1939, pp. 84 ff, on "Recht und Mythos" and further literature mentioned there.

the pernicious influence which poetry, harmony of language, has very often exercised upon moral maxims, Bentham analyzes, among other examples, the famous maxim *Fiat justitia, ruat coelum*, a maxim which Hegel analyzes in a similar way in his *Grundlinien der Philosophie des Rechts*, 1821. As did Hegel later, surely independently, Bentham pointed out that this maxim is unfortunately "as full of extravagance" and of indefensible extravagance "as of harmony" of language.[88]

But be this as it may, Bentham insists that all these principles, the principle of caprice, the phantastic principle or the principle of sympathy and antipathy represent "rather a principle in name than in reality," than an objective "standard for itself"; according to him, apart from the principles of utility and asceticism, any other principle on which moral systems are built up is in truth a "negation of all principle"; all such principles must in the last resort refer to the moralist's "internal sentiments"[89] of sympathy and antipathy, of caprice, although the phrases used in these systems may differ widely.

The principles of asceticism and of utility alone appeal to a palpable "external standard"[90] of right and wrong in morals, namely, to pleasure and pain. All the others try to work without it and take counsel only of "the fine feeling of the soul . . . not . . . overborne and tyrannized by the harsh and rugged dictates"[91] of "external" experiences of pain and pleasure. But Bentham insists that these "fine feelings of the soul" have to be recognized as vague, and that they evidently lead back to arbitrary sympathies and antipathies. It is only the terminology of this

[88] *Op. cit.*, chap. II, sect. II, note of January 1789. Compare Hegel, *Werke* (1833), vol. VIII, §136, §130 (*Grundlinien der Philosophie des Rechts*, ed. by Georg Lasson, 1911, pp. 319, 109): "Man kann von der Pflicht" und dem Recht "sehr erhaben sprechen, und dieses Reden" macht "das Herz weit"; aber "das Recht . . . ist . . . nicht das Gute ohne das Wohl (fiat justitia soll nicht pereat mundus zur Folge haben)." Compare Bentham, *The Limits of Jurisprudence Defined*, ed. by Everett, 1945, p. 284: "Though heaven were wrecked, let justice be adhered to. Heaven may always be preserved." Compare Hegel: "Ein schlechtes Recht ist es, wobei die Welt zu Grunde geht." This last sentence is to be found in the especially valuable lecture notes taken by Heinrich Gustav Hotho, the editor of Hegel's lectures on aesthetics in the edition of Hegel's works, 1832 ff, who attended Hegel's lecture on "Grundlinien der Philosophie des Rechts" in the winter of 1822-23.

The manuscript of these lecture notes was in the possession of the late Dr. Heinrich Levy, Woodbrooke College, Birmingham, England and has not been published hitherto. I am much indebted to the late Heinrich Levy for having permitted me to quote this peculiarly characteristic Hegel passage.

[89] Bentham, *Introduction*, 1789, chap. II, sect. 12.

[90] *Ibid.*, chap. II, sect. 14.

[91] Bentham, *Introduction*, chap. II, sect. 13.

ethics of "fine feelings" which generally obscures this fact. There exists an extraordinary "variety of phrases" among these moralists meant to conceal from the world, and if possible from themselves, this very general pretended "self-sufficiency."[92] Bentham, therefore, goes through a long list of such ethical terms and tries to show in every case, in a few words, why such "phrases" do not offer any really fundamental basis for moral judgment.

MORAL SENSE, COMMON SENSE, THE UNDERSTANDING IN MORALS

First, there is presupposed by many moralists, such as Shaftesbury and Hutcheson, the existence of a so-called moral sense which is said to be capable of telling us what is ethically right.[93] In truth, this is, according to Bentham, a simple surrender of all moral decisions to the arbitrary power of individual sympathy and antipathy.[94] Throughout the centuries it becomes more and more manifest that the moral sense of different moralists leads in decisive concrete questions to quite different or opposite results. Thus, in most disputed moral problems, we lose all firm ground in basing our valuations on the moral sense of the individual, since the voice of the moral sense enunciates different convictions in different individuals.

This is a very summary but, I think, not an unfair criticism of the weakness of all moral sense doctrines. If, nevertheless, this analysis of Bentham makes no impression on his opponents, it is because representatives of the moral sense theories practically all reject an ethics of consequences, and urge the major ethical relevance of motives, human dispositions, of duty and moral rightness, independent of beneficial consequences. Unfortunately, it is only later that Bentham gives his very considered reasons for rejecting this part of the moral sense theories.

On lines fundamentally similar to those on which he criticizes the moral sense, Bentham rejects the theory of "common sense" in morals. For this theory is, so to speak, but a kind of popular edition of Shaftesbury's more aristocratic doctrine of the moral sense. Thomas Reid and James Beattie presuppose the same moral sense as do Shaftesbury and Hutcheson.[95] They offer it only in a more common costume "leaving

---

[92] *Ibid.*, sect. 14, note.

[93] Bentham himself does not mention any moralists in this and the following analyses, though he obviously has specific names in mind.

[94] Bentham, *Introduction*, 1789, chap. II, sect. 14, note, no. 1.

[95] Actually Thomas Reid speaks of our moral faculty and of the moral sense as well as of common sense in morals, see T. Reid, *Essays on the Active Powers*

out" the word *moral*, and "putting in *common*, in the room of it"; but the matter remains the same.

As Bentham good-humoredly adds, at first sight the common sense seems to be better than the moral one. "For a moral sense, being a new thing, a man may feel about him a good while without being able to find it out: but common sense is as old as the creation; and there is no man but would be ashamed to be thought not to have as much of it as his neighbours." Further, in another shrewd and amusing psychological observation, Bentham says that the assumption of common sense in morals "lessens" not only the grudge of the democrat against the pre-supposition of the aristocratic moral sense, but it lessens also the individual responsibility for the moral judgment. "For when a man gets up upon this ground, in order to anathematize those who differ from him, it is not by a *sic volo sic jubeo*, but by a *velitis jubeatis*."[96] Moralists of this type, that is, are convinced that "a sense of some kind or other" which they call common sense "is possessed by all mankind."[96] But the inherent difficulty is again this: if these champions of common sense in morals realize that many other moralists, by reason of their common sense, advocate exactly opposite moral ideas, all they can do is to assure us that the common sense of their opponents has to be "struck out of the account as not worth taking."[97] Thus, paradoxically, the belief in so-

---

of Man (this work appeared only one year before Bentham's *Introduction*, in 1788), p. 238 (ed. Hamilton, p. 588a): "Our moral faculty may, I think, without impropriety be called the Moral Sense"; compare p. 236 f, essay III, chap. VI. Reid states with emphasis that he agrees with Shaftesbury and Hutcheson on this point.

As to the subject matter proper cf. James Beattie, *An Essay on the Nature and Immutability of Truth in Opposition to Sophistry and Scepticism*, 1820 (first published in 1770), e.g. p. 151: "Common sense declares, that a being possessed of perfect knowledge can no more entertain such a sentiment . . . that . . . cruelty, injustice, and ingratitude are worthy of reward and praise . . . than I with my eyes open can just now avoid seeing the light."

[96] Bentham, *Introduction*, 1789, chap. II, sect. 14, note.

[97] Thomas Reid: *Essays on the Active Powers of Man*, 1788, p. 370, Essay V, Chap. I, seems to hint that all differences "about a first principle" in morals can be removed by an "appeal . . . to . . . Common Sense." On the other hand Reid admits that "there may be, and there are, beings who have not the faculty of conceiving moral truth." Nevertheless Reid thinks, certainly without justification, that this fact presents no greater difficulty in morals than in mathematics; "and he declares himself satisfied with the firm belief that no defect, no error of understanding, can make what is true to be false" (Essays on the Active Powers of Man, 1788, pp. 492 f, Essay V, chap. VII). James Beattie, *An Essay on the Nature and Immutability of Truth*, 1820 (first ed. 1770), p. 151, says even more explicitly: "If a created being were to think that virtue which we think vice, and

called common sense in morals cannot secure the belief in common, universally valid truths.

Third, we are in no better situation, if we replace the moral sense or the common sense by the understanding. In his *Review of the Principal Questions in Morals* reprinted and newly appreciated by Oxford moralists in 1948, Richard Price had taught that the standard of moral right and wrong is simply given by our understanding and its intuition of truth.[98] According to Bentham, no such phrases enable us to get beyond the principle of sympathy and antipathy.

For Price cannot deny that in morals other men's understanding often arrives at conclusions different from his; and, as we may add, differences of judgment in ethics are more disconcerting than in physics, since—in contrast to the physicists—for moralists such as Price no reference to observable facts is available in their ethical reasoning. When, thus, the understanding leads men to quite opposite moral convictions, it is of course futile for ethicists like Price to say of their opponents: "so much the worse for them, it is a sure sign they are either defective or corrupt."[99]

---

that vice which we think virtue, what would be our notions of his intelligence? Should we not, without hesitation, pronounce him irrational, and his opinion an absurdity? The absurdity indeed is conceivable, and may be expressed in words that imply no contradiction; but that any being should think in this manner, and yet not think wrong, is to us as perfectly inconceivable, as that the same thing should be both true and false." What James Beatty thought "inconceivable" is, according to Charles L. Stevenson, *Ethics and Language*, 1944, p. 267, the specific character of ethical judgments. They "can be true or false."

Bentham's criticism of Reid's and Beattie's theories is to be found in his *Introduction*, 1789, chap. ii, sect. xiv, note.

[98] See R. Price, *A Review of the Principal Questions in Morals*, 1787 (the first edition of this work appeared in 1757, the latest in 1948, with a comment by D. Daiches Raphael, a former pupil of E. F. Carritt) e.g. p. 58: "We have a power immediately perceiving right and wrong . . . this power is the Understanding"; p. 59: "It is undeniable that many of our ideas are derived from our *Intuition* of truth, or the discernment of the natures of things by the understanding. This therefore *may* be the source of our moral ideas"; pp. 66 f: "Our ideas of right and wrong belong to the understanding, and denote real characters of actions"; p. 69: "The more we enquire, the more indisputable, I imagine, it will appear to us, that we express necessary truth, when we say of some actions, they are right; and of others, they are wrong."

[99] See R. Price, *A Review of the Principal Questions in Morals*, 1787, e.g. p. 463: "There is no object in nature so monstrous as a reasonable being . . . living in contradiction to the remonstrances of his understanding . . . and opposing himself to the obligations of truth and righteousness"; p. 373 f: "Wickedness, . . . a defective regard to virtue . . . is the violent and unnatural state of the mind;

Such a dictatorial pronouncement is nothing but a manifestation of subjective sympathies and antipathies. It certainly cannot serve as a principle of objective ethical inquiry.

FITNESS IN SAMUEL CLARKE'S AND C. D. BROAD'S ETHICS

Fourth and fifth, Samuel Clarke's assumptions of a special "Fitness of Things" and of an eternal, immutable "rule of right"[100] promise us, it is true, an objective, universally valid criterion in ethics; but they again give evidence only of the individual, subjective "sentiments,"[101] the individual likes and dislikes[102] of the moralists who apply such principles.

As the concept of *fitness* or *fittingness* is still used in the discussion of utilitarian ethics by H. Sidgwick and, particularly, by Professor C. D. Broad and Professor A. C. Ewing,[103] I should like to air briefly my doubts as to whether the concept of fittingness has played a happy role

---

the deposition of the reason." Bentham criticizes Price in his *Introduction*, 1789, chap. II, sect. 14, note, no. 3.

[100] See Samuel Clarke, *A Discourse Concerning the Unchangeable Obligations of Natural Religion and the Truth and Certainty of the Christian Revelation*, 1724, e.g. p. 83: We are "forced to deduce" the "obligation of these Things" (such as the principle that "Compacts ought to be faithfully performed, and Obedience to be duly paid to civil powers") "intirely from the eternal Reason and Fitness of the Things themselves antecedent to, independent upon, and unalterable by all Humane Constitutions whatsoever"; p. 95: "The nature indeed and Relations, the Proportions and Disproportions, the Fitnesses and Unfitnesses of Things are eternal and in themselves absolutely unalterable. . . . At the same time . . . all such moral Obligations as are the result of the necessary Proportions and Relations of things, are likewise His positive Will and Command"; pp. 50, 65: "The rule of Right," the "eternal Rule of Equity . . . is That right Reason . . . which can neither be wholly abrogated nor repealed in any part of it."
Samuel Clarke speaks also explicitly of the perversity of the attempts at denying the validity of his eternal rule of right and the fittingness of things in the following way: " 'Tis the greatest Absurdity and Perverseness in the World for Creatures indued with Reason to attempt to break through and transgress this necessary Order and Dependency of things" (*A Discourse Concerning the Unchangeable Obligations of Natural Religion*, 1724, p. 52). As to Bentham's criticism of Clarke see *Introduction*, 1789, chap. II, sect. 14, notes 4 and 5.
[101] Bentham, *Introduction*, 1789, chap. II, sect. 14, note 4.
[102] *Ibid.*, sect. 14, note 5.
[103] A. C. Ewing, *The Definition of Good*, 1947, p. 132, states that he "borrowed" the term "fittingness" from Broad. He, too, regards "fittingness" as a basic moral concept and—differing to some extent from Ross and Broad—he even holds (*ibid.*, p. 190) that "it is fittingness which we must consider in discussing the ultimate reasons which put us under a moral obligation to do some things rather than others." It seems to me, therefore, that my criticism of Broad which follows in the text can, with some modification, be extended to Ewing's use of the term "fittingness."

in ethical analysis. It seems to me that this concept is not only ambiguous in Samuel Clarke, as Bentham noticed, but that it is still ambiguous in its present usage.

Fitness or fittingness as such, fittingness in general, means every kind of aptitude or adequacy of something to something else. Professor Broad, however, defines fittingness or unfittingness as "a direct ethical relation between an action or emotion and the total course of events in which it takes place."[104] From this it follows that he cannot have in mind the ethically indifferent sense of the term fittingness; and so we have to find out first what meaning he attributes to his term.

Professor Broad says: "It is quite easy to give examples. If I am asked a certain question and answer it in a certain way I may be answering that question truly but my answer may lead to subsequent false inferences. It might then be said that this answer was fitting to the initial phase, but was unfitting to subsequent phases in the course of events as modified by it. It would then become a question whether a true answer, or a lie, or silence was a most fitting action on the whole, given the initial phase."[104] Now I think it is by no means easy to see whether in these examples the term "fittingness" is used in a purely ethical sense, or whether it expresses, as the term does according to the Oxford Dictionary, a kind of mixture between neutral and ethical aptitude.[105] But although this is not easy to determine, it seems to me evident that in both cases the introduction of the term fittingness does not clear up the ethical issues in question; rather, it helps to confuse them.

(A). If we take the term in its strictly ethical sense, we come to this result: According to Professor Broad, it is possible to believe that there exists "a direct relation" of ethical fittingness between telling a lie and a situation in which right inferences are likely to be drawn from this lie, provided that from the corresponding true answer false inferences would have been drawn. In passing, it might be noted that to call this "a direct ethical relation" is giving a somewhat strained meaning to the concept of *direct*. But apart from this, if we were capable of ascertaining the ethical character of this relation by intuition, I must say, according to my knowledge of the history of ethics, that this would mean a simplification of ethical problems in comparison with which the most

[104] C. D. Broad, *Five Types of Ethical Theory*, 1930, p. 219.
[105] *A New English Dictionary on Historical Principles*, Oxford, 1901, vol. IV, gives only very few examples illustrating the *ethical* meaning of "fitting" and "fittingness" (see, above all, the quotation from Josiah Shute, *Sarah and Hagar*, 1649); the majority of the examples demonstrate the use of the term in its neutral sense.

naïve types of ethical intuitionism are harmless. Utilitarians go so far as to say that intuitionism over-simplifies by maintaining that a true answer is ethically fit to the initial phase of every course of events. But to say that, by intuition, we even know that a lie is ethically fit to a certain phase of events, is, indeed, an over-simplification of the most controversial problems of ethics which cannot be repaired by any of the later complicated inferences which Professor Broad draws from this first intuited statement.

Yet, granted for argument's sake that it were legitimate to cut the Gordian knot at the beginning, granted it were justified to say that, according to a direct intuition, a lie is ethically fitting to a certain phase of events—what does this insight teach us with regard to the main problem of ethics, the question of moral rightness?

Professor Broad says: "It seems to me that the rightness or wrongness of an action in a given initial situation is a function of its fittingness in that situation and its utility in that situation."[106] We have to estimate "total rightness from total fittingness and total utility."[107] And Professor Broad grants that, therefore, "the intuitionist will have to moderate his claims very greatly. He will be confined to statements about *tendencies* to be right and *tendencies* to be wrong" and about "strong tendencies" to be right or wrong.[107] Doubtless, as Professor Broad admits himself, this is a very limited knowledge.

But the point is: do we really need the introduction of the term "ethical fittingness" in order to obtain these modest results? If this is all we can say about moral rightness, I think it evident that we can do without any reference to ethical fittingness. Professor Broad does not tell us how to estimate total rightness from total fittingness and total utility; and in fact, it seems hopeless to expect satisfactory information from any ethical intuitionism on this point. Professor Broad teaches us to speak only of *tendencies* to be right or wrong, and of strong tendencies to be right or wrong, but not of rightness itself. Yet from these completely vague instructions, it is certainly justifiable to call the tendency of an act right as well as wrong, whenever some or even one of its consequences are useful or not useful, no matter whether this act is ethically fitting for all or some or none of its consequences. If, however, *all* consequences of an act are useful, then we are certainly permitted to say that this act has a *strong* tendency to be right, although

---

[106] C. D. Broad, *Five Types of Ethical Theory*, 1930, p. 221.
[107] *Ibid.*, p. 222.

197

this act were ethically unfitting even for all its consequences;[108] and, vice versa, if *all* consequences of an act are mischievous, then this act has a *strong* tendency to be wrong, even if the act is ethically fitting for all aspects of all phases of its consequences. That is to say, the concept of ethical fittingness is nowhere needed in these reflections.

In other words, these statements on moral rightness are so indeterminate that any restrained utilitarianism is in a position to give precisely the same amount of information; and the reference to ethical fittingness is then a redundant complication. It is true that in his remarks on ethical fittingness Professor Broad gives far more direct instruction than utilitarians are able to give. But then, he limits the validity of this teaching so decisively that, in the upshot, the doctrine of ethical fittingness loses its whole ethical relevance; and this, apart from our general reflections, may also be illustrated by one example given by Professor Broad.[109]

If we compare the whole of his doctrine on moral rightness with certain types of vague utilitarianism or ethical intuitionism, we may say: Professor Broad's theory starts with very far-reaching (yet highly questionable) statements about ethical fittingness. But, just in time, he waters down its daring (yet innocuous) propositions to such an extent that, in the end, he safely arrives at the same conclusions as any eclectic utilitarianism or intuitionism does *without* his roundabout routes. This result, however, is so perplexing that I find it difficult to assume such an acute thinker as Professor Broad did actually think of *ethical* fittingness in these analyses.

(B). Although, of course, I cannot prove this, I am inclined to suppose that according to customary speech he had in mind a kind of *combination* of ethically neutral fittingness and ethical fittingness. But, unfortunately, even then I think that his concept of fittingness can be

[108] In one of his examples, it is true, Professor Broad gives up his main principle and speaks not only of tendencies of acts to be right but of rightness itself, when he says "that a sane person judges it right, though regrettable, to do an act which is unfitting if this be the only means open to him of avoiding a course of events which from their qualities and their mutual relations would be intrinsically very evil" (see C. D. Broad, *Five Types of Ethical Theory*, 1930, p. 221 f). But I do not wish to lay weight on this inconsistency, although, even if Professor Broad's statement is isolated from his main line of thought, no reason is to be found for it. Moreover that example of Professor Broad's reveals the complete superfluity of the term *ethical fittingness*. If even an act, which is entirely unfit, is nevertheless morally right, provided that it is not mischievous, then at least in this case utility or intrinsic goodness is the sole criterion of moral rightness; and ethical fittingness is no factor at all in this estimate of rightness.

[109] See the example analyzed in the previous note.

clearly seen as superfluous and even as misleading in moral philosophy.

Illustrating this by Professor Broad's examples, we have to say: Certainly it is undeniable that sometimes silence or a lie may fit the purpose of avoiding false inferences, which otherwise would have been drawn from a true answer; and it is further undeniable that a true answer fits in general the purpose of transmitting truth. Both these statements, however, concern simple facts free from any ethical valuation or other ethical meaning. How, then, do they receive the ethical relevance they are said to possess?

There is obviously presupposed the validity of the premise that the transmission of truth is moral. But, unfortunately, even this premise tacitly brought in is not sufficient to allow us to decide, or even to discuss, "the question" of *ethical* fitness with regard to the subsequent phases of the above mentioned course of events. Naturally, we are allowed to discuss the ethically indifferent question whether under certain circumstances a lie may prevent the drawing of false inferences, or whether this will be unlikely. But, according to its very nature, no debate of this kind can give us any instruction about the *ethical* fittingness of the lie in question, particularly if ethical fittingness is distinguished from ethical usefulness as is done here.

If we want to debate the ethical fittingness of a lie to a certain situation, we deal with something besides ethically neutral questions. Above all, we have to raise and to solve the following very different problems: Is it a moral action to prevent false inferences at all costs, even at the cost of a lie? Are such lies generally moral? Or if not, which of them are ethically justifiable? Or must we remain skeptics on all these points? Or lastly, is it the case that no general and no specified rules concerning moral rightness are available?—which Professor Broad suggests as the wisest and the truly scientific conclusion.[110] Whatever we may answer here, these highly controversial problems have to be solved first, independently of the answer to the question as to whether a lie can actually prevent a false inference in a certain phase of a course of events. Only after having answered both these types of questions, can we speak of the ethical fittingness of a lie to a certain stage in a course of events.

But Professor Broad, at best, simplifies the problem of ethical fittingness by limiting it in fact to a discussion of ethically neutral fitness, and

[110] See C. D. Broad, *Five Types of Ethical Theory*, 1930, p. 222. "It is very doubtful whether any general rules can be given for balancing one kind of fittingness against another or for balancing fittingness on the whole against utility on the whole" and for estimating moral rightness by the latter procedure.

by hoping that this kind of fitness, quite independent of moral rightness and usefulness, possesses nevertheless an original "direct" ethical meaning. The truth, however, is that the ethically neutral sense of fitness as such can never receive an ethical meaning in such deductions except by a fallacy.

We are in no way entitled to speak of the *ethical* fittingness of a lie to the prevention of false inferences from a true answer, before we have reached a conclusion concerning the moral rightness of that lie—even if it were a skeptical conclusion. And after having arrived at such a conclusion, we do not need to speak about mere fittingness of that lie. For then not only the moral *fittingness* of this lie is justified but its total morality.

Professor Broad warns the moralist against identifying ethical fitness with ethical rightness. But as we can see in his example, his speaking of the ethical fitness of a lie, apart from the moral rightness of this lie, simply means the neglect of the essential ethical problem which is here under examination. For the main subject of controversy is on this point necessarily a problem of moral rightness, and not of fitness, namely, the question whether it is morally right to lie in order to prevent false inferences from a true answer, or whether a lie is even then a moral wrong. The concept of fittingness serves here only as a cloak for the neglect of the cardinal moral problem. *In consequence* of the confusion between ethical and non-ethical fittingness, the concept of fittingness seems to possess some significance besides that of moral rightness; without this confusion the problem of ethical fittingness has to be transferred completely to that of moral rightness, if not to that of ethical usefulness.

Instead of this, apart from that type of fitness which concerns the ethical fittingness to a certain phase of a course of events, Professor Broad finds it essential to mark out a second type of ethical fittingness, namely, the fittingness to a certain factor of a certain phase of a course of events; and he illustrates this "complication" by the following example: "I may be an elector to an office, and one of the candidates may have done me a service. To prefer him to a better qualified candidate would fit one aspect of the situation, since it would be rewarding a benefactor; but it would be unfitting to other factors in the situation, since it would be an act of bad faith to the institution which was employing me as an elector and an act of injustice to the other candidates."[111] In these deductions again, I think the concept introduced into

[111] *Ibid.*, p. 219.

ethics is on the one hand unnecessary and, on the other hand, even obscures the true ethical questions at issue.

Certainly, if electing a benefactor is a fitting reward for him, then
electing him fits one aspect of the situation, provided that the rewarding
of a benefactor is aimed at. This *logic* teaches us, and not *ethics*. But
obviously, Professor Broad wishes to demonstrate far more. He argues
thus: if electing a benefactor is a fitting reward for him, then his election
fits ethically at least one aspect of the situation. But this conclusion is
by no means permissible. We can arrive at this conclusion only if we
presuppose one more premise which is left out here, namely, the presupposition that rewarding a benefactor is morally right. In short, every
judgment on ethical fitness concerns a relation dependent on ethical
rightness. Or, in other words: contrary to Professor Broad, fittingness as
being dependent on ethical rightness is no direct ethical relation. And
fittingness, understood as independent of ethical rightness or ethical
usefulness, is no ethical relation at all.

In order to demonstrate this as concretely as possible with regard to
Professor Broad's example, we can say: Ethically it does not fit even one
aspect of the situation to prefer the better qualified candidate to my
benefactor in an election, unless it is first ascertained that "an act of bad
faith to the institution which was employing me as an elector" is immoral. For it is by no means a matter of course that even an act of bad
faith is unethical. On the contrary, if for instance we are dealing with
an institution of criminals, then it may be our moral duty to do an act
of bad faith to such an institution; and then it would not fit any aspect
of the situation to elect the better qualified candidate; but the least
qualified might be preferable in order to make the work of the institution ineffective.

It is true that it is an act of good faith to an institution to prefer the
election of a better qualified candidate to that of a personal benefactor;
and therefore this act fits one aspect of the situation. But this kind of
fitness is ethically entirely neutral. There is no "direct" way which leads
from this ethically indifferent fittingness to the ethical one. Yet exactly
this way Professor Broad has gone. He thinks a certain act must be
ethically fit at least to one factor of a situation simply because this act
fits a demonstration of good faith. But this conclusion is illicit. The only
correct conclusion is the tautological statement that an act which fits a
demonstration of good faith to a certain institution is fitting to this
demonstration. If we wish to know more and to arrive at Professor

Broad's conclusion we need, first, some kind of reference to the moral rightness of the act in question.

If we may be permitted to formulate his views in this manner, even Professor Broad makes such a reference to moral rightness in two ways. But both ways are impassable except by the help of fallacies. The first of these two types of fallacies we have already sufficiently characterized. It is the inference of the moral rightness of an act simply on the ground of existing convention. The fallacy is as follows: it is conventionally agreed that an act of good faith to an institution is moral; therefore, even the critical moralist can be assured of its morality, for all laws of existing moral convention are actually valid in ethics. I should like to call this paralogism the naturalistic fallacy of convention because its specific characteristic is the unpermitted identification of the facts of a conventional "ought" with the value of a universally valid "ought." This fallacy of convention seems to me deeply rooted in the ethical intuitionism here examined.

The second fallacy involved is this: Professor Broad finds that we are able to "estimate" the moral rightness or wrongness of an act as a "function" of its fittingness and its utility by "balancing fittingness on the whole against utility on the whole,"[112] although such a calculation must remain of only rough approximate correctness. It seems to me, however, that such a calculation cannot be carried out in any way, not even in the roughest manner. Wherever we want to base moral rightness on utility and fittingness, we are first obliged to distinguish between morally neutral utility and fittingness on the one hand and ethical utility and fittingness on the other.

Bentham recognized this and made this distinction with regard to the concept of utility by stating, in his utility principle, that only that useful action is morally right which effects the greatest possible amount of happiness. After having introduced such a concept of morally right utility, Bentham was able to deal with the problems of the *ethical* fittingness of every factor of every phase of the consequences of such an act. These problems considered as problems of ethical utility appear in Bentham in his analyses concerning the intended and the real consequences of acts, and concerning the degree of consciousness by which different intentions are accompanied. As we shall see later, in these analyses Bentham deals with morally right fittingness as a constituting element of morally right utility.

[112] *Ibid.*, pp. 222, 221.

Professor Broad wishes to go quite a different way. He excludes, first, all reference to questions of moral rightness; and he hopes, nevertheless, to be able to infer the moral rightness of an act—more or less precisely—by balancing its total fittingness against its total utility. But according to the very nature of moral rightness (acknowledged by intuitionists as well as by consistent utilitarians) any such inference from neutral fitness to ethical rightness is a fallacy. And any inference from ethical fittingness to ethical rightness reveals itself as entirely void of ethical information. For if an act ethically fits a phase of events, it must be ethically right as to this phase; and if the act is ethically right as to this phase, it must ethically fit it. No distinction between ethical fittingness and ethical rightness is, therefore, justifiable—i.e. the introduction of the concept of ethical fittingness in addition to that of rightness is completely superfluous or even confusing.

The only inference which remains open in this connection is the inference from utility to moral rightness; and this is the basic argument of the utilitarian. The utilitarian is, therefore, fully entitled to reject any inference from an alleged ethical fittingness or from neutral fitness in addition to utility.

Professor Broad states with superior resignation that, in the attempts to find out the moral rightness of an act, "we are soon reduced to something analogous to those perceptual judgments on very complex situations which we have constantly to make in playing games of skill. . . . But, if it is so, it is so."[113] In spite of its resignation, I think this judgment is still too optimistic. For if we follow this doctrine, and estimate the moral rightness of an act by balancing its total fittingness against its total utility, we come not only to less definite judgments than Bentham but to no legitimate ethical judgment at all, despite the introduction of a morally neutral—or morally biased—concept.

Thus, to smile at "the sweet simplicity of Utilitarianism"[114] (that is, at Bentham's elaborate analyses concerning all ethical elements of acts, including his minute inquiries into the relations between the fitness and utility of all possible factors and phases of the consequences of acts) and to introduce, instead of these analyses, fittingness as a direct ethical relation seems to me a striking example of seeing the mote in one's brother's eye.

NATURAL JUSTICE, RIGHT REASON AND SIMILAR PRINCIPLES

Sixth and Seventh, we find in Bentham's list of principles adverse to

[113] *Ibid.*, p. 222 f.   [114] *Ibid.*, p. 223.

utility the mention of the law of nature and all the phraseology connected with it, Natural Justice, Right Reason, Natural Equity, Good Order, the Law of Reason. But as Bentham has already given his detailed criticism of the law of nature in his unpublished *Comment on the Commentaries*, he contents himself here with classifying the law of nature among the applications of the principle of sympathy and antipathy.

According to Bentham, the "chapters and sections of the Law of Nature" contain in truth no more than what seems morally right and wrong to the individual sentiments of those moralists who champion the belief in an ethical law of nature;[115] and the "pretended Law of Nature" thus represents a very "vague expression . . . , productive of a multitude of inconveniences."[116] This is certainly a paradoxical rejection of the law of nature. It paradoxically tends to demonstrate why the "immutable, objective" law of nature has, in truth, a more subjective character than the "subjective" principle of utility.

But Bentham's way of arguing is here in complete harmony with the fuller analysis of this question given in his *Comment on the Commentaries*. Briefly speaking, in this earlier writing too, Bentham insisted that the whole natural law as summarized in the main rules of Justinian consists only of what, according to the "sentiments" of the legislator Justinian, is considered to be morally right. If such a critical analysis of the law of nature is rejected, then, as the *Comment on the Commentaries* added, only a formalistic interpretation is left to the "censorial" moralist, viz. the law of nature can then be understood only as the tautological teaching that what ought to be done ought to be done.

Eighth, after having characterized the law of nature and the law of reason as untenable ethical theories, Bentham directs a similar criticism against William Wollaston's moral theory. In fact, Wollaston, whom Herder counts among the greatest moralists of his century,[117] delineated a doctrine which comes comparatively near to that of the law of nature. He, too, tried to give ethics a more objective basis than the subjective moral sense, or any other sense or moral sentiments, can offer.

To this effect, Wollaston states in his *Religion of Nature Delineated*,

[115] Bentham, *Introduction*, 1789, chap. II, sect. 14, note No. 6.

[116] Bentham, *Introduction*, 1823, vol. I, p. 33, chap. II, sect. 14, note and vol. II, p. 223, chap. XVI, sect. 62, note to IX. Cf. vol. II, p. 265, chap. XVII, sect. 27, note, on "the pretended law of nature, an obscure phantom."

[117] See J. G. Herder, "Adrastea," Band II, *Werke*, ed. Suphan, 1885, Band 23, S. 147.

1722, that moral evil consists in the practical contradiction of a theoretically true proposition. *"Whoever acts as if things were so, or not so, doth by his acts declare, that they are so, or not so;* as plainly as he could by words, and with more reality. And if the things are otherwise, his acts contradict *those propositions,* which assert them to be as they are."[118] "When a man lives, as if he had the estate which he has not, or *was* in other regards (all fairly cast up) what he *is not,* what judgment is to be passed upon him? Doth not his whole conduct breathe untruth? May we not say (if the propriety of language permits), that he *lives a lye?*"[119] *"Moral good and evil are coincident with right and wrong.* For that cannot be good, which is wrong; nor that evil which is right."[120] "If A steals a book from B, which was pleasing and useful to him, it is true A is guilty of a crime in not treating the book as being what it is, the book of B, who is the proprietor of it and one whose happiness partly depends upon it."[121] Is it possible to prove the validity of moral truths in these rather artificial ways? Bentham denies it, and I think it can be shown in detail why he is right in doing so.

Unfortunately, it is not true that all theoretically true propositions "denied . . . by deeds"[122] "signify"[123] immoral acts. Moreover, often such denials do not signify immorality, even if the act in question is measured by Wollaston's own moral standards. And vice versa, there are many theoretically true propositions whose assertions "by deeds" do not "signify" any acts which Wollaston himself would be able to regard as moral on the ground of his Christian ethical convictions. It is, therefore, characteristic that moralists who think in such vague terms (as denial by deeds or by practical reason), Wollaston as well as Kant and others, have always taken refuge in two interesting omissions in order to save their theories: either they did not take into account an indefinitely large number of theoretically true propositions, or they excluded a corresponding number of denials and assertions by deeds.

Suppose, for instance, that "this is a poor man" is a true proposition, and that I deny this "by deeds,"[122] by giving him so much that he is

---

[118] W. Wollaston, *The Religion of Nature Delineated,* 1759, p. 16.
[119] *Ibid.,* p. 13. [120] *Ibid.,* p. 29.
[121] *Ibid.,* p. 31. Of course, this example given by Wollaston contains not one, but at least two theoretical propositions; and the second one (referring to the usefulness of A.'s book) points obviously to an implicit presupposition of the ethical principle of utility, a presupposition which apparently was not noticed by Wollaston himself.
[122] W. Wollaston, *The Religion of Nature Delineated,* 1759, p. 6.
[123] *Ibid.,* p. 10.

no longer poor. Then, according to Wollaston's theory, my deeds would have to be called immoral. And so Wollaston is obviously at much pains to attain the opposite result by putting his "true" proposition in the following question-begging way: "If I, being of ability to afford now and then something in charity to the poor, should yet *never* give them anything at all, I should *then* certainly deny the condition of the poor to be what it is, and my own to be what it is: and thus truth would be injured."[124] On the other hand, if there is, for instance, the theoretically true proposition "this is my enemy," then an assertion of this proposition by deeds would lead us to the moral necessity of hating and persecuting this enemy. Wollaston, however, in accordance with Christian morality, does not acknowledge this. He does not approve of hating the enemy or disapprove of charity. Thus, in order to protect his theories on these points, he simply leaves out of consideration all those true propositions whose conformation would be immoral in his view, or those whose negation would be in his opinion moral. But, in this way neither the love of an enemy nor aid given to the poor can be "demonstrated" as confirmation of true propositions or denial of wrong ones. Neither "practical" affirmations, nor practical contradictions of indefinite numbers of theoretically true statements, can tell us what is ethically right or ethically wrong.

Strangely enough, the use of Wollaston's argument has not become quite extinct even up to the present day. Kant presented an extremely refined version of it. But what Professor Paul Weiss offers as the foundations of his new ethics is almost identical with Wollaston's basic idea in morals. Professor Weiss, too, assures us that we meet with certain concrete ethical truths whose denial would be a philosophical absurdity, for instance the "truth . . . it is wrong wantonly to kill one's friend, for, to deny this, is to commit the absurdity of maintaining that it is either right or indifferent to reduce values unnecessarily."[125]

As in the case of Wollaston, one could certainly subscribe to the ethical validity of Professor Weiss' statement on the murder of a friend, if only there were any legitimate possibility of excluding all those cases in which the application of this "philosophically true" statement runs into insurmountable difficulties. Was Brutus' wanton killing of his friend

[124] *Ibid.*, pp. 24 f. In fact, the very learned Wollaston (quoting the patristic writers, such as Lactantius, p. 42, Clemens Alexandrinus, p. 51, and even the Jewish scholastic Joseph Albo, p. 39, and the Hebrew Comment on the Bible by Rashi, p. 11, refers in his examples to such propositions only whose assertion or denial by deeds asserts beforehand the ethical propositions he wishes to maintain.

[125] P. Weiss, *Nature and Man*, 1947, p. XIX.

Caesar wanton—in at least one of the possible meanings of the word—
and therefore evidently immoral, as the immoral Mark Anthony and
some devoted friends of the "dictator" thought? Or was it a great moral
achievement, as the moralist Cicero said? And Hitler's killing of his
friend Röhm—thought to be extremely wanton by leading S.A. men—
was this immoral? Or was it, perhaps, the only action of the German
tyrant of which even his stanchest opponents could morally approve?
Wherever Wollaston or his contemporary followers infer the validity of
concrete ethical propositions, they owe this result not to the employment
of any objective criterion of moral right and wrong, but only to the
subjective "principle of sympathy and antipathy," to their arbitrary
choice of certain examples and the arbitrary exclusion of others.

Ninth, according to Bentham the use of the principle of sympathy
and antipathy is again perceptible in the "doctrine of election." Whoever counts himself among "the number of the Elect," whoever tells the
world that he is informed by God himself of what is morally right,
speaks, of course, in the opinion of the atheist Bentham exclusively
from his own sympathy and antipathy.

Tenth, Bentham remarks that repugnancy to nature, if regarded as a
standard of moral evil, is but one of the "different . . . words" used for
disguising the principle of antipathy and has no more scientific value
than the principles of moral sense or common sense. "Unnatural, when
it means anything, means unfrequent"; but if for instance "the practice
of exposing children, established among the Greeks and Romans" is
called unnatural, then unnatural certainly does not mean unfrequent;
for just "the frequency of such acts is . . . the great complaint"; unnatural, therefore, means in this case nothing, "nothing, I mean which
there is in the act itself. All it can serve to express is, the disposition
of the person who is talking of it: the disposition he is in to be angry
at the thought of it. Does it merit his anger? Very likely it may"; but
whether and why it does or no, this is the question.[126] This question,
however, cannot be answered by the assertion that the matter in dispute
is repugnant to or in accordance with nature. For what is considered to
be at variance with nature by one moralist is considered to be con-
cordant to nature by the other, and vice versa. Thus, here again, the
subjective principle of sympathy and antipathy has the last word.

[126] Bentham, *Introduction*, 1789, chap. ii, sect. 14, note: compare Bentham,
Traités de Législation civile et pénale, ed. Dumont, tome i, 1820, p. 128.

In all its ten different applications, the principle of sympathy and antipathy evidently does not provide an objective standard of moral right and wrong. It only pretends to do so by "couching"[127] its argument in seemingly objective terms. The ten different applications of the principle of sympathy serve "as a cloak, and pretence, and aliment to despotism: if not a despotism in practice," at least "a despotism . . . in disposition."[127] The principle of utility, however, does not conceal its "subjective" character, related to pleasure and pain, but it has none the less an objective estimate of pain and pleasure in view.

Bentham does not deny that e.g. advocates of the theory of moral sense generally have intentions "of the purest kind," but in spite of these excellent intentions, these moralists easily become "a torment" either to themselves or to their fellowmen. If they are "of the melancholy cast" they sit "in silent grief . . . , if of the irascible," they "declaim with fury and virulence against all who differ from" them; and if such a man happens "to possess the advantages of style, his book may do a considerable deal of mischief before the nothingness of it is understood."[126] Bentham, however, tried to show the reasons for such nothingness. He admits that the dictates of the principle of antipathy "will frequently coincide with those of utility. . . . For what more natural or more general ground of hatred" and antipathy "to a practice can there be, than the mischievousness," the lack of utility "of such practice"?[128] None the less, this principle of antipathy "is far . . . from being a constant ground: for when a man suffers" and feels antipathy "it is not always that he knows what it is he suffers by. A man may suffer grievously, for instance by a new tax, without being able to trace up the cause of his sufferings to the injustice of some neighbour, who has eluded the payment of an old one."[128] The principle of utility, however, obliges us to seek after the objective causes of our sufferings and antipathies and thus, in this regard also, it moves on firmer ground than do subjective and often unmotivated or curable antipathies.

The principle of antipathy and its various applications often lead to error on the side of severity as well as on the side of leniency. Especially frequent are the errors on the side of severity. Bentham mentions, for instance, a quarrel in Russia in which the government had taken part on the ground of antipathy, and in which some thousands of persons lost their lives only because they used a different number of fingers in making the sign of the cross.[129] As to the instances of error on the

[127] Bentham, *Introduction*, 1789, chap. II, sect. 14, note.
[128] *Ibid.*, sect. 15. [129] *Ibid.*, sect. 16, 17.

side of leniency, Bentham has promised to give some examples of this kind. But in the sections of his work to which he refers for this purpose none is to be found.

Aside from this, the following incongruity might be noticed: Bentham originally wanted to characterize the principle of asceticism as the single strict opponent of the utility principle, whereas later on he wanted to subordinate all other principles adverse to that of utility under that of sympathy and antipathy. Also, the reference to the will of God had already been located among the ten applications of the sympathy and antipathy principle under the title "Doctrine of Election." Obviously, he never quite abandoned the conviction that "the theological principle" is, in fact, "not a separate principle"[130] in morals. Nevertheless, he devotes a special section to this principle, mentioning that it is always one or other of the three above mentioned principles presenting itself in another shape.

However, in this discussion of the theological principle, he only repeats certain arguments against the Divine Law which he had already expounded more fully in his *Comment on the Commentaries*. He points out again that the will of God, as revealed in the sacred writings, can nowhere literally be referred to in the details of private conduct. For the will of God "is universally allowed, by the most eminent divines of all persuasions to stand in need of pretty ample interpretations; else to what use are the works of these divines? And for the guidance of these interpretations, it is also allowed, that some other standard must be assumed . . . We may be perfectly sure that whatever is right is conformable to the will of God: but so far is that from answering the purpose of showing us what is right, that it is necessary to know first whether a thing is right, in order to know from thence whether it be conformable to the will of God."[131] The will of God or God's pleasure that is to say, cannot be thought to be prior to the principle of utility, or asceticism, or sympathy and antipathy. On the contrary, in moral and theological valuations, one of these principles must necessarily precede as the true—though concealed—standard of right and wrong.

Bentham admits that "in point of fact" people may often derive their "notions of right and wrong" in morals from the principle of asceticism, or from the theological principle, or from one of the many other applications of the sympathy principle, or from a mixture of these different principles, or even from principles or mixtures of principles some of which are not mentioned in Bentham's list; and he further grants that,

---

[130] *Ibid.*, sect. 18.   [131] *Ibid.*, sect. 18.

again "in point of fact," these notions of moral right and wrong may be justified "by a person reflecting within himself" on quite other grounds than the ground of utility; "I do not care"[132] about this. For here again, as in the *Fragment on Government*, Bentham insists that all these questions relating to points of fact, relating to actual moral feelings or even to actual moral justifications, are not the decisive ethical questions. Not any such point of fact, but the point of right alone is of final import. The actual ethical problem here involved consists in the censorial question: how can human actions be morally justified "in point of right," and not how are they justified "in point of fact."

Bentham is well aware that actions are frequently considered to be moral in spite of their mischievous character. But he answers arguments of this kind: "if duty means anything, that is moral duty, it is your duty . . . to abstain from" a mischievous act "and more than that, if it is what lies in your power, and can be done without too great a sacrifice," it is your duty "to endeavour to prevent it. It is not your cherishing the notion of it in your bosom, and giving it the name of virtue, that will excuse you."[133] On the other hand, very often an action is actually condemned as immoral in spite of its useful character. Bentham is tolerant enough to make allowance for this by stating that you may detest such a useful action "within yourself as much as you please; that may be a very good reason (unless it be also a useful one) for your not doing it yourself"; but as he goes on to say, "if you go about, by word or deed, to do anything to hinder 'the man who does a useful deed' or make him suffer for it, it is you, and not he, that have done wrong: it is not your setting yourself to blame his conduct, or branding it with the name of vice, that will make him culpable, or you blameless. Therefore, if you can make yourself content that he shall be of one mind, and you of another, about that matter, and so continue, it is well: but if nothing will serve you, but that you and he must needs be of the same mind, I'll tell you what you have to do: it is for you to get the better of your antipathy, not for him to truckle to it."[134]

Thus, Bentham here excludes two sorts of questions from his ethical analyses as unessential: first, the reference to actual *private* justifications of the morality of acts and the condemnation of their immorality; second, the reference to actual *public* justifications of the morality of acts

[132] *Ibid.*, chap. ii, sect. 14, 2nd edition, 1823, vol. i, p. 33.

[133] Bentham, *Introduction*, 1789, chap. ii, sect. 14, note, 2nd edition 1823, vol. i, p. 33.

[134] Bentham, *Introduction*, 1789, chap. ii, sect. 14, note, 2nd edition, 1823, vol. ii, p. 34.

and the condemnation of their immorality. The material question is not one concerning actual public or private ethical reasoning about acts; it is this: why *ought* such and such acts to be done? In this way, Bentham's classical distinction between the censorial and the expository problem in morals is here again placed in a new light.

Underestimated Consistency of Bentham's Argument. Is the Criminal's Pleasure Morally Evil?

Bentham never identified duty or the moral good with what people actually think to be duty or the moral good. He carefully avoided this type of most widespread "naturalistic fallacy." He never identified the *ought* with natural mental events, such as *actual thoughts about the ought*. Nor did he commit another naturalistic fallacy, namely, that good has the same meaning as pleasant. Bentham has taught not this but something very different, viz. that pleasure is a good thing, which is not denied even by the overwhelming majority of anti-hedonists.

We are here, therefore, left with only two differences between Bentham's theory and common anti-hedonism: that according to Bentham pleasure *qua* pleasure is always good, and that pleasure is the sole good thing, while, e.g. according to Sir David Ross, pleasure is sometimes evil and "there are other things than pleasure which we think to be good."[135] If, however, anti-hedonism thinks that these statements of Sir David are self-evident, it forgets that they are so only on the ground of common morality.

But Bentham criticizes customary morality throughout. In the strictest contrast to common anti-hedonism, he consistently tries to demonstrate (1) why only pleasure can be ultimately considered to be good and (2) why every pleasure, even the pleasure felt by the criminal, is morally good, *qua* pleasure.

With the first point we have already dealt at some length. As to the second point, Bentham criticized customary morality perhaps in the most considered and severest way in the following deductions of the second chapter of his *Introduction*: Even "the most abominable pleasure which the vilest of malefactors ever reaped from his crime" must not be reprobated in itself; in strict consequence of the utility principle even such a loathsome pleasure would not be evil "if it stood alone"; but "the case is that it never does stand alone," yet "is necessarily fol-

[135] W. D. Ross, *The Meanings of "Good,"* in *Travaux du IXe Congrès International de Philosophie*, Fascicule XI, 1937, p. 79.

lowed by such a quantity of pain (or what comes to the same thing, such a chance for a certain quantity of pain) that the pleasure in comparison of it is as nothing."[136] "It is only upon . . . the principle of asceticism . . . and not from the principle of utility, that the most abominable pleasure which the vilest of malefactors ever reaped from his crime would be to be reprobated if it stood alone."[136] However we may style this estimate of the pleasure felt during the execution of a crime, whether we call it immoralism, moral liberalism or moral criticism, methodologically and substantially this is certainly one of the most original ideas of Bentham.

The Limits of Jurisprudence Defined repeat this basic statement of Bentham's utilitarianism in almost literally the same formula: "The most sordid pleasure which the vilest malefactor ever reaped from his crime (suppose it but pleasure) would not be to be reprobated, *if it stood alone.*" Bentham calls this statement here an "impregnable truth" and, then, partly correcting himself, "a *postulatum* . . . , in matter of censure and approbation, . . . the only *postulatum* I do assume"; and he adds that there are "two standards to one or other of which I refer in everything I advance. For matter of fact I appeal to the experience or observation of those within whose cognizance it lies. For matter of censure or approbation I appeal solely to this principle."[137] It is, in my opinion, not only this basic "censorial" statement which can be called a *postulatum* in ethics. The whole utility principle has, in truth, the function of a *postulatum* within a scientific philosophy of morals or—as Bentham characterizes the utility principle even more appropriately in a MS hitherto unpublished—the utility principle is the basic "hypothesis" of any scientific ethics; and observations of pleasure and pain are the only means of verification in such a science. In any case, however, Bentham rightly emphasizes that this statement about the morality of any "pure" pleasure of the criminal is of fundamental importance to the whole structure of his ethical system.

Anti-hedonists generally assume that the "pleasure of cruelty" even *qua* pleasure is bad, and "that it would have been better that it should not have existed."[138] I, for one, should hesitate to criticize nature and creation in this way. Perhaps even on this point God and nature are wiser than anti-hedonists. If cruel persons must exist, why should that be a better world in which, other things being equal, criminals would

---

[136] Bentham, *Introduction*, 1789, chap. II, sect. 4.
[137] Bentham, *The Limits of Jurisprudence Defined*, ed. by Everett, 1945, p. 115 f.
[138] W. D. Ross, *The Right and the Good*, 1930, p. 151.

not even enjoy their cruelty? Is it psychologically possible that they would do anything cruel if they did not enjoy it in some way? And is it not enough for the moralist to condemn the cruel deed and to see how naturally limited the pleasures of pathological, i.e. of every, cruelty are?

H. W. B. Joseph expatiates on these questions in the following way: "A surgeon compelled by his profession, in the days before anaesthetics, to inflict pain on his patients, if he had taken pleasure in watching their pain, would have lived a life the worse for this pleasure, in a world the worse for his feeling it. I do not mean merely that his character would have been bad; that would have been so if he had sought pleasure this way but failed to feel it. I mean that a world where men found, as well as sought, pleasure from inflicting suffering on others would be made worse, not better, by the occurrence of the pleasure sought."[139] Compared with Bentham's realistic facing of facts, Mr. Joseph's "moralistic" reflections seem to me based on cosmological speculations as colorless and unwarranted as they are psychologically primitive and obviously, in the main, inspired by wishful thinking. Are there any surgeons who feel no pleasure in watching a pain of their patients which they have to consider as indispensable and useful in the end? Should a physician not enjoy his skill, even if this skill unavoidably inflicts pain on his patients? There may be many surgeons who share Mr. Joseph's opinion, and like to picture the ideal man or even the average man as being quite free from any direct or sublimated aggressiveness. This opinion, however, reveals it seems to me a rather uncritical and far too simple separation between selfish and unselfish aggressiveness in human nature.

Of course, so far as the surgeon inflicts needless pain on his patients, he should be called a criminal not only from the moral but also from the juristic point of view. But in this case, too, it is the *consequence* of his pleasure-seeking, viz. the production of needless pain, which makes his action a moral crime; it is not his pleasure-seeking and pleasure-feeling. For he may have this pleasure-feeling in common with the morally most conscientious surgeon, who avoids all needless infliction of pain and yet "enjoys" the infliction of unavoidable useful suffering in preference to false sentimentalism.

The common assumption of morally bad pleasure is, in my view, mistaken mainly for three reasons: First, anti-hedonists argue that it makes every cruel deed worse if the cruel man enjoys it, and less evil if he did not enjoy it at all. But to the psychologist it is obvious, it seems

[139] H. W. B. Joseph, *Some Problems in Ethics*, 1931, pp. 90 f.

213

to me, that the cruel man always enjoys his deed to some extent; and it is psychologically without any meaning to speculate about a world in which the criminal would commit crimes without enjoying them in any way.

Second, though it makes no sense psychologically to believe in an infliction of pain which is not enjoyed by the inflicter at least to some extent, it is perfectly legitimate to separate methodologically the inflicting of pain from the enjoyment of this infliction. Anti-hedonists, unfortunately, lay much stress on the former hypothesis which is psychologically preposterous, and completely neglect the latter methodological abstraction which is ethically of fundamental importance.

Third, the failure to take into consideration the latter methodological abstraction is obviously caused by moral prejudice. But precisely the necessity of removing this prejudice makes the performance of that abstraction ethically essential. It is in no way justified to suppose uncritically that the pleasure of the criminal is, even *qua* pleasure, methodologically inseparable from and infected by the consequences of this pleasure. It is perfectly sufficient to have the moral badness of cruel deeds ultimately grounded in their consequences, without having the criminal's pleasure affected by this badness. His pleasure as pleasure is good, or at the worst innocent, as long as it is methodologically separated from his inflicting of pain; and this methodological abstraction can free us from moral prejudices which lead to most embarrassing complications in any theory of morals. At any rate, morally dogmatic statements about the badness of certain pleasures *qua* pleasures can in no wise invalidate the critically weighed hypothesis concerning the moral goodness of all pleasure in itself.

Bentham's analyses of the criminal's pleasure show, quite clearly, I think, that he is prepared to revise both certain final convictions and the ways of reasoning of customary morality. F. H. Bradley, discussing the immorality of adultery, thought it impossible to demonstrate the immorality of this or other crimes by mere reference to the quantities of pleasures involved.[140] He even thought that "the Hedonist does not want the question raised."[141] This seems to me an entirely misleading statement. For Bentham has raised this question in several connections and put the greatest emphasis on it. In an unpublished manuscript, he attempted to give an especially lengthy proof of the immorality of adul-

---

[140] F. H. Bradley, *Ethical Studies*, 1876, pp. 97 ff (essay III).
[141] *Ibid.*, p. 101.

tery, though this analysis is combined with the proof of some other theses.[142]

It is regrettable that many of the best discussions of utilitarian ethics omit exact references to Bentham,[143] and that anti-hedonists prefer to criticize a type of radical hedonism constructed by themselves. Many of the arguments still raised against hedonism would have to be modified or completely abandoned if they had taken notice of the fourth section of the second chapter of Bentham's *Introduction*, and of corresponding arguments of his *Table of the Springs of Action*.

Final Observations on Anti-Hedonistic Principles

Because of his consistent application of the utility principle, and on the ground of his brief but pregnant characterization of the principles adverse to that of utility, Bentham concludes these reflections with the following simple and resolute statement: other principles or mixtures of principles "in abundance . . . may be the reasons why such and such an act *has* been done: that is the reason or causes of its being done: but it is this (the principle of utility) alone that can be the reason why it might or ought to have been done. . . . The principle of utility neither requires nor admits of any other regulator than itself"[144] in the whole field of morals. Leslie Stephen thought that, especially in the criticism of his contemporary opponents, Bentham had "hit the nail pretty well on the head."[145] I believe that many points of these rough analyses are

[142] See Appendix V of the present book, Bentham MSS, University College, London, Portfolio 96, Folder 6, sheets 128-131.

[143] It is quite characteristic of the general misinterpretation of Bentham's thought that even L. A. Selby-Bigge's well known Oxford Selections from *British Moralists* (1897), I, 345, omit this section in the reprint of Bentham's *Introduction* and turn immediately from chapter II, sect. 3, to sect. 9, thus omitting exactly what Bentham calls the only basic *postulatum* of his moral philosophy.

[144] Bentham, *Introduction*, 1789, chap. II, sect. 19. Bowring in his edition of the *Introduction* in Bentham's *Works*, 1843, part I, pp. 11b ff inserted here chapter V of the introductory part of Dumont's edition of Bentham's *Traités de Législation*, 1820, pp. 25 ff (*The Theory of Legislation*, translated by R. Hildreth, pp. 15 ff). But I shall analyze this chapter of Dumont's edition in its proper place in my report on the *Traités*.

[145] Leslie Stephen, *The English Utilitarians*, 1900, vol. I, p. 241. In his *Kritik des Hedonismus*, 1898, p. 87 ff, Heinrich Gomperz, too, stresses the importance of Bentham's discussion of anti-hedonistic principles in morals and—what was rather rare at that time—he considers Bentham a greater ethicist than J. S. Mill. Like most critics of utilitarianism, however, Gomperz excludes from his reflections the evaluation of Bentham's doctrine of motives and its connection with the utility principle. Mainly for this reason he was not able to do full justice to Benthamism.

in need of supplementary discussion, and there are a number of defects on minor points, as I have tried to show. But despite the imperfection of Bentham's argument in detail, on the whole this second chapter of his *Introduction* seems to me a remarkable attempt to illustrate the important paradox that those theories which pride themselves on giving immediate, intuitive and absolute ethical knowledge lead us, in truth, to a complete relativity of moral judgment—a relativity with regard to the basic principles (moral sense, law of nature, command of duty and the like), and with regard to the application of these principles.

Still, it is commonly believed in modern ethics that certain concrete values or moral rules—essentially independent of any reference to pleasure and pain—are empirically or a priori given and that their moral validity is secured without any further investigation. How widespread this belief is, may be seen from even a fugitive glance at numerous writings of contemporary moralists such as Louis Lavelle,[146] Gérard Petit,[147] Dominique Parodi,[148] Emanuel Leroux,[149] André Lalande,[150] Edmond Goblot,[151] G. E. Moore,[152] A. E. Taylor,[153] W. D. Ross,[154] H. W. Joseph,[155] C. D. Broad,[156] E. F. Carritt,[157] H. A. Prichard,[158] W. M. Urban,[159] Gor-

[146] Louis Lavelle, *Introduction à l'ontologie*, 1947, p. 106 on "la hierarchie des valeurs," pp. 95 ff: "la valeur exprime dans le relatif sa relation avec l'absolu."

[147] Gérard Petit, *L'homme contemporain et le problème moral*, 1943, e.g. p. 378 f: "La certitude de la pensée pratique réglant de près, immediatement l'action singulière, aura un caractère propre qu'elle tient de la nature distincte de la vérité dans son ordre."

[148] D. Parodi, *La conduite humaine et les valeurs idéales*, 1939, pp. 17 ff.

[149] Emmanuel Leroux, "La pluralité des valeurs éthiques," in *Travaux du IXe Congrès International de Philosophie*, fascicule XI, pp. 65 ff.

[150] A. Lalande, *La psychologie des jugements des valeurs* (Travaux de l'universite égyptienne) 1929, pp. 10 ff, p. 27 on "Le caractère a priori des valeurs spirituelles."

[151] Edmond Goblot, *La logique des jugements de valeur*, 1927, e.g. pp. 7 ff, 93.

[152] G. E. Moore, "Reply to My Critics," in *The Library of Living Philosophers*, ed. by P. A. Schilpp, 1942, pp. 554 ff and much more definite teachings of this kind in Moore's earlier writings.

[153] A. E. Taylor, e.g. "Science and Morality," in *Philosophy*, London, 1939, vol. XIV, p. 29.

[154] W. D. Ross, *Foundations of Ethics*, 1939, e.g. pp. 2 ff; W. D. Ross, *The Right and the Good*, 1930, p. 19: "The human mind . . . has in fact an *a priori* insight into certain broad principles of morality."

[155] H. W. Joseph, *Some Problems in Ethics*, 1931, e.g. pp. 104 ff.

[156] C. D. Broad, *Five Types of Ethical Theory*, 1930, pp. 218 ff.

[157] E. F. Carritt, *The Theory of Morals*, 1928, e.g. pp. 136 ff.

[158] H. A. Prichard, "Does Moral Philosophy Rest on a Mistake?" in *Mind*, 1912, pp. 27 ff.

[159] W. M. Urban, "Value Propositions and Verifiability," in *The Journal of*

don S. Jury,[160] W. G. Everett,[161] Nicolai Hartmann,[162] Max Scheler,[163] Giulio Preti,[164] Ortega y Gasset,[165] Francisco Larroyo,[166] and Aníbal Sánchez Reulet[167]—authors who are all, in one way or the other, significant representatives of various national or philosophical trends in contemporary thought.

If ethics were in possession of a system of concrete, definitely valid rules, then, of course, moral philosophy could be restricted to the task of finding out whether a moral sense or our common sense, a law of nature, or some self-evident moral principles, some moral values or something else dictates these ethical rules. But the truth is that no such concrete definitely valid rules exist. The fascist, for instance, on nearly every occasion of his life must feel bound by self-evident ethical obligations completely different from those which are of binding force to a pacifist and the "system" of immediately intuited duties of the fascists may stand Professor Ewing's[168] "coherence test" as well as the system of the pacifists. Both the fascist and the pacifist may appeal to the moral sense or to the law of nature, to intuited values or to *prima facie* duties; but their common sense or the law of nature, their intuited values or their *prima facie* duties give them different or even diametrically opposite instructions. This Bentham wished to show. He wanted to illustrate the irrelevance of the traditional dispute between the different types of intuitional dogmatic ethics. For this debate leaves the main

---

Philosophy, 1937, pp. 589 ff. Cf. especially W. M. Urban, *Fundamentals of Ethics*, 1930, pp. 159 ff and Urban, "Axiology," in *Twentieth Century Philosophy*, ed. by D. D. Runes, 1943, e.g. pp. 66 ff.

[160] G. S. Jury, *Value and Ethical Objectivity*, 1937, e.g. p. 252: "Value exercises peculiar compulsion upon us as an ultimate form of validity"; p. 251: "The absoluteness of value in its normative or imperative mode" must not be "obscured."

[161] W. G. Everett, *Moral Values*, 1918, e.g. pp. 182 ff.

[162] N. Hartmann, *Ethik*, 2. Auflage, 1935, Seite 139 ff, 336 ff.

[163] M. Scheler, *Der Formalismus in der Ethik und die materiale Wertethik*, 2. Auflage, 1922, Band 1, Teil 11, e.g. pp. 507 ff.

[164] G. Preti, *Fenomenologia del valore*, 1942, p. 88.

[165] José Ortega y Gasset, "¿Que son los valores?" in *Revista de Occidente*, Madrid, 1923, e.g. pp. 62 ff: "El conocimiento de los valores es absoluto y cuasi matemático."

[166] F. Larroyo, *La filosofía de los valores*, Mexico, 1936, vol. 1, e.g. pp. 196 ff.

[167] Aníbal Sánchez Reulet, "Ser, valor y existencia," in *Papers and Abstracts of the Second Inter-American Congress*, 1947, e.g. p. 103: "Si el hombre tiene mundo y actua en un mundo objetivo . . . es porque reconoce y afirma, al mismo tiempo, valores objetivos."

[168] On A. C. Ewing's "coherence test" see his *The Definition of Good*, 1947, pp. 203 ff.

problem of any critical ethics untouched. Moreover, it is based on the false assumption that this problem has been solved beforehand.

On the other hand, consistent utilitarianism acknowledges that one has to deal first with a marked relativity of concrete ethical judgments, and precisely this concession makes it better equipped to overcome this complete relativity of concrete ethical valuations. For, like all types of empiricism, consistent hedonism permits the sound use of observation, empirical comparison, hypotheses, and empirical verification in finding out and judging "the good things."

As regards the old struggle between dogmatic metaphysics and the empirical philosophy of nature, the superiority of empirical methods is largely recognized. In ethics, we still have, I think, to learn the same lesson, and Bentham is one of the very few moralists who have contributed to the development of these superior methods in morals.

THE DIFFERENT KINDS OF PLEASURE
AND PAIN

In the third chapter dealing with the four sanctions, or "sources of pain and pleasure," we are again on ground already familiar from the *Fragment on Government* and the *Comment on the Commentaries*. But Bentham offers us no mere repetition of results already obtained; he presents them with at least some supplementation. In both the *Fragment on Government* and the *Comment*, only three sorts of sanctions are enumerated: the political, the religious and the moral.[169] In the *Introduction*, rightly, a fourth sanction is mentioned as the "groundwork," the basis of all others,[170] namely, the physical; and this whole analysis of sanctions is contrasted with the analysis of moral principles which precedes it: while at first pain and pleasure had been taken into account "in the character of *final* causes" of human actions, now a view has to be taken of them "in the character of *efficient* causes or means."[171] Pain and pleasure play, and have to play, the part of *final* causes within ethical *principles*, and they have to play the part of *efficient* causes in the way of moral *sanctions*.

[169] Bentham, *Works*, 1843, part II, p. 293b; Bentham, *A Comment on the Commentaries*, ed. by Everett, 1928, p. 95.
[170] Bentham, *Introduction*, 1789, chap. III, sect. 11.
[171] *Ibid.*, sect. 1.

The word "sanction" itself is derived from Latin, as Bentham mentions, and according to a quotation of the Latin grammarian Honoratus Maurus Servius (the commentator on Virgil), it is connected with "*sanguis*, blood: because among the Romans with a view to inculcate into the people a persuasion that such or such a mode of conduct would be rendered obligatory upon a man . . . certain ceremonies were contrived by the priests: in the course of which ceremonies the blood of victims was made use of."[172] Sanction thus signifies, in the first place, "the act of binding" and, second, from this "by a common grammatical transition, anything which serves to bind a man."[173] In truth, pain and pleasure solely are such binding forces—pain and pleasure caused by four different powers. Therefore, four sorts of sanctions have to be distinguished: "If it be in the present life, and from the ordinary course of nature, not purposely modified by the interposition of the will of any human being, nor by any extraordinary interposition of any superior invisible being, that the pleasure or the pain takes place or is expected, it may be said to issue from or to belong to the *physical sanction*. If at the hands of a particular person or set of persons in the community, who under names correspondent to that of *judge*, are chosen for the particular purpose of dispensing it, according to the will of the sovereign or supreme ruling power in the state, it may be said to issue from the *political sanction*. If at the hands of such *chance* persons in the community, as the party in question may happen in the course of his life to have concerns with, according to each man's spontaneous disposition, and not according to any settled or concerted rule, it may be said to issue from the *moral* or *popular sanction*. If from the immediate hand of a superior invisible being, either in the present life, or in a future, it may be said to issue from the *religious sanction*."[174] "A suffering which befalls a man in the natural and spontaneous course of things" may be styled a *calamity*, but the same suffering inflicted by one of the three other sanctions is commonly called a *punishment*; in the case of a suffering caused by an immediate act of God people also use the phrase a "*judgment*, instead of saying, a . . . judgment formed . . . by the Deity."[175] Further, all pleasure and pain belonging to the physical, political, or moral sanctions "must . . . be experienced, if ever in the *present* life"; it is only pleasure and pain issuing from the *religious* sanction which "may be expected to be experienced either in the

[172] *Ibid*., sect. 2, note.   [173] *Ibid*., sect. 2, note.
[174] *Ibid*., sect. 3-6.   [175] *Ibid*., sect. 8, 9, note.

219

present life or in a *future*."[176] Naturally, of what kind these pleasures and pains of a future life may be we cannot know; for they "lie not open to our observation."[177] So far as we have to do with this present life, however, the physical sanction is altogether the groundwork of the political, the moral, and the religious. It is included in each of the three others; it may "operate . . . independently of *them*," whereas none of them "can operate but by means of this. In a word, the powers of a nature may operate of themselves; but neither the magistrate, nor men at large, *can* operate, nor is God in the case in question *supposed* to operate, but through the powers of nature."[178] All these statements while certainly useful are rather small corrections and enlargements of definitions already known from Bentham's earlier writings.

Moreover, E. Albee is right in warning us against thinking that, as is often assumed, the enumeration of these four sanctions is a specific achievement of Bentham. As a matter of fact, much the same list of four moral "obligations" is to be found in John Gay's *Preliminary Dissertation Concerning the Fundamental Principle of Virtue or Morality*, where we read: The moral "Obligation is evidently founded upon the Prospect of Happiness. . . . This obligation may be considered four ways, according to the four different manners in which it is induced: first, that Obligation which ariseth from perceiving the natural Consequences of things, i.e., the Consequences of things acting according to the fix'd Laws of Nature, may be call'd NATURAL. Secondly, that arising from Merit or Demerit, as producing the Esteem and Favour of our Fellow Creatures, or the contrary, is usually stiled VIRTUOUS. Thirdly, that arising from the Authority of the Civil Magistrate, CIVIL. Fourthly, that from the Authority of God, RELIGIOUS."[179] These definitions of four sanctions are thus no more original with Bentham than the formulation of the utility principle.

[176] *Ibid.*, sect. 7.

[177] *Ibid.*, sect. 10.

[178] *Ibid.*, sect. 11. In his *The Limits of Jurisprudence Defined*, ed. by Everett, 1945, p. 224, Bentham, however, omits the physical sanction because, as he says here, the legislator has to take into account only those sanctions "which are under the influence of intelligent and voluntary agents; viz.: the political, the moral, and the religious sanctions."

[179] John Gay, *Preliminary Dissertation concerning the Fundamental Principle of Virtue or Morality*, prefixed to Edmund Law's translation of William King's (Archbishop of Dublin) *An Essay on the "Origin of Evil*," 4th edition 1758, section ii, "concerning obligation" p. xxviii; compare E. Albee, *A History of English Utilitarianism*, 1902, p. 128; or cf. in J. M. Robertson, *A Short history of Morals*, 1920, p. 360, the reference to Gay and Locke.

Temporary Denial of the Pleasures of the Mind in the Unpublished Criticism of Maupertuis

The relation between the different sanctions is certainly better set out in Bentham's *Introduction* than in his *Fragment* and his *Comment*. The physical sanction is here rightly characterized as the fundamental one. Sometimes, however, Bentham overemphasized the importance of one part of the physical sanction. In an unpublished manuscript discussing Maupertuis' *Essai de philosophie morale*, Bentham went so far as to maintain that all pleasures and pains are solely those of the body. Though he obviously completely abandoned this thesis later, it still deserves, I believe, a brief discussion.

In these critical notes on Maupertuis, Bentham introduces himself as asking Maupertuis; "You make no pleasures of the mind? Yes, says he [Maupertuis] but I do."[180] Bentham, however, analyzing the reasons for the ethical condemnation of adultery and bribery, concludes that all ethical inquiries have to refer ultimately to pleasures and pains of the body, not to those of the mind. These reflections were obviously written down before the composition of the *Introduction*, and they are noteworthy at least with reference to the following points:

First, on the whole the differences among the four sanctions are less clearly marked out here than in the *Introduction*. The moral sanction appears in this manuscript in twofold form; the physical is too vaguely differentiated, while in truth all the sanctions are reduced to one part of the physical sanction, namely, the physical sanction of the body. On the other hand, the example used in this manuscript explains the differences among moral, political and religious sanctions in even greater detail than does the example in the *Introduction*.[181]

Second, it is well brought out again that ideas of pleasure and pain, being at work within the different sanctions and ideas of sanctions, need not be consciously in the minds of actors. It is sufficient if they are, or have been, consciously in the thought of that person whose example

[180] Bentham MS, *hitherto unpublished*, University College, London, Portfolio 96, Folder vi, sheets 128-131. This MS, obviously written about 1776, is printed at full length as Appendix V of the present book.

[181] The example used in the *Introduction* (chap. iii, sect. ix) for the illustration of the differences among the four sanctions is consumption of a man's goods. If such a consumption of goods is caused by an accident, it represents a physical sanction; if it is caused by the political magistrate, it is a political sanction; if it is caused by the want of assistance of neighbors, it is a popular sanction; and if caused by God, it is a religious sanction.

the agent follows, either as permanently inspired or as occasionally influenced by this example.[182] This remark again refutes certain charges made against the "narrow-mindedness" of Bentham's rationalism. As we have seen in the *Fragment* and in the first two chapters of the *Introduction*, Bentham admits without hesitation that many actions, even the majority, are actually not performed because of any rational considerations about their utility.[183] On the contrary, they are executed because of non-rational likes and dislikes. In fact, only in a few of our actions do we think consciously and rationally of pain and pleasure or of one of the four sanctions.

Moreover, in the majority of cases the average man merely imitates the example of other persons without any further thought. But the morally decisive point is: on closer scrutiny we always discover, according to Bentham, that beyond the conscious non-rational likes and dislikes, or beyond the conscious imitation of other persons, any action must be governed lastly, "secretly . . . but unavoidably"[184] by a reference to the thought of pain, pleasure and the four sanctions—a thought taking place either in the moral agent himself or, more distinctly, in the persons who first inaugurated such actions as models.

In his unpublished remarks on Maupertuis, Bentham further tried to resolve all kinds of pleasure and pain into mere feelings of the body. Maupertuis, on the one hand, had called attention to the fact that "tous les plaisirs et toutes les peines appartiennent à l'âme."[185] On the other hand, he was willing to term all pleasures and pains caused by the interference of exterior objects in the usual way "plaisirs et peines du corps"; only pleasures and pains arising without such influence he called "plaisirs et peines de l'âme."[186] These pleasures of the mind, in his view, "se reduisent à deux genres de perception; l'un qu'on éprouve par la pratique de la *justice*, l'autre par la vue de la *vérité*. Les peines de l'âme se reduisent à marquer ces deux objets."[187] In contrast to this, Bentham attempts to show in his unpublished criticism of Maupertuis that these

---

[182] See Bentham MS, *hitherto unpublished*, University College, London, Portfolio 96, Folder VI, sheet 131; Appendix V of the present work, p. 293 f.

[183] Bentham, *A Fragment on Government*, chap. I, §45; *Introduction*, 1789, chap. I, sect. 14; chap. II, sect. 15.

[184] Bentham, *A Fragment on Government*, chap. I, §45.

[185] Maupertuis, *Oeuvres*, tome I, 1756, p. 207 (*Essai de philosophie morale*, chap. III).

[186] *Ibid.*, p. 208.   [187] *Ibid.*, p. 212.

or other pleasures or pains of the mind do not exist, but only pleasures and pains of the body.

In the *Introduction* itself, however, Bentham avoided this far-reaching thesis;[188] and this restriction was certainly wise. For, as he remarks himself in the *Introduction*, "granting, for argument's sake," that "the mind be but a part of the body, it is at any rate of a nature very different from the other parts of the body."[189] The pleasures of the body differ, at least as given phenomena, from the pleasures of the mind; and even if we are inclined to think that any pleasure or pain of the mind may be finally resolvable into and interpreted as a pleasure or pain of the body, or as a remembrance of such feelings,[190] the way in which this reduction may be realizable is at least not yet well enough known to confirm such hypotheses.

For the establishment of an objective ethics, the reduction of all pleasures and pains to feelings of the body is, in any case, not essential. All that is needed is that the differences which exist between the pleasures or pains of the body, and the pleasures or pains of the mind, can at least roughly be compared with each other quantitatively by a common measure, despite their qualitative differences.

MEASUREMENT OF PLEASURE AND PAIN

ACCORDING to an unpublished Bentham MS, the fourth chapter of the *Introduction* is likewise connected with a problem occasionally touched upon by Maupertuis, namely, the measurement of pain and pleasure. Maupertuis had already spoken in his *Essai de philosophie morale* of two elements or dimensions in pleasures and pains, viz. their duration and their intensity. "Dans chaque moment heureux ou malheureux, ce n'est pas assez de considérer *la durée*; il faut avoir égard à

---

[188] See e.g. *Introduction*, 1789, chap. XVI, sect. 11, note, 2nd edition, 1823, vol. II, p. 65, where Bentham speaks of pleasures of the mind apart from those of the body, although he adds that pleasures of the mind "result from the action of an object of sense . . . by association."

[189] Bentham, *Introduction*, 1789, chap. VI, sect. 30, 2nd edition, 1823, vol. I, p. 95.

[190] Sigmund Freud in his *New Introductory Lectures on Psychoanalysis*, 1939, p. 99, subscribes in some measure to a similar view in saying that "frightening instinctual situations can in the last resort be traced back to external situations of danger."

la grandeur du plaisir, ou de la peine; j'appelle cette grandeur *intensité.*"[191]

Concerning this passage in Maupertuis, Bentham explicitly confesses in an unpublished MS: "I thought I had made a sort of discovery, when it had occurred to me that the quantity of Happiness and Unhappiness in any given subject was to be calculated upon these dimensions; and had drawn up a few propositions upon that principle. I was much surprised upon turning over the works of that ingenious Philosopher to find the idea anticipated. Beyond these two dimensions indeed he does not go. The tract in which it occurs for all the useful and original hints it contains is but little known in this country; it has not I believe been translated into our language. The truth is the positions in it for the most part are as false as they are uncomfortable: which may serve to account for the little notice that has been taken of it."[192] That, however, Bentham did not publish these confessions is comprehensible. For this problem of the measurement of pleasures and pains was ultimately treated by Bentham far more thoroughly than by his predecessors such as Hobbes, Hutcheson, Beccaria, Hartley and Maupertuis.

Just as Bentham was far from being the first who formulated the utility principle or who gave definitions of four moral sanctions, so he is as far from being the first who coped with the problem of the measurement of pleasure and pain. Perhaps we should go back even to Plato[193] or Epicurus[194] to find the inaugurators of such trends of thought.

Among English predecessors of Bentham in the seventeenth century, Hobbes speaks of three of the "dimensions" of pleasure and pain, later enumerated by Bentham, namely duration, intensity, extension, in the following way: Bona et mala si comparentur, majus est, caeteris paribus, quod est diuturnius,

[191] Maupertuis, *Oeuvres*, tome I, 1756, p. 194 (*Essai de philosophie morale,* chap. I).

[192] Bentham, *unpublished* MS, University College, London. Portfolio 27, Folder 6, sheet 128; compare a similar short reference to Maupertuis in Bentham MSS published by E. Halévy, *La formation du radicalisme philosophique*, tome I, p. 406 (not to be found in the English translation of this work).

[193] See e.g. Plato: Protagoras 357 A, B: ἐπεὶ δὲ δὴ ἡδονῆς τε καὶ λύπης ἐν ὀρθῇ τῇ αἱρέσει ἐφάνη ἡμῖν ἡ σωτηρία τοῦ βίου οὖσα τοῦ τε πλέονος καὶ ἐλάττονος καὶ μείζονος καὶ σμικροτέρου καὶ πορρωτέρω καὶ ἐγγυτέρω ἄρα πρῶτον μὲν οὐ μετρητικὴ φαίνεται, ὑπερβολῆς τε καὶ ἐνδείας οὖσα καὶ ἰσότητος πρὸς ἀλλήλας σκέψις.

[194] See Epicurus, *Epistula ad Menoeceum* 129 f ed. C. Bailey 1926, p. 88: Πᾶσα οὖν ἡδονὴ διὰ τὸ φύσιν ἔχειν οἰκείαν ἀγαθὸν, οὐ πᾶσα μέντοι αἱρετή· καθάπερ καὶ ἀλγηδὼν πᾶσα κακόν, οὐ πᾶσα δὲ ἀεὶ φευκτὴ πεφυκυῖα. τῇ μέντοι συμμετρήσει καὶ συμφερόντων καὶ ἀσυμφόρων βλέψει ταῦτα πάντα κρίνειν καθήκει. And compare *ibid.* p. 335 Dr. Bailey's explicit reference to the "Utilitarian calculus of pleasure."

ut totum parte.—Et quod, caeteris paribus, vehementius, ob eandem causam. Differunt enim magis et minus ut majus et minus.—Et, caeteris paribus, quod pluribus bonum, quam quod paucioribus. Nam generalius et specialius differunt ut majus et minus.[195]

Hutcheson, in his *Inquiry concerning Moral Good and Evil*, says: "The applying a mathematical Calculation to *moral Subjects*, will appear perhaps at first extravagant and *wild*; but some Corollarys, which are easily and certainly deduce'd below, may shew the Conveniency of this Attempt, if it could be farther pursu'd";[196] and he speaks of different and *"equal Degrees of Happiness*," of "the *Number* of *Persons* to whom the Happiness shall extend"[197] and of *"Addition* to the happiness" and *"Diminution"* in it.[198] But there can be no doubt that Hutcheson did not compare consistently, and did not believe in the possibility of a consistent comparison of different pleasures and pains in exclusively quantitative terms. He also brings in the different qualitative "dignity" of persons or pleasures,[199] as John Stuart Mill did later on.

W. R. Scott, in his monograph on Hutcheson, speaks of two rather unknown authors who also may be regarded as champions of the introduction of a hedonistic calculus,[200] both contemporaries of Hutcheson; one is *Archibald Campbell*,[201] the other an anonymous writer whom Scott thinks he can

[195] Hobbes, *Works*, ed. Molesworth, *Opera Philosophica quae latine scripsit*, vol. II, 1839, p. 102 f, *De homine*, caput XI, 14 (The reference to Hobbes given by E. Halévy, *La formation du radicalisme philosophique*, tome I, 1901, p. 277 f is not quite correct).

[196] F. Hutcheson, *An Inquiry into the Original of Our Ideas of Beauty and Virtue*, Treatise II, concerning Moral Good and Evil, 1729, sect. III, XV, p. 197.

[197] *Ibid., Treatise II, Concerning Moral Good and Evil*, 1729, sect. III, VIII, p. 179.

[198] *Ibid.*, sect. III, VI, p. 177.

[199] See F. Hutcheson, *An Inquiry into the Original of Our Ideas of Beauty and Virtue*, Treatise II, concerning Moral Good and Evil, 1729, sect. III, VIII, p. 179 f. Compare E. Halévy's references to similar passages in Hutcheson's *System of Moral Philosophy*, Book II, chap. VII (E. Halévy, *La formation du radicalisme philosophique*, tome I, 1901, p. 283). Cf. further W. R. Scott, *Francis Hutcheson*, 1900, p. 280, where Scott hints even at some differences between the first and the later editions of Hutcheson's *Inquiry*, so far as the hedonistic calculus is concerned.

[200] See W. R. Scott, *Francis Hutcheson*, 1900, p. 106 ff.

[201] Campbell: *An Enquiry into the Original of Moral Virtue, wherein it is shewn (against the author of the Fable of the Bees, etc.) that Virtue is founded in the Nature of Things, is unalterable and eternal, and the great Means of private and publick happiness. With some reflections on a late book, intitled, an Enquiry into the Original of our Ideas of Beauty and Virtue*, 1733, pp. 275 ff. The first edition of this work appeared in 1728 under the title Ἀρετὴ Λογία *or, an Enquiry into the Original of Moral Virtue* and under the name of Alexander Innes, D.D. Preacher-Assistant at St. Margaret's, Westminster. Alexander Innes is however not a "prête-nom d'Archibald Campbell," as Halévy assumed (*La formation du radicalisme philosophique*, tome I, 1901, p. 283), but it is the name of the writer who

identify with *John Gay*,[202] the same John Gay whose definitions of four moral sanctions and whose general utilitarian ideas we have already met with. Both these thinkers distinguish between duration and degrees of a feeling which should be multiplied in order to receive the total amount of the value of a pleasure or a pain in question.[203] Campbell suggests adding or subtracting from such a result the value of painful or pleasant "Consequents" of the said pleasure or pain.[201] Moreover, the anonymous writer adds one point which is not mentioned even in Bentham's analysis: he distinguishes within "the intenseness of pleasure" the quantity of good in the object from the degrees of susceptibility in the person affected.[204] Yet, although this is in a certain way an enrichment of the analysis at issue, evidently it cannot alter the calculation of the final, total degree of intensities of feeling; and on the whole, the idea of a felicific calculus is, in those older authors, less developed than in Bentham, apart from the fact that there is no evidence that Bentham knew them.

As to *Beccaria's* attempts at measuring ingredients of pains, Bentham himself indicated clearly the amount of his indebtedness to this predecessor in

---

contributed a prefatory introduction to this first edition of the work, "a prefatory Introduction in a letter to the Author of the Fable of the Bees."

[202] See *An Enquiry into the Origin of the Human Appetites and Affections, shewing how each arises from Association, with an account of the entrance of moral evil into the world. To which are added some remarks on the independent scheme, which deduces all obligation on God's part and man's from certain abstract relations, truth* &c., Lincoln, 1747 (reprinted in *Metaphysical Tracts by English Philosophers of the Eighteenth Century* ed. Samuel Parr, 1837), p. 168 f.

[203] As the work of the anonymous writer is of special interest, I think it may be even worth enlarging Scott's quotation, *An Enquiry into the Origin of the Human Appetites and Affections*, 1747, p. 168 f: "All pleasure is relative to the faculty perceiving it, and is in compound ratio of its intenseness and duration. Hence, in equal degrees of intenseness, the pleasure is as the duration; and in equal durations, the pleasure is as the intenseness. Consequently, when the intenseness of one pleasure is to the intenseness of another, as the duration of *this*, is to the duration of *that*, the pleasures, strictly speaking, are equal, and it is perfectly indifferent whether of them be chosen, provided man's existence is commensurate to each, and the enjoyment of neither of them incompatible with the enjoyment of others. Whence we see, that an infinitely small pleasure may be preferable to an infinitely great one, provided the duration of the former surpasses the duration of the latter in a greater ratio than the intenseness of one exceeds the intenseness of the other. This shews us it may be many times prudent to postpone a very great pleasure to a very small one, supposing their durations bear little or no proportion to each other. . . . The intenseness of pleasure depends on the quantity of good in the object, and the degrees of susceptibility in the person affected. When the susceptivities therefore of two persons are the same, the intenseness is as the quantities of good in the object; and in equal quantities, the intenseness is as their susceptibility."

[204] *An Enquiry into the Origin of the Human Appetites and Affections*, 1747, p. 169.

the following way: "It was from Beccaria's little treatise on crimes and punishments that I drew, as I well remember, the first hint of this principle, by which the precision and clearness and incontestableness of mathematical calculation are introduced for the first time into the field of morals—a field to which in its own nature they are applicable with the propriety no less incontestable, and when once brought to view manifest, than that of physics."[205]

Finally also, Hartley distinguishes carefully between "degree and duration" within the experiences of "Happiness and misery";[206] and he even speaks of the special tendencies of pain and pleasure to "procure" other—similar or opposite—feelings,[207] that is, he speaks, though not in the same terminology, of Bentham's dimension of fecundity. Apart from this, however, as we have already seen, Hutcheson as well as Beccaria and Hartley knows and acknowledges—at least implicitly—the existence of another "dimension" of pleasure and pain, viz. their "extension" mentioned in their formulas of the greatest happiness principle. But while all these moralists discuss the problem of the different "elements or dimensions of pleasure and pain" only in passing, Bentham gives it a far more central position and detailed treatment.

Bentham distinguishes not only two or four elements of pain and pleasure, as his predecessors did, but he enumerates seven such ingredients or dimensions of the value of pleasure and pain: intensity, duration, certainty or uncertainty, propinquity or remoteness, fecundity, purity and extent.[208] And the meaning of these terms is perhaps most simply characterized in the following mnemonic rhymes "framed . . . not long after the publication of the first edition" of the *Introduction* and printed first in the second edition, in 1823:

> Intense, long, certain, speedy, fruitful, pure—
> Such marks in pleasures and in pains endure.
> Such pleasures seek, if *private* be thy end:

[205] Bentham: *Works*, 1843, vol. III, p. 286b, 287a, IV: Elements or dimensions of value in regard to pleasures and pains (Appendix to the essay on "Nomography," written between 1811 and 1831) compare Bentham MS Portfolio 27, quoted by E. Halévy, *La formation du radicalisme philosophique*, tome I, 1901, p. 291: "To M. Beccaria . . . I owe . . . the consideration of the ingredients in the value of punishment, which put me upon extending the application of it to pain and pleasure." Compare, however Appendix II of the present book, where Bentham tells us that only after his reading Beccaria did he discover how Maupertuis "some years prior to . . . Beccaria" had proceeded on the same idea. As to Beccaria's calculus of the duration of pains, see e.g. "Dei Delitti e delle Pene," §16.
[206] D. Hartley, *Observations on Man*, 1810, 5th edition (first ed. 1749), part II, chap. IV, sect. 3, prop. 88, p. 407-409.
[207] *Ibid.*, part I, chap. I, sect. 2, prop. 14, corol. 10 (1749), 1810 (fifth ed.) part I, p. 86.
[208] Bentham, *Introduction*, 1789, chap. IV, sect. 4.

227

If it be *public*, wide let them *extend*.
Such *pains* avoid, whichever be thy view:
If pains *must* come, let them *extend* to few.[209]

As Bentham adds, if pleasures and pains are "considered each of them by itself" then only their intensity, duration, certainty or uncertainty, propinquity or remoteness can come into account; but, estimating the whole tendency of an act or event by which pleasure or pain are produced, we have to consider apart from the first four properties the next two, namely, the fecundity and the purity of these pleasant and painful feelings.[210] The fecundity of such a feeling means "the chance it has of being followed by sensations of the *same* kind: that is, pleasures, if it be a pleasure: pains if it be a pain"; and its purity means "the chance it has of *not* being followed by sensations of the *opposite* kind, that is pains if it be a pleasure: pleasures, if it be a pain."[211] Only if a number of persons are taken into account "with reference to each of whom the value of a pleasure or a pain is considered," then the *extent* of pleasures or pains has also to be taken into consideration, that is, the number of persons who have such pleasures and pains.[212] If nothing else, this enumeration of the dimensions of pleasure and pain should protect Bentham from the common suspicion of having paid attention only to the greatest numbers.

The numbers of persons concerned appears in Bentham's enumeration only in the last, the seventh place. And needless to say, the most consistent philosopher of the utility principle never used his ethical principle in the superficial sense of placing any kind of happiness of any majority above the happiness of any minority, without caring for the intensities of pains and pleasures experienced by these minorities. Bentham, not by chance, gives intensities of happiness and suffering the first place in his felicific calculus. To overlook this in any criticism of his moral arithmetic would be as mistaken a criticism as if one were to suspect him of judging the wealth of a man only by the credit side of his account and neglecting the subtraction to be made by taking into consideration the debit side.

With regard to final moral judgments, Bentham can describe the process of the utilization of his seven "properties" of pleasure and pain as follows: "Begin with any one person of those whose interests seem most immediately to be affected by it: and take an account 1. Of the

---

[209] Bentham, *Introduction*, 2nd edition, 1823, chap. IV, sect. 2, note.
[210] Bentham, *Introduction*, 1789, chap. IV, sect. 2-3.
[211] *Ibid.*, sect. 3.   [212] *Ibid.*, sect. 4.

value of each distinguishable *pleasure* which appears to be produced by it in the *first* instance. 2. Of the value of each *pain* which appears to be produced by it in the *first* instance. 3. Of the value of each pleasure which appears to be produced by it *after* the first. This constitutes the fecundity of the first *pleasure* and the *impurity* of the first *pain*. 4. Of the value of each *pain* which appears to be produced by it after the first. This constitutes the *fecundity* of the first *pain*, and the impurity of the first pleasure. 5. Sum up all the values of all the *pleasures* on the one side, and those of all the pains on the other. . . . 6. Take an account of the *number* of persons whose interests appear to be concerned; and repeat the above process with respect to each. . . . Take the *balance*; which, if on the side of *pleasure*, will give the general *good tendency* of the act, with respect to the total number or community of individuals concerned; if on the side of pain, the general *evil tendency*, with respect to the same community."[213] The same process is applicable to both pleasure and pain, in whatever shape they appear, whether they be "called good . . . or profit . . . or convenience, or advantage, benefit, emolument, happiness, and so forth: to pain whether it be called evil . . . or mischief, or inconvenience, or disadvantage, or loss, or unhappiness, and so forth."[214]

Defending himself against the charge of artificial rationalization Bentham grants that the process just described should not be expected to be "strictly pursued previously to every moral judgment, or to every legislative or judicial operation."[215] But he insists that if such a process is to be followed with any hope that it will approach the character of exactitude, it must be pursued on approximately such lines.[215] And in a long MS only partly published by Halévy,[216] he gave further detailed instructions on how to elaborate this application of a hedonistic calculus. Yet Bentham frankly admitted that his moral arithmetic does not represent in his eyes "a novel . . . theory."[217] He even thinks that some kind of felicific calculus is and always was commonly in use. As he mentions, even in considering the pleasures derivable from the possession of an estate, we all calculate in such ways: we think of the length or shortness of the time, of the nearness or remoteness of the time, and of the certainty or uncertainty[218] of our coming into possession of the pleasures in question.

---

[213] *Ibid.*, sect. 5.   [214] *Ibid.*, sect. 7.   [215] *Ibid.*, sect. 6.
[216] See the full publication of this MS (University College, London, Portfolio xxvii, folder No. 5, sheet 32-40) in appendix IV of the present book. John Laird has called attention to the general importance which should be attributed even to the incomplete publication of this MS (see J. Laird: *The Idea of Value*, 1929, p. 326 ff).
[217] Bentham, *Introduction*, 1789, chap. iv, sect. 8.   [218] *Ibid.*, sect. 8.

Thus, apparently, Bentham himself was scarcely so convinced of the originality of the hedonistic calculus as E. Albee, who says in his *History of English Utilitarianism* that "the one important respect in which Bentham departs from his predecessors is in his dubious attempt to reduce ethics to moral arithmetic, in the grimly literal sense."[219] But, Albee adds, this "cannot be regarded as a real advance in ethical theory."[219] On the contrary, Albee is convinced that the introduction of a consistent felicific calculus in ethics represents a disastrous retrogression even within the development of utilitarianism. And on this question, from the days of John Stuart Mill, there has been an almost general agreement of opinion among moralists and historians of philosophy.

Very little is gained by William L. Davidson's observation that "a 'sum of pleasures' . . . may not adequately represent the whole situation, if we demand mathematical precision and exhaustive analysis; but it is the best practical standard . . . , a standard that men constantly employ."[220] Strangely enough, such avowed anti-hedonists as W. D. Ross and McTaggart explicitly argue in favor of the commensurability of pleasures and values; but as anti-hedonists they are by no means willing to ascribe to this argument the same ethical importance as Bentham. McTaggart maintains for instance that "a calculus of values, or, for example of pleasures" is "theoretically possible"; yet that "nothing can be good but pleasure and nothing evil but pain . . . this limitation of good and evil is held—as I think rightly—to be indefensible."[221]

To me exactly the opposite seems to be obvious. There is certainly no reason for the sweeping optimism of the first part of McTaggart's statement and every reason for the "limitation" in the second part. As to the feasibility of the measurement and even of the comparability of ordinary and of subtle feelings, there are obviously far greater difficulties to be overcome than Ross, McTaggart or Bentham have mentioned. However, that the "limitation" of good and evil to pleasure and pain is not only justifiable but the only appropriate basis for ethical reasoning seems to me well demonstrated by Bentham's life-work.

[219] E. Albee, *A History of English Utilitarianism*, 1902, p. 190.

[220] W. L. Davidson, *Political Thought in England, The Utilitarians from Bentham to J. S. Mill*, 1916, p. 70.

[221] J. M. E. McTaggart, *The Nature of Existence*, 1927, vol. II, pp. 448 f. And see W. D. Ross, *The Right and the Good*, 1930, p. 144.—The physiologist Rudolf Wagner, *Der Kampf um die Seele vom Standpunkt der Wissenschaft*, 1857, p. 94 and Franz Brentano, *Vom Ursprung sittlicher Erkenntnis* (English transl. by Cecil Hague), 1902, p. 89, note 40, had earlier based their objection to any exact measurement of "psychical phenomena" on the authority of Karl Friedrich Gauss.

On this point again, I feel myself in far reaching, though not absolute agreement with Professor C. I. Lewis' most recent observations on Bentham's ethical method. Contrary to anti-hedonism and to "emotive . . . skepticism,"[222] Professor Lewis emphasizes that "a mainly valuable contribution of Bentham and his school lay in their intent to repudiate alien and external criteria of goodness in favor of the immanent ideal of a life to be found good in the living of it."[223] But apart from this fundamental agreement with hedonism, Professor Lewis has subjected the felicific calculus of the *Introduction* to a criticism which is, so far as I can judge, more instructive and, in the end, more constructive than any other treatment of the problem in the vast Bentham literature.

Two minor points of criticism of Bentham are mentioned in a footnote of his *An Analysis of Knowledge and Valuation*. As to the relation between fecundity and purity of pleasure or pain in Bentham, he says: "We do not in fact have two dimensions here but only two names for a single one: a painful consequence of a *pain* being called fecundity, and a painful consequence of a *pleasure*, impurity; and a pleasure being called fecund if followed by other pleasure, and impure if followed by pain."[224] One certainly may admit that purity signifies only, so to speak, the "positive" fecundity of a feeling and impurity its "negative" fecundity; the introduction of two dimensions, purity and fecundity, does not deserve more consideration than should be given to a distinction between length and shortness of a duration. No less readily one may concede that the *chance* of pure and impure consequences "belongs under the dimension of certainty or uncertainty of the consequence, and should be separated from the degree or amount of pleasantness or painfulness in it; which last alone should be included under fecundity or impurity"[225] Bentham himself would probably have granted the correctness of this critical musing on his theme.

Another minor objection raised by Professor Lewis, however, seems to me considerably less conclusive. He says that "with respect to propinquity and remoteness . . . one cannot be sure whether" Bentham "means us to assign to nearer pleasures a higher value just on that account, or whether he has in mind that nearer pleasures are in general more certain. But if it is this latter consideration which is the pertinent one, then he is merely repeating under this head of propinquity or remoteness what is already taken into account under the head of certainty or uncertainty. It is to be feared that what he intends is the

[222] See C. I. Lewis, *An Analysis of Knowledge and Valuation*, 1946, p. VIII.
[223] *Ibid.*, p. 494.   [224] *Ibid.*, p. 489.   [225] *Ibid.*, p. 489.

231

anomalous conception that, although we should rationally be concerned about the future, we should be less concerned about it according as it is more remote—and this quite independently of the greater doubt which attaches to the more remote in general."[226] As far as I can see, the reason for Bentham's introduction of the dimensions propinquity and remoteness can hardly be called an "anomalous conception." The greater doubt which attaches to the more remote in general rightly deserves to be distinguished from the degrees of certainty of concrete cases in the near and remote future.

If a number of large, healthy maple trees are standing quite close to my house, it is certain that left to themselves one of them, within the next three hundred years, will crash down onto the house and cause pain. Nevertheless I should not hesitate to live in that house despite the certainty of the danger, as soon as I properly take its remoteness into account. But if there is only the slightest probability that one of the trees will damage the house within the next month, I had better cut down the tree. Despite the high uncertainty of the danger its nearness makes it alarming. If a statesman knows for certain that, within the next five hundred years, the present rate of coal consumption of his country will lead to the exhaustion of the coal mines of the nation, he will not insist on slowing down coal consumption; but he will do so if there is even the slightest chance of a shortage of coal reserves for the coming year. The highest degree of certainty of pleasure or pain thus becomes irrelevant if coupled with the highest degree of remoteness; and the slightest degree of certainty becomes important if coupled with the slightest degree of remoteness. These examples demonstrate, I think, the desirability of distinguishing between higher certainty in general and that higher certainty which is due merely to the propinquity of an expected feeling.

Expected feelings become, it seems to me, not only generally but always less certain in consequence of their remoteness. I myself or others concerned may die the next minute. I cannot think it unjustified, therefore, to point to this specific significance of remoteness and propinquity, although remoteness and propinquity are important only as factors influencing the degrees of certainty of an event. In other words, the dimension of certainty can be subdivided into certainty generally determined by a law of nature and certainty as affected by the special determination of the time of the occurrence of the event.

Far more important, however, are the major arguments used by Pro-

[226] *Ibid.*, p. 492 f.

fessor Lewis against the possibility of an exact felicific calculus. Briefly speaking, his main criticism is directed against Bentham's neglect of the *Gestaltcharakter* of our emotional experiences. Human feelings are not merely aggregates or heaps of satisfactions which can be counted together according to the simple arithmetic rules of addition or subtraction. Our emotional experience is "cumulative and consummatory."[227] "The value attaching to a whole of experience is not independent of the values realized in its constituent parts, but neither is it determined by them without reference to the manner of their composition."[228] Feelings are experienced in an "organic relationship to one another."[229] The constituent feelings of an emotional whole "interpenetrate and qualify one another by the temporal and other relations"[228] which they have to one another. One might argue that Bentham probably intended to meet at least part of these objections by introducing his dimensions of purity and fecundity of feelings. But in any case, as Professor Lewis makes amply clear in his extensive scrutiny of the felicific calculus of the *Introduction*, if "the pleasure we *find* in the experience combining" two feelings does "not accord with the result of summing them,"[230] we have to abandon only this kind of algedonic calculus and certainly not our reliance on the main principle of ethical empiricism—the principle that "values in direct experience are data which must be accepted as found."

Numerous contemporary attempts have been made at a correct measuring of feelings by Walter Whately Smith, Cambridge, England,[231] Bertha B. Friedman,[232] Columbia University, New York, Douglas Freyer,[233] and, as Dr. Leslie Dunlap, Library of Congress, informs me, American industrialists have recently developed even "hedonic price indexes."[234] None of the attempts of this kind known to me seem satisfactory. But this certainly does not mean that any comparatively correct assessment of the value of our feelings as organic wholes is a priori impossible.

[227] *Ibid.*, p. 496.
[228] *Ibid.*, p. 495.
[229] *Ibid.*, p. 503.
[230] *Ibid.*, p. 491 f, 503.
[231] Walter Whately Smith, *The Measurement of Emotion*, 1922, pp. 31 ff on the psycho-galvanic reflex, the reaction time measured and Jung's reproduction test.
[232] B. B. Friedman, *Foundations of the Measurement of Values; the Methodology of Location and Quantification*, 1946.
[233] Douglas Freyer, *The Measurement of Interests*, 1931.
[234] See *Dynamics of Automobile Demand*, ed. by General Motors Corporation, 1939, based on papers presented at a Joint Meeting of the American Statistical Association and the Economic Society in Detroit, Michigan, December 27, 1938, especially A. T. Court's essay on "Hedonic Price Indexes with Automotive Examples," *ibid.*, pp. 99-117 and Louis A. Bean's discussion of this paper.

Even Professor Lewis' severe criticism of Bentham's felicific calculus finally arrives at the conclusion: although value estimates of emotional wholes "must depend on that kind of envisagement we would suggest by . . . some manner of synthetic apprehension . . . , and this does not have the character of discursive judgment, nevertheless in crediting what is thus synthetically envisaged, discursive judgments of the past and future are relied upon and correctness of them is implied. By the same token, value-assessments so arrived at are capable of confirmation in indefinite degree, in the general manner in which the historically reportable and the predictable can be corroborated or disconfirmed. . . . If by reason of the difficulties of it, we should seek to avoid such value-assessment of experiential wholes, then we shall find that quite impossible, since it is indispensable to any attempted rational direction of life and of our action."[235] Especially as far as the direct measurement of pleasure and pain is concerned, this seems to me the soundest evaluation of the issue presently available.

In other writings differing from the approach of the *Introduction*, Bentham pointed mainly to the possibility of an indirect measurement of pleasure and pain, as we shall see later. But in this respect, too, the difficulties of a precise estimate are obviously greater than in the case of the indirect measurement of heat and color sensations. For, popularly speaking, the causes of the perceptions of heat or color are physical events expressing themselves by physical, measurable movements of the mercury or electro-magnetic waves. The causes of pleasure and pain, however, are mental events, preconceived, intended or avoided pleasurable and painful activities.

To measure the pleasure value of these activities by the measurable amount of money which would cause men to engage in these activities is, in many cases, not possible, as Bentham himself realized. And as other methods of measuring have not yet been found, there is only one indirect way of measurement left open: the inference from performed pleasurable activities to the strength of the preconceived pleasure feelings connected with these activities. If we do not want to abandon any rational understanding of human behavior, we are entitled to conclude that any chosen pleasurable activity is caused by a stronger feeling of preconceived satisfaction than its alternatives. Of course, this provides us only with the possibility of measurement of pleasure feelings connected with performed acts. Nevertheless insights of this kind are certainly not valueless in ethics.

[235] C. I. Lewis, *An Analysis of Knowledge and Valuation*, 1946, pp. 508, 506.

Ethics could be called, in a certain sense, "medicina mentis." Just as the physician generally cannot direct the cure of an ailing body with the same precision as an engineer the building of a bridge so, in a similar way, the moralist must try to obtain the best possible, probable value-assessment of all the satisfactions and dissatisfactions involved in a certain moral issue. This task is "as inescapable as it is difficult."[236]

Professor A. J. Ayer and Professor L. J. Lafleur, in their latest publications, both confirm this view in principle, though they stress exactly the opposite aspects of the matter. Professor Ayer thinks that "Bentham's process of 'sober calculation' " is a "myth."[237] But in the end, he admits that though "our estimates of what it is that people 'really' want and how far they are satisfied are bound to be somewhat rough and ready, . . . I think that by observing people's behaviour one can become reasonably sure that their general adherence to certain rules of conduct would on the whole promote the satisfaction of their wants and it is just the discovery and application of such rules that Bentham's principle of utility recommends."[238] Professor Lafleur, on the other hand, insists that "felicific quality is precisely quantified regardless of the evident fact that our knowledge of the quantities is highly imperfect and that we do not even possess unit values in which to attempt to measure them."[239]

In any case, the felicific calculus of Bentham's *Introduction* does not present a fully satisfactory solution of the difficulties in question. In his later years, Bentham had obviously given up the over-optimistic confidence of his youth in this respect. Yet with the fall of the hedonic calculus, as it stands in the *Introduction*, the foundations of consistent hedonism are not endangered to any greater extent than the foundations of medicine by the insight that medicine is not a science of the same precision as physics or inorganic chemistry. In ethics, as in medicine, our judgment is in general as far removed from strict exactness as from total uncertainty. In fact, merely "intuitive estimates" of the intensities of feelings and the influence of joy and grief are taken more and more into consideration in contemporary psychosomatic medicine. But these estimates of the strength of emotions do not make medicine mere guesswork any more than ethics. It would be, therefore, more than

---

[236] *Ibid.*, p. 510.

[237] A. J. Ayer, "The Principle of Utility" in *Jeremy Bentham and the Law*, ed. by G. W. Keeton and G. Schwarzenberger, 1948, p. 258.

[238] *Ibid.*, p. 259.

[239] L. J. Lafleur, in his introduction to a new edition of Bentham's *An Introduction to the Principles of Morals and Legislation*, 1948, p. xiv.

folly to exchange the lack of mathematical precision in hedonism for the dogmatism and complete ambiguity of the self-styled "exactness" and self-evidence of anti-hedonistic principles.

BENTHAM'S *TABULA AFFECTUUM* AND THE CONCEPTS OF VIRTUE AND VICE

E. ALBEE has urged against Bentham that, in the *Introduction*, there is no attempt at "a systematic treatment of the particular virtues";[240] and this seems to be correct at first glance. In truth, however, Bentham deliberately refrained from giving a list of definitions of virtues, and in place of this list he offered in the fifth chapter of his *Introduction* a most characteristic substitute, namely, a long list of the different kinds of pleasures and pains, the experience of which is, in his theory, the constitutive element of all virtues and vices.

He explains all this in the preface of his *Introduction* as follows: "In addition to the analysis . . . of . . . the terms pleasure, pain, motive and disposition," the *Introduction to the Principles of Morals and Legislation* "ought to have given a similar analysis of the not less extensive, though much less determinate, ideas annexed to the terms emotion, passion, appetite, *virtue, vice,* and some others including the names of the particular *virtues* and *vices.* But as the true, and, if he conceives right, the only true ground-work for the development for the latter set of terms, has been laid by the explanation of the former, the completion of such a dictionary, so to style it, would, in comparison of the commencement, be little more than a mechanical operation."[241] This observation is, I think, fully justified, if viewed from the critical presuppositions of Bentham's ethical system. Albee's criticism is merely derived from without, ignoring the well considered basis of Bentham's theory.

Bentham insists right from the start of his ethical reasoning that the ambiguous concepts of virtues and vices have to be broken up into their unambiguous constitutive elements, i.e. into the different kinds of pleasures and pains out of which virtuous and vicious motives are formed. It is, therefore, of no relevance if a critic accuses Bentham of neglecting

[240] E. Albee, *A History of English Utilitarianism*, 1902, pp. 182 f.
[241] Bentham, *Introduction* (Oxford edition) p. vii (*Works*, 1843, part 1, p. 2a) (Italics are mine).

the systematic treatment of the particular virtues yet does not mention the reasons which Bentham gave for this neglect.

However, it would certainly be a mistake to overrate the value of Bentham's catalogue of pleasures, as well as the originality of his list of sanctions. Bentham himself gives at least a hint of not feeling sure whether his table of possible pleasures and pain is complete and satisfactory. All he states is that "the several simple pleasures of which human nature is susceptible, *seem* to be as follows: 1. The pleasures of sense. 2. The pleasures of wealth. 3. The pleasures of skill. 4. The pleasures of amity. 5. The pleasures of a good name. 6. The pleasures of power. 7. The pleasures of piety. 8. The pleasures of benevolence. 9. The pleasures of malevolence. 10. The pleasures of memory. 11. The pleasures of imagination. 12. The pleasures of expectation. 13. The pleasures dependent on association. 14. The pleasures of relief. The several simple pains *seem* to be as follows: 1. The pains of privation. 2. The pains of the senses. 3. The pains of awkwardness. 4. The pains of enmity. 5. The pains of an ill-name. 6. The pains of piety. 7. The pains of benevolence. 8. The pains of malevolence. 9. The pains of the memory. 10. The pains of the imagination. 11. The pains of expectation. 12. The pains dependent on association."[242] Bentham gives assurance that this catalogue is "the result" of an analysis of the subject "taken upon an exhaustive plan"; but he "thought it better to discard" this analysis "as being of too metaphysical a cast."[243] And unfortunately, there is no apparent principle which would guarantee its completeness.

Moreover, there are several points in his table with which psychologists would scarcely be able to agree. It is hardly an adequate estimate when he characterizes *ennui* as a feeling of absence of the pleasures of novelty and of all other kinds of pleasure, and when he denies that it is "a positive pain of itself."[244] It comes, I think, much nearer to truth to say that ennui is not only absence of all pleasures but that it is, especially among the unintellectual masses and average people of all types, a severe form of actual suffering. Schopenhauer's characterization of

[242] Bentham, *Introduction*, 1789, chap. v, sect. 2, 3 (Italics are mine).
[243] *Ibid.*, sect. 3 note.
[244] *Ibid.*, sect. 22 note. The *Traités de législation*, ed. Dumont, tome I, 1820, "Principes de législation," chap. vi, sect. 2, p. 42 (*The Theory of Legislation*, ed. Hildreth, 1896, p. 27) go so far as to say that also the want of pleasures of love is not attended with positive pain, except when there is disappointment. "Quelques tempéramens pourroient en souffrir, mais la continence en général est une disposition au plaisir, qui n'est rien moins qu'un état pénible."

Langeweile[245] as a kind of suffering as depressing as pain itself is obviously more true than Bentham's definition. And similarly, "loss of power" can hardly be interpreted as only one of the many kinds of pains of privation, of mere absence of a pleasure,[246] as it is regarded by Bentham. It seems to me a much more capital pain, even if viewed from outside any ethics of power.

On the other hand, Bentham himself remarks that he does not wish to insist on the adequacy of all details of his scheme. He himself suggests that minor incongruities could be regarded as due to "questions of words,"[247] as unessential. It is certainly needless to refer to all the circumstantial descriptions he gives of the details of the pleasures of the different senses, of the pleasures of wealth and skill and so forth.[248] All these particulars are either ethically unimportant or they need no comment.

Historically, however, Bentham's detailed *tabula affectuum* has to be ranked high in the long succession of similar doctrines starting with that of Aristotle in his *Rhetoric*,[249] and leading through Spinoza's classical description of emotions up to modern analyses of feelings such as that of L. T. Troland.[250] All these descriptions acknowledge pleasure and pain as the sole essential elements of emotions; they explain the large variety of feelings exclusively by the accession of different accom-

[245] See A. Schopenhauer, *Die Welt als Wille und Vorstellung*, Band I, Buch 4, §57, translated into English, 1896, vol. I, p. 404: "Ennui is by no means an evil to be lightly esteemed; in the end it depicts on the countenance real despair." Cf. *Aus Schopenhauer's Handschriftlichem Nachlass*, edited by Julius Frauenstädt, 1864, p. 447: Die beiden "grossen Feinde des menschlichen Glücks sind *Schmerz* und *Langeweile*."

[246] Bentham, *Introduction*, 1789, chap. v, sect. 25 note.

[247] *Ibid.*, sect. 22, note 2.

[248] *Ibid.*, sect. 4 ff. One of the notes of this list contains one of the few indications which allow the assumption that Bentham did not completely refuse the belief in a personal God; see the end of the note of chapter v, sect. 33, under II, 4; cf. Bentham, *Works*, 1843, part 15, p. 196a, where God is characterized as an "inferential real entity."

[249] See Aristotle, Τέχνη Ῥητορική e.g. B 1383 b: "ἔστω δὴ αἰσχύνη λύπη τις ἢ ταραχὴ περὶ τὰ εἰς ἀδοξίαν φαινόμενα φέρειν τῶν κακῶν"; *ibid.* B 1385 b: "ἔστω δὴ ἔλεος λύπη τις ἐπὶ φαινομένῳ κακῷ φθαρτικῷ ἢ λυπηρῷ τοῦ ἀναξίου τυγχάνειν"; *ibid.* B 1387 a:"τὸ νεμεσᾶν . . . ἐστι λυπεῖσθαι ἐπὶ τῷ φαινομένῳ ἀναξίως εὐπραγεῖν."

[250] See L. T. Troland, *The Fundamentals of Human Motivation*, 1928, pp. 273-306, especially p. 300 about the relation of his "hedonism of the past" to "the usual hedonisms of the present and the future." Compare Rex Knight in his review of Paulhan's *The Laws of Feeling*, *Mind*, 1931, p. 254 f: "There is now an increasing tendency to hold that pleasure and pain are the only modes of feelings." Or cf. *Bentham's Theory of Legislation*, ed. by Ogden, 1931, notes, p. 501 f.

panying ideas; whereas the opponents of this psychology of emotions, such as Descartes,[251] Wilhelm Wundt and others,[252] presuppose a certain number of original feelings apart from pleasure and pain. Bentham's *tabula affectuum* has hardly been mentioned anywhere in the history of psychology;[253] but, in my opinion, it equals Spinoza's analysis as regards the clinical, naturalistic objectivity of its expositions.

PROBLEMS OF "MORAL PHYSIOLOGY"

IN THE sixth chapter of his *Introduction*, Bentham gives a second seemingly "dry"[254] catalogue of terms, a list of 32 "circumstances influenc-ing" moral "sensibility," that is, 32 causes creating special dispositions of behavior within the morally relevant actions of men. And although he provides here "some sort of analytic view"[255] which has led him to single out and to put in order this variety of circumstances, he con-fesses here again that he cannot pretend to have exhausted his subject. This list is again unsatisfactory in details and is not sufficiently illus-

[251] See Descartes, *Les Passions de l'Âme*, seconde partie, "Du Nombre et de l'Ordre des Passions et l'Explication des six Primitives"; Descartes, *Passiones Animae*, Artic. LXIX: "Non dari nisi sex primitivas passiones . . . nimirum Admira-tionem, Amorem, Odium, Cupiditatem, Laetitiam et Moerorem; et caeteras omnes componi ex quibusdam harum sex, aut earum esse species."

[252] See W. Wundt, *Grundzüge der physiologischen Psychologie*, 1911, Band III, S. 210 ff or W. Wundt, *Outlines of Psychology*, 1907, p. 91 f, where also six "fundamental feeling qualities" are distinguished, viz., "pleasurable and unpleasur-able," "arousing and subduing . . . feeling qualities" and feeling qualities of "strain and relaxation," compare *ibid.*, pp. 182, 194.

[253] Even D. Bidney's recent *Psychology and Ethics of Spinoza* (1940), which lists thinkers and statesmen following the line of Spinoza's theory of emotions, does not mention Bentham. Nor is Bentham referred to in most of the best known histories of psychology. Neither George Sidney Brett, *A History of Psychology*, 3 vols., 1912, 1921; W. B. Pillsbury, *The History of Psychology*, 1929; Adalbert Ford, *The Story of Scientific Psychology*, 1932; Max Dessoir, *Abriss einer Ge-schichte der Psychologie*, 1911; Otto Klemm, *Geschichte der Psychologie*, 1911; Guido Villa, *La psicologia contemporanea*, 1899; Friedrich Harms, *Geschichte der Psychologie*, 1879; nor Théodule Ribot, *La psychologie anglaise contempo-raine*, 1870, have anything to say about Bentham. The two volumes of James Mark Baldwin's *History of Psychology*, 1913, once mention the name of the founder of the utilitarian school and Charles Edward Spearman, *Psychology down the Ages*, two volumes, 1937, quotes (vol. I, p. 178) from Bentham's *Table* but he does not do justice either to the historical importance of Bentham's theory of emotions.

[254] Bentham, *Introduction*, 1789, chap. VI, sect. 6, note.

[255] *Ibid.*, sect. 46.

trated by examples, as Bentham himself admits. "History and biography," he concedes, ought to have been "ransacked" in order to render this catalogue more "amusing" and "intelligible"[256]—a rather frank concession that many-sidedness of historical perspective is not one of the special virtues of his writings.

Bentham apologizes for this defect in his exposition. As he says in passing, he thought it inadvisable that a single chapter of his book should swell into a considerable volume through references to historical and other examples; therefore he confined himself to "dry and general instruction." Nevertheless, he seems to me right in saying that the task undertaken here by him is "if not absolutely the most difficult task, at least one of the most difficult"[257] in morals, namely, the establishment of a kind of "moral physiology." This is, indeed, an important and "new subject."[257] This "moral physiology" has to show how morally neutral circumstances of the individual body and mind of man may, in many cases, acquire relevance in moral valuations; and these circumstances have to be understood and taken into account not only by the jurist but also by the moralist. But of course these analyses cannot shake the absolute validity of the general principle of morals, the principle of utility.

There is no inconsistency in the employment of a universal principle of morals if it is applied with due regard to the differences of health, strength, age, sex, and similar circumstances of individuals. No matter whether we have to do with an ethics of pure intentions or with one of consequences, ethical judgments which neglect the physiological conditions under which men act are necessarily ill-considered.

In order to save ethics from such precipitate moral valuations, ethical naturalists have sporadically referred to these problems of a moral physiology. Bentham, however, wished to give a comparatively exhaustive list of all circumstances influencing moral sensibility on empirical grounds (not, as Spinoza did, in connection with the metaphysical nature of

[256] *Ibid.*, sect. 6, note.

[257] *Ibid.*, sect. 6, note. That questions of physiology should be taken into account in ethics is explicitly stressed also by John Dewey, *Human Nature and Conduct*, 1930, p. 295 f: "Everything that can be known of the human mind and body in physiology, medicine, anthropology and psychology is pertinent to moral inquiry." Cf. Paul Weiss, "Towards a Cosmological Ethics," *The Journal of Philosophy*, Nov. 24, 1938, p. 649: "An adequate theory of ethics can not neglect a consideration of the natural circumstances and situations in which actions occur. . . . This entails not only a knowledge . . . of the body, but also of the world in which that body finds its material and the conditions for its public actions."

God) and so he applied here the following scheme: in the first place, these circumstances "may be distinguished into *primary* and *secondary*: Those may be termed primary, which operate immediately of themselves: those secondary, which operate not but by the medium of the former. To this latter head belong the circumstances of sex, age, station in life, education, climate, lineage, government and religious profession: the rest are primary. These again are either conate or adventitious: those which are conate are radical frame of body and radical frame of mind. Those which are adventitious are either personal, or exterior. The personal, again, concern either a man's disposition, or his actions. Those which concern his disposition concern either his body or his mind. Those which concern his body are health, strength, hardiness, and bodily imperfection. Those which concern his mind, again concern either his understanding or his affections. To the former head belong the circumstances of quantity and quality of knowledge, strength of understanding, and insanity. To the latter belong the circumstances of firmness of mind, steadiness, bent of inclination, moral sensibility, moral biases, religious sensibility, religious biases, sympathetic sensibility, sympathetic biases, antipathetic sensibility, and antipathetic biases. Those which regard his actions are his habitual occupations. Those which are exterior to him regard either the things or the persons which he is concerned with; under the former head come his pecuniary circumstances; under the latter, his connexions in the way of sympathy and antipathy."[258] In this way Bentham speaks of 32 such circumstances influencing moral sensibility, namely: health, strength, hardiness, bodily imperfection, quantity and quality of knowledge, strength of intellectual powers, firmness of mind, steadiness of mind, bent of inclination, moral sensibility, moral biases, religious sensibility, religious biases, sympathetic sensibility, sympathetic biases, antipathetic sensibility, antipathetic biases, insanity, habitual occupations, pecuniary circumstances, connexions in the way of sympathy, connexions in the way of antipathy, radical frame of body, radical frame of mind, sex, age, rank, education, climate, lineage, government, religious profession.[259] Here again, however, it does not seem to me necessary to reproduce all the particulars, added by Bentham in order to explain the meaning of his 32 terms.

Only a few characteristic details may be touched upon. Bentham here comes back to the problem of the relations between body and mind as

[258] Bentham, *Introduction*, chap. vi, sect. 46; compare chap. vi, sect. 34, sect. 6.
[259] Bentham, *Introduction*, 1789, chap. vi, sect. 6.

regards the expression of emotions by "external indications," and he finds that the quantity of pleasure and pain felt by a man may perhaps be measured best by his pulse. For "man has not the motions of his heart at command as he has those of the muscles of his face."[260] But Bentham does not overrate this suggestion of his and does not pursue the matter any further.

On the contrary, as a critical moralist he warns us against measuring the degree, the "quantity" of feelings by external indications such as the "number of moments spent in crying" or "the quantity of the tears. ... Oliver Cromwell, whose conduct indicated a heart more than ordinarily callous, was as remarkably profuse in tears."[261] Although it may be denied that Cromwell was more than ordinarily callous, at least the general psychological observation made here by Bentham certainly corresponds to the facts.

Bentham shows himself further to be a judicious observer by emphasizing that all external expressions of human feelings, even the pulse, express only that a man is affected; but "they cannot express in what manner, nor from what cause. To an affection resulting in reality from such or such cause, he may give an artificial colouring, and attribute it to such or such another cause. To an affection directed in reality to such or such a person as its object, he may give an artificial bias, and represent it as if directed to such or such another object. Tears of rage he may attribute to contrition. The concern he feels at the thoughts of a punishment that awaits him, he may impute to a sympathetic concern for the mischief produced by his offence."[262] As so often elsewhere, Bentham is specially successful in unmasking hypocritical moral feelings of the type just mentioned.

In addition, psychologically and ethically valuable remarks of a more positive nature are scattered in this moral physiology, for instance, when Bentham declares that "the first pleasure issuing from your own bosom as it were from a radiant point, illuminates the bosom of your friend: reverberated from thence, it is reflected with augmented warmth to the point from whence it first proceeded; and so it is with pains. This is one reason why legislators in general like better to have married people to deal with than single; and people that have children than such as are childless. It is manifest that the stronger and more numerous a man's connexions in the way of sympathy are, the stronger is the hold which the law has upon him. A wife and children are so many pledges a man

[260] *Ibid.*, sect. 33, note.   [261] *Ibid.*, sect. 33.   [262] *Ibid.*, sect. 33, note.

gives to the world for his good behaviour."[263] In this way, the supposed ethical egoist Bentham sings a very sincere praise of sympathy and benevolence. What this song of praise lacks in poetical fire it seems to me to gain by its shrewd and sober juristic observations.

On the other hand, some particulars given here are of rather questionable value, at least if judged by the standard of modern science, for instance, Bentham's assumption that "the health of a female is more delicate than that of the male,"[264] or that "in hot climates men's health is apt to be more precarious than in cold."[265] Statements of this type can hardly be accepted today without supplementary limitations. Yet the discussion of these questions is not only of importance in the fields of medicine and anthropology, it is no less essential in jurisprudence. Moreover, a kind of moral physiology is, in my opinion, a main desideratum of any critical, objective ethics.

THE ARRANGEMENT OF BENTHAM'S ANALYSIS OF ACTS, AND THE ARRANGEMENT OF THE WHOLE CONTENTS OF THE *INTRODUCTION*

After having marked out the problem of a moral physiology, i.e. the questions concerning general, remote "circumstances influencing sensibility," Bentham sets out to view the particular elements of actions, the intentional-

---

[263] *Ibid.*, chap. VI, sect. 26; cf. chap. XI, sect. 42 (under Rule 4): "The general and standing bias of every man's nature is therefore, towards that side to which the force of the social motives would determine him to adhere. This being the case, the force of the social motives tends continually to put an end to that of the dissocial ones; as, in natural bodies, the force of friction tends to put an end to that which is generated by impulse. Time, then, which wears away the force of the dissocial motives, adds to that of the social." Here again the "ethical egoist" Bentham underrates perhaps the strength of egoistic and dissocial motives, as the eighteenth century generally did to an even larger extent. See E. Halévy's discussion of "le principe de la fusion des intérêts" in his *La formation du radicalisme philosophique*, 1901, e.g. pp. 16 ff. I think, however, Halévy's views unsatisfactory on this point, at least so far as the basis of Bentham's ethics is concerned.

[264] Bentham, *Introduction*, 1789, chap. VI, sect. 35.

[265] *Ibid.*, sect. 39. In Dumont's edition of Bentham's *Traités de législation*, 1802, chap. IX, "Des principes généraux de législation" is devoted to the same questions. Bowring, therefore, in his edition of Bentham's *Introduction* inserted after chapter VI a translation of section III of this chapter IX of Dumont's edition. But Bowring did not give the exact reference to Dumont's text.

ity, the motives of acts, the distinctions to be made between different kinds of acts, and finally the ethical problem of the consequences of human actions. But though the arrangement of this material is in general quite perspicuous, in several details the systematic order is not brought out and not preserved with sufficient care; and by such details the structure of the whole scheme has occasionally been obscured.

It would be natural to expect Bentham to treat the problems connected with the intentionality and the motives of acts immediately after his discussion of the remote "circumstances influencing sensibility," and then to go on to analyze the actions themselves and their consequences. Instead, he first gives an analysis of the different classes of acts themselves, and then goes back to the problems of intentions and motives. Moreover, in the seventh chapter of the *Introduction* he even mixes a general survey of the arrangement of all these different problems with the detailed discussion of one of them—that concerning the actions themselves and the circumstances in which they are done.

I shall try to clear up this disorder and attempt to separate distinctly the survey of the whole contents of the *Introduction* from the discussion of only one portion of the subject.

The general survey of the main subjects of the *Introduction* sketched here is this: In the first chapter the principle of utility is introduced, with its reference to pleasure as the sole "good thing," pain as the sole evil. In the 2nd chapter it is shown why no principle adverse to that of utility can represent a consistent standard of moral valuations. In the 3rd chapter, four different sources of pain and pleasure are distinguished as the four possible sanctions. In the fourth chapter, the problem of the measurement of pleasure and pain is dealt with. In the fifth chapter, the different kinds of pleasure and pain are described; and beginning with the sixth chapter, the analysis of human acts and their different elements or accompanying circumstances are set out. In the sixth chapter itself, we are given the general, remote circumstances influencing moral sensibility and action; in the seventh chapter, the acts themselves and the particular circumstances in which they are done; in the eighth chapter, the general intentions of acts, that is, the ideas of the consequences of acts, so far as these ideas are preconceived before the acts; in the ninth chapter, the degree of understanding and of consciousness connected with the intention; in the tenth chapter, the particular motives which make the consequences of an act attractive, which thus decisively give birth to the act and which in no wise are identical with the intention of the act; in the eleventh chapter, the particular, permanent dispositions of men are discussed, so far as they are revealed in actions in contrast to the transient motives and intentions of these acts; in the twelfth chapter, the consequences, especially the mischievous consequences, of acts are analyzed with regard to their ethical importance; the thirteenth chapter deals with the cases unmeet for punishment, cases which are also unmeet for moral blame, at least to a certain extent; for though these last four chapters starting with the thirteenth concern especially juristic problems, they are of high importance for Bentham's ethics too; in the fourteenth chapter the proportion between punishment and offenses is discussed; in the fifteenth chapter, the properties to be given to a "lot" of punishment; in the sixteenth chapter, a very long systematic register of all possible main kinds of offenses is laid down; and in the seventeenth chapter, the chief characteristics of ethics and of jurisprudence are described and a line of demarcation drawn between ethics and legislation.

THE ANALYSIS OF ACTS: THEIR DIFFERENT ELEMENTS AND ACCOMPANYING CIRCUMSTANCES

Aside from this foreshadowing of the whole contents of the *Introduction*, the seventh chapter contains a detailed classification of actions in general and the circumstances in which they are performed. First, acts are here distinguished as positive and negative. By positive acts or "acts of commission . . . are meant such as consist in motion or exertion: by negative" acts or "acts of omission . . . such as consist in keeping at rest; that is, in forbearing to move or exert one's self in such and such circumstances. Thus, to strike is a positive act: not to strike on a certain occasion a negative one."[266] But, true to the critical character of his ethics, Bentham warns us also here against trusting in "the form of the discourse made use of to express" whether an act is positive or negative. "An act which is positive in its nature may be characterized by a negative expression"[267] and vice versa. Thinking back, for instance, to the problem of sanctions against political aggressors which was so much discussed immediately before the Second World War, one can see how much language may mislead the moral judgment. As long as one remains under the spell of the linguistic expression of the matter, one must of course be under the impression that the application of sanctions is a positive act of punishment; in truth, however, it is essentially a negative act, the refusal to finance political crimes. And Bentham's own examples, "the not revealing a conspiracy," the not thinking of paying a tax,[268] are simpler yet equally instructive illustrations of his point.

[266] Bentham, *Introduction*, chap. VII, sect. 8.
[267] *Ibid.*, sect. 10.   [268] *Ibid.*, sect. 8, note.

Bentham's ethical criticism is thus, even on this formal point, of both theoretical and practical interest. As he again and again emphasizes, the critical moralist must avoid at all costs what Nietzsche called "seduction" by linguistic peculiarities or by grammar.[269] Not only the premature praising or blaming of human motives is a source of great error; even a mistake as regards the positive or negative character of acts may lead to grossly false conclusions in morals. Logical positivism and semantics have made us more and more aware of pitfalls of this kind in the theories of nature. In the theories of morals warnings against these traps are even today especially needed, as the credulity in the holiness of language is here much higher and the taking of a word for a phenomenon almost the rule.

Second, acts are distinguished by Bentham as external and internal. "By external, are meant corporal acts; acts of the body: by internal, mental acts; acts of the mind. Thus, to strike is an external or exterior act: to intend to strike, an internal or interior one."[270] Acts of discourse, however, are a sort of mixture of external and internal acts; they are external acts, but as external in "no ways material . . . any farther than as they serve to express the existence of internal"[271] acts.

Further, Bentham distinguishes between transient and continued acts, between a repetition of acts and a habit,[272] between indivisible and divisible, between simple and complex acts, between material and immaterial, exculpatory and aggravative circumstances[273] accompanying acts, and between consequences of acts which are related to the acts themselves in the way of conjunct influence.[274]

The meaning of such divisions and subdivisions is aptly illustrated in this chapter by means of examples, one of them being especially graphic. Just as Pascal said in his *Pensées* that the history of the world would have had another course if Cleopatra's nose had had a different shape,[275] so Bentham tries to exemplify the multitude of remote, extravagant circumstances which can influence historical acts. He states, for instance, that there can be found a connection even between the famous cackling of a goose on the Roman Capitol in 390 B.C. and the murder of Henry IV of France 2,000 years later in 1610 A.D.[276] Nevertheless, most

---

[269] See F. Nietzsche, *Jenseits von Gut und Böse*, e.g. §34.
[270] Bentham, *Introduction*, 1789, chap. VII, sect. 11.
[271] *Ibid.*, chap. VII, sect. 12.　　[272] *Ibid.*, sect. 16-18.
[273] *Ibid.*, sect. 19 f, 23, 27.　　[274] *Ibid.*, sect. 24.
[275] See Pascal, *Pensées*, première partie, article IX, XLVI: "Si le nez de Cléopâtre eût été plus court, toute la face de la terre aurait changé."
[276] See Bentham, *Introduction*, 1789, chap. VII, sect. 26, note.

of these divisions and subdivisions are of minor importance or self-explanatory or they concern jurisprudence rather than ethics. They, therefore, need no special mention.

It need only be observed that Bentham repeats here his admonition neither to "harass ourselves" with unsolvable doubts, nor one another with interminable disputes, and to "be aware of the ambiguity of language."[277] Thus, freedom from the tyranny of language is shown by Bentham to be of the highest value everywhere in ethics. But with regard to most of the definitions of this chapter, this freedom can be obtained in a comparatively easy way.

Intentionality

Bentham's discussion of intentions and their ethical relevance is to be found in the eighth chapter. It too at first deals rather with definitions than with answers to ethical questions. The meaning of the distinctions between the different kinds of intentionality and unintentionality[278] laid down here may be elucidated in the shortest and simplest way by going through the one example used by Bentham, in which he shows all the different possible variations of intentionality and unintentionality in relation to one and the same act, namely, the injury of William II by Sir Walter Tyrrel during a stag-hunt by a wound of which this king of England died. With regard to this one act, according to Bentham, we are able to distinguish at least nine different kinds of intentionality in which the act could have been done.

First, we may suppose that "Tyrrel did not so much as entertain a thought of the king's death; or, if he did, looked upon it as an event of which there was no danger. In either of these cases the incident of his killing the king was altogether unintentional. 2. He saw a stag running that way, and he saw the king riding that way at the same time: what he aimed at was to kill the stag: he did not wish to kill the king: at the same time he saw, that if he shot, it was as likely he should kill the king as the stag: yet for all that he shot, and killed the king accordingly. In this case the incident of his killing the king was intentional, but obliquely so. 3. He killed the king on account of the hatred he bore him, and for no other reason than the pleasure of destroying him. In this case the incident of the king's death was not only directly but ultimately intentional. 4. He killed the king, intending fully so to do; not for any hatred he bore him, but for the sake of plundering him when

---

[277] *Ibid.*, sect. 20.   [278] See also *ibid.*, chap. ix, sect. 17, note.

dead. In this case the incident of the king's death was directly intentional, but not ultimately: it was mediately intentional. 5. He intended neither more nor less than to kill the king. He had no other aim nor wish. In this case it was exclusively as well as directly intentional: exclusively, to wit, with regard to every other material incident. 6. Sir Walter shot the king in the right leg, as he was plucking a thorn out of it with his left hand. His intention was, by shooting the arrow into his leg through his hand, to cripple him in both those limbs at the same time. In this case the incident of the king's being shot in the leg was intentional: and that conjunctively with another which did not happen; viz. his being shot in the hand. 7. The intention of Tyrrel was to shoot the king either in the hand or in the leg, but not in both; and rather in the hand than in the leg. In this case the intention of shooting in the hand was disjunctively concurrent with regard to the other incident, and that with preference. 8. His intention was to shoot the king either in the leg or the hand, whichever might happen: but not in both. In this case the intention was inexclusive, but disjunctively so: yet that, however, without preference. 9. His intention was to shoot the king either in the leg or the hand, or in both, as it might happen. In this case the intention was indiscriminately concurrent, with respect to the two incidents."[279]

Bentham calls further attention to the fact that, naturally, the more stages in which an act is unintentional "the more apparent it will commonly be that it was unintentional with respect to the last. If a man, intending to strike you on the cheek, strikes you in the eye, and puts it out, it will probably be difficult for him to prove that it was not his intention to strike you in the eye. It will probably be easier if his intention was really not to strike you, or even not to strike at all."[280] Finally, Bentham wishes to push his analysis of the different kinds of intentionality even to such a degree of minuteness as to consider (1) "the quantity of matter" that may be moved in consequence of a certain intention, (2) "the direction in which it moves: and (3) the velocity with which it moves."[281] Bentham admits that "these disquisitions are apt to appear trifling";[281] nevertheless, the minute analysis of the various relations between intentions and consequences of acts is of importance, though the principal emphasis in his ethics is laid on the consequences of intentions and not on intentions themselves.

The ethical relevance of intentions is decisively limited in Bentham's theory of morals. To what extent this is the case we learn particularly

[279] *Ibid.*, chap. VIII, sect. 11.   [280] *Ibid.*, sect. 12.
[281] *Ibid.*, sect. 5, note.

from his statement that, properly speaking, "the will or intention"[282] must not be styled good or bad. Neither intentions, that is, merely intended consequences of acts, nor motives of acts can be regarded as good or bad in themselves.[283] Good or bad are epithets genuinely applicable only to the *actual* effects, the actual consequences of acts, in as much as they refer ultimately to pleasure or pain.[284] How daring these statements are may best be illustrated by their comparison with the views of traditional morality, or even more clearly with Kantian ethics. Kant saw goodness and badness solely as bound up with the motives and intentions of acts, while the consequences of acts, pain and pleasure, are for him ethically irrelevant. Bentham, in deliberate opposition to the main tradition of modern moral thought, denies that the intentions and motives of acts are good or bad independently of the consequences of these acts. Only the consequences of acts are, in his opinion, the seat of good and evil; this he tries to demonstrate later in detail.

At best, the consciousness, the knowledge of the circumstances which are relevant to the intended consequences, can be called relatively good. For without the instinctive or explicit knowledge of these circumstances the attainment of the intentions in question is highly endangered, and is realizable only by chance. The prudent and careful understanding of these circumstances is, therefore, according to Bentham, comparatively good; the imprudent, careless misinterpretation of these circumstances is relatively bad.

In this way Bentham again opposes Kantian and traditional ethics. For Kant, seeing moral valuations rooted exclusively in motives and intentions, denies that prudent or even careful consciousness of the

---

[282] See *ibid.*, chap. IX, sect. I.

[283] As to intentions see Bentham, *Introduction*, 1789, chap. VIII, sect. 13: "It is frequent to hear men speak of a good intention, of a bad intention. . . . It is indeed of no small importance, when properly understood: but the import of it is to the last degree ambiguous and obscure. Strictly speaking nothing can be said to be good or bad, but . . . pain or pleasure or . . . things that are the causes or preventives of pain and pleasure." As to motives see *ibid.*, e.g. chap. X, §2, sect. 11: "To speak of . . . good or bad motives is far from being . . . accurate," although "it is common." It is true that in chapter VIII, e.g. sect. 13, and chap. IX, e.g. sect. 15, Bentham speaks occasionally of the goodness or badness of motives, but later in the tenth chapter he corrects himself explicitly and he also explains in chapter X, sect. 13, why he had formerly accommodated himself to the common inaccurate usage of language.

[284] See *ibid.*, chap. VIII, sect. 13: "Strictly speaking nothing can be said to be good or bad, but either in itself; which is the case only with pain or pleasure: or on account of its effects; which is the case only with things that are the causes or preventives of pain and pleasure."

empirical circumstances is of any decisive relevance to the morality of human acts. Bentham, however, insists that "to the title of consciousness" of circumstances of actions "belongs what is to be said of the goodness or badness of a man's intention, as resulting from the consequences of the act";[285] and he tries to clear up in his ninth chapter the reasons why he counts the consciousness of the circumstances, rather than the mere intention, among the factors relevant to morality.

Consciousness of Circumstances and Its Ethical Relevance to Intentions

What makes an act morally good or bad can, according to Bentham, never be based on the mere intention of the agent. For it is generally almost impossible to ascertain the true intention of an agent even after he has performed his action. In any case, the intended consequences of an act are of necessity nothing but possibilities—or impossibilities. Only the actual consequences of acts can be valued as realities. The actual consequences of our deeds are bound to turn out to be very different from our intentions whenever the circumstances in which these intentions are to be executed have been heedlessly or rashly overlooked.

Therefore, Bentham puts the ethical emphasis on the consciousness or ignorance of facts which accompanies our intentions, not on the mere intentions themselves. For it is this knowledge or ignorance of the circumstances which ultimately shapes the transformation of intended consequences into actual consequences.

For all these reasons, the consistent realism and empiricism of Bentham places the principal weight on the *realization* of intentions, on the *real consequences* of acts and on the "perceptive faculty,"[286] the knowledge of facts, which makes possible the proper actualization of intentions. In comparison with these factors of reality, Kant's pure will and all the mere intentions of men, so difficult to ascertain, do not count with Bentham. In his realistic ethics, even so far as intentions are concerned, it is only facts and the consciousness of facts which are of definite moral relevance.

Making further use of his example of the preceding chapter, Bentham therefore carefully defines the following types of consciousness or nonconsciousness within the intentions of acts: "10. Tyrrel intended to shoot in the direction in which he shot, but he did not know that the king was riding so near that way. In this case the act he performed in shoot-

---

[285] *Ibid.*, chap. VIII, sect. 13.   [286] *Ibid.*, chap. IX, sect. 1.

ing ... was *unadvised*, with respect to the *existence* of the circumstance of the king's being so near riding that way. 11. He knew that the king was riding that way: but at the distance at which the king was, he knew not of the probability there was that the arrow would reach him. In this case, the act was *unadvised,* with respect to the *materiality* of the circumstance. 12. Somebody had dipped the arrow in poison, without Tyrrel's knowing of it. In this case the act was *unadvised* with respect to the existence of a *past* circumstance. 13. At the very instant that Tyrrel drew the bow, the king, being screened from his view by the foliage of some bushes, was riding furiously, in such manner as to meet the arrow in a direct line: which circumstance was also more than Tyrrel knew of. In this case the act was *unadvised*, with respect to the existence of a *present* circumstance. 14. The King being at a distance from court could get nobody to dress his wound till the next day; of which circumstance Tyrrel was not aware. In this case the act was *unadvised*, with respect to what was then a future-circumstance. 15. Tyrrel knew of the king's being riding that way, of his being so near, and so forth; but being deceived by the foliage of the bushes, he thought he saw a bank between the spot from which he shot, and that to which the king was riding. In this case the act was *mis-advised*, proceeding on the *mis-supposal* of a *preventive* circumstance. 16. Tyrrel knew that everything was as above, nor was he deceived by the supposition of any preventive circumstance. But he believed the king to be an usurper: and supposed he was coming up to attack a person whom Tyrrel believed to be the rightful king, and who was riding by Tyrrel's side. In this case the act was also *mis-advised*, but proceeded on the mis-supposal of a *compensative* circumstance."[287] Bentham himself is, of course, aware that all these concepts of advisedness, unadvisedness and misadvisedness especially concern the jurist and he therefore tries to clear up explicitly the relation existing between such terms and corresponding notions of the Roman law, such as inscitia, error, dolus.[288] But I think he is right in stating that all these definitions concerning the consciousness of circumstances are "capable" of "constant application, as well to moral discourse as to legislative practice."[289] Certainly, their relevance in ethics is too often kept out of sight.

How intimately these discussions are connected with capital problems of moral responsibility is to be seen from the following definitions and arguments. "An act which is unadvised, is either *heedless*, or not

[287] *Ibid.*, chap. IX, sect. 9 (Italics partly mine).
[288] *Ibid.*, sect. 17.   [289] *Ibid.*, sect. 18.

heedless. It is termed heedless, when the case is thought to be such, that a person of ordinary prudence, if prompted by an ordinary share of benevolence, would have been likely to have bestowed such and so much attention and reflection upon the material circumstances, as would have effectually disposed him to prevent the mischievous incident from taking place: not heedless, when the case is not thought to be such as above mentioned."[290] And further, "what heedlessness is in the case of an unadvised act, rashness is in the case of a misadvised one. A misadvised act . . . may be termed rash, when the case is thought to be such, that a person of ordinary prudence, if prompted by an ordinary share of benevolence would have employed such and so much attention and reflection to the imagined circumstance, as, by discovering to him the non-existence, improbability, or immateriality of it, would have effectually disposed him to prevent the mischievous incident from taking place."[291]

In a Bentham manuscript hitherto unpublished, the relation between unadvisedness and the immorality of acts is illustrated by the following example: "An act which is unadvised with respect to any material circumstances is more or less culpable in proportion to the *obligation* which a man is under to inform himself of that circumstance. . . . Thus a man of ordinary circumspection and benevolence will be more cautious how he fires a gun than how he handles an ax: altho' an ax may chance to fly out of his hand and kill a man: he will also be more cautious how he gives a shove at the brink of a precipice than on plain ground: although a shove even on plain ground may chance to throw him down and even kill him."[292]

From all these statements on advisedness and misadvisedness, Bentham draws the radical conclusion that, if the consequences of acts are mischievous at least in two cases, it does not matter ethically whether their intentions or even their motives are good or bad: "1. in the case of unadvisedness with respect to any of the circumstances on which the mischievousness of the consequences depended; 2. in the case of misadvisedness with respect to any circumstances, which, had it been what it appeared to be, would have served either to prevent or to outweigh the mischief."[293] In these cases as in others, according to Bentham, the consequences of acts alone count decisively in morals, not

[290] *Ibid.*, sect. 5.   [291] *Ibid.*, sect. 12.
[292] Bentham MS, University College, London, Portfolio 27, Folder 12, sheet 80, pp. 1 f, written about 1780.
[293] Bentham, *Introduction*, 1789, chap. IX, sect. 16.

the so-called good or bad intentions and motives. Nevertheless, also, the ignorance of circumstances has sufficient weight to transmute good and bad intentions or motives into innocent, neutral ones.[293] Ignorance of facts can change not only bad intentions into innocent ones but it also changes good intentions into at best neutral intentions.

In other words, here as elsewhere, common conventions of language do not impair the consistency of Bentham's ethical thought. And this consistent self-emancipation from conventional terminology enabled him to arrive at extremely sound ethical conclusions. His opponent Kant, however, reasoning in agreement with common ways of speaking, arrives on all these points at most paradoxical results, denying altogether the ethical relevance of pleasure and pain and the relevance of knowledge to produce pleasant or mischievous consequences of acts. It seems to me a lasting merit of Bentham that, in contrast to Kant, he fully recognized the importance of the knowledge or ignorance of facts in morals. How essential this insight is even from a quite opposite ethical point of view may be seen for instance from H. A. Prichard's inquiry into the problem *Duty and Ignorance of Fact*, published in 1932.

Motives

THE DISTINCTION BETWEEN MOTIVE AND INTENTION
AND THE DIFFERENT KINDS OF MOTIVES

The next chapters of the *Introduction*, chapters X-XII, not only form the central portion of the book but they also yield the pith of the matter; and chapter X on motives contains, perhaps, the most original analyses of the whole volume. Before one is able to enter upon these analyses, however, it requires some care to find out the precise meaning attached to the term *motive*, especially in its contrast to *intention*.

In the ninth chapter of his *Introduction*, Bentham had already tried to illustrate the difference between intention and motive, although he admitted that the two terms are "intimately connected,"[294] and though he had previously used them incidentally without explanation of their difference in meaning. Then, however, in order to show the distinction between intentions and motives he used the following example in a later section: "Out of malice a man prosecutes you for a crime of which he believes you to be guilty, but of which in fact you are not guilty. Here the consequences of his conduct are mischievous: for they are mischievous to you at any rate, in virtue of the shame and anxiety which you

[294] *Ibid.*, sect. 13.

are made to suffer while the prosecution is depending: to which is to be added, in case of your being convicted, the evil of the punishment. To you therefore they are mischievous; nor is there anyone to whom they are beneficial. The man's *motive* was also what is called a bad one: for malice will be allowed by every body to be a bad motive. However, the consequence of his conduct, had they proved such as he believed them likely to be, would have been good: for in them would have been included the punishment of a criminal, which is a benefit to all who are exposed to suffer by a crime of the like nature. The *intention* therefore, in this case, though not in a common way of speaking the motive, might be styled a *good* one."[295] Unfortunately, this example does not satisfactorily clear up the difficulties at issue. For Bentham does not assume that there exist any motives which can be called "constantly good or constantly bad"; and "even malice . . . taken by itself, is good,"[296] as he tries to show later in detail.

We have to look for further information on motives in the special chapter devoted to their discussion. Here the following definition is given: "By a motive, in the most extensive sense in which the word is ever used with reference to a thinking being, is meant anything that can contribute to give birth to, or even to prevent any kind of action."[297]

Of motives in this largest sense, Bentham excludes from his ethical analyses all those motives which "rest in the understanding merely, without exerting any influence in the production of acts of the will." For those "purely *speculative* motives," according to Bentham, do not "exercise any influence over . . . pain or . . . pleasure," and "therefore . . . we have not here any concern" with them.[297] Whether Bentham is right in assuming that there are any motives of thought which have no influence at all on pain and pleasure, or any connection with them the psychologist may doubt. If, say, theoretical reasoning must be separated methodologically from any combination with feelings, it does not follow that speculative thinking or even mathematical thought is not connected with emotions in reality. On the contrary, there obviously is no act of understanding whatever which is not intermixed with feelings of pain and pleasure, and which is incapable of forming a motive influencing the will. Therefore, Bentham's exclusion of speculative motives in ethics—made despite his reservations on this point in chapter X, section 8—are hardly capable of being justified within a complete analysis of moral motives. Motives resting in metaphysical or mystical thought

---

[295] *Ibid.*, sect. 15.
[296] *Ibid.*, chap. x, §2, sect. 10, note.
[297] *Ibid.*, §1, sect. 2.

and, at first sight, merely speculative, may have a marked though unnoticed influence on feelings of pleasure and pain. It seems to me, therefore, more difficult than Bentham thought to distinguish definitely between speculative and "practical" motives. Nevertheless, of course, only motives which in one way or another win practical influence are of concern in ethics.

Within these practical motives, Bentham discriminates first between motives in the proper sense—those which actually "move" a man to act—and motives in the improper sense—those which only determine a man to forbear to act, and which perhaps would better be called "determinatives"[298] or, as we would say in the language of modern psychology, inhibitions.

Further, Bentham draws a distinction between motives in the figurative and in the unfigurative or literal sense. A motive in the figurative meaning of the term is a "fictitious entity," "a passion, an affection of the mind," such as avarice, indolence, malice or benevolence; a motive in the literal sense is, in contrast to all fictitious general objects, a really existing particular incident from which an act takes its rise,[299] such as concrete feelings of pleasure and pain.

Within these real incidents, a distinction may again be made between "*internal* perceptions . . . of pleasure or pain" and "*external events* . . . the happening whereof is regarded as having a tendency to bring about the perception of such pleasure or pain."[300] And further there is a difference between "motives in *esse*" (the *esse* including past existence) and "motives in prospect."[301] These last five divisions of minor importance may again be illustrated best by an example given by Bentham himself: "A fire breaks out in your neighbour's house: you are under apprehension of its extending to your own: you are apprehensive, that if you stay in it, you will be burnt: you accordingly run out of it. This then is the act: the others are all motives to it. The event of the fire's breaking out in your neighbour's house is an external motive, . . . in esse";[302] and under this "term *esse* must be included as well *past* existence, with reference to a given period, as *present*."[303] "The idea or belief of the probability of the fire's extending to your own house, that of your being burnt if you continue, and the pain you feel at the thought of

---

[298] *Ibid.*, §1, sect. 3, note. Sigmund Freud in a talk I had with him a few months before his death endorsed the opinion that the term *inhibition* is an adequate modern equivalent for Bentham's term *determinative*.

[299] *Ibid.*, §1, sect. 4.   [300] *Ibid.*, §1, sect. 5.   [301] *Ibid.*, §1, sect. 6.
[302] *Ibid.*, §1, sect. 6.   [303] *Ibid.*, §1, sect. 7, note 2.

such a catastrophe, are all so many internal events, but still in esse: the event of the fire's actually extending to your own house, and that of your being actually burnt by it, external motives in prospect: the pain you would feel at seeing your house a burning, and the pain you would feel while you yourself were burning, internal motives in prospect."[302]

But "of all these motives," that which stands "nearest to the act, to the production of which they all contribute, is that internal motive in *esse* which consists in the expectation of the internal motive in prospect: the pain or uneasiness you feel at the thoughts of being burnt. All other motives are more or less remote."[304] As to that motive which stands nearest to the act, however, Bentham admits that "it is in all cases difficult, and in most cases unnecessary, to distinguish between objects so intimately connected as the posterior possible object which is thus looked forward to, and the present existing object or event which takes place upon a man's looking forward to the other";[305] that is to say, it is difficult to determine whether it be the expectation of being painfully "burnt, or the pain that accompanies that expectation, that is the immediate internal motive spoken of"[306] which prompts to action. Moreover, "it may . . . perhaps . . . be questioned whether they are distinct entities"; at any rate the solution of both questions is immaterial.[306] And Bentham further admits that the other kinds of motives are often "so intimately allied, that it will . . . be not always material, to avoid confounding them as they have always hitherto been confounded."[306]

But he insists that "in all this chain of motives, the principal or original link seems to be the last internal motive in prospect: it is to this that all the other motives in prospect owe their materiality and the immediately acting motive its existence. This motive," however, "is always some pleasure or some pain; some pleasure which the act in question is expected to be a means of continuing or producing: some pain which it is expected to be a means of discontinuing or preventing"; therefore, Bentham finally states that "a motive is substantially nothing more than pleasure or pain, operating in a certain manner."[307]

MODERN CRITICISM OF BENTHAM'S CONCEPTS OF "MOTIVE" AND "INTENTION"

If, now, we wish to characterize the essence of Bentham's definitions we may, I think, say that the *intention* of an act is the idea of the con-

[304] *Ibid.*, §1, sect. 7.   [305] *Ibid.*, §1, sect. 6.
[306] *Ibid.*, §1, sect. 7, note.   [307] *Ibid.*, §2, sect. 9.

sequences of this act preconceived before the act. The *motive* which gives birth to or prevents this act is the concrete, particular feeling of pleasure or pain which the act is expected or feared to provide, or it is a general state of feeling which impels or prevents an act of this kind.

Similarly, Professor John Dewey says: "Intention is *what* a man means to do; motive is the personal frame of mind which indicates *why* he means to do it. Intention is the concrete aim or purpose; the results which are foreseen and wanted. Motive is the state of mind which renders these consequences, rather than others, interesting and attractive."[308] Dewey, as well as J. H. Muirhead, has commented on this utilitarian distinction between motive and intention; but though this seems to be at first sight a criticism, it is not so in reality.

Professor Dewey observes, in contrast to Bentham, that "ordinary speech" using "motive and intention interchangeably" is after all correct, since such terms as ambition, revenge, benevolence, patriotism, justice, avarice signify, indeed, "both motives and aims."[309] Yet Bentham himself does not deny that motive and intention are in fact always closely combined. Nevertheless, he thinks they can and should be methodologically separated despite their union in such terms as ambition; and I believe that this suggestion of Bentham is of considerable value.

The German term *Gesinnung* combines the meaning of motive and intention even more closely than any English term. But exactly this combination of different meanings in one term (*Gesinnung*) seems to me responsible for a considerable amount of ambiguity and confusion

---

[308] J. Dewey and J. H. Tufts, *Ethics*, 1914, p. 247; compare James Mill, *A Fragment on Makintosh*, 1835, sect. iv, p. 164, where Mill speaks of intentions as "calculations" of consequences; compare A. K. Rogers, *Morals in Review*, 1927, p. 305: "By intention Bentham means primarily the objective aimed at or desired; but for practical purposes it includes also the entire group of consequences which are before the mind of the agent when he acts, or which might have been recognized by him had he used ordinary caution and judgment"; p. 306: "By a motive, on the other hand, Bentham intends to distinguish the *cause* of the intention, as a desire for this or that particular sort of pleasure moving the will to action; whether we are to take its motive force as lying in the prospect of a future pleasure, or, with Locke, in the present uneasiness of desire, Bentham, with his usual indifference to the finer points of analysis sets aside as a merely verbal query." A completely confused account of Bentham's definitions of intentionality, motives, dispositions and consequences is to be found in J. Watson, *Hedonistic Theories from Aristippus to Spencer*, 1895, pp. 154-156. Nor are the few remarks correct which R. A. Tsanoff (in his very attractive *The Moral Ideals of our Civilization*, 1942, p. 493) devotes to Bentham's teaching on intentions.

[309] J. Dewey and J. H. Tufts, *Ethics*, 1914, p. 248.

in the extremely broad domain of morals influenced by this German *Gesinnungsethik*. The term *Gesinnung* is most useful as long as a mainly intuitive, emotional understanding of ethical issues is intended. But the same term tends to obscure any ethical analysis which tries to specify as accurately as possible the different ethical relevances of the elements of acts.

J. H. Muirhead mentions that, at least in John Stuart Mill, the motive is a feeling, and that "the feeling, as feeling, has no moral quality whatsoever."[310] But this again would be no criticism of Bentham. For, according to Bentham, no moral quality should be attributed to motives in themselves. It is only traditional anti-hedonism which dogmatically presupposes that motives in themselves are the very seat of good and evil.

COMPARATIVE IRRELEVANCE OF MOTIVES

After having described the essence of motives and of their different kinds Bentham proceeds to investigate the moral relevance of motives, i.e. the cardinal problem of whether and in what sense, motives can determine the goodness or badness of actions. This is the topic of the second paragraph of this tenth chapter, the discussion of which starts in section ten of the chapter; and it is obviously a mistake that the title of this §2, which reads "no motives either constantly good or constantly bad," appears over section nine instead of section ten.

As to the matter itself, Bentham admits here again that it is indeed "common . . . to speak of actions as proceeding from *good* or *bad* motives"; and in the first section of this chapter he himself had even given the impression of accepting as an acknowledged truth that "every kind of act whatever . . . is apt to assume a different character . . . according to the nature of the *motive* which gives birth to it."[311] But now he states explicitly that these expressions are "far from being . . . accurate."[312] On the contrary, according to Bentham, it is by no means the motives of an act that can determine whether this act is good or bad.

The Jewish prophets and the New Testament once brought about a decisive revolution in morals. They took away the moral emphasis from the consequences of human acts which are, after all, to a large extent not under the control of men but in the hands of fate. At least since the time of the Old Testament, and especially in such moralists as Abe-

---

[310] J. H. Muirhead, *The Elements of Ethics*, 1921, p. 64 and see pp. 62 ff.
[311] See Bentham, *Introduction*, 1789, chap. x, §2, sect. 11 and §1, sect. 1.
[312] *Ibid.*, chap. x, §2, sect. 11.

lard[313] and Kant, it became more and more a moral commonplace that what morally counts is not the visible effects of a man's acts but only his invisible motives. For epistemological reasons, Bentham is completely opposed to this dominant trend of Western morality.

According to Bentham, if motives are called good or bad it can only be "on account of their effects: good, on account of their tendency to produce pleasure, or avert pain: bad, on account of their tendency to produce pain, or avert pleasure."[314] No motives are "either constantly good or constantly bad,"[315] but "the case is, that from one and the same motive and from every kind of motive, may proceed actions that are good, others that are bad, and others that are indifferent."[314] This annihilation of the moral relevance of motives in themselves is certainly one of the most radical points of Bentham's doctrine. It is the point on which his teaching is, in truth, identical with radical immoralism; and so it is not by chance that, in connection with this theory of motives,[316] he defends to a certain extent the immoralism of Mandeville, Helvétius and La Rochefoucauld.

But Bentham was not contented with the establishment of any dogmatic doctrine of motives. He critically based his doctrine on reasons, and tried to explain even the psychological causes which led to opposite common convictions.

He begins as follows: "Let a man's motive be ill-will; call it even malice, envy, cruelty; it is still a kind of pleasure that is his motive: the pleasure he takes at the thought of the pain which he sees, or expects to see, his adversary undergo. Now even this wretched pleasure, taken by itself, is good: it may be faint; it may be short: it must at any rate be impure: yet while it lasts, and before any bad consequences arrive, it is as good as any other that is not more intense."[317] To refute this argument seems to me difficult, as it is clearly confined to the valuation of the evil-doer himself. I think it can hardly be denied that nature—more generous on this point than moralists—does, indeed, reward the more or less pathological offender for other sufferings by some pleasure felt in giving way to his criminal motives. And there is no reason for

[313] See Petrus Abaelardus, *Ethica seu liber dictus: Scito te ipsum* in *Petri Abaelardi Opera*, ed. by Victor Cousin, Paris, tome II, 1859, e.g. p. 611: "Opera . . . omniaque in se indifferentia, nec nisi pro intentione agentis bona vel mala dicenda sunt" or *ibid.*, p. 604: "Nec . . . in opere, sed in intentione meritum operantis vel laus consistit."

[314] Bentham, *Introduction*, 1789, chap. x, §2, sect. 12.

[315] *Ibid.*, §2.

[316] *Ibid.*, §2, sect. 13, note.   [317] *Ibid.*, §2, sect. 10, note.

a critical moralist to call the pleasure felt in these motives evil, if this pleasure is viewed in isolation from the consequences which the offense has for the offender and for other persons.

We may say that the total human disposition which feels itself stimulated by criminal motives is, on the whole, less pleasant even to the offender than other dispositions would be if he could acquire them. And this point is touched upon by Bentham on other occasions.[318] The pleasure of the criminal is doubtless a disvalue to his victim and to society as a whole. But equally doubtless, it is scientifically dogmatic and morally prejudicial to deny that the pleasure felt in giving way to criminal motives is a value to the offender himself, however much he may regret the consequences this pleasure may cause to him and to others. If we insist that even this isolated hedonic tone of a so-called criminal motive is evil, we can do so only by begging the question as to the whole complex of ethical problems involved.

Further, Bentham's statement that the hedonic tone of a criminal motive is in itself good is much more consonant with psychological facts than is the morally biased or merely tautological judgment that even the pleasure felt in having a criminal motive is criminal, and therefore evil. It is hardly to be assumed that a criminal would not enjoy his criminal motives, even if his pleasure were soon afterwards followed by penitence. Psychology is certainly correct in stating that pleasure is felt as a good thing even by masochists and ascetics. At any rate, the combination of these psychological statements with contrary theses in ethics and pedagogy present great, if not insuperable, difficulties.

According to Bentham, "pleasure is in *itself* ... the only good ... setting aside immunity from pain" and "pain is in itself an evil; ... indeed ... the only evil; or else the words good and evil have no meaning."[319] Certainly, if one takes into account the wording of only the second part of this passage it again seems to imply the so-called naturalistic fallacy in ethics, i.e. it seems to suggest the untenable identification of *good* with *pleasant* by definition. But this interpretation of Bentham's text is excluded by the first part of his sentence. For here even the strictest requirements of the exposers of naturalistic fallacies[320] are met, that is, good is here not defined as pleasant, but *the* good is declared to be pleasure in reality. And that pleasure is the only good in reality can

---

[318] See e.g. Bentham's ethical analysis of hatred in his *Traités de législation civile et pénale*, ed. by Dumont, tome I, 1820, "Principes de législation," chap. XI, p. 86 f.

[319] Bentham, *Introduction*, 1789, chap. X, §2, sect. 10.

[320] See G. E. Moore, *Principia Ethica*, 1903, e.g. p. 18.

indeed be demonstrated if, as Bentham assumes, all the seemingly different goods can ultimately be compared with each other on the ground of one common quality, namely, pleasure, i.e. the hedonic tone necessarily characteristic of every experience of goodness.

Be this as it may, a second inquiry made by Bentham is quite independent of the validity of the last far-reaching thesis, and it is of even greater value, viz. Bentham's analysis of the reasons which lead to the common uncritical belief in constant good and bad motives. For the almost universal confusion which exists on this point, the main responsibility lies, in his view, in "a certain perversity of structure which prevails more or less throughout all languages" and which can be described in the following way: "To speak of motives, as of anything else, one must call them by their names. But the misfortune is, that it is rare to meet with the motive of which the name expresses that and nothing more. Commonly along with the very name of the motive is tacitly involved a proposition imputing to it a certain quality; a quality which, in many cases, will appear to include that very goodness or badness, concerning which we are here inquiring whether, properly speaking, it be or be not imputable to motives. To use the common phrase, in most cases, the name of the motive is a word which is employed either only in a *good sense*, or else only in a *bad sense*."[321] In other words, an impartial, unbiased examination of the goodness or badness of a motive is commonly nipped in the bud by the imperfection of human language.

In all languages, most of the words which are names of motives include in their meaning the qualification of goodness or badness; and we do not possess sufficient neutral names of motives. The existing languages thrust upon us numerous terms of motives which seem to be unprejudiced only to the uncritical mind; in truth, they are far from being ethically objective. Thus, the judgment on the moral value of a motive is in general already given along with the introduction of its name before any objective examination of its actual moral character can start. The choice of these names of motives is bound to the stock of terms which the languages place at the disposal of the moralist, and which are, alas! inextricably tied up with an uncontrolled moral valuation of those motives.

We therefore find Bentham speaking in different connections of the

[321] Bentham, *Introduction*, 1789, chap. x, §2, sect. 13.

"imperfection of language,"[322] the "material deficiency" of language,[323] the "intractable"[324] character and even of the "perversity of structure"[325] prevailing throughout all languages. In truth, the fundamental point is, in my view, not that language is "perverse" or "imperfect" but that this imperfection of language is the reflection and expression of common moral prejudices. As Bentham hints, "such is the fate of science, and more particularly of the moral branch; the distribution of things must in a great measure be dependent on their names: arrangement, the work of mature reflection must be ruled by nomenclature, the work of popular caprice."[326] Leaving aside the influence which genuine ethical insight has had on language, it is only too true that the terminology both of ethical motives and of offenses has often been greatly distorted through popular caprice, or the shortsighted dictates of social and private interests.

Indeed, it is characteristic of all times of moral reform or revolution such as those which saw the origin of Judaism, of Christendom or the European Renaissance, that it becomes necessary to revise the existing terminology of moral motives inherited from previous epochs, to withdraw the predicate of goodness from certain motives and to attribute it to others, or to withdraw the predicate of badness from certain motives and to ascribe it to others which up to that time had stood in highest repute.

Most characteristic in this respect is, for instance, the Christian attitude toward φιλοτιμία, the love of distinction, and humility. Early Christian morality took away moral praise from the one and condemned it as secular desire or will to power, while it praised the opposite to φιλοτιμία, namely, humility, which hardly enjoyed great esteem in the ancient Greek and Roman world.[327] In a like sense, Marcus Aurelius, for instance, strongly condemned any disassociation from "civic reason," from the "political logos," by which one would become an "exile" and an outcast from the world,[327a] while in the early Christian literature, in Basilides and Clemens of Alexandria,[327b] exactly the feeling of being

---

[322] *Ibid.*, §2, sect. 13, note 2.　　[323] *Ibid.*, §2, sect. 7, note 2.
[324] *Ibid.*, §2, sect. 13, note 3.　　[325] *Ibid.*, §2, sect. 13.
[326] *Ibid.*, chap. xvi, §1, sect. 10 note.
[327] In the First Epistle to the Thessalonians 4:11, for instance, Paul completely revalues the value of φιλοτιμία by commanding: φιλοτιμεῖσθαι ἡσυχάζειν, "Put your ambition in being quiet."
[327a] Marcus Aurelius, Τῶν εἰς ἑαυτὸν βιβλία, IV, 29.
[327b] Clemens Alexandrinus, Στρωματεῖς IV, Cap. xxvi, 165, 3 ed. by Kirchenväter-Commission der Preussischen Akademie der Wissenschaften, vol. II, 1906,

an "alien in the universe" is exalted as the mark of election. This moral and historical problem, called by Nietzsche *Umwertung der Werte*, is in fact also faced by Bentham. Moreover, he dealt with it in a more acute and emotionally sounder way than Nietzsche.

Bentham lets us see here that, even more important than the discovery or the creation of *new* values, is the *neutrality* with which the existing table of valuations has to be examined and freed from precipitate qualifications. In consequence of their neglect of this point, the average legislators and moralists, according to Bentham, are to be compared with botanists who have so contrived the classes of plants that no truly "common characters could be found for them,"[328] or with architects who cannot "distinguish a dwelling-house from a barn."[329] Bentham, however, made continuous efforts throughout his life to carry through an *Umwertung der Werte* in such a way as to replace all question-begging nomenclature by a strictly neutral and appropriate one. For he regarded this as the fundamental prerequisite to any objective inquiry into morals. Even new dogmatic *Umwertungen der Werte* are no substitute for Bentham's critical system of morals.

In his critical approach to the problem of motives, Bentham insists that "*there is no such thing as any sort of motive which is a bad one in itself: nor, consequently, any such thing as a sort of motive, which in itself is exclusively a good one.*"[330] He therefore uses, both here and later, in his *Table of the Springs of Action*, two very valuable devices to free ethics from a prejudiced and inadequate terminology of motives: first, where only good or only bad denominations of motives exist, he introduces the missing qualification; thus he speaks not only of piety (as a commonly good motive), but also of bad piety, not only of love of honor in the traditional good meaning of the word, but also of bad love of honor. Second, he sometimes totally lays "aside the old phraseology" and invents a relatively "new one"[331] by introducing a neutral combina-

---

p. 321: ἐντεῦθεν ξένην τὴν ἐκλογὴν τοῦ κόσμου ὁ Βασιλείδης εἴληφε λέγειν ὡς ἂν ὑπερκόσμιον φύσει οὖσαν. To my knowledge, as yet, no reference has been made for this purpose to these illuminating passages in Christian and Roman literature of the first two centuries of the Christian era.

[328] Bentham, *Introduction*, 1789, chap. xvi, sect. 58 note.

[329] Bentham, *Introduction*, 1823, chap. xvii, sect. 29 note, vol. ii, p. 276 (addition in the 2nd edition of the *Introduction*).

[330] Bentham, *Introduction*, 1789, chap. x, §3, sect. 29; cf. chap. x, §2, sect. 10 (Italics partly mine).

[331] *Ibid.*, chap. x, §2, sect. 13. C. L. Stevenson in his *Ethics and Language*, 1944, p. 245, makes a somewhat similar suggestion by stating that "emotive mean-

tion of two new terms instead of one old term with its fixed positive or negative accent of moral valuation. For example, instead of the negative term lust he frames "the neutral expression, sexual desire: instead of the word avarice, by putting together two other words also in common use, he may frame the neutral expression, pecuniary interest . . . rejecting altogether the terms, of which the import is infected by adventitious and unsuitable ideas."[332] For "this perverse association of ideas cannot, it is evident, but throw great difficulties in the ways of the inquiry now before us."[331]

Bentham is perfectly aware of the probability that his reform of the ethical terminology of motives and offenses may "excite contempt" or even "indignation."[333] He admits that to "fabricate" new names in morals is an "unpleasant remedy," and throws one to a certain extent "upon the mercy of his readers." He grants later that his new names of offenses consisting of two or even "three words brought together, in a language too which admits not, like the German and the Greek, of their being melted into one, can never be upon a par, in point of commodiousness, with those univocal appellatives which make part of the established stock."[333] Nevertheless, all these "inconveniences" caused by the imperfection of current language are certainly less important than the main requirements of an objective theory of ethics.

It is true that the bulk of mankind has no interest in strictly objective valuations but would prefer, knowingly and unknowingly, biased ones. In connection with this fundamental psychological observation, Bentham explains very well two characteristic features of the common table of springs of action: first, the surprising abundance of names for bad motives and second, the numerical excess of names for good motives over neutral names.

The average person is, indeed, inclined to refer actions far more frequently to bad than to good motives. Or, as Bentham points out as a keen though pessimistic discerner of human nature, "ever ready to depreciate the character of their neighbours, in order, indirectly to exalt their own, . . . the bulk of mankind . . . will take occasion to refer a motive to the class of bad ones as often as they can find one still better,

---

ing can be neutralized, for instance, by balancing a particular laudatory term with a particular derogatory one." But the context of Stevenson's observation is rather different from Bentham's.

[332] *Ibid.*, §2, sect. 13, note.
[333] *Ibid.*, sect. 13 and chap. XVI, sect. 56 (second edition, 1823, vol. II, p. 215).

to which the act might have owed its birth. Conscious that his own motives are not of the best class or persuaded that if they be, they will not be referred to that class by others; afraid of being taken for a dupe, and anxious to show the reach of his penetration; each man takes care, in the first place, to impute the conduct of every other man to the least laudable of the motives that can account for it: in the next place, when he has gone as far that way as he can, and cannot drive down the individual motive to any lower class, he changes his battery, and attacks the very class itself. To the love of reputation he will accordingly give a bad name upon every occasion, calling it ostentation, vanity, or vainglory. Partly to the same spirit of detraction, the natural consequence of the sensibility of men to the force of the moral sanction, partly to the influence of the principle of asceticism, may, perhaps, be imputed the great abundance of bad names of motives, in comparison of such as are good or neutral: and, in particular, the total want of neutral names for the motives of sexual desire, physical desire in general, and pecuniary interest."[334] Just as, for example, Schopenhauer[335] observes that there exist much richer and more colorful descriptions of hell than of heaven, so Bentham could rightly note that there are more bad names of motives than good ones.

Moreover, Bentham went further and found out—again rightly—that in common language next to the multitude of bad denominations of motives comes the number of good ones, while the number of neutral ones is the smallest of the three. For the average man, hardly ever free from uncontrolled emotion, dislikes most to think of motives in neutral names, and he even prefers to presuppose in human actions high-flown, extravagantly good motives rather than neutral ones. "The superior abundance ... of good names in comparison of neutral ones"[336] demonstrates this manifestly. So much the more must scientific ethics try to deliver us from these common prejudices, precisely because these biases are deeply rooted in man and are endorsed by the enormous authority of human language.

Bentham admits that there exist minor differences among the different languages, and he adds that "the language of a people on these points may, perhaps, serve in some measure as a key to their moral sentiments."[336] But, of course, if this is the case, it makes only the more

---

[334] Bentham, *Introduction*, 1789, chap. XI, sect. 17, note.

[335] *Arthur Schopenhauers Sämtliche Werke*, ed. by Paul Deussen, e.g. vol. I, 1911, p. 368.

[336] *Introduction*, 1789, chap. XI, sect. 17, note.

urgent the need for freeing ethical language from national prejudices and other questionable valuations.

In what intricate ways moral thinking is confused by the common terms of motives, Bentham has finally demonstrated in a masterly way by the following deduction: common morality denounces lust, cruelty, avarice as motives which are always bad. But why? The truth is "that when I say," lust, cruelty and the like are bad motives, these are propositions that merely concern the import of the words lust and the like; "and which would be false if transferred to the other words used for the same motives, sexual desire, . . . displeasure and pecuniary interest. . . . Hence we see the emptiness of all those rhapsodies of common-place morality, which consist in the taking of such names as lust, cruelty, and avarice, and branding them with marks of reprobation: applied to the *thing*, they are false; applied to the *name*, they are true indeed, but nugatory."[337] Would you do a real service to mankind, show them the cases in which sexual desire *merits* the name of lust; displeasure, that of cruelty; and pecuniary interest, that of avarice."[338] These few sentences embody, in a specially concentrated form, some of the most important results of Bentham's critical method in ethics; and they remain valuable even independent of the validity of his utilitarian doctrine.

Apart from other defects of common ethical argument already mentioned, common ethical reasoning shows us with particular clearness the dangers of thinking merely in words, independent of reality, in analytic judgments instead of synthetic ones[339]—a danger against which

[337] It is perhaps noteworthy that the term *nugae* is also a favorite expression of Spinoza and used by him often in similar connections, see e.g. Spinoza's "Cogitata Metaphysica," appendix of Spinoza's *Renati Des Cartes Principia Philosophiae*, Pars I, cap. VI, §5, Pars II, cap. III, §5.

[338] Bentham, *Introduction*, 1789, chap. x, §3, sect. 30.

[339] That Kant thought the contrast between "analytic" and "synthetic" means the contrast between judgments maintained on the ground of mere definitions (= analytic) and judgments referring to real facts (= synthetic), is clear e.g. from the following declaration: "Ein bloss analytischer Satz" ist der, "der . . . kein anderes Prädikat seinem Subjekte beilegt, als aus diesem durch den Satz des Widerspruchs entwickelt werden kann. Wenn man mit blossen Begriffen spielt, um deren objektive Realität einem nichts zu tun ist, so kann man viel dergleichen täuschende Erweiterungen der Wissenschaft sehr leicht herausbringen, ohne Anschauung zu bedürfen, welches aber ganz anders lautet, so bald man auf vermehrte Erkenntnis des Objekts hinausgeht," d.h. auf synthetische Urteile (*Kants Gesammelte Schriften*, ed. Preussische Akademie der Wissenschaften, 1912, Band 8, Seite 236 ff, "Über eine Entdeckung nach der alle neue Kritik der reinen Vernunft durch eine ältere entbehrlich gemacht werden soll," 1790).

Kant had emphatically warned in the field of metaphysics, but unfortunately not with the same emphasis in that of morals.

What Bentham has shown here holds, however, not only for motives but also for affections, virtues and vices, as he explicitly states: "here, as elsewhere, it may be observed, that the same words which are mentioned as names of motives, are also many of them names of passions, appetites, and affections; fictitious entities, which are framed only by considering pleasures or pains in some particular point of view. Some of them are also names of moral qualities. This branch of nomenclature is remarkably entangled: to unravel it completely would take up a whole volume."[340] To this we may even add that all that is said here about motives and moral qualities applies also to the modern concept of intrinsic moral values.[341] Thus, independently of any decision for or against hedonism, Bentham's doctrine of motives seems to me in no respect out of date.

Specifically hedonistic ideas are naturally dominant in Bentham's "catalogue of motives," while the principle of utility and its psychological corollaries were but seldom touched upon in his ethical analysis of the moral motives. Merely in passing he remarked there that when a motive "is spoken of as being used in a good sense, all that is necessarily meant is this: that in conjunction with the idea of the object it is put to signify, it conveys an idea of *approbation*: that is, of a pleasure or satisfaction, entertained by the person who employs the term at the thoughts of such object. In like manner, when a word is spoken of as being used in a bad sense, all that is necessarily meant is this: that in conjunction with the idea of the object it is put to signify, it conveys an idea of *disapprobation*."[342] But obviously, this interpretation of the meaning of goodness and badness, which reminds us rather of Hume's ethics, is not accepted by Bentham. For he adds explicitly that, according to the utility principle, ideas of approbation and disapprobation have to be "grounded . . . on . . . the opinion of the *goodness*" or badness "of the object in question";[342] and this goodness or badness must refer ultimately to the pleasant or painful consequences of the act whose motive is in question. "For a man to be governed by any motive, he must in every case

---

[340] Bentham, *Introduction*, 1789, chap. x, §3, sect. 26, note.

[341] Compare D. Baumgardt, "Some Merits and Defects of Contemporary German Ethics," *Philosophy (The Journal of the British Institute of Philosophy)*, 1938, pp. 183-195.

[342] Bentham, *Introduction*, 1789, chap. x, §2, sect. 13.

look beyond that event which is called his action; he must look to the consequences of it: and it is . . . in this way that the idea of pleasure, of pain . . . can give birth to it."[343] Therefore, Bentham's whole list of motives is arranged in close correspondence to the catalogue of pleasures and pains given in chapter V of his *Introduction.*

Bentham starts this enumeration of the motives of acts with that group of motives which are usually called, in a bad sense, sensual—corresponding to the pleasures and pains of the senses. But faithful to his program, he refuses to accept this traditional biased terminology and, instead of sensuality, speaks of physical desire.[344] Names for those motives resulting from the pleasures of the senses and used in a good sense are, he points out, unfortunately not at our disposal: we have only vituperative denominations such as "greediness, voraciousness, gluttony . . . lickerishness . . . daintiness"[345] or "lust, lasciviousness."[346] Therefore he stresses the necessity of introducing instead of these terms the neutral designations "love of the pleasures of the palate"[345] and "sexual desire."[346] The love of wealth as motive of action also possesses a large number of derogatory names such as "avarice, covetousness, rapacity . . . , niggardliness" and only some few relatively appreciative terms such as "economy and frugality."[347] Bentham, therefore, again insists that in order to avoid inconsiderate moral valuations, both contrary kinds of qualifications must be avoided, and solely by the use of a neutral term such as pecuniary interest[347] can ethical analysis be conducted in an objective way.

The same applies to motives of servility and benevolence; the derogatory term as well as its relative counterpart "benevolence" must be replaced by the neutral term "the desire of ingratiating one's self."[344] In the same way all prejudicial designations of motives such as the love of honor, charity, and public-spiritedness or pride, vanity, false honor, ostentation, have to be recognized as question-begging significations of one and the same neutral motive: that is, the love of reputation.[348] Correspondingly, ambition and lust of power are, neutrally seen, only love of power.[349] Devotion, piety, superstition and fanaticism are, neutrally named, religious zeal; "a man holds a cow by the tail while he is dying. On the Thames the motive would in this case be deemed contemptible, and called superstition. On the Ganges it is deemed meritorious, and called piety."[350] But it is, in both cases, simply religious enthusiasm; and

---

[343] *Ibid.,* §1, sect. 6. [344] *Ibid.,* §3, sect. 14. [345] *Ibid.,* §3, sect. 15.
[346] *Ibid.,* §3, sect. 16. [347] *Ibid.,* §3, sect. 19. [348] *Ibid.,* §3, sect. 22.
[349] *Ibid.,* §3, sect. 23. [350] *Ibid.,* §3, sect. 24.

thus neutral terminology can immediately educate to ethical tolerance. In the same way, compassion and partiality have to be styled, in a neutral way, "sympathy . . . , good-will";[351] and wrath, hatred, cruelty, revenge, malice are, neutrally termed, "neither more nor less" than antipathy; even if we speak, in this connection, of ill-will—instead of antipathy—we use a term no longer strictly neutral but one "leaning a little to the bad side."[352] Cowardice and courageous self-defense are, neutrally judged, nothing but one and the same motive: self-preservation.[353] Indolence and love of liberty are both "love of ease"; and we may add that, while it is indeed justifiable to call the love of ease[354] a motive, it is a somewhat odd term for a motive.

Bentham himself did not pretend to guarantee the completeness of his catalogue of motives. For "to make sure of rendering it so, the only way would be, to turn over the dictionary from beginning to end: an operation which, in a view to perfection would be necessary for more purposes than this."[355] And, as we shall see later, in his *Table of the Springs of Action*" Bentham has considerably enlarged the catalogue of motives which he listed in the *Introduction*. So much the less is it necessary to be exhaustive on this point. Only certain conclusions drawn from the analyses of this catalogue of motives are important.

Bentham summarizes these conclusions in the following way: As to the effects of motives, "it appears . . . that these are sometimes bad, at other times either indifferent or good: and this appears to be the case with every sort of motive. If any sort of motive then is either good or bad on the score of its effects, this is the case only on individual occasions and with individual motives; and this is the case with one sort of motive as well as with another. If any sort of motive then can, in consideration of its effects, be termed with any propriety a bad one, it can only be with reference to the balance of all the effects it may have had of both kinds within a given period, that is, of its most usual tendency."[356] It is only under such stipulations that Bentham allows the common characterization of motives as good or bad.

Bentham admits, for example, that a motive may be styled good or bad with some "safety and propriety . . . when the intention it gives birth to is a good one" or a bad one; but he adds at once that the intention itself can only be called good or bad "according to the material con-

[351] *Ibid.*, §3, sect. 25.   [352] *Ibid.*, sect. 26.   [353] *Ibid.*, sect. 27.
[354] *Ibid.*, sect. 28.   [355] *Ibid.*, sect. 13, note.
[356] *Ibid.*, chap. x, §3, sect. 29 (Italics omitted).

sequences that are the objects of it."[357] Thus again, in truth, the goodness or badness of an action can be determined neither by its motives
nor by its intentions but exclusively by its material consequences. "So
far is it from the goodness of the intention's being to be known only
from the species of the motive. But from one and the same motive, as
we have seen, may result intentions of every sort of complexion whatsoever . . . according to the material consequences that are the objects"[358]
of them.

Further, Bentham concedes that "if it were necessary to apply such
denominations as good, bad and indifferent to motives, they might be
classed in the following manner: . . . in the class of good motives might
be placed the articles" with the epithet purely social, namely the motives
of good-will and perhaps also the articles with the epithet semi-social,
namely the motives of love of reputation, desire of amity, religion; in
the class of bad motives might be located the article with the epithet dissocial, namely the motives of displeasure, antipathy; and in the class
of indifferent motives may be listed the articles with the epithet self-
regarding, namely the motives of physical desire, pecuniary interest,
love of power, self-preservation, as including the fear of the pains of
the senses, the love of ease and the love of life.[359] But here again, Bentham does not forget to add that "this method of arrangement . . . cannot but be imperfect; and the nomenclature belonging to it is in danger
of being fallacious."[360]

So Bentham in one direction goes perhaps further than all other ethical apologists of asocial motives. True, he is not a greater radical
than moralists of such different types as Spinoza, Herder, Comte or
Nietzsche.[361] He insists exactly as they do that the self-regarding mo-

[357] *Ibid.*, §3, sect. 33.　　　　[358] *Ibid.*, §3, sect. 33.
[359] *Ibid.*, §3, sect. 31, 34, 35.　　[360] *Ibid.*, §3, sect. 32.
[361] See e.g. Spinoza, *Ethica*, Pars IV, propositio XX: "Quo magis unusquisque
suum utile quarere, hoc est suum esse conservare, conatur et potest, eo magis
virtute praeditus est"; J. G. Herder, "Briefe zu Beförderung der Humanität,
10. Sammlung," 1797, *Werke*, ed. Suphan, Band 18, S. 285: "In der Menschennatur
. . . wirken . . . das Prinzipium . . . des Eigennutzes" und "des moralischen
Sinnes . . . lebendig zusammen"; A. Comte, *Cours de philosophie positive*, 1839,
tome IV, cinquantième leçon, p. 553: "Si donc on pouvait supprimer en nous la
prépondérance nécessaire des instincts personnels, on aurait radicalement détruit
notre nature morale au lieu de l'améliorer, puisque les affections sociales, dès-lors
privées d'une indispensable direction, tendraient bientôt, malgré cet hypothetique
ascendant, à dégénérer en une vague et stérile charité, inévitablement dépourvue
de toute grande efficacité pratique"; F. Nietzsche, *Zur Genealogie der Moral*,
1887, I. Abhandlung, §2: "Heute herrscht das Vorurteil, welches moralisch, un-

tives "can no more be left out of the moral estimate" than the purely social ones.[362] But though in his results Bentham is perhaps no more radical, in his argument he is far more judicious and critical than other well-known defenders of dissocial motives; for he does not limit his task to a dogmatic vindication of asocial motives.

He explains how the purely social motive of sympathy may often do harm if it becomes partiality, and how even the dissocial motive of antipathy may be most valuable if it expresses itself as justice. He therefore warns again and again that the whole common division of motives into good social ones and bad dissocial ones is highly imperfect and contains great dangers. In contrast to these half-true traditional valuations of motives, he repeats the paradoxical thesis that any motive, taken by itself and seen in complete isolation, could be called good.[363] For it offers at least some small amount of pleasure; did it not do so, it could not work as a motive. All pleasure, however, taken by itself is good. And on the other hand, not taken by itself, no motive is either constantly bad or constantly good.[364] Motives can be called good or bad only with reference to their effects in each individual instance.

GRADATION OF VALUE OF MOTIVES

This radical, reforming doctrine of the comparative irrelevance of motives is also of decisive importance in the discussion of an "order of pre-eminence" among motives, a further capital problem of modern ethics. This problem, or at least a quite similar one, is called in German ethics, in F. E. Beneke, Nietzsche, Scheler and Nicolai Hartmann that of the *Rangordnung der Werte*.[365] For, as Bentham points out, it is in gen-

---

egoistisch, désintéressé als gleichwertige Begriffe nimmt, bereits mit der Gewalt einer fixen Idee."

[362] Bentham, *Introduction*, 1789, chap. x, §3, sect. 32. "For," as he adds, what would otherwise "become of the species?" Only in "a system in which the business of life might be carried on" without self-regarding motives could the species survive, but not "in the actual constitution of human nature." Scientific ethics, however, has to deal with our present conditions of life.

[363] *Ibid.*, chap. x, §2, sect. 10 and §2, sect. 10, note.

[364] *Ibid.*, chap. x, §2; §3, sect. 29; §3, sect. 33.

[365] See F. E. Beneke, *Grundlinien des natürlichen Systems der praktischen Philosophie*, 1837, Band I, S. 248, 87 f; Beneke, *Grundsätze der Civil- und Criminal-Gesetzgebung aus den Handschriften des engl. Rechtsgelehrten Jeremias Bentham*, 1830, Band I, S. 58 f. See F. Nietzsche, *Jenseits von Gut und Böse*, 1885-86, e.g. §268. See M. Scheler, *Der Formalismus in der Ethik und die materiale Wertethik*, e.g. Teil I, 1913, S. 106, 103 ff; Teil II, 1916, S. 609. See N. Hartmann, *Ethik*, 1935, Zweiter Teil, Kapitel 28 ff. Compare the "Rangordnung der Pflichten" in Franz Volkmar Reinhard's *System der christlichen Moral*, Band II, 1805, S. 167 ff, S. 171.

eral "the same words which are mentioned as names of motives . . . of passions . . . and . . . also as names of moral qualities,"[366] i.e. of virtues or values.

Be this as it may, Bentham's discussion of the "order of pre-eminence among motives" seems to me superior to that of his successors, at least with regard to its general methodological attitude, though not as regards the detail of psychological and "phenomenological" descriptions. "Taken in a general view,"[367] like later moralists Bentham speaks of an ethical scale of motives and herewith indirectly of a scale of values. But though he is by no means a moral skeptic, he denies far more strictly than his successors of the last century that any definite gradation of ethical motives can be established which could be called valid in concrete application; and he gives reasons why this is the case.

Bentham admits that, roughly speaking, the motive of good-will, of benevolence, the "purely social"[368] value is the highest; for its "dictates . . . are surest of coinciding" with those of Bentham's ethical criterion, the principle of utility.[369] Nevertheless, he insists that even the "purely social" value cannot be considered to be the highest under all circumstances.

An act may have the purely social value in view, it may be governed by the motive of pure benevolence; yet if the consequences of this act run counter to the interest of a numerous assemblage of persons, and if the consequences of another benevolent act prejudice the interest of a much smaller number of people, then little or nothing is gained by insisting that both acts had the highest possible value in view, namely, benevolence. For, in spite of this, one of them may be merely "partial benevolence" and must rank much lower than the other, even lower than acts not having benevolence but "merely" justice in view. And Bentham speaks of "partial benevolence" even in cases in which the interests of a more numerous assemblage of persons are "not present . . . to a man's mind, or, if present, make no impression."[370]

Thus, the statement that benevolence or any other motive should be called the highest value in any case does not answer any ethical question. For such statements cannot show us which are the exceptions to the rules expressed by them. And as these rules themselves are vague, any attempt at establishing a strict "order of pre-eminence among motives" or values must remain a hopeless task.

[366] Bentham, *Introduction*, 1789, chap. x, §3, sect. 26, note.
[367] *Ibid.*, §4, sect. 36.   [368] *Ibid.*, §3, sect. 35.   [369] *Ibid.*, §4, sect. 36.
[370] *Ibid.*, §4, sect. 37.

Therefore, Bentham contents himself with giving some few simple hints as to why he puts benevolence first, the love of reputation second, and the desire of amity third in his by no means obligatory gradation of values and motives. His main points are that benevolence governs actions even in secret to the extensive happiness of others, while love for reputation does so in general only in public; and the desire of amity concerns the happiness of a less extensive number of people than even the love of reputation.[371] Fourth in his scale, after benevolence, the love of reputation and the desire of amity, Bentham ranks religion—certainly on a very low grade in comparison with the place held by religion in practically all ethical systems before and after Bentham down to the twentieth century.[372] But in speaking of religion, Bentham thinks only of the variety of religious confessions, and of the votaries of these faiths; he admits that the dictates of religion would coincide even with those of the highest motive, viz. of benevolence, "were the Being, who is the object of religion . . . supposed to be as benevolent as he is supposed to be wise and powerful. . . . Unhappily, however . . . among the votaries of religion (of which number the multifarious fraternity of Christians is but a small part) there seem to be but few (I will not say how few) who are real believers in his benevolence. They call him benevolent in words, but they do not mean that he is so in reality. They do not mean, that he is benevolent as man is conceived to be benevolent . . . , benevolent in the only sense in which benevolence has a meaning" in Bentham's critical, empirical thought. And as the votaries of religion "bear in their minds . . . but too often the idea of malevolence" in "holy wars and religious persecutions,"[373] Bentham places the religious motive only after the desire of amity, while the last two places in the scale of motives are taken by the self-regarding and the dissocial.

But to demonstrate again how rough and unsure any gradation of motives must be, Bentham winds up this debate by emphasizing that even antipathy, displeasure—the morally lowest motive in the whole scale—may be in many circumstances of higher value than the ethically highest motive, namely, good-will, benevolence. If antipathy vents itself "against a man, on account of a mischief supposed to be done by him to the public," it may be of far higher value than even "good-will,

---

[371] *Ibid.*, §4, sect. 38 f.

[372] *Ibid.*, §4, sect. 40 and see e.g. in contemporary ethics, in Scheler or Spranger, religion occupying the first degree in the scale of values; see e.g. M. Scheler, *Der Formalismus in der Ethik und die materiale Wertethik*, 1913-16, Teil I, S. 103 ff, Teil II, S. 609 and E. Spranger, *Lebensformen*, 1925, S. 236 ff.

[373] Bentham, *Introduction*, 1789, chap. x, §4, sect. 40.

the exertions of which are confined to an individual."[374] For all such reasons, Bentham refuses to set up a definite order of moral pre-eminence among motives; and this shows again the consistency of his critical, censorial method.

For any presupposition of a definite gradation of moral motives always has been, and is still, a significant source of uncritical dogmatism in ethics. In isolation from the discussion of the consequences of action, no valid scale of moral motives can be established.

CONFLICT AMONG MOTIVES AND CLAIMS

Another problem which cannot be satisfactorily approached in abstraction from the other ingredients of action is that of the conflict of motives. Modern moralists have generally defended the opposite view and Bentham has unfortunately dealt with this topic in an even more cursory way than with that of the scale of moral motives. Nevertheless, the main line of his argument is brought out clearly enough.

If a man "is . . . acted upon at the same time by the force of diverse . . . contending motives," by the mere examination of the motives in question it cannot be decided which one of the contending motives is ethically preferable.[375] Moreover, it cannot be ascertained which motives actually govern an action, unless "a multitude of questions" are answered beforehand,[376] questions concerning the whole intellectual horizon within which such or such motives alone can be active.

Bentham illustrates this by the following example: "Crillon, a Catholic (at a time when it was generally thought meritorious among Catholics to extirpate Protestants), was ordered by his king Charles IX of France, to fall privately upon Coligny, a Protestant, and assassinate him: his answer was 'Excuse me, Sire; but I'll fight him with all my heart.' "[376] Were religious motives in operation here? "The answer is, Yes, if his [Crillon's] notion was, that it was God's pleasure he should comply with . . . the dictates . . . of the sovereign." Was the love of reputation among the contending motives? "Yes, if it was his notion that the world would expect and require that he should comply with them: No, if it was not"; was the motive of benevolence governing Crillon? "Yes, if it was his notion that the community would upon the whole be the better for his complying with them: No, if it was not."[376] But even if it can be definitely ascertained which motives were involved in the conflict and which not, no instruction can be obtained in this way about the ethical preferableness of one or another of these motives.

[374] *Ibid.*, §4, sect. 42.   [375] *Ibid.*, §5, sect. 43 ff.   [376] *Ibid.*, §5, sect. 45.

For, as "it has been shown . . . there is no sort of motive but may give birth to any sort of action."[377] And "what is here said about the goodness and badness of motives, is far from being a mere matter of words"; it is needed "for the sake of dissipating . . . prejudices."[378] As a matter of fact, by a mere discussion of moral motives, in isolation from the analysis of the consequences of acts, none of the cardinal problems concerning moral motives can be dealt with satisfactorily—neither the question of the ethical gradation of motives and virtues, nor that of the moral conflict among motives, nor even that of an unbiased neutral denomination of motives and values. To many moralists, it has seemed as if Bentham had here avoided one form of ethical one-sidedness only to favor another. He refused, as he was entitled to do, to value motives and intentions isolated from the consequences of acts; and instead of this, as we shall see later more fully, he placed in the center of moral importance only the consequences of acts. Nevertheless, as we shall also see later, he never went so far as to deny a certain amount of ethical relevance to motives which are analyzed in combination with their effects. It is only the moral significance of motives and intentions analyzed in complete isolation from the valuation of the consequences of acts which he denied.

Comparative Irrelevance of Human Dispositions

Lastly, Bentham did not limit his denial of moral relevance to motives in themselves or to mere intentions, but he extended it also to mere human dispositions. "In the foregoing chapter it has been shown at large, that goodness or badness cannot, with any propriety, be predicated of motives. Is there nothing then about a man that can properly be termed good or bad, when, on such or such an occasion he suffers himself to be governed by such or such a motive? Yes, certainly: his *disposition*. Now disposition is a kind of fictitious entity, feigned for the convenience of discourse, in order to express what there is supposed to be *permanent* in a man's frame of mind, where, on such or such an occasion, he has been influenced by such or such a motive, to engage in an act, which, as it appeared to him, was of such or such a tendency."[379] But "it is with disposition" as with intention and motive or "with everything else: it will be good or bad" solely "according to its effects: according to the effects it has in augmenting or diminishing the happiness of the community."[380]

[377] *Ibid.*, §5, sect. 44.   [378] *Ibid.*, §5, sect. 46.   [379] *Ibid.*, chap. XI, sect. 1.
[380] *Ibid.*, sect. 2.

According to the wide meaning which Bentham rightly attributes to the term ethics or morals, he even mentions here that kind of disposition which influences a man's "own happiness," namely, his firm and sound or his frail, infirm disposition.[380] This kind of disposition concerns ethics only in its widest meaning and it hardly concerns jurisprudence at all; therefore, there "needs not much to be said here" about it.[380] But it seems to me that a firm or frail disposition of the actor is, in fact, a fundamental part of his ethical disposition; it causes not only his happiness or unhappiness, but from this base it also influences his whole conduct so essentially that it certainly should not be forgotten in any discussion of moral or of good or bad dispositions.

Further, as regards the legislator, human dispositions augmenting the *happiness* of others can be assigned by him only to "a hitherto . . . little calculated . . . branch of law, which might be styled the remuneratory."[380] Thus, the most important questions of penal law and ethics which are left are those relating to human dispositions causing *mischief* to others.

But Bentham makes it clear from the beginning that it is perhaps even less possible to speak of absolutely bad dispositions than to speak of definitely bad motives or intentions. All that can be said is, first, that a man is of a bad disposition when "he is *presumed* to be more apt to engage . . . in acts which are *apparently* of a pernicious tendency, than in such as are apparently of a beneficial tendency: of a meritorious or beneficent disposition in the opposite case."[381] For from observation of one single act of a person we can infer only "the probable existence (past or future) of a number of . . . similar acts . . . of the same person."[382] Second, as to dispositions, we have to reckon not with the character which actions turn out to possess but with the inference from the character they *appear* to possess to the actor; and we have to take into account also "unconsciousness and missupposal" of circumstances combined with the acts in question.[383] In judging the true intentions of the agent, the critical moralist must not neglect any of these factors. If an act appeared to the actor likely to be mischievous, and it proved in the upshot innocent or even beneficial, the disposition of the man has nevertheless to be called bad, in as much as its tendency *appeared* to him bad and vice versa. But none of these inferences can be exact.

THE DANGER OF HYPERMORALIZATION

In yet another important direction Bentham cautions the moralist

[381] *Ibid.*, sect. 3. [382] *Ibid.*, sect. 4. [383] *Ibid.*, sect. 5.

against premature conclusions, especially as to the badness of dispositions or an alleged leniency of moral standards in general. Bentham warns us against "hypermoralization," just as Herder did independently of Bentham some few years after him and Sigmund Freud a century later.

"Wer die Menschheit hypermoralisiert, hat sie exmoralisiert," wrote Herder in 1800 in his *Kalligone*; and Freud emphatically and illuminatingly stated the case against "ethical narcissism" as follows: "Dem ethischen Narzissmus des Menschen sollte es genügen, dass er in der Tatsache der Traumentstellung, in den Angst- und Strafträumen ebenso deutliche Beweise seines sittlichen Wesens erhält wie durch die Traumdeutung Belege für Existenz und Stärke seines bösen Wesens. Wer, damit nicht zufrieden, 'besser' sein will, als er geschaffen ist, möge versuchen, ob er es im Leben weiter bringt als zur Heuchelei oder zur Hemmung."[384] Bentham, the jurist, however says less solemnly but no less instructively: "to exalt weakness to a level with crimes, is a way to diminish the abhorrence which ought to be reserved for crimes. To exalt small evils to a level with great ones, is the way to diminish the share of attention which ought to be paid to great ones."[385] This problem of hypermoralization deserves much more attention than it has found hitherto.

It is only too widespread a prejudice that some ethical rigorism can hardly do any harm and that only what Kant branded as ethical "latitudinarianism"[386] is dangerous. Idealistic ethics has again and again emphasized that man is by his very nature so much inclined to fall short of high ethical standards that these ethical ideals can hardly be placed high enough. As Bentham, Herder and Freud realized, exaggeration of this kind is not only a bad service to ethical truth; it is also educationally most objectionable.

Not only aesthetics, as Schiller thought, but ethics itself has to reject any kind of ethical super-rigorism. Hypermoralization does not lead to a raising of ethical standards. On the contrary, it widens the gulf between ethical theory and practice; it encourages moral insincerity, or it creates an almost equally dangerous moral discouragement in sensitive souls.

[384] J. G. Herder, *Kalligone*, 1800, *Werke*, ed. by Suphan, 1880, Band XXII, S. 276; S. Freud, *Kleine Beiträge zur Traumlehre* 1925, S. 71.

[385] Bentham, *Introduction*, 1789, chap. XI, sect. 2, note.

[386] See Kant, *Die Religion innerhalb der Grenzen der blossen Vernunft, Kants Gesammelte Schriften*, ed. by Preussische Akademie der Wissenschaften, Band VI, 1907, p. 22.

DIFFICULTIES IN THE MORAL EVALUATION OF HUMAN DISPOSITIONS

Whether examining moral standards in general, or only inferences of concrete human dispositions in concrete human actions, it is most essential to guard against ethical rigorism as well as against moral all-for-givingness. As far as human dispositions are at issue, it is certainly unjustifiable from the psychological and ethical standpoint to presuppose criminal dispositions where only frail ones should be assumed. It is even dangerous to do so from the pedagogical and political point of view. And of course also the opposite procedure, the attitude of undiscriminating moral forgivingness, is ethically detrimental and scientifically indefensible.

The fundamental insight which is needed here is the knowledge of the difficulties involved in all inferences of human dispositions. These inferences are in general by no means precise, and they can hardly ever be exact. Therefore, the definite judgment on the morality of a man's action cannot be made dependent either on his presumed disposition or even on his motive; it must be based essentially on the intended and the actual consequences of his act. Bentham illustrates this in detail by the following reflections: If the consequences of a man's act are bad or if its tendency, that is, the intended consequences are bad, then the man's disposition is at least "dubious," even if his motive is "the purely social one of *good-will*."[387] For however much benevolence may be the motive of his act, if it concerns only a confined group of people, if it is not "enlarged benevolence" and if it has mischievous effects, then the man's "disposition . . . may be a mischievous or a meritorious one, as it happens."[388] Again, if the tendency of the act is bad and the motive is a semi-social one, the *love of reputation*, then the disposition of the actor remains dubious, "more or less good or bad"; for the motive cannot give sufficient instruction about the goodness or badness of the human disposition at issue. Obviously far more essential is the greater or lesser mischievousness of the intended consequences of the act, and the degree of coincidence of the moral sanctions with the standard of "enlightened benevolence . . . that is . . . of utility."[389] Further, if the tendency of a man's act is bad and the motive is the semi-social one of *religion*, the man's disposition is even more dubious. It depends on whether the consequences of the act are more or less mischievous, and whether "the religious tenets of the person in question approach more

---

[387] Bentham, *Introduction*, 1789, chap. XI, sect. 12.
[388] *Ibid.*, sect. 13, 12.　　　　　[389] *Ibid.*, sect. 18.

or less to a coincidence with the dictates of utility," that is, of enlightened benevolence.[390] Only "where the tendency of the act is bad, and the motive . . . is of the *self-regarding* kind" is "the disposition indicated" a bad one,[391] and so much the more of course "where . . . the motive is the *dissocial* one of malevolence."[392] Nevertheless these reflections show distinctly how untenable are inferences of good dispositions from good motives in the case of actions whose tendency is bad.

On the other hand, where the tendency of an act is good, even the dissocial motive of *ill-will* cannot afford any indication of a definitely bad disposition of the actor. This has been illustrated by Bentham in an ingenious example; and it is the choice of such examples illuminating crucial complications in morals which shows us in Bentham the subtle psychologist and the moralist close to concrete life. "You have detected a baker in selling short weight: you prosecute him for the cheat. It is not for the sake of gain that you engaged in the prosecution; for there is nothing to be got by it; it is not from public spirit: it is not for the sake of reputation; for there is no reputation to be got by it: it is not in the view of pleasing the Deity: it is merely on account of a quarrel you have with the man you prosecute. From the transaction, as thus stated, there does not seem to be any thing to be said either in favour of your disposition or against it. The tendency of the act is good: but you would not have engaged in it, had it not been from a motive which there seems no particular reason to conclude will ever prompt you to engage in an act of the same kind again. Your motive is of that sort which may, with least impropriety, be termed a bad one: but the act is of that sort, which, were it engaged in ever so often, could never have any evil tendency; nor indeed any other tendency than a good one. By the supposition, the motive it happened to be dictated by was that of ill-will: but the act itself is of such a nature as to have wanted nothing but sufficient discernment on your part in order to have been dictated by the most enlarged benevolence. Now, from a man's having suffered himself to be induced to gratify his resentment by means of an act of which the tendency is good, it by no means follows that he would be ready on another occasion, through the influence of the same sort of motive, to engage in any act of which the tendency is a bad one. The motive that impelled you was a dissocial one: but what social motive could there have been to restrain you? None, but what might have been outweighed by a more enlarged motive of the same kind. Now, because the dissocial motive prevailed when it stood alone, it by no means

---

[390] *Ibid.*, sect. 22, 23.   [391] *Ibid.*, sect. 10.   [392] *Ibid.*, sect. 25.

follows that it would prevail when it had a social one to combat it."[393]
The moral impartiality and subtlety of such deductions seem to me to
be representative. It may happen more frequently than we imagine that
a very praiseworthy zeal for justice is caused, to a large extent, by the
bad motive of personal hatred against one or several unjust persons.
Therefore, it is certainly the fairest and wisest conclusion which can
be drawn in these and similar cases not to praise and not to condemn
human dispositions before all the detailed questions mentioned here
are taken into account. Until these questions can be answered with sufficient care on the ground of unequivocal observations, the judgment
about the moral character of a human disposition has to be suspended.

If this be the case even as regards an obviously bad motive such as
antipathy, how much the more must it be so with regard to the neutral
motives of the self-regarding type. Where the intended consequences
of an act are good and the motive is an *egoistic* one, such as pecuniary
interest or physical desire, there is nevertheless no reason for inferring
the actor's disposition to be bad.[394] The disposition in question has to remain in doubt in this case. Where, however, the tendency of an act is
good and the motives are of semi-social or purely social character, such
as those dictated by *religion*, by *love of reputation* or by *benevolence*,
in all these cases it is of course allowable to presume a man's disposition
to be good,[395] and so to infer from the predicate of the motive the same
predicate of the disposition. On the whole, this analysis of moral and
immoral dispositions certainly shows how relevant the tendencies of
acts are, that is, the "certain . . . or the probable . . . consequences"[396]
of acts, and how much less the moral character of motives allows any
conclusions as to the good or bad character of dispositions.

The difficulties in measuring degrees of the morality of dispositions,
however, are no less considerable. Bentham speaks in this connection
of seducing and of tutelary motives, and of "the strength of a temptation" (correspondent to the strength of a restraint or an inhibition).[397]
A seducing motive is a motive which prompts a man to engage in a
mischievous act; a tutelary motive is a motive which restrains a man
from engaging in such an act.[398] And all social motives (such as good
will, love of reputation, desire of amity, the religious motive) may be
considered on the whole to be "standing tutelary"[399] motives. It follows,

[393] *Ibid.*, sect. 24. [394] *Ibid.*, sect. 9. [395] *Ibid.*, sect. 21, 17, 11.
[396] *Ibid.*, sect. 2. [397] *Ibid.*, sect. 29, 40. [398] *Ibid.*, sect. 29.
[399] *Ibid.*, sect. 31-34.

therefore, that the strength of a "temptation . . . is as the sum of the forces of the seducing to the sum of the forces of the occasional tutelary motives . . . after deducting the force of the social,"[400] that is, of the standing tutelary motives.

Now jurisprudence is only concerned with the measurement of the depravity of dispositions, not with their meritoriousness; and as Bentham—in contrast to the title of his book—assures us here that he is "in the present work" solely interested in penal law,[401] he lays down only the following four rules concerning the measurement of the badness of dispositions:

"Rule 1. The strength of the temptation being given, the mischievousness of the disposition manifested by the enterprise, is as the apparent mischievousness of the act." For example "it would show a more depraved disposition, to murder a man for a reward of a guinea . . . than to obtain the same sum from him by simple theft: the trouble he would have to take, and the risk he would have to run, being supposed to stand on the same footing in the one case as in the other. Rule 2. The apparent mischievousness of the act being given, a man's disposition is the more depraved, the slighter the temptation is by which he has been overcome."[402] For instance, "it shows a more depraved and dangerous disposition, if a man kill another out of mere sport . . . than out of revenge . . . or in the view of self-preservation."[402] To these two rules (in which a relatively determinate degree of bad disposition is concluded from a given character of temptation and a given badness of the act) Bentham adds a third rule, in which again a relatively fixed degree of bad disposition is inferred from a given temptation, from the badness of the act, and from the fixed degree of deliberation with which the act is accompanied. This rule (No. 4 in Bentham) reads: "where the motive is of the dissocial kind, the apparent mischievousness of the act, and the strength of the temptation, being given, the depravity is as the degree of deliberation with which it is accompanied. . . . Thus it shows a worse disposition, where a man lays a deliberate plan for beating his antagonist, and beats him accordingly, than if he were to beat him upon the spot, in consequence of a sudden quarrel: and worse again, if, after having had him a long while together in his power, he beats him at intervals, and at his leisure."[402] All these three rules show us a certain determinable correspondence between degrees of the morality of dispositions on the one hand, and degrees of temptations or consciousness accompanying actions on the other.

[400] *Ibid.*, sect. 40.   [401] *Ibid.*, sect. 26.   [402] *Ibid.*, sect. 42.

Finally, however, in a fourth rule (in his enumeration No. 3) Bentham makes it clear that given the badness of an act, from a stronger temptation a less depraved disposition can by no means be inferred. "The apparent mischievousness of the act being given, the evidence which it affords of the depravity of a man's disposition is the less conclusive, the stronger the temptation is by which he has been overcome." For instance, "if a poor man who is ready to die with hunger, steal a loaf of bread, it is a less explicit sign of depravity, than if a rich man were to commit a theft to the same amount."[403] But all that can be said "in this case . . . is, that the evidence of depravity is . . . the less conclusive: it is not said that the depravity is positively the less. For in this case it is possible, for anything that appears to the contrary, that the theft might have been committed, even had the temptation been not so strong."[403] We are, that is, not able to attain in this case any strict conclusiveness; and the same applies to the corresponding inference of a meritorious disposition where good consequences of an act co-exist with slighter temptations.

Taking all this together, we see constantly confirmed how all ethical judgments have to be based primarily on the analysis of facts, particularly on the character of the consequences of acts. The moral character of motives and human dispositions is certainly of importance within the total valuation of acts, and it has to be explored as far as this is in any way possible. But, performed independently of the valuation of the consequences of acts or independently of the objective circumstances of the consciousness of the actor, all moral valuation of mere intentions, of mere motives and human dispositions, must be considered to be ethically futile.

Primary Ethical Importance of Consequences of Acts

This conclusion of the chapters on intentionality, motives and human dispositions is illustrated once more—from the other side—by Bentham's analysis of the consequences of acts. As he now tells us explicitly, the consequences of acts or their tendency is that "article which forms the concluding link involving in it the materiality of the whole . . . chain of causes and effects"[404] hitherto analyzed. Bentham, it is true, wishes to confine himself on the whole to the analysis of the mischievous con-

---

[403] *Ibid.*, sect. 42, rule 3.

[404] *Ibid.*, chap. xii, §1, sect. 1. In his *The Concept of Morals*, 1937, pp. 117-120, Professor W. T. Stace defends with particularly instructive arguments the utilitarian's treatment of the consequences of an act as a genuine part of the whole action.

sequences of acts, obviously again because this part of the inquiry is of primary concern to the jurist. But it is of particular importance in ethics too, and Bentham himself mentions that "the investigation might, by a process rendered obvious by analogy, be extended to the consequences of an act of a beneficial nature."[405] Therefore, not only the jurist will find material of interest in this chapter; it concerns also the moralist who has to expand its results to the analysis of good consequences of acts.

Within the mischievous consequences of an act, we must begin, according to Bentham, by distinguishing between "two . . . parcels: the one containing . . . the *primary* mischief . . . sustained by an assignable individual, or a multitude of assignable individuals," the other containing the *secondary* mischief sustained by a multitude of unassignable individuals or the whole community.[406] Within the primary mischief, we have then to distinguish between the original and the derivative one. The *original* one is confined to any assignable person who is a sufferer in the first instance, the *derivative* mischief is that share of suffering which may befall other assignable persons only in consequence of the mischief undergone by the persons first injured.[407] The secondary mischief "may frequently consist of two other shares": the first is a pain of apprehension, namely, the "*alarm*" produced within an unassignable multitude by the primary mischief;[408] the other share is the "*danger*," the chance of suffering pain which an unassignable multitude may stand exposed to.[409]

The meaning of all these different "shapes" in which mischievous consequences of acts may appear can be illustrated by the following example: You are robbed on the road. The pain you suffer on the occasion of losing money constitutes the original branch of the primary mischief. Two or three creditors of yours who expected you to pay them with that money are disappointed. These mischiefs make up the derivative branch of the primary mischief. An unassignable number of people,

---

[405] *Ibid.*, chap. xii, §1, sect. 18, note. It is somewhat of a paradox that the corresponding consideration given to good effects of acts (which concerns ethics alone, not both jurisprudence and ethics) is to be found in Bentham-Dumont's *Traités de législation*, tome i, "Principes de législation," chap. x, 1820, p. 81 f, although this question has scarcely anything to do with the title of this treatise; and on the other hand Bentham's *Introduction to the Principles of Morals and Legislation* does not contain the analysis of good effects of acts, although this problem concerns the subject matter mentioned in the title of this work, namely morals. Nevertheless, this is hardly of great importance.

[406] *Ibid.*, chap. xii, §1, sect. 3. [407] *Ibid.*, sect. 4.
[408] *Ibid.*, sect. 5, sect. 18. [409] *Ibid.*, sect. 5.

on this occasion, call to mind the danger which they stand exposed to in traveling. "This constitutes the first part of the secondary mischief, resulting from the act of robbery; viz. the alarm."[410] Another unassignable number of people, however, do not only conceive themselves to incur a chance of being robbed, in consequence of the robbery committed upon you, but they do really incur such a chance. "This chance . . . constitutes the remaining part of the secondary mischief of the act of robbery; viz. the danger."[410] And "some acts of robbery may produce alarm without danger: others danger without alarm,"[411] while both alarm and danger may result from robbing the same or different persons.[412] Certainly, all these divisions and subdivisions may seem at first sight of little or no inner relevance, as they refer only to palpable facts and to gross, externally manifest feelings.

But it was Bentham's express intention to base ethical judgment only on the observation of manifest pleasure and pain. In this way, he made every possible effort to free ethics and jurisprudence from reference to vague moral sentiments and equivocal concepts. Any criticism of Bentham which leaves this out of consideration is, therefore, missing the mark. Bentham takes especial pride in the fact that he is able to characterize moral and juristic concepts by having recourse solely to his plain terms of pleasant and mischievous consequences of acts.

Making use of such terms, he defines punishment, for instance, as an act whose primary consequences are attended with a mischief but whose secondary consequences may be beneficial to such a degree as even greatly to outweigh the mischief of the primary and whose secondary mischief, that is, the alarm and the danger, extends no farther than to such persons as are under temptation to commit an act which the primary mischief is "expedient" to prevent.[413] Bentham has further classifications of the "shapes" of mischievous consequences of acts, classifications based on their cause or their simple or complex, their positive or negative, their private, public or semi-public nature.[414] But it is not necessary to enumerate and to explain all these definitions, partly because they are of more interest to the jurist than to the moralist, partly because they are self-explanatory and primarily because they do not concern Bentham's main line of analysis.

---

[410] *Ibid.*, sect. 6.   [411] *Ibid.*, sect. 12.

[412] *Ibid.*, sect. 13. On "le mal du troisième ordre" and other subdivisions see Bentham-Dumont, *Traités de législation*, 1820, tome I, introductory part, chap. x, p. 81, and the analysis of the *Traités* in the second part of the present book.

[413] Bentham, *Introduction*, 1789, chap. XII, §1, sect. 14.

[414] *Ibid.*, §1, sect. 15.

THE INFLUENCE OF INTENTIONS, CONSCIOUSNESS, MOTIVES, AND DISPOSITIONS
ON THE DIFFERENT "PARCELS" OF CONSEQUENCES OF ACTS

The central theme of Bentham's ethical inquiry is, as the *Introduction*
shows, his analysis of the relations observable between the consequences
of acts and all the previously mentioned elements, concomitants and
antecedents of actions. After the main ethical relevance has been secured for the consequences of acts, it is, therefore, nevertheless essential
to look back and ascertain to what extent intentions, motives, dispositions and the degree of consciousness accompanying the intentions are
of ethical importance.

As to intentions and consciousness influencing the different "parcels"
of the consequences of acts, Bentham distinguishes six cases, starting
with complete unintentionality, ending with completely conscious intentions and providing, in this way, the best possible concrete illustration of the difficult questions at issue.

Case 1. "Where the act is so completely unintentional, as to be altogether *involuntary*," the act "is attended with no secondary mischief
at all."[415] For example, a bricklayer working on a house gives a fellow-
workman "a violent push, in consequence of which the second bricklayer falls upon a passenger and hurts him"; in this case it is plain that
nothing can give other people who may happen to be in the street the
least reason to apprehend any danger from the man who fell, whatever
there may be with regard to the man who pushed him.[416] For no danger
can be caused by a completely unintentional act of the falling bricklayer;
only the intentions of the workman who did the pushing can produce
such secondary mischief.

Case 2. "Where the act, though not unintentional, is *unadvised*, in-
so-much that the mischievous part of the consequences is unintentional,
but the unadvisedness is attended with heedlessness. In this case the act
is attended with some small degree of secondary mischief, in proportion
to the degree of heedlessness. A groom being on horseback and riding
through a frequented street, turns a corner at a full pace, and rides over

[415] *Ibid.*, §2, sect. 20.
[416] *Ibid.*, sect. 20. With regard to alarm, the other "share" of secondary mischief,
see Bentham's restrictions of his statements in question in chap. XII, §2, sect. 19.
He explains here that the alarm is immediately governed not by the real state
of intentions, but by their *apparent* one; "it is governed by the real only in as far
as the apparent happens, as in most cases it may be expected to do, to quadrate
with the real."

a passenger, who happens to be going by."[417] It is plain that the secondary mischief caused in this case by the act of the groom, the alarm, danger and the like produced by this act is less or greater according to the degree of heedlessness shown by the groom. That is, in this case, too, there is a certain definable relation between the intentions of acts and their secondary consequences in the form of possible danger.

And the same applies to the three other cases of relations between intention, consciousness on the one hand, and the different branches of consequences of acts on the other. Case 3. "Where the act is *misadvised* with respect to a circumstance, which, had it existed, would *fully* have excluded or (what comes to the same thing) outweighed the primary mischief: and there is no rashness in the case. In this case the act is attended with no secondary mischief at all. . . . Case 4. Where the act is misadvised with respect to a circumstance which would have excluded or counterbalanced the primary mischief *in part*, but not entirely: and still there is no rashness. In this case the act is attended with some degree of secondary mischief, in proportion to that part of the primary which remains unexcluded or uncounterbalanced. . . . Case 5. Where the act is misadvised with respect to a circumstance, which, had it existed, would have excluded or counterbalanced the primary mischief entirely, or in part: and there is a degree of *rashness* in the supposal. In this case, the act is also attended with the farther degree of secondary mischief, in proportion to the degree of rashness. . . . Case 6. Where the consequences are completely intentional, and there is no mis-supposal in the case. In this case the secondary mischief is at the highest."[418] Thus, the result of the analysis of all these cases is that intention and consciousness are by no means "articles" of acts which are ethically unrelated to, or could be described in complete isolation from, the analysis of the different consequences of acts. Moralists only too often fail to take this into account. In truth, the kind of intention and consciousness with which an act is done is of well definable influence, and therefore recognizable in the consequences of acts, viz. in the secondary consequences of the act which are, therefore, rightly distinguished by Bentham from the primary ones. And so it becomes manifest again why, in every consistent theory of morals, it must be the consequences of acts which constitute the element of the highest moral import. The intentions and consciousness accompanying intentions are of only secondary influence and if isolated from the analysis of the consequences they are of no clearly determinable relevance at all.

[417] *Ibid.*, chap. XII, §2, sect. 21.   [418] *Ibid.*, sect. 22-25.

Even more dependent on these consequences is the moral character of motives of acts, although this too is denied by common moral theories. But Bentham makes clear here, in a new and detailed way, that even the best motive cannot obliterate a secondary mischief if it has caused pernicious primary consequences, nor can the worst motive render an act morally bad if its secondary consequences are beneficial though its primary consequences are pernicious.

The first case is illustrated by the following example: Had a son of Ravaillac, the murderer of Henry IV, "merely on the score of filial affection (that is of a very good motive) put him to death in order to rescue him from the severer hands of justice, the motive, although it should . . . in case of punishment have made such rescuer an object of pity, would hardly have made the act of rescue a beneficial one."[419] The second case is illustrated by Bentham by this common experience: the secondary consequences of the prosecution of offenses are morally good, but the motives are, nevertheless, generally of the dissocial or self-regarding kind.

It is extremely rare that prosecutions are undertaken "from the sole influence of public spirit, uncombined with the least tincture of self-interest or ill-will."[420] Whenever this is the case, "it must be acknowledged to be a proceeding of the heroic kind," and "acts of heroism are in the very essence of them, but rare: for if they were common, they would not be acts of heroism"; yet "prosecutions for crimes are very frequent."[421] All the same, though such proceedings are generally brought about by motives of self-interest or even antipathy, their secondary consequences, and with them the whole of such actions, must be acknowledged to be good.

Certainly, worshipers of heroism who believe, paradoxically, even in a common heroic attitude of large communities, will dislike Bentham's rather cool-headed and prudent psychological observations on heroism. But since he, the great practical idealist, is by no means willing to deny the existence of heroism, I think his dispassionate and considerate statements on the subject come nearer the truth than those of his opponents in psychology and ethics.

Yet even if Bentham's attitude towards heroism had to be abandoned completely, his general characterization of the relations between motives and consequences of acts holds; and this alone is here the decisive point. For doubtless there exist—no matter whether frequently or seldom—certain prosecutions of crimes undertaken from motives of self-interest or antipathy against the offenders; and despite such dissocial motives,

[419] *Ibid.*, sect. 26, note.   [420] *Ibid.*, sect. 27, note.   [421] *Ibid.*, sect. 27, note.

the whole of such undertakings must be called morally good. On the other hand, even the best motive, benevolence, cannot make an act of bad consequences a morally good one, as Kant for instance attempted paradoxically to maintain.

At best, the motive can cause an aggravation of the secondary mischief of an act. But it is very characteristic that "it is not from the worst kind of motive . . . that the secondary mischief of an act receives its greatest aggravation."[422] A pernicious act, when committed through the worst motives, "through vengeance, or otherwise through displeasure," causes not nearly such mischievous secondary consequences as the same pernicious act when committed from less reprehensible motives, such as physical desire, the love of wealth, the love of ease and other self-regarding but not dissocial motives.[423] For, as Bentham explains rightly, the purely dissocial feelings of ill-will, vengeance, antipathy are—if not less strong and less frequent—certainly less constant than the most frequent, common motives of self-interest.[423]

Thus the secondary mischief, alarm and danger produced by acts which are motivated by the most common and constant motives of self-interest is greater than the alarm and danger caused by the same acts motivated by worse, but rarer and less constant motives, such as ill-will. And if even the motive of religion effects mischief, it must produce worse secondary mischief than the worst motive, ill-will; for although the motive of religion is in general thought to be far better morally than ill-will, vengeance and antipathy, the motive of religion is more constant than ill-will and therefore more dangerous.[424] Wherever the motive of religion gives birth to mischievous acts and becomes religious fanaticism, it will be morally more pernicious than even the most dissocial motives because of its constancy and its special intellectual blindness. For, as Bentham remarks ironically, the religious fanatic is not able to see that he is fighting against intellectual adversaries who "think, or perhaps only speak, differently upon a subject which neither party understands";[425] he does not realize that there would be even more heretics if there were more thinkers.[426] Religious "fanaticism never sleeps: it is never glutted: it is never stopped by philanthropy; for it makes a merit of trampling on philanthropy: it is never stopped by conscience: for it has pressed conscience into its service. Avarice, lust, and vengeance, have piety, benevolence, honour: fanaticism has nothing to oppose it."[425]

[422] *Ibid.*, sect. 28, 29.　　[423] *Ibid.*, sect. 33.　　[424] *Ibid.*, sect. 34.
[425] *Ibid.*, sect. 34, note.　　[426] *Ibid.*, chap. xi, sect. 23.

Even if one does not approve the whole tenor of this diatribe against religious fanaticism, which is common and typical of the spirit of the eighteenth century, independent of these psychological observations on fanaticism, the ethical result of these analyses of motives and consequences of acts stands on its own feet.

It is a paradoxical truth carefully explained here that the morally worst motive, ill-will, produces less secondary evil than the ethically better motive, self-interest, because it is less constant and on the whole, less frequent. And it seems equally paradoxical that the morally better motive of religion causes more secondary evil than ill-will; for the religious motive works more perniciously than even ill-will by reason also of its greater constancy or, better, through its reinforcement of the constancy of self-regarding motives. All these paradoxes, however, provide new and instructive illustrations of Bentham's main thesis that the consequences of acts, i.e. especially their so-called secondary consequences, are the morally most important part of all elements of acts.

The same applies, lastly, to the relations between moral dispositions and consequences of acts. Bentham had already treated this matter in the eleventh chapter on dispositions. He therefore merely repeats here that the "apparent" dispositions of a moral agent cannot inform us with any precision about the moral goodness or badness of his acts.[427] This can be done solely by the character of the primary and secondary consequences of these acts. Whatever is dependent on the apparent disposition of the agent can form nothing but an aggravation or diminution of the secondary goodness or badness of these acts in proportion to the meritoriousness or depravity of the apparent character of the agent; but it is not possible to determine exactly the degree of such an aggravation or diminution. From the apparent moral or immoral disposition of the agent, no precise inference can be drawn regarding the moral character of the primary and secondary consequences of the act.

Herewith ends Bentham's long and subtle study of the moral act, its different "articles," their relations to each other and their ethical relevance. Strange as it may seem, in the literature on Bentham the importance which should be attributed to these analyses—at least within the borders of the Utilitarian system—has been extraordinarily underrated or even overlooked. E. A. Albee, in his history of Utilitarianism, does

[427] *Ibid.*, chap. XII, §2, sect. 35.

not mention them at all; and even Leslie Stephen does no justice[428] to them in detail and barely outlines their major tendencies.

The most common objections against these analyses are that they contain only a rough, mechanical psychology which never was up to date, and has been definitely out of date for more than a hundred years; and that they distort all ethical discussion by forcing an uncongenial legal doctrine upon it leading to a "completely external . . . , essentially inadequate view of morality."[429] Both these lines of argument seem to me a very inadequate criticism.

First, Bentham is by no means primarily concerned with accurate, exhaustive psychological analyses; he certainly separated elements of acts from each other which psychologically belong closely together. But he separated them only methodologically, not definitely; he separated them only to show, in this way, the different ethical relevance of each of these elements.

The results of Bentham's analyses are, therefore, in principle independent of the detail of his psychological teachings.

Second, Bentham tried to show everywhere that the vagueness of common ethical terminology and reasoning can only be overcome by the introduction of the more exact language of jurisprudence; and this makes it obvious that the problems of the jurist and the moralist are to a large extent identical. It is a commonplace to say that the jurist cannot find out with certainty the character of the moral motives and moral dispositions of men, but that the same concession made by the moralist would take all meaning out of ethics. Bentham, however, shows in detail why the same concession has to be made in morals as in Law; for the moralist, like the jurist, cannot find himself in possession of any precise knowledge of motives and dispositions of moral agents.

From this critical insight, Bentham went on to an important positive finding: he cleared up a considerable number of well-grounded relations between motives, dispositions and intentions on the one hand, and the different parts of consequences of acts on the other, relations which must appear rather paradoxical to common, vague moral sentiments. Yet only by way of Bentham's analyses can the age-old fundamental difficulties of ethical method be removed; they cannot be overcome by the dogmatic assumption that motives and dispositions are intrinsically

[428] See Leslie Stephen, *The English Utilitarians*, 1900, I, p. 256 f in the brief chapter on Bentham's doctrine of sanctions; compare *ibid.*, II, pp. 324 ff on motives in James Mill; *ibid.*, III, pp. 309 ff on motives in J. S. Mill.
[429] *Ibid.*, III, p. 311.

good or bad, i.e. that their goodness or badness is self-evident and independent of the consequences of acts inspired by them. Nor can Bentham's fundamental insights be rivaled by the ethical skepticism of the logical positivists or the most recent semi-skepticism which assigns to the central assertions of ethics only an emotive, non-assertive meaning.

It is, therefore, a deplorable misconstruction of Bentham's line of thought that his "juristical" start from the analysis of consequences of acts should be made responsible for his reaching an "essentially inadequate . . . external . . . view of morality."[430] For epistemological reasons, Bentham deliberately took as his starting point the clear juristic concept of effects of acts in order to free ethics from the more refined, but vague "internal" method of approach.

Especially through his detailed analyses of internal motives, dispositions and intentions, Bentham could make clear why these elements of acts are of less moral relevancy than the most material part of the "articles" of acts, namely, the consequences of actions, the pain or pleasure produced by them. At the same time, however, his well considered analyses of the different factors of acts also give the most fundamental justification for his principle of utility. They show us why not vaguely explorable motives and dispositions but only the evident consequences of acts, namely, pleasure and pain, can provide us with a workable criterion of good or bad.

Bentham's *doctrine of motives is, therefore, not "a logical deduction" from his assumption of the principle of utility,*[431] as Leslie Stephen assumes, but *on the contrary the validity of the utility principle is deduced from that doctrine.* The ethical validity of the greatest-happiness principle is not simply presupposed by Bentham in narrow-minded dogmatism, as is commonly supposed; it receives its ethical legitimation particularly through these analyses of the ethical factors of acts.

ETHICS AND ITS RELATION
TO JURISPRUDENCE[432]

After his discussion of the principle of utility and the principles adverse to it, his account of pleasure, pain and their measurement, and

[430] *Ibid.*, p. 311.　　　　[431] *Ibid.*, I, p. 256.
[432] In Bowring's edition of the "Introduction," *Works*, 1843, part 1, p. 83a, this chapter is numbered xv. The chapter numbered XIII in Bowring's edition, *ibid.*,

after the long analyses of the ethical elements of action bringing out again the decisive moral importance of pleasure and pain, Bentham comes to the discussion of the *"artificial"*[433] consequences of acts, namely, legal punishments. These are, indeed, in the main juristical questions. Nevertheless, even they are largely interspersed with inquiries of specifically ethical interest and, therefore, we must give at least some attention to them.

It is, of course, interesting to the moralist to see how Bentham in his theory of punishment, too, strictly adheres to the principle of utility, and how he therefore rejects the principle of mere expiation. In so far as punishment does not serve the greatest happiness of the greatest number, it cannot be approved in jurisprudence any more than in ethics.

As "all punishment is mischief . . . , upon the principle of utility, if it ought at all to be admitted it ought to be admitted only in so far as it promises to exclude some greater evil. . . . It is plain therefore, that in the following cases punishment ought not to be inflicted. 1. Where it is *groundless*: where there is no mischief for it to prevent; the act not being mischievous upon the whole. 2. Where it must be *inefficacious*: where it cannot act so as to prevent the mischief. 3. Where it is *unprofitable*, or too *expensive*: where the mischief it would produce would be greater than what is prevented. 4. Where it is *needless*: where the mischief may be prevented or cease of itself, without it: that is, at a cheaper

p. 76a, consists of different chapters inserted from Bentham-Dumont, *Traités de législation civile et pénale*, 1802, translated into English, viz. the chapters VII, IX-XIII of tome II, première partie of Dumont's edition (in Hildreth's edition of Bentham's *Theory of Legislation*, 1896, p. 251 f, 256-266). For also these chapters of the *Traités* discuss the problem of alarm caused by offenses. And the chapter numbered XIV in Bowring's edition is the translation of chap. XI (not II as Bowring says) of the introductory part, the "Principes de législation," vol. I, of Bentham-Dumont's *Traités de législation civile et pénale* (in R. Hildreth's edition of Bentham's *Theory of Legislation*, 1896, pp. 54-59). This chapter deals with "Raison pour ériger certain actes en délits." But it is in fact scarcely understandable why Bowring inserted in his edition just these chapters of the work edited by Dumont. He could have chosen instead of them or in addition to them other chapters of Dumont's book dealing with the corresponding problems of Bentham's *Introduction*, for instance Bentham-Dumont, vol. I, introductory part, "Principes de législation," chap. X, 1820, p. 75: "Analyse du bien et du mal politique.—Comment il se répandent dans la société" or tome II, première partie, chap. VIII, "L'influence des motives sur la grandeur de l'alarme." We shall, therefore, discuss the content of these insertions of Bowring's edition only in connection with the whole of Dumont's work from which they are taken.

[433] See Bentham, *Introduction*, 1789, chap. XII, sect. 36.

rate."[434] Thus no punishment whatsoever "ought to be allotted merely" to the purpose of "vindictive satisfaction."[435] Moreover, neither the theory of expiation nor even the unqualified theory of the deterrent influence of punishment is accepted by Bentham, and again the only reason is his strict adherence to the principle of utility.

Bentham even declares in this connection that punishment ought not to be inflicted in case the services of a delinquent were of extraordinary value; for it "would be to deprive the community of the benefit of those services";[436] and this would be unprofitable, incompatible with the rules of the utility principle. Further, as Bentham emphasizes, "no man can be so good a judge as a man himself, what it is [that] gives him pleasure or displeasure"; therefore, in a case in which a person whose interest an act "concerns gave his *consent* to the performance" of this act, "this consent, provided it be free, and fairly obtained, is the best proof that can be produced, that, to the person who gives it, no mischief, at least no immediate mischief, on the whole, is done."[437] And if no mischief on the whole is done, then Bentham insists that the act just characterized ought not to be punished although such an act might, on some occasions, be said to be mischievous. This again is certainly an ethically interesting application of the utility-principle. And it is also of interest to the moralist to see how impunity is demanded here even for "disseminating pernicious principles in matters of *duty*."[438] This misuse of the freedom of thought ought not to be punished, according to Bentham, because it is possible to find a remedy "at a cheaper rate"; Bentham is convinced that, for the purpose of combating error of this kind "the pen is the proper weapon . . . , not the sword."[439] Thus, here once more a question which is of equal importance juridically, politically and morally is answered solely by the application of the utility principle.

As to the different sorts of pleasure and pain, it is urged that the physical pain produced by the legislator, by the political sanction, is the most constantly effective type of pain. Pain and pleasure caused by love of reputation or religion are far more variable; they may have very different effects in different times and places, although on particular occasions their influence may be greater than that of any punishment "which the legislator is able, or at least which he will think proper to apply."[440] Thus, in the field of mere jurisprudence, Bentham again con-

---

[434] *Ibid.*, chap. XIII, §1, sect. 2 and 3.   [435] *Ibid.*, §1, sect. 2, note.
[436] *Ibid.*, §4, sect. 16.   [437] *Ibid.*, §2, sect. 4.   [438] *Ibid.*, §5, sect. 17.
[439] *Ibid.*, §5, sect. 17.   [440] *Ibid.*, §3, sect. 11, note.

firms his statement that physical pleasure and pain are the fundamental phenomena most constant at all times and places. To these phenomena, therefore, the whole system of morals can be referred as to its firmest Archimedean point. Not a so-called universal, categorical imperative a priori can provide us with the constant standard of good and evil; the most constant criterion we possess is the fact a posteriori, that physical pain can never be desired for its own sake, while pleasure can.

In chapter XIV on "the proportion between punishment and offences" again only a few remarks are of specific ethical relevance; but as they concern the problem of measurement in morals, they too are of importance. Following a favorite procedure of his, Bentham draws this parallel between a problem of physics and one of morals: "To say . . . as authors of great merit and great name have said, that the punishment ought not to increase with the strength of the temptation, is as much as to say in mechanics, that the moving force or *momentum* of the *power* need not increase in proportion to the momentum of the *burthen*."[441] In other words, according to Bentham, "the punishment must rise with the strength of the temptation"; and the contrary of this maxim "would be as cruel to offenders themselves, as it would be subversive of the purposes of punishment."[442] For, if the punishment were not to increase with the temptation, the offender would suffer the more since he would have weaker tutelary motives for the encouragement of his moral disposition,[443] and society would have to endure more pain upon the whole. Only in this way, by representing punishment as a benefit to the offender and to the community, could Bentham be said to be an adherent of a modified theory of the deterrent influence of punishment.

Further, by this example taken from jurisprudence, Bentham tries again to illustrate one of his major ethical doctrines: if we judge of the moral value of acts by looking only at the disposition of the actors, as is usually done, we shall be misled by the vagueness of such principles deriving in the last resort from mere antipathy or sympathy for the actor. In place of this, we must take into consideration above all the con-

[441] *Ibid.*, chap. xiv, sect. 8, note.   [442] *Ibid.*, chap. xi, sect. 43.
[443] Bentham adds wittily in this connection that as according to the Anglo-Saxon laws the life of a king in those days was worth exactly 7,200 shillings and "for two hundred shillings you might have killed a peasant . . . an earl Godwin, or a duke Streon, could have bought the lives of a whole dynasty," and "it is plain, that if ever a king in those days died in his bed, he must have had something else, besides this law, to thank for it," see *Introduction*, chap. xiv, sect. 8, note.

sequences of acts in terms of pleasure and pain; moreover, we must calculate as far as possible the exact amount of pain and pleasure caused by human actions in everyday life as well as by sentences of the court. If a man "for giving you ten blows, . . . is punished no more than for giving you five, the giving you five of these ten blows is an offence for which there is no punishment at all: which being understood, as often as a man gives you five blows, he will be sure to give you five more, since he may have the pleasure of giving you these five for nothing."[444] Therefore, Bentham demands that the amount of pain caused by punishment must be in exact proportion to the amount of pain whose production should be prevented by the threat of punishment. In this way, any use of the Deterrence Theory is strictly subordinate to the rules of the utility principle.

Bentham admits that he may be thought to have carried his "endeavours at proportionality" too far on this point; but as apart from "Montesquieu . . . hitherto scarce any attention has been paid to it," he thinks that "in such a matter . . . excess seemed more eligible than defect."[445] For it is easier to retrench a part of a discipline which seems superfluous than to invent the whole.

In this connection, Bentham defends once more the value of a moral calculus. "There are," he writes, "some, perhaps, who, at first sight, may look upon the nicety employed in the adjustment of such rules, as so much labour lost: for gross ignorance, they will say, never troubles itself about laws, and passion does not calculate. But the evil of ignorance admits of cure: and as to the proposition that passion does not calculate, this, like most of these very general and oracular propositions, is not true. When matters of such importance as pain and pleasure are at stake, and these in the highest degree (the only matters, in short, that can be of importance) who is there that does not calculate? Men calculate, some with less exactness, indeed, some with more: but all men calculate. I would not say, that even a madman does not calculate. Passion calculates, more or less, in every man: in different men, according to the warmth or coolness of their dispositions: according to the firmness or irritability of their minds: according to the nature of the motives by which they are acted upon."[446] Certainly these reflections do not give the main reasons why in every science quantitative has to be preferred to qualitative thought. Nonetheless, even the fact mentioned here

---

[444] *Ibid.*, chap. xiv, sect. 12, note.   [445] *Ibid.*, sect. 25, note.
[446] *Ibid.*, sect. 28.

is of import. As a matter of fact, even in ethics we think far more in quantitative terms than is generally admitted.

In 1781, at the time of the printing of his *Introduction,* Bentham seemed to grant that neither certainty nor proximity of pleasure and pain can be measured with sufficient accuracy. At least he there spoke only of a *certain* "proportionable addition"[447] which has to be made to the magnitude of a punishment in order to outweigh its uncertainty and remoteness. But he did not specify the exact proportion and calculation in question.

It is, however, interesting to see that, apparently soon afterwards, he got rid of such doubts relating to the extension of measurement to ethics and jurisprudence. He writes as follows in an as yet unpublished manuscript which was, according to E. Halévy, composed about 1782, and which was obviously worked out only after the printing of the *Introduction* in 1781: "The numbers expressive of" a pleasure's (or a pain's) "magnitude and those expressive of its proximity" or its remoteness "must be multiplied together and not barely added" or subtracted. Suppose the magnitude of one pleasure to be 27 and that of another to be 3, and suppose that the first pleasure by reason of remoteness to be reduced to $\frac{2}{3}$ of its original magnitude (that is lessened by $\frac{1}{3}$) and the second pleasure in consequence of its remoteness to be reduced to $\frac{1}{3}$ of its original magnitude (that is lessened by $\frac{2}{3}$), then we have to reckon in this way: "To multiply a whole number by a fraction is to multiply it by the *numerator* of the fraction and divide the product of that multiplication by the *denominator.* 27 then multiplied by $\frac{2}{3}$ or in other words $\frac{2}{3}$ of 27 is 18: and 3 multiplied by $\frac{1}{3}$, or in other words $\frac{1}{3}$ of 3 is 1. The value then of the greater pleasure will be to that of the lesser, as 18 is to 1. The number expressive of the magnitude of the pleasure supposing it to be present must be magnified by the fraction expressing what it loses in value on the score of its remoteness not simply added: for the deduction to be made on this account applies equally to every portion of it. If the fraction expressive of the alteration made in its value by this circumstance instead of being multiplied into the number expressive of its magnitude were added to it, the value of it would be increased by this circumstance instead of lessened. The value of the greater pleasure would be 27 and $\frac{2}{3}$ instead of 18: that of the lesser 3 and $\frac{1}{3}$ instead of 1."

"After the same manner it may be shown, that the number expressive of the magnitude of the pleasure is to be multiplied by the fraction ex-

[447] *Ibid.,* sect. 16.

pressive of its degree of certainty, not added to it."[448] These deductions give obviously a more detailed and a more far-reaching application of the moral calculus than any other we possess in Bentham's published works. However unsatisfactory we may find the particulars of these attempts, the introduction of subtler but similar methods into ethics is certainly most desirable—a task "as inescapable as it is difficult."[449] However much qualitative terms may be thought to be noble, more poetically expressive and in accordance with common sense, there can be no doubt that no precision of knowledge whatsoever can be attained by their use.

The topic with which chapter XV of the *Introduction* deals is again specifically juristical, viz. "the properties to be given to a lot of punishment." But once more, points of ethical significance are to be noted. All that Bentham says about the relation between quality and quantity of punishment as a kind of pain applies also to the relations existing between quality and quantity of pain and pleasure in general; and Bentham's statement that quality has to "be regulated by ... quantity"[450] is, therefore, of general ethical relevance.

Bentham, that is, denies no more the existence of different qualities of pain and pleasure than he denies the existence of different qualities of punishments which are a characteristic kind of pain. But he lays the utmost stress upon the fact that in a scientific theory of ethics dealing with judgments on the qualities of pain and pleasure, it is necessary to estimate the different qualities of these feelings in some way in terms of quantities.

Also, the problem of retaliation is of interest in this respect. As we have already had occasion to observe, retaliation in the sense of expiation has no place in Bentham's system. Retaliation "in the proper and exact sense of the word" should be called simply that "mode of punishment

[448] Bentham MS, *unpublished*, University College, London, Portfolio 27, Folder 5, sheet 40, pp. 5, 8. E. Halévy published other parts of the series of MS to which the sentences just quoted belong (see E. Halévy, *La formation du radicalisme philosophique*, tome I, 1901, pp. 398 ff). But Halévy omitted the passage just quoted, although he recognized that it is of vital interest for the historian of philosophy. In 1918 Professor W. C. Mitchell referred to Halévy's quotations in *Political Science Quarterly*, June 1918, vol. xxxiii, p. 165, in an essay on Bentham's felicific calculus, and so in 1929 did Professor J. Laird, *The Idea of Value*, p. 326. Yet as neither Professor Mitchell nor Professor Laird published this MS in full, I have placed it in Appendix IV of the present book.
[449] See C. I. Lewis, *An Analysis of Knowledge and Valuation*, 1946, p. 510.
[450] Bentham, *Introduction*, 1789, chap. xv, sect. 1.

which of all others bears the closest analogy to the offence,"[451] that type
of punishment "which is constituted by the circumstance of identity in
point of damage"[451] and which is therefore of highest "exemplary . . .
characteristicalness."[452] If retaliation, then, is "not too expensive," if it
does not produce "superfluous and needless pain,"[453] then and only then
is it practicable as having the highest degree of characteristic efficacy.[454]
But in most cases, retaliation is, according to Bentham, not "frugal"
enough, not sufficiently free from the infliction of superfluous pain[455] to
be the appropriate mode of punishment. And in all cases, he rejects it as
a metaphysical basis for the justification of punishment. The sole legitimate basis for the moral vindication of punishment must remain the
"empirical" principle of utility.

In the very long sixteenth chapter, Bentham undertakes the "arduous
task"[456] of giving the most complete possible list of classes of offenses.
And here again there are some few remarks of general philosophic and
ethical import scattered through the large juristical discussions of these
analyses. Bentham, here as everywhere, makes a great deal of the exactness of his method of logical bipartition,[457] of the "bifurcate,"[457]
"dichotomous"[458] method of division of generic terms; and he therefore
points out that "to understand a thing, is to be acquainted with its
qualities or properties. Of these properties, some are common to it with
other things; the rest, peculiar. But the qualities which are peculiar to
any one sort of thing are few indeed, in comparison with those which
are common to it with other things. To make it known in respect of its
difference, would, therefore be doing little, unless it were made known
also by its *genus*. To understand it perfectly, a man must therefore be
informed of the points in which it agrees as well as of those in which it
disagrees, with all other things. When a number of objects, composing
a logical whole, are to be considered together, all of these possessing
with respect to one another a certain congruency or agreement denoted
by a certain name, there is but one way of giving a perfect knowledge
of their nature; and that is, by distributing them into a system of parcels, each of them a part, either of some other parcel, or, at any rate, of

[451] *Ibid.*, chap. xv, sect. 8. [452] *Ibid.*, sect. 10, 7.
[453] *Ibid.*, sect. 7. [454] *Ibid.*, chap. xv, sect. 7.
[455] *Ibid.*, §1, sect. 11, sect. 8. [456] *Ibid.*, chap. xvi, §1, sect. 1, note.
[457] Bentham, "Essay on Logic" (written between 1811 and 1831), *Works*, 1843,
vol. viii, p. 264b, compare *Chrestomathia*, 1816, p. 319, *Works*, 1843, part xv,
p. 107b.
[458] Bentham, "Essay on Logic," *Works*, 1843, vol. viii, p. 253b.

the common whole. This can only be done in the way of *bipartition*, dividing each superior branch into two, and but two, immediately subordinate ones; beginning with the logical whole, dividing that into two parts, then each of those parts into two others; and so on. These first-distinguished parts agree in respect of those properties which belong to the whole: they differ in respect of those properties which are peculiar to each. To divide the whole into more than two parcels at once, for example into three, would not answer the purpose; for, in fact, it is but two objects that the mind can compare together exactly at the same time. Thus then, let us endeavour to deal with offences; or rather, strictly speaking, with acts which possess such properties as seem to indicate them fit to be constituted offences."[459] With similar applications of his bifurcate "two-pronged"[460] method, Bentham was thereafter engaged throughout his lifetime.

In his *Introduction*, he goes so far as to declare that, "if there be anything new and original in this work, it is to the exhaustive method so often aimed at that I am indebted for it."[461] This praise of the "logical mode"[462] of bifurcate divisions seems to me exorbitant. It is true that such a systematic order of the terms of a science "fixes and propagates the discovery of truth" and, vice versa, "the discovery of truth leads to the establishment of order."[463] But Bentham's insistence on the censorial method in ethics, his drawing of parallels between natural and moral sciences and his reform of biased terminology in morals are, I think, of far higher merit than his lists of dichotomous divisions and subdivisions.

Within these extremely long lists of juristical offenses, we again find especially valuable hints on the necessity of reforming ethical language. As Bentham exclaims here with marked regret, "the distribution of things must in a great measure be dependent on their names: arrangement, the work of mature reflection, must be ruled by nomenclature, the work of popular caprice. . . . Such is the fate of science, and more particularly of the moral branch";[464] and thus he frequently struggles

---

[459] *Ibid.*, chap. xvi, §1, sect. 1, note.

[460] Bentham, *Works*, 1843, vol. viii, p. 291b ("Essay on Logic").

[461] Bentham, *Introduction*, 1789, chap. xvi, §2, sect. 16, note; he himself admits however here that he had reluctantly "to deviate in some degree from the rigid rules" of his new method, as "new instruments are seldom handled at first with perfect ease."

[462] Bentham, *Chrestomathia*, 1816, p. 319.

[463] Bentham, *Introduction*, 1789, chap. xvi, §4, sect. 58, note; 2nd edition, 1823, vol. ii, p. 219.

[464] *Ibid.*, chap. xvi, §1, sect. 10, note; 2nd edition, 1823, vol. ii, p. 62 f.

throughout this chapter with the tyranny and one-sidedness of everyday language in morals on behalf of scientific, unprejudiced terminology.[465] It is solely "gross ignorance" which "descries" no difficulties on this point, "imperfect knowledge finds them out and struggles with them: it must be perfect knowledge that overcomes them."[466]

Further, the distinction between pleasures and pains of the body and those of the mind comes up again. All the difference is that, in the production of the pleasures and pains of the body, "the pleasure or pain may result immediately from the perception which it accompanies: in the production of those of the mind, it cannot result from the action of an object of sense, any otherwise than by *association*; to wit, by means of some connexion which the perception has contracted with certain prior ones, lodged already in the memory."[467] Here, as in several other places, a certain distinction is recognized to exist between feelings of the body and of the mind.[468] However, although Bentham admits that there is a difference between the two kinds of emotion, this difference in his view, is a small one. For the pains and pleasures of the mind, like those of the body, are said to result ultimately from objects of the senses; they result only from prior perceptions of objects of the senses by the way of association.

Under the head of "multiform offences," the moral and juristic problem of falsehood receives a specially characteristic treatment in this chapter. In accordance with the main result of his analyses of moral acts, Bentham once more emphasizes that the consequences of an act contain the material element of the morality or immorality of the whole action. And in connection herewith, he even declares that "falsehood, take it by itself, consider it as not being accompanied by any other material circumstances nor therefore productive of any material effects, can never, upon the principle of utility, constitute any offence at all."[469] This statement goes even further than the roughly corresponding one concerning "abominable" crimes. As to the most "sordid" crimes, Bentham had only declared that the pleasure which the vilest of malefactors ever reaped from them would not "be to be reprobated," if it stood

[465] See e.g. *ibid.*, chap. xvi, §2, sect. 24, note, 2nd edition, 1823, vol. ii, p. 90; chap. xvi, §2, sect. 27, note, 2nd edition, vol. ii, p. 108 f; chap. xvi, §4, sect. 56, 2nd edition, vol. ii, p. 214 f; chap. xvi, §4, sect. 58, note, 2nd edition, vol. ii, p. 218.
[466] *Ibid.*, chap. xvi, §1, sect. 1, note.
[467] *Ibid.*, §2, sect. 11, note.
[468] Compare *ibid.*, §2, sect. 27, 2nd edition, 1823, vol. ii, p. 118, or *ibid.*, §3, sect. 33, where also "pain of body" is distinguished from "pain of mind."
[469] *Ibid.*, §2, sect. 24, 2nd edition, 1823, vol. ii, p. 90.

alone; and he added that it never stands alone.[470] Now it is true that, in contrast for instance to the pleasures of murder, the pleasures of falsehood can be thought to stand comparatively alone. Nevertheless, it seems to me to overshoot the mark to say that falsehood is sometimes no moral offense at all because it can sometimes stand alone. Falsehood, too, like murder, never stands alone in fact.

Bentham is, I think, right in insisting that there are white lies which are ethically justifiable. There are certainly cases in which it is morally allowable to conceal the truth rather than reveal it, especially where the lives of others are concerned. But this does not mean that a lie can ever be regarded as completely innocent. The disposition to lie shows at least an ominous weakness in the liar or a kind of abnormality in his relations to those near him, so that in the general account of different elements of acts it cannot be completely neglected as a source of possibly dangerous effects of the liar's future actions.

Inserted among the long list of juristic offenses, there remain to be noted some further ethical details of general significance. Under the head "semi-public offences of mere delinquency," Bentham speaks for instance of the immorality and the punishableness of transgressions against minorities. Even "menacement . . . denouncing vengeance against persons of particular denominations: for example Jews, Catholics, Protestants, Scotchmen, Gascons, Catalonians"[471] and calumniation of such persons is characterized here as a semi-public offense of mere delinquency.

The law of patrimony is morally justified by Bentham because it seems to him more natural to place "the legal power in the same hands which are beyond comparison the more likely to be in possession of the physical";[472] and that the husband was the slave of the wife "has perhaps never been exemplified."[473] Obviously, Bentham never thought of the possibility of a historical period of matriarchy.

On the other hand, the slavery of women existing "in many barbarous nations" is definitely condemned by Bentham; it is evident that on the principle of utility the interest of both, husband and wife, "ought alike to be consulted: since in two persons, taken together, more happiness

[470] See *ibid.*, chap. ii, sect. 4 and see *The Limits of Jurisprudence Defined*, ed. by Everett, 1945, p. 115 f.

[471] Bentham, *Introduction*, 1789, chap. xvi, §2, sect. 24, note; 2nd edition, 1823, vol. ii, pp. 128 f, 130.

[472] *Ibid.*, §3, sect. 40, note; 2nd edition, 1823, vol. ii, p. 151.

[473] *Ibid.*, sect. 51; 2nd edition, 1823, vol. ii, p. 183.

is producible than in one."[474] If a pretended inferiority of women has been taken as a reason for placing the female sex in a state of perpetual wardship, then "this is not the only instance in which tyranny has taken advantage of its wrong, alleging as a reason for the domination it exercises, an imbecility, which, as far as it has been real, has been produced by the abuse of that very power which it is brought to justify."[475] Also on other occasions, as we shall see, Bentham has shown himself an energetic advocate of the rights of women.

Yet naturally, not only the serfdom of women but slavery altogether is condemned by Bentham, and this as early as 1780 at the first opportunity he had to deal with the problem—more than half a century before the emancipation of slaves in England. He speaks of the "wretched" spots upon the earth exhibiting still "the spectacle of . . . unlimited slavery";[476] he attacks Aristotle and his division of mankind into freemen and born slaves, a doctrine only built upon "the prejudice of the times";[475] and he urgently hopes that the condition of slavery "unhappily not yet at an end" is "but however verging . . . towards extinction."[477]

The fitness of the utility-principle for the ultimate moral standard is anew illustrated here by the following observations: "There is no man who is so sure of being *inclined*, on all occasions, to promote your happiness as you yourself are, . . . neither is there any man who upon the whole can have had so good opportunities as you must have had of *knowing* what is most conducive to that purpose."[478] What circumstance belonging to any action can be more interesting, or rather what other circumstance belonging to it can be at all interesting to a man, "than that of the influence it promises to have on his own happiness, and the happiness of those who are about him?"[479] And beyond the egoistic interests it is also the principle of utility (and the list of offences ordered in accordance with it) which can show us "the necessity of every defalcation, which, for the security and prosperity of each individual, it is requisite to make from the liberty of every other."[480] This

[474] *Ibid.*, chap. xvi, §3, sect. 51; 2nd edition, 1823, pp. 183, 184.
[475] *Ibid.*, chap. xvi, §3, sect. 44, note; 2nd edition, 1823, vol. ii, p. 165.
[476] *Ibid.*, chap. xvi, §3, sect. 42; 2nd edition, 1823, vol. ii, p. 158.
[477] *Ibid.*, chap. xvi, §2, sect. 26, note; 2nd edition, 1823, vol. ii, p. 103; compare chap. xvii, §1, sect. 4, note; 2nd edition, 1823, vol. ii, p. 235.
[478] *Ibid.*, chap. xvi, §2, sect. 44; 2nd edition, 1823, vol. ii, p. 163.
[479] *Ibid.*, chap. xvi, §4, sect. 57; 2nd edition, 1823, vol. ii, p. 217.
[480] *Ibid.*, chap. xvi, §4, sect. 59; 2nd edition, 1823, vol. ii, p. 219.

last application of the utility principle especially shows how conscious Bentham was that the greatest happiness principle can by no means promise unlimited pleasure to every individual but also requires sacrifices.

Contrasting with the prevailing radicalism of Bentham's ethics, two remarks may characterize the far-reaching cautiousness and circumspection of Bentham's thought. First, a brief but important glance at the difficult question of moral accountability and the diagnosis of insanity. "By what means . . . is to be ascertained whether a man's intellect" is in a state of insanity "or no? For exhibiting the quantity of sensible heat in a human body we have a very tolerable sort of instrument, the thermometer; but for exhibiting the quantity of intelligence, we have no such instrument. It is evident, therefore, that the line which separates a quantity of intelligence which *is* sufficient for the purposes of self-government from that which is *not sufficient*, must be, in a great measure arbitrary. . . . The Legislator has no other expedient than to appoint some particular person or persons to give a particular determination of the question, in every instance in which it occurs according to his or their particular and arbitrary discretion."[481] Bentham sees no other way "to cut the gordian knot" of such problems, and he obviously regrets this. So much the more does he recommend, in agreement with progressive modern thought, the careful examination of every individual case, to be carried out not only by judges but also by medical experts.

Second, though Bentham was convinced that the legal and the moral views of countries and ages are, from the nature of things, in a great measure the same, he admits that certain possible differences should be acknowledged. "That the legal interest of different ages and countries have nothing in common, and [that] they have everything, are suppositions equally distant from the truth."[482] This significant statement certainly contradicts the common judgment on Bentham as a rigid, blind internationalist, apriorist and dogmatist.

In the last chapter of the *Introduction* on "limits between private ethics and the art of legislation" Bentham deals again, and this time even more fully, with the relations between ethics and jurisprudence,

---

[481] *Ibid.*, chap. xvi, §3, sect. 44; 2nd edition, 1823, vol. ii, pp. 164 f, 166.
[482] *Ibid.*, §4, sect. 56; 2nd edition, 1823, p. 216. Compare Bentham's "Essay on the Influence of Time and Place in Matters of Legislation," *Works*, 1843, part i, pp. 169-191 (Bentham-Dumont, *Traités de législation civile et pénale*, 1820, vol. iii, pp. 113-179). This essay is entirely devoted to the same question.

another topic of significance for his whole ethical outlook. Here he goes so far as to term legislation but one out of two branches of ethics in general, and to give to the science which is commonly styled ethics the name of private ethics.[483] This unusual nomenclature would be of as little importance as, for instance, Herbart's calling ethics a part of aesthetics,[484] if Bentham had not combined with his uncommon terminology some original and valuable corrections of the common distinction between jurisprudence and morals.

Bentham finds the distinctions usually drawn between ethics and jurisprudence as futile as those generally made between criminal and civil law. As he points out in an appendix to his work, added in January 1789, every civil code must contain, apart from "mere masses of expository matter," a large number of imperatives of the penal code; and vice versa, the penal code must necessarily involve "the imperative matter of the whole number of civil laws" along with its punitive laws and masses of expository matter.[485] But be this as it may, Bentham insists that jurisprudence is to be distinguished from ethics much less than is commonly done, and in a considerably different way.

"Ethics at large," that is, both legislation and ethics, may be defined as the "art" or "science" of "directing men's actions to the production of the greatest possible quantity of happiness, on the part of those whose interest is in view."[486] On the ground of this principal definition, Bentham tries to show how intimately private ethics and legislation go hand in hand on all decisive points. For "private ethics has happiness for its end: and legislation can have no other. Private ethics concerns every member, that is, the happiness and the actions of every member of any community that can be proposed; and legislation can concern no more."[487] Thus "the end they have, or ought to have in view, is of the same nature," further also, "the persons whose happiness they ought to have in view, as also the persons whose conduct they ought to be occupied in directing are precisely the same"; and finally, even "the very acts they ought to be conversant about, are . . . in a *great measure* the same."[488]

---

[483] Bentham, *Introduction*, 1789, chap. xvii, §1, sect. 2, 3.

[484] See J. F. Herbart, *Sämtliche Werke*, ed. by Hartenstein, 1850, vol. i, S. 124 (*Lehrbuch zur Einleitung in die Philosophie*), and vol. viii (*Allgemeine praktische Philosophie*).

[485] Bentham, *Introduction*, 1789, chap. xvii, §2, sect. 29, appendix nos. xvii, xviii; 2nd edition, vol. ii, p. 273.

[486] *Ibid.*, chap. xvii, §1, sect. 2, 20.

[487] *Ibid.*, §1, sect. 8.   [488] *Ibid.*, §1, sect. 8.

There are only slight differences between these two branches of ethics: what commonly is called ethics has only to do with "directing a man's own actions."[489] Legislation, however, has to deal with directing the actions of other human beings (and if only a temporary directing is in question, we have to speak of administration, if the human beings are non-adults, we have to speak of education).[490] There is, on the whole, only one "field for the exclusive interference of private ethics" in full contrast to legislation, namely, those "cases where punishment would be unprofitable."[491] Ethics, to the exclusion of jurisprudence, has to deal chiefly with that comparatively small number of cases where the evil of punishment would exceed that of offense. But even within the realm of these cases, as Bentham adds, it has to be shown carefully whether those acts in question are really pernicious; acts performed by those persons who are only in danger of being involved in the punishment designed for the persons committing such acts should not come under the censure of legislation or even ethics.[491] Moreover, in all cases where punishment would be inefficacious, the jurisdiction of ethics also is, at least in practice, of limited effect. For "it is evident, that, if the thunders of the law prove impotent the whispers of simple morality can have but little influence."[492] If all these points are taken into account, the field fit for the exclusive application of ethics and unfit for legislation is, according to Bentham, much smaller than is commonly believed.

Bentham arrives at this conclusion not only by narrowing the province of ethics, but also by extending the limits of law "a good deal farther than they seem ever to have been extended hitherto."[493] He puts forward the valuable suggestion that a considerable number of rules of beneficence commonly abandoned to ethics should come under the more effective jurisdiction of the law. In all "cases where the person is in danger, why should it not be made the duty of every man to save another from mischief, when it can be done without prejudicing himself, as well as to abstain from bringing it on him? . . . A woman's head-dress catches fire: water is at hand: a man, instead of assisting to quench the fire, looks on, and laughs at it. . . . A quantity of gunpowder lies scattered about a room: a man is going into it with a lighted candle: another knowing this, lets him go in without warning. Who is there that in any of these cases would think punishment misapplied?"[494] Moreover, Bentham thinks that even actions which come under such vague no-

---

[489] *Ibid.*, §1, sect. 3.   [490] *Ibid.*, §1, sect. 4, 5.   [491] *Ibid.*, §1, sect. 12.
[492] *Ibid.*, §1, sect. 11.   [493] *Ibid.*, §1, sect. 19.
[494] *Ibid.*, §1, sect. 19 and sect. 19, note.

tions as rudeness or ingratitude may be brought under the control of law, if an age is enlightened enough to overcome the difficulties which may arise on this point.[495] So for two reasons, by confinement of ethics and by enlargement of the law, Bentham favors a marked contraction of "private" ethics.

Even more important is another unusual finding laid down in connection with his new demarcation line between ethics and law. In general, moralists urge that ethics must proclaim a larger number of altruistic duties than law, and must allow a smaller number of egoistic rights than jurisprudence. Bentham, however, includes in ethics particularly a man's duties to himself; and as "the quality which a man manifests by the discharge" of these duties to himself is that of prudence, duties concerning prudence form an essential part of ethics, according to Bentham.[496] This is another proof of his freedom from the traditional overestimation of altruism.

To emphasize the duties of unselfishness is doubtless of far-reaching educational value. In ethics proper, however, I believe it has more confusing than beneficial effects. Certainly, it is not the business of legislation to counsel men as to duties toward themselves. But after Helvétius had done this in passing,[497] Bentham explains in great detail why prudence must be an essential ingredient of morality, and why the duties to oneself must form a subject matter for ethics. The duties of probity, however, and even those of beneficence, concern jurisprudence far more than is generally assumed; and "with regard to that branch of probity which is opposed to offences against property, private ethics depends in a manner for its very existence upon legislation."[498] On the other hand, in so far as there are reasons for consulting the happiness of others from egoistic motives, ethics has also to deal with problems of beneficence.[499] Measured by the yardstick of conventional ethics and traditional jurisprudence, these statements about the subject matters of the two moral sciences must appear almost perverse. The wide-spread criticism of these "perversities" seems to me, however, irrelevant if, as usual, it does not take into account the reasons by which Bentham justifies his "distortions" of the main ethical topics.

[495] *Ibid.*, §1, sect. 4.
[496] *Ibid.*, §1, sect. 6, 20.
[497] See e.g. Claude Adrien Helvétius, *De l'esprit*, discours II, chap. VI, *Oeuvres complètes*, 1818, tome I, p. 73: "La parfaite probité n'est jamais le partage de la stupidité."
[498] Bentham, *Introduction*, 1789, chap. XVII, §1, sect. 18, 19.
[499] *Ibid.*, §1, sect. 7.

In a very sensitive, humane way, the last chapter of the *Introduction* extends the application of the utility principle to include animals. Throughout his life, Bentham had a warm sympathy for the animal kingdom. He even "encouraged . . . the mice to play about in his workshop," being fond of mice and fond of cats, although "it was difficult to reconcile the two affections";[500] and in his old age, he seems to have been in close touch with the movements for the protection of animals founded at that time in England.

Among the Bentham MS in University College, London, is preserved an invitation for a service on Sunday July 12, 1829 sent to Bentham by "The Committee of the Society for the Prevention of Cruelty to Animals" and signed by its meritorious Hon. Secretary Lewis Gompertz.[501] But as early as in his *Introduction*, Bentham did not forget to mention duties to animals, as the following observation shows: "Animals . . . stand degraded into the class of *things*" owing to "the insensibility of the ancient jurists. . . . Under the Gentoo and Mahometan religions, the interests of the rest of the animal creation seem to have met with some attention . . . is there any reason why we should be suffered to torment them? Not any that I can see. Are there any why we should *not* be suffered to torment them? Yes, several . . . [The day has been, I grieve to say in many places it is not yet passed, in which the greater part of the species, under the denomination of slaves, have been treated by the law exactly upon the same footing, as, in England for example, the inferior races of animals are still. The day *may* come, when the rest of the animal creation may acquire those rights which never could have been withholden from them but by the hand of tyranny.] The French have already discovered that blackness of the skin is no reason why a human being should be abandoned without redress to the caprice of a tormentor. It may come one day to be recognized, that the number of the legs, the villosity of the skin, or the termination of the *os sacrum*, are reasons equally insufficient for abandoning a sensitive being to the same fate. What else is it that should trace the insuperable line? Is it the faculty of reason, or, perhaps, the faculty of discourse? But *a* full-grown horse or dog, is beyond comparison a more rational, as well as a more conversable animal, than an infant of a day, or a week, or even a month old. But suppose the case were otherwise, what would it avail? The question is not, Can they reason? nor, Can they *talk*? but, Can they

---

[500] Bentham, *Works*, 1843, part xxi, pp. 80b, 81a.
[501] See Bentham MS, University College, London, Portfolio 109, Folder 15, sheet 328.

suffer?"[502] On the other hand, it is true, his arguments are less strong where he tries to justify the killing of animals. All he asserts here is that animals "have none of those long-protracted anticipations of future misery which we have. The death they suffer in our hands commonly is, and always may be, a speedier, and by that means a less painful one, than that which would await them in the inevitable course of nature. If the being killed were all, there is very good reason why we should be suffered to kill such as molest us: we should be the worse for their living, and they are never the worse for being dead."[502]

Even if attention is given to these qualifications made by Bentham, it is probably correct to agree with Georg von Gizycki that Bentham was the first moralist to insist on the rights of animals.[503] According to Thomas Fowler, he was at least "amongst the first."[504] At any rate, Schopenhauer's famous plea for sympathy for the animal creation uses pros and contras quite similar to those of the *Introduction*. But Schopenhauer seems to me far less convincing than Bentham, both in his metaphysical reasoning and in his charges against the Old Testament,[505] which he accused of having inspired the European contempt of animals.

[502] Bentham, *Introduction*, 1789, chap. xvii, §1, sect. 4 and sect. 4, note.

[503] G. von Gizycki, *Die Ethik David Humes in ihrer geschichtlichen Stellung*, 1878, p. 231.

[504] T. Fowler, *Progressive Morality*, 1884, p. 193.

[505] See A. Schopenhauer, *Die beiden Grundprobleme der Ethik*, ii. *Über das Fundament der Moral*, §19, No. 7 (*Sämtliche Werke*, ed. by J. Frauenstädt, 1877, Band iv, S. 238 ff) and *Parerga und Paralipomena*, Band ii, §179. These passages were written more than half a century after the *Introduction*, obviously without knowledge of Bentham's similar remarks. It is most puzzling that Schopenhauer should make the Jews responsible for Western Christian insensibility toward the animal kingdom. For it was precisely an English Jew, Lewis Gompertz who, in cooperation with Bentham, first successfully fought on a large scale against cruel treatment of animals.

In order to justify his anti-Semitism on this point, Schopenhauer quotes the Old Testament, Proverbs, chap. xii, verse 10: "Der Gerechte erbarmt sich seines Viehs." But the original Hebrew text of this passage contains absolutely nothing of human pride toward animals, as Schopenhauer assumed on the ground of Luther's translation of the passage. The Hebrew text of Proverbs shows all the warmth of feeling and understanding for the "soul" of the dumb creature which Schopenhauer missed in the Old Testament. In contrast to many Christian authors of modern times, the Old Testament uses the same term for the soul of man, נֶפֶשׁ as for that of allegedly "soulless animals," and the Old Testament characterizes the proper attitude of man toward the animal not as a supercilious mercifulness but as a feeling of the same depths and quality as that between man and woman. It is Luther and men of the sixteenth and seventeenth centuries such as Descartes who displayed pride toward animals and even degraded them into the class of things. Bentham's discussions of these questions show very favorably

Finally, in this last chapter of the *Introduction,* in the course of a discussion of the different branches of jurisprudence, Bentham touches again on the most important point of his ethical method. The chief division which he demands here is neither the distinction between criminal and civil law nor that between local and national or between national and international law, although the term *international* was first introduced into common usage by him and has since then "taken root in the language."[506] The principal distinction drawn here by Bentham remains that between expository and censorial jurisprudence. He therefore vigorously attacks, in this connection, Grotius and Puffendorf as well as Burlamaqui and even Montesquieu because they did not distinguish between expository and censorial problems, between "what law *is*" and "what it *ought* to be." They all neglected this classical distinction between moral problems and those differences in which this fundamental division expresses itself, namely, the differences between historical and juridical, between political and ethical inquiries or between manners and laws; "they seem hardly to have settled the matter with themselves."[507] Bentham, however, emphasizes the capital importance of a "uniformly censorial"[507] method; it is one and the same censorial method which is to him of equally great value in jurisprudence and the whole field of ethics. This and some similar tendencies are, therefore, stressed once more in a special appendix to his last chapter and in a special preface to his whole work, both not written until about nine years after the composition of the work itself, i.e. in January 1789.

against Schopenhauer's argument, both as regards historical insight and the expression of underlying moral indignation.

[506] See Bentham, *Introduction,* 1823, chap. xvii, §2, sect. 25, note, vol. ii, p. 262 and compare Oxford Dictionary under the term *International.*

[507] Bentham, *Introduction,* 1789, chap. xvii, §2, sect. 27, note. An especially witty travesty of Grotius' account of utilitarianism is given in Bentham's *The Limit of Jurisprudence Defined,* ed. by Everett, 1945, p. 117 f. Bentham reports here that, in his *De jure belli et pacis,* prolegomena §16, Grotius strongly objects to Carneades' view that "Utility . . . is the mother of Justice and Equity." But despite the marked protest to this "genealogy," after "an investigation which is not altogether the clearest," Grotius, according to Bentham, cannot but admit that utility is, after all, "a distant relation to . . . Justice and Equity," i.e. to "natural Law," namely, it is "first cousin to its Great-Grandmother." See *ibid.,* p. 118, where even "our own Lord Coke in his Commentary on Littleton" is reported to have granted that the *"argumentum ab inconvenienti"* and "the argument *ab utili et inutili"* hold the tenth and fifteenth places among the twenty "fountains . . . of the Law . . . from whence . . . Littleton and Coke" draw their arguments.

THE APPENDIX TO CHAPTER XVII AND
BENTHAM'S PREFACE TO THE *INTRODUCTION*
WRITTEN IN 1789

BENTHAM's appendix to chapter XVII deals, to a large extent, with juristical questions, among others the difficulties concerning the distinction between criminal and civil law which we have already mentioned. Ethically, however, it is important to see with what energy Bentham distinguishes again between the so-called *logical*, the *ideal*, the intellectual whole of a law and the "physical" element of it, that is, between the ideal, moral validity of a law and its "physical" existence as a statute,[508] in short, between that part of the law which is approachable only by censorial investigation and that which is an object of mere expository inquiry.

In a similar connection, Bentham's criticism of the Bills of Rights enacted by American States such as Virginia, North Carolina, Massachusetts and Pennsylvania is of special interest.[509] Two years before the First Congress of the United States adopted its Bill of Rights, Bentham condemned the epistemological vagueness on which all the great "Declarations of the Rights of Men" were based at the end of the eighteenth century. Evidently, throughout his mature life, he was in hearty and complete agreement with the liberal, progressive tendencies of the European and American "Déclarations des Droits de l'Homme."[510] But he thought that their philosophical basis, the "obscure phantom" of a "pretended law of nature,"[511] was unsatisfactory and weak.

In the various bills of rights, inalienable liberty is, for instance, guaranteed in close combination with protection of property. But, Bentham asks, how can this be managed? Unfortunately, there must occur only

---

[508] Bentham, *Introduction*, 1823, chap. XVII, appendix, vol. II, p. 267.

[509] *Ibid.*, chap. XVII, appendix no. XXVII, vol. II, p. 277.

[510] W. L. Davidson, *Political Thought in England: the Utilitarians from Bentham to J. S. Mill*, 1916, p. 78 like P. A. Palmer, "Benthamism in England and America," in the *American Political Science Review*, 1941, p. 858, found it "surprising" that Bentham combined "extreme radicalism" with his opposition to the doctrine of natural rights. But Davidson rightly added that both Bentham's extreme radicalism and his opposition to the philosophy of natural rights might be understood as "the logical outcome of his leading principle of maximum happiness."

[511] Bentham, *Introduction*, 1823, chap. XVII, §2, sect. 27, note.

too many cases of conflict in which the protection of property can be obtained only by a certain loss of liberty, namely, by the imprisonment of thieves; or vice versa, the liberty of all can be obtained only by the toleration of theft, i.e. by sustaining certain losses of property and abolishing the punishment of theft.[512] In short, these bills of rights maintain demands which exclude each other but, as Bentham adds, they show too that "with men who are unanimous and hearty about *measures*, nothing so weak but may pass in the character of a *reason*: nor is this the first instance in the world, where the conclusion has supported the premises, instead of the premises the conclusion."[512] Consistent ethical reasoning, however, requires a higher degree of epistemological precision than is generally to be found among political, juristic and ethical advocates of the law of nature.

Keeping this in mind, Bentham concludes his whole book with the paraphrase of a striking anecdote told by Helvétius: "Leaning on his elbow, in an attitude of profound and solemn meditation, '*What a multitude of things there are*' (exclaimed the dancing-master Marcel) '*in a minuet!*'—May we now add?—*And in a law*."[513] In contrast to so many acute but necessarily dry disquisitions in Bentham's work—this is certainly the graceful bow of a man of the world at the end of a great scientific work.

Like the appendix to the last chapter, Bentham's preface to his work written about the same time (1789) deals mainly with problems of ethical and juristic method.[514] "Referring to universal experience as their immediate basis," there exist, according to him, some axiomatic statements on pleasure and pain which "require only to be developed and illustrated in order to be recognised as incontestable, . . . for ex-

[512] *Ibid.*, chap. xvii, appendix no. xxvii, vol. ii, p. 277 f.

[513] *Ibid.*, chap. xvii, appendix no. xxvii, vol. ii, p. 279, and compare C. A. Helvétius, *Oeuvres complètes*, 1818, "*De l'esprit*," discours second, chap. i, tome i, p. 42: "Marcel, la main appuyée sur le front, l'oeil fixe, le corps immobile, et dans l'attitude d'une méditation profonde, s'écrie tout à coup, en voyant danser son écolière: Que de choses dans un menuet!"

[514] In his preface to the *Introduction*, 1823, vol. i, p. xiii, Bentham tells us also how he "found himself once unexpectedly entangled in an unsuspected corner of the metaphysical maze. . . . Questions that will be found at the conclusion of the volume" made serious difficulties, for example the question "wherein consisted the identity and completeness of a law?" C. K. Ogden in his *Bentham's Theory of Fictions*, 1932, p. xx, asks: "What was this unsuspected corner?" The answer, I think, must be searched for above all on p. xii f of the preface and in the appendix.

ample ... *a loss falls the lighter by being divided. —The suffering, of a person hurt in gratification of enmity is greater than the gratification produced by the same cause.* These ... have the same claim to the appellation of axioms, as those given by mathematicians under that name."[515] Similar statements on emotions, passions, appetites, virtues, vices can, in his opinion, be easily derived from the axioms on pleasure, pain, motive and disposition; and "the completion of ... so to style it ... a dictionary" concerning virtues, vices and passions "would, in comparison with the commencement" concerning pain and pleasure, "be little more than a mechanical operation."[516] Therefore, on the whole, Bentham cherishes the firm belief that "the present publication ... may do ... the office which is done, by books of pure mathematics to books of mixed mathematics and natural philosophy."[517] Certainly, from the viewpoint of method, this would be *the* decisive service to be done for ethics.

Although Bentham realizes that his *Introduction* must unavoidably be found ... dry and tedious ... by the bulk of readers,"[518] he flatters himself that, at least, his book containing, so to speak, the "occult" body of his doctrine, will be found to be as consistent with his more popular teachings as the occult doctrines of ancient philosophers are contradictory to their popular writings.[517] Moreover, Bentham ventures to hint that his work may boldly challenge comparison with the most influential work on scientific method which antiquity has produced, Aristotle's logical *Organon*, and that it is of even greater importance for practice. "There is or rather there ought to be, a *logic* of the *will*, as well as of the *understanding*: the operations of the former faculty are neither less susceptible, nor less worthy, than those of the latter, of being delineated by rules. Of these two branches of that recondite art, Aristotle saw only the latter: succeeding logicians, ... have concurred in seeing with no other eyes. Yet so far as the difference can be assigned between branches so intimately connected, whatever difference there is, in point of importance, is in favour of the logic of the will. Since it is only by their capacity of directing the operations of this faculty, that the operations of the understanding are of any consequence ... one example amongst a thousand that might be adduced in proof of this assertion, may be seen in the note which terminates this volume."[519] "Such then were the dif-

[515] Bentham, *Introduction*, 1823, vol. I, p. v, note.
[516] *Ibid.*, preface, vol. I, p. iv f.   [517] *Ibid.*, preface, vol. I, p. viii.
[518] *Ibid.*, preface, vol. I, p. vi.
[519] *Ibid.*, preface, vol. I, p. xiv. This last remark refers obviously to Bentham's analysis of the American "Bills of Rights."

ficulties: such the preliminaries; . . . a new branch to add to one of the most abstruse of sciences."[520] In such ways, Bentham again and again attaches the utmost weight to precision in ethical method, uttering, at the end of his preface, a still very timely warning against all those many moralists who, from the familiarity of moral terms, infer the facility of a science of ethics. "Truths that form the basis of political and moral science are not to be discovered but by investigations as severe as mathematical ones, and beyond all comparison more intricate and extensive. The familiarity of the terms is the presumption, but it is a most fallacious one, of the facility of the matter. Truths in general have been called stubborn things: the truths just mentioned are so in their own way . . . they will not compress themselves into epigrams. They recoil from the tongue and the pen of the declaimer. They flourish not in the same soil with sentiments. They grow among thorns; and are not to be plucked, like daisies, by infants as they run. Labour, the inevitable lot of humanity, is in no track more inevitable than here."[521] It is in this way, by facing the special difficulties of a scientific method in ethics, that Bentham aspired to become a Newton and even a modern Aristotle of moral philosophy, the creator of a logic of the will as a counterpart to Aristotle's logic of the understanding.

FINAL ESTIMATE OF BENTHAM'S *INTRODUCTION*

Does Bentham's *Introduction* make good in any way such high ambitions? This is in general denied emphatically by the historian of English utilitarianism, E. Albee, who confines his analysis of Bentham's ethics to a very brief report on some of the best known passages of the *Introduction* and the *Deontology*, and who reserves only half of one chapter of his work for Bentham, while he devotes the other half to William Paley whom he values far more highly.

About the end of the eighteenth century such a judgment was perfectly comprehensible. It represented the point of view of Cambridge University which, very soon after the appearance of Paley's *Principles of Moral and Political Philosophy* (1785), adopted this work as a textbook; and even Bentham's friend, George Wilson, found "many things" in Paley's book so like Bentham, "and so out of the common road,"

---

[520] *Ibid.*, preface, vol. i, p. xv.   [521] *Ibid.*, preface, vol. i, p. xvi.

that he suspected Paley had seen Bentham's *Introduction* which had been printed (although not published) five years before Paley's work came out.[522] In the twentieth century, however, it seems to me that disparagement of Bentham in favor of Paley should receive attention at best on the ground of its paradoxical character and as a curiosity of intellectual history.

The following are the main points of Paley's unsystematic and edifying commonplace[523] utilitarianism: "I am inclined to believe that happiness consists I. in the exercise of the social affections,"[524] not "in the pleasures of the sense,"[525] "II. in the exercise of our faculties, either of body or mind . . . in the pursuit of some engaging end. . . . III. happiness depends upon the prudent constitution of habits";[526] and this is explained by the following rather questionable argument: "A beggar, with the appearance of extreme distress, asked our charity. If we come to argue the matter, whether the distress be real, whether it be not brought upon himself, whether it be of public advantage to admit such applications, whether it be not to encourage idleness and vagrancy, whether it may not invite impostors at our door, whether the money can be well spared, or might not be better applied; when these considerations are put together, it may appear very doubtful, whether we ought or ought not to give any thing. But when we reflect, that the misery before our eyes excites our pity, whether we will or not; that it is of the utmost consequence to us to cultivate this tenderness of mind . . . soon stifled by opposition: when this, I say, is considered, a wise man will do that for his own sake, which he would have hesitated to do for the petitioner's; he will give way to his compassion, rather than offer violence to a habit of so much general use."[527] "IV. Happiness consists in health."[528] "Virtue is *the doing good to mankind, in obedience to the will of God, and for the sake of everlasting happiness.*"[529] It is true

[522] Bentham, *Works*, 1843, part xix, p. 195a, letter from George Wilson to Bentham, November 30, 1788. On the other hand, Wilson found "many things . . . really puerile" in Paley's work.
[523] Paley himself claimed to be only "something more than a mere compiler" and he comforted himself with the assumption that the subject matter, ethics itself, allows no place for discovery or invention; see W. Paley, *The Principles of Moral and Political Philosophy* (1785), 1793, vol. i, p. xxiv f.
[524] *Ibid.*, vol. i, book i, p. 32 (chap. vi on "Human Happiness").
[525] *Ibid.*, vol. i, p. 22 f. [526] *Ibid.*, p. 36.
[527] W. Paley, *The Principles of Moral and Political Philosophy* (first edition, 1785), 1793, vol. i, book i, p. 44 (chap. vi on "Human Happiness").
[528] *Ibid.*, vol. i, book i, p. 39 (chap. vi on "Human Happiness").
[529] *Ibid.*, book i, p. 41 (chap. vii on "Virtue").

that Paley, like Bentham and other utilitarians, gives the definition: "whatever is expedient is right. It is the utility of any moral rule alone which constitutes the obligation of it."[530] Moreover, as Bentham did in his *Introduction*, Paley reduced all the best known criteria of morality in his epoch to the criterion: happiness. "The fitness of things," the conformity to reason and nature, the conformity to truth, to the will of God, all these different criteria of morally right actions are reducible to happiness, to public happiness, "happiness upon the whole."[531] But the decisive difference here is that, according to Bentham, for precision's sake all the vague moral standards of non-utilitarians have to be abandoned because they do not allow unequivocal application. According to Paley, however, *all* the very different criteria of morality can and should be used. For "they all ultimately coincide"; they all "mean" the same.[532] Paley is obviously neither interested in, nor is he even aware of, the fact that in ethics it is methodologically of crucial importance whether the fitness of things, or the conformity to reason or nature or the will of God, or public happiness is considered to be the standard of moral right and wrong. He declares himself satisfied with the uncritical, dogmatic assumption "that moralists . . . commonly meet in their conclusions; that . . . they enjoin the same conduct, prescribe the same rule of duty, and, with a few exceptions, deliver upon dubious cases the same determinations . . . , from whatever different principles they set out."[532] This is in fact, both methodologically and with regard to material ethical teaching, a complete reversal of Bentham's doctrine in spite of all external similarities.

Finally—and this elucidates another point of fundamental difference between Bentham's and Paley's ethics despite apparent identities—it is true that prudence is, according to both these moralists, an attribute of moral value. Acts of prudence and of duty ultimately coincide. Bentham stated this in the *Introduction* and in even greater detail in his later work, and gave many considered and idealistic reasons for this statement. Paley, on the other hand, offers merely the following answer to this question: "the only difference is this; that in the one case we consider what we shall gain or lose in the present world; in the other case,

[530] *Ibid.*, book II, p. 70 (chap. VI on "Utility").
[531] *Ibid.*, book II, p. 54 f (chap. I on "The Question, Why Am I Obliged to Keep my Word? Considered").
[532] *Ibid.*, book II, p. 55 (chap. I on "The Question, Why Am I Obliged to Keep my Word? Considered").

we consider also what we shall gain or lose in the world to come."[533] This kind of argument is certainly, not only in point of method but also in point of religion,[534] of a considerably lower type than Bentham's discerning deductions.

Primarily, however, if we look back at Bentham's long acute analyses of the moral elements of acts, at the chapters on intentionality, consciousness, motives, disposition, and the consequences of actions to which he calls special attention in the preface of the *Introduction*,[535] then the conviction will be forced upon us that nothing but a rather personal dislike of Bentham's "style and method,"[536] and of his moral arithmetic,[537] can lead to a higher valuation of Paley's over Bentham's ethics. In spite of the shortcomings of his psychology, and a certain positivistic narrowness of his intellectual horizon, Bentham's minute inquiries into the moral constituents of acts represent not only a most valuable preparatory work to a modern "phenomenology" of these elements, but they also give a careful ultimate justification of the principle of utility.[538] It

[533] *Ibid.*, vol. I, book II, p. 61 (chap. III on "The Question, Why Am I Obliged to Keep my Word? Resumed").

[534] Even theologians such as F. D. Maurice prefer Bentham's view on this point to that of Paley, see F. D. Maurice, *Moral and Metaphysical Philosophy*, 1873, vol. II, p. 605: "We cannot think that Bentham would have been more useful if, like Paley, he had adopted a notion about the will of God to help out the weaknesses of his Utilitarian motives"; T. R. Birks, *Modern Utilitarianism*, 1874, p. 236, attributes a greater "merit" to Paley's utilitarianism than to that of Bentham, because Paley "seeks to include . . . the personal, the social and the religious element which must be combined in a just and comprehensive view of Moral Science." But Birks, too, thinks that "the manner" in which Paley's utilitarianism combines these elements is "artificial and unsound."

[535] Bentham, *Introduction*, 1823, vol. I, p. vii.

[536] See E. Albee, *A History of English Utilitarianism*, 1902, p. 175; *ibid.*, p. 168: Paley's "tone throughout the *Principles* is really admirable, as compared with that of Bentham in his corresponding works"; compare *ibid.*, p. 176: the tendency toward violent polemics "is so disagreeable a feature" of the later works of Bentham; *ibid.*, p. 148 f: Bentham, "that arrogant writer . . . did so much to bring the doctrine" of Utilitarianism "into needless discredit."

[537] *Ibid.*, p. 190, Bentham's reduction of ethics to "moral arithmetic . . . cannot be regarded as a real advance in ethical theory, but quite the contrary."

[538] Cf. with Bentham's subtle discussions on this point e.g. the inanity and vagueness of the following pronouncements of Paley, *The Principles of Moral and Political Philosophy* (1785), 1793, vol. I, book II, chap. VI on "Utility," p. 70: "Actions in the abstract are right or wrong according to their *tendency*; the agent is virtuous or vicious, according to his design. Thus, if the question be, Whether relieving common beggars be right or wrong? we inquire into the *tendency* of such a conduct to the public advantage or inconvenience. If the question be, Whether a man remarkable for this thought of bounty, is to be esteemed

is these analyses which provide the fundamental proof of the theorem that only the *reference* to the consequences of acts, not *inferences* of dispositions and motives, can serve as a precise ethical criterion.

This ruling doctrine and its meticulous justification, however, is certainly not all that deserves the renewed attention of contemporary moralists. No matter whether one agrees or disagrees with Bentham's teaching on the gradation of values, i.e. the "order of pre-eminence among motives," with his ideas of a moral physiology, or his doctrine of the conflicts among motives and claims, the historian of ethics must realize that a proper approach to these cardinal questions is by no means an achievement of the late nineteenth or the early twentieth century. A much earlier work has already faced these problems in the eighteenth century with a profound critical resolution: Bentham's *Introduction to the Principles of Morals and Legislation.*

There is no gainsaying the fact that Bentham's conception of happiness is crude. Bentham, like Plato, did not allot any philosophical value to poetry[539] or to simple belief in religious dogmas. But, unlike Plato, he did not display any intimate knowledge and understanding of the "poetical," the finest manifestation of the human soul. Further, though he is right in excluding reference to divine law in scientific ethics, he is undoubtedly mistaken in his scornful attitude toward religion and his undervaluation of the place of religion in our intellectual life as a whole. Nevertheless, all this does not detract from the value of his acute new insight into questions of ethical method.

Of course, if we conceive ethics as an art and not a science, we can dispense with such insight. Dante's *Divina Commedia* and Goethe's *Faust,* both works of art, are permeated by moral *Weltanschauung,*

---

virtuous for that reason? we inquire into his *design,* whether his liberality sprung from charity or from ostentation."

[539] See e.g. Bentham MS, hitherto unpublished, University College, London, Portfolio 106, Folder 7, sheet 1, column 8: "Marginal outline of plan of Irish education": "Poetry—no more reason for teaching it than chess or cards"; compare Philarète Chasles, *Oeuvres,* tome 1, 1876, pp. 161 ff: "Mon jeune ami me dit 'Bentham, je songe . . . à transformer en *écoles chrestomatiques* la maison de Milton, le berceau de *Paradis perdu*! Seriez vous encore sensible aux délicatesses idéales et poétiques que le monde vante? Tant pis pour vous! . . . Je ne méprise pas Milton, mais il appartient au passé, et le passé ne sert à rien.'" P. 163: "Bentham a-t-il réellement imprimé à l'esprit humain une impulsion nouvelle? Non. Algébriste de la science sociale, il n'accorde rien aux inconsequences de notre nature. . . . Voilà l'erreur du XVIIIe siècle tout entier, la déification de l'homme et l'apothéose de la raison."

though they are not scientific ethics. But I do not think that Kant's *Critique of Practical Reason* and similar modern theories can or should be appraised as art. These writers obviously aspire to argue scientifically. If, however, such is not their purpose, they must in any case employ scientific methods in order to show why, for instance, Bentham is not a consistent scientific moralist either. For whoever criticizes the poetical character of a certain work must needs do it by aesthetic criteria. Likewise, whoever sets out to criticize the scientific character of an ethics must employ scientific criteria. Such criticism of Bentham, it seems to me, has never been carried on aptly; and I do not think that it can be done convincingly.

Bentham's insistence upon the scientific character of his ethics, however, does not mean that he denies the original connotation of the concepts morally good or bad, and that he identifies them with other non-ethical conceptions. Bentham never defined morally good simply as pleasurable. He did not nullify the fundamental basis of ethical investigation by this paralogism. It is true that, in his polemic against absolute ethics, his formulas often come near this dangerous identification of morally good with pleasant. But in context, it is evident that his theory avoids nothing more carefully than the confusion of "is" and "ought to be."

John Grote defines an ideal as "something which we ought to aim at or try to produce"; and on the basis of this definition, he rejects "utilitarianism in all its forms," because, while it "disclaims idealism," it "borrows a great deal which belongs to idealism alone."[540] The answer to this criticism is that Bentham did not disclaim idealism in the sense of this definition. Bentham admittedly borrowed a great deal which belongs to idealism in this sense.

Expressed in the language of modern ethics, Bentham quite agrees that ethical judgments are value judgments and that they are to be distinguished from all judgments concerned solely with the given. Just as *true* judgments about existing reality are by no means identical with every kind of ordering our observations of this reality, so ethical

[540] John Grote, *Examination of the Utilitarian Philosophy*, 1870, p. 3. Unlike John Grote, Professor Edgar S. Brightman in his *Moral Laws*, 1933, p. 196, indicates, I think pertinently, that Bentham "appeals to the principle of ideal control by judgment" without contradicting his consistent adherence to ethical empiricism. Similarly E. Cassirer emphasized the universal, ideal validity of ethical judgment which Bentham could rightly maintain, despite his full regard for the empirical relativity of ethical beliefs in various lands and epochs of history, see E. Cassirer, *Axel Hägerström*, 1939, p. 73 f.

judgments are not identical with every kind of ordering feelings of pleasure.

Bentham frankly admits, e.g. in his *Fragment on Government*, that the ethical hedonist cannot escape the variability of man's value judgments any more than the scientist can escape the variability of man's judgment about nature. There is no man made theory which is not open to controversy. But there is a decisive difference between theories based on highly disputable generalizations of particular facts and theories which critically refer to indubitable concrete experiences.

Bentham, therefore, insists that any sound controversy in ethics must refer to a criterion which ultimately allows verification by evident, observable facts such as neutral feelings of pleasure. Just as the natural sciences need ultimate reference to neutral observations which are made independently of any theoretical utilization, so ethics needs the reference to experiences of morally good and wicked men which are neutral in their relation to ethical interpretation. Whatever may be the difference between ethics and natural science, there seems to me to be none on this head.

I think it could be shown in greater detail why it is one of the soundest tendencies of English and American ethics to draw a careful parallel between natural science and moral philosophy. As long as we insist on absolute knowledge in ethics—in contrast to the "relative" knowledge conveyed by physics—we shall be disappointed. For obviously, there are no absolute insights obtainable by finite beings either with regard to natural or ethical laws. As long as we expect ethics to provide us with an absolute and simple guide, if only in regard to the main decisions of morals, we shall find neither this nor any humbler substitute for it. Under all circumstances, the concept of morals has to undergo a capital transformation in this respect, even as the concept of physics has already undergone similar transformations. Only a road similar to that trodden in wise restraint by natural scientists for the last three hundred years can lead past the dangers of ethical nihilism and relativism on the one hand, and false pride in absolute knowledge on the other.

Even Kant felt compelled to build up his *Critique of Practical Reason* in close analogy to his theory of nature, laid down in his *Critique of Pure Reason*. Regrettably, Kant in the end abandoned this parallel. But perhaps from nowhere else can we learn more for the construction of a truly critical ethics than from Bentham's method.

Anti-hedonism avers that, by intuition, we possess valid concrete ethical judgments unrelated to pain and pleasure. If this were the case, Bentham's elaborate theory of morals would indeed seem to the philosopher as superfluous and artificial or misleading as Newton's theory of colors generally appears to the painter or the psychologist. Consequently, consistent hedonism would have to be rejected as an entirely inadequate analysis of our intuited ethical judgments, just as modern astronomy would have to be rejected as an entirely inadequate analysis of our observations of the movements of celestial bodies. But the obvious truth is that we do not possess any concrete intuited ethical judgment whose validity is not disputed. Therefore, to construct ethical doctrines on the basis of such unproved judgments means to cease ethical inquiry at the point where Bentham starts.

In fact, while the astronomy of the middle ages could refer to the authority of the senses, common anti-hedonism can refer to a large extent to nothing more than ethical sham evidence. This can hardly be denied now, when millions of men in Germany and Italy believed for years in the self-evidence of certain moral truths which are diametrically opposite to the kind of ethical truths which the rest of mankind believed or pretended to believe to be self-evident. Thus, we either have to find means similar to those of Bentham which shall enable us to build on firmer ground than on that of "self-evident" anti-hedonism; or if this is impossible, we should at least have the courage to confess that, compared to the present state of affairs in ethics, the natural science of scholasticism was highly exact.

FRENCH INTERLUDE

Dumont's Edition of the *Traités de législation
civile et pénale*

FRENCH INTERLUDE

Dumont's Edition of the *Traités de législation civile et pénale*

<hr>

Brief Characterization
of the Nature of Dumont's Editorial Work

Bentham's large work of ethical importance following the publication of his *Introduction* differs widely from its predecessor in style, though the subject is practically the same. The reason is that these three volumes of *Traités de législation civile et pénale* were not published by Bentham himself, but were edited in his own lifetime, in 1802, by Pierre Etienne Louis Dumont de Genève[1] "d'après les manuscrits confiés par l'auteur." This best known of the Dumont editions was translated or rather partly re-translated first into English in 1864 by the American lawyer, historian and moralist, Richard Hildreth.[2]

[1] Bentham in his pamphlet *To the Citizens of the Several American United States* (written in 1817 on the suggestions of Lord (Henry) Brougham, President Madison, Albert Gallatin, Simon Snyder, Governor of Pennsylvania, Letter No. VIII) calls Dumont Stephen Dumont, translating Etienne by the English Stephen (see Bentham, *Works* 1843, part VIII, p. 479a).

A comparatively detailed biography of Dumont is to be found in the second volume of Friedrich Eduard Beneke's *Grundsätze der Civil- und Kriminalgesetzgebung, aus den Handschriften des englischen Rechtsgelehrten Jeremias Bentham,* herausgegeben von Etienne Dumont, nach der 2. verbesserten und vermehrten Auflage bearbeitet und mit Anmerkungen versehen von F. E. Beneke, 1830. A *Notice biographique sur la vie et les écrits* de M. Dumont by the botanist Augustin Pyramus de Candolle had already appeared in 1829 and contains references to Dumont's collaboration with Bentham on pp. 9-15. For further references to French biographies of Dumont see E. Silberner's "Un manuscrit inédit de David Ricardo sur le problème monétaire," in *Revue d'histoire économique et sociale,* Paris, 1940, p. 196 f; and especially Bernard Gagnebin's essay on "Jeremy Bentham et Etienne Dumont" in *Jeremy Bentham Bicentenary . . . Lectures delivered on . . . 8 June 1948, . . .* London . . . University College, 1948, pp. 31-55. Gagnebin mentions *ibid.,* p. 49, that Bentham amused himself by calling the *Traités* "Dumont's *Principles.*" The following analysis of the *Traités* tries to determine to what extent this characterization of the work was justified.

[2] On Richard Hildreth and the odd fact that "one of the most widely read volumes of jurisprudence in the English language should be the work of an American translating from the French of a Swiss pastor who had published over 60 years previously" see C. K. Ogden, *The Theory of Legislation by J. Bentham,* 1931, pp. L f, XXXI. Hildreth's translation into English as well as Beneke's translation into German follow the text of the second edition of Dumont's work in 1820.

On Hildreth, the moralist, see D. Baumgardt, "The Forgotten Moralist: Richard

Dumont, friend and secretary to Mirabeau, later "membre du conseil représentative de Genève," also put into shape ("rédigea") and edited other writings of Bentham, such as the *Théories des paines et des récompenses* in 1811, the *Traité des preuves judiciaires* in 1823, and the *Tactique des assemblés législatives, suivie d'un traité des sophismes politiques* in 1816. Only a sketch of this later work was published by Bentham himself in 1791, and the original text of the "Sophismes anarchiques," freed of Dumont's alterations, was first printed in Bowring's edition of Bentham's *Works* in 1843, after Bentham's manuscripts of these "Anarchical Fallacies" had been lost at the time of Bingham's, James Mill's and Francis Place's edition of Bentham's *The Book of Fallacies*.[3] So much again, on the very strange ways in which Bentham's writings were published.

There can be no doubt that Bentham is considerably indebted to Dumont's editorial activities; for they brought about the first rise of the wide interest taken in Bentham outside England, on the European continent, and in the Americas. But there can be equally little doubt that, with the best intentions, Dumont gave Bentham's manuscripts a somewhat dubious attractiveness.

In editing the manuscripts he continually tried to make them readable for a much wider public than Bentham himself, because of his more acute and complicated type of thought, could ever have reached. Dumont himself declared: "Je n'ai pas traduit les mots, j'ai traduit les idées."[4] And later he specified: "J'ai beaucoup abrégé, mais j'ai souvent ajouté au texte."[5] "Il fallait . . . éclaircir des parties obscures . . . et rem-

---

Hildreth's Theory of Morals" in *Ethics*, vol. VII, no. 3, April 1947, pp. 191-198; Martha M. Pingel, *An American Utilitarian, Richard Hildreth as a Philosopher*, 1948; Paul A. Palmer, "Benthamism in England and America" in *American Political Science Review*, October 1941, pp. 863 f; B. F. Wright, Jr., *American Interpretations of Natural Law*, 1931, pp. 267 f. On Hildreth, the historian, see Arthur M. Schlesinger, Jr., "The Problem of Richard Hildreth" in *New England Quarterly*, June 1940; Alfred H. Kelly, "Richard Hildreth" in *The Marcus W. Jernegan Essays in American Historiography*, 1937. Compare further the biographical and bibliographical material on Hildreth in Louis S. Friedland "Richard Hildreth's Minor Works" in *Papers of the Bibliographical Society of America*, 1946, pp. 126-150 and Donald E. Emerson, Richard Hildreth, 1948.

[3] See E. Halévy, *The Growth of Philosophic Radicalism*, 1928, p. 536 f.

[4] Bentham-Dumont, *Traités de législation*, 1802, tome I, p. ix (discours préliminaire).

[5] Bentham-Dumont, *Traités des preuves judiciaires, ouvrage extrait des manuscrits de M. Jérémie Bentham, jurisconsulte anglais par Et. Dumont*, 1830, tome I, p. xi.

plir les lacunes, que l'auteur avoit laissées."[6] In truth, however, Dumont has not by any means clarified Bentham's text on all points. On the contrary, as compared with Bentham's original manuscripts, Dumont's simplification of the original argument frequently betrays a deplorable lack of precise reasoning.

E. Halévy has shown how Dumont modified the irreligious passages and "tones down Bentham's style."[7] Halévy did not approve of these editorial measures taken by Dumont, because he thought them scarcely compatible with the duties of an editor. He believed, however, that very happy and justifiable modifications are made by Dumont on many points where Bentham, as Halévy writes, "s'était livré à des abstractions trop profondes," aux "formes trop scientifiques," "à une métaphysique, je ne dirai pas trop subtile, mais trop aride."[8] But Halévy whose work was mainly political and economic showed in his Bentham analyses scarcely more interest in philosophic subtlety and precision than Dumont himself.

It seems to me that C. K. Ogden does not overstate the case when he notes that Dumont was rather "obtuse when any of the subtler problems of analysis had to be glossed over in the interest of the wider public for whom he so successfully catered"; and Ogden proves the point by printing a hitherto unpublished manuscript of Bentham's, preserved in the Library of Geneva University, in which Bentham puts together corrections of Dumont's text: these show Dumont's obvious misunderstanding of his theory of fictions.[9] Further, how much less penetration and daring there is in Dumont, when compared with Bentham, may be concluded from the contrast between Bentham's manuscripts and Dumont's text given on p. 26f of the present book. All this is practically admitted in a letter written by Dumont immediately before his death— showing how much he preferred the more popular points of Bentham's *Introduction* to the detailed complicated analysis of the elements of actions.[10] By comparing chapter XII of Bentham's *Introduction* with large parts of the text of Dumont dealing with the same questions, and in-

[6] *Oeuvres de Bentham*, jurisconsulte anglais, Bruxelles, 1829/30, tome I, p. 1; cf. *Traités de législation*, 1802, tome I, p. vii (discours préliminaire).
[7] E. Halévy, *Le radicalisme philosophique*, 1901, tome I, pp. 375 ff. "Dumont atténue les passages irréligieux . . . il . . . apaise le style de Bentham." Compare Jean Marie Guyau, *La morale anglaise contemporaine*, 1879, partie I, chap. I, p. 3, note 3.
[8] E. Halévy, *Le radicalisme philosophique*, 1901, tome I, p. 377.
[9] See C. K. Ogden, *Bentham's Theory of Fictions*, 1932, p. xxix f.
[10] See Bentham, *Works*, 1843, part XXI, p. 24.

serted as chapters XIII and XIV in Bowring's edition of the *Introduction* in Bentham's works, even the reader who consults no more than Bowring's English texts can see to what an extent Bentham's analyses are more lucid and systematic than those of Dumont.

Finally, Dumont himself expressed the wish that Bentham bring out an English publication of his manuscripts, aside from Dumont's French editions, in order "to satisfy readers of different powers."[11] Dumont had to report, in 1822, that "lorsque je publiai à Londres, en 1811, la *Théorie des peines et des récompenses*, M. Bentham exigea de moi de déclarer dans la préface qu'il ne voulait en aucune manière être responsable de ces ouvrages, extraits de manuscrits qu'il n'avait ni achevés ni revus."[12] In the later part of his life Bentham is even reported to have said that Dumont "does not understand a word of my meaning."[13] This certainly should not be taken too literally. At least the first fruit of Dumont's extended editorial work, his *Traités de législation*, have exercised such a large influence that a comparatively detailed account of them must be given here, although the formulations of the text may often be an inadequate reproduction of Bentham's thought.

A Less Critical Approach to the Utility Principle

Like Bentham's *Introduction*, the *Traités de législation* start with a discussion of the principle of utility. It is admitted that the "principe de l'utilité, énoncé vaguement, est peu contredit . . . Mais . . . on n'attache pas à ce principe les mêmes idées . . . il n'en resulte pas une manière de raisonner conséquente et uniforme."[14] In other words, here again it is granted that the principle of utility was widely accepted before Bentham's time. But it is denied that there had been any consistent application of the principle before Bentham. A sign of consistent application of the utility principle is seen especially in Bentham's formation of a thoroughgoing "arithmétique morale."[15] Quite possibly, the term *moral arithmetic* was introduced by Dumont and not by Bentham himself.

In connection with the utility principle, however, the *Traités* define

---

[11] See E. Halévy, *The Growth of Philosophic Radicalism*, 1928, p. 521 and Add. MSS British Museum 33, 542 f., 39; Dumont on April 3, 1795: pour "satisfaire des lecteurs de differentes forces."

[12] Bentham-Dumont, *Tactiques des assemblées législatives*, deuxième edition revue et augmentée, 1822, p. xv (discours préliminaire).

[13] Bentham, *Works*, 1843, part XIX, p. 185b.

[14] Bentham-Dumont, *Traités de législation*, 1802, tome I, p. 1.

[15] *Ibid.*, p. 2.

good and bad far less circumspectly than the *Introduction*. They dog-matically state from the start: "Mal c'est peine, douleur ou cause de douleur, Bien, c'est plaisir ou cause de plaisir."[16] In his annotated copy, it is true, Dumont had added in the margin in ink that "bad" includes every "cause d'absence de plaisir" and good every "cause d'absence de douleur."[17] But this marginal note can, of course, not free these defini-tions from the stigma of dogmatism and lack of critical justification.

At least on one characteristic point, it should be admitted, a strictly coherent usage of the greatest-happiness principle is here developed in an even more detailed way than in the *Introduction*. In his *Introduction*, Bentham had already mentioned that, in his extensive classification of offenses arranged by the standard of the utility principle, he was forced to conclude that usury did not "merit a place" in this catalogue of of-fenses; for if the consent to commit this offense is unfairly obtained, it "amounts to fraud," and if it is unfreely obtained, it is equivalent to ex-tortion. From this he inferred that usury must in no wise be counted among the genuine offenses but should be considered merely a spurious one.[18] Thus, the composition of the *Defence of Usury* owed its origin primarily to the difficulty that Bentham experienced in attempting to find a place for that "imaginary" offense in a list of offenses drawn up strictly according to the greatest-happiness principle.

In the *Traités* this observation concerning usury is boldly generalized and laid down in the following way: "Si le partisan du Principe de l'Utilité trouvoit dans le catalogue banal . . . des délits quelque action indifférente, quelque plaisir innocent, il ne balanceroit pas à transporter ce prétendu delit dans la classe des actes légitimes; il accorderoit sa pitié aux prétendus criminels, et il reserveroit son indignation pour les pré-tendus vertueux qui les persécutent. . . . S'il trouvoit aussi . . . dans le catalogue banal des vertus, une action dont il résultât plus de peines que de plaisirs, il ne balanceroit pas à regarder cette prétendue vertu comme une vice; il ne s'en laisseroit point imposer par l'erreur générale; il ne croiroit pas légèrement qu'on soit fondé à employer de fausses vertus

---

[16] *Ibid.*, p. 3.

[17] *Unpublished marginal note* by Dumont. I owe the insight into the few mar-ginal notes of Dumont's copy of the *Traités* to the kindness of the present owner of these volumes, M. Jean Graven, Professeur à la Faculté de Droit, Université de Genève, Switzerland. He was good enough to send me photostats of the passages in question and to allow me their quotation. Apart from the present quotation, these passages have, however, no ethical relevance.

[18] See Bentham, *Introduction*, chap. xvi, sect. 35 note, vol. ii, 1823, p. 139 and *ibid.*, the preface, vol. i, p. vii f: *Works*, 1843, vol. i, p. 118, chap. xviii and p. iii.

pour le maintien des véritables."[19] On this point the *Traités* are, for once, more radical than the *Introduction* and this remark shows with special clearness how even the classificatory work done by Bentham is not intended to serve the mere purpose of classification, but is ultimately directed by critical, censorial tendencies to a thoroughgoing reform in the field of legislation and morals.

Like the *Introduction*, the *Traités* try to demonstrate that it is impossible to give the principle of utility too great an extension,[20] while the adverse principles allow no consistent application at all. However, all these discussions at the beginning of the *Traités*, and particularly chapters II and III of the introductory part, are little more than small fractions of the text of the *Introduction* translated into French. There are very few additional remarks: the Stoics are mentioned among the philosophical adherents to the principle of asceticism while, strangely enough, among the religious advocates of that principle only the Jansenists are referred to. Against the defenders of asceticism, who inconsistently ask God for a happy future life, the *Traités* argue that, obviously, one cannot see what pledges we have for the goodness of God in another life if he has forbidden the enjoyment of this one.[21] A long note, in all probability added by Dumont, contains quotations from the philosophical ascetics Pliny and Seneca and from Diderot's "Vie de Sénèque."[22] Richard Hildreth, in his translation of Dumont's work, rightly omitted these references, since they are rather awkwardly and arbitrarily chosen.

The principle of sympathy and antipathy is treated here with even more disapproval than in the *Introduction*. It is not only termed "un principe . . . d'imagination et de goût," "un principe despotique et capricieux,"[23] but also "anarchique."[24] On the other hand, the *Traités* considerably cut down the most important critical discussion of the ten best known moral systems which, according to Bentham, are based

[19] Bentham-Dumont, *Traités*, 1802, tome I, p. 5 ("Principes généraux de législation," chap. I), compare the less radical remark on this point in a similar discussion, *Introduction*, chap. II, p. 15, note, vol. I, 1823, p. 35, where Bentham allows one to detest publicly virtuous acts, i.e. useful acts "within yourself as much as you please" and only forbids to "go about, by word or deed to do anything to hinder" others to do them.

[20] *Ibid.*, 1802, tome I, p. 15: "Il est impossible de . . . donner . . . au principe de l'utilité . . . trop d'etendu" (Hildreth, p. 9).

[21] *Ibid.*, tome I, p. 7 (Hildreth, p. 5).

[22] *Ibid.*, p. 8 f.

[23] *Ibid.*, pp. 16 and 31; compare *Introduction*, chap. II, sect. 14, note, vol. I, 1823, 32; chap. II, sect. 11 note, vol. II, pp. 21 f, 26.

[24] Bentham-Dumont, *Traités de législation civile et pénale*, 1802, tome I, p. 31.

on a disguised principle of sympathy and antipathy. Instead of this lacuna, which is epistemologically rather regrettable, some few psychological remarks are offered as to the causes of antipathy in moral judgment, such causes being "repugnance of sense, . . . wounded pride, . . . power controlled, weakened . . . confidence in the future, disappointment in the desire of unanimity and envy."[25] Finally, these psychological remarks are followed by the quite original aperçu that a man born with an organ of pleasure which the rest of mankind did not possess would be pursued as a monster[26] because of the envy and antipathy he would excite.

Some "trifling" epistemological objections to the utility principle are answered here in a rather dogmatic, though graphic fashion. The identification of utility and virtue is brought about simply by dismissing the common contradistinction between virtue and utility as a perversion of language. This "perversion" is corrected without any further justification by the statement: There is no opposition between virtue and interest; on the contrary, virtue is nothing but a sacrifice of a lesser interest to a greater, "of a momentary to a durable, of a doubtful to a certain."[27] In a similar way, any fundamental contradistinction between politics and morals is rejected. As virtue and utility both have to deal with happiness, so have morals and politics: the only difference is, that in politics the happiness of large communities is at issue, while in morals the happiness of individuals is considered. But to assume a cardinal opposition between these two disciplines is similar to supposing that the rules of arithmetic, true for large numbers, are false for small ones and vice versa.[28] So whatever is morally bad cannot be politically good and what is morally good cannot be politically bad. It obviously escaped the attention of the *Traités* that the utility principle interpreted in this manner presupposes the utopian belief in a natural harmony of all human desires. Understood in such a way, the principle of utility can certainly not be defended as a workable criterion in ethics.

The further defense of the principle of utilitarianism is limited here to a few rather meager remarks. We are asked to remember that the principle of utility itself cannot be made responsible for false applica-

---

[25] See *ibid.*, tome I, pp. 11 ff, 16 ff. Hildreth in his influential edition of the *Traités*, translated on p. 11 Dumont's phrase "Désir de l'unanimité trompé" simplp as "the desire of unanimity." In consequence of this inadequacy, the meaning of this paragraph seems to me quite obscured in his rendering.

[26] *Traités*, 1802, tome I, p. 19 (Principes de législation, chap. III, sect. 2).

[27] *Ibid.*, p. 26 (Hildreth, p. 16).   [28] *Ibid.*, p. 27 (Hildreth, p. 16).

tions of its prescriptions. If a man calculates badly, it is not arithmetic which is at fault—it is himself. One, therefore, ought not to hold utility responsible for mistakes which are contrary to its nature, and which, as a matter of fact, it alone is able to rectify. Machiavelli misapplied utility—a fact which, at least according to the *Traités*, was revealed by Frederic II in his *Anti-Machiavel*. If, however, people think it dangerous to make everyone the judge of his own utility, i.e. of his moral duties, the *Traités* answer that on any other assumption man would not be a rational agent. He who cannot judge of what is agreeable to him is less than a child: he is an idiot. Virtue is neither degraded nor weakened by being represented as an effect of reason, and being explained in an intelligible and simple manner. Whoever refuses to acknowledge the rational principle of utility, and takes refuge in irrational, vague feelings of sympathy and antipathy, must fall into a vicious circle of sophistry. "Je dois tenir ma promesse. Pourquoi? parce que ma conscience me le prescrit. Comment savez-vous que votre conscience vous le prescrit? parce que j'en ai le sentiment intime. Pourquoi devez-vous obéir à votre conscience? parce que Dieu est l'auteur de ma nature, et qu'obéir à ma conscience, c'est obéir à Dieu. Pourquoi devez-vous obéir à Dieu? parce que c'est mon premier devoir. Comment le savez-vous? parce que ma conscience me le dit, etc. Voilà le cercle éternel d'où l'on ne sort jamais: voilà la source des opiniâtretés et des invincibles erreurs. Car si l'on juge de tout par le sentiment, il n'y a plus moyen de distinguer entre les injonctions d'une conscience éclairée, et celles d'une conscience aveugle. Tous les persecuteurs ont le même titre. Tous les fanatiques ont le même droit."[29] Rather optimistically, the *Traités* suppose that even Epicurus and Seneca agree essentially in morals, although Epicurus alone, of all the ancients, is said to have the merit of clearly grasping the true source of morals.[30] In any case, according to the *Traités*, the true philosopher cannot deny that "le bonheur seul possède une valeur intrinsèque."[31] The ascetic principle, however, is adapted only to monks, the principle of sympathy and antipathy to inferior moralists—the man of the world and the multitude.[32]

Surveying this whole line of argument one must conclude that the *Traités* approach the analysis of the utility principle far less critically than the *Introduction*. They take much less care to show why principles

[29] *Ibid.*, pp. 29 ff ("Principes de législation," chap. v); (Hildreth, p. 17 f).
[30] *Ibid.*, p. 29 (Hildreth, p. 17).
[31] *Ibid.*, p. 25 ("Principes de législation," chap. iv); (Hildreth, p. 15).
[32] *Ibid.*, p. 16 ("Principes de législation," chap. iii, sect. i); (Hildreth, p. 10).

inconsistent with utility do not fit the requirements of a scientific ethics. But while the *Traités* are more dogmatic, they occasionally compensate for their epistemological defects by a historical reference, or by a perceptive psychological observation.

While, in the *Introduction*, the list of the different kinds of pains and pleasures follows the characterization of the four sanctions, in the *Traités* the order is reversed. Here it is not the sanctions as "sources of pain and pleasure" which are first dealt with; the way leading from the discussion of the different "efficient causes" to the different "final causes"[33] has been abandoned, and it is the fourteen or, in the second edition, the fifteen different classes of pleasure and pain as "final causes" which are first enumerated. In the *Introduction*, only fourteen kinds of pleasant and unpleasant feelings were mentioned;[34] but that new type of pleasure which is added in the second edition of the *Traités*, "le plaisir de l'intelligence,"[35] hardly represents an essential or indispensable supplement to the catalogue of 1789—itself not absolutely satisfactory. "Le plaisir de l'intelligence" could easily be classified under the head "les plaisirs de l'adresse," and these "plaisirs de l'adresse" could be divided into pleasures of manual and of intellectual skill.

On the other hand, from the enumeration of the different kinds of pain in the *Introduction*, one sort has been dropped in the *Traités*, "the pains dependent on association." No reason is given for these alterations in the *Traités*; and, after all, they are of slight importance. As to the general exposition of ideas the work of Bentham-Dumont shows no divergence from the *Introduction* on all these points. Practically the same applies to the chapters on the sanctions and the measurement of pain and pleasure. It may, however, be worth noting that, in the *Introduction*, Bentham betrays the attitude of a skeptic, or at least of an agnostic, toward the religious sanction, while Dumont admonishes us that none of the four sanctions ought to be rejected—all should be employed and directed to the same end with equal emphasis.[36]

In the chapter "De l'estimation des plaisirs et des peines," it is granted that moral calculation is a very slow matter; but it is not necessary to recommence this calculation upon every occasion. When one has be-

[33] See Bentham, *Introduction*, 1789, chap. III, sect. I.
[34] *Ibid.*, chap. V, sect. 2.
[35] *Traités*, tome I, "Principes de législation," chap. VI, sect. I. In the second edition of 1820 "le plaisir de l'intelligence" appears as the tenth, inserted between the ninth and tenth types of pleasure of the first edition.
[36] *Traités*, 1802, tome I, p. 49 ("Principes de législation," chap. VII).

come familiar with the process and has acquired that justness of estimate which results from it, it is possible to compare the sum of good and evil with such promptitude that one is scarcely conscious of the steps in calculation; we perform many arithmetical calculations in the same manner, almost without knowing it. But, disregarding this fact, the salient point is that, in compensation for its slowness, moral calculation—or moral arithmetic—represents the only precise method in ethics, "au lieu que ce qu'on appelle Sentiment est un aperçu prompte, mais sujet à être fautif."[37] This is, again, a simple but fair presentation of the problem at issue. It clearly shows the disadvantage and the cardinal superiority of moral calculation as compared with the dogmatic reference to conventional moral feelings or conventional moral duties and values alleged to be elementary moral "facts."

Within the field of ethical arithmetic, the *Traités* speak of pains as expenses and of pleasures as income.[37] This analogy—the comparison of pains with expenses—appears frequently also in Bentham's later writings; and one of the difficulties involved on this point is perhaps best clarified in a MS *hitherto unpublished* which, in all probability, was composed at about the same time as the *Introduction* and the *Traités*. Bentham explains here that: "The expression 'value of pain' may to some appear rather a harsh one. The term 'value' it is not usual to apply to objects other than what are supposed to produce pleasure, to objects other than what are desirable. But either this we must have for objects that are the objects that are the contrary or none at all: for there is no other that corresponds to it applicable to them. The license for using it in this sense is therefore a license justified by necessity: nor is it by any means an unexampled one. Mathematicians speak without scruple of the *values* of their x and y: tho' x and y are often made to signify debts: objects as anyone can witness not at all desirable. Perhaps the word *importance* might (be made to) answer the same purpose; at least in many cases."[38]

The necessity of representing pains as negative values in the moral calculus can certainly lead to no insuperable difficulty. Within the whole problem of a moral arithmetic, this question has no special relevance

---

[37] *Ibid.*, p. 52 ("Principes de législation," chap. VIII). In the 2nd edition of the *Traités* in 1820 a misprint occurs on p. 49: chap. VII instead of chap. VIII.

[38] Bentham MSS, hitherto unpublished, University College, London, Portfolio 27, Folder 5, sheet 30, p. 7, note b, written probably about 1778 according to Professor Charles W. Everett. A corresponding reflection see Bentham MSS, University College, London, Portfolio 27, Folder 5, sheet 39, p. 4, note (hitherto unpublished).

and is of little consequence; but it is understandable that Bentham, with his refined linguistic conscience, felt uneasy in speaking of pains as values in the sense of negative values. Nevertheless, he was obviously aware that the felicific calculus is beset with much greater intricacies.

The discussion of circumstances influencing sensibility, the topic of chapter VI of the *Introduction*, again has its "counterpart" in the *Traités*; and it is introduced there by one of the parallels between morals and natural science which Bentham is so fond of drawing. "Lyonet fit un volume in 4°. sur l'anatomie d'une chenille: la morale n'a pas encore eu d'investigateur si patient et si philosophe."[39] Further, the theoretical and practical importance of these problems of a "moral physiology" is here illustrated by a historical reference, the type of reference for which Dumont had a special fondness. Joseph II, emperor of Austria, one of the most enlightened princes of the eighteenth century, had to admit on the eve of his death that he would have been less unfortunate in his great moral and legal reform work if he had known how to respect the prejudices, the inclinations and the other circumstances which influenced the sensibilities of his subjects.[40] Also within this catalogue of terms, the circumstances influencing sensibility, a few changes take place, in comparison with the *Introduction*. As the first of these circumstances, preceding even "health," appears "le tempérament,"[41] this being perhaps a concession to the popular doctrine of the different human temperaments as the foundation of all circumstances influencing sensibility; and further, with some justification, the list of these primary circumstances is simplified and reduced from 32 items to only 15, while the catalogue of secondary circumstances remains completely unchanged and is even illustrated by some of the same examples.

Beginning with chapter X of the "Principes de législation" the *Traités* no longer follow the succession of the topics of the *Introduction*. All the fundamental analyses of human actions in general, of intentionality, of consciousness, of motives, of dispositions are here omitted, and are only occasionally mentioned later in a much briefer and more popular form. Chapter X of the *Traités*, immediately after the chapter on sensibility, discusses the problem of consequences of actions; and here too the rea-

[39] *Traités*, 1802, p. 54 ("Principes de législation," chap. IX, sect. I; Hildreth, p. 33).
[40] *Ibid.*, p. 78 ("Principes de législation," chap. IX, sect. III; Hildreth, p. 47).
[41] *Ibid.*, chap. IX, sect. I, p. 55 (Hildreth, p. 33).

soning is less acute than in chapter XII of the *Introduction*. Yet there are a few interesting amplifications on the general line of thought.

The *Introduction* spoke only of primary and secondary mischief. But in the *Traités* we find also "un ... mal du troisième ordre"; aside from the alarm and the danger which make up secondary mischief, this evil of the third order is the effect of long-lasting alarm and danger weakening the active faculties of men and discouraging them in the face of continued alarming crimes.[42] Further minor distinctions are introduced here between a permanent and an evanescent evil, between extended evil concerning a greater number of persons and divided evil concerning numerous people only to a limited extent.[43] Finally, not only the evil, but also the good consequences of actions are taken into account in the *Traités*, though they have much less to do with legislation than with ethics. The good of the second order is in contrast to alarm and danger "de confiance et de sûreté"; the good of the third order, in contrast to discouragement and depression, is "cette énergie, cette gaîté de coeur, cette ardeur d'agir qu'inspirent les motifs rénumératoires"[44]— that gaiety of heart which, according to Epicurus and, strangely enough also to Kant,[45] is the most significant companion of moral action.

It certainly speaks in favor of the thoroughness of Eduard von Hartmann's Bentham studies that he recognized even in the *Traités*—despite their lack of epistemological acuteness—that Bentham's distinction between consequences of the first, second, and third order are "besonders wertvoll und folgenreich."[46] But in the end, unfortunately, Hartmann too did no more justice to the merits of Bentham's critical method than English historians of utilitarianism. He found the whole of J. S. Mill's and Bentham's ethics "klar, plausibel und gefällig" at first glance but especially Mill "seicht und confuse ... bei näherer kritischer Prüfung."[47]

In once again drawing a parallel between natural science and ethics, the *Traités* correctly conclude that these distinctions between good and evil of different orders can furnish us a means of breaking down the

---

[42] *Ibid.*, p. 86 ("Principes de législation," chap. x); (Hildreth, p. 52 f).

[43] *Ibid.*, p. 83 f; Hildreth, p. 51.   [44] *Ibid.*, p. 86; Hildreth, p. 53.

[45] See I. Kant, *Metaphysik der Sitten*, Metaphysische Anfangsgründe der Tugendlehre, *Werke*, ed. Ernst Cassirer, Band VII, S. 310. As to Bentham's high appreciation of Epicurus compare also *Traités*, tome I, 1802, "Principes de législation," chap. v, p. 29: "Epicure, il est vrai, a seul parmi les anciens le mérite d'avoir connu la véritable source de la morale." But that a prelude to the idea of the moral calculus is also to be found in Epicurus' theory of a συμμέτρησις of pleasures and pains was obviously not known either to Bentham or his followers.

[46] E. von Hartmann, *Phänomenologie des sittlichen Bewusstseins*, 1879, p. 611.

[47] *Ibid.*, p. 607.

mixed whole, made up of the consequences of an act, in the same way
as other means help us to break down the mixed metals in order to
discover their intrinsic value and their precise quantity of alloy.[48] But,
though these distinctions between good and evil consequences of different orders are here enlarged, these additions do not increase the
epistemological value of the discussion. At any rate, the epistemological
reasons for making any of these distinctions are much more cogently
brought forth in the *Introduction*.

The same applies, above all, to the important chapter XI, which deals
with the final moral judgments of acts from the "censorial" point of
view. It is true that the necessity of a strictly critical attitude in ethics
is most eloquently made clear on this point. The author asks: "Pourquoi
convient-il d'ériger certaines actions en délits?" (and we may add, why
is it appropriate to praise certain acts as moral?) "Tout le monde est
d'accord; soit. Mais sur quoi est fondé cet accord? Demandez à chacun
ses raisons. Vous verrez une étrange diversité de sentimens et de principes: vous ne la verrez pas seulement parmi le Peuple, mais parmi les
Philosophes. Est-ce du tems perdu que de chercher une base uniforme
de consentement sur un objet si essentiel?" To this the author replies
thus: "L'accord qui existe n'est fondé que sur des préjugés, et ces préjugés varient selon les tems et les lieux, selon les opinions et les cou-
tumes. On m'a toujours dit que telle action étoit un délit, et je pense
qu'elle est un délit. Voilà le guide du Peuple et même du Législateur.
Mais si l'usage a érigé en délits des actions innocentes, s'il fait considérer
comme graves des délits légers, comme légers des délits graves, s'il a
varié partout, il est clair qu'il faut l'assujétir à une règle, et non pas le
prendre pour règle lui-même. . . . Je me suppose étranger à toutes nos
denominations de vice ou de vertu, . . . l'homme que le préjugé flétrit
comme vicieux, celui qu'il préconise comme vertueux sont pour le moment égaux devant moi. Je veux juger le préjugé même, et peser dans
cette nouvelle balance toutes les actions, afin de former le catalogue de
celles qui doivent être permises et de celles qui doivent être défendues."
But in spite of this brillant exposition of the critical attitude in morals,
the *Traités* fall back to complete dogmatism at the upshot of their argument. They simply say: "Je suis appelé à considérer les actions humaines
uniquement par leurs effets en bien ou en mal."[49] Since this is stated

[48] Bentham-Dumont, *Traités de législation*, 1802, tome I, "Principes de législation," chap. x, p. 84. H. Hildreth, *The Theory of Legislation* by Jeremy Bentham,
1864, p. 52.
[49] *Ibid.*, p. 89 f ("Principes de législation," chap. xi); (Hildreth, p. 54 f).

without further qualification, it is nothing but an unwarranted dogmatic statement.

If Bentham had no more to say on this point, his theory would be as uncritical an ethics of the consequences of acts as the theory of his opponents is an uncritical ethics of motives. In fact, however, in his analyses of the elements of human acts in the *Introduction*, Bentham carefully demonstrated why, in our criterion of moral right and wrong, we can ultimately refer only to the consequences of acts, and not to motives or to human dispositions and character. In Dumont's presentation of Bentham's doctrine, these analyses stating the minor relevance of motives are completely separated from the study of the consequences of acts: they appear in the *Traités* only much later. From the methodological standpoint this could not help but have a detrimental effect. The reference to the consequences of acts as the ultimate ethical standard is, in this way, deprived of its critical foundation.

The Analyses of Rape and Hatred

Aside from these grave methodological defects, the importance of the different order of the consequences of acts is illustrated in an ingenious and impressive way by a few particularly pertinent examples. Thus the *Traités* speak of rape—and it is not denied that in this case an evil of the first order happens "par une plaisanterie grossière et puérile. Quoi qu'on puisse dire à cet égard, nier l'existence de ce délit et en diminuer l'horreur, les femmes les plus prodigues de leur faveurs n'aimeront pas qu'une fureur brutale les leur ravisse."[50] Nevertheless, it is emphasized that, taking into account the universality of the desire that gives rise to rape, the evil of the first order caused by this desire must be considered essentially smaller than the evil of the second order, the alarm, the feelings of insecurity of women and husbands. It is solely because of this feeling of alarm that whole nations have interested themselves in quarrels; and the close confinement of women owes its origin perhaps to an epoch of troubles, when the feebleness of laws had multiplied disorders of this kind and spread a general terror.[50]

Similar, but even more perceptive, psychological and ethical details are elucidated in the *Traités* by a fascinating analysis of hatred. The pleasure felt by the hater, and the pain of the first order caused by him, are contrasted with each other and morally interpreted in the following way: "J'ai conçu, n'importe comment, de l'inimitié contre vous. La pas-

[50] *Ibid.*, p. 94 (2nd edition, 1820, p. 88 f); (Hildreth, p. 57).

sion m'égare: je vous insulte, je vous humilie, je vous blesse. Le spectacle de votre peine me fait éprouver au moins pour un tems un sentiment de plaisir. Mai pour ce tems même, peut-on croire que le plaisir que je goûte soit l'équivalent de la peine que vous souffrez? Si même chaque atôme de votre peine pouvoit se peindre dans mon esprit, est-il probable que chaque atôme de plaisir qui y correspond, me parût avoir la même intensité? et cependant ce ne sont que quelques atômes épars de votre douleur qui viennent de présenter à mon imagination distraite et troublée: pour vous, aucun ne peut être perdu: pour moi, la plus grande partie se dissipe toujours en pure perte. Mais ce plaisir, tel qu'il est, ne tarde pas à laisser percer son impureté naturelle. L'humanité, principe que rien peut-être ne peut étouffer dans les âmes les plus atroces, éveille un remords secret dans la mienne. Des craintes de toute espèce, crainte de vengeance soit de votre part, soit de tout ce qui est en liaison avec vous, crainte de la voix publique, craintes religieuses, s'il me reste quelque étincelle de religion, toutes ces craintes viennent troubler ma sécurité, et corrompent bientôt mon triomphe. La passion est fanée, le plaisir est détruit, le reproche intérieur lui succède. Mais de votre côté, la peine dure encore et peut avoir une longue durée. Voilà pour des blessures légères que le tems peut cicatriser. Mais que sera-ce dans les cas où par la nature même de l'injure, la plaie est incurable; lorsque des membres ont été tronqués, des traits défigurés ou des facultés détruites? Pesez les maux, leur intensité, leur durée, leurs suites, mesurez-les sous toutes leurs dimensions, et voyez comme en tout sens le plaisir est inférieur à la peine. Passons aux effets du second ordre. La nouvelle de votre malheur répandra dans tous les esprits le poison de la crainte. Tout homme qui a un ennemi, ou qui peut avoir un ennemi, pense avec effroi à tout ce que peut inspirer la passion de la haine. Parmi des êtres foibles qui ont tant de choses à s'envier, à se disputer, que mille petites rivalités mettent sans cesse aux prises les uns avec les autres, l'esprit de vengeance annonce une suite de maux éternels. Ainsi toute action de cruauté produite par une passion dont le principe est dans tous les coeurs, et dont tout le monde peut souffrir, fera éprouver une alarme qui continuera jusqu'à ce que la punition du coupable ait transporté le danger du côté de l'injustice, de l'inimitié cruelle. Voilà une souffrance commune à tous; et n'oublions pas une autre peine qui en résulte, cette peine de sympathie que ressentent les coeurs généreux, à l'aspect des délits de cette nature."[51] This seems to me one of the most naturalistic and, at

[51] *Ibid.*, pp. 91 ff (2nd edition, 1820, pp. 86 ff; Hildreth, p. 56 f). Compare Bentham, *Works*, 1843, vol. III, p. 226b. It is astonishing to learn that, in the face

THE *TRAITÉS DE LÉGISLATION*

the same time, one of the most moving demonstrations of the immorality of hatred in the history of ethics.

Taken as a whole, and expressed in the provocative language of moral arithmetic, this proves that hate is necessarily uneconomic. It lies in the nature of hatred that the aggressor can enjoy only a puny amount of the pain suffered by his victim. Even the hater himself can never reap the largest part of the fruit of his doings, let alone the losses to be endured by the object of his passion. So hatred must always be bought at much too high a price.

Sound as it is, this apparently cool and sober calculation is, I think, accompanied by the most noble, "idealistic" feeling. It seems to me a classical example of how to combine realistic, objective reasoning with profundity of emotional understanding.

Further Popularization of Fundamentals in the Introductory Part of the *Traités*

From these analyses we are led, again rather abruptly, to two quite different topics—one of them the last theme of the *Introduction*—the discussion of the borderline separating morals from jurisprudence. Here again we find some watering down of the radicalism of Bentham's argument. The *Introduction* had dared to state that both jurisprudence and private ethics are parts of "ethics at large." The *Traités*, however, content themselves with the much more conservative statement: "La législation a bien le même centre que la morale, mais elle n'a pas la même circonférence."[52] Further, the *Traités* assure us that "c'est la morale et surtout la religion qui forment . . . le complément nécessaire de la législation et le lien le plus doux de l'humanité."[53] No parallel can be found, in the radically secular *Introduction*, for this conciliatory attitude toward religion and the modest role ascribed to ethics. With regard to the moral rights of animals, finally, the outlook of the *Traités* is again somewhat different from that of the *Introduction*. It is true that also in Dumont's work we meet with the intention to legislate for the

---

of such Bentham passages as these and others, Sir William David Ross could say in his *Foundations of Ethics*, 1939, p. 75: "The principle 'do evil to no one' is more pressing than the principle 'do good to everyone' except when the evil is very substantially outweighed by the good. . . . It is strange that . . . this consideration has been overlooked by the utilitarians."

[52] *Traités*, 1802, tome I, p. 98 f ("Principes de législation," chap. XII; 2nd edition, 1820, p. 93; Hildreth, p. 60).

[53] *Ibid.*, p. 106 (2nd edition, p. 100; Hildreth, p. 65).

welfare of non-human creation.[54] But the reasons forbidding gratuitous cruelty to animals are confined, in the *Traités*, to one which really refers only to men.

Here, as in Kant, we are told the condemnation of animal torture is a means of cultivating benevolence toward men, "ou du moins . . . un moyen . . . de prévenir cette dépravation brutale qui, après s'être jouée des animaux, a besoin en croissant de s'assouvir de douleurs humaines."[55] In comparison with this narrow, anthropocentric argument, which is not found in the *Introduction*, the corresponding reflections in Bentham's earlier work certainly give witness to infinitely more profound magnanimity.

The end of the introductory essay in the *Traités*, which runs comparatively parallel with the content of the *Introduction*, is a brief assortment of main types of false reasoning on the subject of morals and legislation. Without systematic order, ten such different types of theories are mentioned. In the case of four of these theories, it is difficult to recognize any difference in the heads under which they appear; and much material from the *Fragment on Government* is repeated almost word for word.

First, the criticism of the antiquity of a law is put here in a mild, propitious manner. It is agreed that the antiquity of a moral custom may create a prejudice in its favor; it is denied only that antiquity can, in itself, justify a moral law: antiquity can only smooth the way to its practical acceptance. Its validity, however, must be founded solely on its utility; and if its utility cannot be demonstrated, the law must be regarded as ethically invalid.[56] But, as we have seen, all these questions are far more carefully dealt with in the first great critical work of Bentham's youth, especially in the *Comment on the Commentaries* in the chapters on Common Law. Here only six lines are dedicated to them.

In close connection with this false argument concerning antiquity we find the "reproach of innovation."[57] Actually both types of reasoning have the same end in view: the second merely forbids the contrary of

---

[54] *Ibid.*, p. 107 (2nd edition, p. 101; Hildreth, p. 66); compare *Traités*, tome II, p. 309 f ("Principes du code pénal," chap. XVI, Culture de la bienveillance).

[55] *Ibid.*, tome I, p. 107 (2nd edition, p. 102; Hildreth, p. 66). Compare precisely the same argument in Kant's *Metaphysik der Sitten*, Metaphysische Anfangsgründe der Tugendlehre, §19, §17; and cf. *Eine Vorlesung Kants über Ethik*, ed. by Paul Menzer, 1924, p. 302 f.

[56] *Traités*, 1802, tome I, p. 109 ("Principes de législation," chap. XIII); 2nd edition, p. 104; Hildreth, p. 67.

[57] *Ibid.*, p. 110.

what the first states as the only legitimate rule. While the first demands the grounding of all valid law on antiquity, the second declares that a law not based on antiquity is not valid. But in this case again—it is, in the enumeration of the *Traités*, case three—the "illegitimacy" of innovation is much more fully discussed in Bentham's earlier writings than in the seven lines devoted to it in the *Traités*.

The same applies to case two, the scientifically untenable recourse to Divine Law in morals. The ambiguity of Divine Law is illustrated by reference to its completely different interpretation in Bossuet and Algernon Sidney. While Sidney saw in the Old Testament a glorification of democracy, Bossuet holds that it develops the ideal of autocracy.[58] Doubtless, in this respect too, the *Comment on the Commentaries*, with its extensive discussion of Divine Law, is much richer in its argument.

Fourth, by references to Montesquieu, Beccaria and Rousseau, the *Traités* try to show why an arbitrary definition cannot form the reason for the validity of a law. Montesquieu had defined laws as "des rapports éternelles."[59] Yet such a definition is so vague, it speaks in such general terms, that the definition is far more obscure than the thing to be defined, "La définition . . . redouble . . . ces ténèbres . . . qu'elle . . . devoit dissiper."[60] The quotation from Beccaria is unfortunately not correct. In rejecting torture as a means of discovering the guilt or innocence of an accused person, Beccaria does not abstractly state that the effect of torture is to confound all relations:[61] he concretely marks out which relations are confused, and makes it clear why they are confused.[62] Therefore, to censure Beccaria in this respect seems to me without justification. According to the *Traités*, however, Beccaria's, Montesquieu's and Rousseau's definitions of a law are equally arbitrary. For, as we are told, if only the expression of Rousseau's "volonté générale" were a true law, no law would exist at all, except the laws of the Republic of San Marino: in such a small community alone could the true general will be properly expressed. (The still existing republic of San Marino near Rimini in Italy, one of the oldest states of Europe, has even today no more than about 15,000 inhabitants. Incidentally, I was informed in 1930, when I visited the town of San Marino, that not even there does a general political will exist: only the heads of families have the right to vote.) At

[58] *Ibid.*, p. 109 f (2nd edition, p. 104 f; Hildreth, p. 67 f).
[59] Montesquieu, *De l'Esprit des Lois*, 1749, livre I, chap. I, p. 2 f.
[60] *Traités de législation*, 1802, tome I, p. 111 (2nd edition, 1820, p. 106; Hildreth, p. 68).
[61] *Ibid.*, p. 112 (2nd edition, p. 106 f; Hildreth, p. 69).
[62] See Beccaria, *Dei delitti e delle pene*, ed. R. Palmerocchi, chap. XII, p. 42 f.

any rate, according to Bentham, no adequate reasons for the universal validity of laws can be based on these "arbitrary" definitions of the meaning of a law.

These arbitrary definitions are as inappropriate in ethics and jurisprudence as the three ensuing items criticized by the *Traités*. The first of these three, and the fifth of all the items mentioned in this list of the *Traités*, is the use of metaphors. There is an explicit reference to Blackstone as a lover of those metaphors and allegories which give birth to false images and produce the same effect as false ethical reasoning. When, for instance, Blackstone represents the law as a castle, the *Traités* ask trenchantly: are presently existing laws perhaps to be regarded as castles inhabited by robbers?[63] In other words, allegories may be employed in exactly the opposite sense to the meaning given them by their inventors; and this shows clearly enough that they have no place in any scientific ethics.

Sixthly, "fictions" are here characterized as even more misleading than metaphors. A fiction is defined in the *Traités* as "un fait notoirement faux, sur lequel on raisonne comme s'il étoit vrai."[64] This definition of *fiction* obviously does not cover the meaning given this term later by Bentham, as a result of his elaborate linguistic and logical studies;[65] and in all probability, by about 1800, Bentham had already ceased to assume that fictions are in themselves notoriously false.[66] But be this as it may, both the polemics launched by the *Traités* on this point hold good, the attack on Cocceiji's fictions as well as that on the fiction of a moral "corruption of blood,"[67] a fiction used by certain English lawyers. Moreover, Prussian law under the Nazis deserved such a criticism even more than in Cocceiji's days.

Under the same head of fictions, mention is made of the important concept of the social contract. But on this point, too, the argument of the *Fragment on Government*, Bentham's youthful work, is on the whole more elaborately developed. In their criticism of Rousseau's interpretation of the "contrat social," the *Traités* repeat only the weakest

[63] Bentham-Dumont, *Traités de législation civile et pénale*, 1802, tome I, p. 112 f ("Principes de législation," chap. XIII, §5); (2nd edition, p. 108; Hildreth, p. 70).
[64] *Ibid.*, p. 114 (chap. XIII, §6); 2nd edition, p. 109; Hildreth, p. 71.
[65] See C. K. Ogden, *Bentham's Theory of Legislation*, 1931, notes, p. 514 f; compare C. K. Ogden, *Bentham's Theory of Fictions*, 1932.
[66] See Bentham's letter to Dumont, May 21, 1802, first partly published from Bentham MSS at the Library of Geneva University by C. K. Ogden in his *Bentham's Theory of Legislation*, 1932, p. xxx.
[67] *Traités*, 1802, tome I, pp. 114 ff (2nd edition, p. 109 f; Hildreth, p. 71).

of the objections in the *Fragment*. It consists of the following critical questions: "Dans quelle langue est . . . cette convention universelle . . . rédigée? Pourquoi a-t-elle été toujours ignorée? Est-ce en sortant des forêts, en renonçant à la vie sauvage que . . . les hommes, ont eu ces grandes idées de morale et de politique, sur lesquelles on fait porter cette convention primitive?"[68]

John Locke's theory of the social contract is held to be more specious, because there are monarchies in which the sovereigns assume certain obligations upon their accession to the throne, as Locke wishes them to do. However, even such a contract is but a fiction.[69] For, even if the prince is free to accept or to refuse certain conditions on the part of his subjects at the beginning of his reign, the multitude of his subjects could not have refused their consent without endangering their lives: therefore, they cannot be considered morally bound by a so-called social contract.

Even more false is Hobbes' interpretation of the social contract. For, as the *Traités* point out, it cannot be argued that men deposited all power in the hands of a prince and voluntarily renounced their natural liberty because such liberty produced nothing but evil and the idea of resisting the prince would imply the contradiction of resisting one's self; on the contrary, as the *Traités* emphasize, monarchism and despotism have originated everywhere through violence and false religious ideas.[70] Nowhere was it built up on a fictitious contract between people and government. If Rousseau's version of the theory of the "Contrat social" has been comparatively little criticized so far, the reason is obviously that men do not usually quibble about the logic of a system if the system supports what they would like to see established, in this case liberty and equality.[70] These last few arguments are not developed in the *Fragment on Government* and deserve, therefore, to be noted as a supplement to the discussion which this topic received in the earlier publication.

Besides metaphors and fictions, a third related term appears here—in the whole list of false reasoning, the seventh case—namely, fancies. As such a fancy, the *Traités* mention only "raison éternelle," and illustrate this false reasoning by reference to certain statements of Cocceiji—statements concerning the right of a father over his children, which is allegedly grounded on eternal reason. In criticism of this "fancy," the

[68] *Ibid.*, p. 118 (2nd edition, p. 113; Hildreth, p. 73). Compare Bentham, *A Fragment on Government*, 1776, chap. i, §2.
[69] *Ibid.*, p. 118 f (Hildreth, p. 73 f).   [70] *Ibid.*, p. 118 (Hildreth, p. 73).

Traités pick Cocceiji's arguments to pieces point by point. First, Cocceiji's *"Code Frédéric"* states that the right of a father over his children is founded on eternal reason, since they are born in his house. But the *Traités* reply that it is impossible to speak in this connection of an eternal reason, because the children of travelers are often born on board a vessel, in a tavern, or in the house of a friend; and children of a domestic, in the house of the master. Second, according to Cocceiji, the right of a father over his children is based on his being the chief of the family. But this again, according to the *Traités*, does not apply to a child born in a house in which an elder brother of the father or his patron is the chief. Third, according to Cocceiji, eternal reason decides that the father should have right over his children because they are born of his seed and are a part of his body. Yet again the *Traités* object: if this is the basis of the father's right, it ought to put the power of the mother far above that of the father.[71] In this graphic fashion, the *Traités* illustrate the ambiguity of such a priori principles as eternal reason, reason in itself.

The *Traités*, also, perform a useful function by attacking the decisive defects which such principles reveal: even if their absolute validity were granted for argument's sake, even if it were possible to apply these a priori principles unequivocally, and with the utmost consistency, they would prove to be ineffective in morals for another reason. For, in this case, they would form principles of such rigidity that no ethical life could develop under their rule.

If, under an eternal law, "le fils appartient naturellement au père," then it is impossible to annihilate this right, no matter how unhappy it renders the son or how little the father may deserve it.[72] The *Traités* draw, therefore, at least implicitly, the following valuable conclusion: merely formal principles a priori, such as eternal reason, are too flexible, too ambiguous in their common use. If, however, their equivocal application is prohibited, they become too rigid. That is, they fail from whatever point of view one may analyze their function in morals.

The utility principle, however, "ne s'appliquant qu'à l'intérêt des parties, se plie aux circonstances et s'accomode à tous les besoins."[72] That is, an ethics built up on the principle of utility is equally far removed from the sweeping relativism which does away with all principles, and the rigid absolutism which is completely blind toward changing facts. Theories which entirely ignore the weight of changing facts are, in morals,

[71] *Ibid.*, p. 120 f ("Principes de législation," chap. XIII, §7; Hildreth, p. 74 f).
[72] *Ibid.*, p. 122 (Hildreth, p. 76).

no more scientific than theories which speak of facts alone and neglect all interpretation of facts by principles.

Eighth, the principle of antipathy and sympathy makes another appearance in the *Traités*, though we have already heard a great deal about it in chapter XIII. But here we meet with an interesting qualification of the earlier argument. Like the *Introduction*, the *Traités* emphasize consistently that the moralist and the legislator can never be allowed to build up their theories on their sympathies and antipathies. But the *Traités* now add that even in the form of prejudices, the sympathies and antipathies of the *people*, unlike those of their *judges*, must be taken into account. "Oter une jouissance, une espérance, toute chimérique qu'elle est, c'est faire le même mal que si on ôtoit une jouissance, une espérance réelle."[73] In the calculation of pleasures and pains, prejudices and sympathies, as well as antipathies of all types, must be counted as real feelings and should by no means be dismissed arbitrarily. Only in his final moral valuations must the moralist exclude any sympathy and antipathy of his own which comes into conflict with the one categorical principle of general utility.

In other words, the moralist and the legislator must reckon with the sympathies and antipathies of men most carefully, as long as they only observe the emotional life of those they wish to judge. But, in their final judgment of the morality of human actions, the legislator and the moralist are never allowed to remain the slaves of the prejudices of those they judge. At this point they must free themselves from mere sympathy and antipathy.

To many statesmen and moralists, however, the reference to popular prejudices serves rather as a pretext than as a principle of moral judgment. The real motives of such statesmen are the same prejudices as those of the people whom they have to judge and whom they have to educate to value more useful pleasures. To Bentham, however, the whole result of his earlier reflections remains intact. No personal sympathy and antipathy, independent of or in contrast to the utility principle, must enter the final judgment of the moralist. But, as we learn now, this by no means involves the necessity of excluding impartial observation of other people's sympathies and antipathies. On the contrary, it includes this necessity, and it includes, also, the obligation to help people by political and general education to free themselves from harmful prejudices and to help them acquire, instead, the most useful sympathies

[73] *Ibid.*, p. 123 ("Principes de législation," chap. xiii, §8; Hildreth, p. 76).

and antipathies, after the moralist has impartially decided what these most pleasant, useful emotions are.

Ninth, under the head "Pétition de principe n'est pas raison" we meet again with ideas very familiar to us from Bentham's criticism of Blackstone.[74] Blackstone had inferred that the British Constitution represents a combination of the three different virtues of monarchy, aristocracy and democracy, because this constitution is a combination of these three forms of government. But, as in the *Fragment on Government*, Bentham asks: Was the union of these three types of government perhaps a union of their three different faults? Evidently, this question was not asked because it escaped attention that the whole argument merely begs the question: What should have been demonstrated had already been presupposed. It was taken for granted that the British constitution had only good qualities. Further, under the same head appears once more the criticism of the social contract which had appeared under head 6;[75] and this shows once again the absence of any methodical arrangement. Moreover, here too the argument itself adds nothing to those already mentioned in the *Fragment on Government*.

Tenth, the *Traités*, too, deal with the "imaginary" law of nature; but again, this is not done on any higher level of discussion than in *A Comment on the Commentaries*. Three points, however, are clearly marked out. First, in the theory of natural law in ethics, despite all appearance to the contrary, it is sentiments of pleasure or pain, it is inclinations and not laws which are called laws of nature. But this is to set language in opposition to itself. Laws are certainly not identical with inclinations; on the contrary, they are made for the purpose of restraining inclination.[76] "Les parens sont disposés, . . . sont inclinés . . . à élever leurs enfans, les parens . . . sont obligés . . . doivent élever leurs enfans: voilà deux propositions différentes. La première ne suppose pas la seconde; la seconde ne suppose pas la première."[77] This is another instance in which Bentham shows how clearly he separates "ought" from "is."

It is far more justifiable to blame the majority of advocates of natural law for their confusing "ought" and "is" than to criticize Bentham on that account. Only a few defenders of the Law of Nature, such as Kant and Fichte, maintain a strict differentiation between "ought" and "is."

---

[74] *Ibid.*, p. 127 f ("Principes de législation," chap. XIII, §9); 2nd edition, p. 121; Hildreth, p. 79. Cf. *A Fragment on Government*, 1776, chap. III, p. 20, scholium.

[75] *Ibid.*, p. 131 f (2nd edition, p. 124 f; Hildreth, p. 81 f).

[76] *Ibid.*, p. 133 ("Principes de législation," chap. XIII, §10); 2nd edition, p. 126; Hildreth, p. 83.

[77] *Ibid.*, p. 134 (Hildreth, p. 83 f).

But what is commonly called a law of nature, or a natural right, in ethics is in fact no law at all, i.e. it is nothing which "ought" to be; it is only an "is," an existing inclination, i.e. the contrary to all actual law; and "comment peut-on s'entendre avec un langage qui confond sous le même terme deux choses aussi distinctes?"[78] Why confuse clear language by the contradictory use of such metaphors as natural laws, and such metaphors as natural rights, which are only derivations from other metaphors? The second argument which the *Traités* use against the theory of the Law of Nature is this: according to Montesquieu and Blackstone for instance the natural law commands the father to support his children; and this "has caused the establishment of marriage which points out the person who ought to fulfill this obligation."[79] But if, in truth, a law of nature would command the father to support his children, then there would be no need for propping up this natural law by any laws of the state. The law of the state concerning the support of children would then be completely superfluous. "It would be kindling a torch to add light to the sun."[80] On the other hand, if laws of the state concerning the support of children are indispensable, then the corresponding law of nature proves its inutility, as it commands the same laws but not strongly enough.[81] This argument had already been developed in the *Comment on the Commentaries* in even richer detail.

The third argument used here against the law of nature is the following: one would suppose that, if there is a law of nature, nature has not dictated its laws without reason. But if so, would it not be safer, shorter and more persuasive to give us that reason directly, instead of urging upon us the will of an unknown legislator as itself an authority?[82] This reason for any law of nature is, according to the *Traités*, nothing but utility. It is true that utility has often been understood in a narrow sense and, having lent its name to most immoral actions, it has appeared contrary to morality. It thus became degraded and acquired a mercenary reputation: courage is now needed to restore it to honor. But there is no other way to ground morality firmly than to ground it on utility, on the empirical observation of all those facts conducive to the greatest possible utility. "Ne m'en croyez pas, croyez-en l'expérience, et surtout la

[78] *Ibid.*, p. 135 (Hildreth, p. 84).

[79] *Ibid.*, p. 133 f (2nd edition, 1820, p. 127; Hildreth, p. 83; Blackstone, "Commentaries," book 1, chap. 16).

[80] Bentham-Dumont, *Traités de Législation*, 1802, tome 1, p. 133 (Hildreth, p. 83).

[81] *Ibid.*, p. 135 (2nd edition, 1820, p. 127; Hildreth, p. 84).

[82] *Ibid.*, p. 139 (2nd edition, 1820, p. 131 f; Hildreth, p. 86 f).

vôtre."[83] If two actions have to be judged as regards their morality, only one procedure will do: we must calculate the pleasant and unpleasant effects of these two lines of action by careful empirical observation. Morally good or morally better is that action which promises the greater happiness. But the program of a consistent empiricism in ethics is certainly more instructively developed in the *Comment* than in the short final sentences of this rather summary and unmethodical polemic against ten types of false ethical reasoning.

The Arrangement of the Later Parts of the *Traités*

The remaining part of the first volume and the two other volumes of the *Traités* deal, according to their subtitles, mainly with juristic, political and also economic questions. The first volume in the first edition contains, in its later part, a treatise entitled "Vue générale d'un corps complet de législation." The second volume contains "Principes du code civil" and "Principes du code pénal." The third volume contains a "Mémoire" concerning one of Bentham's favorite ideas, the construction of a Panopticon, a reform prison; an essay on "La promulgation des lois"; another article entitled *"De l'influence des tems et des lieux en matière de législation."* All these treatises appear in an enlarged form also in Bowring's edition of Bentham's works.

In the *Traités*, 1802, tome II, pp. 1-236[84] cover the *Principles of the Civil Code* of Bentham's *Works*, 1843, vol. I, pp. 301-358. Only the appendix of this treatise which Bowring added in his edition of Bentham's works is lacking in the *Traités*.

Tome II, 1802, pp. 237-290[85] of the *Traités* cover adaptions from the *Introduction to the Principles of Morals and Legislation*, 1789, chapter XVI on the division of offenses, chapter XII on alarm and danger as the consequences of mischievous acts, chapter VIII on intentionality, chapter X on motives.

Tome II of the *Traités*, 1802, pp. 291-379[86] cover the *Principles of Penal Law* in Bentham's *Works*, 1843, vol. I, pp. 367-388.

Tome II of the *Traités*, 1802, pp. 380-434 and Tome III, 1802, pp. 1-199[87] are an extract from the *Rationale of Punishment* in Bentham's *Works*, 1843,

[83] *Ibid.*, pp. 138 ff ("Principes de législation," chap. XIII, §10); Bentham, *The Theory of Legislation*, ed. R. Hildreth, 1864, p. 86 f.

[84] In the later editions of the *Traités*, tome I, pp. 88-236 (*The Theory of Legislation*, by J. Bentham, translated by Hildreth, 1864, pp. 93-236).

[85] In the later editions of the *Traités*, tome II, pp. 1-53 (Hildreth, pp. 239-266).

[86] In the later editions of the *Traités*, tome II, pp. 54-138 (Hildreth, 1864, pp. 271-321).

[87] In the later editions of the *Traités*, tome II, pp. 139-379 (Hildreth, 1864, pp. 322-472).

part II, pp. 397-580. (Especially tome III, 1802, pp. 24-199[88] follows closely *Works*, part II, pp. 538-580.)

Tome III of the *Traités* contains in all editions a number of essays which are not to be found in the translation of the *Traités* by Hildreth. Aside from these essays this third volume gives in the first edition part of the *Principes du code pénal*, but in place of this the later editions contain the essay *Vue générale d'un corps complet de législation* which the first edition had printed in the first volume.

This essay, the *Vue générale d'un corps complet de législation*,[89] covers the first thirty-three chapters of *A General View of a Complete Code of Law* in Bentham's *Works*, 1843, part V, pp. 155-209. Chapter XXXIV of this treatise, *Works*, part V, pp. 209 f. is not to be found in Dumont's edition.

The essay on the Panopticon in the third volume of the *Traités* is an extract from Bentham's three writings on the Panopticon, printed in 1791 and reprinted in Bentham's *Works*, 1843, part VII, pp. 37-172. This *Mémoire sur un nouveau principe pour construire des maisons d'inspection, et nommément des maisons de force* was sent by Bentham in 1791 to Garran de Coulon.[90]

The essay *Promulgation des raisons des lois*, tome III of the *Traités*, 1802, pp. 273-301,[91] covers Bentham's *Works*, 1843, part I, pp. 155-163. Its English title is *Essay on the Promulgation of Laws and the Reasons thereof*. The appendix to this essay, tome III of the *Traités*, 1802, pp. 302-321, an appendix entitled *Code pénal. Titre particulier*, is to be found in English in Bentham's *Works*, 1843, part I, pp. 164-168 under the head *Specimen of a Penal Code*.

Tome III of the *Traités*, 1802, pp. 323-395[92] cover Bentham's *Works*, 1843, part I, pp. 169-194, the *Essay on the Influence of Time and Place in Matters of Legislation*.

Part of the confusion in the arrangement of the *Traités* has been cleared up by C. K. Ogden in his introduction to Hildreth's edition of Bentham's *The Theory of Legislation*, 1931, p. XXXVIII. But I hope that I have been able to elucidate a few more of the inconcinnities Ogden did not explain.

As I shall give a summary view of the ethical thought in Bentham's later juristic, economic and religious writings, I think it sufficient to mark out only a few ethically relevant points in those parts of the *Traités* which do not deal explicitly with fundamental questions of ethics.

[88] In the later editions of the *Traités*, tome II, pp. 193-379 (Hildreth, pp. 371-472).
[89] In the later editions of the *Traités*, tome III, pp. 185 ff; in the first edition of the *Traités*, 1802, tome I, pp. 141-361.
[90] See *Traités*, 1802, tome III, p. 203.
[91] In the later editions of the *Traités*, tome III, pp. 69-112.
[92] In the later editions of the *Traités*, tome III, pp. 113-179.

Ethical Observations Related to the Principles of Civil Law, Penal Law and Politics

The main ends of civil law are listed in the *Traités* under four heads. They are (1) to provide subsistence, (2) to produce abundance, (3) to favor equality and (4) to maintain security—all four ends representing only applications of the general principle of utility.[93] Liberty is not ranked among these principal objects of the happiness of civil society because, in Bentham's view, both personal and political liberty are to be regarded as concomitants of security.[94] Among the four objects in which public happiness consists, subsistence ought to be preferred to abundance and security to equality.[95] Nevertheless, more care is bestowed here on the defense of abundance than of equality. For, although abundance is often condemned by being called luxury, it is abundance alone which can provide mankind, in case of wars and all sorts of accidents, with the needed reserves of subsistence.[96] Absolute equality, however, according to the *Traités*, is a utopianism, whether it is equality in personal and civil rights or in economic rights.

It is impossible to give the son the same rights as the father in his father's house, to give the maniac the same rights to imprison others as others have to imprison him.[97] Above all, the attempt to establish absolute equality of possessions would, in Bentham's opinion, completely prejudice the pre-eminent good, security. In fact, as he points out, if equality of property could exist for a day, the revolutions of the next day would overthrow it. The introduction of a community of goods, carried through by small groups in the first effervescence of religious zeal, has, in his eyes, led to nothing but unhappiness, laziness, distrust, and the breakdown of all the benefits of free competition. Accordingly, not perfect equality of wealth, but only the diminution of inequality ought to be the moral aim of society.[98] It is true that, in his

---

[93] Bentham-Dumont, *Traités de législation civile et pénale*, 1802, tome II, pp. 6 ff, "Principes du code civil," première partie, chap. II (2nd edition, pp. 150 ff; Bentham, *A Theory of Legislation*, ed. by Richard Hildreth, 1864, p. 96 f).

[94] *Ibid.*, p. 8 (2nd edition, tome I, p. 152; Hildreth, 1864, p. 97).

[95] *Ibid.*, p. 9 f, "Principes du code civil," chap. III (2nd edition, tome I, p. 153 f; Hildreth, p. 98).

[96] *Ibid.*, p. 16, "Principes du code civil," chap. V (2nd edition, tome I, p. 160; Hildreth, p. 101).

[97] *Ibid.*, p. 11 (2nd edition, tome I, p. 155; Hildreth, p. 99).

[98] *Ibid.*, pp. 48 ff, "Principes du code civil," première partie, chap. XI (Hildreth, p. 120 f). Compare *ibid.*, "Principes du code civil," seconde partie, chap. VI, pp. 169 ff: "Intercommunauté des biens.—Ses inconveniens."

later writings, Bentham upholds essentially the same economic view. Yet the tenor of his later argument is more academic and disinterested and smacks less of political eloquence and propaganda than Dumont's popularizing version. Karl Marx and Friedrich Engels obviously knew only Dumont's editions of Bentham's writings; and so it is, in all probability, Dumont's rendering of Bentham's text which evoked their harsh criticism of Bentham as a leading, typical "bourgeois," as "ein Genie in der bürgerlichen Dummheit."

It would lead us too far afield, were we to discuss here, in any detail, Bentham's views on economics and politics, his defense of the right of property against Beccaria,[99] his suggestions on limiting the testamentary power in order to create a more just distribution of goods in the least violent and revolutionary manner,[100] his doctrine of slavery,[101] of the poor law system,[102] of inflation and deflation, "l'élévation forcée du taux des monnois" and forced reduction of the rate of interest,[103] of the relations between state and religion,[104] between state and arts,[105] of the

[99] *Ibid.*, p. 37 f, chap. IX (2nd edition, tome I, p. 181 f; Hildreth, p. 114).

[100] *Ibid.*, pp. 52 ff, chap. XII (2nd edition, tome I, p. 195; Hildreth, p. 122).

[101] *Ibid.*, p. 53, chap. XII (2nd edition, tome I, p. 196; Hildreth, p. 122 f). Even as regards the abolition of slavery the *Traités* recommends only "une operation lente," but not treading justice under foot for the sake of introducing a new social order. That nevertheless the *Traités* plead for accelerating the emancipation of slaves, as do the other writings of Bentham, see *Traités*, 1802, tome II, pp. 179 ff, "Principes du code civil," troisième partie, chap. II. Compare Bentham, *Works*, 1843, part v, p. 41b ("Manual of Political Economy," chap. III, §2, note): "Gradual abolition and intermediate modification of those personal obligations which come under the head of slavery."

[102] *Ibid.*, tome II, "Principes du code civil," première partie, chap. XIV, sect. I, pp. 59 ff (2nd edition, tome I, pp. 202 ff; Hildreth, pp. 127 ff).

[103] *Ibid.*, tome II, "Principes du code civil," première partie, chap. XV, §2 and 3, pp. 81 ff (2nd edition, tome I, 1820, p. 223 f; Hildreth, p. 140 f).

[104] *Ibid.*, tome II, "Principes du code civil," première partie, chap. XIV, sect. 2, pp. 69 ff (2nd edition, tome I, 1820, pp. 212 ff; Hildreth, p. 133 f). See e.g. p. 69 f: "Les Ministres de la religion . . . rendroient de vrais services à l'Etat, moins ils seroient sujets à ces maladies des dogmes et des controverses, qui naissent de l'envie de se distinguer, et de l'impuissance d'être utile. Il faut diriger leur activité et leur ambition vers des objets salutaires pour les empêcher de devenir malfaisantes. Sous ce rapport, ceux même qui ne reconnoîtroient pas les bases de la sanction religieuse, ne pourroient pas se plaindre qu'on les fît contribuer aux frais de son entretien, puisqu'ils participeroient à ses avantages. Mais s'il y avoit dans un pays une grande diversité de cultes et de religions, et que le Législateur ne fût pas gêné par un établissement antérieur ou des considérations particulières, il seroit plus conformé à la liberté et à l'égalité d'appliquer à l'entretien de chaque Église, les contributions de chaque Communauté religieuse."

[105] *Ibid.*, tome II, "Principes du code civil," première partie, chap. XIV, sect. 3, pp. 71 ff (2nd edition, 1820, tome I, pp. 214 ff; Hildreth, pp. 135 ff). See e.g. p. 74

rights of minorities,[106] of the law on guardianship[107] and of matrimonial laws.[108] However, in the midst of these problems concerning the civil law a few remarks are dropped which are of greater importance, because they throw new light on some main points of Bentham's moral theory.

IMPARTIALITY WITHIN THE ALGEDONIC CALCULUS

Rightly and quite emphatically Bentham warns us here against basing moral judgments on feelings which men ought to have instead of those which they really have. "Il est absurde de vouloir démontrer par des calculs, qu'un homme doit se trouver heureux, lorsqu'il se trouve malheureux . . . il est absurde de raisonner sur le bonheur des hommes

---

(Hildreth, p. 136): "On pourra s'occuper des Comédiens, des Peintres et des Architectes, quand on aura dédommagé les individus des pertes occasionnées par les guerres, les délits et des calamités physiques, quand on aura pourvu à la subsistance des indigens: jusque-là cette préférence accordée à de brillans accessoires sur des objets de nécessité, ne sauroit être justifiée." Here, as elsewhere, Bentham does not show himself a very judicious expert on matters of arts, not even on questions of the social and political function of the arts.

[106] *Ibid.*, tome II, 1802, "Principes du code civil," première partie, chap. XV, §4, pp. 83 ff (2nd edition, tome I, pp. 224 ff; Hildreth, pp. 141 ff). See e.g. p. 83 (Hildreth, p. 141): Il y a "des vexations exercées sur une secte, sur un parti, sur une classes d'hommes, sous le prétexte vague de quelque délit politique, en sorte qu'on feint d'imposer la confiscation comme une peine, lorsqu'au fond on a institué le délit pour amener la confiscation. L'histoire présente plusieurs exemples de ce brigandage. Les Juifs en ont été souvent les objets: ils étoient trop riches pour n'être pas toujours coupables"; p. 85 (Hildreth, p. 143): "L'envie n'est jamais plus à son aise que lorsqu'elle peut se cacher sous le masque du bien public; mais le bien public ne demande que la reforme des places inutiles, il ne demande pas le malheur des individus réformés." Or see *Traités de législation*, 1802, tome II, "Principes du code pénal," première partie, chap. XI, p. 271 f (Hildreth, p. 258): "Moins une partie . . . étoit hors d'état de se défendre, plus le sentiment naturel de compassion devoit agir avec force. Une loi de l'honneur, venant à l'appui de cet instinct de pitié, fait un devoir impérieux de ménager le foible, d'épargner celui qui ne peut pas résister. Premier indice d'un caractère dangereux, foiblesse opprimée."

[107] Bentham-Dumont, *Traités de législation*, 1802, tome II, "Principes du code civil," troisième partie, chap. III, pp. 192 ff (Hildreth, pp. 209 ff).

[108] *Ibid.*, chap. V, chap. IV, pp. 202 ff, 198 ff (Hildreth, pp. 215 f, 213 ff). Compare *ibid.*, "Principes du code civil," seconde partie, chap. III, "Autre moyen d'acquérir—succession," article premier, p. 142 (Hildreth, p. 178; 2nd edition of the *Traités de législation*, 1820, tome I, p. 279): "Point de distinction entre les sexes: ce qui est dit par rapport à l'un, s'étend à l'autre. La part le l'un sera toujours égale à la part de l'autre Raison. Bien de l'égalité.—S'il y avoit quelque différence, elle devroit être en faveur de plus foible, en faveur des femmes qui ont plus de besoins, moins de moyens d'acquérir et de faire valoir ce qu'elles ont. Mais le plus fort a eu toutes les préférences. Pourquoi? Parce que le plus fort a fait les lois."

autrement que par leurs propres désirs et par leur propres sensations."[109]
This is, no doubt, a most useful warning against drawing the distinction
between *is* and *ought* at the wrong point in ethics, i.e. between moral
and immoral pleasures and pains instead of drawing the line between
more pleasure and more pain.

Expressed in a more explicit way, this statement of the *Traités* says:
all legal and moral *ought* has to be based on a calculation of pleasures,
on the surplus of happiness in such a calculation; but it would be a fundamental mistake to ground this calculation on pleasures which ought
to be pleasures, instead of those which are actually felt as pleasures. To
base the moral arithmetic on feelings which men ought to feel would be
a most flagrant begging of the question; for the knowledge of what we
ought to do, or what we ought to feel, is the final aim and end of scientific ethics, not its presupposition. Any utilitarianism that introduces
a basic distinction between qualitatively higher and lower pleasures
evades the issue without noticing it.

Strangely enough, contemporary French existentialism is, on this
point, far more consistently utilitarian than J. S. Mill in his polemics
against Bentham. Simone de Beauvoir frequently expressed Bentham's
ideas in this regard with remarkable emphasis. "L'homme ignorant et
désherité a, lui aussi, des intérêts à défendre; lui seul est compétent pour
décider de ses espoirs et de sa confiance."[110] "La joie, . . . le bien d'un individu ou d'un groupe d'individus mérite d'être pris comme un but
absolu de notre action; . . . nous ne sommes pas autorisés à décider a
priori de ce bien."[111] "Il n'aide rien à la libération des hommes qu'un
clochard prenne plaisir à boire un litre de vin . . . Cependant . . . vouloir
l'homme libre . . . c'est vouloir le dévoilement de l'être dans la joie de
l'existence; . . . il faut que la joie d'exister soit affirmée en chacun, à
chaque instant . . . L'économie de temps, la conquête du loisir n'ont
aucun sens si le rire d'un enfant qui joue ne nous touche pas."[112] In
contrast to Bentham, Simone de Beauvoir rejects any "tranquille calcul
mathématique" in these questions of judging human pleasures.[113] But
she evidently agrees that, in our moral judgments of the value of human pleasures, we have first to take these pleasures seriously for what
they are, not for what they ought to be.

[109] Bentham-Dumont, *Traités de législation*, 1802, tome II, "Principes du code
civil," troisième partie, chap. II, p. 181 (Bentham, *The Theory of Legislation*, ed.
R. Hildreth, 1864, p. 202).

[110] S. de Beauvoir, *Pour une morale de l'ambiguité*, 1947, p. 196.

[111] *Ibid.*, p. 198 and compare p. 199.   [112] *Ibid.*, p. 189 f.

[113] *Ibid.*, p. 207.

In a similar way, Bentham insists that no "ought," and no discrimination between morally higher and morally lower qualities, must be used before a morally neutral calculation of simple facts has been carried out. Any premature introduction of a moral valuation in the calculus of pleasures makes the whole calculus superfluous, because then the moral judgment is uncritically based on those dogmatic valuations, instead of on an impartial calculation of neutral facts. Unless the moral "ought" is consistently based on a calculation of neutral, factual feelings, and not on other moral beliefs, the whole method of moral arithmetic is deprived of its very meaning.

As the *Traités* point out in another connection, "il faudroit avoir un thermomètre moral."[114] This seems to me a happy analogy to ward off some common misinterpretations of Bentham's ideas about an indirect measurement of feelings. For the analogy shows that, as in the case of a thermometer, the indirect measurement may consist in the reduction of certain phenomena (which are to be described and to be interpreted) to other phenomena with a common denominator—phenomena which differ only as to the shares they possess of the common measure. It is necessary to make perceptible "tous les degrés de bonheur ou de malheur"[114] as degrees of happiness or misery, which differ only quantitatively, not qualitatively,[115] from each other, just as do the degrees of heat on the scale of a thermometer. Although normal temperature and high fever represent, qualitatively, quite different states of health, the thermometer indicates these differences in exclusively quantitative terms, that is, in a much more precise way than any qualitative description could do.

Whether this measurement of pleasure and pain can ever be carried out in a completely satisfactory and precise manner is a question which the *Traités*, more than many other writings of Bentham, seem to place in doubt. They explain the importance and the difficulties of these problems of a "mental pathology" in the following way: "Pathologie est un terme usité en médecine mais il ne l'est pas dans la morale, où il est également nécessaire. J'appelle *Pathologie* l'étude, la connoissance des

[114] *Ibid.*, tome II, p. 18, "Principes du code civil," chap. VI (2nd edition, tome I, p. 162; Hildreth, p. 102).
[115] In my essay "Über einige Hauptmethodenfragen der modernen Ethik von Kant bis zur Gegenwart," in *Logos*, ed. by Richard Kroner, Band XIX, 1930, pp. 377 ff, I still shared the common prejudice that J. S. Mill's opposition to Bentham's thesis of the comparability of qualitatively different pleasures means "einen—wenn auch nicht zu überschätzenden—Fortschritt."

sensations, des affections, des passions et de leurs effets sur le bonheur. La législation, qui jusqu'ici n'a été fondée en grande partie que sur le terrain mouvant des préjugés et de l'instinct, doit enfin s'élever sur la base inébranlable des sensations et de l'expérience. Il faudroit avoir un thermomètre moral, qui rendit sensibles tous les degrés de bonheur ou de malheur. C'est un terme de perfection qu'il est impossible d'atteindre, mais qu'il est bon d'avoir devant les yeux. Je sais qu'un examen scrupuleux du plus ou du moins, en fait de peine et de plaisir, paroîtra d'abord une entreprise minutieuse. On dira qu'il faut agir en gros dans les affaires humaines, et se contenter d'une vague approximation. C'est le langage de l'indifférence ou de l'incapacité. Les sensations des hommes sont assez régulières pour devenir l'objet d'une science et d'un art. Et jusque là, on ne verra que des essais, des tâtonnemens, des efforts irréguliers et peu suivis. La médecine a pour base des axiomes de pathologie physique. La morale est la médecine de l'âme: la législation en est la partie pratique: elle doit avoir pour base des axiomes de pathologie mentale."[116] This is not too confident, too self-assured a statement. Nevertheless, as we see, the *Traités* consider any hedonic measurement attainable, however imperfect, as infinitely firmer than "the quicksands of prejudice and instinct" on which ethics has built up its theories so far.

In contrast to ordinary moral theories, and in at least partial agreement with Kant, Bentham did not acknowledge any fundamental difference between the method of ethics and that of natural science. On the contrary, as we saw, he tried to hint as often as possible at strict analogies between the procedures of inquiry in both fields. Even more, however, he rejects any discrepancy between the results of moral and political science, or between pure theory and practice in morals—on this point in full agreement with Kant.[117] As the *Traités* point out, "ce qu'on appelle injuste en morale ne peut-être innocent en politique."[118] Clas-

---

[116] Bentham-Dumont, *Traités de législation*, 1802, tome II, "Principes du code civil," première partie, chap. VI, p. 18 f (2nd edition, 1820, tome I, p. 162 f; Hildreth, p. 102). Compare *ibid.*, p. 28 (2nd edition, tome I, p. 172; Hildreth, p. 109): "Ce n'est qu'avec beaucoup de patience et de méthode qu'on parvient à réduire en propositions rigoureuses une multitude incohérente de sentimens confus."

[117] See I. Kant, "Über den Gemeinspruch: Das mag in der Theorie richtig sein, gilt aber nicht für die Praxis," 1793 (*Kants Gesammelte Schriften*, ed. by Königliche Preussische Akademie der Wissenschaften, Erste Abteilung, Band VIII, S. 289 ff), containing a special polemic against Hobbes' and Moses Mendelssohn's ways of contradistinction between ethics and interior as well as exterior politics.

[118] Bentham-Dumont, *Traités de législation civile et pénale*, 1802, tome I, p. 76,

sical education is, according to Bentham, responsible for the common propagation of the contrary conviction. In contrast to the praise accorded by the Romans to the most immoral political actions, Bentham always insists on the very idealistic—and realistic—view that no antagonism between morals and politics can be admitted without denying the very end of both, the happiness of mankind.

Bentham goes even one step further in his denial of any dissension between moral theory and practice. He observes well: "Des hommes bien intentionnés pensent qu'on ne doit ôter à la bonne morale aucun de ses appuis, lors même qu'il porte à faux. Cette erreur revient à celle des devots, qui ont cru servir la religion par des fraudes pieuses: au lieu de la fortifier, ils l'ont affoiblie, en l'exposant à la dérision de ses adversaires. Quand un esprit depravé a triomphé d'un faux argument, il croit avoir triomphé de la morale même."[119] This argument, too, seems to me sound and important. One of the main roots of moral skepticism is certainly the discovery of unsound or even deceptive reasoning in morals, the acquaintance with false arguments which are, nevertheless, said to be of practical moral value in spite of their theoretical deficiency.

Uncritical, unthinking zeal has done as much harm to the good cause of moral reasoning as to that of religion. Dogmatic, uncritical presuppositions in ethics do not strengthen its persuasive power or its educational value. Too often they lead the bold, inquiring, scientific mind to complete ethical nihilism.

In the field of penal law, as we have pointed out, the *Traités* touch on a number of problems which, without any visible reason, were removed from their proper place in the introductory part of the work. We find here chapters on intentions and motives of actions which are, in the *Introduction,* closely connected with the analysis of the other elements of action and should be linked up with them also in the *Traités.* On the other hand, the analysis of mischievous consequences given in the introductory part of the *Traités* in the first volume, and those given in the chapters on penal law in the second volume, are not in complete accord. And, in addition to these inconsistencies, certain problems of civil law appear here again giving new evidence of the correctness of Bentham's

---

"Principes du code civil," première partie, chap. xv (2nd edition, 1820, tome I, p. 218; Hildreth, p. 137).

[119] *Ibid.,* tome II, "Principes du code civil," troisième partie, chap. v, sect. I, p. 211 (2nd edition, tome I, p. 345; Hildreth, p. 221).

opinion that it is hardly possible to draw any sharp line of demarcation between a civil and a penal code.[120]

As to the elements of actions, we find nothing new here. On the contrary, in the chapter on "intention" it is explicitly granted that this difficult subject is not dealt with here exhaustively.[121] As a matter of fact, in comparison with the masterpiece of analysis on intentions in the *Introduction*, the corresponding remarks of the *Traités* are scanty; and much the same applies to the chapter on motives. This chapter merely summarizes the results of the corresponding inquiry of the *Introduction*, and, although it embellishes them with some popular examples, it does not work out the whole problem as methodically as its model.

With regard to the motives of actions, the *Traités* simply state: "On parle vulgairement des motifs comme étant bons ou mauvais. C'est une erreur. Tout motif, en dernière analyse, est la perspective d'un plaisir à se procurer ou d'une peine à éviter. Or, le même motif qui porte en certains cas à faire une action réputée bonne ou indifférente, peut en d'autres cas porter à une action réputée mauvaise. . . . Un homme pieux fonde un hôpital pour les pauvres, un autre va faire le pélerinage de la Mecque, un autre assassine un Prince qu'il croit hérétique; leur motif peut être exactement le même, le désir de se concilier la faveur divine, selon les opinions différentes qu'ils s'en sont formées. Un géomètre vit dans une retraite austère et se livre aux travaux les plus profonds, un homme du monde se ruine . . . par un faste excessif, un prince entreprend une conquête et sacrifie des milliers d'hommes à ses projets . . . ; tous ces hommes peuvent être animés par un motif exactement semblable, le désir de la réputation. . . . On pourroit examiner ainsi tous les motifs, et l'on verroit que chacun d'eux peut donner naissance aux actions les plus louables comme aux plus criminelles. Il ne faut donc pas regarder les motifs comme exclusivement bons ou mauvais. . . . Pour juger une action, il faut regarder d'abord à ses effets, abstraction faite de toute autre chose. Les effets étant bien constatés, on peut en certains cas remonter au motif, en observant son influence sur la grandeur de l'alarme, sans s'arrêter à la qualité bonne ou mauvaise que son nom vulgaire . . . semble lui attribuer. Ainsi le motif le plus approuvé ne sauroit transformer une action pernicieuse en action utile ou indifférente; et le motif le plus condamné

---

[120] See Bentham, *Introduction to the Principles of Morals and Legislation*, 1789, chap. XVII, sect. 1.

[121] Bentham-Dumont, *Traités de législation civile et pénale*, 1802, tome II, p. 258, "Principes du code pénal," chap. VI (2nd edition, tome II, p. 20; Hildreth, p. 251).

ne sauroit transformer une action utile en action mauvaise. Tout ce qu'il peut faire, c'est de rehausser ou de rabaisser plus ou moins sa qualité morale:... Observons qu'on ne doit s'arrêter à la considération du motif, que dans le cas où il est manifeste et pour ainsi dire palpable. Il seroit souvent bien difficile d'arriver à la connoissance du vrai motif ou du motif dominant, lorsque l'action a pu être également produite par différens motifs, ou que plusieurs ont pu coopérer à sa formation. Il faut se défier, dans cette interpretation douteuse, de la malignité du coeur humain, et de la disposition générale à faire briller la sagacité de l'esprit aux dépens de la bonté. Nous nous trompons même de bonne-foi sur les mouvemens qui nous font agir; et relativement à leurs propres motifs, les hommes sont des aveugles volontaires tout prêts à s'emporter contre l'oculiste qui veut lever la cataracte de l'ignorance et des préjugés."[122] All this is certainly in line with the teaching of the *Introduction* on motives. Nevertheless, at least epistemologically, it is not the whole of the story given there. Even worse, despite the general disbelief in bad motives in themselves which is expressed here, in a later part of the "principes du code pénal" three pernicious desires are enumerated[123] which, at least by implication, are said to be bad motives in themselves: malevolent passions, the appetite for strong drinks and idleness.

Primarily, it is interesting to see how the later chapters of the *Traités*, in their popularizing tendencies, couple the *Introduction's* doctrine of motives with quite different traditional teachings having only an apparent similarity. Confining itself strictly to methodological considerations, the *Introduction* arrived at the conclusion that every human motive is good in itself, if judged without reference to the consequences brought about by that motive.

The *Traités* avoid such provocative, almost paradoxical, theses which flatly contradict common ethical assumptions; they content themselves with saying that "motives ... ought not be regarded as exclusively good or bad."[124] Moreover, from these ethical-*epistemological* problems the *Traités* immediately shift to the entirely different *psychological* problem of whether the human heart contains prevailingly good or bad motives; and the *Traités* decide "que le coeur humain n'a point de pas-

---

[122] *Ibid.*, tome II, pp. 263 f, 266 f, "Principes du code pénal," première partie, chap. VIII (2nd edition, tome II, pp. 25 f, 27 f; Hildreth, pp. 253 f, 256).

[123] *Ibid.*, p. 27, quatrième partie, chap. IV (2nd edition, tome II, p. 219 f; Hildreth, p. 373).

[124] Bentham, *The Theory of Legislation*, ed. by R. Hildreth, 1864, p. 373.

357

sion absolument mauvaise. Il n'est aucune qui n'ait besoin d'être dirigée, aucune qu'on doive détruire. Lorsque l'Ange Gabriel préparoit le Prophète Mahomet pour sa divine mission, il lui arracha du coeur une tache noire qui contenoit la semence du mal. Malheureusement cette opération n'est pas practicable dans le coeur des hommes ordinaires. Les semences du bien et les semences du mal sont inséparablement mêlées. Les inclinations sont gouvernées par les motifs. Mais les motifs sont toutes les peines et tous les plaisirs, toutes les peines à éviter, tous les plaisirs à poursuivre. Or, tous ces motifs peuvent produire toutes sortes d'effets, depuis les meilleurs jusqu'aux plus mauvais. Ce sont des arbres qui portent des fruits excellens ou des poisons, selon l'exposition où ils se trouvent, selon la culture du jardinier, et même selon le vent qui règne et la température du jour. La plus pure bienveillance, trop reservée dans son objet, ou se méprenant dans ses moyens, produira des crimes. Les affections personelles, quoiqu'elles puissent devenir occasionellement nuisibles sont constamment les plus nécessaires, et malgré leur difformité, les passions malveillantes sont tout au moins utiles, comme moyens de défense, comme sauve-gardes contre les invasions de l'intérêt personnel. Il ne s'agit donc de déraciner aucune des affections du coeur humain, puisqu'il n'en est aucune qui ne joue son rôle dans le système de l'utilité."[125] In any case, the *Traités* insist "que le coeur humain ne renferme point de perversité originale et incurable."[126] In this popularizing manner the *Traités* substitute a rejection of the religious dogma of original sin for a quite different type of inquiry—an acute epistemological-ethical analysis concerning the criterion of morality or immorality in motives.

Yet it is only this epistemological-ethical analysis carried out in the *Introduction* on which Bentham based his whole theory of morals. It is only this critical rejection of the uncritical doctrine of bad motives in themselves which can provide a justification for the radicalism of Bentham's ethics of consequences. The religious belief in the non-existence of originally bad motives can never form an adequate equivalent for Bentham's critical analysis of motives. For these analyses concern something entirely different: the subordinate role which the mere evaluation of motives must play in the formation of any ethical judgment.

[125] Bentham-Dumont, *Traités de législation civile et pénale*, 1802, tome III, pp. 27 ff, "Principes du code pénal," quatrième partie, chap. IV (2nd edition, 1820, tome II, p. 219 f; Hildreth, p. 373 f).

[126] *Ibid.*, tome III, p. 191, "Principes du code pénal," quatrième partie, chap. XXII (2nd edition, tome II, p. 371; Hildreth, p. 467).

Only in a note do the *Traités* point to the desirability of a neutral nomenclature of motives. This note tells us that such an unbiased terminology can avoid many seeming paradoxes of language in ethics, for instance, our speaking of good motives which are, nevertheless, causes of evil actions and our speaking of evil motives which are, nevertheless, the causes of good acts.[127] But this timid note is certainly a poor substitute for the bold and searching deductions which the *Introduction* offers on the subject; and the *Traités* themselves admit they do not wish to enter into "une discussion plus profonde sur les motifs."[128] The final exposition of the problem of motives is given only by Bentham's *Table of the Springs of Action* in 1817.

As in the "principes du code civil," we find in the "principes du code pénal" of the *Traités* the discussion of a great multitude of juristic and political topics in no systematic order and with numerous repetitions. No examination of details from these discussions is necessary for our exposition of Bentham's ethics. I shall content myself with the mere mention of Bentham's condemnation of tyrannicide,[129] his far-reaching defense of divorce,[130] his dispraise of gambling,[131] his indulgence toward dueling,[132] his suggestions of insurances against offenses,[133] his estimate

---

[127] *Ibid.*, tome II, p. 266, "Principes du code pénal," première partie, chap. VIII (2nd edition, tome II, p. 28; Hildreth, p. 255).

[128] *Ibid.*, p. 265 f (2nd edition, tome II, p. 27; Hildreth, p. 257).

[129] *Ibid.*, tome II, p. 287, "Principes du code pénal," première partie, chap. XIV (2nd edition, 1820, p. 50; Hildreth, p. 268).

[130] *Ibid.*, tome III, p. 50, "Principes du code pénal," quatrième partie, chap. V, sect. 3 (2nd edition, tome II, p. 240; Hildreth, p. 387): "On doit autoriser le divorce sous les restrictions convenables. Au lieu d'un mariage rompu dans le fait, et qui ne subsiste qu'en apparence, le divorce conduit naturellement à un mariage reel." (The discussion of this topic is to be found under the following head: "Faire en sorte qu'un désir donné se satisfasse sans préjudice, ou avec le moindre préjudice possible.") Compare in the "Principes du code civil" the head "Du mariage," *ibid.*, 1802, tome II, pp. 202 ff, troisième partie, chap. V, sect. 2 (2nd edition, tome II, pp. 346 ff; Hildreth, p. 221).

[131] *Ibid.*, 1802, tome III, p. 33, "Principes du code pénal," quatrième partie, chap. IV (2nd edition, tome II, p. 223; Hildreth, p. 377): "J'exclus seulement les jeux de hasard." Compare *ibid.*, tome III, p. 118, chap. XV (2nd edition, tome II, p. 305; Hildreth, p. 425); compare in "The Principles of the Civil Code," Hildreth, p. 106.

[132] *Ibid.*, 1802, tome II, p. 348, seconde partie, chap. XIV (2nd edition, tome II, p. 108; Hildreth, p. 302); further *ibid.*, tome III, p. 43 f, quatrième partie, chap. V, sect. 1, no. 3 (2nd edition, tome II, p. 234 f; Hildreth, p. 383 f; Bentham, *Works*, 1843, part II, p. 380 f). In later years, however, Bentham pleaded for the prevention of dueling by legislation and gave the following reasons for it: "Mere insensibility to danger of pain and death is a virtue which man possesses in jointtenancy with the bull, the bear and their challenger—the dog. . . . In former days

of coffee and tea as more moral beverages than the inebriating liquors,[134] his general explanation of punishment as a cure which should be reduced as far as possible to pecuniary compensation,[135] his frequent defense of the character of Negroes and Jews against misinterpretation,[136] his rejection of too ascetic an observation of Sunday,[137] his fight against

---

I thought I saw some benefits from . . . propensity to duelling . . . and committed the mention of them to writing; . . . on further consideration I have arrived at the persuasion that they amount to little, if anything, and that, at any rate, they are, in a prodigious degree, outweighed by the mischievous effects" (Bentham, *Works*, 1843, part xxi, p. 14a, Letter to the Duke of Wellington of March 22, 1829); compare a note in Bentham's Memorandum-Book of 1821, *Works*, 1843, part xx, p. 530b: "Duelling.—The man who values himself on his personal courage independently of the application made of it, values himself on that which is possessed in a higher degree by a dog, especially, when he is mad." Compare C. K. Ogden's notes to his edition of Bentham's *The Theory of legislation*, 1931, p. 532 f. Still in the "Rationale of Judicial Evidence" apparently less marked rejections of dueling are to be found, see e.g. Bentham, *Works*, 1843, part xiii, p. 22a, note, book v, chap. iv, §2 and *ibid.*, part xiv, p. 413b, book ix, part 3, chap. iv, §3. Bentham's most cogent condemnation of dueling is perhaps to be found in his *Deontology*, 1834, tome ii, pp. 309 ff, where he objects especially to the fact that dueling places the "innocent on a level with the guilty."

[133] Bentham-Dumont, *Traités de législation civile et pénale*, 1802, tome iii, pp. 196 ff, "Principes du code pénal," quatrième partie, chap. xxii (2nd edition, tome ii, pp. 376 ff; Hildreth, pp. 470 ff).

[134] *Ibid.*, tome iii, pp. 32, 31, chap. iv: "L'Introduction des liqueurs non enivrantes, dont le café et le thé sont les principales . . . est l'introduction d'un amusement innocent. . . . Ces deux articles, que des esprits superficiels seront étonnés de voir figurer dans un catalogue d'objets moraux, sont d'autant plus utiles, qu'ils viennent directement en concurrence avec les liqueurs enivrantes" (2nd edition, tome ii, pp. 225, 224; Hildreth, p. 376).

[135] *Ibid.*, 1802, tome iii, p. 191, "Principes du code pénal," quatrième partie, chap. xxii (2nd edition, tome ii, p. 371; Hildreth, p. 467).

[136] *Ibid.*, tome iii, p. 126, "Principes du code pénal," quatrième partie, chap. xxvi (2nd edition, tome ii, p. 311 f): "Le voyage de Mungo-Park, en Afrique, a répresenté les Noirs sous le point de vue le plus intéressant; leur simplicité, la force de leurs affections domestiques, la peinture de leurs mœurs innocents, a augmenté l'intérêt public en leur faveur. Les écrivains satiriques affoiblissent ce sentiment. Quand on a lu Voltaire, se sent-on dispose en faveur des Juifs? S'il avoit eu plus de bien-veillance à leur egard, en exposant l'avalissement où on les tient, il auroit expliqué les traits les moins favorables de leur caractère, et montré le remède à côté du mal." Compare 2nd edition, 1820, tome ii, p. 39, "Principes du code pénal," première partie, chap. xi, obviously an apology of the Marranos, the Jewish lip-Christians in Lisbon (Hildreth, p. 261). This note about the Jews at Lisbon is *not* to be found in the first edition of Bentham-Dumont's work (see *ibid.*, tome ii, p. 276).

[137] *Ibid.*, 1802, tome iii, pp. 35 ff, "Principes du code pénal," quatrième partie, chap. iv (2nd edition, 1820, tome ii, p. 226 f; Hildreth, p. 378 f).

the "fiction cruelle" of a moral corruption of blood,[138] his defense of
the rights of bastards,[139] his analysis of the moral perversion of states,
in which it is more dangerous to lend aid to justice than to take arms
against it, possibly more dangerous to witness a crime than to commit
it,[140] his reflections on poverty, benevolent societies and public charity,[141]
his struggle for limitation or even disuse of capital punishment.[142] Even
the minute details of these discussions sometimes throw a certain light
on concrete moral tendencies in Bentham, and they reveal the character
and the greatness of his law reforms. Nevertheless, more elaborate consideration of them is not the task of this book.

Once again arithmetic is called in to aid the establishment of a balance between offenses and punishments. But the *Traités* warn us not
to overrate the applicability of algebra on this point. "Il ne faut pas
s'attacher à l'esprit mathématique de la proportion au point de rendre
les lois subtiles, compliquées et obscures. Il y a un bien supérieur; c'est
la brièveté et la simplicité. On peut encore sacrifier quelque chose de la
proportion si la peine en devient plus frappante, plus propre à inspirer

[138] *Ibid.*, 1802, tome II, p. 396, "Principes du code pénal," troisième partie,
chap. IV (2nd edition, 1820, tome II, p. 355; Hildreth, p. 332): "Corruption du
sang. C'est une fiction cruelle des Jurisconsultes qui ont inventé cette absurde théorie pour déguiser l'injustice de la confiscation. Le petit-fils innocent ne peut
hériter du grand-père innocent, parce que ses droits se sont altérés et perdus en
passant par le sang du père coupable. Cette corruption du sang est une idée fan-
tastique: mais il y a une corruption trop réelle dans l'esprit et le coeur de ceux
qui se déshonorent par ces sophismes atroces." That Bentham, in criticizing the
cruel fiction of a moral corruption of blood, by no means fought against mere
ghosts of the distant past, especially of the Spanish Inquisition (see e.g. F. Ayde-
lotte in *The American Historical Review*, vol. XLVIII, no. 1, October 1942, p. 11 f)
is now evident from the fact that this cruel fiction saw its most ignominious
resurrection in Nazi- and Fascist-legislation of the twentieth century.
[139] *Ibid.*, tome III, p. 397 (2nd edition, tome II, p. 355; Hildreth, p. 332).
[140] *Ibid.*, tome II, p. 284, "Principes du code pénal," première partie, chap.
XIII; Hildreth, p. 266.
[141] *Ibid.*, 1802, tome III, pp. 126 ff, "Principes du code pénal," quatrième partie,
chap. XVI; 2nd edition, 1820, tome II, p. 312 f; Hildreth, p. 430 f. Compare "Principes du code civil," première partie, chap. XIV, sect. 1, *ibid.*, 1802, tome I, pp. 64 ff;
2nd edition, 1820, tome I, p. 208 f; Hildreth, p. 130 f.
[142] *Ibid.*, 1802, tome II, pp. 429 ff, "Principes du code pénal," troisième partie,
chap. XI; 2nd edition, 1820, tome II, p. 187 f; Hildreth, pp. 353 ff. Compare *ibid.*,
1802, tome III, p. 195, "Principes du code pénal," quatrième partie, chap. XXII;
2nd edition, 1820, tome II, p. 374 f; Hildreth, p. 470: "Soyez difficile à croire à
cette necessité de la mort." Compare *ibid.*, 1802, tome III, p. 123, chap. XVI; 2nd
edition, tome II, p. 309; Hildreth, p. 428: "Des lois sanguinaires ont une tendance
à rendre les hommes cruels."

au peuple un sentiment d'aversion pour les vices qui préparent de loin des délits."[143] On the other hand, wherever exact calculation of damage is possible, it is strictly required; and even tables of natural deterioration which stolen articles may undergo (dead or living objects) is thought to be required in a library of justice.[144] Primarily, however, we are assured that whatever constitutes a part of human happiness is worthy of becoming the subject of a lawsuit, even if this happiness is based on a very odd taste. Since enlightened and philosophic benevolence has to sympathize with tastes very different from its own, and since it is imagination which gives value to the objects esteemed most precious, the *Traités* deem it by no means ridiculous that a canary bird, a rusty lamp or a Dutch tulip should become the object of a lawsuit.[145] For, as we have already seen, the moral calculus has to take into consideration only those pleasures which men actually enjoy, not those which they ought to enjoy.

It is the very essence of the moral calculus to base moral valuations on a comparison of facts, and not on other valuations. Only after ethics has carried out its task can education begin to help men improve their ways of pleasure seeking so as to procure more and lasting pleasure. Without ethics, however, pedagogy would be without any guide to determine the direction in which education should take place.

The ethical attitude toward animals is, in the "principes du code pénal," as well as in the "principes du code civil," grosser, more callous than in Bentham's other writings. The "code pénal" repeats the statement of the "code civil," that cruelty toward animals has morally to be condemned because it is an incentive to cruelty toward men.[146] And another reason, certainly on no higher moral level, is given here for the same ethical prescription, namely, to soften the lot of animals, be-

[143] *Ibid.*, 1802, tome II, p. 389, "Principes du code pénal," troisième partie, chap. II; 2nd edition, 1820, p. 147; Hildreth, p. 327.
[144] *Ibid.*, 1802, tome II, p. 328, "Principes du code pénal," seconde partie, chap. XII; 2nd edition, 1820, tome II, p. 91; Hildreth, p. 291.
[145] *Ibid.*, 1802, tome III, p. 118, "Principes du code pénal," quatrième partie, chap. xv; 2nd edition, tome II, p. 305; Hildreth, p. 425. Compare *ibid.*, tome I, p. 107, "Principes de législation," chap. XII; 2nd edition, 1820, tome I, p. 102; Hildreth, p. 66, and compare similar observations in Simone de Beauvoir's *Pour une morale de l'ambiguité*, 1947, pp. 103 ff.
[146] *Ibid.*, 1802, tome III, p. 118, "Principes du code pénal," quatrième partie, chap. xv; 2nd edition, tome II, p. 305; Hildreth, p. 425. Compare *ibid.*, tome I, p. 107, "Principes de législation," chap. XII; 2nd edition, 1820, p. 102; Hildreth, p. 66.

cause they labor for us and supply our wants.[147] One should, however, not exaggerate the difference which exists on this point between Bentham's writings: the *Traités* even draw a parallel between the lot of animals and that of slaves. Yet the *Traités* certainly do not deepen the argument of the *Introduction* on this point.

Like other parts of the *Traités*, the "penal code" reveals a comparatively moderate attitude toward religion. It is not a religious unbeliever or an agnostic who speaks here, as is the case in other writings of Bentham, but an enlightened religionist of the eighteenth century, a representative of a religion of moral reason. "La religion elle même . . . est bonne . . . autant qu'elle est l'auxilaire de la vertu"; but any sacrifice of virtue to religion has to be rejected.[148] "Une vérité claire de morale ne s'ébranle point, mais la croyance d'un dogme est plus au moins chancelante."[149] "L'irréligion au contraire (je répugne à prononcer le mot d'*athéisme*)[150] s'est manifestée de nos jours sous les formes les plus hideuses de l'absurdité, de l'immoralité et de la persécution. Cette expérience suffit pour montrer à tous les bons esprits dans quel sens ils doivent diriger leurs efforts. Mais si le Gouvernement vouloit agir trop ouvertement pour favoriser cette direction salutaire, il manqueroit son but. C'est la liberté de l'examen qui a corrigé les erreurs des siècles d'ignorance, et ramené la religion vers son véritable objet. C'est la liberté de l'examen qui achevera de l'épurer et de la concilier avec l'utilité publique."[151] The main services which religion may render to morality are, in the eyes of this enlightened Christendom, moral instruction adapted to the most numerous class of society, consolation for the woes inseparable from humanity, and a means of exciting benefi-

[147] *Ibid.*, 1802, tome III, p. 124, "Principes du code pénal," quatrième partie, chap. XVI; 2nd edition, 1820, tome II, p. 310; Hildreth, p. 429.

[148] *Ibid.*, 1802, tome III, p. 137, "Principes du code pénal," quatrième partie, chap. XVIII; 2nd edition, 1820, tome II, p. 322; Hildreth, p. 436. Compare Bentham, *Works*, 1843, part XIX, p. 146a, the following more radical aphorism of Bentham's Commonplace Book, written about 1785: "Judging God to be a vain and proud and jealous being, like themselves, some men imagine that flattery and humiliation will give him pleasure . . . hence, in a word, the exaltation of so called religion above morality. Of religion, which, with respect to God, the object of it, is universally allowed to be useless and which, with respect to men, is useful, no otherwise than as promotive of morality."

[149] *Ibid.*, 1802, tome III, p. 138; 2nd edition, tome II, p. 323; Hildreth, p. 437.

[150] This remark on atheism is omitted in Hildreth's edition (see *Traités*, 1802, tome III, p. 142; and see Hildreth, p. 439).

[151] *Ibid.*, p. 142 f.

cence.[152] Whether this was actually the religious creed of Bentham about 1800, or how far it is only that of Dumont, is difficult to decide.

Bentham and Ethnological Relativity
"De l'influence des temps et des lieux en matière de législation"

The whole third volume of the later editions of the *Traités* has not been published by Hildreth in his translation of Bentham-Dumont's work. This third volume has contained, in all French editions since 1820, a long essay dealing with Bentham's "Panopticon"—his plans to construct new types of prisons—and a still lengthier treatise "Vue générale d'un corps complet de législation" while in the first edition the second item is to be found only in the first volume of the *Traités*. Both these treatises, especially the first, are not of basic ethical interest; and besides, both are to be found translated into English in Bowring's edition of Bentham's works. Therefore, in discussing the whole of Bentham's later thought, we shall have occasion to refer to the ideas of these essays in the enlarged treatment they received at the hands of the older Bentham.

To a very brief article, "De la promulgation des lois. De la promulgation des raisons des lois," we have already referred in another connection.[153] So there is left for brief review only one interesting essay, "De l'influence des temps et des lieux en matière de législation," whose main ethical thesis is easily recognizable in the title itself.

In this treatise particularly, Bentham proves to be one of the most clear-sighted forerunners of the nineteenth century's ethnological school in ethics. Of course, his anthropological knowledge was still limited by the standards of his time, the rambling reports which explorers of the eighteenth century had brought home from the lands of primitive and exotic peoples. And yet, he presents his ethnological material so graphically that it supports his main theses extremely well.

Through numerous examples, he makes plain how greatly time and space influence the moral customs of men. The moral convictions of early primitive tribes are quite different from those of modern highly civilized societies; and even in modern times, there is an overwhelming difference between the moral outlook of exotic peoples of the Far East or the tropics and the peoples of western civilization. As Bentham points

---

[152] *Ibid.*, 1802, tome III, p. 143, "Principes du code pénal," quatrième partie, chap. XVIII; 2nd edition, 1820, tome II, p. 328; Hildreth, p. 440.

[153] See the present work, pp. 25-29.

out, even the feeling of shame, among a number of primitive communities, is not bound to their sexual organs but to their organs for eating;[154] and, accordingly, such a feeling of shame gives rise to very different moral conceptions.

The lesson to be drawn from all such historical and anthropological observations is well expressed by a remark in the "principes du code pénal," which in the first edition of the *Traités* is also to be found in the third volume of the whole work. "Sur les points de morale, où il y a des questions contestées, il est bon de consulter les lois des différentes nations. C'est pour l'esprit une manière de voyager. Dans le cours de cet exercice, on se dégage des préjugés locaux et nationaux, en faisant passer en revue devant soi les usages des autres peuples."[155] All this sufficiently proves, I think, how much freer Bentham was from the prejudices of his nation and his age than is commonly granted by historians of philosophy or jurisprudence.

Even today, moralists are generally far less willing than Bentham to admit that there is a basic relativity of concrete moral maxims in different civilizations. Again and again, it is maintained, in contrast to Bentham, that the universal validity of many concrete moral rules cannot be overthrown even by what seems the most graphic diversity of moral customs.

Professor Brand Blanshard, for instance, tried to demonstrate this in a specially striking way as follows: The primitive Fijians killed their parents. But even this practice, which "makes us shudder," does not indicate that the "underlying scale of values" of the Fijians was different from our own.[156] The difference lies only in certain theoretical views connected in the two cases with exactly the same basic ethical values. The Fijians believed that unless a person dies young, he will be condemned to a wretched existence of decay in afterlife. Because of

---

[154] Bentham-Dumont, *Traités de législation civile et pénale*, 1802, tome III, p. 340 f, "De l'influence des temps et des lieux en matière de législation," chap. I, no. 8; 2nd edition, tome III, p. 129 f; *Works*, 1843, tome I, p. 176a.

[155] *Ibid.*, 1802, tome III, p. 58, "Principes du code pénal," quatrième partie, chap. v; 2nd edition, tome II, p. 248; Hildreth, p. 393. Compare in connection with this statement the general admonition to blush at the spirit of family, at that spirit of caste, or party, of sect or profession which militates against the love of country and that unjust patriotism which glories in the hatred of other nations. See *ibid.*, 1802, tome III, p. 128, "Principes du code pénal," quatrième partie, chap. XVI; 2nd edition, 1820, tome II, p. 314; Hildreth, p. 431: "Le plus beau model est tracé dans ce mot de Fénelon qui peint son coeur: Je prefère ma famille à moi, ma patrie à ma famille, et le genre humain à ma patrie."

[156] See B. Blanshard in *Preface to Philosophy*, ed. by W. P. Tolley, 1946, p. 125.

this creed, they killed father and mother when both were still in their prime. But apart from this creed which differs from ours, our and their scale of values are exactly the same. "We think that we should cherish our parents and concern ourselves about their interests. So did they. We think such concern should display itself in securing those parents' happiness. So did they. It was the very fact that their values and filial attitudes were so similar to ours that made them adopt an outward custom so very different."[156] It seems to me, however, that the strain which such ethical analyses impose on the interpretation of relevant facts makes Professor Blanshard's argument untenable.

Contemporary anthropologists, it is true, ascribe filial affection to the primitive Fijians.[157] But philosophers such as C. D. Broad and A. C. Ewing are hardly mistaken in calling all such psychological speculations on "babies" and "primitive savages . . . of the weakest kind known to science."[158] How often have Freudians been blamed for drawing psychological inferences without sufficient evidence! And certainly it sounds paradoxical to many ears that Freud ascribed even to civilized children hostile feelings toward their parents, although these children present their parents with very pleasant gifts on Father's and Mother's Day. The inference of such hostility, however, serves after all to make more understandable a comparatively coherent chain of strange but evident reactions in many children. Is the inference to the Fijians' filial affection less paradoxical than the Freudian inferences? And is the compensation for this paradoxical inference also some more coherent understanding of other types of behavior of the Fijians?

The *Encyclopaedia Britannica* counts the primitive Fijians "among the most notorious of the Pacific island cannibals" and Frazer's *Golden Bough* reports—in connection with Fijian customs—that in Raratonga (or Rarotonga, not so far off from the Fiji islands) "as soon as a son reached manhood, he would fight and wrestle with his father for the mastery, and if he obtained it he would take forcible possession of the farm and drive his parent in destitution from home."[159] One can readily grant that cannibalism (though this needs much further explanation) may go hand in hand with filial love and love of dogs with the slaughter of millions of men. But can one prove the existence of altruistic feelings in all men by the vague inference to filial devotion even in Fijians, and

[157] See e.g. Robert Briffault, *The Mothers*, 1927, vol. I, p. 147.
[158] See A. C. Ewing, *The Definition of Good*, 1947, p. 24.
[159] James George Frazer, *The Golden Bough*, part III, "The Dying God," 1930, p. 191.

can one ignore all those primitive customs which argue against this type of inference?

Further, it was obviously the Fijians and other primitives themselves who created their strange creeds about afterlife. It is, therefore, certainly one-sided to explain the behavior of these primitives by reference to their creeds alone rather than to attempt to explain both the creeds and the behavior by their functional interrelationship. If, however, the latter is done, and the cannibalism of the Fijians is taken into account along with their custom of killing men in their prime, the altruistic purity of those cannibalistic filial feelings may appear in an even more questionable light than before.

And finally, if we would nevertheless attribute to those primitives truly altruistic feelings, despite their cruel customs, and if we think that these feelings are all that counts morally, this must lead to more and only too familiar absurdities. The civilized son who would not especially care for his parents but did not kill them would, then, obviously be far less moral than the Fijian who murders his parents out of a love morally sanctified despite its disastrous results.

For all these reasons, it seems hardly appropriate to insist that all men, even the Fijians and the Hitlers, have factually the same scale of values and it is impossible to demonstrate this by their filial affection or their love of animals. But even if it were granted to anthropologists and moralists that all men agree in their basic factual evaluations, this would certainly not be the way to guarantee the desirability and moral validity of these factual evaluations.

Bentham fully admitted that there is complete diversity of concrete moral evaluations. As a truly objective observer of human life he did not think it justifiable to presuppose that the filial or similar attitudes are morally the same in all men and all epochs of history. He did not even assume that all men approve of his supreme ethical principle of the greatest happiness of the greatest number. All he insisted on is that this principle is entitled to figure as the most comprehensive and least capricious criterion for judging the morality of human behavior. As such, however, this criterion does not stand in need of any belief in the factual recognition of basic concrete values by all men.

In common with practically all leading men in the late eighteenth century, Bentham, in the *Traités*, shows a highly optimistic outlook on human progress, an unshakable confidence in the reformative power of human reason and knowledge. "On parle avec regret de l'âge d'or, de l'âge, où l'on ne savoit rien";[160] but this is an error; according to the *Traités*, the diffusion of knowledge in an advanced civilization is, on the whole, definitely beneficial to the development of higher morality. "Quelques écrivains ont pensé ou paru penser que moins les hommes ont de connoissances, mieux ils valent—que moins ils ont de lumières, moins ils connoissent d'objets qui servent de motif au mal ou de moyens de le commettre. Que les fanatiques aient eu cette opinion, je ne m'en étonne pas, vu qu'il y a une rivalité naturelle et constante entre la connoissance des choses réelles, utiles et intelligibles, et la connoissance des choses imaginaires, inutiles et inintelligibles. Mais cette manière de penser sur le danger des connoissances, est assez commune dans la masse du genre humain."[161] Experience, however, teaches us something very different: "Les plus grands crimes sont ceux pour lesquelles le plus petit degré de connoissance est suffisant; l'individu le plus ignorant en sait toujours assez pour le commettre."[162]

And yet, in spite of his rationalism, Bentham has nothing in common with the great a priori reasoners of the eighteenth century. It is true that throughout he maintains his confidence in reason; he distrusts all passionate, non-rational thought which, according to him, is in ethics bound up with the blind principle of sympathy and antipathy.[163] Cool, rational judgment is Bentham's ideal in ethics, in contrast to all non-rational emotional thinking. But, despite his belief in reason, he resists the common temptation to rationalize in ethics by mere arguments a priori. He builds up a rational theory in morals, yet this theory carefully takes into account all types of non-rational feelings of pleasure and pain.

[160] *Ibid.*, 1802, III, p. 16 ("Principes du code pénal," quatrième partie, chap. II); 2nd edition, 1820, II, pp. 207, 206; Hildreth, p. 366.

[161] *Ibid.*, 15 f (2nd ed., II, 208; Hildreth, p. 367).

[162] *Ibid.*, p. 17 (Hildreth, p. 367).

[163] See *ibid.*, 1802, III, p. 16 ("Principes du code pénal," quatrième partie, chap. II; 2nd ed., p. 207; Hildreth, p. 366 f): "En jugeant de la grandeur des délits, on a plus suivi le Principe de l'Antipathie que celui, de l'Utilité." "L'Antipathie regarde plus à la dépravation apparente du caractère, indiqué par le délit, qu'à toute autre circonstance. C'est aux yeux de la passion le point saillant de chaque acte, en comparaison duquel l'examen strict de l'Utilité paroît toujours froid." Compare *ibid.*, III, p. 198 (Principes du code pénal, quatrième partie, chap. XII; 2nd ed., p. 378; Hildreth, p. 472): "Ce n'est pas les brillantes sociétés du monde qu'on veut intéresser à une formule presque arithmétique, c'est à la pensée des hommes d'État qu'on la présente." But that this coolness of the final judgment does not mean dullness of the ultimate aims of utilitarian morality may be inferred from the last words of the "principes du code pénal" (*ibid.*, p. 199; Hildreth, p. 472): "Voilà l'objet de cette science politique, franche et généreuse, qui ne cherche que la lumière, qui ne veut rien d'exclusif, et qui ne connoit point de moyen plus sûr de perpétuer ses bienfaits, que d'y faire participer toute la grande famille des nations."

How unusually far Bentham went in this respect, how objectively and impartially he weighed emotions and prejudices of moral conviction opposite to his own, may be learned, above all, from a remark in one of his later writings. Here he grants that even a system of moral teachings entirely opposite to his own could present itself as a comparatively coherent system of morality. He calls this system "the wolf's bible," in contrast to his own doctrine, "the shepherd's bible."[164] Thus, a century before Nietzsche, Bentham coined terms that are equivalent to Nietzsche's terms, master-and-slave-morality. Personally, I should prefer Bentham's terminology, because it seems to me more objective than Nietzsche's.

Although himself a rationalist, Bentham tried to do full justice to all those vital problems which are commonly neglected, even by leading representatives of rationalistic ethics. These are the crucial questions concerning all those worlds of moral ideas which are nationally, historically or religiously different from the Judaeo-Christian morality of western civilization.

Moralists of the eighteenth and early nineteenth centuries either tried to minimize these differences or they simply dismissed moral ideas of other civilizations as pagan or barbarous. Far more than even Herder and other non-rationalists of the eighteenth century, Bentham anticipated the course which European ethics was to take in the French and English ethnological school up to Durkheim and Westermarck on the one hand, and Friedrich Nietzsche on the other.

Bentham fully recognized the weight of ethnological facts in ethics as well as the weight of that alarming fact—a consistent master-morality. But there is even more to be learned from him. Even Dumont's edition of the *Traités* shows, I think, impressively how successfully Bentham took into account both the relativism of the anthropologists and the absolutism of ethical universalists.

Of course, aside from logic, we can never speak of absolutely valid principles but only of principles valid in so far as human insight and human knowledge carry us. But taking this into account, I believe that Bentham—far more than Lévy Bruhl or any other representative of anthropological or universalistic, of empirical or aprioristic ethics— showed us how, on the relativity of existing moral ideas, ethical judgments, nevertheless, can be based which are of universal validity so far as human insight, in physics and in ethics, is entitled to speak of any universal validity.

[164] Bentham, *Works*, 1843, vol. i, p. 291 (*Defence of Economy against the Right and Honourable Edmund Burke*, 1817, section v; second edition, 1830).

MATURITY
The Ethical Analyses in the Later Writings

MATURITY

The Ethical Analyses in the Later Writings

MANIFEST divergencies exist as to the value of the different phases of Bentham's lifework. Charles W. Everett, Charles M. Atkinson, Leslie Stephen, James Mackintosh, Francis Place and others think much less of Bentham's later writings than of the works of his youth, and this for at least two reasons: because of the complexity and intricacy of his later style, and because the later publications and manuscripts are, to a considerable extent, nothing but the completion of plans sketched in his earlier years.[1] On the other hand, C. K. Ogden, J. H. Burton and John Neal make out a strong case for the importance of the neglected works of the later period.[2] It is not difficult, however, to achieve a comparative reconciliation between such apparently divergent views.

[1] See C. W. Everett, "Bentham's Anti-Senatica," *Smith College Studies in History*, XI, no. IV, 1926, p. 220: "The *Fragment on Government*, the *Introduction to the Principles of Morals and Legislation* and the *Defence of Usury* ... are still read. His later works are generally consulted only by the determined scholar who will bear with the form for the matter"; C. M. Atkinson, *Jeremy Bentham, His Life and Work*, 1905, pp. 28 f: "Eminent critics have affirmed that throughout Bentham's writings there are numberless passages which in point of wit, eloquence and expressive clearness have rarely been excelled in the works of any writer of our language: his close ingenious reasoning provides constant and useful exercise for the mind while his wealth of apt illustration, drawn from an infinite variety of sources ... enlivens the dullest topic. At the same time ... men who assuredly would not be deterred from the study of Bentham by the mere abstruseness of his subject matter have often been repelled by the difficulties of his later style." Leslie Stephen, *The English Utilitarians*, 1902, vol. I, p. 272: "Nobody could write more pointedly or with happier illustrations than Bentham in earlier years. . . . Afterwards . . . Bentham's style becomes tiresome"; James Mackintosh, *A general View of the Progress of Ethical Philosophy Chiefly during the Seventeenth and Eighteenth Centuries*, Philadelphia, 1834, p. 210 f: In his early works Bentham's style was "clear, free, spirited," in his later years his language became "obscure and repulsive," though "many passages . . . retain . . . the inimitable stamp of genius." Or see G. Wallas, *Francis Place*, 1898, pp. 84 f: Place complains in a letter to James Mill on October 20, 1817, that Bentham's "Codification Papers" oblige the reader to study not only the subject itself but also "the phraseology of the author" and he hoped that temperate criticism might lead Bentham to improve his way of writing. To this James Mill replies in a letter to Place on November 6, 1817, that "there is no one thing upon which he [Bentham] plumes himself as his style and he would not alter it, if all the world were to preach to him till Domesday."

John MacDonell, in his article on Bentham in the *Dictionary of National Biography*, vol. IV, 1885, p. 278b, dates the "deterioration" of Bentham's style from "about 1810."

[2] J. H. Burton, *Benthamiana*, 1863, pp. ix f: "There is a great difference between

It is true that the foundations of all the moral and juristical teachings of Bentham were laid in the writings of his youth. But beyond all doubt, his later doctrine on logic and many details of his later ethical and juristical thought deserve equal attention; their value, and the value of the scrupulous exactitude of his later style, have often been regrettably underrated.

A TABLE OF THE SPRINGS OF ACTION

It is very significant that the only work by Bentham dedicated specifically to ethics and not edited by someone else bears the title *A Table of the Springs of Action*.[3] For it is in the analysis of human springs of action as developed in this small pamphlet that Bentham provides the whole of his teaching with a carefully hewn foundation stone. Only here does his doctrine of the moral motives, and with it his entire utilitarianism, receive its final "censorial" grounding. Therefore it seems to me that a systematic exposition of Bentham's ethics should start, not with a dogmatic reference to the principle of utility, as is usually done, but with the theory of moral motives that contains Bentham's attempt to justify his utilitarianism critically.

the author's earlier and his later works. At an early period of his life he had a vivid and teeming fancy . . . he possessed, to an eminent degree, the faculty . . . to send forth his philosophy to the world, illustrated and attractively adorned . . . as he advanced in life, . . . he allowed the most remarkable feature of his mind— his power of abstract reasoning to master the others. . . . Much has been said of the intricacy and obscurity of the sentences in his later works. That they are complex is in many instances true; but that they are obscure and dubious, is so much the reverse of the fact . . . that all the apparent prolixity arises from the skill with which the author has made provision that no man shall have a doubt of what he means to say." Compare the praise of Bentham's later style by an anonymous writer whose "general preface" is in some copies of Bentham's *Works* prefixed to volume I of the edition of 1843, or C. K. Ogden, *Bentham's Theory of Fictions*, 1932, pp. xxx f. Finally see John Neal in his biographical notice on Jeremy Bentham in his edition of Bentham-Dumont's *Principles of Legislation*, Boston, 1830, p. 39: "For people who are not acquainted with his early works to complain of all his late works for not being clear is about as absurd as it would be for a man who had never studied his multiplication table, to find faults with a treatise on fluxions for not being as intelligible . . . as a newspaper essay." But compare *ibid.*, p. 38 and p. 39, note.

[3] The work was printed in 1815 but first published only in 1817; see Charles W. Everett in E. Halévy, *The Growth of Philosophic Radicalism*, 1928, p. 528. Jan Hendrik Jacobus Antonie Greyvenstein's *Het Sociale Utilisme van Bentham*, 1911, is one of the few Bentham analyses which refer to the "Springs of Action" even in passing, see *ibid.*, p. 84 f.

Bentham's principal ideas about the subject had already been sketched in the *Introduction*, particularly in the chapters on motives and dispositions. But in *A Table of the Springs of Action* and in other works of the later period, the doctrine of the *Introduction* receives an especially valuable supplementation.

Before entering upon these ethical analyses proper, however, Bentham lays down a number of refining definitions and explains that, exactly speaking, ethics cannot deal exhaustively with motives but, at best, with springs of action. Under this latter "denomination those objects and considerations alone are included in this Table which, in their operation on the will, act as it were in the way of immediate contact"; under the name of motives, however, all those considerations have to be included "which act on the will no otherwise than through the understanding"; and of those motives "no book could comprise the catalogue."[4] Thus —more carefully than in the *Introduction*—the motives acting on the will through the understanding are, in 1817, excluded from the ethical analysis. Only the springs of action are taken into account, because they are in immediate contact with the will and represent the ethically decisive part of men's motives. The science which has these springs of action for its subject—independent of their relation to ethics—is called by Bentham "psychological dynamics"; and, within this science, pleasure and pain appear in the character of means, whereas everywhere else pleasure and exemption from pain "fall to be considered . . . in the character of ends."[5] As to the nature of pleasure and pain, however, there exists, according to Bentham, widespread confusion in psychology as well as in ethics. There is an almost general belief that there are dozens of emotions which are essentially different from pleasure and pain but actually their names are essentially synonyms for pain and pleasure. Therefore Bentham emphasizes right from the beginning how useful it is to have long lists of these synonyms for pleasure and pain which allow us to recognize that all these numerous synonyms do not denote anything essentially different from our two fundamental emotions.

Bentham mentions no fewer than fifty-five terms of pleasure: gratification, enjoyment, fruition, indulgence, joy, delight, delectation, hilarity, merriment, mirth, gaiety, airiness, comfort, solace, content, satisfaction, rapture, transport, ecstasy, bliss, joyfulness, gladness, gladfulness, gladsomeness, cheerfulness, comfortableness, contentedness, happiness, blissfulness, felicity, well-being, prosperity, success, exultation, triumph,

[4] Bentham, *Works*, 1843, vol. I, p. 205a, no. a; p. 208b, no. m.
[5] *Ibid.*, p. 205a, b.

amusement, entertainment, diversion, festivity, pastime, sport, play, frolic, recreation, refreshment, ease, repose, rest, tranquillity, quiet, peace, relief, relaxation, alleviation, mitigation. And even higher is the number of pains, sixty-seven in all: vexation, suffering, mortification, humiliation, sorrow, grief, mourning, concern, distress, discomfort, discontent, dissatisfaction, regret, anguish, agony, torture, torment, pang, throe, excruciation, distraction, trouble, embarrassment, anxiety, solicitude, perplexity, disquiet, disquietude, inquietude, unquietness, discomposure, disturbance, commotion, agitation, perturbation, disorder, harassment, restlessness, uneasiness, discontentedness, anxiousness, sorrowfulness, sadness, weariness, mournfulness, bitterness, unhappiness, wretchedness, misery, infelicity, melancholy, gloom, depression, dejection, despondence, despondency, despair, desperation, hopelessness, affliction, calamity, plague, grievance, misfortune, mishap, misadventure, mischance.[6] The enumeration of all these synonyms, however, is by no means a matter of mere terminology. On the contrary, these lists provide a particularly striking confirmation of the consistency of Bentham's thought.

Consistent anti-hedonists deny, for obvious reasons, that such springs of action as dissatisfaction and despair or amusement and blissfulness, refreshment and ecstasy, ease and exultation, have, even psychologically speaking, anything in common. Anti-hedonists generally draw a sharp line of demarcation between religious and sensual, bodily and spiritual pleasures or pains.[7]

At least since the days of Pascal—to whom Max Scheler and Nicolai Hartmann explicitly refer in this respect[8]—the belief in absolute qualitative differences between human feelings has formed the very basis of anti-hedonist ethics. Bentham's critical ethics, however, rejects this psychological thesis right from the beginning.

Bentham does not deny that the moralist, with his different terms for

[6] *Ibid.*, pp. 205b, 206a.
[7] See e.g. the emphatic protest of Max Scheler against any attempt to bridge over the contrast between sensual, vital, spiritual and religious pleasure or pain in Max Scheler, *Der Formalismus in der Ethik und die materiale Wertethik* (1921), p. 108: Die religiösen Zustände "Seligkeit und Verzweiflung . . . sind . . . von Glück und Unglück ganz . . . unabhängig," p. 107: unabhängig auch von "geistiger Freude und Trauer," von "vitalem Froh- und Unfrohsein" und vom "Genuss des Angenehmen" oder Widerwillen gegen das Unangenehme. Cf. Dietrich von Hildebrand, "Die Idee der sittlichen Handlung," in *Jahrbuch für Philosophie und Phänomenologische Forschung*, ed. by E. Husserl, vol. iii, 1916, e.g. pp. 164 ff; "Sittlichkeit und ethische Werterkenntnis," *ibid.*, vol. v, 1922, p. 463 ff.
[8] M. Scheler, *Der Formalismus in der Ethik und die materiale Wertethik*, 1921, p. 22; N. Hartmann, *Ethics*, 1932, vol. ii, p. 31.

emotions, tries to characterize feelings of very different intensities and connotations. But Bentham denies, I think justly, that the ethicist is allowed to start his inquiry by using appellations of feelings which do not contain strictly neutral psychological distinctions but, instead, contain moral differentiations under the cover of seemingly neutral psychological terms.

In the *Introduction*, Bentham had already protested against the use of ethically biased terminology for *motives*. In the *Table*, however, he enlarged this protest in such a way that, in addition, the terms for any *emotions* which play a part in human motives or in the consequences of actions must, according to him, be freed from ethical partiality. Every human feeling must be understood to be nothing but a type of pleasure or pain, no matter how morally noble or mean it may appear at first glance and in whatever intensity or shade of pleasure or pain it may represent itself to the observer.

It is an extremely pernicious, though widespread, confusion between psychological and ethical issues when the psychologist *qua* psychologist dares to distinguish, e.g. between a (morally) low feeling of contentedness and a (morally) noble feeling of elevated inner tranquillity or between a (morally) low emotion of uneasiness and a (morally) moving deep sadness. Any psychologist who insists that such distinctions between pleasures or pains express basic differences between our emotions is no longer a neutral psychological observer; he is already a biased moralist.

The psychologist *qua* psychologist is never entitled to make ethical distinctions. This is exclusively the business of the moralist. The task of the psychologist is exclusively to describe feelings, not to evaluate them morally. If the psychologist nevertheless introduces moral evaluations to his descriptions of feelings, he ceases to give adequate and correct descriptions. His mere "descriptions" are, then, highly controversial.

The psychologist of a small highly civilized democracy, such as Denmark or Holland, may, thus, describe certain sentiments of an artist or scholar as a superior joyous serenity while, to the psychologist of a great aggressive industrial state, the same sentiments appear as a cheaply introverted self-gratification; the psychologist of a primitive rustic community may characterize the melancholy of a poet as sheer self-pity, while the same melancholy appears to the literary critic of a great metropolis as the finest flower of the inner suffering of a great writer.

To base our ethical teaching ultimately on such characterizations of feelings (even if these feelings are not immediate springs of actions) is worse than to base our judgment of the climate of a country on the completely divergent observations of Eskimos and Central-African negroes.

In comparison with this fundamental discussion of the synonyms for pleasure and pain, other introductory remarks made here by Bentham are certainly of minor importance. It is noticed here for instance that most of the leading terms employed in ethics, such as the springs of actions, are fictitious entities instead of actual objects. But although they are not actual objects, fictions are in the *Table* no longer regarded as non-entities, as they were in the two critical comments on Blackstone forty years earlier. Fictions are now held to be useful, indispensable instruments for human language and even human thought; confusion, error, endless dissension and hostility arise only if, as is commonly done, such fictions are thought to be real objects.[9] It is this concept of fiction—fiction considered as a legitimate means of human speech and human reflection—to which Bentham adheres throughout his later thought.

Apart from this logically characteristic point, a number of further ethically relevant explanations and definitions are here introduced. A distinction is drawn between "positive good (understand pathological good)" that is, physical and mental good, which is either pleasure itself or a cause of pleasure, and negative good, which is "either exemption of pain, or a cause of such exemption. In like manner, positive evil is either pain itself or a cause of pain: negative evil, either loss of pleasure or a cause of such loss."[10]

A further distinction is made between pleasures operating as springs of action and pleasures remaining inert. Inert pleasures derived, for instance, from a recollected landscape, can give birth to action only in a remote way by means of some different pleasure as, in the mentioned example, by "the pleasurable idea of the pleasurable sensation expected from that . . . view."[11] Therefore, though no pleasure is capable of operating as a motive except through imaginations, only expected pleasures, not recollected ones, can be actuating motives.[12]

Finally, expositions of the terms "interest," "desire," "aversion," "want," "hope," and "fear" are given. Bentham admits that none of these appellatives have any superior genus.[13] Nevertheless, he tries to explain them by means of synonyms, and by showing their place in the succession of those psychological phenomena which can be observed when human actions are performed. So he states that, if a man is acting in order to possess a good, "1. He has felt himself to have an interest

[9] Bentham, *Works*, 1843, I, p. 205a; 211a, §1.
[10] *Ibid.*, p. 206b, nos. 10, 11, 14.   [11] *Ibid.*, p. 207a, no. 18, 19.
[12] *Ibid.*, no. 5, no. 19.   [13] *Ibid.*, p. 209a, no. 11.

in the possession of that same good. 2. He has felt a desire to possess it. 3. He has felt an aversion to the idea of his not possessing it. 4. He has felt the want of it. 5. He has entertained a hope of possessing it. 6. He has had before his eyes the fear of not possessing it. 7. And the desire he has felt of possessing it has operated on his will in the character of a motive, by the sole operation, or by the help of which, the act exercised by him, as above, has been produced."[14] All these are more or less acceptable and useful new contributions to the psychology of utilitarian ethics.

One remark of this kind, however, should be particularly noted in the age of psychoanalysis. This is Bentham's regret that there does not exist in the language a substantive which expresses the contrary of "motive," that is, a tendency to restrain action in the sense in which a motive produces action.[15] As a matter of fact, up to Bentham's time only adjectives such as "restrictive" could be used for this purpose, but a corresponding noun was unknown in psychological terminology. Today the need which Bentham felt has been met. The important term he missed was introduced to psychology by Johann Friedrich Herbart[16] and has gained a central place in the theories of Sigmund Freud through whom the term has become common in the language of every day life. This term is inhibition.

Expanded Criticism of the Ethics of Motives

However, none of the above mentioned psychological expositions form the main topic of Bentham's *A Table of the Springs of Action*. The principal subject is ethical, and concerns the "censorial" characterization of motives, i.e. the judgments of ethical approbation or disapproval on the springs of action.

Far more fully than in the *Introduction*, Bentham shows in the fourteen parts of his Table and in the ensuing "explanations" and "observations" why practically all the common ethical appellatives of motives are,

[14] *Ibid.*, no. 9.

[15] *Ibid.*, p. 208b, no. 7; compare *ibid.*, VI, 257a: an appropriate term for these causes which produce "inaction" is as much needed as the term *motive* which signifies those causes which produce action (*Rationale of Judicial Evidence*, book I, chap. XI, §1).

[16] In Herbart's psychology, however, the term *Hemmung* has a far more intellectualistic connotation than in Freud (see J. F. Herbart, *Lehrbuch zur Psychologie*, 1816, II. Teil, §126 ff; *Psychologie als Wissenschaft, neu gegründet auf Erfahrung, Metaphysik und Mathematik*, 1824-25, §37 ff; J. F. Herbarts *Sämmtliche Werke*, ed. by G. Hartenstein, 1850, vol. V, pp. 17 ff, 319 ff.

from an exact, censorial point of view, completely misleading. As he describes the problem now in detail, in practically all moral characterizations of motives the following erroneous procedure takes place: quite neutral psychological entities are not characterized neutrally, but "on account of some *accidental* effect which, on this or that occasion, has been observed to be produced by the *desire*, the whole corresponding group, of *psychological* entities—*pleasure, interest, desire, motive*—are, on all occasions, by the undistinguishing and uneludible force of" a condemnatory or laudable "appellative involved in one common and undistinguishing censure."[17] Wherever a eulogistic or a dyslogistic denomination of a human motive is used, there the possibilities of using an opposite appellative are covered and kept out of sight.[18] Therefore, before any motive is characterized by a vituperative predicate, a proof should first be given that the corresponding laudatory predicate is out of place. Such a proof, however, is usually not given. "Applied to the . . . springs of action, and in particular to pleasures and to motives . . . impassionate appellatives form no inconsiderable part of the ammunition employed in the 'ethical' war of words. Under the direction of sinister interest and interest-begotten prejudice they have been employed in the character of fallacies or instruments of deception by polemics of all classes: by politicians, lawyers, writers on controversial divinity, satirists, and literary censors."[19] And this uncritical employment of biased ethical names for motives is the more dangerous, because performed in a manner often hidden from the judging moralist himself, not to mention his hearer or reader.

"Having, without the *form*, the *force* of an assumption—and having for its object, and but too commonly for its effect, a like assumption on the part of the hearer or reader—the sort of allegation in question, how ill-grounded so ever, is, when thus masked, apt to be more persuasive than when expressed simply and in its own proper form: especially where, to the character of a *censorial* adding the quality and tendency of an *impassionate* allegation, it tends to propagate, as it were by contagion, the passion by which it was suggested. On this occasion, it seeks and finds support in that *general* opinion, of the existence of which the eulogistic or dyslogistic sense, which thus, as it were by adhesion, has connected itself with the import of the appellative, operates as proof."[20] "True it is" that in all questions of ethics "the species of psychological

[17] Bentham, *Works*, 1843, vol. I, p. 209b, no. 4.
[18] Bentham, *Works*, 1843, p. 209b, no. 4.
[19] *Ibid.*, p. 210a, no. 4, no. 5.   [20] *Ibid.*, p. 209b, 210a, q, no. 3.

entity" which is usually looked for "in the first place is the motive."[21] But by referring to the commonly condemnatory or laudatory motives no objective moral judgment can be obtained.

Two main objections have been raised to Bentham's fourteen lists of eulogistic and dyslogistic names of motives in his *Table of the Springs of Action*. First, these lists have been said to be not exhaustive and, second, they are said to contain motives which do not represent psychologically simple elements but very complex psychological entities. Both these objections are justified from the standpoint of the psychologist. On the other hand, Leslie Stephen is certainly right in pointing out that the addition of several concepts which J. S. Mill missed, such as moral duty or conscience, would have spoiled all the consistency of Bentham's argument.[22] Moreover, Bentham was not interested in giving an exhaustive list of the psychological elements of motives. He was exclusively interested in giving a list of motives which are of fundamental importance ethically and whose ethical implications are, in general, critically misunderstood. Such ethically significant motives, however, ought not to be elementary concepts from the point of view of the psychologist. If seen from this angle, with all its rich enumeration and confrontation of one-sided moral characterizations, this *Table* is perhaps the most instructive signpost, the most objective warning signal against uncritical moralizing that we possess in ethical literature.

Bentham has given the fourteen parts of his *Table*, apart from their ordinary names, very picturesque and baroque titles, which, though rather unusual, are in their own manner attractive, and in their colorfulness are similar to the terms of Bacon's *Novum Organon*. Bentham, for example, speaks here of motives of the alimentary canal or motives of the palate and the bottle, of motives of the sexual appetite or of the sixth sense, of sensual motives, of pecuniary motives or motives of the purse, of motives of power or of the scepter, of motives of curiosity or of the spying-glass, motives of amity or of the closet, motives of good repute or of the trumpet, religious motives or motives of the altar, motives of sympathy or of the heart, motives of antipathy or of the gallbladder, motives of labor or of the pillow, motives of self-preservation and self-regarding motives.

The great care and scrupulousness with which Bentham has collected the different shades of moral blame and praise in these denominations of motives is of the highest value for seeing through the moral fallacies

---

[21] Bentham, *Works*, 1843, vol. I, p. 211a.
[22] Leslie Stephen, *The English Utilitarians*, 1900, vol. I, pp. 252 ff.

which everywhere, in ethics as in daily life, are built up by the uncritical use of these terms. The overwhelming majority of moralists apply such eulogistic as well as dyslogistic terms to precisely the same actions without noticing it. For this very reason Bentham again stresses his conclusion that it is impossible to erect any judgment of moral approbation or disapprobation on the observation of human motives alone.

For, if we praise an act because of its moral motive or condemn it on account of its immoral one, we have not pronounced any critical judgment at all. We have stated only a hidden tautology. We give the impression of providing sufficient justification for our judgment of the act. But in fact we only repeat a foregone conclusion arrived at by our quite arbitrary choice in naming the motive of the act. This choice is the only decisive basis of our judgment and it is an entirely uncritical choice dictated by forms of bias unchecked or even unnoticed.

If we aim at a truly objective judgment of an act arising from a certain motive, no simple praise or blame of this motive will do; only a careful consideration of the factual pleasure and pain produced by that motive can secure objective validity for our moral judgment. "Destitute of reference to the ideas of pain and pleasure, whatever ideas are annexed to the words virtue and vice amount to nothing more than that of groundless approbation or disapprobation. All language in which these appellatives are employed, is no better than empty declamation."[23]

Whether Bentham goes too far in this criticism of a biased naming of moral motives may briefly be considered by confronting his theory with that of one of the ablest anti-hedonists, F. H. Bradley. Bradley admits, seemingly in agreement with Bentham, that "the casuist must have little ingenuity, if there is anything he fails to justify or to condemn" with regard to moral motives. "Cowardice is prudence and a duty, . . . theft is economy, . . . courage rashness and a vice, and so on." From there, however, Bradley goes on to say: "But the ordinary moral judgment is not discursive. It does not look to the right and left. . . . When the case is presented, it fixes on one quality in the act. . . . Point out to a man of simple morals that the case has other sides than the one he instinctively fixes on, and he suspects you wish to corrupt him."[24] I think that on this, as on other points, Bradley's censure of hedonism has an exceedingly shaky foundation.

The weakness of Bradley's argument is not too visible only because, in his discussion of the ethical ambiguity of motives, he includes an an-

[23] Bentham, *Works*, 1843, vol. I, p. 211b.
[24] F. H. Bradley, *Ethical Studies*, 1927, p. 197 note.

swer to quite a different question—a question which has merely a sham similarity to the major ethical problem at issue.

A psychologist may agree with Bradley's observation that people often give up good moral intentions and good motives after they think the case over "discursively," and realize the flexibility of the ethical interpretation of motives. But this psychological fact should never be confused with the moralist's requirement for adequate, consistent reasoning about motives.

In other words, it is psychologically correct that people often are intellectually confused and morally imperiled when they realize the complexity of any judgment on motives. But this does not mean that the moralist too must get confused and imperiled, and should, therefore, ignore possible intellectual pitfalls in order to save his integrity.

Certainly, no layman should be morally obliged to argue about scientific ethics, particularly if he is of such low intellectual capacity that his discursive reasoning may endanger his morals. Yet this is no excuse for rejecting moral reasoning altogether. If a professional moralist or the plain man starts to think about morality, he may, of course, err in his discursive thinking. But he may err no less profoundly in relying on wrong moral intuitions.

Therefore, the only fair advice to be given on moral thinking is to think its problems out and to think rightly. But the expectation that moral truth can be arrived at simply by stopping discursive thinking is far too optimistic and dogmatic an expectation. Moreover, this expectation is in flagrant contradiction to the facts.

If discursive reasoning about motives leads to no firm grounding of moral judgment, as Bradley grants, we must look for a firmer basis of ethics by referring to other, less vague elements of human actions. But we cannot have the slightest hope that pure intuition concerning the ethical character of motives can free us from the embarrassment caused by the discursive interpretation of these intuitions. It is evident that not only a fascist's discursive reasoning about motives but his discursive *and intuitive* characterization of motives will flatly contradict all the moral intuitions of a pacifist. Thus, in contrast to Bradley, I think it is clear that every kind of primary reference to *motives* leads us astray in ethics, as Bentham pointed out. It is by no means, as Bradley thought, only the discursive interpretation of motives which is misleading.

In contrast to Bradley, Kenneth Burke values as a special achievement the fact that Bentham made the moralist conscious of the relativity of all ethical judgment of motives.[25] But Burke's appraisal also fails to do full justice to Bentham. If Bentham had done no more than draw the attention to the relativity of valuations of motives, he would deserve at least part of Bradley's censure; he would have remained only a radical skeptic and negativist in ethics. But Bentham supplemented his criticism of the ethics of motives by a positive moral theory of the consequences of acts. The mere analysis of motives, taken by themselves, leads either to relativism and skepticism, or to an uncritical dogmatism in ethics. Only in so far as attention is focused on the consequences of acts can the basis be secured for a positive critical theory of morals.

John Dewey, however, despite his emphasis on Bentham's "consequences theory"[26] has, I think, also failed to take into account the whole of Bentham's doctrine. Like Bentham, Dewey declines all ethics "identifying morals with the purification of motives" and with "edifying character";[27] and he adds: "The insistence of utilitarianism that we must become aware of the moral quality of our impulses and states of mind on the basis of the results they effect and must control them—no matter how 'good' they feel—by their results, is a fundamental truth of morals."[28] But Dewey insists that, as fundamentally as he agrees with Bentham's polemics against any mere "attitude theory"[29] in ethics, Bentham's mere "consequences theory" seems to him no less one-sided. Again and again Dewey pleads for a higher synthesis of Bentham's teaching with the "attitude theory" of Kant.

He, therefore, primarily stresses the point that, after all, in reality, in life, there is no strict separation between motives and consequences brought about by these motives. The "error . . . lies in trying to split a voluntary act which is single and entire into two unrelated parts," the one termed "inner," the other, "outer"; the one called "motive," the other, "end."[30] To this the answer is, in my opinion, that doubtless, in reality, the motive is intimately connected with the effects which it produces. But, for epistemological reasons, it is nevertheless indispensable to separate the motive from its effect, methodologically, as indispensable

[25] See K. Burke, *Permanence and Change*, 1935, pp. 239 ff, 244 f. In his *A Grammar of Motives*, 1945, p. 284, Burke narrows even this limited praise of Bentham's *Table* and shows himself even less aware of the constructive tendencies of Bentham's critical theory of motives.
[26] See J. Dewey and J. H. Tufts, *Ethics*, 1908, part II, chap. XII, §2, p. 229.
[27] J. Dewey, *Human Nature and Conduct*, 1930, p. 280.
[28] Dewey and Tufts, *Ethics*, 1908, chap. XIII, §2, p. 252.
[29] *Ibid.*, p. 241.
[30] *Ibid.*, chap. XII, conclusion, p. 237. Cf. J. Dewey, *Human Nature and Conduct*, 1930, p. 43; Dewey and Tufts, *Ethics*, 1932, pp. 184 ff.

as it is in a chemical analysis of water to separate the hydrogen from the oxygen. For only by this separation of chemical elements can we demonstrate that there are always two parts of hydrogen to one part of oxygen in water; and only by a methodological separation of motives from their consequences can one show that it is solely the usual, prevailing or the actual *consequences* of motives which determine the moral value of a motive and an act. No motive and no act can be properly judged in ethics without reference to its effects, pleasure and pain. But these consequences, pleasure and pain, can be said to constitute the elements of everything morally good or bad. For these reasons, it seems to me that only Bentham's allegedly one-sided emphasis on consequences and not Dewey's attempt to overcome this "one-sidedness" is epistemologically justified.

Of no motive can any "clear idea . . . be entertained, otherwise, than by reference to the sort of pleasure or pain which such motive has for its basis: viz. the pleasure or pain, the idea and eventual expectation of which is considered as having been operating in the character of a motive."[31] "On this basis must also be erected, and to this standard must be referred—whatsoever clear explanations are capable of being suggested, by the other more anomalous appellatives . . . , such as emotion, affection, passion, disposition, inclination, propensity, . . . moral quality, vice, virtue, moral good, moral evil."[32] "To a truly enlightened as well as sincerely benevolent mind it will appear that, on each individual occasion, it is by the probable balance in the account of utility, whether of pleasure or of pain, that the judgment, whether it be of approbation or of disapprobation, ought to be determined."[33] But "take away pleasures and pains, not only happiness, but justice and duty . . . , obligation and virtue" and all the many laudatory and vituperative springs of action—all of which have been "so elaborately held up to view as independent of them [viz. pain and pleasure]—are so many empty sounds."[34] Thus the principle of utility, referring all moral predication consistently to terms of pain and pleasure, receives in the *Table* an even more extensive critical explanation and justification than in the earlier writings of Bentham.

Along with this fundamental idea concerning motives go some few other remarkable inquiries into details of this doctrine. As to the as-

[31] Bentham, *Works*, 1843, vol. I, p. 211a.
[32] *Ibid.*, vol. I, p. 211b.   [33] *Ibid.*, vol. I, p. 209b, no. 4.
[34] *Ibid.*, p. 206b, no. 15.

sumption of the motive of "actual disinterestedness," Bentham comes to the seemingly paradoxical decision that disinterestedness exists as an interest, as a motive, but there is no absolute disinterestedness, no "disinterestedness, properly speaking"; no human act ever has been or ever can be "disinterested . . . in . . . the original and only strictly proper sense" of the word.[35] For, "the absence of *all* interest" is a "state of things which consistently with voluntary action is not possible."[36] "There exists not ever any voluntary action which is not the result of the operation of some motive or motives: nor any motive which has not for its accompaniment a corresponding interest, real or imagined."[36] As we shall see later more distinctly, Bentham denies the possibility of an absolutely free will in the sense of a will which is empirically unconditioned by motives and corresponding interests.

If this is correct, and even if the law of causality is considered a merely heuristic principle for the understanding of human actions, then indeed "the most disinterested of men is not less under the dominion of interest than the most interested. The only cause of his being styled disinterested is—its not having been observed that the sort of motive (suppose it sympathy for an individual or a class of individuals) has as truly a corresponding interest belonging to it, as any other species of motive has. Of this contradiction between the truth of the case and the language employed in speaking of it, the cause is—that, in the one case, men have not been in the habit of making—as in point of consistency they ought to have made—of the word interest that use which in the other case they have been in the habit of making of it. At the same time by its having been as properly and completely and indisputably the product of interest as any other action ever is or can be, whatsoever merit may happen to belong to any action to which, in the loose and ordinary way of speaking, the epithet disinterested would be applied, is not in any the slightest degree lessened."[36] In other words "in the case where sympathy is the motive, there is . . . not . . . less need of —nor even less actual demand for—such a word as interest than in the case where the motive and interest are of the self-regarding class. . . . Witness these expressions among so many . . .—a man in whose behalf I feel myself strongly interested . . . in whose fate—in whose sorrows— I take a lively interest."[37] All these statements evidently show that Bentham on this point was not as blind as he is often charged with being.

---

[35] Bentham, *Works*, 1843, vol. I, p. 211b, §2, p. 212a.
[36] *Ibid.*, vol. I, p. 212a.
[37] Bentham, *Works*, 1843, vol. I, p. 212a.

He by no means denied the existence of altruistic feelings; in fact, he admitted them explicitly. But he went further, and insisted that, though the objects of these inclinations are other persons rather than ourselves, these inclinations must have a motive, and this motive, the cause of these extra-regarding inclinations, can be, in the last analysis, only self-regarding interest. Bentham did not fall into the error which Broad attributes to Hobbes, the error of identifying the object of altruism with its cause: he clearly distinguished the two concepts from each other.

C. D. Broad criticizes Hobbes, because Hobbes overlooked the fact that the objects of altruistic feelings are other persons than the altruistic subject; Hobbes mixed up the subject in which altruistic feelings exist with the objects which such feelings concern.[38] Wherever such a confusion takes place, it naturally leads to grave fallacies.

But the main consequence to be drawn from this wrong criticism of altruism is not, as Broad says, the simple acknowledgment that altruistic feelings exist having as objects other persons than ourselves. The principal conclusion to be drawn is that even those feelings which have other persons as objects must be of "egoistic" interest for the subject having these altruistic emotions. Broad, therefore, stresses only another one-sided view, different from the view he criticizes in Hobbes but no less a half truth. Bentham, however, did justice to the two sides of the problem of disinterestedness, as we shall see later, in even greater detail.

The Disproportion between the Number of Dyslogistic, Eulogistic and Neutral Terms of Motives

Further, Bentham enters, in the *Table*, into a minute discussion of the psychologically and ethically interesting question of why there should be an obvious disproportion between the number of dyslogistic, eulogistic and neutral attributes of motives. The old complaint of pessimists is certainly not ill-founded: Even Dante's and Milton's language is much richer and more glowing in its pessimistic, vituperative, dark colored terms than in expressions of moral agreement and optimism. There is hardly any tongue on earth which is not better fit for the description of death and condemnation than of beatitude and bliss.

But Bentham is not content with such vague generalities which commonly lead to general pessimism; he approaches the same subject in a far more concrete, differentiating fashion. First he shows in detail in his lists of motives how large the majority of dyslogistic terms is within his

[38] C. D. Broad, *Five Types of Ethics*, 1930, pp. 65 f, 63, 64.

careful enumeration of the different names for these springs of action. If we count them together in his *Table*, the proportion is, roughly speaking, 197 dyslogistic terms to 56 eulogistic ones. Dealing with the motives of sympathy the *Table*, it is true, contains a majority of laudatory names. But even here there is no scarcity of vituperative terms; and in most of the other lists of the *Table*, we find a definite deficiency of laudatory ones.[39] The number of ethically neutral appellatives enumerated by Bentham is about 64; but, as he adds explicitly, in no case does there exist any abundance of neutral names.[40] Moreover, practically none of these neutral names are in common, ordinary use. Bentham had to coin artificial neutral terms in order to eradicate one of the main roots of uncritical reasoning in ethics.

Further, Bentham finds that there are eight types of motives in which "men in general do not derive any advantage, one man from what is done by another, for the satisfaction of those several desires";[41] and this is the reason why in these cases no *eulogistic* terms are commonly used in moral discussions. These eight types of motives, for which no eulogistic terms are generally in use, are "(No. 1.) Desire of food and drink. (No. 2.) Sexual desire. (No. 3.) Physical desires in general. (No. 5.) Desire of power. (No. 6.) Curiosity. (No. 12.) Love of ease. (No. 13.) Desire of self-preservation. (No. 14.) Personal interest in general."[41] If someone acts on any of these eight motives, others generally see in it no advantage for themselves; and as ethical reasoning is commonly dominated by interests, not by an impersonal love of objective truth, it is quite comprehensible why no eulogistic terms are usually available for these motives. True, as Bentham adds, it may be doubted whether men, in satisfying their sexual desire, do nevertheless not offer some advantage to the objects of their desire. But Bentham answers that this doubt has no real foundation,[42] for it results from confusing sexual desire with love.

In four groups of motives Bentham finds eulogistic appellatives to be abundant. These are "(No. 8.) Regard for reputation: (No. 9.) Fear of God: (No. 10.) Good-will towards men"[43] and with certain necessary, supplementary explanations—to be pointed out later—also (No. 4.) love of the matter of wealth. The reason for this fact is, again, that of all these "desires there is not one which is not common for one man to behold an advantage to himself, in the creating and increasing, in

---

[39] Bentham, *Works*, 1843, vol. I, pp. 202, 213a, 212b.
[40] *Ibid.*, vol. I, p. 213b.   [41] *Ibid.*, vol. I, p. 212b.
[42] *Ibid.*, vol. I, pp. 212b f.   [43] *Ibid.*, vol. I, p. 213.

the breasts of other men."[43] Advantage has, in this as in other cases, led to the creation of a terminology which appropriately expresses these human interests but which is not an expression of impersonal impartiality.

Want of *dyslogistic* ethical appellations does nowhere exist; and the cause or reason for this is once more the general interest of men. For "there exists not any species of desire such that by the pursuit of it, i.e. of the object of it, it does not frequently happen that one man's interest is opposed and his desires frustrated by the interests and corresponding desires and pursuits of other men."[44] Therefore ethical discussion is, as regards all human motives, amply provided with dyslogistic terminology; and it is not necessary, in explaining this fact, to take refuge in a general pessimistic philosophy of life.

There is only one case in which a majority of eulogistic, rather than dyslogistic, denominations can be found. This is in the case of the motive of sympathy; but this, too, follows from what has been said above. For the motive of sympathy conflicts least with the interests of other men. On the other hand, a special abundance of dyslogistic attributives can be observed in relation to the motive of sexual desire. The causes for that "may be seen in 1. the intensity of the desire, 2. its aptitude to enter into combination with others . . . 3. the importance of the consequences with which the gratification of it is liable to be attended, 4. the varieties of ways in which the interests of different persons are liable to be put in opposition to each other by the force of it," for instance, in the experiences of rivals, husbands and gallants, parents or other guardians and wards, legislators, moralists and divines.[44] Though sexual desire is the indispensable basis of the preservation of the species, especially numerous invectives are directed against it simply because it is likely to come into opposition with a particularly large number of the interests of other men. A considerable abundance of dyslogistic, as well as eulogistic, terms exist in another field of marked emotional interests—in the field of the motives of the purse. Here, in general, the interests of men are equally divided according to their interests in disbursement or non-disbursement by certain persons;[45] and so it is not surprising to see in this case an equal abundance of eulogistic and dyslogistic motives at work in ethical judgment.

An *abundance* of *neutral* terms cannot be found in any case. The cause is that "seldom, comparatively speaking, has a man occasion to speak of a motive as operating or of a desire etc. as having place in any human breast—whether his own or any other—without feeling an in-

[44] *Ibid.*, vol. 1, p. 213a.   [45] *Ibid.*, vol. 1, p. 213.

389

terest in presenting it either to the approbation or to the disapprobation of those for whose ear or eye his discourse is intended."[45] Thus practically everywhere, the existing interests of men favor and forward the creation of biased terminology and prevent a neutral one. The want of neutral appellations is so considerable that in eight types of motives no neutral denominations exist at all; they have to be formed artificially by a combination of two words. These types of motives are "(No. 2.) Sexual desire: (No. 3.) Physical desire in general: (No. 4.) Love of money, or rather of the matter of wealth: (No. 5.) Love of power; unless Ambition, as well as Aspiringness, be regarded as purely neutral: (No. 6.) Desire of Amity: (No. 7.) Regard for reputation: (No. 12.) Love of Ease: (No. 14.) The desire corresponding to Personal interest at large."[45] In these cases the want of neutral appellatives can perhaps be somewhat remedied by the combination of a faintly dyslogistic word with a eulogistic adjunct such as "noble ambition" or "generous pride."[46] Upon other desires, however, such as drunkenness or malignity, such a quantity of odium is heaped that their combination with a eulogistic adjective is impossible, at least in the eyes of Bentham.[45] He obviously had no knowledge of the paradoxical language of mystics or psychologists who speak of divine drunkenness or creative malignity.

On the whole, however, this detailed comparison of the frequency of eulogistic, dyslogistic and neutral motives is certainly far more than the tedious, pedantic play with words which it may seem at first view and which it is commonly thought to be to this day. I do not know any more systematic and more enlightening proof of the partiality of common ethical judgment than this analysis of motives in Bentham.

The Substitution or Masking of Motives and other *Motifs* of the *Table*

It is human interest, not impartial ethical valuation, which in everyday language determines even the coining of terms for motives. This again is to be inferred from Bentham's observations on what he calls the substitution and the covering or masking of motives.

Neither moralists nor psychologists can deny that seldom does it happen that a man's "conduct stands exposed to the action of no more than one motive. Frequently indeed—not to say commonly—does it happen that on one and the same occasion it is acted upon by a number of motives"[47] acting even in opposite directions. So for example, love of jus-

---

[46] *Ibid.*, vol. I, p. 214. [47] *Ibid.*, vol. I, p. 218a.

tice consists of the component elements of the desire for self-preservation, of sympathy for a single individual liable to become a sufferer by injustice, sympathy for the community at large, but also of antipathy to profiteers of injustice and unjust judges. The love of liberty consists of the desire of self-preservation, sympathies for the community and the sufferers from misrule, but also of antipathies against tyrants, against profiteers of tyranny and of love of power.[48]

In the moral characterizations of such complex motives, the following forgeries or falsifications are commonly practiced willingly or unwillingly: either one motive out of a complexity of springs of action is selected and all others are kept out of sight and covered or masked by it; or, if no motive within the given complexity is suitable for this purpose, then an invented motive may be substituted in place of the actual ones.[49]

If friends judge the act of a friend, they will try to mask the whole combination of his assailable motives by a sufficiently respected one. If adversaries judge the act of an adversary, they will try to cover all his comparatively "good" motives by a "bad" one. But if friends, in the act of a friend, cannot find a sufficiently respected motive "then, instead of the actual motive, some such other motive will be looked out for and employed as being sufficiently favourable shall, by the nearness of its connexion with the actual one, have been rendered most difficultly distinguishable from it. To speak shortly, if the actual motive do not come up to the purpose, another will in the account given of the matter be substituted to it: or, more shortly still, the motive will be changed. And so vice versa in the case of enmity."[50]

Both the eulogistic or dyslogistic covering and the eulogistic or dyslogistic substituted motives are termed by Bentham "covering motives" or "fig-leaves . . . employed . . . for the unseemly parts of the mind."[51] As such springs of action are mentioned, for instance, the desire of having children as a covering expression for sexual desire; the love of good cheer, the love of a social bowl as a substitute for the interests of the palate and of the bottle; love of country, love of mankind, philanthropy, love of duty, sense of duty—all these five terms are named as covering motives for love of power; industry, or the desire of labor, as "coverings" for the desire of the matter of wealth; sympathy and gratitude as substitutes for the desire of amity; public spirit and love of justice as coverings for antipathy or even the will to persecution.[51]

[48] *Ibid.*, p. 210b.
[49] *Ibid.*, vol. I, p. 218a, §8 and p. 218b.
[50] *Ibid.*, p. 218b.
[51] *Ibid.*, pp. 218b, 219.

In this connection, Bentham goes so far as to declare that love of duty and the desire of labor, taken by themselves, are "impossible motives," "contradictions in terms."[52] For, as he says, duty has to be understood as synonymous to "obligation . . . and . . . it . . . is not possible . . . that a man should derive any pleasure from" and feel any love for "any such thought as that of being forced to it."[53] Similarly, according to Bentham, "labour . . . taken in its proper sense . . . , labour considered in the character of an end" is never qualified to produce a desire, but always an "aversion," ease, not labor is the object which men are striving for.[54] Further, as to the desire for having children, Bentham thinks that at least "to indigent parents" a child before birth can scarcely be an object of desire.[53] The tenability of these last statements may be doubted. Labor, I think, can indeed be loved not only as a means, but as an end, though not as an ultimate end and not "without any view to anything else."[54] But the same applies to wealth and to other ends named as legitimate by Bentham; and Bentham himself, throughout his life, provides a good example of the possibility of love of labor as a relative end.

Aside from these minor points, Bentham has, I think, succeeded in his main task of illustrating the methods used by common partiality in the ethical denominations of motives. It does not matter whether this bias is caused by "inborn . . . indigenous . . . weakness" of the intellect or by adoptive intellectual weakness or by sinister interest, or by a mixture of intellectual and volitional depravity, by "interest-begotten prejudice" (conscious or "not self-conscious").[55] This partiality has, in any case, given birth to a "speculative" and a "practical error of the very first importance,"[56] to an error which pervades all ethics of pure motives or values. It is the fundamental error of assuming that the moral goodness or badness of an act can be impartially and objectively ascertained by the character of its motive, independent of the consequences of the act.

Repeating briefly some of his remarks on alarm and danger[57] and other reflections of the *Introduction*[58] Bentham develops the main theme of his chief earlier work even more fully in the *Table*. "Proper subjects of the attributives good and bad are" according to him "consequences,

---

[52] *Ibid.*, vol. I, pp. 219a, 214a. [53] *Ibid.*, vol. I, p. 219a.
[54] *Ibid.*, p. 214a. [55] *Ibid.*, vol. I, p. 217b.
[56] *Ibid.*, vol. I, p. 215a. [57] *Ibid.*, vol. I, p. 216a.
[58] See e.g. *ibid.*, vol. I, p. 206b, no. 14, the acknowledgment of genuine pleasures and pains of the mind apart from those of the body; or *ibid.*, vol. I, p. 206a, no. 8, the enumeration of the seven elements of value of pleasure and pain.

intentions ... intentions considered in respect of the consequences which at the time of the intention a man actually had or at least . . . is supposed to have had in view. . . . These, together with the acts, which the intentions in question are considered as having been directed to the production of, or as having a tendency to produce, will . . . be seen to be the only subjects to which, in the character of attributives, such adjuncts as good and bad can either with speculative propriety or without danger of practical error . . . be attached."[59] The predicates good and bad may be attributed also to habits without too much danger of misinterpretation. To dispositions, inclinations and propensities the attributes good and bad are often ascribed "in practice";[60] but in theory great caution must be used in making such attributions. To motives, however, to pleasures and pains, to interests, desires and aversions the predicates good and bad "cannot without impropriety be attached";[60] and they ought never to be attached to them in the strict, absolute sense in which the great majority of moralists employ them.

As Bentham adds, in contrast to the common ethical estimation of motives, "if goodness were to be measured by necessity to human existence, . . . of all motives, actual or imaginable, the very best . . . would be the motives that correspond respectively to the desires of food and drink . . . and to sexual desire. . . . Yet, to any such desire as that of eating or drinking, by those by whom so much is said of good motives and so much stress is laid upon the degree of goodness of a man's motives, admittance would scarcely have been given into their list of good motives: and as to sexual desire, taken by itself, so bad a thing is it commonly deemed in the character of a motive, or even in the character of a desire, that all the force which it is in the power of human exertion to muster has, to a great extent, been employed in the endeavour to extinguish it altogether. Under the general name of self-regarding interest . . . are comprisable the several particular interests corresponding to all the several motives that do not belong either to the social class . . . or the dissocial class."[61] To attach to this self-regarding interest, commonly called selfishness, any good epithet would be generally thought to be "a contradiction in terms"; but if you "weed out of the heart of man this species of interest with the corresponding desires and motives, the thread of life is cut and the whole race perishes."[61] On the other hand, interests and motives commonly provided by the best "letters of recommendation," such as fear of God, and love of reputation can become the

[59] *Ibid.*, vol. i, pp. 216b, 217a.   [60] *Ibid.*, p. 217a.
[61] *Ibid.*, vol. i, p. 216a.

393

source of religious persecution, of infanticide, of conquest, this "aggregate of all the crimes and . . . the mischiefs that man is capable of committing or suffering"; and even sympathy may be evil, if not extended "to the whole sensitive race, all species included, present and future."[62] All these lines of reasoning lead, therefore, to the same conclusion: goodness or badness of motives does not depend on the motives themselves; it "depends altogether upon the direction in which, on each occasion, they act, upon the nature of the effects, the consequences, pleasurable or painful of which they become efficient causes or preventives."[63] If, however, according to traditional moral views, only so-called good motives were to be cultivated while so-called bad motives, such as "selfishness," were to be combated or extirpated, this manipulation could be compared, according to Bentham, with the ingenious prescript of putting into a watch only regulators, "but not one main spring."[64] This repeated defense of self-regarding interests and Bentham's general tendency of contemplating human motives as neutrally as lines, planes or bodies, has some marked similarity to Spinoza's ethical thought.

Bentham's general agreement with Spinoza is perhaps even more marked in his conception of free will, so far as he touches on this large problem in his *Table*. Like Spinoza, Bentham believes in *libera necessitas*, that is, he explicitly states with Spinoza that we are allowed to call human actions free or necessary with equal right. "Employ the term free will—to the exclusion of the term free will, employ the term necessity . . . the language so employed will not be found to be expressive of any real difference."[65] According to Bentham any human "action is . . . the result of that one motive or that group of simultaneously operating motives of which, on that same occasion, the force and influence happen to be the strongest."[65] This is indeed Spinoza's doctrine of *libera necessitas*, but without anything of the background of Spinoza's metaphysics. On the contrary, Bentham's ideas on free will are as thoroughly rooted in empirical ground as his whole theory of motives and self-interest, and all this is developed by him without any traceable or probable influence from Spinoza's ethics.

We should not allow the modest title of Bentham's work, *A Table of the Springs of Action*, to deceive us. By dint of the seemingly pedantic method of cataloguing hundreds of terms for motives, and by

[62] *Ibid.*, vol. I, pp. 214a, 216b. [63] *Ibid.*, vol. I, p. 216b.
[64] *Ibid.*, p. 215b. [65] *Ibid.*, p. 218a.

means of only a few accompanying explanations, Bentham gave part of the foundations of his ethical thought a pregnant, striking, and classical formulation.

BENTHAM'S LATER JURISTIC, ECONOMIC AND RELIGIOUS WRITINGS

Free Will in These Writings

The problem of moral motives, as well as that of free will, appears in Bentham's later thought again in another connection; and these scattered reflections also deserve at least some brief attention. As for free will, the "Rationale of judicial Evidence" proclaims explicitly "It is by experience we are taught that, as in the case of every other modification of human conduct . . . no action is ever performed without a motive."[66] This assurance is, however, certainly as laconic as it is epistemologically unsatisfactory. The law of causality may be regarded as an indispensable heuristic principle for psychological research, as a principle a priori or as a general statement based on induction; but the law of causality is certainly not taught us by mere empirical observation.

As we saw from a letter written in 1789,[67] Bentham gave no thought to the epistemological difficulties of the problem of free will. He saw no need for any belief in free will, at least not within *his* ethics. His ethical reflections presuppose the law of causality as a sufficiently well established principle of empirical science; and metaphysical beliefs in which free will might have its place were, he felt, not his concern.

He admits, it is true, that the application of the law of causality is far more complicated in the field of morals than in the field of physics. "Prone as is the human mind to the making of hasty and imperfectly grounded inductions on the field of physical science, it cannot but be much more so in the field of psychology and ethics in which is included the field of politics; commonly not only is the collection made of influencing circumstances incomplete, but uninfluencing circumstances and even obstacles are placed in the station of and held up to view in the character of principally or even exclusively operating causes. Thus su-

[66] Bentham, *Works*, 1843, vol. VI, p. 242a ("Rationale of Judicial Evidence," first printed in 1827).
[67] See *ibid.*, vol. X, p. 216.

perior is the density of the clouds which overhang the relation between cause and effect in the field of morals as compared with the field of physics. Two concurring considerations may help us to account for this difference—1. The elements of calculation being in so large a proportion of the psychical class—such as intentions, affections and motives— are in a proportional degree situated out of the reach of direct observation. 2. In the making of the calculation the judgment is in a peculiar degree liable to be disturbed and led astray by the several sources of illusion, by original intellectual weakness, by sinister interest, by interest-begotten prejudice and by adopted prejudice."[68] "Amongst psychological facts no such close conformity is commonly observed as amongst physical facts. They are not alike open to our observation; nor in so far as they have happened actually to be observed, has the result of the observation been such as to warrant the supposition of a degree of conformity equally close."[69] But all this concerns essentially the application of the law of causality and not the validity of the law itself. The strict causation of all human acts is generally not contested by Bentham.

The most cautious and skeptical attitude toward the validity of general causation is perhaps to be found in the following deductions of the *Rationale of Judicial Evidence*, first published in 1827: "The sort of internal perception of consciousness we all feel of what is called the freedom of our will is of itself sufficient to put a negative upon the application of any such term as impossibility to any of the facts which present themselves as flowing from that source. To assert the impossibility of any given act, is to assert the necessity of the opposite act; and, in a proposition asserting the necessity of this or that act on the part of any human agent, a denial of the freedom of his will is generally understood to be involved."[70] In other words, as we seem never able to apply the concepts of impossibility and necessity to the causation of actions, we seem to be never entitled to presuppose the absolute validity of the law of causality in the field of human behavior and we should, therefore, not deny the possibility of free will altogether. Nevertheless, even in this connection Bentham goes on to say: "Examined to the bottom this consciousness of the freedom of our will would, it is true, be found to amount to neither more or less than our blindness as to a part, more or less considerable, of the whole number of joint causes or concurrent circumstances on which the act of the will and with it the con-

[68] *Ibid.*, vol. VIII, pp. 209b, 210a ("Ontology," written in 1813-1814 and 1821).
[69] *Ibid.*, part XIII, p. 114a ("Rationale of Judicial Evidence").
[70] *Ibid.*, part XIII, p. 114a.

sequent physical acts depend: nor is this the only instance of a false conception of power growing out of impotence."[70] Thus the belief in free will is even here, at least, partly reduced to ignorance and partly to vanity signifying the futile striving for power in powerless creatures.

In a comparatively similar way Bentham points out "that it is only by a sort of misconception and verbal illusion that such attributes as necessity, impossibility, probability, improbability are considered and spoken of as if they were attributes and properties of the events themselves"; and then he adds: "the only sort of fact of which they are really and truly indicative, is the disposition of our mind, of our own judgment to be persuaded, with a greater or less degree of assurance, concerning their existence or non-existence: to entertain an assurance, more or less intense that at the place in question, at the time in question the fact in question was or was not in existence."[71] These reflections might be construed to admit the assumption of causality as a heuristic principle of research; in any case, they show that Bentham rejected causality as a law ontologically established in nature. Bentham, it is true, sees no way to exclude the ontological *possibility* of freedom, but he finds no room in psychological and ethical analyses for any *affirmation* of free will. In the field of empirical research he, at any rate, does not take into account indeterminism.

Bentham, of course, admits that man in general is by no means "perfectly conscious of his own mind and aware of the moments and directions of the incessantly fluctuating forces that are operating on him."[72] On the contrary "this is not the case with one man in a million, in any the least degree; nor perhaps with any man in perfection."[72] The motive a man is actuated by is frequently "secret to himself . . . the rare case is not that of his not knowing, but that of his knowing it. It is with the anatomy of the human mind as with anatomy and physiology of the human body: the rare case is not that of a man's being unconversant, but that of his being conversant with it. The physiology of the body is not without its difficulties: but in comparison of those by which the knowledge of the physiology of the mind has been obstructed, the difficulties are slight indeed. Not infrequently, as between two persons living together in a state of intimacy, either or each may possess a more correct and complete view of the motives by which the mind of the other, than of those by which his own mind, is governed. Many a woman has in this way had a more correct and complete acquaintance

[71] *Ibid.*, vol. VII, p. 114.
[72] *Ibid.*, "The Rationale of Reward," 1825, p. 351 (*Works*, 1843, vol. II, p. 266b).

with the internal causes by which the conduct of her husband has been determined, than he has had himself."[73] On this point, we see once more how little of a mere rationalist Bentham is as regards the psychology of the human will, how much he has in common with modern theories concerning the limits of rational thought and the power of the subconscious or unconscious forces of the human mind.

Bentham does not deny that causes of human actions are often "of atomical . . . and almost invisible . . . force."[74] But to these psychological concessions he repeatedly adds such dogmatic declarations as the following: "No action whatsoever" is "without a motive," without a cause.[74] "Minute, it is true, minute in the extreme is the quantity of pleasure or pain requisite and sufficient to the formation of a desire; but still it is not the less true—take away all pleasure and all pain, and you have no desire. . . . No act of the will can take place but in consequence of a correspondent desire; in consequence of the action of a desire in the character of a motive."[75] "Every . . . sort of action must have its inducement."[76]

Finally in a MS on sex published by C. K. Ogden in 1931, Bentham combines particularly clearly the stress laid on strict causation with that on causation by pleasure: "Unless attended with pleasure" an operation "never is performed."[77] And Bentham illustrates this by reference to rather earthy and radical examples, the sexual enjoyment obtained by pigs and, above all, that obtained by pederasts in homosexual intercourse: "Enjoyment from such a source? exclaims the man to whom it really is or to whom it seems good to represent it as being a source of disgust and horror. But unless it was really an enjoyment, all the effects of which history and observation join in showing it to be productive, would be effect without a cause. Considered in the character of an object of sexual appetite, the sow is to me an object of abhorrence; there-

---

[73] Bentham, *The Book of Fallacies*, 1824, p. 372 f (*Works*, 1843, part IV, pp. 477b, 478a).

[74] Bentham, *Works*, 1843, vol. VI, p. 259a ("Rationale of Judicial Evidence," book I, chap. XI, para. 2). Cf. already Part II of the Introduction to the Principles of Morals and Legislation published by Charles W. Everett under the title *The Limits of Jurisprudence Defined*, 1945, p. 53: "Without a motive no such thing as action"; *ibid.*, p. 154 note: "No man acts without a motive; no man acts against a preponderant mass of motives."

[75] *Ibid.*, vol. VIII, pp. 280b, 280a ("Logic," Appendix A, written between 1811 and 1831).

[76] *Ibid.*, part VIII, p. 398b ("Draught of a Code for the Organization of Judicial Establishments in France with Critical Observations on the Draught proposed by the National Assembly Committee," 1790).

[77] Bentham, MS on Sex published in *The Theory of Legislation* ed. by C. K. Ogden, 1931, p. 477.

fore she is and always must be to the father of her pigs. Such is the logic, which should make a merit of denying the name of a sense of enjoyment to an appetite the gratification of which has been sought by such multitudes at the risk and frequently to the sacrifice of life."[78] Broadly speaking, therefore, a more or less critical assumption of strict causality prevails in Bentham's psychological and ethical analyses.

It is extremely rare that he admits the possibility of free will as existing in a world in itself. He did not wish to regard free will as impossible if seen from the point of view of an absolute ontology which aspires to speak of things in themselves. But he excluded the assumption of free will from any scientific interpretation of empirical phenomena in physics and ethics. Moreover, according to some of his remarks, he thought we learn from immediate experience that free will does not exist; and it is to experience that he turns throughout his work as the highest source of certainty.

Empirical Observation and the "Ought" in Ethics

In his *A Comment on the Commentaries* Bentham had already avowed himself a consistent empiricist; and in his later thought this stand gains further and even increased emphasis. Experience remains to him "the foundation of all our knowledge and of all our reasoning— the sole guide of our conduct, the sole basis of our security."[79] "Consult experience, man's faithful and steady guide; and behold on how simple a ground the case stands. In children, at an early age, the reliance on assertion is strongest: why?—Because at that age experience is all, or almost all, on one side. As age advances that reliance grows weaker and weaker: why?—Because experience is acquired on both sides—experience certifying the existence of falsehood as well as that of truth."[80] "A theory is . . . no farther good than in so far as its indications receive, as occasion serves, the confirmation of experience."[81] "Experience, observation and experiment—these are the foundations of all well-grounded medical," moral and "legislative practice."[82] "It is

[78] Bentham, MS on Sex; see Bentham, *The Theory of Legislation* ed. by C. K. Ogden, 1931, p. 493.
[79] Bentham, *Works*, 1843, vol. vi, p. 241b; *Rationale of Judicial Evidence*, 1827, book i, chap. vii, §2.
[80] *Ibid.*, vol. vi, p. 241a.
[81] *Ibid.*, part vii, p. 177a ("Panopticon versus New South Wales," written in 1802).
[82] *Ibid.*, vol. iii, p. 224a, 224b (Pannomial Fragments, written at sundry times, some of the latest sheets are dated June 1831).

with rules of morality and propositions in psychology as with [juristi-cal] laws: when the indication of reasons and these reasons grounded on experience is regarded as unnecessary, any one man is as competent to the task of making them as any other."[83] "In the whole human race, considered at all periods of its history, the knowledge of particulars has preceded that of generals"[84] and it ought to precede it in any scientific investigation. Perhaps the most careful analysis of experience as the source of all beliefs and certainty is given in this passage: If "you ask me . . . what is that ulterior and deeper or highest cause that causes experience to be the cause of belief?—you ask me for that which is not

[83] *Ibid.*, vol. VI, p. 238b.

[84] *Ibid.*, vol. VIII, p. 282a ("Logic," Appendix B, sect. I. Completely on the ground of empiricism remains also Bentham's so-called method of bipartition within the classification of generic terms. This "bifurcate" (vol. VIII, p. 264b), "dichotomous" (vol. VIII, p. 253b), compare *Chrestomathia*, 1816, p. 319, *Works*, 1843, part xv, p. 107b or "two pronged method" (*ibid.* vol. VIII, p. 291b, "logic," Appendix B, sect. III) is well illustrated in the *Chrestomathia* in the following way: "Entities are either real or fictitious: real, either perceptible or inferential: perceptible, either impressions or ideas: inferential, either material, i.e. corporeal or immaterial, i.e., spiritual. From the observation, by which, for example, the words duties and rights are here spoken of as names of fictitious entities, let it not for a moment so much as be supposed, that, in either instance, the reality of the object is meant to be denied, in any sense in which in ordinary language the reality of it is assumed. One question, however, may be ventured to be proposed for consideration, viz., whether, supposing no such sensations as pleasure or pain, duties would not be altogether without force, and rights altogether without value?" (*Chrestomathia*, 1816, pp. 338 ff, *Works*, VIII, pp. 126a, 126b note); or compare the following lucid survey of entities according to the "exhaustively" dichotomous "mode of division" (*Chrestomathia*, 1816, p. 319), a survey of unknown date, written obviously not before 1810 and not published hitherto: "Entities are either Real or Fictitious. Real are either Material or Mental. Material are either substances or motions. Mental are either perceptions or sensations. Perceptions are either Impressions or Ideas (see Hume). Sensations are produced from some perceptions, not from all. Qu: is a Volition a thing distinct from a sensation, Volitions are no other way distinguishable from one another but by the Events which are the objects of them. An operation is an assemblage of acts simultaneous (contemporary) and (or) succedaneous but if succedaneous uninterrupted. An occupation (in the sense in which it is of the Class of real Entities) is an assemblage of operations although interrupted. An act is a motion resulting from Volition or it is a motion of a being endow'd with volition this to take in Involuntary as well as Voluntary Acts. Fictitious entities are feigned in imitation of real ones. Correspondent to each Species of Material real entities is a fictitious one. Fictitious Entities then are either fictitious Substances or fictitious Operations. Instances of fictitious Substances are Qualities, Vowels, Dispositions, anything which not being a Substance is said to act or which a man is said to hear. Instances of fictitious operations are to have, to love, to teach, to read." (Bentham MSS, University College, London, Portfolio 106, Folder 2, sheet 2.)

mine, nor anybody's, to give; you require of me what is impossible. It may probably enough have appeared to you that what you have been doing, in putting to me that question, amounts to no more than the calling upon me for a proposition, to be delivered to you on my part. But the truth is, that, in calling upon me to that effect, you have yourself, though in an obscure and inexplicit way—you have yourself, whether you are aware of it or no, been delivering to me a proposition— and a proposition which, if my conception of the matter be correct, is not conformable to the truth of things. The proposition I mean is, that— over and above, and distinct from, those objects which you have in view, in speaking of the words experience and belief, of which the first represents the cause, and the other the effect—there exists a distinct object, in the character of an ulterior and higher cause, which is the cause of the causative power, exercised by that first-mentioned cause: such is the proposition which is comprehended and assumed in and by your interrogative proposition beginning with the word why: but, to my judgment of the matter, this indirectly advanced proposition presents itself as erroneous. For, upon looking for such supposed distinct object, as the archetype of, and thing represented by, the word cause, as now, on the occasion of this second question employed by you, it does not appear to me that any such object exists in nature. If ever it should happen to you to have discovered any such archetype, do me the favour to point it out to me, that I may look at it and examine it. Till you have done so, it will not be in my power to avoid considering as erroneous the proposition which you have been delivering to me in disguise."[85] This is certainly a circumstantial but an interestingly minute explanation of why Bentham sees in experience the ultimate basis of all knowledge and morals below which no deeper foundations are accessible to us.

Bentham seems, however, to take up a paradoxical attitude for an empiricist. For, as often as he stresses the necessity of strictly empirical methods, just so frequently does he refuse in ethics to substitute the questions concerning the "ought" for those concerning the "is." It is the pursuit of both these apparently irreconcilable tendencies which gives Bentham's ethical method its particular significance and value.

As in his first published essay in 1770 and in his first book in 1776, he continues in his later ethical thought scrupulously to separate ex-

[85] Bentham, *Works*, 1843, vol. VI, p. 237b ("Rationale of Judicial Evidence," book I, chap. VII, para. 1).

pository from censorial problems. "The law as it is" and "law as it ought to be" are "very different" things.[86] In his *Chrestomathia* (1816) developing the system of divisions and subdivisions of the different branches of learning, Bentham characterizes ethics or morals in the largest sense by the term "thelematoscopic pneumatology," i.e. the doctrine of those spiritual phenomena which concern the will and the manner of conducting one's self in the course of life;[87] and the two main branches of ethics which he here distinguishes from each other are not private and public ethics or jurisprudence and private morality, but censorial and expository ethics. The fundamental difference between these two parts of ethics is here described in the following way: Censorial ethics is that part of moral science which is "expressive of judgment or sentiment or approbation or disapprobation as intended by the author of the discourse, to be attached to the ideas of the several voluntary actions (or same modifications of human conduct) which in the course of it are brought to view; in other words, his opinion in relation to each such act on the question whether it ought to be done, or to be left undone or may, without impropriety, be done or left undone."[88] Therefore, this branch of ethics is also called "dicastic," because it has, so to speak, to fulfill the functions of an objective moral judge, to determine what is morally right ($\delta\iota\kappa\alpha\sigma\tau\eta s$ = the judge); and in contrast to this, the other branch of ethics is nothing but expository, that is to say "simply exegetic . . . or enunciative, viz. in so far as, without bestowing any such mark of approbation, disapprobation or indifference, the discourse has for its object the stating what in the opinion of the author has on each such occasion actually come to pass, or is likely to have come to pass, or to have place at present, or to be about to come to pass in future—i.e. what act is on the occasion in question most likely to have been done, to be doing, or to be about to be done."[89] This definition of expository ethics represents, however, in my view no improvement in comparison with earlier definitions of the *Fragment* and the *Introduction*. For what Bentham here styles expository ethics is psychology, not ethics at all, even in the largest modern sense of the word; and similarly awkward, or even inaccurate, seems to me Bentham's further illustration of the contrast between

---

[86] Bentham, *The Book of Fallacies*, 1824, p. 117.
[87] Bentham, *Chrestomathia*, 1816, pp. 204, 197. *Works*, 1843, part xv, p. 89 f.
[88] Bentham, *Works*, 1843, part xv, p. 93b.
[89] *Ibid.*, part xv, p. 92 f (*Chrestomathia*, 1816, p. 212 f).

dicastic and exegetic ethics when he says[90] that in censorial, dicastic ethics "the discourse is immediately addressed . . . to . . . the volitional . . . faculty" of the human mind; in exegetic, expository ethics, however, the discourse applies itself immediately to the intellectual faculty.

Nevertheless, it remains characteristic that all the other divisions of ethics mentioned in this connection contain both a dicastic and enunciative, expository part. Bentham divides ethics further into "genioscopic, i.e. general matters regarding and idioscopic, i.e. particular matters regarding"; and genioscopic morals he also terms theoretical, speculative, while idioscopic is called practical; further he distinguishes "apolioscopic i.e. political-state-not-regarding, viz. private ethics" from polioscopic, i.e. political-state-regarding[91] i.e. political ethics.

But all these and other divisions of ethics, law and politics fall under the "first" and most important division into a censorial and an expository branch, which have to be distinguished clearly within every part of all other divisions, while the other divisions are granted to be in general less definite.[92] For Bentham, therefore, the division of ethics into an enunciative and a dicastic branch is everywhere the most fundamental and determinate one within his manifold classifications of the different parts of morals.

To the historian of philosophy, it is instructive to see that Bentham felt most indebted on this point to David Hume. As he declares in his "Commentary on Mr. Humphrey's Real Property Code" in 1826, "by David Hume in his Treatise on Human Nature the universality of this practise of confounding the two so different objects (. . . the is and the ought to be . . . the το ον and the το δεον) . . . was first held up to view."[93] And even more explicitly in the appendix of his *Chrestomathia* he says: "By David Hume in his Treatise on Human Nature the observation was for the first time, it is believed, brought to light—how apt men have been on questions belonging to any part of the field of Ethics to shift backwards and forwards, and apparently without their perceiving it, from the question what has been done to the question what ought

---

[90] *Ibid.*, part xv, p. 93b.

[91] Bentham, *Chrestomathia*, 1816, p. 214 f, *Works* (1843), part xv, p. 94a.

[92] Bentham, *Works*, 1843, part xv, p. 94a, see e.g. "The deeper it (genioscopic ethics) descends into particulars, the more plainly it will be seen to belong to the idioscopic." Or see *ibid.*, part xv, p. 95b note: "Between such discourses as are regarded as being the results or products of the exercise of legislative power and such as are not regarded in that light . . . the line of separation remains, even to this day, altogether unsettled and indeterminate."

[93] *Ibid.*, vol. v, p. 389b.

to be done and vice versa: More especially from the former of these points to the other; . . . to every eye by which those two objects have not been completely separated from each other the whole field of ethics . . . must ever have been—yes, and ever will be—a labyrinth without a clue."[94] The history of philosophy can, to some extent, approve this high estimate of Hume's work. For it is indeed Hume's merit that, within empiricism, he stressed the importance of the "ought," of the validity of laws, often more clearly than even the rationalism of the seventeenth and eighteenth centuries had done; and he did so not only in epistemology but also in ethics.

BENTHAM'S EMPIRICISM AND THE DECLARATION DES DROITS DE L'HOMME

The high practical importance which has to be attributed to a strict distinction of *is* and *ought* is further illustrated by Bentham in his criticism of the French "Déclaration des droits de l'homme." Again and again he asks in his "Anarchical Fallacies": what is the real meaning of *can* and *cannot* in numerous articles of this declaration of the National Assembly and that of Sieyès? "Is it . . . to speak of what *is* established or of what *ought* to be established"? As he points out, in the proposition of article I "Social distinctions cannot be founded but upon common utility" the word *cannot* has in truth three different meanings: "in the first . . . it makes appeal to observation . . . in regard to a matter of fact: in the second it is an appeal to the approving faculty of others in regard to the same matter of fact" and in the third it means even "a violent attempt upon the liberty of speech and action on the part of others by the terrors of anarchical despotism, rising up in opposition to the laws."[95] So "can" and "cannot" in the French Declaration of Rights have such different meanings that "they resemble that instrument which in outward appearance is but an ordinary staff, but which within that simple and innocent semblance conceals a dagger. These are the words that speak daggers."[96]

In any case, "can" and "cannot" are, in the moral declarations of the French Revolution, "ambiguous and envenomed" words;[97] and "the same confusion of that which it is supposed *is*, with that which it is conceived

[94] Bentham, *Chrestomathia*, 1816, p. 346, note (*Works*, 1843, part xv, p. 128, note).

[95] Bentham, *Works*, 1843, part IV, p. 499b (Anarchical Fallacies being an Examination of the Declarations of Rights issued during the French Revolution).

[96] *Ibid.*, part IV, p. 500a (analysis of article I of the Declaration decreed by the Constituent Assembly in France).

[97] *Ibid.*, part IV, p. 504b (analysis of article III) 507a.

ought to be" is demonstrated to exist by Bentham in the first and third as well as in the fourth and fifth of the articles of the French "Déclaration."[98] And in the analysis of the seventh and eighth articles also the employment of the "improper" "insurrection-inviting" word *can* is criticized by Bentham, because it covers *is* as well as *ought* and covers even the nullification of all law (which is opposed to this *can*).[99] The terms *can* and *cannot* "leave it continually in doubt" in the documents of the French Revolution whether they "mean solely to declare what shall be the state of the law after the moment of the enactment of this declaration, or likewise what has been its state previous to that moment";[100] and because unambiguous, proper terms are available, the use of such equivocal terms is not only "silly,"[101] but it is even "a moral crime"[102] in consequence of their "mischief-making and anarchy-exciting import." The whole theory of natural rights which is based on this confusion of "is" with "ought" is, according to Bentham, to be compared with "hunger" but "not bread"; or, better, "natural rights is simple nonsense . . . nonsense upon stilts. But this theoretical nonsense ends in . . . mischievous nonsense."[103] This is certainly blunt language. In using it, however, Bentham doubtless did not intend to denounce the progressive political tendencies which the theory of natural rights has often served. What he wished to denounce was the epistemological ambiguity of this theory. In fact, in consequence of its vagueness about "is" and "ought," the theory of natural rights may work in favor of political anarchy as well as progress or even in favor of political reaction. But, in any case, the moralist's vagueness on this point definitely undermines the possibility of consistent ethical inquiry.

Even for the characterization of different national characters Bentham occasionally used a reference to the distinction of *is* and *ought to be*. So he remarks once on the French that "on the subject of chemistry Europe has . . . adopted with . . . admiration . . . the systematic views . . . of the French nation"; "on the subject of the fundamental principles of government" the same nation has produced "execrable trash,"[104] particularly because the French confused what *is* not, with what *ought* not to be and what is legally void. The Germans Bentham reproaches

[98] See *ibid.*, part IV, p. 505b (analysis of article IV) p. 507a (analysis of article V).
[99] See *ibid.*, part IV, pp. 510a, 512a.
[100] *Ibid.*, part IV, p. 530a (Observations on parts of the Declaration of Rights as proposed by Citizen Sieyès).
[101] *Ibid.*, part IV, p. 530b.   [102] *Ibid.*, p. 524b.
[103] *Ibid.*, p. 501a (Anarchical Fallacies).
[104] *Ibid.*, p. 521b (Anarchical Fallacies, conclusion).

because they were even "interdicted from inquiring into things as they ought to be" and because they "can only inquire about things as they were."[105] But these two remarks are not to be taken too seriously; the last one appears as only a desultory apperçu in conversation.

Where, we must ask now, is there any room left for the *ought* in a consistently empirical science? Where can an *ought* be found within a strictly empirical theory of morals? For the answer to this question, Bentham's *Comment on the Commentaries* had already prepared ample material. But, certainly, the complexity of the problem demands some further elucidation.

The answer to this question may perhaps best be summarized in the following way: Within a strictly empirical system of morals even the *ought to be* must ultimately be referred to a kind of *is*, but to another kind of *is* than the *is* of already existing *oughts*. Even more simply, the *ought* can never be grounded on any given, existing rules of that which ought to be, it has to be founded on a judgment concerning quite different empirical facts. Or still more concretely, the *ought* cannot be built up on existing moral valuations, but only on a comparison of the amount of expected feelings, i.e. on psychological facts, bound up with the effects, the consequences of planned actions.

THE "OUGHT" IN BENTHAM AND IN "TIME-HONORED" ETHICS

These results of Bentham's methodological reflections are certainly at complete variance with "time-honoured" ethics. Sir David Ross rightly described this time-honored method as that of Plato, Aristotle and Kant, who all based their ethical investigation on "common knowledge," on "common opinions" about morality, or on the moral judgments of "wise" men.[106] Indeed the ethical dogmatists of all times have followed this line of thought; and Kant too remained an ethical dogmatist despite his intention to write a "critique" of practical, ethical reasoning.

All these dogmatic moralists comforted and still comfort themselves with the belief that there is in morals a *consensus omnium*, a common consent or at least an agreement among all those men whom these moralists condescend to consider wise; and all the existing differences

---

[105] *Ibid.*, part xx, p. 562b (A conversation between Bentham and Bowring about the year 1827). Compare another unfavorable judgment concerning the Germans, at least the ancient Germans, *ibid.*, vol. ii, p. 254.

[106] W. David Ross, *Foundations of Ethics*, 1939, pp. 1 f.

are, according to ethical dogmatism, only the result of "different perspectives"[107] in facing the same truth.

Fortified by such prejudices, and ignoring such fundamental differences as those between master morality and slave morality or other moral codes, these dogmatic moralists have indeed one great advantage over their opponents. Like the dogmatic metaphysicians of older times, with their belief in things in themselves and in a world of thousands of inexplicable qualities, dogmatic anti-hedonists keep much closer to the prejudices of language and to those of the plain or the "wise" man. Methodologically, this advantage comes to the fore, above all, in their assertion that they alone distinguish consistently between *ought* and *is*, strictly in compliance with the spirit of modern and ancient languages.

Again like the old metaphysical dogmatists, these dogmatic moralists, in complete accord with common ethical terminology, cut off any connection between the world of truth and that of verifiability through empirical observation. All this seems to give their method, at first glance, a definite superiority over Bentham's. For Bentham is not at all in agreement with the common terminology of morals; and he does lead back to empirical facts in spite of all his sharp distinction between *ought* and *is*, between valid truth and facts. Dogmatic anti-hedonists, however, seem to remain in the realm of the *ought* from the beginning to the end of their ethical inquiry; and they are very fond of showing off their methodological superiority over the "confused, naturalistic" view of every possible type of hedonism.

But is their method really as consistent as they suppose? Is the plain man's moral insight into the "ought" of equal trustworthiness with his mathematical judgment, his perceptions, or even the judgment on his likes and dislikes, as manifested in his actions? The mathematician, the physicist and even the psychologist can check the judgment of the plain man by something different from that judgment. But the dogmatic moralist has nothing in hand apart from such judgments. He is completely at a loss, the moment he discovers that his investigation is based on nothing but judgments, beliefs and moral codes which are of a highly controversial character, and do not allow us to distinguish between the ethically right and wrong judgments of the plain man. It is certainly no comfort at all to coddle oneself with the conviction that none "of the main theories of ethics," even that of millions of Machiavellians, shows "blindness to moral values" and that they all, even the

[107] *Ibid.*, p. 2.

most opposite ones, are at the worst "mis-statements" of the same truth, based at the worst on "some apparently trivial logical error."[108]

In fact, the fundamentals of time-honored ethics reveal themselves not as statements of immediately true insight into the *ought* itself, but as a number of judgments which are factual, just as much as are the basic statements of Bentham's ethics.[109] Anti-hedonistic dogmatists refer to "factual" value judgments of plain and wise men; and Bentham refers to the factual emotions of men. In any case, dogmatic moralists are completely in error if they believe that they are moving, or that they ever can move, in the realm of an immediate insight into a true *ought*, an *ought* without any dependence on an *is*, but applicable to that *is*. The time-honored method of ethics cannot dispense with facts, any more than physicists can[110]—in spite of all assurances or claims to the contrary.

It seems to me that nothing is gained for truth by basing ethical judgments simply on other common ethical judgments. If we do so, we only *seem* to have protected the *ought* from any contact with the *is*. As a matter of fact, we then fall victims to completely unverifiable statements, statements which themselves express therefore no truth, because at best their correctness or incorrectness can never be ascertained.

That is to say, neither the physicist nor the dogmatic metaphysician nor the dogmatic moralist can ever move in the realm of truth without any reference to an *is*. In fact they all refer to some kind of *is*. It is the *type* of "is" to which they refer which makes all the difference. Bentham saw this clearly. He recognized that moralists do not have to make their choice between an absolutely pure "ought" and an "ought" confused with the "is" as his opponents emphasize. The true alternative is, according to Bentham, that between an "ought" which is based on the "is" of unverifiable existing "oughts" or an "ought" which is verifiable by neutral facts, just as the truth of natural laws is verifiable by neutral sense data.

[108] *Ibid.*, p. 2.

[109] Moreover, like Edmund Husserl, Moritz Schlick, R. v. Mises and others, Bentham was inclined to think that every imperative, not only a moral one, is an expression of a hidden assertion concerning a seemingly different *is*, see *Works*, 1843, vol. IX, p. 337 ("The Constitutional Code," book II, chap. x, sect. II, article II). Cf. Husserl, *Logische Untersuchungen*, Band I, 1913, S. 47: Jede "normative" Disziplin muss notwendig "einen von aller Normierung ablösbaren theoretischen Gehalt besitzen"; M. Schlick, *Problems of Ethics*, 1939, pp. 14 f: "Let it be understood . . . that . . . a norm is nothing but a mere expression of fact." R. v. Mises, *Kleines Lehrbuch des Positivismus*, 1939, e.g. p. 399.

[110] See the opposite view in W. D. Ross, *Foundations of Ethics*, 1939, p. 3.

Recognizing this true alternative, Bentham built his "ought" up by reference to a neutral verifiable "is," namely human feelings, and not by reference to unverifiable types of "ought" or "is." Of all these methodological complications he was obviously well aware; and it is evidently for this reason that, again and again in his later thought, he carefully examined all those phenomena on which the rules of the ought are usually built up, viz. the motives of actions or the values directing actions. Disinterestedness, veracity, benevolence and similar motives are the ideas on which, commonly, the validity of moral pre-scripts, of duties and even that of moral ends is ultimately based. Such motives are the main carriers of values, of the "ought" in the moral systems opposed to Bentham's ethics of happiness. Small wonder that a further detailed criticism of the ethics of motives and the defense of the ethics of happy consequences remains a principal subject of Ben-tham's later thought, both from the point of view of method and that of the matter itself. Only if we patiently think out all such implica-tions of Bentham's philosophy, can we understand his seemingly para-doxical emphasis on the *ought* within a consistent ethical empiricism. But as, in general, no attention is paid to these acute justifications of the principle of utility, Bentham's ethical method has been considered paradoxical or—what is worse, yet even more common—it has been ridiculed as hopelessly naïve.

Ethical Ambidexterity of Motives (Fortitude, Liberality and Honor)

In his later thought Bentham consistently adheres to the main re-sults of his doctrine of moral motives, already laid down in his *Intro-duction*, and he frequently refers to these major ideas. But even apart from the *Table of the Springs of Action* valuable supplements to this theory are still given in his later writings. Above all, Bentham is fond of repeating that there is no motive and "no sort of interest that is not capable of being a sinister interest—no sort of interest that is not capable of being a dexter interest."[111] "There is not any species of in-terest—any species of motives to which it may not happen to act in this as well as in the contrary direction."[112] This can be illustrated by many examples and even by concessions of advocates of an ethics of motives, that is by opponents of utilitarianism.

[111] Bentham, *Works*, 1843, part xiv, p. 394a ("Rationale of Judicial Evidence," book ix, chap. iii, para. 1).
[112] *Ibid.*, vol. vi, p. 258a (book i, chap. xi, para. 1).

Even Aristotle granted that, for instance, "fortitude is a virtue or a vice according as applied. You must know the nature of the case in which a man has to give exercise to the quality, before you can decide on its being a virtue or not."[113] This is certainly an original and appropriate observation on the Aristotelian virtue of the mean. In the light of Bentham's critical analysis, Aristotle's teaching takes on a new meaning. Starting to base his ethics dogmatically on an analysis of motives, even Aristotle himself is, according to Bentham, finally compelled to abandon this attempt and to leave the ethical value of every motive in abeyance. What Aristotle can characterize only vaguely as the function of a motive in its extreme, is to him a vice; but the same motive appearing in what he even more vaguely calls a moderate use is to him a virtue.

In short, motives have even in Aristotle's dogmatic ethics of motives no unambiguous ethical character. While Aristotle is generally admired because he graduated the differences between virtues and vices, Bentham's criticism of Aristotle is certainly even more to the point. Bentham rightly emphasizes that this gradation must remain completely vague unless, first, not the virtues and vices of motives are analyzed, but the ends, the consequences of acts, which these motives have in view.

As regards the motive of liberality, Bentham demonstrates that it has to be ethically characterized in three different ways, according to the different actions to which it leads. "Liberality . . . exercised to a good end and at a man's own expense . . . is a virtue . . . exercised by a public functionary at the expense of the public . . . is but another name for waste . . . exercised at the expense of others and without their consent it is a vice."[114] "Murder upon a small scale . . . is not good. Why? Because we are used to see men hanged for it. Murder on the largest scale. Oh, that is most excellent! Why? Because we are used to see men crowned for it."[115] Or finally, as Bentham mentions several times, the love of honor is by no means always a laudable motive. Even when a statesman speaks of honor with "loudness" and "fierceness," leading to war, that is to "homicide . . . and destruction," his love of

[113] *Ibid.*, part xx, p. 582b.
[114] *Ibid.*, vol. ix, p. 267 ("The Constitutional Code," book ii, chap. ix, sect. xv, article 7).
[115] *Ibid.*, part xx, p. 509b (from Bentham's "Memorandum Book," 1818-19). Compare *ibid.*, part xix, pp. 76 f: "Conquest by an individual . . . made in the ancient or modern Eastern manner is robbery in the gross, . . . conquest by a nation" is a glorious deed.

honor is, according to Bentham, no good motive;[116] and besides this, "a sort of honor may be found (according to a proverbial saying) even among thieves. But to regard such honor with complacency, to speak with reprobation of every instance of the absence of it, to speak with eulogium of every instance of the manifestation of it, is indeed a natural enough prejudice, but in some of its consequences a very pernicious one."[117] This ethical ambidexterity of motives is, however, not only characteristic of such motives as honor, liberality or fortitude; it is, as Bentham tries to show time and again, a characteristic even of the most fundamental motives on which anti-hedonists commonly build up their moral theories. It is a characteristic even of the love of truth and of benevolence.

LOVE OF TRUTH AND MENDACITY

Love of truth seems to be an absolutely virtuous motive, morally right in every respect and under all possible circumstances. To Wollaston it was the only virtue embracing all others which are said to be mere manifestations of it. But to Bentham all this is completely misleading.

First, he warns us against assuming that there is mendacity in every case of objectively untrue statements. An objectively incorrect statement is only too often upheld in perfect love of truth and sincerity, even before the court; and above all "psychological facts . . . present" an even "more inviting field to mendacity than is commonly presented by physical facts."[118] Secondly, however—and this is the main point— "mendacity is not a uniform" motive; it changes its color according to the nature and substance of the action "to which it is rendered or endeavoured to be rendered subservient"; so for instance "mendacity employed in drawing down upon an innocent head the destroying sword of justice is murder: murder encompassed with all its correspondent terror. Mendacity employed in the obtainment of money is

---

[116] *Ibid.*, part VIII, pp. 438b, 438a (*Jeremy Bentham to His Fellow Citizens of France on Houses of Peers and Senates*, 1830, para. 7, No. 16, 15).

[117] *Ibid.*, vol. IV, p. 225b (*Panopticon versus New South Wales* or *the Panopticon Penitentiary System and the Penal Colonization System, Compared*, 1802). Compare *Ibid.*, vol. VI, p. 265b: "A sort of honour is to be found among thieves. So it has often been observed, and truly: but this honour is neither more nor less than a disposition to pursue that interest—to be impelled by that detached portion of the general moral force by which the members of the predatory community in question are bound together"; the communities of thieves have "particular interests acting in opposition to the general interest."

[118] *Ibid.*, vol. VI, p. 246a ("Rationale of Judicial Evidence," book I, chap. VIII).

but depredation."[119] But in certain cases mendacity may be a moral duty.

Certainly "there . . . is . . . no . . . mischief which . . . is not producible by . . . falsehood . . . , by a guilty pen or tongue . . . as by the cannon or the sword."[120] "So dishonourable and pernicious to a man is the reputation of habitual or frequent falsity—so honourable and so valuable to him that of never having violated truth—that without the least prejudice to any other individual by even a single departure from veracity it may happen to a man to do irremediable mischief to himself."[121] Thus Bentham casts no doubts upon the far-reaching moral depravity of the motive of mendacity, and on the factual as well as the justly high ethical valuation of the love of truth.

On the other hand, however, he states with the same vigor that in many cases mendacity is a legitimately moral motive; and he leaves ample room for justification of white lies. "Mendacity is not only permitted, but in some cases properly permitted. . . . That cases exist in which a departure from truth is and ought to be either prescribed or at least allowed by the moral or popular sanction considered in its true and largest sense is out of dispute"; and Bentham enumerates three main cases in which untruthfulness is even a moral obligation, one group of cases in which it is at least morally permitted: "1 . . . such are all those . . . cases . . . in which mischief to another would be the certain or probable effect of verity, while from falsity no evil at all or at least no equal evil will with equal probability be the result: as if a madman or assassin with a naked weapon in his hand asks whether his intended victim be not there, naming the place where he actually is. 2. To this same head may belong falsehoods of humanity or beneficence: as when a physician, to save pain of mind, gives hopes which he does not entertain himself. 3. To this same head may be referred what may be termed falsehoods of urbanity which is but humanity or beneficence applying itself to interest of inferior moment: as where on being interrogated by Artifex concerning the degree of estimation in which he holds a production of Artifex—for fear of applying discouragement, Crito gives for answer a degree higher than that which he really entertains: and so in regard to conduct in life, taste and so forth. 4. As to the

---

[119] *Ibid.*, vol. v, p. 220b (*Swear not at all: containing an Exposure of the Needlessness and Mischievousness, as well as anti-Christianity, of the Ceremony of an Oath*, 1817, sect. 14).

[120] *Ibid.*, vol. vi, p. 297a (Rationale of Judicial Evidence," book ii, chap. v, para. 2).

[121] *Ibid.*, vol. vi, p. 267b ("Rationale of Judicial Evidence," book i, chap. xi, para. 5).

cases in which departure from truth is allowed without being prescribed. A footing on which this matter is commonly placed seems to
be that where a man has no right to the information sought by him the
information need not be given to him. But granting, that were probity
or the duty of one man to another the only consideration to be attended
to, a liberty thus ample might and would be allowed—the latitude will
be found to receive very considerable limitation, when those considerations are attended to which concern a man's self-regarding interest,
and belong to the head of prudence."[122] At least the first three types
of ethically required mendacity, the falsehoods of duty, of humanity
and of urbanity, ought also to be sanctioned by religion according to
Bentham,[123] insofar as he does not reject the religious sanction altogether.

John S. Mill, the editor of the first edition of Bentham's *Rationale
of Judicial Evidence* (1827), referred in this connection to William
Paley's treatment of these problems of mendacity. Paley speaks indeed
of an "immediate benefit which you propose by the falsehood" you
tell to a "madman" or a "robber."[124] But it seems to me that Paley's argument is methodologically and materially much inferior to that of Bentham. For Paley simply cuts the Gordian knot by maintaining "that
there are falsehoods which are not lies" and therefore "not criminal"
and that in such instances no promise to "speak the truth is violated
because none was given or understood to be given."[124] As statements
are generally made for the implicit purpose of conveying the truth and
as there is, therefore, no need of an additional promise to this effect,
Paley's argument is certainly no more than a rather cruel trick. The
crucial problem of white lies can not be solved by drawing a line of
demarcation between falsehoods and lies, in the way in which Paley
does this. For lies are certainly lies, no matter whether, before telling
the lie, a promise was or was not given to tell the truth. The explicit
promise to tell the truth marks an aggravating circumstance, but the
lack of this explicit promise cannot transform a lie into a non-lie.

So far as the problem of the white lie is concerned, the sharpest contrast exists between Bentham's ethics of consequences and the whole

[122] *Ibid.*, vol. vi, p. 267b ("Rationale of Judicial Evidence," book i, chap. xi,
para. 5).
[123] *Ibid.*, vol. vi, p. 271a ("Rationale of Judicial Evidence," book i, chap. xi,
para. 7).
[124] W. Paley, *The Principles of Moral and Political Philosophy*, 1793, book iii,
chap. 15, pp. 184 ff.

tradition of the ethics of pure motives. Discussions of the white lie can be followed back at least to Augustine's *De Mendacio* (395 A.D.) and *Contra Mendacium* (420 A.D.)[125] where, as in Kant and Fichte, lying to succor men in peril is said to be immoral under all circumstances.

An especially marked contrast to Bentham's consistent emphasis on the consequences of acts is the weight which German idealistic ethics places on motives; and strangely enough, by chance—or in the case of Kant, perhaps by reference to a common source—Kant and Bentham even use the same examples to illustrate their opposite moral decisions concerning mendacity.

In his essay "Über ein vermeintliches Recht, aus Menschenliebe zu lügen" (1797), Kant, too, speaks of the man who is asked by a dangerous madman or by a murderer to disclose where his victim can be found. Kant refers in this passage to a remark of Benjamin Constant,[126] which was perhaps known to Bentham too. In any case, Kant, according to the principles of his ethics, first compares the moral weight of the two motives which are, in this instance, in conflict with each other, viz. benevolence and love of truth; and he decides then that it is ethically wrong to tell a lie under all circumstances. Nevertheless, in order to justify this decision, he most inconsistently refers to possibly mischievous effects which a lie could produce, a reference which is definitely contradictory to his general principle that the moral value of an act depends entirely on its motive, no matter what its consequences may be.

Though more consistent in its method, and more imposing in its content, in the end Fichte's argument concerning necessary lies seems to me no less questionable than Kant's. Henrich Steffens, the Norwegian philosopher, a student of Fichte and friend of Schelling, has handed down to us in one of the ten volumes of his autobiography an illuminating talk he once had with Fichte about veracity. Steffens tells us: "Als ich hörte, wie er (Fichte) den Satz: man dürfe unter keiner Bedingung eine Unwahrheit sagen, behauptete, wagte ich es, ihm folgendes Verhältnis entgegenzustellen: Eine Wöchnerin ist gefährlich krank, das Kind sterbend, liegt in einer anderen Stube; die Ärzte haben entschieden erklärt, dass eine jede Erschütterung ihr das Leben kosten wird. Das Kind stirbt"; die Frau "fragt nach dem Befinden des eben

---

[125] See *Patrologiae Cursus completus, Series latina prior*, ed. J. P. Migne, vol. XL, 1861, pp. 487 ff, especially pp. 544 ff.

[126] I. Kant, *Gesammelte Schriften*, ed. by Königlich Preussische Akademie der Wissenschaften, Erste Abteilung, Band VIII, 1912, pp. 423 ff, 427.

gestorbenen Kindes: die Wahrheit würde sie töten; soll ich sie sagen?—
'Sie soll,' antwortete Fichte, 'mit ihrer Frage abgewiesen werden.' . . .
'Das heisst,' erwiderte ich, 'auf das Bestimmteste sagen: ihr Kind sei
todt. Ich würde lügen,' rief ich bestimmt, und Thränen traten mir in
die Augen, weil ich mich einer solchen Scene, die ich erlebt hatte, erin-
nerte, und ich nenne ganz entschieden diese Lüge eine Wahrheit, meine
Wahrheit. . . . 'Deine Wahrheit,' rief Fichte entrüstet, 'eine solche, die
dem einzelnen Menschen gehört, giebt es gar nicht; sie hat über Dich,
Du nicht über sie zu gebieten. Stirbt die Frau an der Wahrheit, so soll
sie sterben.' Ich sah die absolute Unmöglichkeit ein, mich mit ihm zu
verständigen."[127] In comparison with such arguments from leading
ethical idealists, Bentham's analyses show, I think, not only more common sense and consistency, but perhaps even more idealism.

Nevertheless, with regard to the falsehoods of humanity and urbanity, Bentham is quite undogmatic, as may be inferred from the following remark: "The wound . . . given by a man to his own reputation"
in consequence of a falsehood of humanity or urbanity "will be the
more severe the more intense and deliberate the averment by which the
truth is violated: and thus it is, that after a falsehood of humanity or
urbanity, uttered with a faint or ordinary degree of assurance, if urged
and pressed, stronger and stronger asseverations being on the other
part called for in proof of the verity of the preceding ones, a man may
for the preservation of his own character find it necessary to give up
the enterprise of humanity or urbanity and declare, after all, the naked
truth."[128] And the same experienced weighing of details is finally revealed in Bentham's remark that to combine imaginary facts in a falsehood requires more pain and more difficulties than to tell the truth;
thus also the love of ease operates in favor of veracity as a physical sanction to which the religious, the moral and the legal sanctions still add
their weight.[129] In any case, the whole of this analysis of veracity and
mendacity speaks again clearly in favor of Bentham's main point—that
not motives but the consequences of acts are of decisive moral relevance,
that "only in consideration . . . of the mischievous effect of which . . .

[127] Henrich Steffens, *Was ich erlebte*, 1841, Band IV, S. 158. Compare another
example of this "stock illustration" of the problem in question in Mark Twain's
"Heaven and Hell," see W. M. Urban, *The Fundamentals of Ethics*, 1930, p. 39 f.

[128] Bentham, *Works*, 1843, vol. VI, p. 267b ("Rationale of Judicial Evidence,"
book I, chap. XI, §5).

[129] *Ibid.*, vol. VI, pp. 262 ff, part XI, pp. 19 ff ("An Introductory View of the
Rationale of Evidence, chap. VII, §4-7).

falsehood . . . is or tends to be productive" can punishment properly be employed[130] or a moral verdict be proclaimed.

EGOISM AND UNSELFISHNESS

Methodologically and materially no less instructive are Bentham's later discussions of self-interest and disinterestedness. As we have already seen, the assumption of an absolutely good motive, the assumption of a sacrifice of all personal interest is according to Bentham psychologically and ethically an untenable presupposition. For, in the strictest sense of the word, self-sacrifice implies a self-contradiction, the assumption of an interest to do something combined with the denial of any interest in the case in question; and further this absolute disinterestedness would imply the annulment of the law of causality. Bentham, however, saw no sufficient reason for such a negation of the validity of causality; and even if psychology could grant the existence of absolute disinterestedness, Bentham would deny that absolute unselfishness is an absolutely good motive.

But as much as Bentham deflated the concept of disinterestedness, he never questioned the obvious fact that there exists a special kind of interest in performing disinterested acts, and this by no means contradicts the denial of the possibility of *absolute* disinterestedness. On the contrary, particularly in his later writings, Bentham frequently gives this assurance: "I admit the existence of disinterestedness in the sense . . . of philanthropy. . . . I do not deny it: I cannot deny it: I wish not to deny it: sorry should I be if it were in my power to deny it."[131] He was well aware that many, misunderstanding him, might reproach him in this manner: "What a picture, old and gloomy-minded man! are you giving us of human nature! As if there were no such quality as disinterestedness—no such quality as philanthropy—no such quality as disposition to self-sacrifice—in the whole species: no such individual as a king taking pleasure in his duty—doing on all occasions his utmost to promote the happiness of his people! Notions such as these! And with proofs to the contrary—proofs so brilliant and so indubitable—all the while before your eyes!"[132] But Bentham answers: "How could I do otherwise than admit . . . all this. . . . My children! I have not far to

[130] *Ibid.*, vol. VI, p. 293b note ("Rationale of Judicial Evidence," book II, chap. v, §1).

[131] Bentham, *Works*, 1843, part VIII, p. 431a, no. 13, II ("Bentham to his Fellow-Citizens of France," 1830).

[132] *Ibid.*, part VIII, p. 430b, no. 10, p. 431a ("Bentham to his Fellow-Citizens of France," 1830).

look for it. Without it, how could so many papers that have preceded this letter have come into existence? I admit the existence of a disposition to self-sacrifice."[133] The sincerity and conclusiveness of such declarations are certainly strong enough to exempt Bentham from the frequently uttered reproach of preaching absolute egoism, and denying the possibility of relative unselfishness.

Bentham's well considered main point is that even disinterestedness must ultimately be caused by a kind of self-interest in the benevolent man impelling him to prefer a comparatively altruistic action to an entirely selfish one. The correctness of this thesis is not denied even by such an avowed antagonist of hedonism as F. H. Bradley. Bradley, too, admits that "no act is ever without a reason for its existence, and the reason is always a feeling of pain or of pleasure or both. We seek what we like and avoid what we dislike; we do what we want, and this is selfish. . . . Deliberately to act without an object in view is impossible; duty is done for duty's sake only when duty is an object of desire; . . . only the thought of what you like or dislike brings with it a practical result. Whether we consider blind appetite or conscious desire or circumspect volition, the result is the same."[134] But Bradley goes on to say that the statement "I do what I want to do is an idle . . . triviality, . . . the barest tautology."[135] The question of the selfish motive in every action is idle, because it is "asking what everybody knows or an attempt to mislead" presupposing that all acts are absolutely selfish. And along with Bradley other moralists dismiss the denial of absolute disinterestedness either as a sophistry or as an immaterial empty phrase. John Dewey calls "the fact" that every living creature acts "as a self" a mere "truism" and warns against transforming this "truistic fact" into the fiction of the creature's "acting always *for* self."[136] James Martineau elaborates on the same theme in the following way: "Most persons would be affected with some surprise and amusement on being told that in their friendships, their family affections, their public spirit, their admiration for noble character, their religious trust, they had a single eye to their own interests and were only using their fellows, their children, their country, their heroes, their God as instruments of their personal pleasure."[137] C. D. Broad even thinks that this doctrine of the

---

[133] *Ibid.*, part VIII, p. 431a, no. 13 ("Bentham to his Fellow-Citizens of France," sect. v).

[134] F. H. Bradley, *Ethical Studies*, 1927, p. 227 (Essay VII).

[135] *Ibid.*, p. 228.

[136] J. Dewey, *Human Nature and Conduct*, 1930, pp. 134 ff.

[137] J. Martineau, *Types of Ethical Theory*, 1891, vol. II, p. 309. Compare *ibid.*,

impossibility of disinterested action, definitely "killed" by Joseph Butler cannot "flourish . . . any longer but among bookmakers and smart
young business men" or "go to America," as all "good fallacies" do
when "they die and rise again as the latest discoveries of the local professors."[138] But these arguments certainly are no genuine demonstrations
of the non-validity of Bentham's doctrine; and Broad himself finally
does not deny that "no action of mine can be completely hostile to self-
love."[139] Thus the most acute criticism of the disbelief in absolute disinterestedness does not concern the incorrectness of this disbelief, but
rather its importance or its inaccurate, misleading formulation.

One should, of course, welcome any warning against common mis-
representations of psychological facts; and it may even be granted that
in an ethics of consequences, the disbelief in absolute disinterestedness
is no matter for special concern. If, in an ethics of *consequences*, absolute unselfishness is excluded, it does not mean the exclusion of the
most important elements of actions: beneficent intentions and consequences of acts. To deny the existence of absolute disinterestedness
concerns only a motive of action; and the motives are not of decisive
ethical relevance in Bentham or in any consistent ethics of consequences.

But it is extremely strange that protagonists of an ethics of motives

---

vol. II, p. 357: "If the end of life is to make the most of its pleasures and minimise
its pains, there is no room for the devotee of compassion, whose heart is irresistibly
drawn to the haunts of sin and misery, and takes on it the burthen of countless
woes besides its own, and bleeds for every wound it cannot heal. Look only at
the countenance of such a one, at the tender depth within the eye, the clear and
thoughtful brow, the sensitive and precarious calm upon the features, and say
whether you are here in presence of the best economist of happiness. If this be the
object of your quest, had you not better go to the resorts of refined and easy life
where there is luxury that hurts no health, and art that adorns the scene without
and the mind within, and alternate industry and gaiety that brighten all the hours,
and neighbourly offices enough just to keep the reproach of selfishness away, and
religious observance enough to mingle a deeper tone and higher sanction with it
all? Here surely we must count up more pleasures and fewer pains than fall to
the lot of the hero of compassion. True it is that he would not exchange his labour
for this rest; not, however, because it is a less happy state; but because it is a state
too happy for a soul once pierced by the sorrows of humanity. Were the hedonistic
rule psychologically imperative upon him, he would be tempted by the exchange,
and quit his vows of service. It is only because it is impossible for him to listen
to it without shame, that he toils on beneath his cross." The answer to this argument is, in my view, that we do more honor to the devotee of compassion and
explain his attitude toward life more adequately, if we assume that he finds happiness in compassion rather than that he misses happiness in having no more of
the average pleasures of ordinary or even highly civilized men.
[138] C. D. Broad, *Five Types of Ethics*, 1930, p. 55.
[139] *Ibid.*, p. 73 f.

should seek to discredit the importance of an insight into the impossibility of absolute self-sacrifice. For great theologians, moralists and the majority of men believe in absolute self-denial as the highest moral motive. This alone should protect Bentham's denial of absolute unselfishness from being called an idle, worthless tautology. Modern psychology in particular, having duly taken into consideration the phenomenon of the pleasure of suffering, can give ample evidence for the fact that making sacrifices can be and always is combined with self-regarding interest. To understand the paradoxical complexion of joyful sacrifices and joyful suffering is, both psychologically and ethically, of high importance. It is by no means a mere problem of words.

If any truism is involved in the analyses of altruistic acts, it is, in my opinion, not to be found where Bradley, Dewey and C. D. Broad suspect it. It seems to me a truism to emphasize that altruistic acts are done for the sake of others. But it is no truism at all to urge that even altruistic deeds must be inspired by some kind of self-interest making them more attractive to the agent than merely selfish ones.

If all this is taken into account, Bentham's utilitarianism can in no way be considered a philosophy of egoism. On the contrary, it is the most consistent philosophy of altruism, provided that three critical limitations are not lost sight of. First, the disinterestedness of an action does not exclude all self-regarding interest of the same action; it includes some personal interest in that action, this interest being the cause of that act. Second, it ought to be acknowledged that self-preference is, in the total life of nature, a far more necessary motive than disinterestedness. Third, neither the motive of self-regard nor that of disinterestedness is, ethically speaking, good or bad taken by itself; and it is in no wise lamentable that extra-regarding interests are much rarer than self-regarding ones.

The first point we have already seen sufficiently discussed in the *Table of the Springs of Action*, and in Bentham's address to his fellow citizens of France. The second point is elucidated in the following statements of his *Constitutional Code*: "In the general tenor of life, in every human breast, self-regarding interest is predominant over all other interests put together. . . . This position may to some eyes present itself in the character of an axiom: as such self-evident and not standing in need of proof. To others as a position or proposition which, how clearly soever true, still stands in need of proof. To deliver a position in the character of an axiom is to deliver it under the expectation that either it will not be controverted at all or that he by whom it is controverted will not, in justification of the denial given by him to it, be able to advance anything by which the unreasonableness of his opinion or pretended opinion will not be exposed. Of this stamp are the axioms laid down by Euclid. In the axioms so laid down nothing of dogmatism will, it is believed, be found. . . . For the satisfaction of those who may doubt" that self-regarding interests are predominant over and much more frequent than extra-regarding ones "reference may be made to the existence of the species as being of itself a proof and that a conclusive one. For after exception made of the case of children not arrived at the age of which they are capable of going alone or adults reduced by infirmity to helpless state, take any two individuals, A and B, and suppose the whole care of the happiness of A confined to the breast of B, A himself not having any part in it and the whole care of the happiness of B confined to the breast of A, B himself not having any part in it and this to be the case throughout, it will soon appear that in this state of things the species could not continue in existence and that a few months, not to say weeks or days, would suffice for the annihilation of it. Of all modes in which for the governance of one and the same individual the two faculties could be conceived as placed in different seats—sensation and consequent desire in one breast, judgment and consequent action in another, this is the most simple. If, as has with less truth been said of the blind leading the blind, both would in such a state of things be continually falling into the ditch; much more frequently and more speedily fatal would be the falls supposing the separation to have place upon any more complex plan. Suppose the care of the happiness of A being taken altogether from A were divided between B and C, the happiness of B and C being provided for in the same complex manner and so on, the greater the complication, the more speedy would the destruction be and the more flagrant the absurdity of a supposition assuming the existence of such a state of things."[140] Even the desire of the matter of wealth as one of the types of self-interest is according to Bentham necessarily far more frequent than any

---

[140] Bentham, *Works*, 1843, part xvii, pp. 5b, 6a ("The Constitutional Code," written in 1821, 1827, published in 1830). Compare *ibid.*, part xvii, p. 192: "Take any two persons . . . Adam and Eve. Adam has no regard for himself: the whole of his regard has for its object Eve. Eve in like manner has no regard for herself: the whole of her regard has for its object Adam. Follow this supposition up: introduce the occurrences which sooner or later are sure to happen and you will see that at the end of an assignable length of time, greater or less according to accident, but in no case so much as a twelvemonth, both will unavoidably have perished" ("The Constitutional Code," book ii, chap. vi, sect. 31, article ix). Compare *The Book of Fallacies*, 1824, p. 393 f.

extra-regarding interests; "the man who desiring to live has no desire
for the matter of wealth exists only in the fancy or rather in the language of shallow declaimers: to desire to live is to desire to eat and to
desire to eat is to desire to possess things eatable."[141] Of "the purity of
motives . . . , the utter absence of every particle of self-regard, of this
immaculate purity each man in the most peremptory manner asserts
the existence in his own instance: deny it or hesitate to admit it, you
offer him an affront—an affront the stain of which he perhaps not unfrequently invites you to permit him to wash away with your blood.
Of the same purity he calls upon you, though perhaps in a tone not
quite so loud to admit, on the part of his . . . supporters. Nor yet, unless
under the smart of some particular provocation or in the ardour of
some particularly advantageous thrust, is he backward in the acknowledgment of the same purity in the breasts of honourable gentlemen on
the other side of the house. By this means while the praise of good
temper and candour is obtained, the price for the purchase of the corresponding acknowledgment on the other side is thus paid in advance.
. . . At the expense of truth (need it be said?) is all this laudation and
self-worship, every atom of it. But the more irrefragably true is the contrary position, the more strenuous is the urgency of the demand for it,"
the wish "to believe in that fabled purity which is not ever true even
where temptation is at its minimum, much less in a situation in which
it is at its maximum. . . . What is the language of simple truth? That in
spite of everything which is *said* the general predominance of self-
regard over every other sort of regard is demonstrated by everything
that is *done*: that in the ordinary tenor of life, in the breasts of human
beings of ordinary mould, self is everything to which all other persons
added to all other things . . . are as nothing."[142] The very truth is that
only "in a highly matured state of society, in here and there a highly
cultivated and expanded mind, under the stimulus of some extraordinary excitement, a sacrifice of self-regarding interest to social interest
upon a national scale has not been without example."[142] "The degree in

[141] *Ibid.*, part XIII, p. 54b ("The Rationale of Judicial Evidence," 1827, book v,
chap. XIII, §1).

[142] *Ibid.*, part XVII, pp. 60b, 61a ("The Constitutional Code," 1830, book I, chap.
IX). Compare *ibid.*, vol. II, p. 482b: "In the few instances, if any, in which throughout the whole tenor or the general tenor of his life a person sacrifices his own
individual interest to that of any other person or persons, such person or persons
will be a person or persons with whom he is connected by some domestic or other
private and narrow tie of sympathy" (*The Book of Fallacies*, 1824, part v, chap. IX,
no. 4, p. 393).

which the predominance of motives of the social or disinterested cast is commonly asserted or insinuated is by the very nature of man rendered impossible."[143] With the help of all such psychological considerations, Bentham tries to show that there are, indeed, overwhelmingly more self-regarding motives than extra-regarding ones, and that, even within extra-regarding motives, a certain amount of self-regard is to be found.

In comparison with these two psychologically important points of Bentham's theory of altruism only his third point is mainly of ethical interest. According to Bentham the motive of egoism and that of unselfishness are neither absolutely good nor absolutely bad. Both are relatively good or bad according to the consequences they lead to. But it is misleading to regard disinterestedness as morally good, self-love as bad. The "general habit of self-preference is so far from being . . . a reasonable cause of regret that the existence of it is an indispensable condition not only to the well-being but to the very being of the human species and should therefore be a cause of satisfaction."[144] "The more correct and complete a man's conception of the subject is, the more clearly will he understand that in this natural and general predominance of personal over every more extensive interest there is no just cause for regret."[145] That is, self-interest is in many cases morally as valuable as unselfishness.

A very simple practical conclusion, which Bentham draws from all these reflections, is the following: As there are extra-regarding motives which cause good effects and are therefore motives of duty, and as there are also egoistic motives which cause good effects, and are therefore motives of ethical interest, true morality recommends the "duty and interest junction principle,"[146] that is, the "connecting a man's interest with his duty,"[147] "to make each man's interest to observe on

[143] *Ibid.*, part IV, pp. 412a, b (*The Book of Fallacies*, 1824, p. 121, part I, chap. V, sect. 2).

[144] *Ibid.*, part XVII, p. 61a ("The Constitutional Code," 1830, book I, chap. IX).

[145] *Ibid.*, part IV, p. 475b (*The Book of Fallacies*, 1824, part V, chap. 3). Compare *ibid.*, part IV, p. 482b, no. 6: "In this general predominance of self-regarding over social interest, when attentively considered, there will not be found any just subject of regret any more than of contestation" (*The Book of Fallacies*, 1824, part V, chap. IX, 1824, p. 393).

[146] *Ibid.*, part XVI, p. 380b (*The Tracts on Poor Laws, Outline of a Work Entitled Pauper Management Improved*, book I, chap. IV, sect. II).

[147] *Ibid.*, vol. VIII, p. 381a (*The Tracts on Poor Laws, Pauper Management Improved*).

every occasion that conduct which it is his duty to observe."[148] "To join interest with duty and that by the strongest cement"[149] has to be the object of the law and of moral conduct. "In the instance of each . . . agent the course prescribed by his particular interest shall on each occasion coincide, as completely as may be with that prescribed by his duty: which is as much as to say, with that prescribed by his share in the universal interest."[150] "All that the most public-spirited, which is as much as to say the most virtuous of men can do, is to do what depends upon himself towards bringing the public interest, that is, his own personal share in the public interest, to a state as nearly approaching to coincidence, and on as few occasions amounting to a state of repugnance, as possible with his private interests."[151] "The notion which insists upon disinterestedness (i.e. the absence of the species of motive most to be depended upon) as an indispensable qualification . . . is a notion respectable in its source, but the most prejudicial in its tendency of any that can be imagined—every system of management which has disinterestedness, pretended or real, for its foundation is rotten at the root, susceptible of a momentary prosperity at the outset, but sure to perish at the long run. That principle of action is most to be depended upon, whose influence is most powerful, most constant, most uniform, most lasting and most general among mankind. Personal interest is that principle."[152] (Bentham, it is true, refers here immediately only to "Pauper management" but, as we may be allowed to infer from the evident philosophical enlargement he gave to his later argument in comparison with the original publication of this writing in 1796, he obviously intended to apply these ideas to the whole field of morality.) "A system of economy" and of ethics built on disinterestedness "is built upon a quicksand."[152] Bentham even takes the risk of saying that because public virtue and fargoing disinterestedness "cannot reasonably be regarded as being so frequently exemplified as insanity . . . , so . . . , as in the case of insanity, it is in what has place in the conduct on the

---

[148] Ibid., vol. VIII, p. 380b.

[149] Bentham, "Management of the Poor," 1796, p. 363. Compare Bentham, Works, 1843, part VII, p. 125b ("Panopticon or the Inspection-House containing the Idea of a new Principle of Construction applicable to any Sort of Establishment in which Persons of any Description are to be kept under Inspection," Postscript, part II).

[150] Bentham, Works, 1843, vol. II, p. 273b (Leading Principles of a Constitutional Code for any State, first published in The Pamphleteer, 1823, sect. II, no. 16).

[151] Ibid., vol. II, p. 475b (The Book of Fallacies, 1824, p. 363).

[152] Ibid., vol. VIII, p. 381b ("The Tracts on Poor Laws").

part of the thousands, and not in what has place in the conduct of one in every thousand, that all rational and useful political" and moral "arrangements will be grounded. Of a state of things thus incontrovertible no sooner is the existence to a certain degree extensively acknowledged than all pretence to this species of purity" of disinterestedness "will be regarded as would an assertion of chastity in the mouth of a prostitute at the very moment of solicitation: regarded as an insult to the understandings of all those to whom it is addressed—and will as such be resented."[153] He who is afraid that putting self-love at the foundation of a moral system would mean the destruction of the system is to be compared with the man who infers that putting a regulating spring into a watch will mean the destruction of the watch.[154]

Even the golden rule of the New Testament is, in Bentham's view, no substitute for the duty and interest junction principle. In the French Declaration of the Rights and Duties of the Man and the Citizen, which appeared in 1795, the golden rule has this rendering: "All the duties of the man and citizen are derived from these two principles engraven by nature in all breasts, in the hearts of all men—Do not to another that which you would not men should do to you. Do constantly to others the good which you would receive from men."[155] Bentham criticizes this golden rule of morality in the following severe manner: "Do as you would be done by, says the abridged expression of . . . this . . . precept, as given by the English proverb. What improvement the precept

---

[153] *Ibid.*, part xvii, p. 61b ("The Constitutional Code," book i, chap. ix). As a kind of mitigation and correction of this gross statement may be regarded the following remark of Bentham's "Nomography": "Were it not for the operation" of the extra-regarding sympathetic sanction, "no small portion of the good, physical and moral, which has place in human affairs would be an effect without cause" (*Works*, 1843, vol. iii, p. 292b, "Nomography or the Art of Inditing Laws," appendix: Logical Arrangements or instruments of invention and discovery, sect. viii).

[154] Compare Bentham, *The Book of Fallacies*, 1824, p. 177. Or cf. *Works*, 1843, part vi, p. 507b: "Address yourself to anyone of the 658" members of parliament "with the exception of some half-hundred or thereabouts . . . tell him that his situation is a trust, that to fulfil that trust is a duty—tell him that the situation of a monarch is a trust—that the Prince Regent has declared it so to be—and that in the hands even of the Prince Regent it never has been, nor even can be a perfect sinecure;—talk to him in any such strain—so you may if you please, but first prepare yourself for a horse-laugh in your face" ("Plan of parliamentary Reform in the Form of a Catechism with Reasons for each Article with an Introduction showing the Necessity of radical and the inadequacy of moderate Reform," 1817, sect. xiv, no. ix of the introduction).

[155] Bentham, *Works*, 1843, vol. ii, pp. 526b, 527a (Declaration of the Rights and Duties of the Man and Citizen, article ii).

has received from the new edition given of it by the anti-christian hand will presently appear. A division is here made of it into two branches, a negative and a positive: the tendency of the negative, placed where it is, is pernicious; the tendency of the positive branch, worded as it is, absurd and contrary to the spirit of the original: the former, for want of the limitations necessary to the application here made of it, is too ample; the latter, by the tail clumsily tacked on to it, is made too narrow. In what country is it that it is the wish of accusers to be accused— of judges to be condemned—of guillotiners to be guillotined?" Only "in topsyturvy-land where cooks are roasted by pigs and hounds hunted by hares";[156] and Bentham concludes this criticism by saying that only "morality, not affecting precision, addresses itself to the heart: law of which precision is the life and soul addresses itself to the head."[157] This final remark, it is true, contradicts all other statements that Bentham has made on morality; and it would seem, therefore, that only his violent polemic against the so-called moral "laws" of this French declaration misled Bentham to speak so derogatorily of ethics in contrast to jurisprudence.

The Alleged Identity of All Men's Interests

The modern French interpretation of Bentham has maintained the widespread notion that his ethics stands and falls mainly on the acceptance of two principles, which are both essentially based on wishful thinking. First, the uncritical belief that enlightened self-interest is by its very nature identical with socially valuable behavior and, second, the almost equally utopian hope that legislation can achieve an artificial identification of socially valuable behavior with the action of even unenlightened self-interest.

Elie Halévy saw in "l'identification artificielle des intérêts . . . le grand problème"[158] or almost the only problem of utilitarian ethics; and André Lalande aptly summarizes this kind of French criticism as follows: "L'utilitarisme oscille historiquement . . . entre deux thèses: 1° l'identité naturelle entre l'intérêt public et l'intérêt bien entendu de chacun; 2° l'identification souhaitable (et partiellement réalisée déjà) de ces deux intérêts différents, par le moyen de législation."[159] Similarly,

[156] *Ibid.*, vol. ii, p. 527a.
[157] *Ibid.*, vol. ii, p. 527b ("*Anarchical Fallacies*, Declaration of the Rights and Duties of Man and the Citizen," article ii).
[158] E. Halévy, *La formation du radicalisme philosophique*, 1901, tome i, p. 24.
[159] A. Lalande, *Vocabulaire technique et critique de la philosophie*, 1947, p. 1154.

Émile Bréhier indicates in a few remarks on Bentham that "il s'agit en somme, au moyen des sanctions, d'identifier l'intérêt egoïste et l'intérêt social qui, sans elles, divergeraient."[160]

René Le Senne enumerates quite a number of characteristics of Bentham's utilitarianism and obviously recognizes also the importance of Bentham's "méditation ininterrompue sur les effets affectifs de nos actes."[161] But he, too, at the end of his instructive analysis, thinks "la conciliation des intérêts . . . le problème le plus important que l'utilitarisme devait étudier."[162] "L'utilitarisme . . . est particulièrement incapable de rendre raison de tous les aspects de la vie morale qui comportent du sacrifice."[163] And already Frédéric Rauh blamed in Spencer's "essays de concilation de l'altruisme et de l'égoïsme cette défiance du désintéressement qui characterise le benthamiste."[164]

In a similar manner, André Cresson assures us that "la proposition centrale du Benthamisme" is the blind belief that "la prudence mène à la bienveillance"; and he adds: "voilà, bien ce qu'il fraudrait prouver,"[165] i.e. can the rules of an "arithmetic of pleasures" ever justify the utopian hope of a natural identity of all human interests? Even the Belgian, Eugène Dupréel, despite his admiration of Bentham's genius for consistency, shares the common French prejudice that Bentham was especially occupied with the "application du principe des intérêts solidaires."[166]

But all these seemingly fatal objections to Bentham's utilitarianism are, of course, not limited to modern French criticism. Carlyle had already given them a well known, simple and striking expression by saying that the problem of all the "cunning mechanisers of Self-interests" was the "insoluble" one: "Given a world of Knaves, to produce an Honesty from their united action";[167] and Leopold von Wiese—like other European and American critics—even implies[168] that Bentham's

---

[160] E. Bréhier, *Histoire de la philosophie*, tome II, 1932, p. 675.
[161] R. Le Senne, *Traité de morale générale*, 1942, p. 228.
[162] *Ibid.*, pp. 228 ff.   [163] *Ibid.*, p. 397.
[164] F. Rauh, *Essai sur le fondement métaphysique de la morale*, 1890, p. 36.
[165] A. Cresson, *Le problème moral et les philosophes*, 1933, pp. 123 ff.
[166] E. Dupréel, *Traité de morale*, vol. I, 1932, pp. 52 ff.
[167] T. Carlyle, "Characteristics," 1831, in *Collected Works*, 1869, vol. VIII, p. 374. Compare Carlyle's essay on "Voltaire," *ibid.*, vol. VII, pp. 238 f: "If every man's selfishness, infinitely expansive, is to be hemmed in only by the infinitely expansive selfishness of every other man, it seems as if we should have . . . a remarkable Chaos, but no habitable Solar or Stellar System."
[168] L. v. Wiese, *Ethik in der Schauweise vom Menschen und von der Gesellschaft*, 1947, Seite 66.

ethical analyses were concentrated merely on the selfish individual, and that only the development of social ideas in the nineteenth century led J. S. Mill to a stronger emphasis on the interests of the community.

All our preceding analyses of Bentham's ethics, however, have, I hope, sufficiently demonstrated that none of the moral ideas just mentioned form the central theme, let alone an indispensable presupposition, of Bentham's theory of morals. The principle of the greatest happiness of the greatest number is essentially the criterion for judging the morality of human behavior; and the setting up of such a moral standard does not presuppose a positive answer to any of the two questions (1) whether the egoistic interests of all men naturally coincide and (2) whether only the lawgiver and the educator can bring about an artificial reconciliation of the diversity of egoistic interests of individuals and groups. On the contrary, these two questions are of ethical interest only after the ethical criterion of the utility principle has explained why —in contrast to the principle of master morality—the reconciliation of human interests is of moral relevance. After the proper moral standard has been set, however, it is by no means decisive for the epistemology of ethics whether—and how far—the reconciliation of interests is brought about by nature or by juristic and educational efforts.

The questions of how the principle of utility can best be used to educate men for the best obtainable reconciliation of their interests with that of society are the great problems of pedagogy and jurisprudence. But in a theory of morals, doubtless, the question of what is moral must be answered first before the educator and the jurist can approach any of the difficulties of applying the right moral standard. In his discussion of the "duty and interest junction principle" and many of his related analyses, Bentham dealt extensively with questions of applied ethics. But he always rightly gave methodological priority to theoretical ethics, i.e. the epistemological foundations of every ethical judgment.

On the other hand, Bentham's distinction between theoretical and applied ethics does not narrow the field of ethical theory in such a way as Professor A. C. Ewing and the contemporary schools of Oxford and Cambridge moralists seek to do. According to Ewing, for instance, philosophical ethics must discuss essentially or almost exclusively the meaning of the term "good," not "what things are good, and it is therefore neither an attempt to command certain values (good things) nor to give advice on the solution of concrete ethical problems. It is a doubtful point how much the philosopher can do in either direction, though he can do something, but anything he does will not be a direct deduction from the analysis of good."[169] In fact, this limitation of theoretical ethics to the common sense analysis of some basic ethical concepts ("good," "ought" and "fitting") would necessarily hold down the task of philosophy and science to a task as limited and—in many respects—as superfluous as that of most tracts on physics in medieval scholasticism.

As long as chemistry felt satisfied with the mere analysis of the common sense meaning and the "essence" of kitchen salt, all the most subtle discussions of scholastics and housewives would certainly have rejected the paradoxical result of that highly artificial scientific method which dares to teach that the "indefinable," "simple," "odorless element salt" is a combination of strong smelling chlorine with inflammable sodium. As long as ethics is essentially limited to the analysis of the meaning of good and morally fitting and the like, it can bring about no adequate understanding of the far more important, paradoxical and complex meaning which these terms take on in the world and in the thought of moral and immoral men of the world. Science and the theory of ethics have achieved little or nothing, if they care only for the common sense meaning of principal terms, and not also for the "material contents"[170] of the things represented by these terms in reality, for the connection of these things with other things and especially for impartial, basic criteria of distinguishing these things from others in reality.

Theoretical ethics must methodologically precede applied ethics in the same sense as physics must precede technology. But in the fields of theoretical ethics more is required than a mere clarification of the shades of the theoretical meaning of some fundamental concepts. If theoretical ethics is limited to a mere analysis of the meaning of basic ethical terms, all the most vital problems of the unprejudiced evaluation of human behavior are evaded; or better to say, the mere analysis of ethical terms generally shares the common prejudice that the decisive moral questions of the distinction between good and bad things and between good and bad behavior in reality are already answered.

This, however, is the common popular obsession that the main problem of distinction between good and bad has been settled since the days of Adam and Eve, and that, as far as reality is concerned, we have to deal essentially or even exclusively with the problems of the best educational applications of definitely fixed altruistic maxims. But this

[169] C. A. Ewing, *The Definition of Good*, 1947, p. 212.
[170] Compare P. Haezrahi, "Some Arguments against G. E. Moore's View of the Function of 'Good' in ethics" in *Mind*, vol. LVII, July 1948, pp. 339 f, although I cannot agree with the details of this essay.

popular view is evidently mistaken and I do not think that Nietzsche is wrong in calling the almost exclusive concentration of the moralists on the ethical importance of altruism "eine fixe Idee."[171] André Lalande, in his criticism of Benjamin Franklin's and indirectly of Bentham's "egoistic ethics," went so far as to maintain: "Franklin disait que si les coquins savaient les avantages de l'honnêteté, ils se feraient honnêtes gens par coquinerie. Cela est possible, mais il resterait un grand fonds de coquinerie dans cette honnêteté-là."[172] But this praise of altruistic motives—as the only carrier of moral relevance—is also tenable only if Bentham's epistemological objections to the mere ethics of motives are disregarded.

Bentham criticized every ethics which bases its evaluations on the mere judging of motives, be they altruistic or egoistic motives; and this epistemological criticism of the common criteria of moral values is independent of, and a logical prerequisite to, all applications of moral criteria to life and history.

Absolutely Good or Bad Motives and Absolutely Good or Bad Men

From his extended analyses of motives, of fortitude, of liberality, of honor, of mendacity and selfishness, Bentham again draws a precise ethical conclusion. This conclusion is that "as to good and evil, neither have the objects respectively signified by those words any value nor the words themselves any meaning but by reference to pain and pleasure."[173] There exists, according to Bentham, no motive and nothing which is absolutely good or absolutely bad independently of its production of pleasure and pain. Also, the supposition of the existence of perfectly ideal men is untenable; for it is scarcely imaginable that the whole conduct of a man has only beneficent consequences and no mischievous ones at all. There are commonly in life only mixtures of good and bad motives or desires, in only relatively good or bad human beings. "All sorts of desires are common to all human beings."[174] With an exception or two not worth dwelling upon, there is "no human bosom that is not

[171] See F. Nietzsche, "Zur Genealogie der Moral" in *Nietzsche's Werke*, 1899, Band vii, p. 305.

[172] A. Lalande, *Précis raisonné de morale pratique*, 1930, p. 8.

[173] Bentham, *Works*, 1843, vol. vi, p. 257a note ("Rationale of Judicial Evidence," 1827, book i, chap. xi, §1).

[174] *Ibid.*, part xiii, p. 54a ("Rationale of Judicial Evidence, book v, chap. xiii §1).

the seat, constantly or occasionally, of every modification of desire."[175] To suppose that there are absolutely good or bad motives and men is only too "vulgar" an error. It is only the narrow-minded crowd which thinks in such terms, it is "men of narrow experience, of hasty judgment and of small reflection—in a word, the bulk of mankind" who have "in a manner but two classes in which to stow a man in respect of merit: they know but of two characters, the good man and the bad man. If then they happen to view a man's conduct in any instance in a favourable light, up he goes among the good men; if in an unfavourable, down he goes among the bad men; and they fix a great gulf between the two. If their opinion with respect to either come to change, as they have no intermediate stages, he is removed from his station with the same violence as he was at first placed in it. But men of observation and cool reflection who have had patience and sagacity to make a narrow search into human nature, learn to correct the errors of this indolent and hasty system; they know that in the scale of merit men's characters rise one above the other by infinite and imperceptible degrees; and at the same time that the highest is distant from the lowest by a much less space than is commonly imagined."[176] Through its connection with the ethical relativity of motives this old and sound psychological insight into the ethically mixed nature of men seems to me to appear in a new light.

No motive can be called absolutely good; that is, according to Bentham, every motive is relatively good, insofar as it produces some satisfaction. But as there is no efficient motive which does not cause at least the pleasant expectation of some pleasure, every motive can be called relatively good; and there is no "class or species of motives to which any such epithet as bad can with propriety be applied."[177] In Bentham's view, even the bloodthirstiness of a murderer has to be called relatively good, insofar as this motive affords him satisfaction. "Whatever act" or motive "affords any the minutest particle of satisfaction, of pleasure or removes or prevents any the least particle of pain is in so far good . . . even in the instance of the most atrocious malefactor that ever lived."[178] For the sake of objective ethical valuation, this insight into the relative goodness of all motives has to be combined with an understanding of the difficulties involved in discovering what are the true motives of a man—difficulties which are great, even if nothing but ethically

[175] Ibid., part XIII, p. 54b.　　[176] Ibid., part II, p. 487a.
[177] Ibid., part IV, p. 415b (The Book of Fallacies, 1824, part II, chap. I, §3).
[178] Ibid., vol. VI, p. 259a ("Rationale of Judicial Evidence," book I, chap. XI, §2, note).

neutral terms are applied, and all biased appellations of motives are avoided.

Bentham rightly stresses that this psychological question also has to be treated with critical circumspection for psychological *and* ethical reasons. For, in contrast to the manifest consequences of acts, "motives are hidden in the human breast."[179] The motives of men are never given in immediate evidence. In every case they have to be inferred; and such inferences are always more liable to error than the analyses of given facts. "Put the same question to a man to whom the springs of action are known and the mechanism of the human mind familiar—he will scorn to pretend to know what is not capable of being known. He will answer" in a certain case "desire of gain, enmity, public spirit; these motives (not to speak of casual ones) any one exclusively, any or all conjunctively, and in any one of the whole assemblage of imaginable proportions—the proportions never the same for two days or two hours together, nor understood, or so much as inquired into, by the individual himself."[180] Particularly "when men of law talk of malice, they do not know what they mean: this, though so short an account, differs little, if anything, from the true one. For discovering what they mean there is one course to be taken and but one; . . . malice is either express or implied. With this distinction at command, if a fancy happens to take you to punish a man as for malice, it is impossible for you to be under any difficulty. Whatever you happen to mean by malice, if you can prove it, you prove it: if you cannot prove it, you imply it."[181] "The field of motives is an open and ample field for the exercise not of mendacity only, but of bias. The tendency of bias is to attribute the greatest share or rather the whole agency in the production of the act to a particular motive, to the exclusion of or in preference to whatever others may have concurred in the production of it. Few indeed that are able, scarce any that are willing to give on every occasion a correct account of the state of the psychological force by which their conduct has been produced. Ask Reus for his own motives—they are the most laudable or in default of laudable, the most justifiable or at least excusable of any that can be found. Ask a friend of Reus for the motives of Reus—the answer is the same. Ask Actor for the motives of Reus—the same gradation, the order only reversed. Ask Reus for the motive which gave birth to the prosecution on the part of Actor—the motive of course is the most odious that can be found: desire of gain, if it be a case which opens a door to gain; if not enmity, though not under that neutral and unimpassioned, but under the name of revenge or malice or some other such dyslogistic name. Ask a friend of Reus or an enemy of Actor—the answer is the same. Ask an enemy of Reus or a friend

[179] *Ibid.*, part iv, p. 415b (*The Book of Fallacies*, 1824, part ii, chap. i, §3).
[180] *Ibid.*, part vi, p. 246b ("Rationale of Judicial Evidence," book i, chap. viii).
[181] *Ibid.*, vol. vi, p. 304a ("Rationale or Judicial Evidence," 1827, book ii, chap. 5, §4).

of Actor—his motive was public spirit, the purest public spirit."[182] It is generally these difficulties of ascertaining the true motives of men, combined with a prejudiced terminology of motives, which lead ethics and psychology astray.

These psychological and ethical considerations are finally enriched again by a list of reasons which commonly induce the uncritical characterization of motives. Bentham finds there may be at stake either an intentional, or even more frequently, an unnoticed "fallacy of confusion," "interest-begotten . . . , authority-begotten . . . , habit-begotten prejudices"[183] or in the case of the imputation of bad motives a fallacy of distrust, in the case of the imputation of good motives a fallacy of obsequiousness.[184] A combination of a great part of such tendencies may be observed in the favorable interpretation of motives of monarchs. In this case, habit-begotten, authority-begotten prejudices, the fallacies of obsequiousness, the interests in adulation, devout superstition and the belief in "ghosts"[185] collaborate, in order to produce the most widespread phenomenon of light-minded praise of dignitaries and superiors in general.

A further very frequent reason for the employment of biased characterization of motives is, according to Bentham the "love of ease," "sloth" which, it is true, in the ancient world was recognized neither as "god nor goddess, not ranking higher than with syrens"; but it is "in our days . . . not . . . the less powerful."[186] "Presuming is" always "shorter than proving."[187] "By implying malice in your bosom, he who knows nothing about you or your case" saves himself and others "the trouble of thinking whether any such thing as malice, whatever be meant by the word, had in your case any existence."[188] "Pronouncing the word conscience" and referring to good or bad motives of one's own or others' actions is "so easy."[189] "Goodness and badness of all qualities experienced or imaginable, these are the very first that would present themselves to notice, these are the very first that would obtain names."[190] Thus, as good and bad are among the oldest terms used in human language,

[182] *Ibid.*, vol. vi, pp. 246a, b (*The Rationale of Judicial Evidence*, book i, chap. viii).

[183] *Ibid.*, vol. iv, p. 557b ("Codification Proposal to All Nations Professing Liberal Opinions," 1822, part i, sect. 7).

[184] *Ibid.*, vol. ii, p. 415b (*The Book of Fallacies*, 1824, part ii, chap. i, §2, 3).

[185] *Ibid.*, part xvii, p. 84a ("The Constitutional Code," book i, chap. xiii).

[186] *Ibid.*, part ix, p. 90b (*The Elements of the Art of Packing as Applied to Special Juries Particularly in Cases of Libel Law*, 1821, part i, chap. vi, §2).

[187] *Ibid.*, part xi, p. 55b ("An Introductory View of the Rationale of Evidence, for the Use of Non-lawyers as well as Lawyers," chap. xii, §12).

[188] *Ibid.*, part xi, p. 55a ("An Introductory View of the Rationale of Evidence," chap. xii, §12, sample 2).

[189] Bentham, *The Book of Fallacies*, 1824, p. 109 (part i, chap. iii, sect. 2).

[190] Bentham, *Works*, 1843, vol. viii, p. 203a ("A Fragment on Ontology," written between 1813 and 1821, chap. ii, sect. 3).

the love of ease tempts us to apply those primitive terms even in the mere description of human motives.

Strange to say, however, with this love of ease may be combined what seems its opposite, the will to power. By blindly imputing certain motives to other persons the will to power generally feels more satisfied than if the judgment were left in abeyance. "Power" is always "more pleasant than impotence."[191] To withhold the passing of any premature moral judgment of human motives or even to confess our ignorance as to the true motive of a certain action—such an objective attitude requires a suppression of moral vanity which many moralists are unable or unwilling to perform.

No less important than vanity are ignorance, intellectual weakness and other sorts of weakness which all influence moral prejudices with respect to human motives. "Home-made" opinions are very rare; "inbred intellectual weakness" is much more frequent.[192] In contrast to common prepossession, Bentham emphasizes that ignorance and narrowness of mind are generally coupled with moral weakness, not with moral strength and innocence. "In the estimation of vulgar prejudice there is a natural alliance between improbity and intelligence, between probity and imbecility. In the estimate of discernment they are differently grouped: improbity and hebetude—probity and intelligence."[193] "Of imbecility—at any rate of self-conscious and self-avowed imbecility—proportionable humility ought naturally to be the result"; but, on the contrary, of imbecility, particularly if it associates itself with blind belief in authority, "of this species of idolatry—of this worshipping of dead man's bones—all the passions the most opposite to humility—pride, anger, obstinacy and overbearingness—are the frequent, not to say the constant accompaniments."[194] Moreover "the thicker the ignorance, the more completely is the furniture of men's minds made up of those interest-begotten prejudices which render them blindly obsequious to all those who with power in their hands stand up to take the lead"[195] and to persuade their followers to believe in the interpretations they give of their own and of others' motives.

In connection with these observations Bentham occasionally ventures to say that moralists and jurists who judge not on the ground of the consequences but only on the ground of the motives of acts have too much "the offender . . . in view . . . , not the community injured by the offense"; they are more directed by antipathy against the actor than by benevolence to-

[191] *Ibid.*, part XI, p. 55b ("An Introductory View of the Rationale of Evidence," chap. XII, §12, sample 2).
[192] *Ibid.*, vol. IV, p. 557b (*Codification Proposal to All Nations Professing Liberal Opinions*, 1822, sect. 7); compare *The Book of Fallacies*, 1824, p. 377.
[193] *Ibid.*, part XIV, p. 393b ("Rationale of Judicial Evidence," book IX, part III, chap. 3, §1).
[194] *Ibid.*, part IV, p. 392a (*The Book of Fallacies*, 1824, part I, chap. I, §2).
[195] Bentham, *The Book of Fallacies*, 1824, p. 54, part I, chap I, sect. 2.

wards the public.[196] "The only species of government which has or can have" the consequences of acts consistently in view, that is, the true aim of all moral acts, "the greatest happiness of the greatest number, is" according to Bentham "a democracy."[197] Moreover, once he even states that all the moralists who do not agree that the beneficial consequences of acts, i.e. the greatest happiness of the greatest number, are alone of decisive moral importance, are either "a set of corruptionists" or "a correspondent set of dupes."[198] All general praise of human motives, however, or general lament about them are nothing but "topics . . . of rhetoric";[199] rhetoric which is an "ever ready prostitute—prostitutes herself to despotism."[200] It is only "the practitioners in the arts of rhetoric (that is, of deception)" who are "fond of skirmishing" on such vague subjects as the general depravity or dignity of human nature and human motives. The conclusiveness of most of Bentham's observations on these points is, I think, hardly imperiled by some of his angry overstatements—or by the many unflattering items he enumerates. It may be said that all these objections concern only the common use of ambiguous terms for motives but not the refined theories of leading moralists. It seems to me, however, that most attractive contemporary ethics suffers from what Bentham revealed as an untenable ambiguity of ethical fundamentals.

Contemporary Existentialism, Bergsonianism and Similar Theories of Motives

As if to challenge Bentham's insistence on an unambiguous theory of motives, Simone de Beauvoir entitled her latest ethical work *Pour une morale de l'ambiguité*. Forcefully bringing out the general trends of contemporary existentialism, she emphasizes that by trial and by intimate experience men have always become aware of their living in a tragic tension and ambiguity between "to be and not to be." Only the philosophers have generally tried—in vain—to evade or to mask this fundamental insight.[201] The true philosopher, however, has to restore it to sight and to protect this basic feature of our existence from distort-

[196] Bentham, *Works*, 1843, part XIV, p. 409a ("Rationale of Judicial Evidence," 1827, book IX, part 3, chap. 4, §1).

[197] *Ibid.*, part XVIII, p. 47a ("The Constitutional Code," book I, chap. IX).

[198] *Ibid.*, part VIII, p. 537a (*Codification Proposal to all Nations Professing Liberal Opinions*, 1822, part I, sect. I).

[199] *Ibid.*, part XIII, p. 115b ("The Rationale of Judicial Evidence," book V, chap. 17).

[200] *Ibid.*, part XVI, p. 521a (*Letters to Count Toreno on the Proposed Penal Code Delivered by the Legislation Committee of the Spanish Cortes*, April 25, 1821, written at the count's request, Letter V). This passage is omitted in the first edition in 1822.

[201] S. de Beauvoir, *Pour une morale de l'ambiguité*, 1947, pp. 12 ff.

ing analyses which, at the cost of truth, aspire to present an essentially ambiguous phenomenon in terms of the rigid unambiguity of an artificial logic.

Looking down on the unambiguous logic of the mere *Verstand*, adopting, to a large extent, the ambiguous dialectical method of Hegel's *Vernunft* and even more markedly the method of Kierkegaard, Simone de Beauvoir emphasizes that there are insoluble tensions and liaisons between subject and object, human consciousness and the world, man and fellowman,[202] things and their human, moral significance,[203] inward and outward life,[204] the will to one's existence and the will to the development of the world,[205] the meaning of an action and the content of that act,[206] the effect of an act and its inner motive.[207] However, the main source of value in these dialectical relations lies for existentialism definitely in the realm of the subject and not in any seemingly given object.

The language and the meaning of such statements certainly go much beyond anything that Bentham or John Dewey or any ethical empiricist has in view when he maintains that, in reality, motive and consequences of an act are closely connected with each other; that both have to be taken into account in our evaluation of the act and that they can be separated from each other only by methodological distinctions.

The ethics of contemporary existentialism seems, thus, worlds apart from any kind of utilitarianism and ethical empiricism. Jean Paul Sartre comprehensibly, therefore, insists that "la psychoanalyse existentielle . . . nous indique la nécessité de renoncer à la psychologie de l'intérêt, comme à toute interprétation utilitaire de la conduite humaine, en nous révélant la signification idéale de toutes les attitudes de l'homme."[208]

---

[202] *Ibid.*, p. 102. [203] *Ibid.*, p. 104. [204] *Ibid.*, p. 107.
[205] *Ibid.*, p. 122. [206] *Ibid.*, p. 212. [207] *Ibid.*, p. 193.
[208] J. P. Sartre, *L'être et le néant, Essai d'ontologie phénoménologique*, 1943, p. 720. Only in his *Situations II*, 1948, pp. 308 f, perhaps under the influence of Simone de Beauvoir, Sartre comes almost as close to the philosophy of the greatest-happiness principle as his disciple came one year earlier. Nevertheless he admits only that "l'arithmétique des plaisirs" can be applied to certain cases but not to those cases in which the attainment of a greater happiness can be bought solely at the price of a *qualitative* deterioration of the character of those who aspire to that greatest happiness. Such a case exists, for instance, if the Communist Party sanctions lying and creates liars and oppressors in order to free society from other oppressors and liars. By this application of the utility principle, Sartre reveals that he illegitimately oversimplifies the function of the principle by linking its application only to the ultimate end of action and by alleging that the utility principle is neglecting the means in favor of the ultimate ends.

Strangely enough, however, and obviously without being aware of it Simone de Beauvoir often comes surprisingly close to the position of consistent hedonism. She reports that a personal acquaintance, a radical Kantian, denied that there is morally any difference between the suffering of one man and that of ten thousand; in opposition to this kind of "Kantian" argument she insists that "il est . . . logique, bien que cette logique implique une scandaleuse absurdité, de préférer le salut du plus grand nombre."[209] She grants that one may say that "aucune multiplication n'a prise sur la subjectivité"; but she concedes to utilitarianism that "pour celui qui a la décision à prendre, les hommes sont . . . donnés comme des objets qu'on peut compter."[209] Again and again, therefore, she emphasizes that every individual pleasure counts, every "joie individuelle et vivante," even the seemingly useless enjoyment of a "lazzarone napolitain" who dozes in the sun or the laughter of a child playing with a balloon.[210]

In this connection, Simone de Beauvoir rejects the views of "l'homme sérieux" and of the national as well as the economic collectivists who discard the pains and enjoyments of the individual.[211] The collectivist is willing to sacrifice everything to mere abstract ideas: "Nation, Empire, Union, Économie etc."; but, as she maintains, "aucune de ces formes n'a de valeur en soi, elle n'en a qu'un tant qu'elle enveloppe des individus concrets."[212] "C'est un des mensonges de l'esprit sérieux que de prétendre donner au mot 'utile' un sens absolu; rien n'est utile s'il n'est utile à l'homme."[213] All this certainly involves no criticism of Bentham's consistent hedonism but rather a confirmation from unexpected quarters.

Even the rejection of the belief in an "identity of the interests of all men" does not mean a refutation of Bentham's utilitarianism. Beauvoir—apparently following the general line of the French interpretation of utilitarianism—thinks that not only John Stuart Mill's but also Bentham's and other types of hedonism are untenable on account of their fallacious supposition that "le véritable intérêt de chacun se confond avec l'intérêt général."[214] But as we have seen, this supposition

---

[209] S. de Beauvoir, *Pour une morale de l'ambiguité*, 1947, p. 159.

[210] *Ibid.*, pp. 189 f.   [211] See *ibid.*, e.g. pp. 71, 202 f.   [212] *Ibid.*, p. 203.

[213] *Ibid.*, pp. 133 f. Compare pp. 70, 156. On p. 111 "le bonheur de l'homme" is called an untenable "terme fixé" along with such concepts as that of "le Savoir absolu," "la perfection de la beauté." But this does not seem to involve any contradiction to the frequent statements on the value of concrete happiness, the relative good and useful, concrete pleasure.

[214] *Ibid.*, p. 157.

by no means forms an indispensable or even an essential basis of Bentham's ethical theory.

Yet despite these points of noticeable agreement between existentialism and hedonism, in tenor and substance their moral teachings remain *toto caelo* different from each other. Simone de Beauvoir grants that what is useful to the individual and pleasant for him is ethically important. But the criterion of moral value—quite unlike that of hedonism—is, she insists, the inner liberty of the individual, the inner sense and not the pleasant results of his acts. "La morale, c'est le triomphe de la liberté sur la facticité."[215] Dieu même était d'accord . . . avec la doctrine existentialiste, puisque, selon le mot d'un prêtre antifasciste, 'il avait un tel respect de l'homme qu'il l'a créé libre.' "[216] And in this respect Jean Paul Sartre seems to be even more radical than the existentialist psychologist Maurice Merleau-Ponty[217] and Beauvoir in rejecting any possible obstacle to the inner freedom of man.[218]

In any case, in full agreement with conventional morality and in full opposition to hedonism, Simone de Beauvoir extols the inner freedom, the inner motives, the inner truth of the act and spurns by comparison the outward results of the act. "La valeur d'un acte n'est pas dans sa *conformité* à un modèle extérieur, mais dans sa vérité intérieure. Nous récusons les inquisiteurs qui veulent créer du dehors la foi et la vertu."[219] The unavoidable result of these romanticizing tendencies, however, is, as in all conventional ethics, that the inner truth of an act, the purity of its motive, necessarily makes the act good, however revolting its consequences may be. Measured by her moral criterion, which so enthusiastically hails the ambiguity of human motives, any "truthful" act must be considered good, even if its consequences drown the world in sufferings.

Simone de Beauvoir, on this point no longer in agreement with conventional morality, consistently and courageously admits that it is legitimate to draw this paradoxical inference from the use of her moral

---

[215] *Ibid.*, p. 64.   [216] *Ibid.*, p. 101.

[217] See M. Merleau-Ponty, *Phénoménologie de la perception*, 1945, pp. 517 ff and the whole chapter "la liberté" *ibid.*, pp. 496 ff. Cf. M. Merleau-Ponty, *La structure du comportement*, 1942, e.g. pp. 300 f. "La conscience transcendentale, la pleine conscience de soi n'est pas toute faite, elle est à faire, c'est-à-dire à réaliser dans l'existence"; p. 304: "Peut-on penser la conscience perceptive sans la supprimer comme mode original . . . ?" etc.

[218] See Jean Paul Sartre, *L'être et le néant*, 1943, especially his discussion of "Liberté et responsabilité," *ibid.*, pp. 638 ff.

[219] S. de Beauvoir, *Pour une morale de l'ambiguïté*, 1947, p. 193.

criterion. Despite her proven abhorrence of Nazi cruelty and the heroic resistance of French existentialists to Nazi terror, she grants that even if an individual is hateful, "haïssable par le sens qu'il a donné à sa vie," he may still evoke sympathy in us, if only his heart, his inner vigor and true conviction are in his motives.[220] Those, however, who lack this "chaleur vivante," the lukewarms of the Gospels, are the real "sous-hommes."[220] "J'ai entendu dire qu'au procès de Nuremberg, Goering exerçait sur ses juges une certaine séduction à cause de la vitalité qui émanait de lui."[220] In contrast to common practice, then, Simone de Beauvoir does not deny the moral ambiguity of good and subjectively "true" motives. Goering and Hitler always remained true to their convictions and, therefore, she does not, as is commonly done, use derogatory names for their motives because the results are abhorrent.

She frankly grants that, though an act may serve entirely abominable ends, its motives, its inner vitality and truthfulness are the only and sufficient carriers of its moral value. This is certainly a far more accurate statement than the only too familiar-sounding assurances to the contrary in hundreds of ethical tracts of ancient and modern times.

But in the light of this honest confession, how little is said in the concluding words of her ethical work in which she assures us that "tout homme qui a eu de vraies amours, de vraies révoltes, de vrais désirs, de vraies volontés, sait bien qu'il n'a besoin d'aucune garantie étrangère pour être sûr de ses buts; leur certitude vient de son propre élan. Il y a un très vieux dicton qui déclare. 'Fais ce que dois, advienne que pourra.' C'est dire d'une autre manière que le résultat n'est pas extérieur à la bonne volonté qui se réalise en le visant."[221] If true desires, that is, true motives are all that is morally relevant and if, nevertheless, these motives can admittedly inspire immoral deeds—as in the case of Goering—is it, then, unjustified to conclude that this ethics and its principle "vouloir la liberté n'est qu'une formule creuse"[222] and that this ethical doctrine is merely "formal and completely incapable of giving any content to that liberty in which it wishes us to engage?"[223]

Although Simone de Beauvoir is determined to defend existentialist ethics against this reproach of formalistic emptiness, this ethics leads indeed to an equally untenable formalism and, despite her beliefs to the contrary,[224] to equal "absurdities" of ambiguity as Kant's formalism and all mere ethics of motives.[225]

---

[220] *Ibid.*, p. 61.   [221] *Ibid.*, pp. 222 f.   [222] *Ibid.*, p. 110.
[223] *Ibid.*, p. 102.   [224] See *ibid.*, p. 180.
[225] For a more detailed analysis of contemporary existentialism and especially

Simone de Beauvoir's "morale de l'ambiguité" has quite a number of points in common with Bergson's ethics of the *élan vital* and the "paradoxes," the ambiguities of his morality of the "open soul."[226]

There are, of course, weighty differences between Bergson's and existentialist ethics. Bergson's *Les deux sources de la morale et de la religion* presents itself, as the title of the work indicates, only as a psychology of ethics; and he speaks less derogatorily of the sources from which the rigid, unambiguous principles of "closed morality" spring up than Simone de Beauvoir speaks of "l'homme sérieux" and his construction of the fixed maxims of a closed society.[227] Certainly her language is far less the language of love in the sense of the New Testament than is the language of Bergson. But Bergson's ideals, in turn, have more of the dynamics of the "élan vital" than of the ascetic retirement and the passive, silent humility preached by so many Epistles of the Apostles; and Bergson, in his only work on ethics, doubtless wished to give more than a mere psychology of the origin of morality.

Like Simone de Beauvoir and Lévy-Bruhl, Bergson definitely implied that there is one approach to moral issues which is superior to all others; unlike Lévy-Bruhl and like Beauvoir, he thinks that the higher morality is not represented by a dispassionate understanding and a rational settlement with existing moral rules, but by a supra-rational creative life in moral paradoxes.

According to Bergson and Beauvoir, this higher supra-rational morality does not look back to statutes and rules fixed by the group in the past, but it looks forward—it is open to the uncertainties of the future, to the risks of free choice. "Être libre . . . c'est pouvoir dépasser le donné vers un avenir ouvert."[228] The free man of higher morality, "est être des lointains, mouvement vers l'avenir, projet; . . . selon le mot de

---

Jaspers', Sartre's and Gabriel Marcel's ethical formalism see D. Baumgardt "Existentialist Ethics in the Light of a New Theory of the Meaning of Life" in *Papers and Abstracts of the Third Inter-American Congress of Philosophy*.

[226] H. Bergson, *Les deux sources de la morale et de la religion*, 1932; on paradoxes, e.g. p. 57; on "l'âme ouverte" and "l'âme close," "morale ouverte" and "morale close," e.g. pp. 33 f, 56 ff, 61 ff. Simone de Beauvoir, too, speaks of "un élan vers l'être," see her *Pour une morale de l'ambiguité*, 1947, e.g. p. 61.

[227] On the "société close," see e.g. H. Bergson, *Les deux sources de la morale et de la religion*, 1932, p. 27 ff on "la société close." Although the ethical world of "l'homme sérieux" in Beauvoir (see *Pour une morale de l'ambiguité*, 1947, pp. 66-77) is not identical with that of Bergson's "closed soul," this world has certainly far reaching similarities with it, especially seen from the point which is essential for our critical evaluation.

[228] S. de Beauvoir, *Pour une morale de l'ambiguité*, 1947, p. 127.

Heidegger . . . il est . . . infiniment plus que ce qu'il serait si on le ré-
duisait à être ce qu'il est."[229] As Edouard Le Roy observes, "the good"
in Bergson's philosophy does not mean a "thing" but rather a "way."[230]
And Bergson as well as French existentialism assure us that the truly
moral and free man is open to the concerns of mankind, the concerns
of "l'humanité entière,"[231] "la fraternité humaine,"[232] "la totalité des
hommes,"[233] and not only to the concerns of a particular community
or nation.

In a similar, though somewhat more traditional Christian vein,
Maurice Blondel distinguishes between "l'objet de la science des
moeurs" and what he calls the "syndérèse morale," a higher ethical
"expérience concrète, *sub specie universi.*"[234] Only the object of the
lower science of morals allows for a completely rational treatment of
its subject matter, namely, the analysis "des préceptes empiriques, des
moralités populaires qui semblent résumer la sagesse des siècles et des
nations."[235] And in a similar way, referring to Blondel's and Léon
Ollé-Laprune's earlier works, Paul Gaultier insists that "l'éthique ne
repose ni sur l'évidence rationelle, ni sur celle des sens, mais sur . . .
une . . . évidence purement intérieure."[236] These inner moral experiences, la liberté, the higher morality of free human actions, Blondel
goes on to say, cannot be subjected to an analysis of scientific precision
similar to the precision possible in the analysis of the empirical, moral
rules of a closed society, which—like other historical phenomena—are
simply given *faits accomplis.*

In the field of the free, truly moral act, it cannot be our task to determine "avec plus de précision et de rigueur la loi des répercussions
nécessaires et les conséquences des actes humains."[237] For the free
action "est un appel et un écho de l'infini: elle en vient, elle y va"; there-

[229] *Ibid.,* p. 143.
[230] E. Le Roy, *Une philosophie nouvelle,* 1912, p. 206: "le bien . . . est une voie
plus qu'une chose."
[231] See H. Bergson, *Les deux sources de la morale et de la religion,* 1932, e.g.
p. 34.
[232] *Ibid.,* p. 55.
[233] S. de Beauvoir, *Pour une morale de l'ambiguité,* 1947, p. 202.
[234] M. Blondel, *L'action,* tome II, 1937, p. 302.
[235] *Ibid.,* p. 300.
[236] P. Gaultier, *L'idéal moderne,* 1908, pp. 47 f.
[237] M. Blondel, *L'action,* tome II, 1937, p. 300. Compare Jean Nabert, *L'expérience intérieure de la liberté,* 1924, where it is especially stressed e.g. on pp. 259 ff
that "nous apercevons la catégorie suprême de la croyance à la liberté . . . dans . . .
l'idée d'une activité infinie" and compare the polemics against Frédéric Rauh's
Études de morale, 1911, *ibid.,* pp. 199 ff.

fore "la science, ici, ne peut être que pratique, c'est-à-dire fondée sur une réelle expérimentation de l'impénétrable complexité de la vie."[237] "Au-dessus de toute éthique naturaliste, utilitaire, sociologique même, et pour rendre possible ces formes subalternes, une morale vraiment morale . . . s'offre donc à nous comme l'extension de ce qu'il y a de plus essentiel à notre vouloir, comme l'oeuvre originale de l'agir humain, comme la production, en l'homme et par l'homme, d'une réalité transcendante à toutes les données et conditions."[238] Judged by the standards of this true, transcendent reality Bentham's utilitarian arithmetic "est une chimère."[239] "Même lorsqu'on se persuade que les conséquences des actions sont seules importantes, rien de plus 'scientifique' que de se détacher de ces conséquences mêmes, pour suivre les indications de la conscience qui sont déjà une leçon de l'action. A la tâche donc, sans nous demander avec une vaine avidité: 'A quoi bon, qu'est-ce que cela vaut?' Les actes sont comme les pierres d'un édifice inconnu, où il est plus beau d'être humblement manoeuvre que de se hausser à faire l'architecte, parce que le plan de l'ensemble échappe à nos yeux, et que les plus communes expériences de la vie pratique restent mystérieuses à notre raison."[240] In other words, in the opinion of Blondel, Bergson and French existentialism, rational unambiguity of moral thought and moral behavior—and especially a rational utilitarian approach to them— can at best be characteristic of the static habits, the lower morality of the closed society and the closed soul.

As Bergson states, only the lower ethics of justice can rationally be formulated in "utilitarian terms" which "faithfully" preserve "its mercantile origins."[241] The creative life of love, the life of the moral hero, "l'appel du héros,"[242] the *imitatio Christi*, the open morality toward the whole of humanity confronts us with formulas "that border on contradiction"[243] any moment we wish to express this higher morality in terms of the lower, the closed group ethics.

In the eyes of all one-sided empiricists and rationalists, this whole distinction between a higher and lower type of morality would be nothing but what Kant ironically once called an untenable "aristocratic" mysticism.[244] Nevertheless, there seems to me no doubt that

[238] M. Blondel, *L'action*, tome II, 1937, pp. 302 f.
[239] *Ibid.*, p. 299.　　　　[240] *Ibid.*, p. 301.
[241] H. Bergson, *Les deux sources de la morale et de la religion*, 1932, p. 70.
[242] *Ibid.*, pp. 29 ff.　　　　[243] *Ibid.*, p. 57.
[244] See Kant's essay "Von einem neuerdings erhobenen vornehmen Ton in der Philosophie," in *Kants gesammelte Schriften*, herausg. v. d. Königl. Preussischen Akademie der Wissenschaften, Band VIII, 1912, pp. 390 ff where Kant denounces

existentialism, Bergsonianism and similar ethical speculations give rich and subtle poetical insights into the ethical meaning of human life.

And yet in our context the decisive question is: Where is there any guarantee in these speculations that the ethics of the higher ambiguous motives of the "free man" can justify acts of generosity, of love, of openness to the brotherhood of man, and that the ambiguous morality of the free and "liberating" élan vital will not vindicate acts of the utmost heroic brutality and bloody world-dictatorship? Without being given any reasons, we are merely assured that exclusively moral, pleasant and valuable results will flow from the "truly free" will of vital actors.

At least as far as all the major issues between master morality and the ethics of generosity are concerned, consistent hedonism can provide an unequivocal criterion of what is morally right and wrong. The criterion is: the morality of sheer power can never satisfy the demands of the greatest happiness of the greatest number while the ethics of justice and mercy can. But wherever consistent hedonism is so slightly thought of and where ambiguous motives are so highly praised as in the half-mystical types of contemporary French ethics, there a complete breakdown of all unbiased criteria of ethical value is unavoidable.

Character and Conduct

As a result of reflections of this kind, Bentham insists that the critical moralist "must unlearn" all rhetoric and biased appellations, all "question-begging appellatives" of alleged moral or immoral motives.[245] Ethics has rigorously to "unteach" this fallacy.[246] Expressed in a different way, or rather applied to somewhat different concepts, this first presupposition of any critical ethics can be formulated in the following way: the moralist has to estimate the character of an actor by his conduct, and not his conduct by his character.

For, the character of a man is, according to Bentham, practically the same as his moral disposition. "*Character* is sometimes used as synonymous to disposition itself; but more commonly for the opinion supposed to be entertained concerning the disposition of the individual in question by such persons as have had more or less opportunity of becoming acquainted with the indications given of it. *Character* is accord-

---

any and all "noble" philosophers who think that by way of genius, "durch einen einzigen Scharfblick auf ihr Inneres," they can achieve more than by rational methodological thinking.

[245] Bentham, *Works*, 1843, vol. II, p. 436a (*The Book of Fallacies*, 1824, part IV, chap. I).

[246] *Ibid.*, vol. II, p. 436b.

ingly on occasion of this sort the word almost exclusively in use: disposition very seldom: the distinction is scarcely an object of notice."[247] All disposition, however, "is produced by motives."[248] "A man is said to be of such or such a disposition, according as it is to the influence of the motives that belong to this or that class that he is considered as being more or less in subjection: reference being made to the degree of influence supposed to be exercised by these same motives over the minds of the generality of the class of persons with whose conduct his conduct is compared. If the motives of the self-regarding class are considered as predominant, a selfish disposition is ascribed to him: if motives of the social class, a disposition of the social benevolent cast: if of the dissocial kind, a disposition of the dissocial or malevolent cast."[249] Accordingly, as we have already seen, to build up moral judgment only on the inferred character of a person, that is, on "pronouncing anything on the disposition" or the moral motives of actions would be "the pronouncing a verdict" or a praise "without evidence,"[250] a "vague and ungrounded vituperation"[251] or eulogy. Judging a man morally on the ground of his implied or self-proclaimed motives alone is, according to Bentham, as mistaken as "looking upon this or that actor as a good man, because he acts well the part of Othello or bad, because he acts well the part of Iago."[252] In this last remark, it is true, Bentham refers mainly to characters who are "self-trumpeters" of their virtue. Nevertheless, it is not an illicit interpretation to suppose that on this point too Bentham had indirectly in mind the general problem concerning the ethical valuation of human characters.

Free from blind radicalism, Bentham admits that "not unfrequently indication of disposition . . . comes in of course along with other and more directly apposite evidence and when it does, it is naturally impressive."[253] But he warns us constantly that, in general, "to take disposition

[247] *Ibid.*, part xiii, p. 56b (*The Rationale of Judicial Evidence*, 1827, Book v, chap. xiii, §2).

[248] *Ibid.*, part xiii, p. 56a.

[249] *Ibid.*, part xiii, p. 56a (Rationale of Judicial Evidence, book v, chap. xiii, §2). Compare *A Treatise on Judicial Evidence*, 1825, p. 176.

[250] See *ibid.*, vol. v, p. 255a (*The King against Sir Charles Wolseley, Baronet and Joseph Harrison, schoolmaster, set down for Trial at Chester, on the fourth of April 1820, Brief Remarks tending to show the Untenability of this Indictment,* 1820).

[251] *Ibid.*, vol. v, 256a (The King against Wolseley and Harrison, 1820).

[252] *Ibid.*, part iv, 412b (*The Book of Fallacies*, 1824, p. 121, part i, chap. v, sect. 2).

[253] *Ibid.*, part xiii, p. 56b ("The Rationale of Judicial Evidence," 1827, book v, chap. xiii, §2).

for the subject of express inquiry, would be to try one cause or perhaps a swarm of causes under the name and on the occasion of an other."[254] For, as a hitherto unpublished MS emphasizes particularly clearly: "What a man's disposition is, can only be presumed,"[255] as is the case with his real motives. Accordingly, Bentham recommends to the moralist and jurist that "no evidence of character, good or bad—no speaking to character, favourably or unfavourably . . . ought to be admitted without power to the judge . . . to allow of time for inquiry into the character of the character-givers themselves."[256] If "ill-disposition," malignity, bad character "are imputed to others . . . without proof . . . let any sincere lover of truth, justice, sincerity declare" whether to the thus judging persons "the imputations would not apply with more justice than to those to whom they are . . . applied."[257] In other words, if moralists tend to infer a stable good or bad character of men instead of observing their changing conduct, Bentham considers this as a proceeding without any value from the viewpoint of the critical moralist.

Bentham readily admits that it may be "scarcely possible . . . to do away completely" with all estimating of men by character instead of conduct. It seems impossible to abolish all question-begging denominations of human motives and dispositions. But in proportion as this "effect on the understanding and through that channel on the temper and conduct of mankind" is achieved "the good effect of the exposure will become manifest."[258] Bentham himself certainly worked hard towards this end; and he spared no effort to make this fundamental point of his doctrine clear.

All moral judgment must be based mainly on the conduct of men, on the results of this conduct, not on men's implied character or their motives. But while stressing this point throughout his work, while stressing the insuperable difficulties of grounding moral valuations on motives, Bentham has not overlooked the complications with which his own theory of consequences is confronted. To determine the amount of

[254] Ibid., part XIII, p. 56a.

[255] Bentham MS hitherto unpublished, bound together with a copy of Bentham's Introduction to the Principles of Morals and Legislation (1789), British Museum, North Library. Compare the Introduction itself, chap. XI, sect. IV.

[256] Bentham, Works, 1843, part XIII, p. 59a ("Rationale of Judicial Evidence," book v, chap. XIII, §4).

[257] Ibid., vol. v, p. 250b (The King against Edmonds and Others, Set Down for Trial at Warwick on 29th March 1820, Brief Remarks Tending to Show the Untenability of This Indictment, 1820).

[258] Bentham, The Book of Fallacies, 1824, p. 220, part IV, chap. I.

pleasure acquired by the effects of actions is certainly difficult; and
Bentham seems to have been aware of these difficulties in his later writings even more than he was in his *Introduction*. He insists, however,
that without reference to empirical happiness or empirical suffering,
any supposition of absolutely good or bad consequences of acts or aims
of life would be as misleading as the assumption of absolutely good or
bad motives and characters. He once illustrated this by saying that
"without discrimination I neither condemn martial law—nor even torture . . . knowing that government throughout is but a choice of evils
I am on every occasion ready to embrace the least of any two, whatever
may be its name"; but "the end . . . must be pure and clear of all objection."[259] In an even bolder statement he went so far as to say that
"whatever act affords any the minutest particle of satisfaction of pleasure or removes or prevents any the least particle of pain is in so far good;
in this case are the great majority of human acts even in the instance
of the most atrocious malefactor that ever lived."[260] This radical consistency of Bentham's ethics of success should never be lost sight of.

Accordingly the supposition of any absolutely good goal of life, different from empirical happiness, the assumption of a metaphysical *summum bonum* is ironically rejected by Bentham. "*The summum bonum*
is a fruit of the tree of pure good upon the taking of which into his
mouth a man experiences at one and the same time every pleasure in
which in the nature of a sensitive being he is susceptible, each in the
highest degree; pains of all sorts at the same time keeping aloof. . . . It
is the kernel of that fruit of which the *philosopher's stone* is the shell. It
was lately found by Baron Münchhausen on the Island of Medemusia
after a careful search made in pursuance of the directions given by Aristotle, Plato and Cicero in whose philosophical repasts—as in the codes of
those universally admired masters of ethical science anybody may see—
it formed a constant article. By Cicero in his Tusculan Questions it has
been made plain to the perfect satisfaction of his Auditor (a most perfectly well-bred young gentleman . . .) that pain is no evil. But the truth
is, as the philosopher confessed to the Baron, that during the whole of
his dialogue they were both of them chewing the summum bonum nut
to which the areca, even when wrapped up in the betel leaf, forms a very

---

[259] Bentham, *Works*, 1843, vol. iv, pp. 211a, b ("Panopticon versus New South
Wales or the Panopticon Penitentiary System and the Penal Colonisation System").
[260] *Ibid.*, vol. vi, p. 259a, note (Rationale of Judicial Evidence, 1827, book i,
chap. xi, §2).

inadequate substitute. The consequence was that all that time to the philosopher and his agreeable young friend pain was no evil whatsoever it may have been and be about to be to the vulgar of that and other ages."[261] So Bentham-like contemporary positivism in ethics[262] discards any metaphysical assumptions and anti-hedonistic, absolutist valuations with regard to ends of human conduct, just as he does with regard to motives.

Later Formulae of and Reflections on the Utility Principle

As we saw, the moral judgment has to be built up mainly on the analysis of men's conduct or, more precisely, on an analysis of the amount of happiness caused by this conduct and judged by the principle of utility. In Bentham's later thought, the validity of the old formula of this utility principle is justified or, perhaps, limited by the following explanation: "If the nature of the case admitted the possibility of any such result, . . . the greatest happiness of all" would have to be "the end aimed at . . . but such universality is not possible . . . thus it is, that to provide for the greatest felicity of the greatest number, is the utmost that can be done toward the maximization of universal . . . felicity."[263]

What seems to be even more important, in his *Constitutional Code*, Bentham limits his justification of the utility principle to an especially narrow range by explaining in great detail: "When I say the greatest happiness of the whole community, ought to be the end or object of pursuit, in every branch of the law—of the political rule of action, and of the constitutional branch in particular, what is it that I express?—this and no more, namely that it is my wish to see it taken for such, by those who, in the community in question, are actually in possession of the powers of Government. . . . In making this assertion, I make a statement relative to a matter of fact, namely that which, at the time in question, is passing in the interior of my own mind; how far this statement is correct, is a matter on which it belongs to the reader, if it be worth his while, to form his judgment. Such then being the desire, truly or falsely expressed by me, but at any rate expressed by me—in his breast has that same desire a place? If so, then may it be worth his while to apply his attention to the course herein marked out by me, under the notion of its being correspondent and contributory, and conducive to the attainment of the same end. On the other hand, if so it be, that that same desire has no place in his breast, on that sup-

---

[261] *Ibid.*, part xv, p. 83a, note (Chrestomathia, appendix, sect. viii).

[262] See e.g. Charles L. Stevenson, *Ethics and Language*, 1944, p. 175: "Whatever may be the meaning of this term [the *summum bonum*] . . . it has always been taken to imply intrinsic value." But such a "conception of ethics" in which emphasis is placed on intrinsic value and the *summum bonum* is not "feasible."

[263] Bentham, *Works*, 1843, vol. ii, p. 269a, note ("Leading Principles of a Constitutional Code for any State," 1823, sect. i).

position, generally speaking, it will be a useless trouble to him to pay any further attention to anything contained in it. . . . In saying, as above, the proper end of government is the greatest happiness of all, or, in case of competition, the greatest happiness of the greatest number, it seems to me that I have made a declaration of peace and goodwill to all men. On the other hand, were I to say, the proper end of government is the greatest happiness of someone, naming him, or of some few, naming them, it seems to me that I should be making a declaration of war against all men, with the exception of that one, or of those few."[264] At first glance, all these statements could be interpreted as the complete abandonment of any objective justification for the utility principle and as a simple confession of a merely subjective predilection for it on the part of the hedonist Bentham.

But any Bentham interpretation of this kind[265] seems to me to lose sight of the facts that even in his youth, Bentham did not claim to offer a strict proof of the validity of the utility principle but only the evidence of its superiority over all rival principles; and that in an unpublished MS he presented the utility principle explicitly as a "hypothesis." Moreover the main reason for his restraint in the *Constitutional Code* was, in all probability, only his wish not to burden his extended legal deductions with any special justification for the validity of the utility principle.

As in his youth, Bentham frequently includes in his old age under his principle of utility a regard for animals, particularly because "an adult quadruped . . . has in him . . . much more morality as well as intelligence . . . than any biped has for months after he has been brought into existence."[266] On the other hand, Bentham occasionally limits the formula of the greatest-happiness principle by adding "for the greatest length of time."[267] But, of course, this qualification of the utility principle had already been taken into consideration in the old list of the seven dimensions of value of pleasure and pain—a list repeatedly mentioned[268] in the later writings. All he did later in this respect was to pay additional attention to some of these dimensions in his formula of the utility principle.

[264] Bentham, *Works*, 1843, vol. IX, pp. 4f ("Constitutional Code," book I, introd., sect. 1).
[265] Such an interpretation is, for instance, advocated in a remark of Laurence J. Lafleur's introduction to a new edition of Bentham's *Introduction*, see *An Introduction to the Principles of Morals and Legislation* with an introduction by L. J. Lafleur, 1948, p. xv.
[266] *Ibid.*, part XX, p. 550a ("Letter to the Editor of the *Morning Chronicle*," March 4, 1825).
[267] *Ibid.*, vol. II, p. 482b (*The Book of Fallacies*, 1824, p. 392, part V, chap. IX).
[268] *Ibid.*, vol. III, p. 287a ("Nomography," appendix: "Logical arrangements or instruments of invention and discovery," sect. IV); compare *ibid.*, vol. III, p. 214a ("Pannomial Fragments," chap. II); *ibid.*, part VIII, pp. 540 ff ("Codification Proposal," 1822, sect. 3).

Again we find in the later works some points already mentioned before implicitly, for instance, a remark on the "relations between the import of the word happiness and that of the word pleasure, pain" and utility: "sole positive element of happiness alias felicity, alias well-being—pleasures and those determinate ones: sole negative element of happiness, exemption from pains and those equally determinate ones. Determinate import thereby given to the word utility, a word necessarily employed for conciseness sake, in lieu of a phrase more or less protracted in which the presence of pleasures and the absence of pains would be brought to view. An action may be considered and spoken of as useful, as conducive to general utility, in proportion to the value of any pleasures which it is its tendency to produce or of any pains which it is its tendency to avert."[269] "A pleasure is single—happiness is a blended result, like wealth."[270] Further, as to the "relation of emotion, affection, passion and humour, to pleasure and pain, and thereby to one another: An act is said to be the result or effect of an emotion, when the motive by which it is regarded as produced is a pleasure or pain considered as transient: of an affection, when it is regarded as the result of a permanent, or say, an habitual state of mind in which sympathy or antipathy towards the object in question and consequently the pleasures and pains corresponding to them are regarded as frequently having place: of a passion—of a state of mind transient or permanent in which the emotion or affection is regarded as being in a high degree of intensity: of a man's humour, when the emotion or affection or passion is regarded as being produced by an incident or sort of incident by which it is seldom or never produced in any other or in more than a few other minds in any degree or in a degree equal to that in which it is produced in the mind in question."[271] Further, "absence of pain" is called "negative good, . . . absence of pleasure—if arising from loss—negative evil"; pleasure, however, is positive good, pain is positive evil.[272] Of course all this is nothing new.

More interesting than these references to the simplicity of the utility principle are the remarks about the difficulties of its correct application. Bentham frequently emphasizes "that to make a right and effectual use of the greatest happiness principle, requires the concurrence of those requisites which are not

[269] *Ibid.*, vol. iii, p. 286b ("Logical Arrangements," written between 1811 and 1831, sect. iii). Compare *ibid.*, vol. iii, p. 241a: "Happiness is a word employed to denote the sum of the pleasures experienced during that quantity of time which is under consideration, deduction made or not made of the quantity of pain experienced during that same quantity of time" ("Pannomial Fragments," written at sundry times up to 1831, chap. ii).

[270] *Ibid.*, part xx, p. 585a (Bowring's Memoranda from Bentham's conversation in the years 1827-28).

[271] *Ibid.*, part xx, p. 509a f (Notes made by Bentham in his Memorandum Book, 1818-19).

[272] *Ibid.*, vol. iii, p. 214a ("Pannomial Fragments," written at sundry times up to June 1831, chap. ii).

always found in company: invention, discernment, patience, sincerity; each in
no inconsiderable degree; while, for the pronouncing of decisions without
consulting it, decisions in the *ipse dixit* style, nothing is required but boldness."[273] In one of his "Letters to the Citizens of the United States" Bentham
proudly points to the fact that "the reasons" his ethics gives for the validity of
moral and juristical laws are "composed . . . of considerations having regard
to the universally exemplified and universally recognised principles of human
nature viz. feelings and desires"; so "these reasons have their anchor . . . prepared in every human breast."[274] Nevertheless he also stresses the other side
of the picture, that even "in its purest possible state of simplicity the law in
every part of it draws upon all men for a portion of labour and intelligence
more than all men have to bestow upon it."[275] Though on this point he particularly referred to the formulation of juristic laws, in accordance with his
general tendencies he obviously did not wish to exclude the implicit reference
to the establishment and formulation of concrete moral laws.

Employing Descartes' *Cogito ergo sum* as a kind of joke Bentham con-
temptuously attacks all ethics and jurisprudence, which in their use of the
utility principle, neglect "close reasoning" and indulge in an "aërial mode of
contestation":[276] "I think; therefore I exist, was the argument of Des Cartes: I
exist; therefore I have no need to think or be thought about, is the argument of
jurisprudence."[277] As intelligence is needed for probity, according to Bentham,[278] so careful and patient reasoning is indispensable for ethical judgment.
To apply in ethics nothing but the simple "principle of common sense or moral
sense or any other purely verbal principle" leads to "dogmatism...ipse-dixitism
. . . to a nonsense ethics."[279] A curious spectacle enough would be, but rather

[273] *Ibid.*, vol. II, p. 463a (*The Book of Fallacies*, 1824, p. 316, part IV, chap. X,
sect. I).

[274] *Ibid.*, part VIII, p. 492b (*Jeremy Bentham, an Englishman, to the Citizens of
the Several American United States*, written in 1817 on the suggestions of Lord
Henry Brougham, President Madison, Albert Gallatin, Simon Snyder, Governor
of Pennsylvania, Letter V). Incidentally, as late as in a memorandum of 1830,
Bentham preferred the United States Constitution to any other type of Government, see *Works*, 1843, vol. XI, p. 62a: "I prefer the English constitution, such as
it is, to non-government, and to every other but the United States' government"—
a point rightly emphasized by Hilda G. Lundin in her "The Influence of Jeremy
Bentham on English Democratic Development" in *University of Iowa Studies in
the Social Sciences*, vol. VIII, number 3, 1920, p. 21.

[275] *Ibid.*, vol. VII, p. 290b ("Rationale of Judicial Evidence," 1827, book VIII, chap.
XIX, §1).

[276] *Ibid.*, part IV, p. 455b (*The Book of Fallacies*, 1824, p. 288, part IV, chap. VIII).

[277] *Ibid.*, part XII, p. 374a ("Rationale of Judicial Evidence," book II, chap. X,
§6).

[278] See *ibid.*, part XIV, p. 393b ("The Rationale of Judicial Evidence," book IX,
part III, chap. III, §1).

[279] *Ibid.*, vol. VI, p. 239 f ("Rationale of Judicial Evidence," book I, chap. VII,
§2). Compare *ibid.*, p. 240, the enumeration of the principles of ipse-dixitism of

more curious than instructive, to see a partisan of moral sense in dispute with a partisan of common sense or two partisans of either of these verbal principles in dispute with one another. Let the common sense of one of them command what the moral sense of another leaves indifferent or forbids; or let the common sense of one of them forbid what the moral sense of another leaves indifferent or commands; or let the like conflict have place between two philosophers of the common sense or two partisans of the moral sense. When each of them has delivered the response of his oracle according to the interpretation put upon it by itself, all argument should, if consistency were regarded, be at an end; as at Lincoln's-Inn exercise where one of the pleaders has declared himself for the widow and the other against her, the debate finishes."[280] At best the application of such principles as that of the moral sense or common sense is equal in value to the application of the Aristotelian logic to physical sciences carried through "for near two thousand years."[281] And this application of Aristotelian logic to physics was always considered by Bentham as something entirely futile. To apply such verbal principles as moral sense, no empirical observation or comparison of observation is needed, but solely "pen, ink and paper"; however, to make up an ethical account on the ground of the principle of utility "requires thought and talent . . . reason . . . and . . . increasing reference to experience—experience of pain and pleasure."[282] On the side of moral dogmatism based on the moral sense, ultimate reference is made to "assertion," to innate ideas and innate propensities, the reference to which should have been scientifically "exploded" forever since the days of John Locke.[283] But the greatest-happiness principle stands on the ground of solid

---

dogmatic presentation of "favorite tenets" (p. 239b): "When by a consideration of any kind a man is determined to maintain a proposition of any kind and finds it not tenable on the ground of reason and experience, to conceal his distress, he has recourse to some phrase in and by which the truth of the proposition is, somehow or other, assumed. Thus in the moral department of science having a set of obligations which they were determined to impose upon mankind or such part of it at any rate as they should succeed in engaging by any means to submit to the yoke—phrases in no small variety and abundance have been invented by various persons for the purpose of giving force to their respective wills and thus performing for their accommodation the functions of a law: law of nations, moral sense, common sense, understanding, rule of right, fitness of things, law of reason, right reason, natural justice, natural equity, good order, truth, will of God, repugnancy to nature." This list of the principle of ipse-dixitism is on the whole a repetition of that of the *Introduction*, chap. ii, sect. xiv. The only new and instructive remark is that Bentham presents here the principle of utility as based on reason and experience and contrasts it with all other moral principles as being manifestations of merely irrational tyrannic will.

[280] *Ibid.*, vol. vi, pp. 239a, b ("Rationale of Judicial Evidence," book i, chap. vii, §2).

[281] *Ibid.*, vol. vi, p. 239a.   [282] *Ibid.*, p. 239 f.
[283] *Ibid.*, p. 240 f.

experience and needs on each occasion to strike a careful "balance . . . in collecting together the several items" of pain and pleasure produced by the consequences of the acts in question and in the instance of each item to pay regard "to the several elements of value, to determine on which side—on that of pleasure or pain, of profit or loss, the difference is to be found."[284] So, by experience and reason, "the tendency . . . to produce more pleasure than pain and consequently to be" morally "right—or more pain than pleasure and consequently to be wrong—is made known and demonstrated."[285] By allowing and requiring such an impartial analysis of the consequences of acts, the principle of utility shows its superiority to dogmatic, anti-hedonistic principles of morality.

To carry out these substantiated, detailed analyses of the consequences of acts, Bentham enumerates not only the good and evil consequences of the first and second order, as he did in his *Introduction*, or three orders of good or evil consequences, as he did in a manuscript edited by Dumont in his *Traités de Législation*,[286] but in one of his later treatises he even speaks of a fourth order of effects with regard to "public rewards" exciting others to perform valuable public service.[287] In other passages of his later writings he returns, however, to the mention of consequences of only three or two orders.[288] In any case, the introduction of these new orders of effects is not of major concern.

In connection with his enlarged list of orders of the effects of actions Bentham occasionally enlarged also his catalogue of sanctions. In his "Introductory View of the Rationale of Evidence," it is true he keeps to the list of

[284] *Ibid.*, p. 238 f.
[285] *Ibid.*, p. 238b.
[286] See Bentham-Dumont, *Traités de Législation*, 1802, tome I, introductory part, chap. x (*The Theory of Legislation*, ed. by R. Hildreth, 1864, p. 49).
[287] Bentham, *Works*, 1843, vol. III, p. 289b (Nomography, appendix: Logical Arrangements, written between 1811 and 1831, sect. VI).
[288] Three orders of effects are mentioned in *Works*, vol. III, p. 230a ("Pannomial Fragments," chap. IV, §5, written between 1829 and 1831). Only two orders of effects are mentioned in *Works*, part XII, p. 535 ("Rationale of Judicial Evidence," 1827, book IV, chap. v, §2). Further, only two orders of effects are enumerated in *Works*, part III, pp. 20b, 123a, b ("Principles of Judicial Procedure with the Outlines of a Procedure Code," chap. III, and chap. XXIII, §4, written mainly between 1820-27 and edited by Richard Doane). Again, only two orders of effects are distinguished in vol. III, p. 358b ("Equity Dispatch Court Bill being a Bill for the Institution of an Experimental Judicatory under the name of the Court of Dispatch, for exemplifying in Practice the manner in which the proposed summary may be substituted to the so-called regular system of procedure and for clearing away by the experiment the arrear of business in the Equity Courts," part I, sect. VI, article 37, written between 1829 and 1831).

the four sanctions he had given in his *Introduction*;[289] and in his *Rationale of Judicial Evidence*, he does the same, distinguishing the physical sanction from the three which he calls psychological sanctions in contrast to the physical one.[290] But in the same essay in which he speaks of four orders of effects, in his *Nomography*, he also adds to the usual number of four sanctions a fifth, the sanction of sympathy,[291] apart from the physical, the moral, the political and the religious sanctions.

This sanction of sympathy falls, according to Bentham, partly "within the description of the physical" one, because the pleasure produced by an action caused by sympathetic affection is the "immediate result" of the action in question "without the intervention of any exterior will."[292] But in contradistinction to the physical and moral sanction, as well as to the political and religious one, Bentham thinks that the sanction of sympathy alone cannot be called a self-regarding sanction and should therefore not be identified with those four others.[293] In a letter to Dumont, dated October 28, 1821,[294] Bentham even reports that he had "discovered" still more sanctions, a retributive and an antipathetic one, and he further divides the political sanction into the legal and administrative one, including both with the physical, the sympathetic, the antipathetic, the moral and the retributive one as the seven human sanctions in contrast to the religious one as the superhuman sanction. But I do not think that it is necessary to attach any special importance to these "discoveries" of Bentham's.

Far more instructive, however, than these formal divisions and sub-divisions is Bentham's rather paradoxical statement that "apppparent justice . . . is the direct end and the immediately important object of the system of procedure,"[295] not real justice.

The vindication Bentham gives of this—at first sight rather repellent—declaration is this: if the decision of a court is not conformable to real justice, but conformable to apparent justice, if a guilty man is acquitted or an innocent man is punished on the ground of the best available apparent justice, then, nevertheless, only a mischief of the first order is produced though a

---

[289] See *Works*, 1843, vol. vi, p. 19a ("An Introductory View of the Rationale of Evidence," chap. vii, §3), and compare *Introduction*, 1789, chap. iii.

[290] *Ibid.*, vol. vi, p. 260b (*Rationale of Judicial Evidence*, 1827, book i, chap. xi, §3).

[291] *Ibid.*, vol. iii, pp. 290a, 291b ("Nomography," appendix: Logical Arrangements, written between 1811 and 1831, sect. viii).

[292] *Ibid.*, vol. iii, p. 291b.

[293] *Ibid.*, p. 292a.

[294] This letter is not to be found in the edition of Bentham's correspondence, *Works*, part xix ff, but only in a note to the edition of the "Introduction" in *Works*, vol. i, p. 14a.

[295] Bentham, *Works*, 1843, part iii, p. 20b ("Principles of Judicial Procedure with the Outlines of Procedure Code," mainly written between 1820 and 1827, chap. iii).

contrast exists to real justice. That is to say, in this case of a violation of real justice only one person or a comparatively small group of persons has to suffer, but the wider public is not alarmed since, by the presupposition of the case, the public is not aware of any injustice. That is, no evil of the second order, concerning a much larger number of people, is involved. If, however, the contrary happens, if the decision of a court is not conformable to apparent justice, but conformable to real justice, then the good or evil of the first order, concerning only comparatively few people, is small, but the mischief of the second order, the alarm caused by the apparent violation of justice, affects a very large public and so represents a much greater evil.[296] Judged by Bentham's own ethical standards, this argument seems to me to underrate considerably the intensity of the pains which every real injustice imposes on the sufferers of the mischief of the first order.

But whatever we may think of the value of these reflections, they place at least two cardinal convictions of Bentham's in a particularly glaring light. They demonstrate how consistently Bentham urges the pre-eminence, the weight of the consequences of acts, in every moral valuation, and how much less relevance he ascribes to all other elements of human conduct. And no less essential is the energy with which he defends the importance of appearance in its relation to "abstract" reality in itself, reality conceived as separated from appearance. "In point of utility," that is of morality, "apparent justice is everything. . . . From apparent justice flow all the good effects of justice—from real justice, if different from apparent, none. . . . Real justice, abstractedly from apparent justice, is a useless abstraction not worth pursuing, and supposing it contrary to apparent justice, such as ought not to be pursued."[297] This is certainly a high valuation to place on appearance in contrast to reality in itself. Reality so far as it is conceived to be totally opposed to the world of appearance is inaccessible to human insight, and therefore irrelevant to the epistemologist Bentham.

This, however, is an attitude which he shares not only with the empiricism of all times, but even with Kant's "Kritik der reinen Vernunft" and to a large extent with Hegel. Though these questions are primarily the concern of jurisprudence, in Bentham they are also of great interest to ethics in general. Of far more obvious ethical importance, however, is Bentham's criticism of two very common sayings, which again refer to the problem of the consequences of acts.

Does the End justify the Means? "Good in Theory, Bad in Practice"

Despite the definite primacy which Bentham attaches to the effects

[296] *Ibid.*, part III, pp. 20 f.
[297] Bentham, *Works*, 1843, part III, p. 21b ("Principles of Judicial Procedure," chap. III).

of acts, his attitude toward the so-called Jesuitic rule about means and ends is one of severe disapprobation. Bentham does not want his doctrine misunderstood in such a way as to attribute all the moral weight to the *ultimate* end of an act regardless of the mischief caused by its precedent consequences.

On the contrary, in full agreement with the general trend of his teaching he explains that the morality of the famous maxim that the end justifies the means may be granted only on three conditions. These three strictly confining conditions are "1. that the end be good. 2. that the means chosen be either purely good, or if evil, having less evil in them than on a balance there is of real good in the end. 3. that they have more of good in them or less of evil, as the case may be, than any others by the employment of which the end might have been attained. Laying out of the case these restrictions, note the absurdities that would follow. Acquisition of a penny loaf is the end I aim at. The goodness of it is indisputable. If by the goodness of the end any means employed in the attainment of it are justified, instead of a penny I may give a pound for it: thus stands the justification on the ground of prudence. Or, instead of giving a penny for it, I may cut the baker's throat and thus get it for nothing: and thus stands the justification on the ground of benevolence and beneficence."[298] In this way Bentham has clearly enough protected his ethics of consequences from the misinterpretation which contends that he justified all bad means in favor of the ultimate effect of an action.

Further—and this time in full agreement with leading idealists— Bentham refused to approve another commonplace in ethics. He emphatically rejects the view that there may be human actions valuable in theory which, nevertheless, are "not the thing for practice"; and vice versa, he denies "that a plan which is essentially incapable of proving good in practice can with propriety be said to be good in theory."[299] Kant too declined to acknowledge any antagonism between theory and practical life in ethics.[300] But it seems to me that here again, Bentham's argument has a sounder basis than that of Kant.

[298] Bentham, *The Book of Fallacies*, 1824, pp. 341 f, part IV, chap. XIII (*Works*, vol. II, p. 470).

[299] *Ibid.*, p. 305, part IV, chap. IX, sect. III (*Works*, vol. II, p. 460a).

[300] See Kant, "Über den Gemeinspruch; das mag in der Theorie richtig sein, taugt aber nicht für die Praxis," 1793, *Gesammelte Schriften*, ed. Königl. Preussische Akademie der Wissenschaften, Erste Abteilung, Band VIII, 1912, S. 273 ff.

Kant, after all, cannot deny that many actions cause mischief in practice, though the moral purity of their motives stamps them with the character of theoretically good actions according to his doctrine. All he did was to add that such mischievous acts have to be called practically good from the moral point of view; and *vice versa*, most beneficent acts have to be characterized in the eyes of Kant as morally bad or morally indifferent, if their motive was morally bad or indifferent. For, in Kant's view, happiness on the one hand and morality on the other are two totally different things; they can never be sought for at the same time at least during man's earthly life.

Bentham, however, pays all due respect to the utility of the consequences of acts right from the beginning of his ethical inquiry. He includes the consideration of the "practical" effects of acts throughout his ethical theory. Accordingly, it is much easier for him to deny the possibility of any conflict between theory and practice than it is for Kant. Bentham can simply declare that, if some plans "have been bad in practice, it is because they have been bad in theory"; it is because "in the account taken of profit and loss, some circumstance that has been necessary to render the plan in question advantageous upon the whole has been omitted."[301] And the same applies to the phrases "too good to be practicable," "too speculative," "too theoretical," "too utopian to be put into practice"—all these words of wisdom, so often used by men of the world, either with "lamentation" or with "a grin of malicious triumph."[302] Bentham, the *moralist*, could feel freer from this conflict between theory and practice than any other moralist in the whole history of philosophy.

Bentham, the experienced political scientist adds, however, that it is indeed "deep sagacity," if "the ruling few" speak of the practical "dangerousness" of utilitarian theories; these theories are indeed dangerous to the ruling few, though beneficial to the many; and it is, therefore, "utopian" to expect from the few an approval of utilitarian theories planned on the basis of the greatest happiness principle.[303] If a law is "promotive of the interest of the many," and if there is "anything in it that is adverse to the interests, the prejudices or the humours of the ruling few, the wonder is, not that it should not have been brought forward before, but that it should be brought forward even now" and

---

[301] Bentham, *The Book of Fallacies*, 1824, p. 306, part IV, chap. IX, sect. III (*Works*, vol. II, p. 460b).

[302] *Ibid.*, p. 309 (*Works*, vol. II, p. 461b).

[303] *Ibid.*, pp. 315, note, 302 (*Works*, vol. II, pp. 463a, note, 459b).

455

that it is not turned down by an "indirect way of brow-beating" of the "man high in office" and by his arrogance covered only "under a thin veil of modesty."[304] For, "none are so completely deaf as those who will not hear—none are so completely unintelligent as those who will not understand."[305] On this account Bentham, in his *Book of Fallacies*, wished to "correct" a statement made in his *Introduction*. He blames the "simplicity" of his mind for having thought (in the work of his youth) that the phrase "dangerousness of the utility principle" was "a gross absurdity"; he now finds that this phrase contains great wisdom in the interest "of the ruling few."[303] In any case, *philosophically* speaking, all arguments against the practical value of good theories are beside the point, particularly if these theories are built up so consistently on the ground of practical beneficence, as is the case with Bentham.

Difficulties and Superiorities of Utilitarian Ethics Confirmed

Though Bentham displays, in all his later writings, a firm belief in the superiority of his theory on the points hitherto mentioned, he is not blind to difficulties of his doctrine as regards the felicific calculus. In his later thought he refrained from any definite, further development of his moral arithmetic. Perhaps his opinions as to the applicability of the moral calculus were, in his later years, even more cautious than he had shown them to be in his *Fragment on Government*.

In his *Rationale of Judicial Evidence* (1827), for instance, he grants that neither the measurement of the force of interests and motives is precisely attainable nor the mensuration of pleasures and pains. "Between the ideas respectively denoted by the words interest, motive, hope, fear, good, evil, pleasure and pain the connection is inseparable. Without motive there is no interest; without hope or fear there is no motive; without good or evil there is no hope or fear; without pleasure or pain there is no good or evil. . . . But . . . it is not with trustworthiness in psychology as with temperature in physics; in which you can say not only, it was cooler yesterday at noon than today at the same hour; but, by observation taken each day on the thermometer, you can express the difference by numbering in each case the degrees. The only state of things in which the force of an interest . . . is susceptible of measurement is that in which the correspondent pleasures or pains have for their

---

[304] *Ibid.*, pp. 114, 116 (*Works*, vol. ii, pp. 410b, 411a).
[305] *Ibid.*, p. 119 (*Works*, vol. ii, p. 411b).

efficient cause an object susceptible of mensuration."[306] In his *Codification Proposal* (1822), he even seems to admit that "unhappily or happily, for quantities of pleasure or pain we have no . . . measures"; only for "weight, extent, heat, light—for quantities of all these articles we have perceptible and expressible measures."[307] But he limits this skeptical remark to the acknowledgment that it is only *direct* measurement of pleasure and pain which is generally not possible in so far as the *intensity* of feelings is concerned. "Considered with reference to an individual in every element of human happiness, in every element of its opposite unhappiness the elements, or say dimensions of value . . . are four: intensity, duration, propinquity, certainty; add, if in a political community, extent. Of these five the first, it is true, is not susceptible of precise expressions; it not being susceptible of measurement. But the four others are."[308] Moreover, though the intensity of pleasure itself is not directly "ponderable or measurable, to form an estimate," it may at least be possible to measure the intensity of a pleasure indirectly by measuring "the source" of it, particularly if this source is the general "representative of pleasure, viz. money."[309] This is a clear indication of the two fundamental limitations to which the moral calculus is naturally subject. The first is that the intensity of a pleasure or a pain is generally not directly measurable. The second is that an indirect measure of the intensity of feelings is possible only in as much as their source can be measured.

However, in his *Rationale of Judicial Evidence* Bentham exempts from these concessions the measurement of two or perhaps only one interest, and that of the corresponding pleasure or pain, viz. that of aversion to labor or at least that of pecuniary interest, i.e. of the direct pleasure of wealth. "Out of all the species of interest it is . . . in two" that they and their corresponding pleasures are measurable, namely in the case of pecuniary interest and the aversion to labor. "In the case of pecuniary interest for example everybody sees that upon a given person (proximity and probability being in both cases the same) the operative force of a sum of £20 will be, practically speaking (though not in mathematical strictness) double that of £10. So in the case of aversion to labour the operative force of a course of labour for two hours will be,

[306] Bentham, *Works*, 1843, part xiv, pp. 567a, 568b ("The Rationale of Judicial Evidence," book x, chap. ii).

[307] *Ibid.*, part viii, p. 541a (Codification Proposal Addressed to All Nations Professing Liberal Opinions, sect. 3).

[308] *Ibid.*, part viii, p. 542a.   [309] *Ibid.*, part viii, p. 540b.

practically speaking, double that of a course of labour of the same sort for one hour and, mathematically speaking, something more. . . . The irksomeness of labour," however, "depending so much more upon the species than upon the quantity as measured by time, and of labour, the same in species as well as quantity, the degree of irksomeness being so widely different to different individuals, in such sort that a quantity of labour which to one man is highly irksome, shall to another be not merely indifferent, but highly agreeable; quantity of labour forms but an imperfect and incompetent subject of mensuration. There remains therefore money as the only efficient cause of interest and pecuniary interest as the only interest the force of which . . . is commodiously measurable. Yet this measuring rule once obtained—by reference to this (by means of the principle of commercial and commutative exchange) cases will happen in which the force of any other species of interest" and pleasure "may by accident become susceptible of mensuration,"[310] as this is illustrated by two examples concerning the pleasures of honor or power and revenge.

Certainly, the analysis of these questions of measurement is in need of far more refinement; Bentham himself, for instance, realized that happiness does not rise with the arithmetical ratio of property, or that of power and other causes of pleasure.[311] But, in spite of all these dif-

---

[310] *Ibid.*, part xiv, p. 569a ("Rationale of Judicial Evidence," book x, chap. ii). The two examples given here are the following: "Suppose two political situations affording honour or power (both or either) without profit: considering each by itself, it may be difficult to form any sort of estimation of the degree of force with which . . . they may respectively operate upon the mind of a given person. But suppose them to have been, each of them, the objects of purchase and sale—the one having been bought and sold for £2,000, the other for £4,000: in this case the force of the interest constituted by them respectively is as susceptible of mensuration as that of an interest constituted by money." Secondly, "for an injury done, or supposed to be done, the party injured prosecutes the supposed injurer. He knows beforehand that . . . he will not, even in the event of his succeeding in the prosecution, receive satisfaction in any pecuniary shape: he understands, on the other hand, that the amount of the expense on his side is not likely to be less than £50. He prosecutes notwithstanding and delivers his testimony. The interest by which he has been engaged to embark on this prosecution is the interest created by that modification of the pleasure of antipathy, called the pleasure of revenge. Here, then, not indeed the exact force of that interest, but the minimum of it is given and expressed in money. It is certain that it acts upon him with a force at least equal to £50—that is to the apprehension of losing £50; since he pays £50 for the purchase of a chance of it. With how much greater a force, does not appear: since it does not appear how much more he would have spent in prosecuting rather than not obtain the pleasure of the revenge" (*Works*, part xiv, p. 569a).

[311] See e.g. *Works*, 1843, part xviii, pp. 14-17 ("Constitutional Code," book i,

ficulties, he was, I believe, not wrong in holding fast to one fundamental conviction: "How far short soever this degree of precision" of the application of the utility principle "may be of the conceivable point of perfection—of that which is actually attained in some branches of art and science—how far short soever of absolute perfection—at any rate in every rational and candid eye unspeakable will be the advantage it will have over every form of argumentation in which every idea is afloat, no degree of precision ever attained, because none is ever so much as aimed at."[312] It seems to me that this is not an unfair account of the high desirability as well as of the great difficulties of a "moral arithmetic."

The difficulties are great. They are, certainly, greater than Bentham had realized or made clear in his *Introduction*. As he admitted in his later writings, the intensity of pleasures and pains is generally not directly measurable, even if their duration, propinquity and certainty are. Apart from that, any measurement of the complicated, intricate feelings of "problematic souls" is a far more entangled task than Bentham ever realized. Moreover, any measurement of pleasure and pain—direct or indirect—is still today far less precise than mensurations in meteorology, not to mention those of exact physics or chemistry. But can we say that any valuable direct or even indirect estimate of the intensity of human feelings is a priori impossible? That is, I think, where the matter stands now.

So much for the later analyses of the elements of action, and the utility principle connected with them. Other moral discussions, however, with which we are already familiar receive in the later writings some supplements also worth noticing. John Locke's "original compact," the original "compact between king and people" is here again characterized as a "fabulous one"

---

chap. III, sect. 5); vol. IV, p. 541, and compare Bentham-Dumont, *Traités de Législation.*

[312] *Works*, 1843, part VIII, p. 542a ("Codification Proposal," part I, sect. 3). It is true, however, that the two following formulations of this conviction, to be found in the same section, are less happily phrased, pp. 542a, 542b: "Till the principle of utility . . . is on each occasion, if not explicitly, implicitly referred to as the source of all reasoning—and arithmetic . . . employed in making application of it, everything that in the field of legislation calls itself reasoning or argument will—say who can in what large proportion—be a compound of nonsense and falsehood; both ingredients having misrule for their effect, after having in no small proportion had it for their object (p. 542a, 542b); 542a: "The footing upon which . . . reasoning is . . . placed by the principle of utility is not only the only true and defensible footing, but the only one . . . on which any tolerable degree of decision can have place: and even in so slight a sketch as the present already it may have been observed how near to mathematical the degree of precision is in this case capable of being made."

and well contrasted with the compact of 1688, the compact between King, Lords and Commons which "was but too real a one."[313] "The origination of governments from a contract is a pure fiction or in other words a falsehood."[314] "Contracts came from government, not government from contracts."[315] Accordingly, as the *Fragment on Government* had already tried to demonstrate, the idea of a "*contrat* social" can never serve as a basic concept of morals and as a substitute for the utility principle.

No less than the original contract, the law of nature is found to be an untenable basis of morals and political philosophy. To the criticism of the French *Déclaration des droits de l'homme*—this most influential concrete application of the natural law—Bentham devoted a special pamphlet, his "Anarchical Fallacies." The emptiness, the tautological or even contradictory character of the general law of nature is here again elucidated in the following deductions: "Nature, say some of the interpreters of the pretended law of nature—nature gave to each man a right to everything; which is in effect but another way of saying—nature has given no such right to anybody. . . . Nature gave . . . to every man a right to everything:—be it so—true; and hence the necessity of human government and human laws to give to every man his own right without which no right whatsoever would amount to anything. Nature gave every man a right to everything before the existence of laws and in default of laws. This nominal universality and real nonentity of right, set up provisionally by nature in default of laws, the French oracle lays hold of and perpetuates it under the law and in spite of laws. These anarchical rights which nature had set out with, democratic art attempts to rivet down and declares indefeasible. . . . In vain would it be said that though no bounds are here assigned to any of these rights, yet it is to be understood as taken for granted and tacitly admitted . . . that they are to have bounds as it is understood will be set them by the laws. Vain . . . would be this apology; for the supposition would be contradictory to the express declaration" of the law of nature "and would defeat the very object which the whole declaration has in view. It would be self-contradictory, because these rights are, in the same breath in which their existence is declared, declared to be imprescriptible. . . . Precious security for unbounded rights against legislators, if the extent of those rights in every direction were purposely left to depend upon the will and pleasure of those very legislators! Nonsensical or nugatory, and in both cases mischievous: such is the alterna-

---

[313] Bentham, *Works*, 1843, vol. IV, p. 447b ("Jeremy Bentham to His Fellow-Citizens of France on Houses of Peers and Senates," sect. XII, no. 19).

[314] *Ibid.*, vol. II, p. 501a ("Anarchical Fallacies being an examination of the declarations of rights issued during the French Revolution," first published in full in 1843).

[315] *Ibid.*, part IV, p. 502a ("Anarchical Fallacies, A critical Examination of the Declaration of Rights, published by the French National Assembly, in 1791," article II, sentence 1).

tive."[316] Contrary to the law of nature, "contrary to every principle of justice, considered in themselves, these expressions are both of them nonsense—mere nonsense. That which they concur in supposing is that a list of principles and a corresponding list of rules, generally recognized as coming under that denomination are in existence: whereas no such lists are capable of being produced by any person by whom the existence of them is thus asserted."[317] "The making of such divisions" as natural, economical, political laws in morals "may be parodied by distributing zoology into the science of chimeras, of horses and of animals!"[318] "If I say a man has a right to this coat or to this piece of land . . . what I assert is a matter of fact. . . . In the case of alleged natural rights no such matter of fact has place—nor any matter of fact other than what would have place supposing no such natural right to have place. . . . A man is never the better for having such natural right: admit that he has it, his condition is not in any respect different from what it would be, if he had it not. . . . If I say a man has a natural right to the coat or the land—all that it can mean, if it mean anything . . . , is that I am of opinion he ought to have a political right to it . . . , he ought to be protected and secured in the use of it. . . . It may . . . be said to deny the existence of these . . . natural . . . rights which you call imaginary is to give a *carte blanche* to the most outrageous tyranny. The rights of man anterior to all government and superior as to their authority to every act of government, these are the rampart and the only rampart against the tyrannical enterprises of government. Not at all—the shadow of a rampart is not a rampart;—a fiction proves nothing—from that which is false you can only go on to that which is false. . . . It is not the rights of man which cause government to be established: on the contrary, it is the non-existence of those rights. What is true is that from the beginning of things it has always been desirable that rights should exist—and that because they do not exist; since, so long as there are no rights, there can . . . be . . . no sources of political happiness. . . . It is the weakness of the understanding which has given birth to these pretended natural rights; it is the force of the passions which has led to their adoption, when, desirous of leading men to pursue a certain line of conduct which general utility does not furnish sufficient motives to induce them to pursue or when, having such motives, a man knows not how to produce and develop them, yet wishes that there were laws to constrain men to pursue this conduct or what comes to the same thing that they would believe that there were such laws—it has been found the shortest and easiest

[316] *Ibid.*, part IV, p. 502 (Anarchical Fallacies).
[317] *Ibid.*, vol. III, p. 388a note ("Equity Dispatch Court Bill," part I, sect. IX, art. 2).
[318] *Ibid.*, part V, p. 157 ("A General View of a Complete Code of Law," published in French in 1802, chap. I, §1).

method to imagine laws to this effect."[319] This last explanation of the origin and the purpose of the law of nature seems to me not only of psychological interest; it also adequately illustrates the function of natural law seen from the angle of consistent hedonism.

"There are . . . no rights contrary to the law—no rights anterior to the law. Before the existence of laws there may be reasons for wishing that there were laws—and doubtless such reasons cannot be wanting, and those of the strongest kind; but a reason for wishing that we possess a right," a natural law, "does not constitute a right. To confound the existence of a reason for wishing that we possessed a right with the existence of the right itself, is to confound the existence of a want with the means of relieving it. It is the same as if one should say, everybody is subject to hunger, therefore everybody has something to eat. . . . Those who govern allege legal rights—the rights of the citizen—real rights: those who wish to govern allege natural rights—the rights of man—counterfeit rights. . . . Those to whom the faculty of making these imaginary laws instead of real laws has been transferred have not much trouble in making them"; natural rights "are made as easily as songs. . . . For the making of real laws talent and knowledge . . . labor and patience are requisite: but for the making of forgeries sources of the rights of man nothing more is required than ignorance, hardihood and impudence. Rights of men when placed by the side of legal rights resemble assignates . . . placed by the side of guineas. . . . Behold the professors of natural law . . . the legislating Grotii: . . . that which the Alexanders and the Tamerlanes endeavoured to accomplish by traversing a part of the globe the Grotii and the Puffendorffs would accomplish, each one sitting in his armchair: that which the conqueror would effect with violence by his sword the jurisconsult would effect without effort by his pen. Behold the goddess Nature!—the jurisconsult is her priest; his idlest trash is an oracle and this oracle is a law. . . . The mystic tree of good and evil, already so interesting, is not the only one of its kind: life . . . , the law resemble it and yield fruits equally mixed. Upon the same bough are two sorts of fruits of which the flavour is opposite—the one sweet and the other bitter. The sweet fruits are benefits of all kinds . . . , rights. . . . The bitter and thorny fruits are burthens, . . . obligations, duties. These products, so opposed in their nature, are simultaneous in their production and inseparable in their existence. The law cannot confer the benefit without at the same time imposing a burthen somewhere; it cannot create a right without at the same time creating an obligation. . . . Benefits being in themselves good, the well-instructed legislator (I mean, directed by utility) would create and confer them freely with pleasure. If it depended upon himself, he would produce no other fruits: if he could produce them in infinite quantity—he would accumulate them in the bosom of society; but as the inexorable law of nature is opposed to this

[319] *Ibid.*, vol. III, pp. 218 ff ("Pannomial Fragments," chap. III).

course and he cannot confer benefits without imposing burthens, all that he can do is to take care that the advantage of the benefit exceed the disadvantage of the burthen and that this advantage be as great, . . . the disadvantage as small as possible."[320] "Jurists in general have not known what foundation to give to obligation. If you inquire what is its principle, you will find the clouds thicken around you. They will talk to you of the divine will—of the law of nature, of conscience, of quasi contract. They will talk of everything except service—the only clear, the only reasonable notion . . . which can serve as a limit and a guide in the establishment of obligations."[321] Good, useful services are the only proper basis for the creation of obligations; and it is the principle of utility alone which can show how "the evil of the obligation should be compensated by the good of the service."[322]

Finally, as we could expect from the analyses of the *Comment on the Commentaries*, the superiority of utilitarian ethics over the common law is, in the later writings, no less emphasized than the superiority over the law of nature. As does the natural law, the common law suffers first from the indeterminateness of its prescripts. "Singularly unfortunate, if not unskilfull must that judge be who out of" the "rich granary . . . of . . . the . . . common, . . . unwritten law fails on any occasion to find that which is most agreeable to his wishes, whatsoever they may happen to be—to his wishes guided, as they cannot but be, by what at the moment he looks upon as being his interest."[323] "Do you know" how the judges make the common law? "Just as a man makes laws for his dog. When your dog does anything you want to break him of, you wait till he does it and then beat him for it."[324] The common law by its very nature "can never . . . be either known or settled."[325] It is entirely "an ex post facto law."[326] "It carries in its hand a rule of wax."[325] It is a most cruel tyrant who punishes "men for disobedience to laws . . . which he had kept them from the knowledge of."[327] So the common law is

---

[320] *Ibid.*, vol. III, p. 221b, 220a ff ("Pannomial Fragments," chap. III).

[321] *Ibid.*, part v, p. 180b ("A general View of a Complete Code of Laws," chap. XIII).

[322] *Ibid.*, part v, p. 181a ("A general View of a Complete Code of Laws," chap. XIII and compare *ibid.*, part v, p. 180a, chap. XII, No. v).

[323] *Ibid.*, part XVI, p. 573b ("Securities against Misrule adapted to a Mahommedan State and prepared with particular reference to Tripoli in Barbary," written between 1822 and 1823, chap. III, sect. II).

[324] *Ibid.*, vol. v, p. 235b ("Truth versus Ashurst or Law as it is contrasted with what it is said to be," written in 1792, but first published in 1823).

[325] *Ibid.*, vol. v, p. 236a.

[326] *Ibid.*, vol. v, p. 546b ("Justice and Codification Petitions being forms proposed for signature by all persons whose desire is to see justice no longer sold, delayed or denied and to obtain a possibility of that knowledge of the law in proportion to the want of which they are subjected to unjust punishments and deprived of the benefit of their rights, Petition for codification").

[327] *Ibid.*, vol. v, p. 547a.

said to be full of ambiguities, not by chance, but intentionally, because it is meant to be a flexible ex post facto law.

Combined with these attacks against the pliable character of common law we find in the later writings an equally stringent criticism of the veneration for its antiquity and a definite disparagement of ancient ethical wisdom in general. The reference to "the wisdom of our ancestors" is mocked at as "Chinese argument," as a "fallacy of authority"[328] incapable of forming any basis for scientific ethics. For, the wisdom of old times is not the wisdom of experienced men, "of gray hairs";[329] it is the wisdom of generations which are in truth youthful in comparison with those of our times. It is "the wisdom of the cradle the maxim of which is: 'not experience, but inexperience . . . is . . . the true mother of wisdom'."[330] The acceptance of such a maxim is to be compared with the official homage done in "Tibet . . . to . . . an infant lying and squalling in his cradle."[331] To the best of my knowledge, such arguments demonstrating the youthfulness of ancient times are first used in the late Renaissance, for instance, in Giordano Bruno's *La Cena de le Ceneri*;[332] but Bentham could scarcely have been acquainted with this literature.

Full of faith in progress, he paints an extremely dark picture of the moral and intellectual level of older times. "It is from the folly, not from the wisdom of our ancestors that we have so much to learn."[333] Bentham even believes "that in comparison of the lowest class of the people in modern times (always supposing them proficients in the art of reading and their proficiency employed in the reading of newspapers) the very highest and best informed class of . . . our . . . wise ancestors will turn out to be grossly ignorant."[334] This is certainly a striking example of the faith of modern enlightenment in its superiority over the dark ages. As Bentham frequently repeats, "few of . . . our ancestors . . . could so much as read and those few had nothing before them that was worth the reading."[335] "Not only devils but ghosts, vampires, witches and all their kindred tribes" have been driven out of modern states "by so cheap an instrument as a common newspaper. . . . The bare smell of printers' ink" was more intolerable to them than "the touch of holy water."[336] "The great utility of a code of laws is to cause both the

[328] *The Book of Fallacies*, 1824, p. 69, part I, chap. II, sect. I.
[329] *Ibid.*, p. 71 (sect. 2).　　　　[330] *Ibid.*, pp. 71, 70.
[331] *Ibid.*, p. 72. In his *Reliable Knowledge*, 1945, p. 558, Professor Harold Atkins Larrabee rightly shares Bentham's rejection of the "Chinese argument."
[332] See Giordano Bruno, *Opera Italiana*, ed. by Giovanni Gentile, Bari, 1925, vol. I, p. 31 (Dialogo primo, Teofilo answering Prudenzio pedante who refers to Job XII, 12) Teo: E soggionge: in molti anni la prudenza . . . voglio dire, che noi siamo piú vecchi che i nostri predecessori."
[333] Bentham, *The Book of Fallacies*, 1824, p. 79 (part I, chap. II, sect. 2).
[334] *Ibid.*, p. 75.
[335] *Ibid.*, p. 237 (part IV, chap. III, sect. 3).
[336] *Ibid.*, p. 77 (part I, chap. II, sect. 2).

debates of lawyers and the bad laws of former times to be forgotten."[337] Even the moral standard of our "barbarian ancestors" was, in the eyes of Bentham, not higher than their intellectual one. "When from their ordinary occupation, their order of the day, the cutting of one another's throats or those of Welchmen, Scotchmen or Irishmen they could steal now and then a holiday, how did they employ it? In cutting Frenchmen's throats in order to get their money; this was active virtue: leaving Frenchmen's throats uncut was indolence, slumber, inglorious ease."[338] But not only earlier epochs of English history are seen by Bentham in this unfavorable light; he thinks no more highly of the flowering of classic Greek enlightenment. He admits once that Aristotle's system of logic is a "monument of human industry and genius . . . , considering its date, justly admired and venerated"; but he, nevertheless, thinks that "Plato . . . this spoilt child of Socrates . . . and Aristotle . . . , notwithstanding all their rivalry . . . concurred in wrapping up the whole field of pneumatology . . . in . . . clouds."[339] On account of their "eloquence" he thinks even less of Plato and Cicero than of Aristotle. To all this impatient and short-sighted account of "ancient wisdom" only one finer observation is added. As Bentham grants, "undoubtedly the history of past ages is not wanting in some splendid instances of probity and self-devotion; but in the admiration which these excite we commonly overrate their amount and become the dupes of an illusion occasioned by the very nature of an extensive retrospect. Such a retrospect is often made by a single glance of the mind; in this glance the splendid actions of several ages (as if for the very purpose of conveying a false estimate of their number and contiguity) present themselves, as it were, in a lump leaving the intervals between them altogether unnoticed."[340] Such illusions, caused by neglect of the laws of intellectual perspective, are indeed very common among historians. But, upon the whole, Bentham is certainly less fair as a critic of past ages than those historians who wrongly idealize the past. He was in no way a historian,[341] and did not wish to be one. He was a moral philosopher and a great reformer.

[337] *Ibid.*, vol. III, p. 207a (A general view of a complete code of laws, chap. XXXII).

[338] Bentham, *The Book of Fallacies*, 1824, p. 238 (part IV, chap. III, sect. III).

[339] Bentham, *Works*, 1843, part xv, p. 120b, p. 120a ("Chrestomathia being a Collection of Papers explanatory of the Design of an Institution proposed to be set on foot under the Name of the Chrestomathic Day-School . . . for the Extension of the New system of Instruction to the higher Branches of Learning for the Use of the Middling and higher Ranks in Life, Appendix No. IV, sect. XVIII).

[340] Bentham, *The Book of Fallacies*, 1824, part I, chap. II, sect. II, p. 78.

[341] See e.g. *Works*, 1843, part v, p. 207a (View of a complete Code of Laws, chap. XXXII): "Historical disquisitions ought not to have place in the general collection of the laws. It is not necessary to cite what the Romans did. If what they did was good, do like them, but do not talk of them."

Emancipation of Women

In accordance with his general reformatory efforts, Bentham is to a large extent a defender of women's rights. In his *Treatise on Judicial Evidence* in 1825 he speaks with indignation of the statute book of the Pays de Vaud, because it says that "the testimony of two women or girls shall be equal and neither more nor less than equal to that of a man"—an enactment which is, according to him, "more humiliating for the legislator than for the sex which was the object of it."[342] "On the ground of the greatest happiness principle . . . the interest of a person of the female sex constitutes as large a portion of the universal happiness and interest as does that of a person of the male sex. No reason can be assigned why a person of the one sex should as such have less happiness than a person of the other sex. Nor, therefore, whatsoever be the external means of happiness, why a female should have a less portion of those same means. If in this respect there were a difference, the principle of equality would require that it should be rather in favour of the female than of the male sex: inasmuch as there are so many causes of suffering which do not attach upon the male and do attach upon the female sex: such as pains of gestation, of parturition, labor of nurturition, periodical and casual weaknesses, inferiority in all physical contests with the male sex and loss of reputation in cases where no such loss attaches upon the male."[343] Bentham further reminds his compatriots of the fact that "in no two male reigns was England as prosperous as in the two female reigns of Elizabeth and Anne."[344] To a considerable extent he defends Queen Mary, and refers to "the choice of a sub-legislature in the Directory of the East India Company" where "females have an equal share with males"—a sub-legislature "governing with absolute sway in subordination to the supreme legislator sixty millions of subjects in British India."[345] All this shows that as to "appropriate probity and appropriate intellectual aptitude . . . if they apply not with propriety to both sexes, it seems not easy to say with what propriety they can be applicable to

[342] Bentham, "A Treatise on Judicial Evidence," 1825, p. 210 note.

[343] Bentham, *Works*, 1843, part xvii, p. 108a ("Constitutional Code," book i, chap. xv, sect. vii).

[344] *Ibid.*, part xvii, p. 108b.

[345] *Ibid.*, part xvii, p. 109a. Compare *ibid.*, iii, 541a ("Catechism of Parliamentary Reform or Outline of a Plan of Parliamentary Reform in the Form of Question and Answer with Reasons to each Article," sect. ii, no. 14). Compare *ibid.*, iii, 567a, note ("Radical Reform Bill with Extracts from the Reasons, Bill intituled Parliamentary Reform Act being an Act for the more adequate Representation of the People in the Commons House of Parliament," sect. iii, art. iv, note).

either."[346] Accordingly, Bentham sees no theoretical reason whatsoever for excluding women from participation in the constitutive or even the legislative and executive power of the state.

Moreover, he goes further, and tries to analyze the psychological background of male prejudice toward women; he dismisses with disgust the "common-place witticism" which statesmen of his time used to show in their dealings with the emancipation of women; and in the common attitude of amusement at the rights of women he sees mainly a tyrannical blindness, and the same dishonest reference to the "non-entity"[347] of the so-called law of nature which he had already branded in relation to other matters.

As regards the rights of women, he even rejects the authority of the much admired Helvétius: "Among certain barbarous or half-civilized nations the services of their warriors have been rewarded by the favors of women. Helvetius appears to smile with approbation at this mode of exciting bravery. It was perhaps Montesquieu that led him into this error. In speaking of the Samnites among whom the young man declared the most worthy selected whomsoever he pleased for his wife, he adds that this custom was calculated to produce most beneficial effects. Philosophers distinguished for their humanity . . . , both of them eloquent against slavery, how could they speak in praise of a law which supposes the slavery of the best half of the human species? How could they have forgotten that favours not preceded by an uncontrolled choice and which the heart perhaps repelled with disgust afforded the spectacle rather of the degradation of women than the rewarding a hero? . . . And if . . . the warrior . . . disdained this barbarous right, was not his generosity a satire on the law?"[348] Such remarks certainly do honor to

---

[346] *Ibid.*, III, 463a ("Plan of Parliamentary Reform," 1817. Sect. VII, §2).

[347] Bentham, *Plan of Parliamentary Reform* (1817), introduction, sect. VII, §2 (*Works*, III, 463b, 464a, note 1-4); see *ibid.* the reference to Charles Fox's speech in 1797 containing the following remark: "I hope, gentlemen will not smile if I endeavour to illustrate my position by referring to the example of the other sex. In all the theories and projects of the most absurd speculation it has never been suggested that it would be advisable to extend the elective suffrage to the female sex. . . . Why but because by the law of nations and perhaps also by the law of nature that sex is dependent on ours."

[348] Bentham, *Works*, 1843, part III, p. 197a (*The Rationale of Reward*, originally printed in 1825, book I, chap. II). Compare with this criticism of Helvétius and Montesquieu Bentham's approval of the following story told by Voltaire: "At the first representation of his tragedies the audience who saw the author in a box with an extremely beautiful young duchess required that she should give him a kiss by way of acknowledging the public gratitude. The victim, a partaker in the general enthusiasm, felt apparently no repugnance to make the sacrifice: and,

Bentham the psychologist as much as they reveal the theoretical consistency of his plans for reform.

Nevertheless, as in the case of radical socialism and the complete abolition of slavery, Bentham hesitated to make concrete radical suggestions, so far as immediate practical reform is concerned. He is afraid that a general "mixture of sexes in the composition of a legislative or executive body" would, in his lifetime, lead "to nothing but confusion and ridicule."[349] As to the introduction of female suffrage, he thinks that "there might be" also "inconvenience upon the whole"; but he seems to grant that on this point the practical difficulties are far fewer than in the case of general admission of women to the legislative and executive power.[350] However, he obviously held even this inauguration of equality of constitutive rights to be "at present" not advisable.

Though he expected that much practical good would arise from the admission of women to political activities, he nevertheless points out that "there is no political state that I know of in which on the occasion of any new constitution being framed I should think it at present expedient to propose a set of legislative arrangements directed to this end. Before the state of the legal system had been made, on almost all other points contributory in the highest degree to the greatest happiness of the greatest number scarcely could any prospect be afforded of its being rendered so as to this. The contest and confusion produced by the proposal of this improvement would entirely engross the public mind and throw improvement in all other shapes to a distance."[351] Thus, though a radical reformer in theory, Bentham hesitated on this point to put his theories immediately into practice. He was, in general, no friend of far-reaching sudden revolutions, which might produce as much or even more confusion than real progress.

Communism

Far more conservative than in the matter of the emancipation of women is Bentham's attitude towards communism. Evidently the problem concerning the relation of the greatest-happiness principle to "equal-

---

without the intervention of the magistrate, we may trust to the enthusiasm of the sex and their passion for distinction, for preferences that may animate courage and genius in their career" (*ibid.*, pp. 197a, 197b).

[349] *Ibid.*, part XVII, p. 108a ("The Constitutional Code," book I, chap. xv, sect. VII).

[350] *Ibid.*, part VI, p. 567a note ("Radical Reform Bill," sect. III, art. IV).

[351] *Ibid.*, part XVII, p. 109a ("Constitutional Code," book I, chap. xv, sect. VII, §1).

ity . . . of wealth" frequently occupied his mind. We have already seen, in the *Traités*, that to him a diminution of economic inequality was the proper ideal of society, but he by no means believed in a revolutionary establishment of the community of goods. Of the four "proper ends of the distributive branch of law," viz. security, subsistence, abundance and equality, it was security and subsistence which he ranked highest; and even abundance—providing reserves for times of need— he thought to be of greater social importance than the "utopian" equality of possessions.

The same teaching, enriched by some instructive supplementary ideas, is met with in the later writings. "In a word it is not equality itself, but only a tendency toward equality, after all the others are provided for, that on the part of the ruling and other members of the community is the proper object of endeavour."[352] "The utmost conceivable equality has place . . . in physics; it applies . . . to weight, measure, time and thence to motion"; but as absolute economic equality is not "an immediate instrument of felicity," only "practicable equality . . . admitting of degrees" ought to be aspired to.[353] Bentham does not omit to mention the old observation that "number for number the certain probative symptoms or circumstantial evidences of infelicity as exhibited on the countenance are at least as frequent in the case of the monarch as in the case of the labourer."[354] Security, which is, in Bentham's view, the most fundamental condition of felicity, ought to be absolutely equal to all. "Where is the man to whom . . . greater or better security ought to be afforded than to any other?"[355] But the same does not apply to equality of property, as in this case even a small increase of happiness of one person can be brought about only by "defalcation made from that of another"; and there is a general "antagony"[356] between equality and the three other ideals of community life, namely, security, subsistence and abundance.

In his *Pannomial Fragments*, Bentham admits that if this were not the case, if only its "effects of the first order" had to be taken into account, then communism ought to be introduced in every country governed by the greatest-happiness principle. "If the effects of the first order were alone taken into account, the consequence would be that on the supposition of a new constitution coming to be established with

[352] *Ibid.*, vol. III, p. 294a, cf. p. 293b ("Logical Arrangements," sect. XI).
[353] *Ibid.*, part XVII, p. 14b ("The Constitutional Code," book I, chap. III, sect. v).
[354] *Ibid.*, p. 15a.   [355] *Ibid.*, p. 15b.
[356] See *ibid.*, p. 16a and *ibid.*, vol. III, p. 293 f.

the greatest happiness of the greatest number for its end in view, sufficient reason would have place for taking the matter of wealth from the richest and transferring it to the less rich, till the fortunes of all were reduced to an equality or a system of inequality so little different from perfect equality that the difference would not be worth calculating."[357] But in reality, according to Bentham the evils of the second and third order caused by communism undermine the security and even the subsistence of a community to such an extent that those evils would completely outweigh the advantage of economic equality. "Evil of the second order—annihilation in the first place of happiness by the universality of the alarm and the swelling of danger into certainty: Evil of the third order—annihilation of existence by the certainty of the non-enjoyment of the fruit of labour, and thence the extinction of all inducement to labour."[357] Of course, all these are familiar arguments. Of interest, however, is the way they are put in systematic order and fitted into the method of Bentham's ethical reasoning.

In his *Constitutional Code*, Bentham enumerates as many as five different degrees of evil consequences necessarily connected with any introduction of equality of possessions: (1) a diminution of pleasure without pain in the case of a very wealthy person deprived of an unknown but small part of his fortune, (2) a pain of privation, if this defalcation made from the mass of property is considerable, (3) a pain of apprehension of ulterior loss, (4) general pain from repression of industry, (5) general pain of insecurity by contagion.[358] All these evil consequences are, for Bentham's utilitarianism, sufficient reasons to justify the statement that "absolute equality in relation to property . . . is not desirable. . . . It is not desirable, because never having had existence in any country at any time it could not have place in any country in future without having been endeavoured to be established in that same country: in which case not only the endeavour, but the very design alone, accompanied with any assurance of its being about to be followed by the correspondent endeavour perseveringly exercised, would suffice to destroy the whole of the value and the greatest part of the substance of the matter thus undertaken to be divided."[359] Apart from that, as he pointed out in the *Traités*, the maintenance of radical communism is also "impossible." "It is not possible, because, supposing it to have place at the commencement of any one day, the operations of that one day

---

[357] *Ibid.*, vol. III, p. 230a ("Pannomial Fragments," chap. IV, §5, 4).
[358] *Ibid.*, part XVII, p. 16a.
[359] *Ibid.*, part XVII, p. 18b.

will have sufficed to have destroyed it before the commencement of the next."[359] Again, these are quite common anti-communistic arguments.

Nevertheless Karl Marx and Friedrich Engels certainly missed the mark in characterizing Bentham as the typical ideologist of anti-socialistic capitalism.[360] As Marx and Engels once admitted, Bentham's "System des wohlverstandenen Interesses" led to the "englischen Kommunismus" of Robert Owen;[361] and certainly, in his later writings, Bentham did not remain a champion of radical, capitalistic free competition, of the laissez faire economy of the eighteenth century. He "gently favoured . . . equality of wealth. . . . The most powerful means of augmenting national wealth are those which maintain the security of properties and which gently favour their equalization."[362] For the sake of "the greatest happiness of the greatest number interested" he again, as he had done in the *Traités*, suggests as the mildest economic reform certain regulations in the executions of wills.[363] He grants that modern hereditary arrangements had been "produced by a state of society such as has no longer any place anywhere," by the feudal system or by even more ancient institutions; and these hereditary arrangements are now "as adverse as possible to equality of distribution," though they were "not wholly destitute of reason" in a primitive state of society, when the necessity of military self-defense even of small groups or families required such hereditary exigencies.[364] Further, in contrast to economic reaction, he pleads for maximizing of wages and for a conditioned minimizing of "the profits of stock."[365] "Equality requires that, though it be at the expense of all the other members of the community, the income of those whose income is composed of the wages of labour be maximized. Reason: of these are composed the vast majority of the

[360] See e.g. Karl Marx, Friedrich Engels: *Historisch kritische Gesamtausgabe*, Erste Abteilung, Band v, 1932, S. 391 f, S. 387; "Das Kapital," 1872, S. 162 (3. Kapitel, 2. Abschnitt, 3).—Oscar Jászi, in an introduction to one of the chapters of Géza Engelmann's *Political Philosophy from Plato to Bentham*, 1927, p. 337, goes so far as to say that "not even Karl Marx unveiled and persecuted in such a conscious and passionate way the abuses of class rule and political exploitations as Bentham did."

[361] Karl Marx, Friedrich Engels: *Historisch kritische Gesamtausgabe*, Erste Abteilung, Band iii, 1932, S. 308 (*Die heilige Familie oder Kritik der kritischen Kritik*, 1845).

[362] Bentham, *Works*, 1843, vol. iii, p. 203b ("View of a complete Code of Laws," chap. xxviii).

[363] *Ibid.*, part xvii, pp. 17a, 17b ("The constitutional Code," book i, chap. iii, sect. 5).

[364] *Ibid.*, part xvii, pp. 17b, 18a.

[365] *Ibid.*, vol. iii, p. 230b ("Pannomial Fragments," chap. iv, §5).

whole number of the members of the community. Exceptions excepted, equality requires that the profits of stock be minimized. Reason: because the net profit of stock is composed of the mass or say portion remaining to the employer of the stock after deduction made of the wages of the labour applied to it. Exception will be—if this supposed case be really exemplified—where the possessors of the wages of labour are so many and the possessors of the profits of stock so few that by a small addition to the one no sensible defalcation will be made from the other."[365] Though this is definite anti-communism, it is, seen from the point of view of the early nineteenth century, at least a vague and abstract program of socialistic reform.

In their polemical treatise against "Bruno Bauer und Consorten," Marx and Engels praised Bentham-Dumont's "Théorie des peines et récompenses."[366] In their "Die deutsche Ideologie" in 1845-46, they acknowledged that Bentham, as well as Helvétius, demonstrated to the "bourgeoisie" that they damage themselves by their "Borniertheit."[367] At the same time, however, Marx and Engels frequently ridicule Bentham.[368] In one of his letters, Engels characterizes "den Kerl" Bentham as "arg langweilig und theoretisch";[369] and Marx went so far as to say that Bentham was nothing but a "genius in the way of bourgeois stupidity."[370] Does the ethical genius of Bentham deserve this judgment from

[366] Karl Marx, Friedrich Engels, *Historisch kritische Gesamtausgabe*, Erste Abteilung, Bd. III, 1932, S. 355 f (*Die heilige Familie*, 1845).

[367] *Ibid.*, I. Abteilung, Band v, 1932, S. 224 (*Die deutsche Ideologie* 1845-46, Das Leipziger Konzil III Sankt Max).

[368] See e.g. *ibid.*, S. 192: "Bentham's Nase . . . muss erst ein Interesse haben . . . ehe sie sich zum Riechen entschliesst."

[369] *Ibid.*, Abt. III, vol. I, p. 18 (Engels an Marx in Brüssel, März 17, 1845).

[370] Karl Marx, *Das Kapital*, 1872, Bd. I, S. 634: Der "Urphilister Jeremias Bentham, dies nüchtern pedantische, schwatzlederne Orakel des gemeinen Bürgerverstandes des 19. Jahrhunderts . . . ist unter den Philosophen, was Martin Tupper unter den Dichtern, Beide waren nur in England fabricirbar. . . . Selbst unsern Philosophen Christian Wolf nicht ausgenommen, hat zu keiner Zeit und in keinem Land der hausbackenste Gemeinplatz sich jemals so selbstgefällig breit gemacht. Das Nützlichkeitsprinzip war keine Erfindung Bentham's. Er reproducirte nur geistlos, was Helvetius und andere Franzosen des 18. Jahrhunderts geistreich gesagt hatten. Wenn man z.B. wissen will, was ist einem Hunde nützlich?, so muss man die Hundenatur ergründen. Diese Natur selbst ist nicht aus dem 'Nützlichkeitsprinzip' zu konstruiren. Auf den Menschen angewandt, wenn man alle menschliche That, Bewegung, Verhältnisse u.s.w. nach dem Nützlichkeitsprinzip beurteilen will, handelt es sich erst um die menschliche Natur im Allgemeinen und dann um die in jeder Epoche historisch modificirte Menschennatur. Bentham macht kein Federlesens. Mit der naivsten Trockenheit unterstellt er den modernen Spiessbürger, speziell den englischen Spiessbürger als den Normalmenschen. Was

another genius who, let us remember, was himself not absolutely free from delusions?

It is true that Bentham was never fully aware of a class struggle, of the economic conflicts between bourgeois and worker, which rapidly developed in his later lifetime. He remained a bourgeois theoretician who had grown up during the years preceding the French Revolution, and had witnessed the passing of feudalism, the passing of the economic conflicts between nobility and the *tiers état*. He, then, saw before his eyes a rather stable economic world, the stability of which he wanted to preserve for the sake of general security. Therefore, if Bentham is viewed historically, it seems to me hardly justifiable to measure the aged friend of Robert Owen, the contemporary of Goethe and Louis XVI, by standards taken from economic observations of the middle of the nineteenth century.

Pacifism

In his pacifism Bentham was during his later years more radical than in his ideas on slavery, emancipation of women and socialism, although his words may often not seem to bear out this statement. The utility principle itself he once characterized as "a declaration of peace and good-will to all men," while "on the other hand, were I to say the proper end of government is the greatest happiness of someone . . . or

---

diesem Kauz von Normalmensch und seiner Welt nützlich, ist an und für sich nützlich. An diesem Masstab beurteilt er dann Vergangenheit, Gegenwart und Zukunft. Z.B. die christliche Religion ist 'nützlich,' weil sie dieselben Missethaten religiös verpönt, die der Strafcodex juristisch verdammt. Kunstkritik ist 'schädlich,' weil sie ehrbare Leute in ihrem Genuss an Martin Tupper stört u.s.w. Mit solchem Schund hat der brave Mann dessen Devise 'nulla dies sine linea' Berge von Büchern gefüllt. Wenn ich die Courage meines Freundes H. Heine hätte, würde ich Herrn Jeremias ein Genie in der bürgerlichen Dummheit nennen" (Kap. 22, 5: Der sogenannte Arbeitsfonds). Apart from Marx's unhistorical depreciation of Christian Wolff, this characterization of Bentham seems to me a classical misjudgment of genius. That what is deemed useful by men, differs in different points of time and of space Bentham grants no less than Marx. In fact he emphasized this at great length in his essay "De l'influence des tems et des lieux en matière de législation." It is certain that in the field of economics Marx infinitely enlarged the insight into these changes of human interests. But Marx neglected quite uncritically a completely different problem, viz: whether the changing interests of man form nevertheless a legitimate basis for moral judgments. On this point far more dogmatic and "unscientific" than Bentham, Marx simply presupposed that the economic happiness of the greatest number is the only legitimate criterion of morality. On this point far more critical than Marx, the seemingly "leather-tongued" B. did, I think, a splendid job in his mountains of piles of "rubbish," "Schundschriften," as I try to show in the present book.

473

of some few . . . it seems to me that I should be making a declaration of war against all men with the exception of that one or those few."[371] At least he constantly demands the immediate abolition of aggressive wars in his later writings.

In the beginning of the chapter on the Defensive Force in his *Constitutional Code*, he emphasizes that the sole object of an army ought to remain defense; "offence and aggression as towards other nations, much more conquest, are repugnant to the essential and leading principles of the constitution delineated by the present Code."[372] The moral right to wage a defensive war, however, is so strictly limited that it almost ceases to exist. For Bentham realizes that a pretense for a war of defense is almost never wanting, no matter whether the enemy is "formidably strong or providentially weak: if formidably strong, too long have we delayed the necessary task of obtaining . . . indemnity for the past and security for the future: if providentially weak, now is the favourable time for taking advantage of his weakness and preventing him from becoming formidable: now has the Lord of Hosts—as the archbishop's prayer will not fail to inform us—delivered the enemy into our hands! Thus, if there be nothing past for which to obtain indemnity, security for the future will, at any rate, be an easy purchase."[373] Instead of wars, Bentham recommends "calling in commissaries" from other nations[374]—a measure which did indeed lead to good results in some recent pre-war experiences.

In this connection, Bentham strongly defends "the unopulent many . . , in a word . . . the class of radicalists" as less aggressive in the case of war "than any that stand above them in the scale of opulence"; for the many "will be greater sufferers"; and this difference existing between different classes of the population, particularly in wartime, is more and more stressed by Bentham in his later years. In his *Observations on the Restrictive and Prohibitory Commercial System*, he mentions the damage done to the many, the have-nots, by the issue of war-

[371] Bentham, *Works*, 1843, part XVIII, p. 5a ("The Constitutional Code," introduction, sect. 1).

[372] *Ibid.*, vol. IX, p. 333b ("The Constitutional Code," book II, chap. X, sect. 1, article 4). Compare *ibid.*, vol. III, p. 611a the distinction made between necessary and defensive war and unnecessary, offensive war for conquest. ("Radicalism not Dangerous," written between 1819 and 1820, part II, sect. 10).

[373] *Ibid.*, vol. III, pp. 439a, b (*Plan of Parliamentary Reform*, 1817, sect. III).

[374] *Ibid.*, part VIII, p. 410a (*Emancipate Your Colonies!* first published for sale in 1830).

money and inflation;[375] and that apart from this point, the necessity of "standing armies" in the European states has always prevented morally needed improvements in the domestic sphere of these nations and has, therefore, primarily hurt the interests of the underprivileged classes.[376] Finally, the predominance of class-interests over actual national interests, marked even in wartime, is pungently illustrated by the following remarks: "By one another monarchs are styled brothers, and on that one occasion they are sincere; for they have a common interest, and that interest is paramount to every other interest. Many a monarch has given up to a brother monarch, and freely too, dominions which he might have kept, if he had pleased. No monarch ever gave up freely to his own subjects an atom of power which in his eyes could be retained with safety. War is a game—a game of backgammon. Between two players at the game of war there is no more enmity than between two players at backgammon. In the breasts of the players at war there is no more feeling for the men of flesh and bone than during the game at backgammon there is on the part of the men of wood for one another or themselves. While to one another all monarchs are objects of sympathy, to all monarchs all subjects are objects of antipathy; of a sort of compound sentiment, made up of fear, hatred and contempt; something like that which women and children are apt to feel for a toad."[377] It is by no means contemptible aid which can, according to Bentham, be given to pacifism by an improvement of moral and political *theories*, particularly by avoiding ambiguous or confused ethical teaching. If "the import of all words, especially of all words belonging to the field of Ethics, including the field of politics, . . . should one day become fixed . . . what a source of perplexity, of error, of discord and even of bloodshed would be dried up!"[378] In this way Bentham's pacifism is closely connected with the whole of his ethical teaching.

Judge and Co. The Church

Finally, a good many of these reflections are accompanied by Bentham's often somewhat monotonous invectives against lawyers, poets

[375] *Ibid.*, part v, p. 100a (*Observations on the Restricted and Prohibitory Commercial System, especially with a reference to the decree of the Spanish Cortes of July 1820*, originally printed in 1821, sect. III).
[376] *Ibid.*, part XVII, p. 58b ("The Constitutional Code," book I, chap. IX).
[377] *Ibid.*, part XVII, pp. 129b, 130a ("The Constitutional Code," book I, chap. XVII, sect. II).
[378] *Ibid.*, part XV, p. 106b ("Chrestomathia," appendix, sect. 12).

and churchmen. Bentham was obviously aware of this monotony: he grants that his polemic against "the fee-fed judge," against "the firm . . . Judge and Co."[379] "it will be said, is merely the ordinary theme of declamation. So it is; but," as he adds, "the declamation is founded on facts."[380] Because of that he fills his writings with accusations of the "private and sinister interest"[381] of jurists. The "lawyer tribe" has no more interest in reform of the law than "highway robbers . . . in a high-way-robbery-preventive code," than "ladies-procuresses . . . in a female-chastity-securing code."[382] As in every science, so in jurisprudence the reformer "becomes the object of a mixture of contempt . . . , jealousy and envy: of contempt insofar as this practice of his is regarded as in-dicative of folly—of jealousy, insofar as his success and thereby his chance of superiority with reference to the persons thus occupied in making observation of him is an object of apprehension—of envy, in-sofar as it is a subject matter of conviction and belief."[383] The "ends of judicature under the fee-gathering system . . . are . . . opposite to the ends of justice."[384] "So far as money is concerned, virtue according to what we have been used . . . to hear and read of at school and at col-lege . . . consists, though not perhaps in doing all together without money, at any rate in taking care not to set too high a value on it. But with all its virtue, or rather in virtue of its very virtue, the aristocracy" and particularly the jurists "will not . . . do a stitch without money. . . . Why? Because in their eyes . . . nothing whatever but money is of any value."[385] "Insofar as concerns justice and veracity, there are two codes

[379] *Ibid.*, vol. vi, p. 267a, vol. v, p. 369a (*Official Aptitude Maximized, Expenses Minimized as shown in the several papers comprised in this volume,* 1830, paper viii: *Indications respecting Lord Eldon including history of the pending judges' salary-raising measure,* originally published in 1825, sect. xvii). Cf. *ibid.*, vol. vii, p. 232b, vol. v, p. 514a (*Justice and Codification Petitions,* 1829, Abridged Peti-tion for Justice, §58).

[380] Bentham, *A Treatise on Judicial Evidence,* 1825, p. 37.

[381] Bentham, *Works,* 1843, vol. vi, p. 42b ("View of the Rationale of Evidence," chap. xi, §6).

[382] *Ibid.*, vol. ii, p. 13 (*Principles of Judicial Procedure,* 1837, chap. ii).

[383] *Ibid.*, vol. viii, p. 242a ("Essay on Logic," written between 1811 and 1831, chap. vi, sect. 4).

[384] *Ibid.*, part xiii, p. 199a ("Rationale of Judicial Evidence," book viii, chap. iii).

[385] *Ibid.*, vol. v, p. 316a (*Official Aptitude Maximized, Expense Minimized,* pa-per vi: *Defence of Economy against the Right Honourable George Rose,* first pub-lished in 1817, sect. viii). As to Bentham's lifelong pride in financial and social independence see, for instance, the story of his relation to Lord Shelburne which he recorded with special relish almost half a century after the event in the preface to the second edition of his *A Fragment on Government* in 1828, *Works,* 1843, vol. i, p. 248b, 249a: when Bentham was a guest of the Earl of Shelburne at

of morality that in this country have currency and influence; viz. that of the public at large and that of Westminster Hall."[386] "The manufacturers of . . . judge-made law,"[387] "law jargon . . . prevent information from being conveyed . . . , secure habitual ignorance or produce misconception."[388] "The knowledge of this jargon has become a cabalistic sign by which the initiated recognise each other; and the obscurities of the language have enabled financiers to deceive the simple up to a certain point with regard to transactions which would otherwise have been at once recognised as nefarious."[389] "It is a rule with all learned English judges to receive evidence in any shape except the only proper one; they leave that to the tallow-chandlers."[390] "The God of Moses was the God of Justice; the God of Judge and Co. the Demon of Chicane."[391] "The savage is mild and placable, compared with the English lawyer. The savage minces or broils his enemy and is satisfied: the lawyer, at a whisper from above, gluts on the child unborn his unprovoked and mercenary cruelty. . . . They have acted as a surgeon would do who having a mad dog tied up should secretly cut . . . the knot that the animal on gaining its liberty might send in to its master a supply of patients. . . . It has been already mentioned as among the intermediate ends of lawyer-craft to corrupt the morals of the people; and among the means to that end, the planting and cherishing in the public breast the love of

---

Bowood in 1781, one night soon after his arrival, he "was met by the Master of the House . . . in a room, on a table in which, the guests used to receive or deposit the lights they had need of in passing to and from their several apartments. . . . 'Mr. Bentham' said he, candles in hand . . . 'what is it you can do for me?' My surprise could not but be visible. Candles still in hand—'Nothing at all, my Lord' said I; 'nothing that I know of. . . . I am like the Prophet *Balaam*: the word that God putteth into my mouth—that alone can I ever speak'. . . . He took this for what it was meant for—a declaration of independence."

[386] *Ibid.*, part XIII, p. 188a ("Rationale of Judicial Evidence," 1827, book VII, chap. v). Compare *ibid.*, part XIII, p. 276a, the reference to the cruel "Christianity of Lord Coke" and his double code of morals and law, one for the treatment of gentiles, the other for that of Jews.

[387] *Ibid.*, vol. VI, p. 65b ("An Introductory View of the Rationale of Evidence," chap. XIV, §7).

[388] *Ibid.*, vol. VII, p. 280a ("The Rationale of Judicial Evidence," book VIII, chap. XVII).

[389] Vol. III, p. 204b (A general view of a complete Code of Laws, chap. XXIX). Compare pp. 241a ff ("Nomography," chap. III, §VIII ff, chap. IV ff).

[390] *Ibid.*, part XIV, p. 531a ("The Rationale of Judicial Evidence," book IX, part VI, chap. I).

[391] *Ibid.*, vol. V, p. 544b ("Abridged Petition for Justice, Supplement which may be added or not to any one of the three or any other proposed Petition," sect. II).

lies."[392] With a power of imagination reminding us of his contemporary Goya, he once remarks that "to the youth of both sexes when flocking to a ball-room or a theatre it has never yet been proposed, as a condition precedent to their admission into those seats of social pleasure and innocent delight, that they should each of them before the delivery of the ticket take a roll in the contents of a night-cart, kept in waiting for that purpose. But an initiation of that sort cannot be more repugnant to the ends that attract the children of gaiety to a theatre or a ball-room than the being rolled, as suitors are, through the mire of mendacity is repugnant to the ends in pursuit of which they find themselves under so unhappy a necessity as that of betaking themselves to that seat of affliction called a court of judicature."[393] If there is monoideism in these "declamations," one is at least compensated for this by the colorfulness of their expression.

Clergymen, naturally, receive no better treatment at the hands of Bentham than jurists. "By those whose power . . . religion has been . . . established or continues to be . . . supported a virtual certificate has been given and continues to be given that in their eyes the system . . . supported is false."[394] "To establish religion, is to establish insincerity: to establish insincerity, is to establish that vice by which not only vice in every minor shape is served and promoted, but vice swollen into the shape of criminality,"[395] and consequently, in his *Constitutional Code,* he devotes a special chapter to the subject "Established Religion—None."[396] "If it be so clearly contrary to the greatest happiness of the greatest number, even in the present life, that a system of opinion on the subject of religion, admitting it to be true, be . . . established, as clearly is it true to regard to the religion of Jesus in particular that the affording such establishment to the religion of Jesus is inconsistent with his will, as evidenced by his own declarations as well as by his own practice. Nowhere is he stated to have directed that to the religion delivered by himself any such establishment should be given. Nowhere, either in terms or in substance has he said—give money to those who say they believe in what I have said or give money to those who teach others to

[392] *Ibid.,* part XIV, p. 436b ("The Rationale of Judicial Evidence," book IX, part III, chap. VII).

[393] *Ibid.,* vol. VII, p. 205b ("The Rationale of Judicial Evidence," book VIII, chap. III, §3).

[394] *Ibid.,* part XVII, p. 93b ("The Constitutional Code," book I, chap. XIV).

[395] *Ibid.,* part XVIII, p. 453b ("The Constitutional Code," book II, chap. XI, note).

[396] *Ibid.,* part XVII, pp. 92 ff.

believe what I have said."[397] Churchmen as well as lawyers live, in Bentham's view, too often on "pious and useful falsehood."[398] If their falsehoods are not conscious, then they are in any event caused by their disinclination toward clear thinking, their love of obscurity or rhetoric.

"Nothing is more troublesome to a man than to be obliged to know what he means: no error so pernicious that he would not rather adopt and give currency to, than load himself with so much trouble. To explain or to inquire what it is a man means, is metaphysics: light is an object of hatred to all owls and to all thieves; definitions under the name of metaphysics to all rhetoricians."[399] Another source of the ready acceptance of falsehoods in law and religion, according to Bentham, is the psychological fact that "downright nonsense" can "become the subject-matter of a severe and inshakeable belief," more severe than even the belief in "improbable matters of facts."[400] "There is no proposition so absurd, no proposition so palpably false in which . . . belief" may not be "declared."[401] "In the field of theology (all history joins in proving it) the attachment manifested by men to an opinion, and in particular by men in power, is strenuous and inflexible in the direct proportion of its absurdity. The effect is the result of the conjoint influence of a variety of causes. . . . With the zealous and sincere: the more palpably and flagrantly absurd the proposition . . . , the greater is the difficulty and thence the apparent merit of the sacrifice . . . of . . . the mind," a sacrifice welcome to "a malevolent and jealous deity. . . . Sincere or insincere: the more palpable the absurdity, the greater is the triumph . . . obtained over those minds from whom an assent, real or apparent, can be produced for it . . . the more gross the nonsense, the more prostrate is the obedience on one part, the more absolute the power on the other."[402] "Unhappily, the power of the will over opinion . . . is but too

[397] *Ibid.*, part XVII, p. 94b.

[398] *Ibid.*, part XIV, p. 572b, note ("The Rationale of Judicial Evidence," book x, chap. II).

[399] *Ibid.*, vol. VII, p. 115b ("The Rationale of Judicial Evidence," book v, chap. XVII); Bentham adds to this remark this: "I hate metaphysics, exclaims Edmund Burke somewhere: it was not without cause." But on many occasions he directs similar aggression not only against statesmen and lawyers, but also against clergymen.

[400] *Ibid.*, vol. VII, p. 111a ("The Rationale of Judicial Evidence," book v, chap. XVI, §10).

[401] *Ibid.*, part XII, p. 557a f ("The Rationale of Judicial Evidence," book IV, chap. VII, §3).

[402] *Ibid.*, part XIII, p. 109, note ("The Rationale of Judicial Evidence," 1827, book v, chap. XVI, §10).

well understood by men in power."[403] "When reason is against a man, a man will be against reason. In this he is consistent: as consistent as he is the contrary, when reason or something that calls itself reason is employed in proving that on such or such a subject reason is a blind guide and that to be directed by her is unreasonable."[404] "When the terrors of which religion is the source, are the instruments employed for inculcating," an "outrageous . . . absurdity . . . the strength of the persuasion thus inspired presents little cause for wonder. . . . The greater the difficulty, the greater is, in case of success, the merit. Hence that most magnanimous of all conclusions, *credo quia impossibile est*. Higher than this the force of faith . . . cannot go. . . . The understanding is not the source—reason is of itself no spring of action: the understanding is but an instrument in the hand of the will: it is by hopes and fears that the end of action is determined."[405] To this large realm of non-rational life in the Church and in religion the scientific ethics of Bentham takes exception. He graphically sums up his account of church history by maintaining that "the history of the church for ages is nothing but a chronicle of lies; pious frauds were consecrated by the highest authority; false miracles, false saints, false relics, . . . false decretals, false donations, false visions and revelations were supported by the testimony of doctors, bishops and the most revered pontiffs. In a word . . . truth seemed to be banished from the earth in the name of that religion which, in itself, is the greatest enemy of falsehood."[406] Even the phrase "The holy mother Church" contains, according to Bentham, as many falsehoods as words; for, it signifies nothing but a multitude of unholy males.[407] He rightly recognized, on this and other occasions, that religion is speaking in poetical symbols expressing emotions rather than rational thought. But from this he blindly infers that poetical and religious language expresses nothing but falsehood.

Poetry and Arts. Religion

In Bentham's attitude toward poetry and the arts as well as religion we get the reverse of his profound critical insights into ethical meth-

---

[403] *Ibid.*, part XIII, p. 108b.

[404] *Ibid.*, vol. VI, p. 242b ("The Rationale of Judicial Evidence," 1827, book I, chap. VII, §2). Compare Helvétius, *Oeuvres complètes*, 1818, tome III, p. 285.

[405] *Ibid.*, part IV, p. 466a (*The Book of Fallacies*, part IV, chap. X, sect. v).

[406] Bentham, *A Treatise on Judicial Evidence*, 1825, p. 34 f.

[407] Bentham, *Works*, 1843, vol. VIII, pp. 249 ff ("Essay on Logic," written between 1811 and 1831, chap. VII, sect. 9).

odology. Like other great rationalists of the present day and of earlier times, he lacked a genuine understanding of art and religion. I do not think that this can be inferred from his remark that poetry is less innocent than the game of push-pin.[408] For the artist himself and the expert on art are likely to agree with that judgment. Poetry and arts influence the emotional lives of men for good or evil far more than sport and games.

But Bentham strikes at the roots of the autonomy of art, when he declares that there is no artistic taste at all "which deserves the epithet *good*, unless it be the taste for such employments which, to the pleasure actually produced by them, conjoin some contingent or future utility: there is no taste which deserves to be characterized as bad, unless it be a taste for some occupation which has a mischievous tendency. . . . All the arts . . . in as much as they constitute innocent employments . . . possess a species of moral utility. . . . They are excellent substitutes for drunkenness, slander and the love of gaming."[409] The fundamental error which Bentham so carefully avoided in ethics traps him in aesthetics: he simply identified beautiful with morally good or subjectively pleasant, while in ethics he had strictly rejected a parallel identification of morally good with subjectively pleasant or truly real. Accordingly, he grotesquely misjudges[410] every defense of higher and purer aesthetic taste and poetical insight.

He regards the "idea of *bad taste*" as "fantastic," and imputes to the reformers of bad taste, such as Addison or Hume, the useless destruction of perfectly harmless, though vulgar amusements.[409] As if the vulgar, aesthetically lower amusements had not at all times been protected and favored by a sufficiently dominating majority of followers, while the higher aesthetic pleasures of true artists and true art historians have barely been tolerated!

As I have tried to show in the analysis of the *Comment on the Commentaries*, Bentham did meritorious work in excluding poetical declamation from scientific inquiry in ethics. Similarly, I think, his rejection of a purely religious or theological basis for scientific ethics is methodo-

---

[408] *Ibid.*, part III, p. 253b ("The Rationale of Reward," 1825, book III, chap. I).
[409] *Ibid.*, vol. II, pp. 254b, a ("The Rationale of Reward," 1825, book III, chap. I).
[410] In my essay "Science, Ethics and Metaphysics" in *Papers and Abstracts of the Third Inter-American Congress of Philosophy*, I tried to indicate more fully how the truth value of poetical and metaphysical insights can be protected along with that of scientific rational truth—and truth in scientific ethics.

logically legitimate and scientifically necessary, as it was once for scientific physics and historiography.

But from this it by no means follows that religion, poetry and art themselves have not their genuine place in the intellectual life of man.[410] In spite of all efforts to the contrary, religion cannot be replaced by science any more than scientific ethics by religion or poetry. The rejection of theonomic ethics and the moral condemnation of Church abuses does not provide the slightest justification for a discredit of religion itself. The scientist who makes religion responsible for religious superstition commits no lesser fallacy than the religionist who condemns science on account of the immoral use of technology.

The extended anti-religious campaign in which Bentham indulged during his later life must count as one of the most short-sighted crusades of this type. Several of these polemical writings appeared pseudonymously, and though it is regrettable from the historical point of view that Bowring did not reprint them in his edition of Bentham's works, not too much of Bentham's scientific work is lost by this omission.

Bentham's dislike of the established church, and his objection to theonomic ethics, should be clearly distinguished from his fight against religion itself. Further, I think that his protest against the exclusion of atheistic witnesses before the courts cannot be proved to be a sign of hostility toward religion. He stood not only for the abolition of religious oaths, but also advocated in a lengthy book Christ's command "Swear not at all"; and he tried to show in detail why "any presumption of improbity which can be afforded by atheism is very slight."[411] If someone confesses to be an atheist, his statement "is either false or true. If false, the supposed cause of the exclusion fails in point of fact: he is not an atheist; he cannot, therefore, with propriety be excluded on the ground of atheism. If the answer be true, the cause of exclusion fails on another ground: the presumption of mendacity, the presumption grounded on the atheism is proved to be erroneous."[412] It does not seem to me anti-religious that he denied the moral or juristical right to punish atheism;[413] for it is obvious that atheism has to be fought by other means than legal penalties. I even hold it perfectly justifiable for him to think that if the propagators of immoral dogmas, of the belief in an

[411] Ibid., part xiv, p. 421a ("The Rationale of Judicial Evidence," book ix, part iii, chap. v, §1).

[412] Ibid., part xiv, pp. 421b, 422a.

[413] Ibid., vol. iii, p. 171b ("A General View of a Complete Court of Laws," chap. vi).

immoral God, in themselves deserve punishment, they should not be punished, because "it is not the sword which destroys errors, but the liberty
of examining them"; and truth is the only proper "antidote to these
poisons."[414] Atheism has, I believe, often been rightly said to be not
incompatible with a truly religious life; and superstition, or low, immoral religion, seems to be indeed a more dangerous enemy of true
religion than is atheism.

That Bentham was himself an atheist can only be inferred. In 1817
he gave this impression to John Quincy Adams, at that time Minister
Plenipotentiary to England, later President of the United States. In
John Quincy Adams' "Memoirs" we read under the date of June 8, 1817:
"Walk with Bentham. He says, Place is an atheist. I fear he is one
himself. . . . The general tenor of his observations . . . was to discredit
all religions and he intimated doubts of the existence of a God . . . he
replied little to my argument, apparently because he saw that my opinions were decided and he did not wish for controversy. He said however
that Place was a professed atheist. . . . I consider him as entertaining inveterate prejudices against all religions. . . . If he had found my sentiments congenial with his own, I have no doubt he would have disclosed his sentiments more fully."[415] But independent of all this, Bentham's understanding of religion remains appallingly limited, his very
approach to it awkward.

"The subject of religion" is "excluded from the list of subjects taught"
in Bentham's "Chrestomathic Day School"; and unless the reasons he
offers for this measure are so many excuses, dictated by diplomacy in the
hard struggle to introduce secular schools, or unless they are honest,
purely administrative considerations, his argument as regards religion
is hardly to the point.[416] He mentions the difficulties his school would
have with parents of many denominations, who all would wish to see
their creed being taught, and he further points to the higher expenses
in the budget of the school; therefore, he thinks, the avoidance of any
"instruction that is repugnant or disrespectful to Religion"[417] would satisfy all possible objections to his point of view.

His rejection of *cacotheism*, of the belief in a God of wrath, in a
"malevolent" God, is, of course, not original: he shares this view with
many representatives of religious liberalism; and he is very profuse on

---

[414] *Ibid.*, vol. III, p. 171a.
[415] John Quincy Adams, *Memoirs*, 1874, vol. III, pp. 563 ff.
[416] Bentham, *Works*, 1843, part xv, p. 41b (*Chrestomathia*, table I, §94).
[417] *Ibid.*, part xv, p. 41 f.

that theme. "Religionists in general" are in his opinion believers in "cacotheism," because to them God has mainly "the qualities . . . of malevolence and maleficence," or at best God is to them benevolent only in name, . . . but . . . malevolent in description."[418] God's "changeful and incomprehensible inclinations" are to "be supposed far more frequently pernicious than beneficial to mankind," and so "the portrait" of God is that of an immoral "capricious tyrant."[419] Obviously, it never occurred to Bentham that the belief in a God of wrath might be a very profound and accurate expression of the experience of the oldest human affliction, human suffering from the cruelty of fate. The belief in a loving *and* chastening God does not interfere at all with the acceptance of the morality of the greatest-happiness principle, though Bentham always presupposed that it necessarily would; on the other hand, the religious belief in a purely loving God in no way excludes the acceptance of a "secular" morality of vengeance and cruelty, as history has often shown and still shows us.

To Bentham's childlike optimism all the more despondent, somber subtleties of a religious *Weltanschauung* simply did not exist. He wrongly saw in these religious speculations merely a superstitious distortion of rational ethical issues and therefore hopelessly confused[420] those religious teachings with these moral questions.

This is again manifest in his discussion of the religious problem of original sin. While in his earlier writings the idea of original sin seems to him simply absurd, he later charges it with being a very "insidious"

[418] *Ibid.*, vol. vi, p. 106b ("An Introductory View of the Rationale of Evidence," chap. xxi, §3). Compare part v, p. 171 ("A General View of a Complete Code of Laws," chap. vi, order ix) and cf. part xiv, p. 423b ("The Rationale of Judicial Evidence," book ix, part iii, chap. v, §2).

[419] Philip Beauchamp (pseudonym for Bentham), *Analysis of the Influence of Natural Religion on the Temporal Happiness of Mankind*, 1822, p. 20. Compare *ibid.*, p. 25: "The vehemence of our praise is . . . not measured by the extent of the kindness bestowed, but by the superiority of the donor to the receiver, and implies only the dependence and disparity of the latter." Therefore the "capricious despot . . . the Deity . . . is yet never described without largest . . . encomiums."

[420] In several recent essays of mine, I briefly tried to indicate how these difficulties can be principally overcome, see D. Baumgardt, "Cultural Bridges in Ethics and the Philosophy of History," in *Approaches to Group Understanding*, ed. by L. Bryson, L. Finkelstein, R. M. Maciver, 1947, pp. 542-552; "Poise and Passion in Philosophy," in *Learning and World Peace*, ed. by L. Bryson, L. Finkelstein, R. M. Maciver, 1948, pp. 358-371; "Toward a Copernican Turn in Ethics" in *Eoon* (Hebrew) ed. by Hugo Bergmann, Martin Buber and Julius Guttmann, vol. i, fasc. i, 1945, and especially "Gesinnungsethik und Erfolgsethik," *Philosophische Studien*, vol. i, Heft 1, 1949, pp. 91-110.

one, a mere gratification of the "anti-social pride and insolence" of ruling classes; "out of the very sink of immorality was this fallacy drawn: a sentiment of hatred and contempt"; with the help of the concept of original sin the ruling few declared, so to speak: "so bad are they in themselves," the ruled many, "no matter how badly they are treated: they cannot be treated worse than they deserve . . . ; of so bad a crew, let us make the best for ourselves. . . . If Nero had thought it worth his while to look out for a justification, he could not have found a more apt one than this."[421] This interpretation of original sin is completely opposite to that of Nietzsche. But, while Nietzsche can claim a certain harmony with the historical facts, Bentham is entirely in error regarding the historical origin of the idea as well as its original meaning.

The concept of original sin did not have its origin within the ruling class of the first century A.D.; it began among persecuted Christians; and certainly neither Nietzsche nor Bentham did justice to the deep and wide-spread emotions of honest self-humiliation and inner suffering which led to the creation of this religious symbol. Such demoniac passions of self-accusation were apparently quite alien to Bentham. Theodor Litt is certainly mistaken in believing that "Bentham sich um die theoretische Begründung . . . des Utilitätsprinzips . . . wenig Sorge macht" but he hardly goes too far in emphasizing that "Benthams Naturalismus . . . psychologisch . . . in einer ungeheuerlichen Verarmung der Erlebniswelt . . . endigt."[422]

In his *Analysis of the Influence of Natural Religion on the Temporal Happiness of Mankind*, published under the pseudonym Philip Beauchamp, Bentham holds it sufficient to give the following definition of natural and revealed religion: "By the term religion is meant the belief in the existence of an almighty Being by whom pains and pleasures will be dispensed to mankind during an infinite and future state of existence"[423]—certainly a very narrow and low concept of religion. From

---

[421] Bentham, *The Book of Fallacies*, 1824, pp. 282 ff (part IV, chap. VII; *Works*, vol. II, p. 454b).

[422] Theodor Litt, "Ethik der Neuzeit" in *Handbuch der Philosophie*, herausgegeben von Alfred Baeumler und Manfred Schröter, Abteilung III, 1931, D, p. 148.

[423] Philip Beauchamp (Bentham), ed. by George Grote, *Analysis of the Influence of Natural Religion on the Temporal Happiness of Mankind*, 1822, p. 3. In this book too, as he had already done in his *Comment on the Commentaries*, he urges (p. 10) that "natural religion furnishes no directive rule whatever" in ethical respect, but also no rule for the happy organization of our life in a "future state of existence"; see e.g. p. 13: "If a man ignorant of medicine is unable to point out a course of life which shall, if pursued in England, preserve him from liability

this definition of religious belief, and from another ethically more instructive consideration, Bentham concludes that by religion "the science of morality . . . , this all important science . . . has been enveloped in a cloud of perplexity and confusion . . . and has become . . . doubtful and embarrassed . . . , destitute of all center and foundation."[424] For, as he explains, up to his time the science of morality had found it "impossible to reduce . . . the practices on which the same epithet of approbation is bestowed . . . to one common principle or to discover any constituent quality which universally attracts either praise or blame. . . . The moralist comparing the various actions to which praise or blame is awarded and finding not the smallest analogy either in the nature or tendency, some being beneficial, others hurtful, others indifferent—is unable to range them under any common exponent, and accordingly sets them down in a catalogue one after another, as distinct and heterogeneous dictates of a certain blind and unaccountable impulse which he terms a moral instinct or conscience. In cases where all men agree in approving or disapproving the same practice, he appeals to this universal consent as an invincible testimony to the justice of the feeling and extols the uniformity of nature's voice: in cases where they differ, he compliments the particular sect or public for whom he writes . . . and bastardizes the rest of mankind as an outcast and misguided race. . . . To this stagnant and useless condition . . . the science of morality . . . has been reduced by the excessive misapplications of praise and blame which religion has to so large an extent occasioned, though other causes have doubtless contributed to the same end."[425] Certainly if religion, of necessity, led to such results, Bentham's criticism would be justifiable. But, in contrast to Bentham, it is doubtless perfectly legitimate to distinguish religion from "superstition" and from "abuse of religion"[426]—no less legitimate than to draw a clear line of

---

to the yellow fever when he goes to Jamaica, how much more boldness is required to prescribe a preparatory course against consequences still farther removed from the possibility of conjecture?" P. 14: "In estimating the chances of life and death, of health and disease, no insurer ever inquires whether the actions of the applicant have been agreeable or disagreeable to the Deity."

[424] *Ibid.*, p. 87 f.

[425] Philip Beauchamp (Bentham), *Analysis of the Influence of Natural Religion on the Temporal Happiness of Mankind*, new edition, 1875, pp. 79 ff, 87 f. *Ibid.*, 1822, pp. 87, 88. Compare *ibid.*, 1822, p. 38: "If . . . piety consisted of a collection of qualities calculated to produce temporal benefit, you would discover the same identity between Pagan and Christian piety, as there is between Pagan and Christian justice or veracity. But the very reverse is most notoriously the fact."

[426] *Ibid.*, p. 2. J. S. Mill reports in his *Autobiography*, ed. by J. J. Cross, for the

demarcation between scientific ethics and uncritical preaching of morality, between science and a criminal use of technology.

In his *Church of Englandism* in 1818 Bentham has no hesitation in maintaining that Jesus' wish at the Lord's Supper "Do this in rememberance of me" was "completely devoid of mystery," that the communion was in no way "designed by Jesus for general imitation," that he never suggested that this "sort of commemoration" should be "practised" by "all nations" or by "every living creature," because it shows its "utter unfitness for that purpose."[427] Thus, in Bentham's view, the symbol of the Lord's Supper has been wrongly "sublimated into a mystery" and "absurdity deduced from it."[428] In a word, he really thinks that he can show the nonsensicalness and preposterousness of this great and ancient religious symbol by stating that "bread, this first of the two supposed necessary instruments of salvation" is inaccessible, for instance, "in the tropical countries" where "some manufactured grain, such as rice . . . has all along occupied the place of this elaborated article of manufacture. Still in narrower . . . limits . . . wine is made"; so wine, "necessary as it is to salvation in England," may it "be dispensed with in Hindostan?"[429] On the ground of these few trivial considerations Bentham obviously thought he had definitely "debunked" a religious sacrament and turned it into ridicule.

In his *Not Paul, but Jesus,* pseudonymously published under the name Gamaliel Smith in 1823, and in his *Summary View of a Work, intituled Not Paul, but Jesus,* Bentham seems to believe sincerely that he could discard the whole of the work of Paul by showing that Paul had used for himself money which he had collected for the use of his congregations.[430] In a strange piece of Bible exegesis, he punctiliously checks

---

first time without alterations or omissions, 1924, p. 49 f, that it was "the searching character" of these anti-religious analyses by Bentham-Beauchamp "which produced the greatest effect on me."

[427] Bentham, *Church of Englandism,* 1818, appendix II, pp. 154 ff, 157 ff.

[428] *Ibid.,* p. 159.

[429] *Ibid.,* p. 160 f.

[430] See Gamaliel Smith Esq. (Bentham), *Summary View of a Work, intituled Not Paul, but Jesus, as exhibited in Introduction, Plan of the Work and Titles of Chapters and Sections,* January 31, 1821, p. 14, appendix, chap. II: "Paul's love of money. Proofs of money received or craved by him"; and see Gamaliel Smith, *Not Paul, but Jesus,* 1823, pp. 378, 395: "Of a particular instance of money obtained by him on a false pretense—namely by the pretense of its being for the use of others when his intention was to convert it to his own use—a mass of evidence we have which presents itself as being in no slight degree probative." Compare *ibid.,* VII: "In the Gospels and Paul's Epistles two quite different, if not

every occasion on which Paul speaks of money; and this fight of an angry lawyer of the nineteenth century against the religious genius of the first century A.D. is, certainly, bizarre beyond all description.

It would not be rewarding to follow the course of these anti-religious discussions and their confusing amalgamation with seemingly moral questions. If Bentham had given us nothing but his anti-religious writings, he would have given us less than Nietzsche's *Antichrist* or Freud's *Die Zukunft einer Illusion*, or even the *Welträtsel* of the zoologist Ernst Haeckel.

---

opposite religions are inculcated; . . . in the religion of Jesus may be found all the good that has never been the result of the compound so . . . unhappily made—in the religion of Paul all the Mischief." Compare *ibid.*, IV, VI and *Summary View of a Work, intituled Not Paul, but Jesus*, 1821, p. 2: Not only "the fathers," but also Paul are "no . . . longer to be regarded as guides either in faith or morals." Compare *ibid.*, p. 3: "In the doctrines" of Paul is "to be found the origin and the cause of no small part—perhaps of the greatest part—of the opposition which that religion with its benevolent system of morals has hitherto experienced." (According to Charles W. Everett's bibliographical notes in E. Halévy's *The Growth of Philosophic Radicalism*, 1928, p. 544, this work was "put together by Francis Place for Bentham as stated in Place's copy in the British Museum.")

GLEANINGS

The *Deontology*

GLEANINGS

The *Deontology*

―――――――

THE only ethical work of Bentham which I do not want to analyze in full is his *Deontology*. This seems, at first glance, a most paradoxical attitude to be taken by a writer on Bentham's theory of morals. For Bentham's *Deontology* is his only large-scale work which deals exclusively with ethics as distinct from jurisprudence. But in fact the *Deontology* is even less the work of Bentham himself than Dumont's edition of the *Traités de législation*.

These two volumes evidently contain a considerable amount of material which has little to do with Bentham's original manuscripts. John Bowring inserted a long chapter on the history of the utility principle, in which he suddenly appears in his own person, quoting only now and then from Bentham. There are, further, many discussions of religious questions in which a far more favorable view of Christendom is taken than in either the earlier or later writings of Bentham; and this shows that there must have been at least a preference given to those "disjointed fragments"[1] of Bentham's notes which were comparatively more in accordance with Bowring's own convictions. Finally we find in the *Deontology* detailed "ethical" admonitions concerning correct behavior in avoiding "the emission of gas from the alimentary canal," in refraining from "smacking . . . lips," from "a bubbling sound" while drawing in liquids, from "chewing with a noise," from "eructation" without covering your mouth with your handkerchief, from "unnecessary delay

――――――

[1] Bentham, *Deontology; or, the Science of Morality*, vol. ii, 1834, p. x. Characteristic of the relation between Bentham and Bowring in this respect and, in itself, a very amiable illustration of religious tolerance is the following story told by Bowring, *ibid.*, 1834, vol. ii, pp. 229 ff. "For two or three years after my acquaintance with Mr. Bentham we had frequent discussions on some points of religious controversy. Certainly on his part there was no diminution of affection towards me; on mine, no diminution of reverence towards him, notwithstanding the unchanged state of our minds on the subject in question, after so many and such long debates. One day, he said to me, 'I shall not change your mind, I see; you will not change mine, you know. If we go on, I shall give you pain, or you will give me pain, and in either case pain to both will be the consequence. We will never talk on this matter again.' Nor did we." Cf. Graham Wallas, *The Life of Francis Place*, 1898, p. 82: "I am for toleration, said Bentham. If every man were to quarrel with every man whose opinions did not on every point whatsoever coincide with his, the earth would not be long burdened with the human race."

in answering letters," the moral advice to avoid excitement by a "deliberate repetition of the alphabet."[2] I shall not venture to decide whether these detailed instructions are also the work of Bowring, or concessions which Bentham made to the more "practical" mind of his secretary, or just senile pedantries of the old Bentham himself.

At any rate, the question of what part of this "desultory and diffuse . . . work"[3] really belongs to Bentham and what part to Bowring can be clarified only by a meticulous comparison of Bentham's original manuscripts with the printed text of the *Deontology*; and even then, many questions may be left unanswered. Leslie Stephen assured us on the ground of his examination of Bentham's MSS that Bowring's edition represents substantially Bentham's own text.[4] But, as Leslie Stephen's whole work shows that he had very little interest in Bentham's unpublished writings, I am not certain whether his comparison of the printed and the unprinted text of the *Deontology* was careful enough, and whether his judgment in this respect can be relied on as final.

Bowring put together his edition out of "small scraps of paper . . . written . . . at times remote from another and delivered into my [Bowring's] hands without order or arrangement of any sort."[5] It is rather difficult to distinguish these original scraps of paper in the 75,000 sheets of Bentham's MSS and it seems to me not at all certain that all these scraps have been preserved. But, as two American scholars have already started to prepare a new edition of the *Deontology* on the ground of these original Bentham MSS, I do not wish to duplicate this painstaking work. I shall give only a brief analysis of Bowring's text which, after all, has a certain historical interest in itself no matter to what extent Bowring has watered down Bentham's original phrasing.

Fundamental Anti-Dogmatism

All we know of Bowring leads us to believe that he was not too much interested in epistemology. Nevertheless, even in his edition of Bentham's *Deontology* papers the epistemological problem of a critical method in ethics plays a dominating part. I take this as confirmation of the correctness of my Bentham analysis, which stresses, above all and from the beginning, the importance of his censorial method.

The *Deontology* hardly gives us any new argument in this respect,

[2] Bentham, *Deontology*, vol. II, pp. 237, 244 f, 239, 248, 168.
[3] *Ibid.*, vol. I, p. 5.
[4] Leslie Stephen, *The English Utilitarians*, 1900, vol. I, p. 314, note.
[5] Bentham, *Deontology*, 1834, vol. II, p. x.

but there are a considerable number of striking and graphic formulations of Bentham's life-long anti-dogmatic ethical convictions. In the beginning of the first chapter of the *Deontology* we read: "He who, on any other occasion should say 'it is as I say, because I say it is so,' would not be thought to have said any great matter: but on the question concerning the standard of morality, men have written great books wherein from beginning to end they are employed in saying this and nothing else. What these books have to depend on for their efficacy, and for their being thought to have proved anything, is the stock of self-sufficiency in the writer and of implicit deference in the readers; by the help of a proper dose of which, one thing may be made to go down as well as another. Out of this assumption of authority has grown the word *obligation* . . . while such a cloud of misty obscurity has gathered round the term, that whole volumes have been written to disperse it. The obscurity, notwithstanding, has continued as dense as before, and it can only be dissipated by bringing in the light of utility. . . . The public legislator, with all his powers, is generally less despotic in his phraseology than the public writer—that self-constituted legislator of the people. He makes laws without giving reasons—laws which generally convey only his sovereign will and pleasure. It is indeed a misfortune that men come to the discussion of important questions predetermined to decide them only in one way. They are pledged, as it were, to their own minds, that certain practices shall be wrong, and certain other practices right. But the principle of utility allows of no such peremptoriness, and requires, before any practice is condemned, that it be shown to be derogatory to human happiness. Such an investigation suits not the dogmatical instructor."[6] But if moral dogmatism "be the standard . . . the opinions of the Inquisition bid fairest of any yet known for being the very perfection of truth and right reason, and morality may be graduated according to the miseries inflicted by persecution. If numbers decide, Idolatry would drive Christianity from the field."[7] Throughout the deductions of the *Deontology* Bentham repeats these warnings against ethical dogmatism and gives reasons for his exhortations. "The law-giver should be no more impassionate than the geometrician."[8] "Mathematicians, so long as they confine themselves within the province of their science,[9] cannot be, and accordingly never have been, other-

[6] *Ibid.*, vol. I, pp. 9 f, 8.   [7] *Ibid.*, vol. I, p. 9.   [8] *Ibid.*, vol. II, p. 19.
[9] This limitation was prophetically wise and cautious in face of contemporary representatives of a German, Aryan mathematics. The whole passage is to be found in *Deontology*, vol. I, p. 26, note.

wise than tranquil. . . . The tranquillity and good temper of a disputant is in proportion to the inward consciousness of the aptitude of his arguments to produce conviction." Seen from this point of view, unhappily, the common moralist compares ill with the mathematician. For it is a complete self-delusion to believe that with "self-evident" demands of "prima facie rightness" (which in different systems of morals flatly contradict each other) we are even "better off"[10] than with self-evident axioms in geometry.

"The words impropriety, unlawfulness, and such like, are flung at particular actions in order to excite odium, as if they were evidence of depravity; such words being, in fact, only a part and portion of that phraseology, by which a man seeks to shelter his own dogmatism from the analysis which the doctrines of utility would apply to it."[11] Most of the talk of common morality on virtues and vices is "characterised by that vagueness which is a convenient instrument for the poetical, but dangerous or useless to the practical moralist."[12] The rhetorician's "object being to put others in a passion, his course is to appear to be in a passion himself"; therefore he repudiates "unexciting" and unexcited language; but it is "logical, and not . . . rhetorical purposes"[13] that *Deontology* wants to serve. Men in general express their moral judgments in "such obscure terms as 'right' or 'fitting,' terms which serve only to express their disapprobation and not the ground of it."[14] "No man, how philosophical, how scrupulous soever, but believes infinitely more propositions upon trust than upon perception: the only difference in this particular between the philosopher and the non-philosopher, or in short between the wise man and the weak is, that the latter rests upon authority conclusively, in the last as well as in the first instance; the former always keeps open the appeal to reason, that is, to his own perceptions. The judgments of the first, upon hearing the report of authority, are provisional; the judgments of the latter are definitive. But of demonstration certain propositions are not susceptible. The proposition that happiness is better than unhappiness cannot be subjected to mathematical proof. But let him who impugns the doctrine impugn our reasonings. It is the only axiom we desire to have taken for granted, and this is to make a very small demand upon confidence or upon credulity."[15] One may add that the greatest-happiness principle implies one more presupposition which is not explicitly mentioned here, viz.

[10] See W. David Ross, *Foundations of Ethics*, 1939, p. 320.
[11] Bentham, *Deontology*, 1834, vol. 1, p. 201.   [12] *Ibid.*, vol. 1, p. 196.
[13] *Ibid.*, vol. 1, p. 36.   [14] *Ibid.*, vol. 1, p. 279.   [15] *Ibid.*, vol. 1, p. 277 f.

the hypothesis that each person's pleasure is ethically as valuable as the same quantum of pleasure felt by any other individual, that a quantum of pain experienced by one individual weighs ethically as much as the same quantum of pain experienced by any other person. But, in any case, Bentham here complies clearly with Henry Sidgwick's demand that utilitarianism ought to characterize the utility principle as an "intuitive" presupposition of its system, as an intuitive "hypothesis," and not as an empirical observation.

The common hypothesis of anti-hedonism is here again exposed as arbitrary. Commonly "good and evil conscience are . . . used to represent the tribunal before which a man tries the merits of his own actions in his own mind, and the recompense or punishment which he attaches to those actions."[16] But the difficulty is that conscientiousness or "the moral sense . . . will just be wanting where it is most wanted—that is, in the case of those who have it not";[17] and, above all, in only too many people "conscientiousness takes a direction opposed to the general well-being."[16] Wherever conscientiousness does this, it certainly makes no sense to call it the source of morality. In all these many cases, conscientiousness is a definite source of immorality "in the very proportion of its influence."[18] So if Sir W. David Ross asks whether there are "not . . . things such as conscientious action whose goodness is matter of general agreement;[19] the answer, I think, has to be No, as Bentham rightly saw, and not Yes, as Ross assumes without any further examination. Even in harmless cases, conscientious action may be said to be at least valueless, if it reveals too much cumbersomeness and a lack of grace.

Moralists ought never to "erect for themselves . . . a high throne . . . in the character of absolute and infallible monarchs"; they should never dictate "to the world below. . . . The wantonness of a political ruler has often been the topic of animadversion; the self-erected arbitrator wielding like the madman in his cell his imaginary sceptre, is, in truth, more egregiously wanton. A certain sense of responsibility—a fear of reaction may control the despotism of an acknowledged tyrant, but where is the control which is to check the waywardness and presumption of the self-elected dictator of morals. . . . In fact to be most useful" the moralist "will be employed somewhat in the character of a scout—a man hunting for consequences—consequences resulting from a particular course—collecting them as well as he can, and presenting them for the

[16] *Ibid.*, vol. I, p. 137.   [17] *Ibid.*, vol. II, p. 73.   [18] *Ibid.*, vol. I, p. 137.
[19] W. D. Ross, *The Right and the Good*, 1930, p. 88.

use of those who may be disposed to profit by his services. His task is humble—his labor is great—his reward can only be the anticipation of good to be done."[20] "To say 'you ought,' is easy in the extreme. To stand the searching penetration of a Why? is not so easy. Why ought I? Because you ought—is the not unfrequent reply; on which the Why? comes back again with the added advantage of having obtained a victory. . . . Even where precepts are founded on good reasons, the development of those reasons is a matter of considerable exertion and difficulty. . . . But to set up laws and precepts is . . . a task to which all men are competent, . . . a task which the foolish indeed are most eager to engage in—for ignorance has no more convenient cloak than arrogance."[21] Deontology "has no purpose to answer by despotic dogmatizing. . . . She consents even to set aside the code of the lawgiver and the dogmas of the divine."[22] The undogmatic "Linnaeus of Natural History has appeared in the world . . . the Linnaeus of Ethics is yet to come."[23] "Have the courage to ask" in morals and be not led astray by "the ordinary phraseology of the world"![24] In the first epoch of mankind virtue was "*vis*," force, courage, and ethics spoke the language of force; in the second epoch morality substituted fraud for ignorance and violence and spoke the language of the fraud of priests and aristocratic lawyers. From these terminologies ethics has to free itself in the third epoch of history, in the epoch of a critical and democratic, international and pacifistic application of utility and justice.[25] Finally, with biblical solemnity and in accord with the genuine benevolence of his character, Bentham tries to dissociate himself from dogmatic moralism in the following expressive way: "The danger of putting forward any proposition as a leading principle, other than that which would maximize felicity, consists in this—that if it coincide with the greater principle it is supererogatory; if it do not coincide, it is pernicious. Any principle that is not subordinate to it may be opposed to it, either diametrically or collaterally. The ascetic principle, if all comprehensive and consistent, may be evidenced as one of direct opposition—the ipse dixit principles of all sorts may be ranked among the indirect opponents. . . . 'He who

---

[20] Bentham, *Deontology*, 1834, vol. i, pp. 30 f, 30.
[21] *Ibid.*, vol. i, pp. 32, 31.   [22] *Ibid.*, vol. i, pp. 159, 158.
[23] *Ibid.*, vol. i, p. 202.   [24] *Ibid.*, vol. ii, pp. 311, 47.
[25] *Ibid.*, vol. ii, pp. 48 ff; compare vol. i, p. 239 f. Nietzsche aimed perhaps, at least partly, at this fundamentally critical spirit of Bentham's ethics in stating that "Bentham fühlte sich als Gesetzgeber, Rée als Beherrschter, . . . als Lehrer von gegebenen Gesetzen," see *Nietzsche's Werke*, ii. Abteilung, Band xiii, 1903, "Unveröffentlichtes aus der Umwertungszeit (1882/83-1888)," S. 222.

is not under me is against me,' may be said with figurative . . . truth by
the Greatest-Happiness Principle. . . . And let not this declaration be
taken as the result of arrogance of disposition: it grows out of the nature of things, and the necessities of the case. Let it not be considered to
bespeak unkindness toward any advocate of the opposite opinions, for
such unkindness is neither its necessary nor even its natural accompaniment."[26] With this leniency toward his ethical opponents, Bentham
combined the most consistent critical radicalism known in the history
of ethics.

Bentham once advised us to banish the term *ought* from the ethical
dictionary; and this suggestion has often been completely misinterpreted.
It is true, Bentham says: "The talisman of arrogance, indolence, and
ignorance, is to be found in a single word, an authoritative imposture,
which in these pages it will be frequently necessary to unveil. It is the
word 'ought' . . . in deciding 'you ought to do this—you ought not to
do it'—is not every question of morals set at rest? If the use of the
word be admissible at all, it 'ought' to be banished from the vocabulary
of morals."[27] H. Rashdall and A. E. Taylor have understood these remarks of Bentham as proving a fatal confusion of value-judgments
with factual statements.[28] I think, however, that the end of this passage
clearly shows the opposite tendencies at work in Bentham's thought.
Bentham goes on to say on the very same page: "There is another
word, which has a talismanic virtue too, and which might be wielded
to destroy many fatal and fallacious positions. 'You ought'—'You ought
not,' says the dogmatist. Why? retorts the inquirer—Why?"[29] In his
Deontology, as in his other writings, Bentham clearly distinguishes
between "ought" and "is." The contrast between these two different
spheres of judgments is not so elaborately brought out here as in the
Fragment on Government but the contrast is by no means overlooked.

Bentham had no intention of banishing the term *ought*, in order to
identify the *ought* with an *is*; all he wanted was to verify every *ought*
by ultimate reference to an *is*. In contrast to this critical foundation of
ethics any reference to an unverified *ought* means grounding morals on
an *is*, namely, on existing moral rules which are believed to be uni-

[26] *Ibid.*, vol. I, p. 330 f.   [27] *Ibid.*, vol. I, p. 31 f.
[28] See H. Rashdall, *The Theory of Good and Evil*, 1907, vol. I, p. 224, and
A. E. Taylor, "The Right and the Good," *Mind*, vol. XLIX, no. 194, April 1940,
pp. 222, 220.
[29] Bentham, *Deontology*, vol. I, p. 32.

versally acknowledged laws while, in fact, these laws frequently contradict each other. By referring to the greatest-happiness principle, however, we can weigh the right of these contradictory claims, and call them to order by means of a comparison of obvious facts, viz. pleasant and less pleasant feelings.

The *Deontology* uses the utility principle in this way and emphasizes, therefore, that "it is, in fact, very idle to talk about duties. . . . A man, a moralist, gets into an elbowchair, and pours forth pompous dogmatisms about duty. . . . 'It is your duty to do this—it is your duty to abstain from doing that'; and this is easy travelling for a public instructor. 'But *why* is it my duty?' And the answer if sifted will be found to be—'Because I bid you—because it is my opinion—my will.' 'Well, but suppose I do not conform myself to this will of yours?' 'O then you will do very wrong'—which being interpreted means, 'I shall disapprove of your conduct.' "[30] "The labyrinth . . . of the human mind . . . is explored" by one clue; "that clue is the influence of interest; of interest, not in that partial and sordid sense in which it is the tyrant of sordid souls, but in the enlarged and beneficent sense in which it is the common master of all spirits, and especially of the enlightened."[31] "To detect the fallacies which lie hid under the surface, to prevent the aberrations of sympathy and antipathy, to bring to view and to call into activity those springs of action whose operation leads to an undoubted balance of happiness, is the important part of moral science."[32]

That the proper use of the utility principle is not always simple, that this principle, even understood as the rule of the pursuit of one's own interest, is exposed to the possibility of ample misuse, is explicitly granted even in the *Deontology*. Certainly, not every man acts with a "correct view . . . to his own interest"; and therefore, "the business of the Deontologist is to bring forth from the obscurity in which they have been buried, those points of duty, in which by the hands of nature, a man's interests have been associated with his enjoyments—in which his own well-being has been connected, combined, and identified with the well-being of others; to give, in a word, to the social, all the influence of the self-regarding motive. He is to use, for the production of the greatest sum of happiness, those elements of happiness which exist in the breast of every man . . . for such an artist, there is no want of work—there can be no want of work, while remediable evil is to be found in the world."[33]

---

[30] *Ibid.*, vol. I, pp. 10, 12.   [31] *Ibid.*, vol. I, p. 101.
[32] *Ibid.*, vol. I, p. 174.   [33] *Ibid.*, vol. I, pp. 12, 23.

In this application of the utility principle, the *Deontology* does not hold out the prospect of absolute mathematical certainty. But at least there is, as we are informed, "the consolation of knowing that, by the application of a right standard, there are few moral questions which may not be resolved, with an accuracy and a certainty not far removed from mathematical demonstration"; in any case "vice may be defined to be a miscalculation of chances: a mistake in estimating the value of pleasures and pains. It is false moral arithmetic."[34] "Weigh pains, weigh pleasures; and as the balance stands, will stand the question of right and wrong."[35] Aristotle, however, and his "Oxford disciples" fail to make clear what is the "quantity of the quality out of which virtue is made,"[36] as Bentham tries to show in detail. In failing to indicate properly what is "neither too much nor too little" in virtue, what is "the proper dose . . . of the moral medicine," the Aristotelian moralists are far less precise not only than mathematicians, but even than physicians; "if a physician treat of disease, he does not satisfy himself with scribbling down their names, but thinks it useful, finds it necessary, indeed, to record their symptoms. Not so our moralist. His virtues are names, without symptoms: he talks of virtue; but how virtue is to be separated from that which is not virtue, forms no portion of his care."[36] These are some of the reasons why Bentham thinks his utilitarianism superior to the essentially qualitative dogmatic characterization of virtues in Aristotle and in the Oxford moralists of his time. Perhaps we may add that something of the same objection still holds good for the Oxford moralists of our time.

Self-Interest and the Morality of Power

On the whole, the utopian belief in a coincidence of all human interests is apparently fostered more in the *Deontology* than in Bentham's other writings; and also the businesslike character of utilitarianism is here perhaps more emphasized than anywhere else. It is not necessary even to open the two volumes; on the title page Bowring promises in the rather questionable style of too persuasive a salesmanship that Bentham's *Deontology* teaches "the harmony and co-incidence of duty and self-interest, virtue and felicity, prudence and benevolence." And the title of the second volume adds that all these harmonies between the

[34] *Ibid.*, vol. I, p. 131; cf. vol. II, pp. 99, 77, 79, 135.
[35] *Ibid.*, vol. I, p. 137.   [36] *Ibid.*, vol. I, pp. 150 ff.

most desirable goods are not only "explained, exemplified" by Bentham's work but also applied there "to the business of life."

It seems that only too often the *Deontology* identifies egoism with virtue, prudence with altruism and builds up its entire reasoning on these flagrant fallacies. Vice appears here particularly frequently as a "spend-thrift," virtue as "a prudent economist that gets back all her outlay with interest."[37] "It cannot be a man's duty to do that what it is his interest not to do. . . . The more closely the subject is examined, the more obvious will the agreement between interest and duty . . . their co-incidence . . . appear"; the immoral action is only "a miscalculation of self-interest"; "if every man, acting correctly for his own interest, obtained the maximum of obtainable happiness, mankind would reach the millennium of accessible bliss; . . . to show how erroneous an estimate the vicious man makes of pains and pleasures is the purpose of the intelligent moralist."[38] If the opinions and conduct of others toward us were indifferent to us, it "would be but a waste . . . to make a sacrifice . . . to obtain their friendly affections";[39] but "by every act of . . . beneficence . . . a man contributes to a sort of fund, a savingsbank, a depository of general good-will, out of which services of all sorts may be looked for, as about to flow from other hands into his."[40] Modesty, courage, mansuetude, friendship, urbanity, liberality and even veracity have to be "subordinate . . . to prudence and benevolence."[41] "Prudence . . . sets its limits to benevolence"; but "those limits do not, on ordinary occasions embrace large space. . . . Prudence makes a sort of commercial bargain. . . . The expenditure is expected to bring back something more than its cost."[42] "It is no more fit to call disinterestedness a virtue in moral economy than to call expenditure a merit in political economy."[43] Seen from the angle of uncritical, idealistic Jewish, Christian or Hindu tradition, this type of ethical language and argument must certainly appear not only repulsive, but also grossly distorted. As long as altruism alone is felt to be, in one way or the other the very heart of moral life, Bentham's *Deontology* must give the impression of being a complete perversion of ethical verity.

Even the *Deontology*, it is true, does not exclude self-denial and sacrifice from ethics altogether. It is stated there that the idea of virtue may sometimes be included in the idea of sacrifice or self-denial. "The terms sacrifice or self-denial are appropriate where virtue consists in the ab-

[37] *Ibid.*, vol. II, p. 28. [38] *Ibid.*, vol. I, p. 11 f. [39] *Ibid.*, vol. II, p. 132.
[40] *Ibid.*, vol. II, p. 260. [41] *Ibid.*, vol. II, pp. 64 ff, 68, 59; vol. I, p. 251.
[42] *Ibid.*, vol. I, p. 208. [43] *Ibid.*, vol. I, p. 165.

stinence from enjoyment."[44] But, as the *Deontology* adds immediately, these terms "are less properly employed where the good sacrificed is of the negative kind and the virtue is found in self-subjection to suffering. . . . It will be obvious that though the idea of virtue may be sometimes included in the idea of sacrifice, or self-denial, yet these are by no means synonymous with virtue, nor are they necessarily included in the idea of virtue. . . . Virtue has not only to struggle with individual inclination, it has sometimes to struggle against the general inclination of the human species, and it is when it triumphs over both that it exists in its highest degree of perfection. In proportion as a man has acquired a command over his desires, resistance to their impulse becomes less and less difficult, till, at length, in some constitutions all difficulty vanishes. . . . The idea of the greater distant suffering has extinguished that of a lesser contemporaneous enjoyment. And it is thus that by the power of association, things which have been originally objects of desire become objects of aversion; and, on the other hand, things which had been originally objects of aversion, such as medicines, for instance, become objects of desire. . . . When things are in this situation, the virtue, so far from being annihilated, has arrived at the pinnacle of its highest excellence, and shines forth in its brightest lustre. Defective indeed would that definition of virtue be, which excluded from its pale the very perfection of virtue."[45] Obviously self-denial and sacrifice mean here nothing but far-sighted self-interest, and at least explicitly, the two terms do not here include altruistic self-denial.

But it should not be lost sight of that, implicitly, the *Deontology* fully allows for the inclusion of altruism when it refers to a disinterestedness from which only one's fellowman gets a manifest benefit. "Nothing that is called virtue is entitled to the name, unless, and in so far as, it is contributory to happiness; the happiness of the agent himself or of some other being."[46] "The sacrifice of interests presents itself abstractedly, as something grand and virtuous, because it is taken for granted that the pleasure one man flings away must necessarily be gathered up by another. And supposing no pleasure were lost in the transfer, and no pleasure gained, it is clear that the whole sum of happiness would continue just as it was, notwithstanding a million shiftings from one possessor to another. But in the commerce of happiness, as in that of wealth the prominent question is, how to make circulation assist production."[47] Moreover both of Bentham's formulae "The greatest happiness of the

[44] *Ibid.*, vol. I, p. 143.
[46] *Ibid.*, vol. II, p. 31 f.
[45] *Ibid.*, vol. I, pp. 143 ff.
[47] *Ibid.*, vol. I, p. 164 f.

greatest number" and "Maximizing felicity" pay attention not only to the interest of the agent who consults the utility principle but also to the interest of all on whom the behavior of the agent has any bearing.

What the *Deontology*, as well as the earlier writings, want to exclude completely is not altruism, but disinterestedness in the shape of absolute self-sacrifice. On this point, Bentham insists here, as elsewhere, that "to escape from one's self, to forget one's own interests, to make unrequited sacrifices and all for duty, are high-sounding phrases, and . . . as non-sensical as high sounding. Self-preference is universal and necessary: if destiny be anywhere despotic, it is here. When self is sacrificed, it is self in one shape to self in another shape, and a man can no more cast off regard to his own happiness . . . than he can cast off his own skin, or jump out of it. And if he could why should he?"[48] "But . . . , cries an objector, where is sympathy? where is benevolence? where is benef-icence? . . . Why urge a man to pursue . . . pleasure . . . that which he is always occupied in pursuing? . . . Answer exactly. . . . To deny the existence of the social affections would be to deny the evidence of all experience. Scarcely in the most brutal savage would they be found altogether wanting. But the pleasure I feel in bestowing pleasure on my friend, whose pleasure is it but mine? The pain I feel at seeing my friend oppressed by pain, whose pain is it but mine? And if I felt no pleasure, or felt no pain, where . . . would be my sympathy?"[49] Yet evidently the commercial toughness of many formulas of the *Deontol-ogy* and the meagerness of explicit consideration given here to altruism have drawn much more attention upon themselves than the more subtle discussion of egoism and altruism in Bentham's "To his Fellow-citizens of France."

Aside from this, the *Deontology* is doubtless far too optimistic in its statements that virtue is almost identical with refined self-interest, en-lightened egoism almost identical with altruism. The *Deontology* con-siderably underestimates the frequency of cases in which altruism does not yield any profit to the altruist, save the gratification afforded by his own benevolence. The *Deontology* equally underrates the frequency of clashes between egoism and considerable, though not absolute, self-sacrifice—those cases in which the interests of others are not only dif-ferent from the manifest profit of the altruist, but even hostile to it; those cases in which altruism means not only no profit, in the common sense of the word, but an obvious loss to the altruist; those many in-

[48] *Ibid.*, vol. II, p. 121.   [49] *Ibid.*, vol. I, p. 83 f.

cidents in which there is neither a harmony between the altruist's egoism and his altruism nor between his egoism and the egoism of others.

But as I have tried to show, methodologically Bentham's ethics of utility is not dependent on any trust in the final concord of human aims or on any underestimation of the importance of self-sacrifice. The belief in an ultimate pre-established harmony among all human interests is by no means an indispensable article in the faith of consistent hedonism.

Only if the positive—and the most valuable—tendencies of Bentham's ethical method are misjudged or overlooked, can his radicalism appear destructive or utopian. On the whole, Bentham's hedonism keeps in line with the soundest tendencies of "naturalistic" ethics when he states:, "There has been among moralists a vehement disposition to shut out the influence of the self-regarding principle from the mind. Why this reluctance to admit, as a motive, that which is and must be the strongest of all motives—a man's regard for himself? Why is not self-love to be brought into the field? It is from a sort of bashfulness—a disposition to consider that principle to which all the actions and passions of men owe their birth, as the *partie honteuse* of our nature."[50] The very term *partie honteuse* of our nature appears also in Nietzsche's *Zur Genealogie der Moral*[51] and exactly in the same evaluative sense. Nietzsche praised it as a special merit of English moralists of the nineteenth century to have done far more justice to the *partie honteuse* of human nature than other European ethicists.

Bentham comes even nearer to a morality of power, or to "immoralism," when he points out that "*Deontology* professes no scorn for that very selfishness to which vice itself appeals. . . . She has no purpose to answer by despotic dogmatising. . . . She surrenders every point which cannot be proved to be beneficial to the individual. She consents even to set aside the code of the lawgiver and the dogmas of the divine. She takes for granted that these cannot be unfriendly to her influences, that neither legislation nor religion are hostile to morality; and she insists that morality shall not be opposed to happiness. Make out to her a case against human felicity, and she is smitten with silence and with helplessness . . . she assumes nothing but that which no man will deny— namely that all men wish to be happy."[52] It is too often forgotten that

[50] *Ibid.*, vol. I, p. 163.
[51] F. Nietzsche, *Zur Genealogie der Moral*, I, I; *Werke*, 1919, Bd. VIII, S. 302.
[52] Bentham, *Deontology*, 1834, vol. I, p. 158 f.

even the seeming desire for unhappiness in the melancholic is a hidden wish which drives him to avoid a greater pain he might have to undergo in a state of seemingly purer happiness.

Therefore, the ethical importance of power and of the self-regarding impulses is so frequently vindicated by Bentham. "Power, in all and every shape, is the sole instrument of morality, and the struggle for it, within the limits of prudence and benevolence, so far from being worthy of reprehension, is perhaps the very strongest of all excitements to virtue."[53] In this way, Bentham fully shares certain sound convictions of a morality of power; but by including benevolence, his hedonism dissociates itself from the one-sidedness of a sheer master-morality as much as from the one-sidedness of uncritical idealistic asceticism.

Last Shifts of Terminology · Historical Notes in the Margin

There are a considerable number of notes in the *Deontology* concerning ethical terminology. But they are of minor interest in themselves and in comparison with the work already done in earlier writings of Bentham. As late as 1826 in his *Commentary on Mr. Humphrey's Real Property Code* Bentham had used the term "deontology" as a "more expressive name" for the whole field of ethics and in his *Chrestomathia* he had explicitly included in "deontology" private and public ethics as well as international law.[54] In the *Deontology*, however, the term is limited to the realm of private ethics exclusive of jurisprudence. "Deontology is derived from the Greek words, το δεον (that which is proper) and Λογια, knowledge—meaning the knowledge of what is right or proper; and it is here specially applied to the subject of morals, or that part of the field of action which is not the subject of public legislation. . . . In a word, Deontology, or Private Ethics, may be considered the science by which happiness is created out of motives extra-legislatorial—while Jurisprudence is the science by which law is applied to the production of felicity."[55] Nevertheless the principle of utility is termed here "the Deontological law"[56] though it certainly applies to jurisprudence too.

---

[53] *Ibid.*, vol. II, p. 51. Though his presuppositions are very different from Bentham's basic argument, like Bentham, the Norwegian Anathon Aall has specially emphasized that "die Rolle, die der Macht in der Moralökonomie zukommt, nur ungenügend angegeben ist" and that "in diesem Punkt für die Erforschung der Moralwissenschaft noch vieles zu tun übrig bleibt"; "Pflicht . . . ist inhaltlich die von dem sozialethischen Gefühl sanktionierte Forderung, dass eine subjektive Machtfähigkeit objektiv verwirklicht werde," see Anathon August Frederick Aall, *Macht und Pflicht*, 1902, p. III f, v, 121 ff and *passim*.

[54] See Bentham, *Works*, 1843, vol. v, p. 389b and vol. VIII, p. 289a, b.

[55] Bentham, *Deontology*, 1834, vol. I, pp. 21, 28.   [56] *Ibid.*, vol. II, p. 30.

As Bowring recounts, Bentham "once thought of proposing the employment of the word *Eudaimonology* to represent the utilitarian doctrines, and *Eudaimonologians* its professors. To those acquainted with Greek the meaning would be sufficiently obvious; but that acquaintance is so rare, that he did not venture to recommend the terms to general adoption. Besides, custom must be departed from in not rendering the word *Eudaemonology*; and in such a shape umbrage might be given to men of pious minds, who would possibly associate with it the idea of a doctrine . . . , of which devils were the subject."[57] The Latin equivalent of Eudaimonology, *Felicitism*, or *Felicitarianism* deserves, according to Bowring, a certain preference over the Greek term. For this and other reasons, he thought the phrase "the *Felicity-maximizing* principle will, perhaps, be found the most convenient of all the terms hitherto employed."[57] In his *Constitutional Code*, Bentham once grants that "if . . . instead of the word *happiness*, the word *interest* is employed, the phrase *universal interest* may be employed as corresponding indifferently to the interest of the greatest number, or to the interest of all."[58] In any case, as Bowring tells us, in his later years "dissatisfaction . . . with utilitarian phraseology gradually increased in Bentham's mind," mainly on the ground of "an observation made to Mr. Bentham by Lady Holland. . . . She said that his doctrine of utility put a *veto* upon pleasure; while he had been fancying that pleasure never found so valuable and influential an ally as the principle of utility. It was clear, therefore, that the word 'utility' not only failed in communicating to other minds the ideas which Bentham attached to it, but that to some minds it communicated ideas wholly different and opposed to them. And true it is that unless the Greatest-Happiness Principle be recognized as the end, the doctrine of utility might be represented as useful to some other end."[59] Therefore "the phrase 'greatest happiness of the greatest number' was . . . employed by . . . Bentham"; and as Bowring adds, this was done first in Bentham's "Codification Proposal"[59] in 1822. As a matter of fact, it was already done in 1776, in Bentham's first book, his *Fragment on Government*; I cannot explain how this could escape Bowring's attention.

Even the term "the greatest happiness of the greatest number" was finally given up by Bentham in favor of the term "Felicity maximizing principle." For, the transfer of a certain fund of happiness from a minority to a majority which is only insignificantly larger may bring about a loss of happiness on the whole; therefore, such a transfer cannot be ethically approved of. To do justice to this fact the term "maximization of felicity" may be more appropriate than that of the greatest happiness of the greatest number.[60] But to clear away misinterpretations of all these formulae which only too

[57] *Ibid.*, vol. 1, p. 320 f.   [58] Bentham, *Works*, 1843, vol. 11, p. 6b.
[59] *Ibid.*, vol. 1, pp. 319, 318.   [60] *Ibid.*, vol. 1, pp. 328 ff.

often occur even greater efforts must be made. Making use of preparatory work done by G. E. Moore, Professor A. J. Ayer pointed out: "The principle of utility is simply this. Let us say that the value of an action is positive if the total quantity of pleasure that it causes to all the persons in any way affected by it is greater than the total quantity of pain; and let us say that its value is negative if the total quantity of pain that it causes is greater than the total quantity of pleasure. If it causes an equal amount of pleasure and pain it may be said to have neutral value. Then, in any case, in which the value of an action A exceeds that of another action B, it may be that both are positive but that the margin is greater in the case of A, or that while A's value is positive B's is neutral or negative, or that A's is neutral and B's negative, or that while the value of both is negative the margin is greater in the case of B. In all these cases let us say, for the sake of brevity, that A produces a greater quantity of happiness than B does. Now the principle of utility is that of any two actions which differ in value, by these criteria, the more valuable is to be preferred. In other words, that action is to be chosen which will cause the greater quantity of happiness in the sense defined. And if the amount of happiness that they will respectively cause is equal then there is no reason for choosing one of them rather than the other."[61] These are certainly welcome clarifications of the meaning of the utility principle. Beyond them, I think, it should be stressed that it cannot be the fundamental problem of a critical ethics to decide whether an act is absolutely moral or absolutely neutral or absolutely immoral. The basic problem can only be the question whether one of several possible acts is more moral than the others. And in this direction even more refinements of Bentham's formulae are certainly desirable.

In contrast to the terminology of the *Introduction* Bentham "in after life" spoke of the "ipse-dixit principle" or of "ipse-dixitism" instead of the principle of sympathy and antipathy.[62] But though this new terminology expresses better what Bentham had in mind in his *Introduction*, the matter itself was certainly lucidly enough formulated in the work of his youth.

Of even less consequence is a casual suggestion of the *Deontology* that the term "well-being" be substituted for the term "happiness" because "happiness ... represents pleasure in too elevated a shape" and only few, "perhaps none,"[63] would admit in his progress through life the enjoyment of happiness.

Finally, a distinction is made in the *Deontology* between social and popular or moral sanction and, within the popular, a differentiation between aristocratic and democratic moral sanctions, while within the political or legal

[61] A. J. Ayer, "The Principle of Utility" in *Jeremy Bentham and the Law*, ed. on behalf of the Faculty of Laws of University College, London, by George W. Keeton and Georg Schwarzenberger, 1948, p. 249.
[62] *Ibid.*, vol. I, p. 322 f.   [63] *Ibid.*, vol. I, p. 78.

sanction a distinction is drawn between its judicial and its administrative branch.[64] The *Deontology* complains that "when we have words in our ears we imagine we have thoughts in our minds,"[65] and that "the general imperfection of language is one of the great impediments to the progress of philosophy . . . as all languages had their birth in a period when moral and intellectual cultivation could only be in their infancy"; therefore, the *Deontology* expresses the hope that "a time will come when morality, like chemistry, will create its own fit nomenclature."[66] Without aping the nomenclature of chemistry Bentham has considerably improved ethical terminology. But his most valuable suggestions in this respect are not to be found in his *Deontology*.

Particularly poor are the historical references which are now and then inserted into the systematic inquiries of the *Deontology*. An interest in the history of philosophy is regarded here not only as valueless, but even as pernicious. To "read modern books less and ancient more" is said to be an almost perverse maxim, or one which betrays more snobbery than genuine intellectual interest.[67] The natural consequence of such an attitude was an amazing ignorance of the history of ethics, and often an almost unbelievable crudeness of historical judgment.

Comprehensibly, this applies less to the immediate forerunners of Bentham's utilitarianism. As in earlier writings, David Hume is praised, because "he brought in the light of utility to show what was the motive and the merit of justice," and his reference to a chimeric so-called "sense of virtue" is at least acquitted of being an invention of "uncandid artifice."[68] His list of virtues is criticized with great fairness.[69] Helvétius is lauded again as "the first moralist who turned with steady eye to the utilitarian principle,"[70] Mandeville's "Fable of the Bees" is not ill characterized as utilitarianism "under a cloud."[71] Of Shaftesbury as well as of Beattie and of Price, it is said once more, with reason, that by introducing the concepts of moral sense, common sense and "moral understanding" they all tried to unite in their "own person the characters of Advocate and Judge."[72] The criticism of Locke and Maupertuis too is as justifiable as it is witty. Their theory "that every action has its source in uneasiness, . . . in ill-being"[73] is certainly not supported by Samuel Johnson's everyday life experience and practice.

But it is, beyond any doubt, bizarre and ludicrous to hear from Bentham in the *Deontology* that "Socrates' contempt for riches was mere affectation. . . . It was only denying to himself the doing the good which riches would have enabled him to do." That Epictetus was an avaricious miser paying

[64] *Ibid.*, vol. I, pp. 90 f, 102.   [65] *Ibid.*, vol. I, p. 257.   [66] *Ibid.*, vol. I, p. 132 f.
[67] *Ibid.*, vol. I, p. 280 f.   [68] *Ibid.*, vol. II, pp. 70 ff; cf. vol. I, p. 256 f.
[69] *Ibid.*, vol. I, pp. 227 ff, 246 ff.   [70] *Ibid.*, vol. II, p. 31.
[71] *Ibid.*, vol. II, p. 24; compare vol. I, p. 105.   [72] *Ibid.*, vol. I, pp. 70 ff.
[73] *Ibid.*, vol. I, pp. 81 f, 80.

"himself with the pleasures of imagination" which were "greater to him than those of actual fruition," is another statement of the *Deontology* not much more pertinent than that about Socrates, or that about Christ, who is said to have justified the moral character of suicide by his sacrificial death.[74] Even less does it pay to listen to the monotonous abuses of Plato, which fill many pages.[75] The only point of interest is that Bentham shares this opposition to Plato not only with our contemporaries, Bertrand Russell,[76] R. H. S. Crossman[77] and Karl Popper[78] but also with some of the greatest naturalists of the seventeenth, nineteenth, and twentieth centuries, such as Spinoza, Karl Marx and Sigmund Freud.[79]

The *Deontology* winds up these attacks on earlier moralists by proposing an *index expurgatorius* of all "the books which have bewildered and betrayed mankind"[80] in philosophy and particularly in ethics. If the *Deontology* itself had carried out this suggestion, the result would certainly have been more of a historical curiosity than a guide through the history of ethics.

Ethics of Consequences and Knowledge of the World

Bentham's criticism of all ethics of motives is perhaps harsher in the *Deontology* than anywhere else, though the presentation of his argument has by no means gained by this. Nevertheless here too the essentially epistemological character of his argument is often well brought out. "It is the idlest of idling to be inquiring into that which has no influence, and forgetting that which has all the real influence upon our condition. . . . After all, we have nothing to do with motives . . . it is the act, and not the motive . . . which . . . is before us," but "the motive . . . is . . . concealed from us."[81] "In the character of a judge, nothing can more assist an honest and a useful decision, than the laying bare all actions as they really are, the tracing consequences as they present themselves in overt conduct; avoiding carefully, on the one hand, all attempts to dive into the unfathomable regions of motives which cannot be known; and, on the other, steering clear of that petty, pharisaical vanity which is so fond of exhibiting itself to the great detriment of the exhibitor."[82] "The search after motive is one of the prominent causes

[74] *Ibid.*, vol. 1, pp. 260 f, 80.   [75] *Ibid.*, vol. 1, pp. 39 ff, 281 f.

[76] See B. Russell, e.g. *Philosophy and Politics*, 1947, p. 13; *A History of Western Philosophy*, 1945, p. 113.

[77] See R. H. S. Crossman, *Plato Today*, 1937, e.g. pp. 275, 278, 282 f.

[78] See Karl Popper, *The Open Society and its Enemies*, 1945, vol. 1, pp. 92, 121 ff, 137.

[79] Compare D. Baumgardt "Über den 'verloren geglaubten' Anhang zu Karl Marxens Doktordissertation" in *Gegenwartsprobleme der Soziologie, Alfred Vierkandt zum 80. Geburtstag*, ed. by Gottfried Eisermann, 1949, p. 114.

[80] Bentham, *Deontology*, 1834, vol. 1, p. 281.   [81] *Ibid.*, vol. 11, p. 154.

[82] *Ibid.*, vol. 11, p. 136 f.

of men's bewilderment in the investigation of questions of morals. The search is grounded on a vague notion that in the spring of action, rather than the act itself, the real quantity and quality of vice and virtue might be found but this is a pursuit in which every moment employed is a moment wasted. . . . Those who dread the light which . . . the radiance . . . of . . . the . . . utility . . . standard . . . throws upon human *actions*, are fond of engaging their votaries in the chase of an inaccessible, wandering will-o'-the-wisp, which they call *motive*—an entity buried in inapproachable darkness, and which, if it were approachable and produceable, would be of no value whatever."[83] This certainly sounds like a much too radical undervaluation of the ethical importance of motives, an underestimation based only on the difficulty of finding out the true character of motives.

But the *Deontology* did not forget to provide some qualification to this seemingly wholesale misjudgment of ethical motives. It grants, at least in passing, that beneficence, a beneficial act, is not virtuous "except in so far as accompanied with benevolence,"[84] i.e. accompanied with the motive of benevolence. But even in this connection and in general, Bentham insists that the motive of "benevolence is not a virtue, any farther than, as occasion serves, it is accompanied with beneficence; if when occasion serves, correspondent beneficence is not exercised, it is a proof that the desire was not in reality, present; or that, if present, it was inoperative; it was so faint as to be of no use. . . . Seed sown is no otherwise of any value than for the crops of which it is productive."[84] This primary relevance of the consequences of acts is stressed again and again for various reasons.

"A man's motives affect nobody until they give birth to action; and it is with the action and not with the motive, that individuals or societies have any concern. Hence, in discourse, let all indications of motives be avoided. This will remove one spring of error and false judgment from the mind of the speaker, and from the minds of the hearers one source of misunderstanding. . . . The pretension which indicates the *motives* of others is almost always futile and offensive. For, if their motive be what we suppose it, and the motive be a praiseworthy one, it will be visible by and in the act; and if the motive be a blameworthy, to denounce it will be but a cause of annoyance to him to whom the motive is attributed . . . if bad motives produce good actions so much the better for society; and if good motives produce bad actions, so much the worse."[85]

This argument concerning the disastrous consequences of the finest motives is often graphically presented in the *Deontology*. "Perhaps there never was a group of more conscientious and well-intending men than the early inquisitors; they verily believed they were doing God service; they were under

[83] *Ibid.*, vol. I, p. 125 f.   [84] *Ibid.*, vol. II, p. 259 f.
[85] *Ibid.*, vol. II, pp. 156, 154.

the influence of motives most religious and pious, while they were pouring out blood in rivers, and sacrificing, amidst horrid tortures the wisest and best of their race."[86] "The most horrible of offences, the most devastating and murderous of crimes, if followed up to their origin, will be found only ... the creation of a misery, intending to prevent a greater misery, but mistaking its purpose and miscalculating its means. And of such mistakes and such miscalculations none has been more prolific than the despotism of benevolent intention. ... Despotism never takes a worse shape than when it comes in the guise of benevolence. ... A man fancies he knows what is best for other men ..."; but "pleasures and pains, the sweets and the bitters of existence, cannot be tried by the taste of another. What is good for another cannot be estimated by the person intending to do the good, but by the person only to whom it is intended to be done. The purpose of another may be to increase my happiness, but of that happiness I alone am the keeper and the judge. ... A belief, an honest belief, that they are under the real influences of benevolence, sometimes leads men to conduct the most intrusive and tyrannical. ... Under the shadow of this fallacy, vast masses of misery have been poured out upon the world, and that with the most benevolent intention."[87] Not what seems to be a good motive in the eyes of an agent can make an act morally valuable, but only what the "victims" of this act can ultimately acknowledge as the beneficial consequence of that act.

As a supplementary reflection to this argument the *Deontology* repeats that in itself no motive is bad, since it secures at least something good, some gratification to the agent; and if it were unable to do this, it would have been unable to induce him to act. "Motive, indeed! As if all motives were not the same—to obtain for the actor some recompense for his act, in the shape of pain averted, or pleasure secured. The motive, as far as that goes, of the vilest is the same as the motive of the noblest, to increase his stock of happiness. The man who murders, the man who robs another, believes that the murder and the robbery will be advantageous to him—will leave to him more happiness than if he had not committed the crime. In the field of *motive*, however, he may make out a case as recommendatory of his conduct, as if he were the most accomplished of moralists."[88] "All motives are abstractedly good; no man has, ever had, can, or could have, a motive different from the pursuit of pleasure or the shunning of pain. ... But be the motives what they may ... it is not on them that the moralist is called to deliver his award. He has to do with conduct—with conduct, when its consequences invade the regions of suffering and enjoyment. He is but a despotic intruder elsewhere."[89] "In so far as the inflicter is concerned, no doubt the infliction of evil is good, for no action can have its source in any other motive. However

---

[86] *Ibid.*, vol. II, p. 154 f.
[88] *Ibid.*, vol. II, p. 155.

[87] *Ibid.*, vol. II, pp. 291, 289, 288.
[89] *Ibid.*, vol. I, p. 126.

enormous the evil may be, and however trifling the pleasure of inflicting it, still that pleasure is good, and must be taken into account."[90] "As to evil without good, that is impossible. . . . The least possible good is . . . that of a gratification to your own ill-will."[91] Archibald Prentice reported a talk he once had with Bentham in which Bentham allegedly confessed to him that he could "not understand how any man could have pleasure in giving pain to others."[92] That Bentham in his *Introduction* and repeatedly in his *Deontology* took exactly the opposite view, shows again with how much reserve the numerous reports about Bentham's naïveté have to be taken.

In the *Deontology* also Bentham gives at least a few of the reasons why throughout the ages the ethics of motives has received so much preference to the ethics of consequences. "Claims to purity, accusations against impurity of motive are dragged about in eternal processions, to excuse, to justify, to laud, to reprove, . . . to condemn. The whole field of action is covered with pretensions on this score indefatigably put forward, constantly appealed to, and seldom grounded on anything better than the usurpation of the motive-denouncer. Why is a habit so baneful to the general well-being so constantly persisted in? In the first place, it is so flattering to the self-regarding affections; it enables the speaker or the writer to set up his own standard of right and wrong; it saves him from the laborious necessity of tracing the consequences of actions; it enables him to take the opinions of others into a region—the region of another man's mind—where those opinions find no light to guide, and men are but too willing from mere love of ease, to allow the usurper to set up his throne of judgment. If a man is to determine as to the value of an action by its consequences, he must study those consequences; he must present them to those whose approval or condemnation of the action he desires to obtain; he exposes himself to contradiction if he misrepresents, to correction if he voluntarily or involuntarily errs. The blanks he leaves may be filled up, the exaggerations he introduces may be cut down; he is, in a word, forced to come into court with his witnesses, and to establish his case by the evidence he can adduce. But if, on the contrary, he can, by his own dictum, proclaim that for the action there was a bad motive or a good motive in the mind of the actor, the judgment is an easy process; its decrees are not complicated by a variety of entanglements. Good and evil present themselves at once, and thus rashness and self-conceit perform functions which belong to reason and philosophy."[93] In the ethical judgment of motives and consequences of acts "two elements become frequently the principal guides: self-presumption and blind deference, qualities which seem somewhat incompatible, indeed; but which unite in mischievous influence;

[90] *Ibid.*, vol. II, p. 279.   [91] *Ibid.*, vol. II, p. 202 f.
[92] Archibald Prentice, *Historical Sketches and Personal Recollections of Manchester*, 1851, p. 384.
[93] Bentham, *Deontology*, 1834, vol. II, p. 44 f.

the deference being, in fact, submission to that species of authority which flatters the self-regarding principle."[94] Thus at least three factors figure here as the reasons for the popularity of the ethics of motives over that of consequences: the vain haste to play the role of the moral judge, the eager acquiescence in the ruling moral standards of one's group, and the love of ease which abhors the difficult scrutiny into the objective effects of human acts.

Like the *Introduction* and the *Table of Springs of Action*, the *Deontology* warns against the use of eulogistic or dyslogistic terminology preceding ethical analysis. For such biased "phrases . . . act upon the mind as stained glasses act upon the visual sense," and the object contemplated assumes a coloring which is not its own; therefore to separate the ethical judgment from the employ of all uncritical "laudatory or condemnatory language" is here rightly called one of the "most important triumphs of mental discipline."[95] "Happiness wherever it is, and by whom ever experienced is the great gift confided" to mankind's "charge . . . this alone—is the pearl of great price."[96] Kant, in his "critical" foundation of ethics, used exactly the same metaphor.[97] But he used it in the opposite sense, concerning the motives and not the consequences of acts. Yet to conclude from this, like most moralists, that Bentham's use of this metaphor has a far less critical basis than that of Kant seems to me entirely unjustifiable even in terms of the text of the *Deontology*. Granting that Kant is far more in harmony with common ethical language (and with the prejudices of common language), granted that the appeal to motives is in common practice held to be of far greater educational value than Bentham's reference to the consequences of acts—neither the maintenance of linguistic nor that of educational conveniences can claim to be a prerequisite for the critical epistemological clarification of ethical fundamentals.

The ethics of motives in its different presentations has generally made, and is able to make, ample allowance for ignorance in matters of worldly as well as theological knowledge. The innocent country girl, "der reine Tumbe," the "guileless fool" the simple, inexperienced mind, the ordinary folk have often been explicitly proclaimed to be the ideal of the moral man.

[94] *Ibid.*, vol. II, p. 47.
[95] *Ibid.*, vol. II, p. 145. Cf. vol. II, p. 283 and p. 194, a terminology similar to that of the "Table."
[96] *Ibid.*, vol. II, p. 272.
[97] See I. Kant, *Grundlegung zur Metaphysik der Sitten*, 1785, §3, translated by J. W. Scott in *Kant on the Moral Life*, 1924, p. 44: "Even if . . . a good will . . . should . . . achieve nothing . . . like a jewel it would still shine by its own light as a thing which has its whole value in itself."

Sharing the age-old belief in the existence of simple, elementary natural laws in morals, Kant emphatically assures us that even "der gemeinste Verstand," the "plainest man," completely "inexperienced in understanding the course of the world"[98] knows in all possible cases very well what is good and what is evil. As recent a thinker as Benedetto Croce, despite some major qualifications, wishes to come to the rescue of the "ideale morale dell' innocenza e de l'inesperienza." He praises the moral importance of that "prima e piú vera visione che fu aperta alla nostra mente" and he extolls in men of genius "questa sublime puerilità . . . questa ottusità che era come la garanzia della loro sensibilità . . . questa debolezza che andava a pieno beneficio della loro forza principale."[99] But Croce admits that the dialectic opposites of innocence and "candidezza," namely, "malizia" and "prudenza" are also of great positive relevance in morals[99] and he grants that the days when innocence was a principal moral ideal have gone.[100] Perhaps even more than in his earlier writings Bentham tried to leave no doubt in his *Deontology* that the old romantic or idealistic praise of innocence and inexperience cannot stand trial by the critical method of a realistic ethics.

Like C. L. Stevenson's emotive ethics,[101] Bentham's utilitarianism insists that knowledge of the world and knowledge of men are an indispensable prerequisite to truly moral decisions. Not only the insight of the psychologist, but also "the experience of the medical adviser, the lessons of the economist, may indeed take place of the counsels of morality."[102] "Fiat experientia, . . . Experimentalize! . . . was the axiom of Bacon . . . Fiat observatio . . . observe! . . . is Bentham's apophthegm."[103] "Vain is the attempt to teach morals by declamation, or to build theories

---

[98] See I. Kant, *The Fundamental Principles of the Metaphysics of Ethics*, translated by Otto Manthy-Zorn, 1938, p. 19, about the end of section 1: "Inexperienced in understanding the course of the world, incapable of being prepared for all that happens in it, I (i.e. the 'plainest man') merely ask myself: Can you will that your maxim becomes a universal law? If not, then it is unsound; and indeed not because of a disadvantage arising from it for you and others." Compare Kant, *Grundlegung zur Metaphysik der Sitten*, ed. Theodor Fritzsch (Reclam), S. 18, 34, 33, 25.

[99] B. Croce, "Frammenti di etica" in *Saggi filosofici*, vol. VI, 1945, p. 146.

[100] *Ibid.*, p. 143.

[101] Charles L. Stevenson, *Ethics and Language*, 1944, e.g. p. 134: "Moral questions may lead one to all fields of inquiry"; pp. 332, 329: "What knowledge is there, indeed, that has *not* a potential bearing on evaluation?" Compare p. 11 f.

[102] Bentham, *Deontology*, 1834, vol. II, p. 85. "Take place of" is, according to *A New English Dictionary*, Oxford, vol. VII, 1909, p. 928b, an archaic phrase meaning "to go before."

[103] *Ibid.*, vol. I, pp. 4, 316.

... opposed ... to ... facts. ..."[104] They who discourse ... on the supposition that man will act in opposition to acknowledged interests, make morality a fable, and law a romance"; any system of morals which "proposes to a man a line of conduct as necessary to be maintained which is not maintainable," any moral idealization which "affects to accomplish what is not accomplishable ... is false and hollow"; it can never be a trustworthy guide through the "ethical labyrinth in which prejudice or interest stronger than prejudice" usually involves man. "The times of the grossest depravity have always been those of the darkest ignorance, and never were examples of enormous and devastating vice more abundant, than in the days when outrageous and useless sacrifices of happiness were most sedulously preached, and most scrupulously practised."[104] "As well were it to preach to wood or to stone" as to an imaginary ideal nature of man, "to motives which cannot be brought into action";[105] but, as Bentham says in a similar context, man generally in "stretching his hand out to catch" ideal "stars ... forgets the flowers at his feet, so beautiful, so fragrant, so various."[106] Man ought, however, to learn that he cannot "choose his position in the world."[107] In morals too he has to accept the place in the universe in which he finds himself and to learn from facts.

Man has to study first which sources of pleasure are "put into his hand" and from which pleasures or ideals he is excluded; and he has then to study the nature of other men; no flattering or distorted portrait will do; were men "still worse, it could not but be useful to study them honestly."[108] To such an unbiased inquiry into human emotions also the *Deontology* tries to contribute by a noticeable number of sound psychological observations.

It may suffice to mention only a few of these aperçus. "Bending, ... cringing or fawning to his superior, the same man is stiff, and even insolent to his inferior. It is an everyday case and a very natural one; for the suffering to which he subjects himself in the one case, he seeks to counterbalance by enjoyments of the same character in the other."[109] "Inattention may create an intenser pain than hatred."[110] "Of all that is pernicious in admiration, the admiration of heroes is the most pernicious and how delusion should have made us admire what virtue should teach us to hate ..., is among the saddest evidences of human weakness and folly. The crimes of heroes seem lost in the vastness of

[104] *Ibid.*, vol. II, pp. 73 ff.　[105] *Ibid.*, vol. II, p. 79.　[106] *Ibid.*, vol. II, p. 52.
[107] *Ibid.*, vol. II, p. 50.　[108] *Ibid.*, vol. II, pp. 50, 73.　[109] *Ibid.*, vol. I, p. 210.
[110] *Ibid.*, vol. II, p. 202.

the field they occupy."[111] "Lying . . . invariably does harm to the liar himself."[112] "Between the intellectual faculties and virtue and vice there exists an intimate relation."[113] Do not refer to "irremediable infirmities . . . and corporeal defects. . . . Derision of organic defects is one of the most cruel forms of pain-giving."[114] The "herd of moralists" thought of sexual desire as does "the surgeon who, in order to cure a pimple, should amputate a limb."[115] "Deal out such liberal encouragement as the case will justify, . . . but . . . if flattery exceed the bounds of truth . . . you may become to . . . the flattered person . . . an object of contempt and dislike."[116] "Excite no expectation that is likely to be disappointed. . . . Your exaggeration of your own ability to serve will . . . lead to diminished affection towards you when that exaggeration is made manifest by the failure of your attempts to serve. Your self-love will leave more vexation from its detected helplessness than gratification from its anticipated influence."[117] "Masks there are which . . . deceive even their wearers."[118] The definitions of envy, jealousy and of liberty (*libera necessitas*) as well as the ethical valuation of anger[119] come particularly near to Spinoza's naturalistic views. But while Spinoza, since the days of Herder and Goethe, has conquered his place among the most venerable sages of naturalism, even learned historians of philosophy are generally not willing to grant Bentham any similar honor.

Bentham's belief that there is "no voice of . . . benevolence, without an echo . . . and that love is the source of love"[120] is hardly naturalistic enough; it is obviously more of an optimistic hope than an observable fact. Nevertheless the whole of Bentham's psychology and ethics can scarcely be accused of indulging in naive, optimistic rationalization of facts.

In the *Deontology*, again, non-conscious, non-rational impulses are taken into consideration to a large extent. It is, according to Bentham, by no means "necessary that a man should be conscious of the existence of the inducement" which impels him to, or prevents him from, an action; "Balaam was stopped by the power of an angel that was invisible to him."[121] Interest commonly "does not attack men's integrity in front but undermines it. . . . It . . . acts in an . . . insensible and

---

[111] *Ibid.*, vol. II, p. 254. [112] *Ibid.*, vol. I, p. 240. [113] *Ibid.*, vol. I, p. 271.
[114] *Ibid.*, vol. II, pp. 227 f, 246. Compare *ibid.*, p. 43. [115] *Ibid.*, vol. II, p. 88 f.
[116] *Ibid.*, vol. II, p. 276. [117] *Ibid.*, vol. II, p. 251. [118] *Ibid.*, vol. II, p. 277.
[119] *Ibid.*, vol. I, p. 221 f; vol. II, p. 97; vol. I, p. 265.
[120] *Ibid.*, vol. I, p. 181 f; vol. II, p. 41. Cf. vol. II, p. 217.
[121] *Ibid.*, vol. I, p. 88.

covert manner. . . . Arguments against the proscribed opinion . . . are thought much of; . . . those in favor of it . . . are received askance, and hustled as it were out of the mind without a hearing."[122] Also the impossibility of repressing dissatisfactions completely by force is recognized: "Enough will not be done by the mere attempt at forcing an annoying thought to vacate the mind; it will infallibly be supplanted by another thought, and the balance of happiness will be between the efforts of the thought which enters and that which makes its exit. . . . Like flakes of snow that fall unperceived upon the earth, the seemingly unimportant events of life succeed one another. As the snow gathers together, so are our habits formed. No single flake that is added to the pile produces a sensible change; no single action creates, however it may exhibit, a man's character; but, as the tempest hurls the avalanche down the mountain, and overwhelms the inhabitant and his habitation, so passion, acting upon the elements of mischief, which pernicious habits have brought together by imperceptible accumulation, may overthrow the edifice of truth and virtue."[123] Observations of this kind are certainly not symptomatic of a blindly rationalistic psychology.

In the whole field of the psychology of the intellect, of will and action, in his interpretation of the mentality of statesmen and jurists, Bentham revealed a penetrating insight into the subtleties of the human mind and gave full tribute to the weight of non-rational impetus. At least one love-letter we possess discloses that passionate, tender personal feelings were not alien to him in his youth.[124] But, as the *Deontology* strongly indicates, his understanding of artistic, poetical, symbolic language and feeling was astonishingly limited. In the *Deontology*, for instance—completely deaf and insensitive to the power of symbolic, aesthetic expression of melodies and colors—he asks if "to you such and such an assemblage of sounds is harmonious and attractive, to another they seem discordant, or they afford no gratification, what mischief results to you, or to mankind, from that difference of opinion?"[125] The meaning of the great religious myth of the lost paradise and all its world-wide symbolic background, is most prosaically explained away by Bentham by the rather silly "ethical" advice that "when the fatal apple was presented to Eve," Eve ought to "have turned her back upon it, or have made a present of it to the first frugivorous quadruped that

[122] *Ibid.*, vol. II, p. 139.   [123] *Ibid.*, vol. II, p. 110; vol. I, p. 269 f.
[124] Bentham, *Works*, 1843, vol. X, p. 277.
[125] Bentham, *Deontology*, 1834, vol. II, p. 215; compare *ibid.*, vol. I, p. 185.

crossed her path."[126] With such blind spots and one-sidedness did the great ethical scientist pay for the many illuminating discoveries he made in ethical methodology; and in these defects of his psychological and ethical understanding, no one should take him as an example. On these points his teaching concerning the nature of pleasure certainly remains inadequate, as on other points it stands in need of essential supplementation.

[126] *Ibid.*, vol. ii, p. 110.

EPILOGUE

Is Benthamism "Bankrupt"?

EPILOGUE

Is Benthamism "Bankrupt"?

========

NOTHING has harmed the study of Bentham's ethics more than the customary patronizing smile at this great moralist's "primitiveness" and alleged superficiality. The childlike simplicity, the cheap radicalism, the lack of educational value and the utopian rationalism of his ethical teaching have been taken for granted to such an extent that during the past four decades no need was felt for any careful re-examination of these pretended deficiencies. F. H. Bradley thought Benthamism a "bankrupt" theory; and Sir W. D. Ross feels sure that hedonism "has . . . not . . . much vitality to-day"; it is, in his view, a "dead or dying horse."[1] Although, as a competent judge in matters of vitality, Oxford philosophy enjoys less authority than in any other respect, no one has so far seriously questioned the validity of Bradley's or Sir David's verdict on Bentham.

Supported by the master's most distinguished student, John Stuart Mill, the common feeling of superiority toward Bentham has deprived us of any detailed analysis of Bentham's theory of morals. During the last century exactly that happened which Bentham's ethics had to fear most: while his political thought and the general influence of his school were discussed at great length, the subtleties of his theory of morals remained unknown. The publication of a few of his London manuscripts has only now begun; and much of his finest ethical thought has remained buried under the very eyes of moralists in the midst of his juristic writings (twenty-two parts of his collected works), in his books edited by Dumont and his anonymously published pamphlets.

It is mainly for this reason that in the present work I have let Bentham speak for himself in a large measure and have given the exact texts of his arguments which have hitherto been hidden in numerous

----

[1] See F. H. Bradley, *Ethical Studies*, 1876, p. 113; W. D. Ross, *The Foundations of Ethics*, 1939, p. 65. Though Bradley and Ross usually speak of hedonism in general, their criticism is certainly meant to include Bentham primarily. Nor is the article, which the London *Times Literary Supplement* dedicated to the 200th anniversary of Bentham's birth, free from this understood superiority feeling over the philosopher Bentham, see *ibid.*, "Bentham Commemorated," issue of February 21, 1948, pp. 101 f.

widely scattered sources, many of them by no means easily accessible. I believe the time has come for contemporary moralists to cease attacking the self-created phantom of a naïve, uncritical visionary or a "boyish" and—senile Bentham.

I do not think that the moral philosophy we need today will be an uncritical adoption of Bentham's theory as it stands. This is precluded by the shortcomings of his psychology, by his extremely narrow religious and metaphysical views and even by many details of his ethical argument itself. My own ethics, at any rate, differs very widely from Bentham's on all these points.

Needless to say that it is only of historical interest to see how far Bentham cherished the naïve hope that altruism is identical with enlightened self-interest, i.e. that there is a complete coincidence among all the different interests of men. He nourished these views to a lesser degree than many of his contemporaries and he explicitly admitted the ethical value of self-sacrifice in certain cases of moral conflicts. But such views in no way form the heart of his ethical theory. Contrary to the general opinion of Bentham's critics, his moral philosophy by no means stands or falls with the acceptance or rejection of these or similar beliefs.

The core of Bentham's ethical theory is his detailed analysis of the different elements of ethical judgment; it is his critical, "censorial" method in ethics; it is the hitherto unappreciated and even unknown extent of his critical approach to the ethical judgment in general. This "censorial" method of Bentham seems to me superior to that of all of our best-known theories of values and to other highly reputable examples of conservative thinking among contemporary moralists.

When I planned to write the second volume of my history of ethics, I shared the common prejudice against the moral philosophy of Bentham and thought that a brief chapter on his utilitarianism could do full justice to the simplicity of his ethical thought, which had already been so generally criticized and seemed so completely inadequate for coping with any of the subtle methodological problems of modern or ancient moral doctrines. After having turned to the sources themselves I felt obliged to write a large volume, instead of the planned chapter. In a time which, in its practice, certainly does very little honor to the "time-honoured" teachings of our ruling ethical schools, it seems to me ill-advised to dismiss Bentham's ethics offhand with the common labels of heretical thought: ethical naturalism, subjectivism, and relativism.

Ethical Relativism, Skepticism and Absolutism

Bentham avoids, with equal consistency, the two principal dangers which ethical methodology has to face: on the one hand the Scylla of ethnological relativism including the "scepsis" of logical positivism and the semi-skepticism of "emotive ethics"; on the other hand the Charybdis of apriorism and modern value absolutism. Especially in his essay "De l'influence des temps et des lieux en matière de législation," Bentham does full justice to the relativity of moral customs and concrete ethical rules; but contrary to common anthropological teaching he denies that these varying moral rules cannot be overruled by one universal ethical principle.

Unlike Lévy-Bruhl or Carnap, he justly recognizes that "une science des moeurs," or a so-called "psychological ethics," cannot be a substitute for ethics. In fact, Lévy-Bruhl's moral science or Carnap's "psychological ethics" is either completely identical with ethnology or psychology, or it is as meaningless a science as psychological physics or ethnological chemistry would be. Bentham wished to teach relativity, but not relativism; scientific ethics, but not science as a substitute for ethics. And unlike emotive ethics he did not think that, by assigning merely the meaning of emotive approval to the principal concepts of ethics, he could save moral thought from subjectivism.

Yet, if anthropological and psychological and emotive theories of morals are too skeptical an ethical teaching, Kantian apriorism and modern value absolutism prove far too rigid. Neither Kant's categorical imperative, nor the multitude of absolute duties and intrinsic values of contemporary ethical schools in England, Germany or France, allow any satisfactory application to ethical reality.[2] All these theories, speaking so much of absolute validity, either remain in their lofty separation from concrete life and cannot say anything of the concrete conflicts of ethical reality or, if they try to do so, lead to the same relativistic chaos of conflicting absolutes, to the same want of a superior, valid ethical criterion which is felt in the relativism of the ethnological school in ethics.

In other words, we may agree, on this point, with Ortega y Gasset: "Esto es precisamente lo que no puede ser: ni el absolutismo racionalista —que salva la razón y nulifica la vida—ni el relativismo, que salva la

[2] As to a detailed criticism of ethical absolutism see D. Baumgardt, *Der Kampf um den Lebenssinn unter den Vorläufern der modernen Ethik*, 1933, Teil I, pp. 3-193.

vida evaporando la razón."[3] Only a universal principle, combined with the careful analysis of human desires and moral customs, can form a proper basis for ethical judgment; and this principle should not be a dogmatic statement but "merely" a hypothetical one—a hypothesis, however, that permits the most coherent and consistent interpretation and evaluation of all the phenomena concerned.

Wolf and Shepherd Morality

While ethical relativism and skepticism at least keep themselves aloof from dogmatic valuations, conservative "time-honoured" ethics gravely exposes itself on this point. In comparison with Bentham's critical method, all the conservative theories of morals, which presently dominate the field, are as dogmatic and uncritical as is Nietzsche's or Machiavelli's or modern fascist ethics.

For propaganda purposes, or for ethical edification, it may be deemed satisfactory to preach democratic or fascist ethics, Judaeo-Christian or "master" morality without comment or justification. As yet it is certainly the rule in every-day life that each of these two ethical parties thinks its axioms self-evident, though the axioms of the two parties completely contradict each other. But, as regards philosophical theories of morals, I think the time has passed when an ethicist can be allowed to assert dictatorially that Judaeo-Christian, Hindu, Buddhist or democratic morals are obviously "slave" morality. And the time is also over when a philosopher is entitled to sit in his armchair and smile at the "fanatics" or "neurotics" who take the "gentle" or the "tough" Nietzsche, or both Nietzsches, seriously. In philosophic ethics, I believe, it will no longer do to revolt in righteous indignation against the barbarians who dare to question the unambiguous and self-evident validity of democratic morals, and the morality of the leading world religions. Nor will it do to exclude Machiavellianism from the discussion, simply on the ground of one's own self-assured social equilibrium and progressive liberalism.

From all the dogmatic systems of morals—from the simple adoption of a "Wolf's Bible," as well as from that of a "Shepherd's Bible"[4] Bentham kept critically away. This position of his is, I think, far more clearly in the tradition of the historically most honored types of ethical discussion than the still fashionable neglect of these questions in our

---

[3] José Ortega y Gasset, *El tema de nuestro tiempo*, 1938, p. 37.
[4] See Bentham, *Defence of Economy against the late Mr. Burke*, 1817, p. 28.

best-known contemporary ethical schools. Plato, in his *Gorgias* and his "Thrasymachos," would hardly have devoted so much energy to refuting the "master" morality if this teaching had been to him only a laughing-stock or some cheap demagogy without any major philosophical relevance.

On the whole, we are today justly inclined to believe that Plato did not take his adversaries (or at least the leading sophists of his day) seriously enough. Modern Platonists seem to me to have so much the less reason for underrating the philosophic relevance of a consistent morality of sheer power. Even Plato in his *Gorgias* could finally defeat the morality of force only by taking refuge in a myth, a myth which to us can serve no longer as a philosophical argument. All the more should modern admirers of Plato hesitate, before they shrug aside this great problem. If one does not wish to accept Bentham's answer to the "master" morality questions, at least one should take some advice from Plato or Bentham and admit that the defense of "herd" morality is a genuine philosophical problem. In fact, in comparison with the age-old world struggle between "master" and "slave" morality, even the most cherished feuds of "time-honoured" philosophical ethics are only insignificant family tiffs.

Foundations and Superstructure of Ethical Systems

Bentham was far more aware of the ethical weight of the problem of Machiavellianism than all the critics he has hitherto had to face. He clearly saw that even the most complicated superstructure of ethical reasoning, built up by believers in *prima facie* duties or in evident values, cannot make up for the epistemological weakness and the provincial self-righteousness of their basic ethical presuppositions. In their subtle fight to decide whether the morality of the Victorian age should be crowned by an ethical doctrine of the right, or of the good, or of "the righter and the better," the most distinguished moralists of the Western democracies have entirely overlooked the fact that Bentham's utilitarianism is more than merely one of the many philosophical defenses of Victorian or pre-Victorian goodness or rightness.

Contrary to these conventional types of ethics, Bentham's consistent hedonism does not take its stand on the level of the old rivalries between dogmatic teleological and dogmatic deontological, formalistic ethics. Innumerable valueless triumphs have been won over this chimera of pseudo-Benthamism. But the writings of Bentham himself reveal that

525

he labored critically on a level far more fundamental than the shaky, dogmatic foundations adopted by conventional ethics. He tried to lay the ground for critical reflection on ethics in general, and did not naïvely presuppose that his concrete ethical beliefs were already secured beyond any possibility of questioning.

Contemporary hedonism, however, is, in its foundations and its total structure, perhaps even weaker than dogmatic anti-utilitarianism. For in its best representatives, anti-hedonism tries at least to compensate for the frailty of its fundamentals by the subtlety of inferences drawn from these fundamentals. Contemporary utilitarianism, however, such as that of Durant Drake and James Mackaye, betrays a complete inferiority to the teaching of Bentham by adopting presuppositions as dogmatic as those of his opponents, by its lack of any critical theory of moral motives and by its total neglect of the problems of power-morality.

Durant Drake, *Problems of Conduct*, 1935, p. 76, dismisses, for instance, any critical analysis of the moral evaluation of love by the dogmatic assertion: "To call love good is not to give an opinion, it is to describe a fact." In fact, the term love expresses a definite evaluation of and opinion about that motive —opinion which presupposes a whole system of other more fundamental moral axioms. It is a matter of highly controversial opinion whether this or that motive deserves to be praised as love or to be blamed as moral weakness, whether it is to be condemned as fanaticism or whether, in certain cases, patriotic hatred is to be thought better than love. The basis of Bentham's critical hedonism—that this or that experience of a person pleases that person—is a truly factual statement, whose correctness must and can be determined only by reference to facts; if necessary, the facts of the person's total behavior. But the proper use of the term "love" presupposes an *opinion* on a certain motive, in Drake's case a favorable evaluation which must be the end but can never be the beginning of an ethical analysis of this motive.

Drake also discards, e.g. *ibid.*, pp. 162, 177, the morality of power, the "wolf's Bible," as the doctrine of mere "cranks" and "unbalanced iconoclasts." Such abuses, however, must naturally become less convincing every day, as power politics becomes steadily more outspoken in an age of global power conflicts. And power politics is certainly entitled to retaliate by the use of other abusive epithets such as hypocrisy, slave morality, herd morality, morality of acquiescence, of decadence or of reaction. But none of these fundamental disputes can be settled on the level of such essentially emotional reactions.

While Drake's dogmatic presentation of utilitarianism nowhere refers to Bentham, James Mackaye's *Logic of Conduct*, 1924, p. 265, is strangely satisfied with rejecting Bentham's critical hedonism because it rests on a merely "convictional foundation." Evidently, Mackaye thinks a sufficient basis for criticizing Bentham is that Bentham allegedly did nothing but "approve of ... the code of utility" in the first chapter of the *Introduction to the Principles of Morals and Legislation*. Mackaye, however, does no more than assure us that the code of utility is, on the strength of simple evidence, the "code of maximum ultimate interest to mankind" and therefore sufficiently justified as *the* moral code, see *ibid.*, e.g. pp. 468, 265. Aside from this, the moral appellations of motives appear no less dogmatically prefixed in the thought of Mackaye than in that of Drake. Mackaye, too, obviously sees no difficulty in calling "all or almost all ... selfish motives ... bad" and unselfish ones good, see *ibid.*, e.g. p. 331 and even p. 344 ff. Nowhere does he take into account the fundamental possibility of giving the same motive contrary moral names, either eulogistic or dyslogistic ones, according to different underlying principles of moral evaluation.

The Ethics of the Plain Man

If the only task of the moralist can be, and should be, the description of what the plain man thinks to be moral then, it is true, Bentham's utilitarianism is the most inappropriate theory which could be offered. If there is anything to which all plain men of different ages and societies will agree, it is that they do not conceive of morality in terms of happiness.

They all refuse to identify moral behavior, *per definitionem*, with the production of happiness. They refuse to commit this "naturalistic fallacy"; and up to this point they are even in agreement with Bentham. The point on which all plain men contradict Bentham is his thesis that the maximizing of happiness is the proper criterion of morality.

If, therefore, the epistemological dogmatism of the plain man were the only proper basis for ethical argument, then it would be indeed "an easy game"[5] to expose the alleged fallacies of Bentham's hedonism. But that the epistemological wisdom of the plain man is sacrosanct in ethics represents such a misleading "conventional fallacy" that even the most elaborate criticism of Benthamism built up on this uncertain ground is valueless.

For the plain man, and the most sophisticated interpreters of his morals, live in an atmosphere of completely *false security* in believing that the different *prima facie* duties and values of their different environments are universally valid and even "more evident" than the axioms of geometry. It may be true that the plain man thinks e.g. an "in-

[5] See, e.g. W. D. Ross, *The Foundations of Ethics*, 1939, pp. 65, 308, 316.

tense malevolence" always worse than a "tepid" malevolence. But is this belief of the plain man a self-evident axiom? The New Testament certainly does not share this opinion of Sir David Ross;[6] for it prefers the wicked to the tepid.

By starting with completely unwarranted axioms, the plain man's ethics must, of necessity, end in relativism of judgment, and not only in that relativity which Bentham teaches.[7] The ethics of the plain man, in different times and communities, must end in real subjectivism of judgment, while the subjective feelings on which Bentham's hedonism is based are neutral, objective, and not arbitrarily changeable facts.

From the point of view of all plain men, the rejection of Bentham's hedonism stands as much to reason and is as natural as their rejection of the concepts of modern chemistry, of physics, and astronomy. What a plain man still means by salt is not a compound of Na and Cl, but the "indefinable" quality salt. What he means by traveling is that he passes towns and villages in his car, not the "absurd, sophisticated" teaching that perhaps towns and villages pass by while his car remains unmoved. What he means by a sunset is that the sun sets, not that the earth moves and we on its surface temporarily lose sight of the sun during our movement. If these plausible ideas of the plain man are deemed the ultimate standard of truth, then Aristotelian physics, medieval alchemy, Ptolemaic astronomy are certainly far "superior" to later scientific theories in these fields.

As does the conscience of the common man so do alchemy, Aristotelian physics, anti-Copernican astronomy, and anti-Benthamism set out confidently, with an evident insight into the true "essence" of a great number of "indefinable" qualities, complicated relations between celestial bodies, chemical elements, *prima facie* duties or absolute values. But in the end, in the concrete cases of reality, all such evident insight into the "good in itself," the "good through and through," the indefinable absolute rightness, and the intrinsic values melts down to something distressingly unrevealing; or, as the most mature anti-hedonistic teaching admits, this evident knowledge of ethical principles turns out to be "highly fallible," if applied to ethical particulars.[8] Moreover, even the

[6] See W. D. Ross, *The Foundations of Ethics*, 1939, pp. 320, 324.

[7] As regards the cardinal difference between an ethics of relativity and ethical relativism, between subjective experiences and a subjectivism of judgment, i.e. a judgment without any objective validity, see the valuable discussion of these concepts in H. Lanz, *In Quest of Morals*, 1941, pp. 87 ff.

[8] See W. D. Ross, *The Foundations of Ethics*, 1939, pp. 321, 316; W. D. Ross, *The Right and the Good*, 1930, p. 42.

principal "infallible" insights in all these branches of knowledge must, to every critical mind, finally appear as a mere agreement in words, and not an agreement with regard to real issues.

The same movement of the sun over the sky seems, on the same day, at one point of the unmoved, flat earth, an evident movement of many more hours than at another point of the same flat planet. The common evident characteristics of gold, immediately given, apply to shiny brass as well as to gold. The plain believer in a purely "natural" ethics of egoism and force can rely on an immediate ethical insight with as much right as the plain believer in the contradictory ethics of unselfishness and absolute love. The defender of Christian values may disparage the virtues of vitality and force a thousand times, as private and public vices; as far as immediate ethical insight is concerned, he is no better off than those who equate virtue with sheer power. The fascist, too, possesses immediate insight into a whole system of absolute values and *prima facie* obligations, all of which are completely contradictory to those of the Christian pacifist. Both are able to believe with equal honesty in the universal validity of their contradictory experiences. Bentham avoided this uncritical generalization of alleged evident insight in ethics.

The Hypothetical Character of the Utility Principle

It is true that anti-hedonism, even in its most subtle types, keeps nearer the language of the plain man than Benthamism. But so long as, even in our Western civilization, pacifism, for instance, is considered by the Quaker as a high virtue, and by the fascist as evidence of a morally most detestable degeneration, there seems to me no reason for thinking slightingly of Bentham's ethics. For Bentham tries to bridge over these far too much ignored contradictions between the "evident insights" of different plain men or geniuses of opposite strain.

This bridging of opposite ethical beliefs is not to be regarded as just another dogmatic teaching, but should be taken—as Bentham presented it in his most mature, and hitherto unpublished statement—as a critical "hypothesis" in ethics. The utility principle must be considered a hypothetical supposition, whose value as a neutral ethical criterion has been elucidated in detail by Bentham, particularly by a minute analysis of the ethical relevance of the different elements of acts and of ethical judgment.

If, according to Bentham's best advice, the hypothetical character of the utility principle is duly taken into account, full justice can be done to one of Henry Sidgwick's most important remarks on hedonistic empiricism. As Sidgwick rightly saw, such a principle as that of maximizing felicity cannot pass as an insight won by purely empirical observation and induction. The fundamental principle of empirical hedonism can by no means be empirically given; it has to be intuitively presupposed as merely hypothetical truth. However, the preferableness of the utility principle to other hypothetical tenets can be demonstrated, if it can be critically shown that the hypothetical utility principle is less capricious and gives a more coherent explanation of ethical phenomena than its rivals.

The present work on Bentham tries, for the first time, to judge Bentham's hedonism from this "censorial" epistemological standpoint—a point of view whose consideration he so often, but vainly, recommended to his followers as well as to his opponents.

Oversimplification and Overcomplication in Ethics

Of the numerous charges brought against Bentham's general methodology, a good many contradict each other and each of these contradictory statements seems to me to miss the mark. Bentham has been accused of oversimplification as well as over-complication even by half-utilitarians.

Many attempts have been made to supplement the "oversimplifying monism" of the utility principle by the principles of moral fitness or rightness, or by a multitude of value principles. As I have tried to show in detail, on several occasions, modern ethicists have been too eager to put their faith in greater and greater specialization of independent moral principles. But they have been less successful in discovering the degree of homogeneousness between seemingly diverse moral characteristics. Doubtless, it is more important that a theory be true than that it be simple; but equally, the fact that Ptolemaic astronomy or Paracelsian alchemy leads, in its results, to more complications than Kepler's or Lavoisier's theories, is no evidence of the superiority of the former. It does not seem justifiable to me that contemporary anti-hedonists should dismiss Bentham's utilitarianism as "child's play," as "a product of the craving for a simple creed," for a simple, "readily applicable criterion."[9] For at the very roots of their own theories these anti-hedonists

[9] See C. D. Broad, *Five Types of Ethical Theory*, 1930, p. 239, pp. 219 ff; W. D. Ross, *The Foundations of Ethics*, 1939, pp. 83, 79 ff; W. D. Ross, *The Right and the Good*, 1920, p. 24.

make use of far too simple ethical intuitions and fall prey to a rather conventional craving for over-simplified absoluteness.

On the other hand, particularly in the nineteenth century, Bentham's critics frequently condemned his overcomplicated calculations in matters of morality. These complications, it was maintained, compared ill with the straightforwardness and simple lucidity of anti-hedonistic intuitivism. Yet again this criticism failed to realize that the seemingly evident principles of moral intuitivism possess only a mock simplicity, a sham evidence, such as the "laws of raininess and the supplementary laws of sunshine" of which F. H. Bradley spoke ironically. Or even more frequently the criticism of Bentham's overcomplications was simply due to the fact that his critics confounded a criterion of morality with explicit reflections accompanying all moral action; and, of course, these objections against hedonism are of no higher value than certain objections which could be made against the value of grammatical rules.

Unquestionably, grammatical rules need not be consulted during a speech, any more than the utility principle during a moral act. A continuous consultation of grammar may even impede any fluent speech, as much as an express detailed calculation along the line of the utility principle may prevent moral action when swift decision is vital; but this is certainly no conclusive objection against either the value of grammar, or the ethical importance of the utility principle.

False Ambition of Precision

The hedonic calculus has also been criticized for rather opposite reasons. Earlier critics took exception to it as an attempt to overrationalize human action. Especially the higher types of human behavior, it was felt, cannot and should not be subjected to an analysis in merely rationalistic mathematical terms. More recent critics agree with Bentham as to the high desirability of a felicific calculus. But, according to them, the whole project must of necessity remain utopian, much as Bentham's tendency to precision and rationalization is to be welcomed.

I do not wish to re-open here the historic question of the details of Bentham's algedonic calculus and wish to refrain from any discussion of its systematic value or disvalue independently of Bentham's analyses. But, broadly speaking, is it not strange that when psychologists report the most complicated intelligence test in one precise quotient, when educators do not hesitate to use exact figures in judging examination papers, even the hope of a future more correct estimate of pleasure feelings should be declared chimeric?

With reference to a number of misapprehensions which traditionally occur at this point, it has to be remembered that the hedonic calculus by no means denies the existence of qualitative differences between different pleasures. But it tries to compare these different qualities by reducing them—or at least their causes or their intended and actual effects —to a common denominator, just as Newton carried out a reduction of color and tone qualities to quantitatively determinable characteristics, without denying that we always experience qualitative differences. And why should what is possible in an analysis of color phenomena be a priori impossible in an analysis of emotions? In this case, too, the task is to make out, in positive and negative quantities of "affective tones," a neutral common denominator which makes possible the comparison of seemingly incomparable qualities of emotion.

Though opposed to Bentham's utilitarianism in general, René Le Senne in principle has given an appropriate interpretation of the tendencies of Bentham's felicific calculus by stating: "Les événements physiques sont aussi des qualités: pourtant les physiciens ont trouvé les moyens de les faire tomber sous la mesure. Le moraliste n'a qu'à s'inspirer de leur exemple."[10] Professor William P. Montague also sees "the missing link in the case of Utilitarianism" in "the inconsistency which resulted from Mill's appeal to a quality other than pleasure for evaluating pleasures."[11] But he, too, thinks that this "gap in the logic of Utilitarianism" can be filled by conceiving that spiritual satisfactions are in the end "not qualitatively alien to sensory desires, though infinitely . . . greater in magnitude."[12]

To Benedetto Croce, it is true, quantitative utilitarianism is, to say nothing worse, an indulging in an "ingegnosa fraseologia. . . . Ma la medisimezza o la simiglianza delle parole non basta a cancellare la pro-

---

[10] R. Le Senne, *Traité de morale générale*, 1942, p. 224.

[11] W. P. Montague in his essay "The Missing Link in the Case of Utilitarianism," *Studies in the History of Ideas*, ed. by the Department of Philosophy of Columbia University, vol. II, 1925, p. 287.

[12] *Ibid.*, p. 289. However, as Professor Montague insists that satisfaction and sensory desires are "incommensurably," though "not qualitatively" different from each other, I do not wish to construe an identity of my view with that of Professor Montague. Obviously, he is not interested in carrying out any concrete comparison or measurement of the qualities of feelings, since he thinks them, after all, incommensurable, despite any lack of essential qualitative difference between them.

fonda distinzione delle cose."[13]· To this, I think however, consistent utilitarianism can reply with at least as much reason that the deep contrast existing between mere ethical *terms* is not sufficient to extinguish the similarity existing between the *realities* which these terms should properly express. But be this as it may, and even if one thinks that W. Whately Smith's Cambridge experiments, B. B. Friedman's and other types of measurement of "affective tones" are so far by no means conclusive, there is another objective viewpoint at our disposal.

In the analysis of our own feelings and those of others, not only our own and others' satisfactions and dissatisfactions should be taken into account. To the exploration of the quanta and the intensities of feelings still another objective approach is open. Primarily, in crucial cases or experiments, the degree of a feeling is best revealed by the trend of behavior which is determined by the pleasure or displeasure in question. We ourselves, and others, may frequently misjudge the degree of a certain emotion if we examine it only by introspection or measure nothing but its physiological concomitant. However, if we closely scrutinize the kind of behavior which has been caused, or prevented, by our emotions, then another unbiased criterion of the strength of those feelings is secured. There is no reason for giving up this criterion as long as we maintain the well-founded hypothesis that every action is determined by a desire which impels the agent, consciously or unconsciously, to perform that particular action more than any other in his power.

In any case, rough comparisons of degrees of pleasure take place daily, as often as the difference between a cold and hot day is detected even without a precise thermometer; and even such rough calculations are, at least, no less exact than the vague and highly disputable utterances on higher and lower degrees of values in contemporary ethics. Further, I think it is by no means a fatal objection against the hedonic calculus if we admit that the moral arithmetic cannot lead in every case to a final positive or negative judgment about the morality of an act. As Professor R. B. Perry justly points out:[14] "That better means more intense and durable pleasure is not disproved by showing that it is extremely difficult to determine which of two pleasures is the more intense and durable, for it may well be that it is extremely difficult to discover which of two objects is the better."

It is only too common an objection to hedonism that it cannot answer the question: What should be done if one course of action prom-

---

[13] Benedetto Croce, *Filosofia della pratica economica ed etica*, 1923, pp. 231 f.
[14] Ralph Barton Perry, *General Theory of Value*, 1926, p. 608.

ises the same amount of happiness as another, but the one can secure only less happiness for more people and the other more intense happiness for fewer? The simple answer to this is that if ever such a case arose neither of these two alternative lines of conduct could be said to be less or more moral. Provided that the more intense happiness of a few is not outweighed by misery and hardships of the many, the more even distribution of the same amount of happiness is—contrary to some common pseudo-democratic belief—not in itself a higher value.

G. E. Moore, A. J. Ayer and—probably more than any other moralist —Georg Simmel[15] have gone into comparatively greater detail on these questions. But none of them—including Bentham—has done sufficient justice to these details. Primarily it has not been sufficiently emphasized that the decisive problem of critical ethics cannot concern the question of absolute morality but only the question: is one of several possible acts relatively more moral than the others or not?

In this connection it is certainly one of the greatest merits of consistent hedonism that it forces the moralist, far more than any other moral teaching, to go into the most conscientious and impartial weighing of complicated emotional details. The main problems of hedonism do not end with the proclamation of the hedonistic principle, as is almost universally believed, but they start with this proclamation.

As to the fallibility of exact estimates of degrees of feeling, however, we may add: it is no reason for rejecting meteorology altogether, if certain meteorological predictions fail in very complicated climates and weather conditions. Meteorology remains, nonetheless, superior to all attempts to explain the rainfall by a command of Jupiter Pluvius—or by a prima facie obligation to work in the fields after rain. Moreover, there are certainly cases of behavior which are equally good or equally bad; and, therefore, it is not the fault of an algedonic estimate if, in these cases, it does not lead to an indictment or a recommendation. In marked cases of morality or immorality, however, a felicific estimate provides a clear justification for the moral standard of the great world religions while consistent anti-hedonism and eclectic, inconsistent eudaemonism completely fail to do so.

The Criminal's Pleasure and the Martyr's Suffering

Of the many objections which have been raised against a consistent

[15] G. Simmel, *Einleitung in die Moralwissenschaft*, vol. 1, 1892, pp. 323 ff.

ethical use of the greatest-happiness principle only two may be considered briefly. They seem to supplement each other effectively: the reference to the criminal's pleasure and the martyr's suffering.

Again and again, it has been called an outright absurdity to term the happiness of the evil-doer ethically good and the suffering of the martyr morally evil; and by these two examples alone any universal use of the utility principle, even its hypothetical employment, seemed to be sufficiently invalidated. For certainly Bentham's and any consistent use of the greatest-happiness principle must count every suffering *qua* suffering as evil and every pleasure *qua* pleasure as good.

Of course, the consistent hedonist will have no difficulty in correcting the widespread error that pleasure must always be the common type of gaiety, and melancholy or even religious despair must always be painful. Miguel de Unamuno, for instance, has sufficiently elucidated what a "most disagreeable effect" and "profound disgust"[16] the "joie de vivre" of a Parisian boulevard produced on him and how happy he felt "in the midst of anguished multitudes clamoring to heaven for mercy."[17] And he is certainly right in denying that this is "a paradox."[16] Consistent hedonism, too, can confirm that this seemingly paradoxical use of the terms *gay* and *disagreeable* does not contradict the hedonistic principle that every kind of pain caused by hilarity is bad and every spiritual enjoyment of "muchedumbres acongojadas . . . que entonen un *de profundis*"[17] is good.

But critical hedonism can and must go even further. There is no doubt that on the ground of common morality the criminal's pleasure appears a priori as ethically bad and the saint's suffering a priori as morally valuable. From the point of a critical ethics, however, this seems to me in no way conclusive. First, who is a criminal or which act is evil is by no means self-evident. Before any such ethical judgment can be passed, this judgment has to be justified by a general criterion of good and evil. For whoever is a criminal on the ground of a consistent "master" morality is generally a saint, if judged by the standard of a morality of altruism and vice versa. Therefore no judgment which itself presupposes ethically controversial judgments can invalidate a hypothetical principle of ethics which, at least, attempts to base moral judgment on morally neutral data. If worst comes to worst the hypothetical prin-

[16] M. de Unamuno, "Sobre la europeización (Arbitrariedades)" in his *Ensayos*, tomo VII, 1918, p. 170.
[17] *Ibid.*, p. 171.

ciple may be termed ethically as much biased as the opposite particular moral judgments on criminals and saints, but not more biased.

Second, the motives which make the condemnation of the criminal's pleasure seemingly justified can be taken into consideration in a far more consistent and critical way if the pains caused or suffered by the criminal or the martyr are methodologically separated from the pleasures acquired or produced by them. There is no cogent reason left for calling the evil-doer's happiness in itself bad, if all pains of others which his acts bring about are clearly marked as ethically bad. And on the other hand no martyr's pain is ethically valuable in itself, unless it is coupled with spiritual or even material blessings for him and others.

If this seems to be too much ethical generosity, too much liberalism or libertinism, it may be asked whether it is in any respect a sign of higher Christian or Jewish morality to insist on the a priori badness of the criminal's pleasure. Is it really evidence of greater morality to prefer a world in which none of the pains caused by the evil-doers were removed and only the pleasure of the criminal had gone? Would it be an ethically worse world in which all the martyr's spiritual and material happiness bought by his pain were preserved but his suffering were removed? Are they self-evident axioms, these statements about the moral badness of the criminal's pleasure and the moral goodness of saintly suffering? Or are these "self-evident" insights perhaps no more than manifestations of certain Puritan prejudices? Anti-hedonists, such as H. W. B. Joseph and W. D. Ross, have certainly done no justice to the critical presuppositions and implications of consistent hedonism at which I just tried to hint.[18]

Fundamental Flaws
of Hedonistic Psychology?

If we turn now—in a similarly incomplete and, unfortunately, most sketchy fashion—from methodological to psychological questions, it certainly must be granted that Bentham's psychology shows nothing of the refinement of psychological studies of the twentieth century. Even

[18] See, e.g. H. W. B. Joseph, *Some Problems in Ethics*, 1931, pp. 90 f; W. D. Ross, *The Right and the Good*, 1930, p. 151. Neither of these authors nor many others take into consideration the obvious fact that, in an ethical analysis, pleasure and pain can be *methodologically* separated from other data of consciousness. They content themselves with the common insight that there is a most intimate *actual* conjunction between the martyr's pain and great bliss and between the criminal's pleasure and much pain.

compared with that of his contemporaries, his psychology was that of a jurist and a political observer, not that of a professional laboratory psychometrist or of a sensitive poet. Regrettably, his illustrations of happiness-sentiments are usually too redolent of the bench or the stock exchange.

In this respect, Bentham's ethics certainly cannot be taken as a model. Aside from this point, what he termed pleasure ought to be termed the hedonic tone or the hedonic color of preconceived or actually experienced states of mind. In this way pleasure, as a concomitant quality of mental experiences, would be protected from being misunderstood as a special kind of mental event, separate from other data of consciousness. If, however, such precautions are explicitly taken, in line with Bentham's implicit statements, I think that all the numberless refutations of hedonistic psychology piled up in ethical textbooks can be shown to fall to the ground.

Friedrich Nietzsche, in agreement with other anti-hedonists, has objected to hedonistic psychology by remarking that "it is not man who seeks pleasure, it's only the Englishman." This criticism does certainly not strike either at the root or at any vital point of Bentham's hedonism. First, in speaking of pleasure as an end, or the end, of human action, Bentham evidently does not have in mind pleasure in general, distinguished from all concrete pleasant or happy or extremely joyful experiences. He thinks only of the hedonic tone of concrete human aims and ends, which alone makes these ends attractive to the human will, just as we mean concrete beef, pork, or mutton when we speak of eating meat, and do not think of meat in the abstract.

Second, if F. H. Bradley or Nietzsche emphasizes that man never strives for ἡδονή, but at best for ἡδέα, Bentham's hedonism is by no means at issue on this point; he cannot be confuted by the statement that every pleasant feeling must have still another "content than its pleasantness."[19] Wherever Bentham speaks of pleasure, he certainly thinks of concrete pleasant activities or states of mind, and not of a special mental event isolated from all others, a separate entity ἡδονη.

Since Henry Sidgwick coined the phrase, much has been made of the so-called hedonistic paradox; and it is paradoxically true that the more we strive explicitly for pleasure, the less we obtain it. Or, as Max Scheler said, in extending this argument, the value of the agreeable, like all the other values we aim at, appears only on the "back of our deeds"

[19] See F. H. Bradley, *Ethical Studies*, 1927, p. 236.

537

and ought not to appear in our intentions.[20] Whoever attempts to realize the value of the pleasant directly in itself, turns out to be a decadent bon-vivant; whoever attempts to realize other values directly, with the sole aim of demonstrating his righteousness, is a sanctimonious pharisee. There is not a special kind of mental events called pleasures, actually detachable from other psychological events; and there are no experiences of values in our intellectual life which could actually be severed from the flow of other experiences.

I should even say that anyone who would believe in the existence of pleasure or values actually, and not only methodologically, separable from concrete pleasant or valuable experiences, would be more than a degenerate *bon-vivant* or a bigoted pharisee: he would be a hopeless Don Quixote.

Such criticism however, it should be clear, does not concern any essential point of Bentham's psychology. He presupposes nothing but the existence of a hedonic tone, or better to say, an algedonic, a "positive or negative affective tone," an affective coloring of our concrete experiences. In this shape, as a "positive affective tone" of mental experiences, pleasure can indeed be verified as the determining factor of human action. Even the voluntary martyr ultimately finds, in the torture he has to undergo, more hedonic attraction than in the desertion of his cause. Nor would malice or revenge take any interest in the suffering of others, unless the idea of this suffering were pleasant to the maligner and the avenger. And if, from the standpoint of an unbiased psychological observer, the pleasantness of these feelings were not outweighed by the sufferings of others which are connected with it, malice and revenge would not be ethically condemnable according to the impartial, critical moralist Bentham.

Finally, H. Rashdall finds a mistaken *hysteron proteron* in hedonistic psychology. For, as he maintains, hedonism "puts the cart before the horse"; in reality the imagined pleasantness is created by the desire, and not, as hedonism assumes, the desire by the imagined pleasantness.[21]

[20] See M. Scheler, *Der Formalismus in der Ethik und die materiale Wertethik*, 1921, p. 22. Cf. Nicolai Hartmann, *Ethics*, translated by Stanton Coit, 1932, vol. II, pp. 31 ff.
As to a critical analysis of hese views see D. Baumgardt, "Some Merits and Defects of Contemporary German Ethics" (*Philosophy, The Journal of the British Institute of Philosophy*, April 1938).

[21] See H. Rashdall, *The Theory of Good and Evil*, 1907, vol. I, pp. 15, 40. Cf. W. M. Urban, *Fundamentals of Ethics*, 1930, p. 78, John Dewey and James H. Tufts, *Ethics*, 1908, p. 271, Bertrand Russell, *A History of Western Philosophy*, 1945, pp. 778 f.

Certainly, if Bentham had assumed that we have first to sit down and to think of a certain pleasantness before desiring it, he would have been wrong. It has readily to be granted that, in the complicated intermixture of imagination, desire and action, no strict line of demarcation can be drawn between a distinct idea of pleasantness and desire, between a hedonic tone as a "causa finalis" and one as a "causa efficiens." Pleasantness may be given as an integral part of desire itself.

All this does not interfere with any essential thesis of Bentham's psychology. All he presupposes is that, in judging actions ethically, we are ·allowed to discuss and compare the hedonic tones of the different ends of acts in methodological abstraction. This, however, in no way implies that, in reality, in the actions themselves, the hedonic tone is psychologically given in disjunction from the act, either before or after the act. Therefore the alleged paralogism, the *hysteron proteron* mentioned above, is by no means an indispensable premise of Bentham's psychology.

Neither the so-called hedonistic paradox, nor the hedonistic *hysteron proteron*, nor the experiences of martyrdom, revenge, and malice are in contradiction with the essential presuppositions of Bentham's hedonism. Even in the field of psychological fundamentals, the objections of oversimplification raised against Bentham's main theses are commonly due to oversimplifications on the part of his critics.

In the nineteenth century Bentham's psychology was perhaps more accused of overcomplication than of oversimplification. The hedonist was especially often ridiculed because he was supposed to carry out so many complicated calculations previous to his acts that he would miss every chance of acting. In truth, Bentham never assumed that every human action must be accompanied by a circumstantial, conscious, rational calculation of consequences. He explicitly granted that, more often than not in our actions, only an intuitive, unperceived calculation of consequences takes place and psychologically no more than this is required by his doctrine. The detailed, rational estimate of all the hedonic effects of our actions is only needed for judging the ethical value of these acts: it is by no means essential for their performance.

Educational and Religious Prejudices

From the viewpoint of pedagogy, of education and religion, perhaps even more objections have been raised against Bentham's ethics than

539

from any other quarter; and again rather opposite arguments have been advanced for this purpose.

Coleridge and Carlyle thought the anti-idealistic, immoral character of Bentham's teaching and personality quite evident. They therefore contented themselves with abusing Bentham and his followers as "paralytic radicals," and believed it "God's mercy . . . that our (philosophic) Jacobins were infidels and a scandal to all sober Christians; had they been like the old Puritans, they would have trodden Church and King to dust—at least for a time." That Bentham and practically all his followers could easily rival the Carlyles and Coleridges *qua* moral characters obviously escaped the attention of these champions of idealistic ethics. Bradley even spoke of a "degradation," a "prostitution" and "bastardisation"[22] of ethics by utilitarianism. Fiery tongues of this brand are fortunately no longer heard today.

On the contrary, more academically minded moralists such as Henry Sidgwick and C. D. Broad see too much "reforming fire," too white a "heat of moral enthusiasm"[23] in Bentham and his successors. But all these *dicta*, which keep hedonism so severely in leading strings, are certainly more representative of the critics' own sentiments than they are of Bentham's teaching. Nevertheless these sentiments too are, in all probability, responsible for the lack of a sufficiently impartial analysis of Bentham's moral theory.

In scores of stock objections to Bentham's hedonism, similar pedagogical or religious scruples are tacitly involved. Preoccupied with the more conspicuous and seemingly more urgent problems of pedagogy, with the contrasts between duty and inclination, between altruistic and egoistic behavior, anti-hedonism generally not only slurs over Bentham's more fundamental methodological inquiries but also fails to note his full recognition of the ethical problem of unselfishness.

It is true that the problem of altruism and that of subduing selfish inclinations has no such central place in Bentham as it does in practically all anti-hedonistic theories. But Bentham himself never taught that personal sacrifices in favor of the greatest happiness of the greatest number are avoidable. Bentham's hedonism is in no way essentially bound up with the assumption of a utopian harmony between all indi-

[22] As to Carlyle and Coleridge, see e.g. A. Seth Pringle-Pattison, *The Philosophical Radicals and Other Essays*, 1907, pp. 25, 11, where apparently Seth Pringle-Pattison does not dissociate himself too resolutely from the opinions of Carlyle and Coleridge; F. H. Bradley, *Ethical Studies*, 1876, pp. 57, 145.

[23] See C. D. Broad, *Five Types of Ethical Theories*, 1930, pp. 157, 238.

vidual and general interests of mankind. It is J. S. Mill and not Bentham who drew very near this illusion and the fallacy of identifying "valuable" with "actually desired."

In textbooks just published Bentham's hedonism is still reproached because it "can produce submission, but not loyalty, conformity, but not devotion; . . . In all the higher motives there is something more than a balancing of pleasures and pains."[24] Certainly, at first glance, Bentham's ethics of consequences seems to pervert and to paralyze the main emphasis which, pedagogically, has to be laid on the motives and not the results of human acts. In the eyes of many anti-hedonists, Bentham's utilitarianism, by a superficial reversion of all progressive educational insight, leads back to a primitive and gross "by their fruits ye shall know them."

Utilitarianism seems to throw to the wolves the greatest educational achievements of a moral "trial of the hearts and reins" brought about by the teaching of the Jewish prophets, of Abelard, Kant, and John Ruskin[25] who taught us to examine above all man's motives, his heart and spirit. But, in truth, Bentham did not underrate the pedagogical importance of a primary appeal to human motives.

What he did was to show why in ethics even motives cannot be judged impartially without references to the consequences of acts, i.e. why in ethics even motives can be judged objectively only as indications of prevalently beneficial or mischievous consequences. The basic importance of this doctrine of motives can, perhaps, best be demonstrated by a thought-experiment supplementing Bentham's teaching. Certainly, for argument's sake, it is entirely within the realm of *logical* possibility to suppose that hatred would prevalently produce more happiness than love. But under these presuppositions it would be evident that, then, hatred could no longer be considered as an "intrinsically" bad motive.

[24] See William Henry Roberts, *The Problem of Choice*, 1941, pp. 149 f. Cf. E. A. Wesley, *Utilitarianism in England during the 19th Century*, 1901, pp. 14 f: "Numbers may stand for definite sums, if we deal with ethical abstractions . . . but for the real flesh and blood creature, with . . . passions they stand for nothing at all"; J. W. Allen, *The Social and Political Ideas of Some Representative Thinkers of the Revolutionary Era*, 1931: "It is fortunate that Bentham is not one of those writers whose every word should be read before we begin to write about them. . . . To read" the "mass" of "his writings would be a waste of time. I have not attempted the task."

[25] See e.g. John Ruskin, *Unto this Last*, 1862, pp. 21 f: "No man ever knew or can know, what will be the ultimate result to himself, or to others, of any given line or conduct. But every man may know . . . what is a just and unjust act."

Under these circumstances, hatred allegedly bad under all circumstances, bad independent of all its consequences, would have to be thought prevalently good. And by a similar thought experiment it becomes manifest that kindness and generosity would have to be deemed bad if prevalently they were to bring about misery.

That is, under all these circumstances the moral value of the motive fully reveals itself as dependent on the consequences of the act whereas the moral value of the consequences is not in the same sense dependent on the motive. It is in vain, therefore, to proclaim on behalf of the ethics of motives that hatred is a priori bad, bad in itself, and love is good by its very essence.

It would be utterly absurd to base the critical moral judgment on any of those "mysteriously evident" characteristics of motives—characteristics which would flagrantly give the lie to the deepest, fundamental, evident experiences concerning happiness and pain. Vice versa, however, it remains entirely consistent to insist that love is good because and in so far as it leads to greater happiness and that hatred is bad only because and in so far as it leads to greater pain.

The educator can stress the moral value of love and disvalue of hatred only *after* the moralist has ascertained that hatred produces on the whole (though not always) far more suffering than happiness and love more joy than pain. Any impatience, however, any short cut taken by pedagogy in the answers to these questions would be disastrous and completely confusing. These impatient answers are disastrous even when extolling blind love which ignores all the demands of justice and undermines, thus, the foundations on which true love can alone thrive; and these direct moral appeals to motives are, of course, even more pernicious when they preach hatred as the only evidence of manliness and virtue and denounce even the understanding of an opponent as a sign of degeneration.

The educator is fully entitled to appeal, first of all, to the motives of men. Without vigorous good motives every individual and every society is in a state of decay. Good motives demand the utmost cultivation by every moral leader of every group of men. But before this cultivation can take place, the epistemology of ethics must have ascertained what the good motives are and why they are good.

Only on the basis of these critical reflections can it be shown why our Judaeo-Christian motives are good and not the motives of sheer power or any type of ethical relativism and nihilism.[26] Our common theories of morals, however, yield far too much to the pressure and the exigencies of uncritical pedagogy. They are but made to order for these educational needs and lack, therefore, any sufficiently firm basis, as this can be provided only by the impartial, critical moralist. Bentham, however, insisted, I think with reason, that ethical inquiry should logically never be made subsequent and subservient to educational practice.

As practical application of any knowledge is always based and must be based on some type of theory, this is no less the case in morals. Only ethics can tell us which educational practice is morally valuable and which is morally valueless.

Certainly it must be granted that the truly "edifying" character of Bentham's ethics is often hidden under cool, sober reasoning of a prevailingly juristic character. But I think it should be no less readily granted that, what Bentham's hedonism lost by its juristic diction, it gained in precision and in a closer approach to the hard realities of life. It was never his intention to degrade moral behavior to the lower level of mere legalism; he endeavored to elevate the theory of morals, so far as possible, to the higher level of juristic exactness.

Last, but not least, Puritanism and the majority of religious beliefs seem to be irreconcilably antagonistic to Bentham's hedonism; and, on the other hand, Bentham's failure to understand the vital, genuine importance of religious life cannot be explained away. But if religion ever had and continues to have meaning, it centers around the "Urerlebnisse," the fundamental experiences of human blessedness and human despair; and, on principle, a consistent hedonism finds it certainly less difficult to include the highest types of pleasure and pain than to exclude them. Too often it has been said that hedonism deals only with "materialistic" feelings and, therefore, degrades ethics. Yet hedonism in itself does not only allow but even demands any possible elevation in this respect. Consistent hedonism does not only permit but even insists on the inclusion of all types of feeling: the whole world of artistic emotion and the truest religious sentiments. If there is, in Bentham's moral philosophy, almost nothing of the religious spirit in the common sense of the word, the gist of his teaching certainly rather invites than forbids its extension toward liberal modern religion.

[26] See D. Baumgardt, "Gesinnungsethik oder Erfolgsethik?" *Philosophische Studien*, Heft 1, 1949, pp. 91 ff, where I am concerned, in greater detail, with these questions of a constructive consistent hedonism.

It has been said by a leading English moralist of the day that, "in the long run," we "will have to choose between Bentham and Kant" in ethics. Be this as it may, there seems to me no doubt that an analysis of Bentham's ethics, far more detailed than any I could give in these brief concluding remarks, can be of decisive consequence not only for writing the history of modern ethics, but also for any systematic ethical reasoning.

Bentham's mummy, preserved at University College, London, suffered in World War II at the onslaught of contemporary barbarians who might have belonged to a pre-Egyptian civilization. Wisely, therefore, the mummy was withdrawn for repair into the Egyptian department of the College's collections, as we were informed in a bulletin of London University of 1940.[27] Bentham himself, in contrast to this with-

[27] The following poem contains, beautifully condensed, a good number of the common prejudices against Bentham and may well serve my critics as a substitute for prose reviews: from H. Bevington, *Nineteen Million Elephants and Other Poems* (Houghton Mifflin Co.), 1950, pp. 33 f. By the kind permission of Helen Bevington.

A BOMB FOR JEREMY BENTHAM (1940)

The teapot he named Dick
And Dapple was his stick.
He cherished pigs and mice,
A fact which will suffice
To hint, from all we hear,
He was a little queer.

They say he cherished men,
Their happiness, and then
Calmly assumed one could
Devise cures for their good,
Believing all men the same,
And happiness their aim.

He reckoned right and wrong
By felicity—lifelong—
And by such artless measure
As the quantity of pleasure.
For pain he had a plan,
Absurd old gentleman.

His final vanity,
Or mild insanity,
Preserved him, in a case,
A sprightly waxen face,
A habit snug upon
His quiet skeleton.

drawal, once humorously said to Philarète Chasles[28] that he would like to return to life each century for a short time, in order to instruct himself as to the fate of his moral theories. I am by no means sure that Bentham would not regard me as far too critical of his philosophy of morals. But I hope, at least, that both he and my severest critics will grant that I offer a fairer and more patient presentation of his ethical teaching than he has been accorded hitherto.

Dispenser of odd knowledge
At University College—
Where surely it was fitting
That Nazis, bent on hitting
A real objective, sent them
A bomb for Jeremy Bentham.

[28] See Philarète Chasles, *Études sur les hommes et les moeurs au XIXe siècle*, 1850, p. 89.

APPENDICES

Appendix I

BENTHAM MS, hitherto unpublished, University College, London, Portfolio 169, Folder 13, page 79.

This manuscript is written about 1780 and contains the report of one of Bentham's dreams in which, as far as I can see, the term *Utilitarian* appears for the first time in Bentham.

"The great name LS" mentioned in this MS is, probably, Lord Shelburne, Marquis of Lansdowne, who about that time and later showed the greatest interest in Bentham, the man and his work. The "man named George" is, probably, King George III.

Dream. The world is persuaded not without some colour (ground) of reason that all reformers and system-mongers are mad: and not without some colour of reason. Formerly they used to live upon grass-hoppers in deserts: walk upon (about) golden thighs or sit upon three legged stools in temples: now they live in garrets: from whence in due time they are removed to Bethlehem. I don't mean such of Judah, but of Moorfields.

My madness has not yet to my own knowledge (consciousness) (as far as I can perceive myself) come beyond a dream. I dreamt t'other-night that I was a founder of a sect: of course a personage of great sanctity and importance. It was called the sect of *utilitarians*.

As I was musing one night (in flew) an angel flew in at my window: I forgot his name—but it would be as [sic] easy to learn it in heaven where he is as well known for the implacable enmity he bears to the demon of chicane as S'Michael is by the battles he has had with Satan. He put into my hands a book which he said he had just been writing with the quill of a phoenix. it was lettered on the back Principles of legislation. I had no occasion to cut it he said as St John did his: all I had to do was to cram it as well as I could down the throats of other people: (they would it had the true flavour of the fruit of the tree of knowledge of good and evil).

One day as I was musing over this book there came out to me crying a great man named LS [?] and he said unto me. what shall I do to be saved? I had forgot continued he: I must not talk of myself—I mean to save the nation? I said unto him: take up my book and follow me.

We walked about (trudged on) a long while without any sort of plan (in rush of adventures), and without knowing of what we were going about (where we were to go first or when and) as in the fashion till we spied a man named George who had been afflicted with an incurable blindness and deafness for many years. I said unto my apostle give him a page of my book that he may read mark learn and inwardly digest it. The man struggled a good deal at first and made a good many faces as much as to say that is from the nastiest stuff I ever tasted in my life: but no sooner was it down than before a man could have said "ekphatos," up came (forth came) out of his bosom seven devils blacker than the blackest of the 3 crows that were raided by the swan in the Tatler and the blackest of all was S——d.

I know him by the mark of the beast which was so visible in his forehead. Immediately the man heard everything that a man could (would) hear and there fell the scales from his eyes and not seeing what better he could do with himself, he also followed us. We had not travelled long before we saw a woman named Britannia lying by the water side all in rags with a sleeping lion at her feet: she looked very pale and upon inquiring we found she had an issue of blood upon her for many years. She started up fresher, faster and more alive than ever: the lion wagged his tail and fawned upon us like a Spaniel.

Appendix II

BENTHAM MSS, University College, London, Portfolio 169, Folder 3, sheet 13, p. 2 (In an old folder marked "Legislaturientes epistolae Brouillons unsent 1774?, 1778?")

According to Professor Everett (who first published the second part of this draft-letter in his *The education of Jeremy Bentham*, 1931, pp. 110ff) this MS was written in 1776. The first part of this draft-letter is addressed to the Empress Catherine II of Russia.

Madame, J'ai l'honneur d'envoyer à votre Majesté un ouvrage que des Magistrats commissionés par elle (éclairés et patriotiques) ont paru chercher.

J'ai vu un article dans la Gazette de Moscou. On désire un éclaircissement (demande des éclaircissemens) (entre autre) sur le sujet des peines. (En) Voilà (Voici) ce que j'ai pu fournir (la dessus).

Citoyen d'un état libre et usant de (exerçant) cette liberté dans toute son étendue, il n'y a que deux souverains (puissances) sur la terre auxquels (auxquelles) j'ai eu quelque espérance de plaire. Celui dont le pouvoir a des bornes manifestement inénarrables et celle à laquelle (in the margin: pour le bonheur du peuple) il n'en faut pas. Si les idées que j'ai fait hazarder (in the margin: J'envoye une copie pour Votre Majesté, j'envoye une autre pour le Roi de Pologne) sont telles que je désire, il faut du pouvoir pour s'en servir. Il n'y a qu'un seul endroit ou (sic) j'ai espéré trouver l'un et l'autre en dose suffisante. Je suis, Madame avec le plus profond respect qu'a jamais animé (ressenti) un coeur libre de votre Majesté le très humble serviteur.

Il y en a sous presse une traduction française. On dit que votre Majesté n'en a pas besoin.

Voici une lettre que je viens d'envoyer à M. Voltaire.

Sir, By the first conveyance that offers itself you will receive a thick volume which very probably you will never read. It is entitled Theory of Punishment. It is part of a work to which if it should be completed I intend to give some such title as Principles of Legal Policy: The object of it is to trace out a new model for the Laws: of my own country you may imagine, in the first place: but keeping those of other countries all along in view. To ascertain what the Laws ought to be, in form and tenor as well as in matter: and that elsewhere as well as here. All that I shall say to recommend it to you is that I have taken counsel of you much oftener than of our own Ld. Coke and Hale and Blackstone. The repose of Grotius and Puffendorf and Barbeyrac and Burlamaqui I would never wish to see disturbed. I have built solely on the foundation of utility, laid as it is by Helvetius. Beccaria has been *lucerna pedibus* or if you please *manibus meis*. Perhaps what I have done may be found but cobweb work. Such as it is however, it is spun out of my own brain. As such I send it to you. It is neither borrow'd nor pilfer'd. I have spent upon it on the whole already about 7 years. I mean to bestow upon it the rest of my days, which at present are somewhat more than a third of yours.

One of the rewards I have been proposing to myself has been your good opinion. Perhaps I am come too soon to attain it: perhaps too late. I have seen with regret the following billet said to have been sent to an intruder perhaps not more impertinent than myself. Octoginta duo annos octoginta duo nobis, veniam peto si non sum visendus sed obliviscendus. My labours have been so tedious that before they are come to an end my best rewards may I fear be lost. Helvetius is gone—years ago my eyes paid a tribute to his memory, and you and d'Alembert are leaving us.

If you should ever find anything to say to me I need scarce tell you that it will be acceptable. Anything directed to Elmsly's the Bookseller (successor to Vaillant) will reach me. I am a Lawyer by profession: and might have been so by practice. My name is precisely as well known to you as that of the meanest inhabitant of Siberia. It is Jeremy Bentham.

Appendix III

BENTHAM's first publication of which the half is reprinted in C. K. Ogden, *Jeremy Bentham, 1832-2032*, 1932, p. 54, a letter "To John Glynn, Esq., Serjeant-at-Law" in *The Gazetteer and New Daily Advertiser*, Monday, December 3, 1770, p. 2, column 1: (London, British Museum, The State Papers Reading Room, Burney Collection 572b).

To John Glynn Esq; Serjeant at Law

You have miserably deceived the expectations of your friends. Law was, at any rate, to be found to disarm government, in this fortunate exigence, of the strength of the able but unwilling. Each vagabond, rescued from the danger of being useful, would be a fresh reinforcement to the squadrons of patriotism: and though every such an one is indeed already her militia-man by birth, yet this important obligation could not but inspire him anew with a tenfold addition of zeal. The Aegis of Liberty was to be held up to cover all, and dazzle the eyes of weak-sighted observers.

The scheme, it must be acknowledged, was not ill-concerted; the merit of serving the nation was happily conciliated with the satisfaction of distressing it. With one hand, Britain was to be pushed headlong into the war, with the other, her hands were to be tied down from providing for her defence: there wanted but a Lawyer to weave the cord; your well tried fidelity left no room to hesitate about the choice.

Messrs. Wedderburn and Dunning were next pitched upon for the purpose. The number thought competent was to be completed; and it was hoped *your* persuasions, joined to the common dissatisfaction against administration, might dispose *them* to adopt an expedient so happily calculated to distress it. The *hopes*, I say, of the patriots, were in those *two gentlemen*; but in *you*, Sir, was their *confidence, their security*.

The event has proved both alike ill-founded; those gentlemen had more honesty, or more discretion, not than there was reason to expect, but than was expected; they move in a sphere unconnected with, and far higher than the vortex which harries you; *their* integrity is a price by much too great for such popularity as *your friends* can give them: an instructive sympathy has taught those *friends* to look for kindred weakness or dishonesty wheresoever they see an opponent of administration; but they are mistaken; wisdom and integrity are distributed, though unequally, among both parties.

They, I say again; have disappointed the expectations of your employers; but *you*, Sir, have betrayed their trust. Was it for this the City gold was poured into your *ready* hand? Is it necessary to tell you, that it was not for to be instructed what the law *is*, that your employers quitted their *legitimate advisers? New laws*, fitted to every variable purpose of sedition, must successively be woven from the cobweb materials of ancient barbarism; work, nor think to carry with you your scruples to the task, or, like *him*, you will be cast off, without *his* integrity to console you.

But I fear I injure you all this while in attributing to you that opinion which your hand has signed. Your learned eloquence, we are told* and authentication is preferred, was actually employed in endeavouring to reconcile your colleagues to a more acceptable doctrine: employed, it seems it was,

* *Public Advertiser*, p. 2, col. 3, 26th Nov.

though employed in vain: those experienced veterans stood firm against the power of that voice, whose allurements no Jury can withstand. Here let me pause a while to admire your conclusion: with loudness you proclaimed that *pressing* was *illegal*: in silence you affixed your seal to its legality.

Mr. *Wilkes*, it is to be hoped, will one day favour us with that *other* picture of your sentiments which he is so happy to possess, of Mr. *Reynolds's* designing; ranged in parallel columns, they will together form no improper appendage to the effigy of your person. The design should be allegorical in conformity to the mysteriousness of your conduct: Janus, for instance, with his double countenance, each crowning its respective column; the one facing the higher world, the other working contrary intimations to the gaping populace below.

With all these materials before it, the world will still find some difficulty in its conception of your conduct. Vouchsafe, therefore, to come forth and extricate us from our perplexity; teach us to whom we are to give credit for your genuine sentiments, yourself or your anonymous apologist? Tell us or let your friend tell us how long it has been the duty of a Counsellor to his clients, to sell them another's judgement when they pay him for his own? Or if you mean hereafter to be more just, tell your consultants, is it by the rule of contraries, or by what other rule they are to interpret your future responses? Flatter not yourself that you shall be any longer permitted to save your credit with your party, by your expedient of a clandestine protestation. I will ask you once for all in their name, is it the opinion you have signed, or its opposite, that is yours? Answer then in pity to their distractions, and let them see whether *discretion* or *they* are henceforward to reckon you for their own.

Yet if I might be permitted to advise, the latter should be your preferable resolve. Discretion and you have long ago shaken hands. Your efforts for reconciliation would be but awkward; *you* have forgotten *her* voice, and *she* would not obey *your* call. You once had the choice between an irreproachable obscurity, and a disgraceful fame; that choice is made; you have passed your rubicon, to continue on your course is not now of choice, but of necessity; pursue on the road of disgrace in the company in which you entered it; adhere to them, and you still have society; quit them, and you wander in abandonment; the paths are past, and it is now too late to regain the station of esteem.

For their sake then, and for yours, make one last effort to reconcile you to the affections of your friends. *Your house* has been miserably divided against itself; nothing now but the most religious unanimity can save you. Command another pilgrimage to a more favourable oracle, and let the response be dictated not by your judgment, but by your wishes; new-model the economy of the *tripod*—Mr. *Secretary Morris*, and perhaps Mr. *Adair*, will think it an honour to give *their signature* to any *leaves* that have been consecrated by *your's*. You need not be disquieted with the apprehension of their permanency; like their equally impostrous archetypes of old, they will indeed be *dispersed*, but, like them, they will be forgotten.

Irenius

Appendix IV

BENTHAM MS dealing in particular detail with the principles of a moral calculus

Of this MS a relatively small part was published by E. Halévy in his *La formation du radicalisme philosophique*, tome I, 1901, pp. 398 ff (not reprinted in the English translation of this work in 1928). Professor John Laird in *The Idea of Value*, 1929, p. 326 calls the extract of this MS published by Halévy "the fullest general account of what Bentham . . . calls "Value of a lot of pleasure or pain: how to be measured." Halévy himself writes (in *La formation du radicalisme philosophique*, 1901, tome I, p. 414): "Tout le manuscrit dont nous extrayons ce fragment présente un intérêt réel pour l'historien de la philosophie et pour le philosophe. Peut-être y aurait-il lieu d'en entreprendre la publication intégrale." This complete text I give here.

According to Halévy the following reflections are writen "aux environs 1782" (*ibid.*, p. 398).

Bentham MSS, University College, London, Portfolio 27, Folder 5, sheet 32, pp. 1 f:

VALUE

One of the Roman Emperors, Nero I think it is, is said to have offer'd a reward to (him who should be) the inventor [omitted: of] a new pleasure. (There are moralists who are more scandalised at this idea of the tyrant, than at all his cruelties). A proposition thus calculated to promote the happiness of mankind (excites more horror in) has met with worse treatment with moralists of a certain stamp than the worst of these cruelties which destroy it. They will tell (answer) you nay: for that the pleasures that a sensualist had in view were indubitably impure. But either the word impure had with them no meaning (that was anything to the purpose) or it meant, in the sense in which I always mean to take it, (the only determinate sense it is capable of) a pleasure of such a nature as to be more frequently than not attended or follow'd by pains more than equivalent to it. But this was certainly no part of the proposal. To one who reasons consistently (consistent reasoner) the quality of a pleasure independent of its quantity is of no account. Every thing that produces pleasure is prima facie good: if it is to be reputed bad, it can only be in virtue of some pain which it produces more than equivalent to such pleasure. The pleasure being incontestable, in order to prove the cause of it to be an evil, it lies upon any one to prove that it is productive of such attendant pain.

Every thing that produces pleasure is good in proportion to the *clear* pleasure it produces: and till it can be shown to produce pain, all the pleasure it is seen to produce ought to be reputed *clear*. This must be eternally true in spite of all prejudices and all declamations to the contrary. . . .* Neither Newton's Laws of nature, nor Euclid's axioms are more incontestable.

[sheet 33, page 1.] Pleasures and pains, how measured

No. I

[In the margin: from p. 1] Under the article of *value*, every observation that can be made with regard to pleasure, applies equally to pain: after this notice, to save words, I shall all along make mention only of pleasure. The limit of the quantity of a pleasure in respect of intensity on the (this) side of diminution is a state of indifference (insensibility): the degree of intensity possessed by that pleasure which is the faintest of any that can be distinguished to be pleasure, may be represented by unity: [In the margin: Such a degree of intensity is in every day's experience] according as any pleasures are perceived to be more and more intense they may be represented by higher and higher numbers: but there is no fixing upon any particular (distinguished) degree of intensity as being the highest of which a pleasure is susceptible.

The limit of the quantity of a pleasure in respect of duration is the least portion of duration that can be assigned (distinguished): suppose a moment. If then a moment be taken for the least portion of time that is distinguishable, it is certain that no pleasure, to exist at all, can last for less than a moment. Such a degree of duration for a pleasure is within every day's experience. But there is no fixing upon any particular number of moments as being the greatest during which any pleasure can continue.

[Sheet 33, p. 3] The quantum of the value of a pleasure in point of proximity has for its limit on the side of increase actual presence. No pleasure can be nearer, no pleasure can, on the score of proximity, be more valuable, than one that is actually present. Pleasures that are actually present are within every day's experience. But there is no fixing upon any number of moments months or years, that shall constitute the greatest interval which can subsist between any present time, and the time at which the event of a pleasure's being enjoy'd is to take place. The greatest possible duration of a man's life were it determined might indeed determine the greatest degree of remoteness of a pleasure as far as a single person were concerned: but in the first place

* These dots are put in by Bentham himself.

the greatest possible duration of a man's life is a quantity that never can be determined; in the next place it often becomes material to consider the pleasure not of a single person only but of many persons in succession.

The quantum of the value of a pleasure in point of probability (certainty, as it is more convenient to call it on the present occasion), has for its limit on the side of increase that absolute certainty which cannot be denied to take place where the pleasure is actually present. No pleasure can be more certain than one that is actually present. But there is no fixing upon any number of chances which shall be the greatest there can be against the event of any pleasure's taking place.

Now then, whole numbers increase continually from a fixed point (unity): fractional numbers decrease continually from the same fixed point. Hence it appears, I imagine pretty plainly, why the degrees of intensity and duration must be express'd by whole numbers: that of proximity and that of certainty by fractions.

[Sheet 34, p. 1. Pleasures and Pains—how measured] So much for the circumstances that are ingredients in the value of a pleasure (as far as concerns) considered as being enjoyed by a single (as far as a) individual (is concerned in it): when a whole community (that is a multitude of individuals), is considered as being concerned in it, the value of it is to be multiplied by the number of such individuals. the [sic] total value of the stock of pleasure belonging to the whole community is to be obtained by multiplying the number expressing the value of it as respecting any one person, by the number expressing the multitude of such individuals. The accession it (a pleasure) receives in value by this circumstance may be denominated its extent.

A pleasure considered as extending itself in this manner through a whole community would hardly in common language be termed a pleasure: it would rather be termed a lot of happiness. [In the margin: A lot of happiness]

So much for the value of a pleasure considered by itself. [In the margin: Fecundity and Purity] Considered with reference to other sensations that may result from the same causes, the value of it may be regarded as susceptible of two other ingredients, fecundity and purity: Fecundity in as far as those causes may be productive of pleasures (sensations of the same kind, to wit): purity in as far as they may be exempt from producing sensations of the opposite kind; to wit pains.

It is evident that the more pleasures in number and value any given pleasure is followed by, the greater will be its value: and the more pains, the less.

[Sheet 34, p. 2] Of the four other ingredients in the value of a pleasure there will be perpetual occasion to make mention under their respective names: the whole system of the ensuing disquisitions in a manner turns upon them. Of these two last there will hardly be special occasion to make mention, at least under these names. For in taking an account of the physiological effects of any mode of conduct the more simple way is to consider the several pleasures and pains it is productive of by themselves: (setting the sum of the pleasures on one side of the account, and on the other, that of the pains.) instead of bringing in all the subsequent pleasures and pains in the lump, by way of appendages to the first. For each of them in order to the obtaining a true estimate of its value, must be examined (considered) under the same four heads under which the value of the first was taken.

[Sheet 34, p. 3] The idea of considering happiness as resolvable into a number of (individual) pleasures, I took from Helvetius: before whom (whose time) it can scarcely be said to have had a meaning. (This is directly contrary to the doctrines laid down in Cicero's Tusculan disputations: which book, like most of the other philosophical writings of that great master of language, is nothing but a heap of nonsense.) The idea of estimating the value of each sensation by analyzing it into these four ingredients, I took from M. Beccaria: gleaning up those several articles from different places in which I saw them made use of in estimating the force and utility of punishments. Considering that punishment is but pain applied to a certain purpose, that the value of a pleasure is (composed of the same articles) susceptible of the same analysis, and that pains and pleasures, and actions in as far as they had a tendency to produce or prevent the one and the other were all that morals and politics (or so much as was of any use or meaning in those sciences) had in view, it seemed to me that such an analysis was the very thing that was wanted as the foundation for a compleat system of moral science. I had already proceeded some length in building upon that foundation when Maupertuis' Essay on Moral Philosophy fell into my hands. That ingenious philosopher whose work is (of a date some years) prior to that of M. Beccaria, proceeds upon the same idea of making such an analysis for his groundwork. He had however pursued it but by halves, omitting to take (not taking) any account of the two articles of proximity and certainty. Besides this omission, he fell into a very melancholy [sheet 34, p. 4] fundamental error, by the wrong turn he gave to his definition of the word pleasure. This led him into a variety of conclusions as false as they are melancholy, which seem to have been the reason of his book having been still less noticed than it deserves. The definition he gives of (the word) pleasure, is so constructed as to exclude from any title to that appellation, every degree of pleasure that falls short of being the highest.

[Sheet 35, p. 1. How to measure Pain and Pleasure] The business of the Legislator is to augment the sum of happiness in a state as much as possible. If the sum of happiness be on any occasion increased, it must be by increasing the sum of pleasures, or diminishing that of pains. This may be done in either of three ways. 1st By introducing a pleasure instead of a pain. 2dly By introducing a less pain instead of a greater pain. 3dly By introducing a greater pleasure in the room of a lesser pleasure. The business then is done, (The effects then are brought about) sometimes by applying pain, sometimes by applying pleasure. Now as to pain the Legislator has many modes and those very certain in their operation of applying at all times directly to the object. With pleasure this is not the case: whenever it were to be applied some (individual period) term or other must be fixed for the operation to be performed: and were even the object a given person, there is no operation whatever which the Legislator could be certain would at any fixed period give him pleasure (produce pleasure in (such) that object).

To produce pleasure therefore the Legislator has but one course to take, which is to lay in a man's way some *instrument* of pleasure, and leave the application of it to himself. By instrument of pleasure we are here to understand anything that goes under the name of a *possession*: whether that possession [sheet 35 p. 2] be a real or fictitious entity. [In the margin: Money the only current instrument of pleasure] Possessions that are real entities are all of them to be found among the several (bodies) substances, that surround us: the value whereof, that is their aptitude (capability) of producing pleasure is measured by that one sort of them which being the pledge and representative of almost all the rest (others) is a means of acquiring them at any time, I mean *money*. Possessions that are fictitious entities, are (either) power (condition) (or) and reputation. Money is also, directly or indirectly a means of acquiring even these.

Now then of these three possessions, money, power and reputation, [in the margin: from the nature of things it can] it is only in small quantities to a few persons and on particular occasions that the two latter are at the disposal of the Legislator. Suppose a fund of money once collected no matter by what means, and every individual in the state may be made to profit by a distribution of money (it): [in the margin: See Hume's essays contra. What Mr. Hume says must be understood with this allowance] such individuals may be *rich* with respect to the individuals of another state; but if any of them are rendered *powerful* or *honourable* in comparison of one another and therefore by their own Government, they must be *powerful* or *honourable* in respect to and at the expense of, one another. Money therefore is the only current possession, the only current instrument of pleasure. When a Legislator then has occasion to apply pleasure, the only way (method) he has of doing it, ordinarily speaking is by giving money. Now then money being the current instrument of pleasure, it is plain by uncontroverted experience that the quantity of actual pleasure follows in every instance in some proportion or other the quantity of money. As to the Law of that proportion nothing can be more indeterminate. [In the margin: In small sums, the quantity of pleasure is nearly as the quantity of money] It depends upon a great variety of circumstances, which however I shall endeavour to collect (in due time) [in the margin: see the next chapter]. Thus much however is true in general, that the more money a man has given him the more pleasure. There are it is true some men to whom the same sum would give more pleasure than to others: to the same man likewise the same sum would give more pleasure at one *time* than at another: and even with respect to the same man and at the same time it is not true where the disproportion is very large between two sums that the proportion between the two pleasures would follow exactly the proportion between the sums. *One Guinea*, suppose, gives a man *one degree* of pleasure: [in the margin: a certain quantity no matter what call it] it is not true by any means that a *million* of guineas given to the same man at the same time would give him a *million* of such degrees of pleasure. Perhaps not a thousand, perhaps not a hundred: who (can say) knows? perhaps not fifty. In large sums the ratio of pleasure to pleasure is in this way less than a ratio of money to money. There is no limit beyond which the quantity of money cannot go: but there are limits, and those comparatively narrow beyond which pleasure can not go. There are men whose pleasure the acquisition of a hundred guineas would carry to this utmost limit: [in the margin: which borders upon distraction;] beyond which (even with) is (lies) pain: a hundred thousand could not carry it farther (beyond). Here then is the quantity of money encreased a thousand fold, and that of pleasure not at all. For all this it is true enough for practice with respect to such proportions (small quantities) as ordinarily occur, that *caeteris paribus* the proportion between pleasure and pleasure is the same as that between sum and sum: it (so much) is strictly true that the ratios between the two pairs of quantities are nearer to that of equality than to any other ratio that can be assigned. Men will therefore stand a better chance of being right by supposing them equal than by supposing them to be any otherwise than equal. They ought therefore, in every case in which no particular reason can be given to the contrary, to be supposed equal, and spoken of as such.

Speaking then in general we may therefore truly say, that in small quantities the pleasures produced by two sums, are *as* the sums producing them. But money is capable of being measured: Any sum of it consider'd as a whole [in the margin: Money is capable of being accurately divided] is capable of being divided into parts, the ratio of which parts one to another may be made evident to the [sheet 36, p. 5] senses to the utmost exactness (degree) that can be required; to wit by (in respect of) bulk and weight. Now to these parts correspond so many degrees of pleasure: and thus it is that under the restrictions above specified we may measure with the utmost exactness any such pleasure as is produced (producible) by money, that is any such pleasure as in general it lies within the province of the legislator to bestow. [In the margin: And therefore is the (only) original measure of such pleasure as it belongs to the Legislator to bestow, and of such pain as is derivable from the same source.]

As pleasure is given by giving money, so is pain by taking it away. This latter fact stands equally uncontroverted, and is equally matter of experience with the former. For correspondent reasons and under correspond [sic] restrictions (it is right to say that) caeteris paribus the (quantity of) money is the just direct and proper measure (and the only proper measure) of that sort of pain which is produced by means of money. But (Now) money, as has been said is the only current and universal means in the hands of the Legislator of producing pleasure. At the same time it is not by any means the only current and universal means of producing pain. With respect to pain it is not an universal means of (in) itself: nor is it even so general as other means which the nature of mankind affords. [In the margin: For to any man money may be given. But from whom who has no money, no money can be taken.] At the same time of producing pain there is another means which is really (strictly) universal: for every man has a body.

Of such pleasure then as is produced by the bestowal of money, and of such pain as is produced by the taking it away, (away of money) money is [sheet 36, p. 6] the direct and proper measure: and (being) not only the measure, but the producing instrument or cause. But of a pleasure or a pain produced by any other cause, money though not the cause may be the measure; if not the direct one, yet an exact and proper one, and the only one such pain or pleasure will admitt [sic] of.

[In the margin: Of other pleasures and pains, though not the *original*, it may be the *assumed* measure.] If of two pleasures a man knowing what they are would as lief enjoy the one as the other, they must be reputed equal. There is a reason for supposing them equal, and there is none for supposing them unequal. If of two pains a man had as lief escape the one as the other, such two pains must be reputed equal. If of two sensations, a pain and a pleasure, a man had as lief enjoy the pleasure and suffer the pain, as not enjoy the first (one) and not suffer the latter, such pleasure and pain must be reputed *equal*, or as we may say in this case, *equivalent*.

If then between two pleasures, the one produced by the possession of money, the other not, a man had as lief enjoy the one as the other, such pleasures are to be reputed equal. But the pleasure produced by the possession of money, is *as* the quantity of money [sheet 36, p. 7. How to measure] that produces it: money is therefore the measure of this pleasure. But the other pleasure is equal to this: the other pleasure thereof is as the money that produces this: therefore money is also the measure of that other pleasure. It is the same between pain and pain; as also between pain and pleasure.

[In the margin: A common measure necessary to enable men to annex the same ideas in point of quantity to the same words.] The use of a common measure is to enable the person who speaks to communicate to any one he is speaking to the same idea of the quantity of any thing he is speaking of as he himself conceives. A common measure must therefore be some instrument the name of which suggests upon being mentioned to both parties an idea of the same quantity. You tell me St Paul's is bigger than the Pantheon:

I agree with you that it is so. This agreement does not hinder our ideas of the proportion of those two bodies from being very different. You may think St Pauls [sic] ten times as big as the other building: I may think it not more than half as big again: You now tell me that St Pauls [sic] contains two millions of cubic feet; the Pantheon but half a million. If I agree with you in this our ideas of the bigness of the respective buildings are now the same. [sheet 36, p. 8. How to measure]. We have found a common measure for them viz: a foot ruler an instrument the use of which is familiar to both of us, and which through the medium of our senses presents us with such ideas of quantity as by experience we always find to be alike. In the same manner if you say it was hotter yesterday at noon than it was to day at the same hour (and I agree with you), our ideas of the heat of the weather at those periods respectively may notwithstanding be very different. But if you say the thermometer stood at 60 yesterday and fell to-day to 50 and I agree with you, our ideas of the heat in this case must be alike.

If then, speaking of the quantity (the respective quantities) of various pains and pleasure [sic] and agreeing in the same propositions concerning them we would annex the same ideas to these propositions, that is if we would understand one another, we must make use of some common measure. The only common measure the nature of things affords is money. How much money would you give to purchase such a pleasure? 5 Pounds and no more. How much money would you give to purchase such another pleasure? 5 Pounds [sheet 37 p. 9. How to measure] and no more. The two pleasures are (must as to you be reputed) equal. How much money would you give to purchase immediately such a pleasure? 5 Pounds and no more. How much money would you give to exempt yourself (immediately) from such a pain? 5 pounds and no more. The pleasure and pain must be reputed equivalent.

[In the margin: It may apply to one kind of pleasure or pain as well as to another] From what source those (such) pleasures or those (such) pains may issue, whether the pleasure (be the pleasure) (consist in) (of) drinking so many bottles of wine, in enjoying the favours of such a woman, in possessing the respect or good will of such a man, in relieving such an object in distress, in doing such a service to one's country or to mankind in general, in revenging one's self in such a manner upon such a person; whether the pleasure be in its consequences productive of pleasure, or of pain or of neither: the pain of pain or of pleasure or of neither (in a word whether they be fruitful, pure, or insulated) are circumstances which so long as the pains or pleasures in question be considered *in themselves* (and without regard to consequences) make no difference with respect to the propriety of speaking of them, as being in money of such a value. If I having a crown in my pocket and not being adry (thirsty), hesitate whether I shall buy a [sheet 37, p. 10. How to measure] bottle of wine (claret) with it for my own drinking, [In the margin: It may apply to one kind of pleasure or pain as well as to another] or lay it out in providing sustenance for a family I see about to perish for want of my assistance, so much the worse for me at the long run: but it is plain that so long as I continued hesitating the two pleasures of sensuality in the one case, of sympathy in the other, were exactly worth to me five shillings: to me they were exactly equal.

I beg a truce here of our man of sentiment and feeling: while from necessity and it is only from necessity, I speak and prompt mankind to speak a mercenary language. [In the margin: Apology for applying it to refined pleasures.] The Thermometer is the instrument for measuring the heat of the weather: the Barometer the instrument for measuring the pressure of the Air. Those who are not satisfied with the accuracy of these instruments must find out others that shall be more accurate, or bid adieu to Natural Philosophy. Money is the instrument for measuring the quantity of pain or pleasure. Those who are not satisfied with the accuracy of this instrument must find out some other that shall be more accurate, or bid adieu to Politics and Morals.

[Sheet 37, p. 1. How to measure] Let no one (man) therefore be either surprised or scandalized if he find me in the course of this work valuing every thing in money. 'Tis in this way only we can get aliquot parts to measure by. If we must not say of a pain or a pleasure that it is worth so much money, it is in vain in point of quantity to say any thing at all about it. There is neither proportion nor disproportion between Punishments and Crimes.

In conformity to this method of considering the subject, it will be proper to settle the import of several expressions we shall have occasion to make use of.

[In the margin: Profit and Loss by a punishment or a crime]

The *pleasure* resulting from any act to the agent may be stiled the *profit of* that act. The *pain* resulting from it, the *loss by* that act. According to the different kinds of pleasures and pains, we may distinguish therefore so many different kinds of profits and losses. Profit accordingly might be distinguished into the sensual kind and the mental: in the latter class we should find pecuniary which includes all that is meant by the word profit in that confined and narrow sense of it which is rather the most common.

[Sheet 38, p. 1. Pleasures and pains how measured] It imports a Legislator as well as every private man to know how to measure the *value* of a pain or pleasure: to know on what circumstances belonging to it the value of it depends. For the more in number the pleasures are which a man is about to enjoy within a given time, and the greater each of them is in value, the number and value of the pains he is about to enjoy within that time being deducted, the greater for that time will be his happiness. [In the margin: The Fasc. p. 1, N°. 1]

The circumstances on which the value of a pleasure depends when considered by itself are these four: viz.

1. Intensity,
2. Duration,
3. Proximity or remoteness,
4. Degree of certainty, that is of certainty, probability or improbability.

The circumstances of intensity and duration belong necessarily and at all times to all pleasures: every pleasure must be more or less *intense*: every pleasure must last for such or such a *time*. These two circumstances taken together form (constitute) what may be properly termed the magnitude of a pleasure. It is indeed common enough to speak of the magnitude of a pleasure when nothing more than the intensity of it is in view. But then the duration of it is [sheet 38, p. 2. Pleasures and Pains—how measured] either neglected, or supposed to be already settled. Of two pleasures that is actually greater than the other which is more intense for the time that they both last. We may accordingly proceed to lay down the following axioms.

1. Of two pleasures, equal in intensity, the magnitude is as the duration.
2. Of two pleasures equal in duration, the magnitude is as the intensity.
3. The magnitude of any given pleasure is as its (number) [sic] intensity multiplied by its duration.*

Next with regard to the circumstances of proximity and certainty. A pleasure, like any thing else, must be either past present, or future. If past, its value is at an end. (as such there can be no further occasion to consider it.) Present it (any one single pleasure) can be only for a very short space of time, without the interruption of indifference, of pains, or of other pleasures) [In the margin: how long soever any thing may continue that is a fund of pleasures.] Future it may be for an indefinite length of time; accordingly there is much more occasion to consider pleasures as future than as present. When once a pleasure is present, no speculations concerning either its remoteness or its uncertainty can have place. It can be in no degree either remote or uncertain. So long as it is yet to come, it must be in some degree remote, and it may be in a greater or less [sheet 38, p. 3. Pleasures and Pains—how measured] degree uncertain. Presence therefore is [at once] the limit at once of remoteness and uncertainty.

The value of a pleasure is the less, the more remote it is. Its remoteness [may be measured with the utmost nicety. It] is measured by the number of moments or other greater parts of time that are to elapse between the time with reference to which the pleasure is considered as being remote, and the time at which it is to be enjoyed. The value of a pleasure considered as present being represented by unity, the value of it considered as remote must be represented by a fraction.

* To speak more accurately, as the number expressive of its intensity multiplied by the number expressive of its duration.

When a pleasure is remote, the value of it will again be less, the less certain it is: (as to speak at full length, the less certain the event is of its happening.) When such an event is not absolutely certain, the degree of its uncertainty, like that of the certainty of any other event is measured by the ratio of the number of the chances there are (is) for its happening, to that of the number of chances there are (is) for it's [sic] not happening.

Concerning the magnitude of the value of a pleasure we may therefore proceed to lay down the following axioms.

Of two pleasures equal in magnitude and not both of them present, the value is as the proximity.

Of two pleasures equal in magnitude and proximity, and not both of them certain, the value is as the degree of certainty.

The value of any given pleasure is as the intensity, duration, proximity [sheet 38, p. 4. Pleasures and pains—their kinds] and certainty multiplied together [a]

Note

At full length thus: the value of any (given) pleasure is to the value of any other pleasure as the product of the numbers representing the intensity duration proximity and degree of certainty of the *one* when multiplied together, is to the product of the numbers representing the intensity duration proximity and degree of certainty of the *other* when multiplied together.

The numbers representing the *intensity* and *duration* of a pleasure, should be whole numbers: those representing it's [sic] remoteness and degree of certainty, fractions; and for this reason. The quantities of intensity and duration of which a pleasure is susceptible have each of them a fixed limit on the side of diminution: they have none on the side of increase. On the other hand the quantities of proximity and degree of certainty of which it [obviously omitted: is] susceptible have each of them a fixed limit on the side of increase; they have none on the side of diminution.

[Sheet 39, p. 1. Pleasures and pains how measured] I am aware that the remoteness of the latter part of the greater pleasure during its continuance is a circumstance that diminishes it's [sic] value: insomuch that a pleasure which spread out if one may so say in point of duration, could not be quite so valuable as a pleasure of the same magnitude that spread out in point of intensity. [But the influence of the circumstance is too trifling to be here insisted on.] Accordingly a hundred a year for *thirty* years (come when it will) is not so valuable as a thousand [omitted: a] year [commencing from the same time] for *three* years.

As to the proportion in which the value of a pleasure is diminished by its remoteness, this will be rather difficult to ascertain. The proportion in which the value of a sum of money that is of a fund of pleasures is diminished by this circumstance is different in different countries, according to the rate of interest.

What has been observed concerning the manner in which the value of a pleasure is affected by the circumstances of remoteness and uncertainty, is far from being a matter of mere speculation. It is exemplified and verified by every day's experience. The value of a sum of money is affected exactly in this manner: and how else is it that a sum of money can be valuable but as a fund of pleasures; or what comes to the same thing of the means of averting pains?

[Sheet 39—p. 2 and 3 empty—, p. 4. Pleasure and Pains—how measured]
[In the margin: Value applied to pains]
Note

Persons at large will be apt, I doubt, to be startled a little when they come to see the word value applied to a pain: the word value in common speech not being usually applied to any other objects than what are looked upon as desirable. It will not however appear extraordinary to any persons who are in the least degree conversant with algebraical speculations: algebraists have as frequent occasion to attribute a negative value to the objects under their consideration, as a positive and where a positive quantity represents a gain, a negative quantity represents a loss. Notwithstanding this warrant I should not have given this unusual sense to the word value if I could have found any other word that was readily susceptible of the neutral import I had occasion to express.

Note

The same difficulty will probably occur to the applying the word *purity* to the exclusion of desirable objects such as pleasures, that I apprehended might occur to the applying the word value to objects undesirable. Nor can I find so good a warrant in this case as in the former. But I have the same plea of necessity for my excuse.

[Sheet 40, p. 5. Pleasures and pains—how measured] The numbers expressive of the intensity of a pleasure and those expressive of its duration, are to be multiplied together, not merely added. For supposing the pleasure to continue all along at the same degree of intensity, every degree of intensity it possesses is carried through every degree of duration: and *vice versa* every degree of duration is extended over every degree of intensity. Accordingly if of two pleasures, the one be *three* times as intense as the other, and likewise continues three times as long, it is not six times only as great, but nine times. The first pleasure (suppose) has three degrees of intensity, and likewise three minutes of duration: the second but one degree of intensity and one minute of duration. The first then during the first minute has three degrees of intensity, that is three times as many as the second: during the second minute it has the same three degrees of intensity over again: which makes it already six times as great as the other pleasure: during the third minute it has the same three degrees of intensity still; which makes it nine times as great.

In like manner the numbers expressive of its magnitude and those expressive of its proximity must be multiplied together and not barely added. The magnitude of the first pleasure is 27, that of the other, 3. At the same time the degree of proximity or remoteness of the first is such as makes [sheet 40, p. 6 is crossed out, p. 7 is blank, p. 8. Pleasures and Pains how measured] it's [sic] value less by ⅓ only than it would have been had the pleasure been present: while the degree of remoteness of the other pleasure is such as makes it less by ⅔ than it would have been had the pleasure been present: [In the margin: leaving it equal to ⅔ of that of a present pleasure of the same magnitude] leaving it equal to ⅓ only of that of a present pleasure of the same magnitude. To multiply a whole number by a fraction is to multiply it by the *numerator* of the fraction, and divide the product of that multiplication by the *denominator*. 27 then multiplied by ⅔ or in other words ⅔ of 27 is 18: and 3 multiplied by ⅓, or in other words ⅓ of 3 is 1. The value then of the greater pleasure will be to that of the lesser, as 18 is to 1. The number expressive of the magnitude of the pleasure supposing it to be present must be magnified by the fraction expressing what it loses in value on the score of its remoteness not simply added: for the deduction to be made on this account applies equally to every portion (particle) of it. If the fraction expressive of the alteration made in its value, by this circumstance instead of being multiplied into the number expressive of its magnitude were added to it, the value of it would be increased by this circumstance instead of lessened: the value of the greater pleasure would be 27 and ⅔ instead of 18: that of the lesser 3 and ⅓ instead of 1.

After the same manner it may be shown, that the number expressive of the magnitude of the pleasure is to be multiplied by the fraction expressive of its degree of certainty, not added to it.

Appendix V

Bentham MS, hitherto unpublished, University College, London, Portfolio 96, Folder 6, sheet 128-131, obviously written about 1776.

I call Pleasure every sensation* that a man had rather feel at that instant than feel *none.*

I call Pain every sensation that a man had rather feel none than feel.

"I call Pleasure, says a celebrated French Philosopher [in the margin: Maupertuis Essai de Philosophie Morale, ch. 1 Oeuvres Tome 1 Lyon 1756 p. 194] Every sensation [in the margin: The word is *"Perception"*—it makes no difference] that a man had rather *feel* than *not* feel. I call Pain, continues he, every sensation that a man had rather *not* feel than *feel.*

* The word "perception" is crossed out here by Bentham.

"Every sensation," he says again, ". . . during which a man would neither wish to sleep, nor *to pass on to any other sensation* every such sensation is a pleasure. The time which such sensation lasts is what I call the *happy moment*. [In the margin: I hope thus much is enough to make an end of the philosophical Romance (?) of which the Moral is Go hang yourself. "Abi cito and suspende te."]

A *moment* he might well call it: nor after this need we be surprised at reading at the head of his next chapter—"that in common life the sum of *evil* surpasses that of good." A melancholy conclusion this: (it must be confessed) and happily as ill-founded as it is melancholy. According to his definitions, especially the last of them, no man should be deemed to have a fortune, but Croesus—No man to have height, but Goliah, or the tallest of the Patagonians —No woman beauty but Venus—No pleasure in short is a pleasure, but the highest a man knows of. He goes on, as one might imagine (for tho' unfortunate in this and some other instances Maupertuis was a mathematician, and if he erred it was with method and precision), he goes on, and says, Every sensation . . . during which a man would wish to sleep or to pass on to any other, every such sensation is a Pain.

Note

I thought I had made a sort of discovery, when it had occurred to me that the quantity of Happiness or Unhappiness in any given subject was to be calculated upon these dimensions; and had drawn up a few propositions upon that principle. [In the margin: I had hit upon this method of analysing (analysis of) our perceptions. The idea of these two dimensions, when it first occurred, seemed new to me: I thought I had made a sort of discovery, when I thought of taking it up as a model to analyze all our sensations by.] I was much surprised upon turning over the works of that ingenious Philosopher to find the idea anticipated. Beyond these two dimensions indeed he does not go. The tract in which it occurrs [sic], for all the useful and original hints it contains is but little known in this country: it has not I believe been translated into our language. The truth is the positions in it are for the most part as false as they are uncomfortable: which may serve to account for the little notice that has been taken of it. The fundamental errors seem to be this I have been taking notice of: and another which I shall have occasion to mention presently.

Yes, says Maupertuis, "The pleasures that a man finds in increasing his riches and his power (pleasures of possession and expectation as I call them) are pleasures, but they are pleasures of the body—How so? because they originate in the body—they suppose the existence of the pleasures of the body, which a man purposes by means of his riches or his power to procure without which they would be themselves no pleasures +ib. 212. Then you make no pleasures of the mind? Oh, yes says he, but I do. [In the margin: They are nothing else than pleasures of the body seen at a distance.] There are just two sorts of them: and I will tell you what they are. One is, the *practise of Justice*. The other is, the *view* [sheet 129, p. 1] of *Truth*. I think it will not need many words to shew that these pleasures, great and real as they are, (or, to speak more accurately sources of pleasures) depend as entirely upon the pleasures of the body, as those which he has allow'd to do so. "As for Justice, continues he very candidly, I don't know very well what to make of it, that's true. Indeed it is not necessary." All that is necessary to mean, and all I mean by practise of it, is, the fulfilling what a man imagines to be his duty, be it what it may."

"No more is it necessary to give an exact definition here of Truth. All I mean by views of truth is, that perception which a man experiences when he is satisfied with the evidence with which things appear to him." For precision's sake I will take his definitions instead of the terms defined: and begin with the pleasure which a man feels at fulfilling what he thinks his duty.

This fulfilling what he thinks his duty is either the doing of some act which he thinks it his duty to do, or the abstaining from some act, which he thinks it his duty to abstain from.

I will take an example from each branch of duty, Private and Public: and inquire whether the pleasure a man has from each of them, does not as much require the existence of the pleasures of the body, as any other does.

To begin with a duty of the Private kind. It is a duty in a man to behave with affection to his wife, and that in preference to any other woman. The man I take for my example is of that opinion. Preferring her society to that of any other woman, he goes on partaking with her, amongst others, of those physical pleasures, which to partake of with another woman (without her consent), would be a breach of duty to her. Thus far, I suppose there is none of that pleasure which consists in the fulfilling of what a man imagines to be his duty, and which has nothing to do, says our Author with the pleasures of the body. The pleasure which a man reaps in repeating an act, must be that which is all along the motive with him to that act. It is too absurd to think of any other motive for the act we are speaking of, than the pleasure which a man would find in it and which men did find in it, before any such word, or such a notion as that of duty came into their heads.

We now suppose him under a temptation to enter into the same course of pleasure with another woman, and he resists it: [In the margin: he has a desire to enjoy it, but notwithstanding he abstains.] Now he has the pleasure of fulfilling his duty; of abstaining from what it is his duty to abstain from.

I should be glad now to know wherein the pleasure he now has consists. It consists not I suppose in the mere consciousness that he is abstaining that he is not doing what by the supposition he would take a pleasure in doing what he has a desire to do: in short in the being under restraint: one might as well lay it down as a general maxim that a man finds a pleasure in thinking that he is going to prison. [Sheet 130] If he abstains from taking the pleasure in question as we suppose him to do, it is I suppose on the four accounts following, some or all of them.

1st. Because he thinks God may be displeased with him.

2. Because he thinks the Law may punish him.

3. Because he thinks he may lose the esteem and good-will of his acquaintance.

4. Because he thinks he may lose the good-will of his wife herself.

To each (every one) of these events, pain is or at least may naturally [in the margin: does probably] appear to him to be annexed: and that a pain originating ultimately in the body.

If the 1st of these be the consideration that governed him, it is plain that the pleasure he finds in fulfilling his duty in this behalf is not (consists not in) the bare reflection that he is fulfilling his duty, but in his reflecting on the pains he avoids by not violating it: Viz: such pains whether in this world or in the next, that he might apprehend from the displeasure of the Deity, at the same time that he reflects on the pleasures that he secures by such conduct; [in the margin: will secure him] viz: such pleasures as he expects from the favour of the Deity. [In the margin: Another observation might here be made. If the pains a man has to apprehend from the displeasure of the Deity are not pains of the body; as the Scriptures seem to intimate, they are at least pains; which man could have no notion of, nor therefore be influenced by, if it were not for the pains of the body.]

If it be the 2^d that governed him, it is plain according to our authors [sic] own account that the pleasure he enjoys is a pleasure originating in the body: for the pleasure of thinking that he exempts himself from the pains inflicted by the Law. Now all these pains are without dispute referable to the body.

If it be either the 3rd or 4th, it is the pleasure of reflecting that he has escaped a pain: the pain of forfeiting the esteem, or if another word pleases better the good will of those about him. Now what is it that esteem is good for? is it good of itself, or of something it procures? That it is good of itself one may allow him after he has told us, how much pleasure a man would find in the esteem of a set of beings he had neither good nor harm to apprehend from; [in the margin: find with Helvetius(?)] the inhabitants of Saturn for example (supposing there are any) or the inhabitants of a drop or two of stale vinegar?

If I ask him what riches or power are good for, he (agrees with us and) has his answer ready—he knows that they afford pleasure [in the margin: may procure him] and the physical sufferances against which they are a defence [in the margin: may ensure him]. To these objects at least, he says it is but too common for men to refer exclusively the benefits of these *means* as he calls them, their riches and their power. They are valuable therefore as means only—for in no other light does he speak of them. And what else they are valuable as means *to* he does not tell us, nor on what other account they are valued, when they are valued as he seems to intimate they may be on another besides this that he has mentioned.

If they are valuable on account of any thing else besides the pleasures of the body they are means to, it must be the pleasures of the mind. But these he has himself reduced to two, the two we have just mentioned above, namely the pleasure of thinking that one is fulfilling one's duty which is that we are now considering: and that of the view of truth, or of being satisfied with the evidence of things as they appear to us.

The last mentioned of these pleasures we are to come to by and by. As to the other, it will hardly [sheet 131] be said that riches and power have any particular tendency to confer it: Nobody ever thought yet of saying that there were not duties to fulfil or that a man was not able to fulfill [sic] his duties as well without as with them.

If riches and power therefore are good for anything it is for the physical benefits they procure. What else than should esteem be good for? Esteem is good, it is a cause of pleasure nobody can doubt of it. It is a means of procuring sometimes physical pleasures directly, at other times riches and power which procure them: nobody can doubt of that neither. We know no instance where it is a source of pleasure but where it may procure them. The cases where we can conceive it as being no source of physical pleasure, we perceive immediately that it can not be the source of pleasure at all. It is not comprised in our author's (catalogue) list of mental pleasures. It follows that it gives pleasure as being a source of physical pleasure and no otherwise.

To which ever of these sources therefore we refer the pleasure that a man takes in fulfilling his duty, it appears that how great soever the pleasures which it confers, it is none strictly speaking of itself. It gives pleasure, because it gives a view of others: but suppose no others to exist, and it would give none.

Hitherto we have considered an instance of private duty: if we take one of public duty, it [in the margin: the question] will stand just upon the same footing.

Let that instance be the refusing of a bribe by a man in public trust. If he finds a pleasure in it it will be on one or other or all of the three first accounts one of the four we assigned before. If we suppose in him a strong affection for his country (a passion tho' not unexampled hitherto unhappily in public men but too rare) and that this was his motive, the gratification of this his pleasure; [in the margin: we must point out the original of a man's love for his country] besides that this pleasure does not appear to be strictly the same with that in question: we must then observe: that 1st the person is conscious of the motives the causes of that affection, in which case he is conscious that they are partly the sense of the physical benefit he in common with the rest of the citizens derives from the condition which it is in, the constitution which it enjoys; a constitution which would be prejudiced by the act we suppose him to abstain from: partly to the sense of the esteem (the honour) that will redound to him in particular from that particular act of patriotic self-denial and from the character which it is necessary he should put it in practice to maintain: in short, to the pain every man must feel after having rendered one course of conduct habitual to him to run at once into a quite opposite one.

Or else he is not conscious of these motives, and then his conduct was the fruit of a good education given him by persons acting under the consciousness of these motives, or from the precepts of some (to come to the last) who were.

Appendix VI

BENTHAM MS, *hitherto unpublished*, University College, London, Portfolio 27, Folder 2, sheet 15, written ca. 1776

Happiness is the end of every human action, of every human thought, how can it, or why ought [sic] to be otherwise? This is for those to say who sometimes seem to struggle to dispute it. If they are serious we will hear them in another place: at present by way of hypothesis (in the margin: it shall be an hypothesis) let us suppose it without dispute.

Further references to Bentham MSS *hitherto unpublished* are to be found on pp. 26f, p. 34, p. 37 (p. 40), p. 43, p. 44, p. 45, p. 55, p. 60 (p. 140), pp. 165f, p. 182, p. 183 (214f), p. 221f, p. 224 (p. 229), p. 252, pp. 296f, p. 307 (Lewis Gompertz MS), p. 317, p. 327 (Etienne Dumont MS), p. 332, p. 400, p. 444.

INDEX

of Names and Subject Matter*

* This index was done in the main by my late wife, Carola Baumgardt, who—faithfully as in all she did—worked on it until her last hour. Her modesty did not permit me to say in this book more of what I owe her.